MICROCOMPUTER SYSTEMS PRINCIPLES
FEATURING THE 6502/KIM

MICROCOMPUTER SYSTEMS PRINCIPLES
FEATURING THE 6502/KIM

R.C. Camp
T.A. Smay
C.J. Triska

Professors
Department of Electrical Engineering
Iowa State University
Ames, Iowa

MATRIX PUBLISHERS, INC.
Portland, Oregon

© Copyright, Matrix Publishers, Inc. 1978

All rights reserved. No part of this book may be reproduced or utilized in any form or by any means, electronic or mechanical, including photocopying, recording or by any information storage and retrieval system, without written permission from the publisher.

10 9 8 7 6 5 4 3 2 1

Library of Congress catalog card number: 78-71522

ISBN: 0-916460-27-4

Production: Patricia Miller
Illustrations: Scientific Illustrators
Printing: Pantagraph Printing
Editor: Merl K. Miller

Matrix Publishers, Inc.
30 NW 23rd Place
Portland, OR 97210

CONTENTS

PREFACE

1 INTRODUCTION TO MICROCOMPUTER-BASED DESIGN   1

Evolution of the Microcomputer/Microprocessor Applications / Engineering Design of Microcomputer-Based Products / Educational Demands Created by the Microprocessor / Objectives of this Book

2 GENERAL ASPECTS OF MICROPROCESSOR-BASED SYSTEMS   13

Microprocessors and Microcomputers / Classification of Computers and Computer Systems / General Features of Microcomputer-Based Systems / Information Flow in Microcomputers / Central Processor Hardware Elements / Addressing Modes / Microprocessor Instruction Sets / Microprocessor Word Length / Symbolism in Digital Computers / Arithmetic Operations in Microcomputers / Interrupts and Subroutines / Technological Factors in Microprocessors

3 THE MCS6502 MICROPROCESSOR AND PERIPHERAL PARTS   69

Introduction to MCS6502 / Programming Model / Data Paths / Concept of Operation of MCS6502 Instructions / Complete Description of Operation Codes / MCS6502 Specifications / Peripheral Interface Chips / Example Problems

4 SOFTWARE AIDS   173

Introduction / The Software Design Process / Elements of Program Translation / Text Editors / Simulators / Special Program Debug Features / In-circuit Emulation / Logic State Analyzers / Prom Programmers

5 MICROCOMPUTER INTERFACING AND SYSTEM DESIGN 243

Introduction / Guidelines for System Design / Miscellaneous Advice on System Design / Interfacing Examples / Input / Output-TTL, Speed, Bits, Serial / Parallel Conversions / Address Maps and Organization / Memory and I/O Selection / System Design Examples

6 INTRODUCTION TO THE M6800 MICROPROCESSOR 299

Introduction / Principal Characteristics / Some MCS6502 and M6800 Differences / M6800 Programming / Electrical Characteristics of the M6800 / M6800 Microcomputer Example / Example Problems

7 INTRODUCTION TO I8080 MICROPROCESSOR 347

Characteristics / I8080 Architecture and Programming Model / Data Paths / I8080 Instruction Set / I8080 Example Program / Electrical Characteristics of the I8080

8 AN MCS6502-BASED MICROCOMPUTER— THE KIM-1 411

Introduction / What is a KIM-1 / The KIM-1 System: (A micro versus a mini) / An Example Program / KIM-1 Memory Map and Table / Machine Code for Example / Entering Example Code into KIM-1 / Execution of Example From the Keyboard / Decimal or Binary Code / KIM-1 Keyboard Key Functions / Operating the KIM-1 via Teletype / Adding an Audio Tape Recorder to the KIM-1 / The KIM-1 Display

APPENDICES

A USER'S GUIDE TO THE MDT 650 461

B OPERATING PRINCIPLES OF THE KIM-1 MONITOR AND ON-BOARD I/O HARDWARE 485

PREFACE

The emergence of the microprocessor as a principal element in the design of electronic systems has generated an acute new educational need. Within the Electrical Engineering Department at Iowa State University, the response to this need has been similar to that at many other institutions, viz., the modification of existing course material and the generation of new course material slanted toward the study of microprocessor principles and applications.

This book has evolved from classroom notes developed for Computer Engineering 437, *Introduction to Microprocessors*, which has been taught at Iowa State for the last three years. Since the emphasis is on hands-on experience, it has been necessary to provide an in-depth examination of the system chosen as the principal laboratory vehicle, the KIM-1 microcomputer available from MOS Technology, Rockwell, Commodore, and Synertek. The authors have attempted to provide an approach to study of the KIM-1 and its microprocessor element, the MCS6502, that will develop understanding capable of easy transfer to other systems, past, present, and future.

Because the role of software development and system integration is considered critical to the design process, considerable material is devoted to examination of the role of microcomputer development systems. The MDT-650 development system is included because of its role in supporting the MCS6502 microprocessor. Although this system will be available to relatively few institutions, it is nonetheless an excellent example of equipment of this type. The transition to newer support equipment, such as the System 65 by Rockwell, should prove easy. A companion to the System 65 is the Intel MDS-800, designed to support the I8080 and I8085 microprocessors. The capabilities and overall usage are similar for these two and most students familiar with either will adapt quickly to the other.

The authors owe a tremendous debt to Professor James W. Nilsson, who played a critical role in pulling together the efforts of the authors and in integrating their rather style-disparate contributions into a manuscript of (hopefully) reasonable coherence. Without his patient guidance and goodnatured exhortations the project would undoubtedly have failed.

The authors also wish to thank J. O. Kopplin, Chairman of the Department of Electrical Engineering, for his continuing encouragement and support of the development of this book.

The authors wish to thank Mrs. Betty Carter for her long-term patience in typing the many manuscript iterations which have occurred during preparation of the book. Thanks also to Mrs. Sherry Smay and Mrs. Jeanne Gehm who assisted during the latter stages of typing.

Finally, thanks to faculty colleagues and students within the Department of Electrical Engineering, Computer Engineering, the Engineering Research Institute, and the Computation Center at Iowa State University for their innumerable contributions in the form of conversation and criticism.

1

INTRODUCTION TO MICROCOMPUTER-BASED DESIGN

1.1 EVOLUTION OF THE MICROCOMPUTER

The term "revolutionary" is rather indiscriminantly applied to such diverse subjects as home-laundry soap, rock music, automobile tires, and other products of contemporary society. We also hear many references to the electronics revolution, the LSI revolution, and the microprocessor or microcomputer revolution. With respect to these latter subjects, the principal act which can be termed truly revolutionary was the invention of the transistor in the late 1940's. Subsequent development of integrated circuits (ICs), medium-scale integrated circuits (MSI circuits), large-scale integrated circuits (LSI circuits),and very large scale integrated circuits (VLSI circuits) has followed a natural evolutionary path, at an admittedly staggering rate.

Figure 1.1-1 is a plot which demonstrates that the number of components per integrated circuit has doubled each year since 1959, the year the planar transistor process, upon which bipolar IC development was based, was introduced by the Fairchild Corporation (Reference 1). It is truly remarkable that this exponential rate of growth has continued over such an extended period of time. If the trend continues until 1979, and it appears that it will, we can expect to have access to monolithic chips containing 2^{20} (about 1 million) components.

Individual *digital* circuits tend to be comparatively simple and tolerant of signal level and component parameter variation. These characteristics, combined with the tendency toward regular, repeated structure in registers, arithmetic units, memory units, and other logical subsystems make digital systems natural candidates for implementation

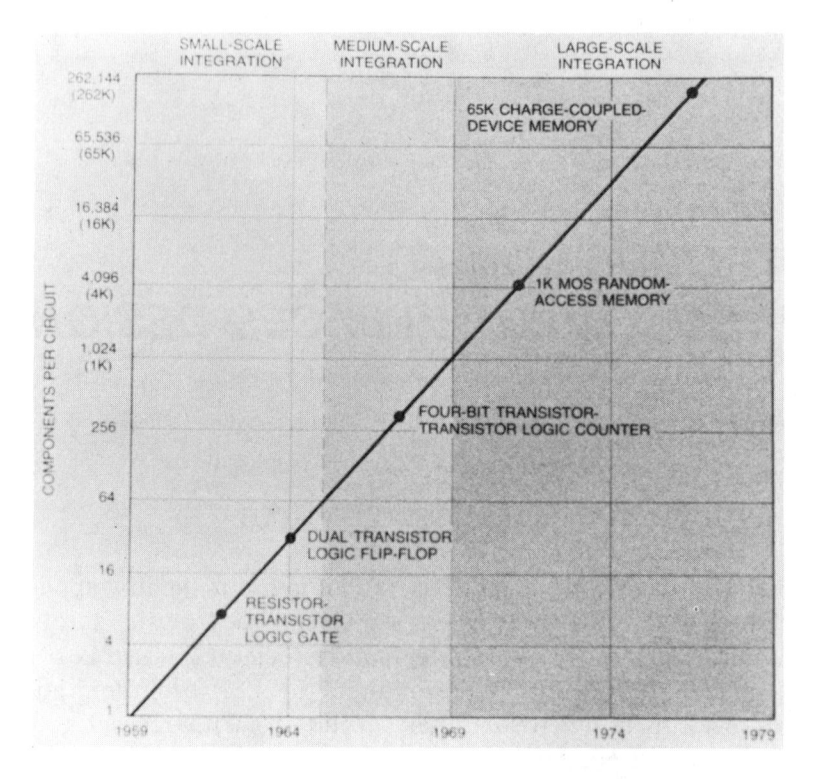

Figure 1.1-1 Evolution of large scale integrated (LSI) circuits
(Courtesy Robert N. Noyce, reference 1)

via LSI technology. Thus, we have observed the development of such components as: IC gates and flip-flops; MSI registers and ALU's; and LSI microprocessors and memory units. At each stage these developments have exemplified the state-of-the-art in semiconductor technology.

The principal impact of the breakneck race of technology is economic. The transistors of the 1950's cost from 50 cents to several dollars each. The ICs of the 1960's were similarly priced, as were the MSI units of the early 1970's. Today a microprocessor containing perhaps 5000 transistors (see Figure 1.1-2) can be bought in single-unit lots for 30 dollars or less. In high-density memory units, transistor costs are between 0.01 and 0.1 cents. Noyce (Reference 1) states that the industrial experience curve supports a prediction of a 100-fold increase in electronic functions incorporated into products by 1986, coupled with a 20 fold decline in cost per function. The impact of this explosion in electronic technology on our lives and on society at large will be staggering enough to warrant the use of the word "revolutionary" in its most literal sense.

Another important by-product of LSI technology is extreme reliability. The failure rate of integrated semiconductor units has tended to be fairly uniform at the package level, regardless of the number of components or functions which comprise the package. Another factor which contributes to system reliability is the economic feasibility of using *redundant* systems or subsystems.

The microprocessor of today, then, is the contemporary result of a tremendously rapid evolutionary process based on the transistor, a fundamental invention barely 30 years old.

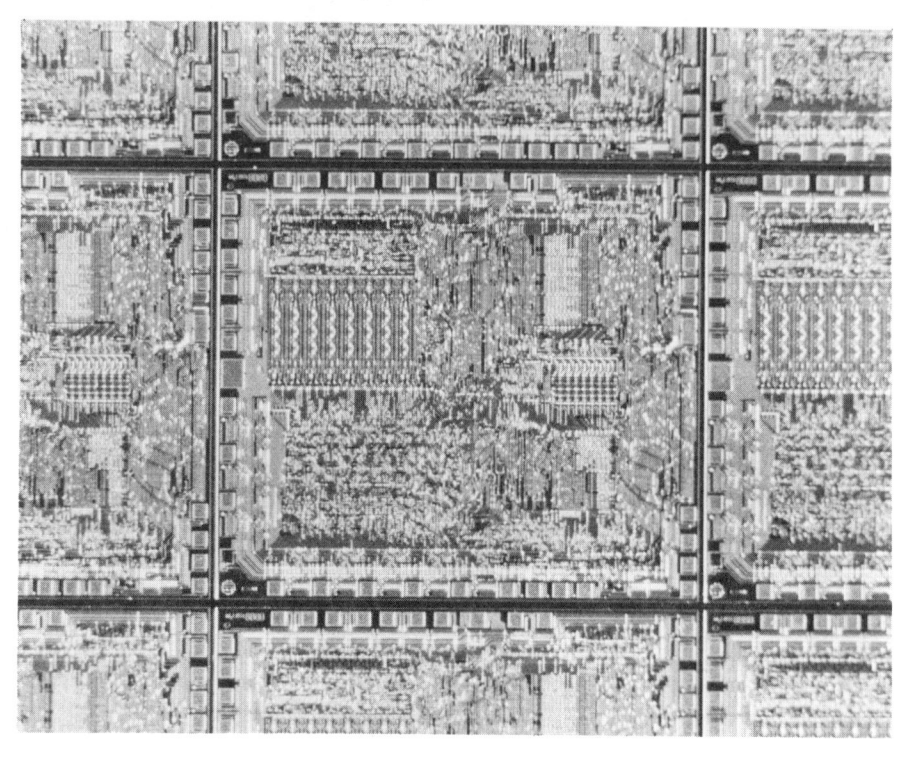

Figure 1.1-2 Photomicrograph of Intel 8080 microprocessor

1.2 MICROPROCESSOR APPLICATIONS

The hand-held calculator and the digital watch, Figure 1.2-1, were among the first products of LSI technology. In each of these cases, the projected market volume was large enough to warrant very large devel-

Figure 1.2-1 The digital watch and the hand-held calculator—products of the LSI revolution

opment costs associated with specialized LSI units. Microprocessors are no less expensive to develop, but their programmable nature makes them adaptable to a variety of diverse applications. Thus, if programming costs can be controlled, the economic benefits of large-volume LSI production can be applied to products whose individual market volumes cannot justify special-purpose LSI chip development.

1.2.1 Categories of Microprocessor Applications

The wide range of microcomputer applications can be roughly divided into three categories. First, there is the type of application in which the microcomputer simply plays the traditional role of its larger and more expensive brother, the minicomputer or large-scale computer. The so-called "personal" computer, Figure 1.2-2, is an example of this type of application. The function provided by the personal computer is in concept much the same as that provided by the industrial or institutional computer, e.g., record-keeping, file storage and retrieval, and capability for execution of user programs directed toward analytical or abstract problem-solving. In the personal computer,

Introduction to Microcomputer-Based Design

of course, the range of such activities is considerably scaled down. We may note, for example, that among the problems deemed suitable for execution on the personal computer are such games as craps, ping-pong, backgammon, Hurkle, Wumpus, and other purely recreational exercises. The implication that the owner of such a system deems such usage to be cost-effective in providing recreational service dramatically illustrates the modified role of the traditional computer system.

As a second major application category, we may consider those situations in which the microcomputer-based system is employed as a substitute for existing non-computerized implementations. Many consumer product applications such as appliance controls, automobile controls, point-of-sale terminals, video games (as pinball replacements), gasoline pumps, and vending machines fall into this category. Digital thermometers, voltmeters, weighing scales, and many other instruments are replacements for existing analog units. In those cases where the

Figure 1.2-2 A typical "personal computer" – The Commodore PET 2001

digital instrument is microprocessor-based, its cost-effectiveness is usually a result of enhanced function rather than of reduced cost.

The third category of microprocessor applications is that of products which are neither conventional data-processing systems, nor digital substitutes for existing nondigital implementations. Example include toys, robots, synthetic organs, and voice recognizers and synthesizers. The distinguishing characteristic of products in this category is that they conceptually require the microprocessor for their existence.

1.2.2 Microprocessor Application Areas

A second way to classify microprocessor applications is by area of application. In each area we may find examples of the three categories discussed in Section 1.2.1. See References 2, 3, 4, and 5 for an excellent overview of microprocessor application areas.

1.2.2.1 Data Processing. Section 1.2.1 mentions the advent of the personal computer as a viable and cost-effective form of data processing for individuals or families. We may expect the personal computer to evolve rapidly, and to become more reliable and less demanding of operator expertise for effective use. Continued development of low-cost and reliable second-level storage will also be necessary if the personal computer is to reach its potential.

In the established area of large-scale data processing systems, the microprocessor finds many applications. "Intelligent" terminals (see Figure 1.2-3) which provide remote editing, formatting, and graphic functions, are generally microprocessor based. Other peripheral units (disks, displays, data collection interfaces, etc.) often contain distributed intelligence in the form of microcomputer-based controllers. Finally, the impact of LSI technology is definitely reflected in the design and operation of high-speed processing units (see References 2 and 6). Microprocessors are not yet suitable for use as central processors in high-performance data-processing systems, but the distinction between microprocessors and high-speed LSI "number-crunchers" will become narrower as the technology continues to develop.

1.2.2.2 Instrumentation. This is a very natural application area for the microprocessor. Processing speed is more than adequate for many instrumentation requirements, and accuracy, analytical power, and decision-making and control capability offer the possibility of tremendous expansion of function relative to nondigital approaches.

Introduction to Microcomputer-Based Design 7

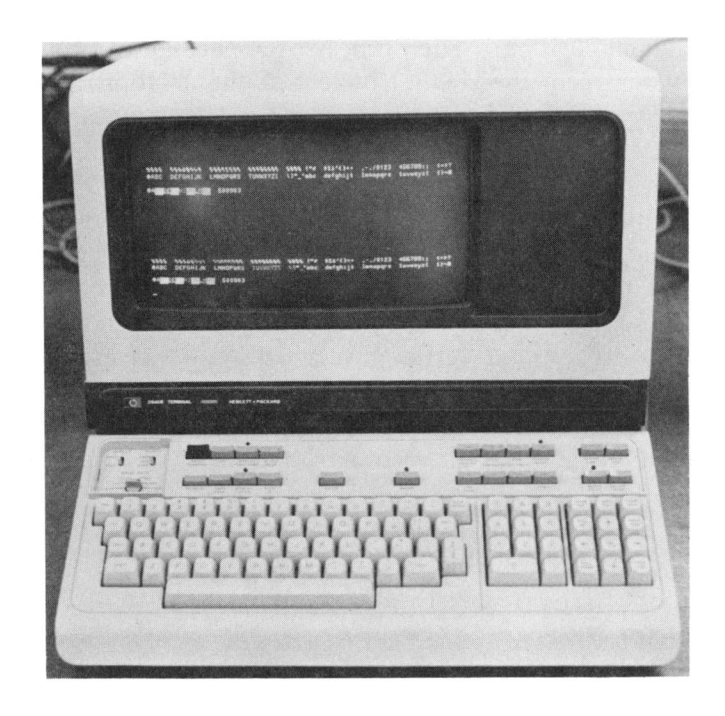

Figure 1.2-3 An "intelligent" terminal—the Hewlett-Packard model 2640B

Digital implementation of a wide variety of metering functions is well established. As the microprocessor is incorporated into digital instrumentation, capability for automatic calibration, data analysis, data recording and transmission, and other manifestations of "intelligence" result. Hewlett-Packard Corporation, for example, has developed a whole family of microprocessor-based instruments which can communicate with each other via a standard interface bus, referred to as the Hewlett-Packard Interface Bus (HPIB), otherwise known as the IEEE 488 bus.

1.2.2.3 Control. This is another area in which the microprocessor offers tremendous promise. Inexpensive microprocessor-based controllers have application to process control, numeric machine control, and other related activities. Dedicated controllers are now available in appliances such as microwave ovens, in automobile fuel-injection, engine timing, and nonskid braking systems, in camera automatic exposure control systems, in home heating/cooling systems, and many other consumer products. We will undoubtedly see hundreds or even thousands of new applications in this area within the next few years.

1.2.2.4 Communication. Microprocessor applications in this area will very likely represent the greatest impact of the microprocessor to our daily lives. Applications in the fields of radio, telephone, and television will intensify the already profound effects of these media on our daily activity. Personal communication applications such as portable telephones and information-transfer devices will allow us to greatly increase our communication capability. Our daily exposure to information in the form of newspapers, radio, telephone, television. books, personal conversations, visual observations, etc., creates a tremendous need for information storage and retrieval mechanisms. Microprocessors and cheap bulk storage mechanisms provide promise for satisfaction of this need, which we presently partially satisfy with copying machines, photographic apparatus, tape recorders, and other information storage implementations.

1.3 ENGINEERING DESIGN OF MICROCOMPUTER–BASED PRODUCTS

1.3.1 The Changing Role of the Engineer

Until recently it has been customary for the design engineer working in the computer field to become something of a specialist. Perhaps he was called a logic designer, a memory designer, a packaging specialist, a printed-circuit specialist, a mechanical designer, or a programmer. In one of these roles, he formed part of a design team which, under the direction of a project engineer or project manager, collectively generated the desired system design.

There are many products under development today which require the support of such a design team, but with the microcomputer has come the need for a new concept of design. Products designed by the approach described above were predicated on acceptance of the high expense of computing systems, and the economic penalties associated with the team design concept were in balance with the ultimate cost (and presumably the benefit) of the product. The inexpensive microcomputer offers promise of correspondingly inexpensive products, but this promise can only be realized if design costs can be reduced somewhat in proportion to production costs, which means that the team design concept can represent an intolerable economic burden in many cases. Exceptions would be those high-volume production situations

Introduction to Microcomputer-Based Design

(automobiles or appliances, for example) where high development costs can be amortized over a very large production volume.

The microcomputer has thus produced a need for engineers who individually can provide the skills of the collective design team. As a minimum requirement, such an engineer would have proficiency in the following areas:

1. *Computer organization* — He should be proficient in the principles which underlie operation of processors, memories, peripheral units, and other digital system components.
2. *Logic design* — He should be proficient in interconnecting IC, MSI, and LSI logic units to provide desired function. Understanding of both logical and physical (electrical and mechanical) constraints is implied.
3. *System interfacing* — He should be capable of selecting and interconnecting such diverse digital and nondigital components as logic units, transducers, optical couplers, analog-to-digital and digital-to-analog converters, etc., to configure appropriate communication paths between the microcomputer and the system in which it is to be integrated.
4. *Software development* — He must possess not only programming skill, but also an appreciation of the costs of programming and of the principles of hardware/software tradeoffs.
5. *Application expertise* — He must not only be a computer specialist, but he must also know enough about the application to which the system is directed to make appropriate design decisions.

Development of the skills listed here is not easily achieved, but the engineer who possesses them will have a guaranteed position in the area of digital systems design. Also, the economic promise of the microprocessor is so great that it will dominate the small computer application area so completely that the demand for "computer designers" will be essentially confined to the limited few organizations engaged in development of either new microprocessor devices or large, high-performance computer systems. An information-processing system that will require the design of a special-purpose processor will rarely occur. Thus, most engineers will be concerned with the applications of microprocessors rather than with their design.

1.4 EDUCATIONAL DEMANDS CREATED BY THE MICROPROCESSOR

Development of the skills enumerated in Section 1.3 represents a significant educational challenge. Among the dilemmas faced by both those who would provide this education and those who have need of this education are the following:

1. A body of general principles, forming a basis upon which continued growth of understanding of new concepts and products can be based, should be a primary goal of development.
2. An appreciation of the role of the various aspects of design relative to system cost must be developed. This involves the necessity for exposing the student to considerable hands-on experience, since the extremely time-consuming and costly process of avoidance, detection, and elimination of "bugs" in the system under design can be taught in no other meaningful way. Unfortunately this requires the student to become somewhat immersed in the particular details of the system chosen as the vehicle for this hands-on activity. Time spent in achieving the required level of detailed operational efficiency of such a system tends to detract from the development of the general principles described in item (1).
3. Since the software design process is of extreme importance, the hands-on opportunities of item (2) are of particular importance in the software area. Once again time spent attaining proficiency in operation of particular software systems can negatively influence the development of general skills.
4. Because the range of applications of microcomputers is so diverse, it is difficult to provide either appropriate hardware or general educational support for more than a few limited examples.

1.5 OBJECTIVES OF THIS BOOK

The educational dilemmas enumerated in the previous section are very real, and any attempt to solve them necessarily requires compromise. This book is intended to provide educational support for the engineer who wishes to engage in microcomputer-based system design, and the degree of compromise reflected herein has been achieved by application of the following philosophical principles:

1. It is both desirable and economically feasible to provide the student with fairly extensive "hands-on" experience in the area of microcomputer-based system design.
2. It is not possible, within the constraints of time or money, to provide extensive hands-on experience in using more than a limited number of contemporary hardware systems. Even if many contemporary systems could be covered, it is impossible to predict the characteristics to be encountered in available systems of a few years hence. Thus, this book will concentrate in detail on only one contemporary system, the KIM-1 Microcomputer, based on the MOS Technology 6502 microprocessor. Chapters 3, 8, and Appendix A treat the 6502 microcomputer development system in sufficient detail to permit the student to become proficient in its use without additional supporting material.
3. Because items (1) and (2) are somewhat contradictory to the stated objective of development of general principle, considerable effort has been made to relate the specific characteristics of the chosen hardware (which is representative of current technology) to general characteristics of microcomputer systems.
4. To aid in the development of general principle, the characteristics of two other microcomputer families (the Motorola 6800 and the Intel 8080) are discussed (in Chapters 6 and 7), and their properties are related to those of the 6502 family. The emphasis in this comparison is on factors which should be considered in evaluation of system capability and suitability for particular applications.
5. The importance of the software design process is reflected in Chapter 4, which discusses software aids to microcomputer-based system design. Once again there is some conflict between operational detail and general principle, but enough representative examples are given to provide a basis for general understanding of the diverse aspects of this process.
6. The problem of interfacing with the microprocessor is addressed in Chapter 5. One again specific examples are given for the student to study and repeat if he desires.
7. Since there is the possibility of considerable variance among the backgrounds of students for whom this book is intended, Chapter 2 is provided as general background and reference material.

BIBLIOGRAPHY

All references in Chapter 1 are taken from the *Scientific American*, September, 1977, special issue on microelectronics.

1. Noyce, Robert M., "Microelectronics."
2. Terman, Lewis M., "The Role of Microelectronics in Data Processing."
3. Oliver, Bernard M., "The Role of Microelectronics in Instrumentation and Control."
4. Mayer, John S., "The Role of Microelectronics in Communication."
5. Kay, Alan C., "Microelectronics and the Personal Computer."
6. Sutherland, Ivan E., and Mead, Carver A., "Microelectronics and Computer Science."

2

GENERAL ASPECTS OF MICROPROCESSOR-BASED SYSTEMS

2.1 MICROPROCESSORS AND MICROCOMPUTERS

Before defining these elements, let us state that the distinctions which form their definitions are really not very important. Furthermore, as the technology races along, we find that today's definition is inadequate tomorrow. Because we must have some meaning for the various descriptive terms we use, however, we will adopt a rather arbitrary and hopefully somewhat standard set of definitions that will suffice.

2.1.1 Microprocessor Definition

A *microprocessor* is a relatively complete digital processing element most often embodied in a single silicon chip. It contains registers, data paths, and control logic which permits execution of conventional machine language programs. The machine language instruction set is in most cases completely defined by this control logic, although there are systems which operate in a microprogrammed mode and therefore do not have a unique assembly-language level instruction set. The chip may contain a clock circuit which provides a central timing reference, although some do not. The chip may or may not have a limited amount of local scratchpad memory, but, at least in the contemporary case, program storage must be externally provided. The cost of a typical microprocessor will be between ten and fifty dollars.

2.1.2 Microcomputer Definition

A *microcomputer* is a module which has as components a microprocessor chip, some amount of memory for both program and data storage, input/output interface chips, a clock, and other logic such as buffers and drivers, all mounted on a printed circuit board. A typical microcomputer may cost between $100 and $500.

2.1.3 Microcontroller Definition

There is a class of single-chip elements which do not exactly correspond to the microprocessor definition. These elements comprise a sort of uniform section, or *bit slice*, comprising typically two to four bits of each register and data path of a typical processor structure. These elements can be laterally cascaded together to form a processor of rather arbitrary size. Because the control function does not lend itself to this type of repetitive structure, it is only represented in primitive form on the chips, and must be augmented by still other special-purpose chips, typically in a microprogrammed manner. This type of bit-slice structure will be herein referred to as a *microcontroller*.

2.2 CLASSIFICATION OF COMPUTERS AND COMPUTER SYSTEMS

Computers, like so many other things, come in a variety of shapes, colors, and sizes. Herein they will be somewhat loosely categorized as large scale systems, minicomputer systems, and microcomputer systems.

2.2.1 Large Scale Computing Systems (Figure 2.2-1)

The full-scale general-purpose computer, so favored by cartoonists and television science fiction writers, typically occupies a large room and is surrounded by card readers, magnetic tape drives, and a variety of other exotic devices. Installation cost may be several hundred thousand or even several million dollars, and a small army of programmers, technicians, and customer engineers is required to maintain the system. The central characteristic of such a system is its role as a "precious resource," with attendant justification of investment in support.

2.2.2 Minicomputing Systems (Figure 2.2-2)

The next level down in the computer hierarchy is the minicomputer. This type of system, physically about the size of a filing cabinet or desk, will tend to be used in a more dedicated role than its larger general purpose relative. It may, for example, be installed in a laboratory

General Aspects of Microprocessor-Based Systems 15

Figure 2.2-1 A modern large-scale computation center

Figure 2.2-2 A typical minicomputer installation

for the purpose of data collection, or in a production facility for the purpose of process control. In most minicomputer-based systems, especially those at the lower end of the cost spectrum, which ranges from about ten thousand up to one hundred thousand dollars, the level of investment cannot support a large staff, and one or two operators must handle the system. It should be noted, however, that many contemporary systems which carry the minicomputer label are extremely sophisticated, associated with a large volume of peripheral equipment, and virtually indistinguishable from those thought of as large scale systems.

2.2.3 Microcomputer Systems (Figure 2.2-3)

The newest class of digital computer is, of course, the microcomputer. It is, as its name implies, small in size (typically occupying a single printed circuit board), low in cost (from one hundred to one thousand dollars) and, with respect to its larger cousins, somewhat limited in processing capability. Its processing capability, however, must not be underestimated, since it surpasses many minicomputers of only a few years' vintage, and the rate of improvement is extremely high.

It is common to define the microcomputer in terms of its technological development, as we did in Section 2.1.2. Thus, we find the term "microprocessor" applied to a single-chip LSI (Large-Scale Integration) unit with the full range of digital computer features (op codes, multiple registers, data transfer paths, multiple addressing modes, interrupt-handling systems, etc.) but lacking the volume of memory needed to properly be called a computer. The microcomputer itself is thus a microprocessor, supported by memory elements and special-purpose I/O chips, all combined in a modular package. This technological definition is, unfortunately, subject to constant revision. We have seen and will continue to see breakneck development of LSI technology, and present projections indicate that, by the early 1980's, it will be technically and commercially feasible to include not only relatively large volumes of memory, but also I/O circuitry and analog-to-digital and digital-to-analog interface elements on the single-chip unit. Is such a unit a microprocessor or a microcomputer?

The answer to this question should probably be "Who cares?" It is, in the future, going to be extremely difficult to maintain a system for classifying computers in terms of technological implementation. Already we see LSI-based minicomputers, such as Digital Equipment Corporation's LSI-11, and, as higher-performance LSI technology

General Aspects of Microprocessor-Based Systems **17**

comes along, even the largest computers will have LSI units as their central processors.

Figure 2.2-3 The KIM-1 — A single-board microcomputer

2.2.4 Economic Classification of Computer Systems

For our purposes it is probably more sensible to characterize the microcomputer in terms of its *economic*, rather than its technological nature. It is this former factor which leads us to speculate on the use of digital computer technique in automobiles, home appliances, and the whole range of consumer and industrial products. It is hard for product manufacturers to resist the allure of the microcomputer, which for only a few hundred dollars promises to exceed the capability of conventionally designed electronics, without the requirement for extensive design in each new application. Each microcomputer must of course be specifically programmed for individual applications.

The promise of the microcomputer is thus its potential for bringing the capability of the digital computer to a whole new spectrum of application areas, principally due to new economic ground rules brought about by LSI technology. If this economic payoff is to occur, however, we must develop new skills in our engineers, so that they can effectively cope with the pressure of the reduced design budget that goes along with the attempt to penetrate low-cost application markets. The lower cost limit on effective use of microcomputer technology in low-volume applications is represented not just by the lowest-cost microcomputer, but by the ability of the single engineer, without extensive outside support, to effectively marshal the skills of both hardware and software technique in achieving a total system design.

2.3 GENERAL FEATURES OF MICROCOMPUTER—BASED SYSTEMS

Microprocessor-based systems contain all the essential ingredients found in any computer-based system, but the relative emphasis on each of these ingredients is often considerably different. Large systems, for example, often reflect an attempt to make optimum use of the central processing facilities, since those facilities represent a large investment. In microcomputer systems, by contrast, the addition of one or more central processors may be of little cost when compared to the equipment to be controlled. Even in single-processor systems, one should not really be concerned whether the system microcomputer is working at maximum capacity or not, unless some of the unused capacity can be devoted to reduction in system hardware.

Figure 2.3-1 illustrates some typical microprocessor-based systems. Some of these systems (the camera exposure control and the automobile fuel-injection system, for example) represent extensive special-purpose microprocessor design effort due to special packaging or power-consumption problems, but the rest could be handled by standard off-the-shelf microcomputers. In this latter case, the design problem thus principally boils down to: (1) selection of a microcomputer system; (2) design of a system interface; and (3) design of programs for system control. These first two steps are described as the *hardware* design, while the latter step is that of *software* design.

Note that, in each of the examples shown in Figure 2.3-1, the operators or users of the system are essentially unaware of the presence

General Aspects of Microprocessor-Based Systems 19

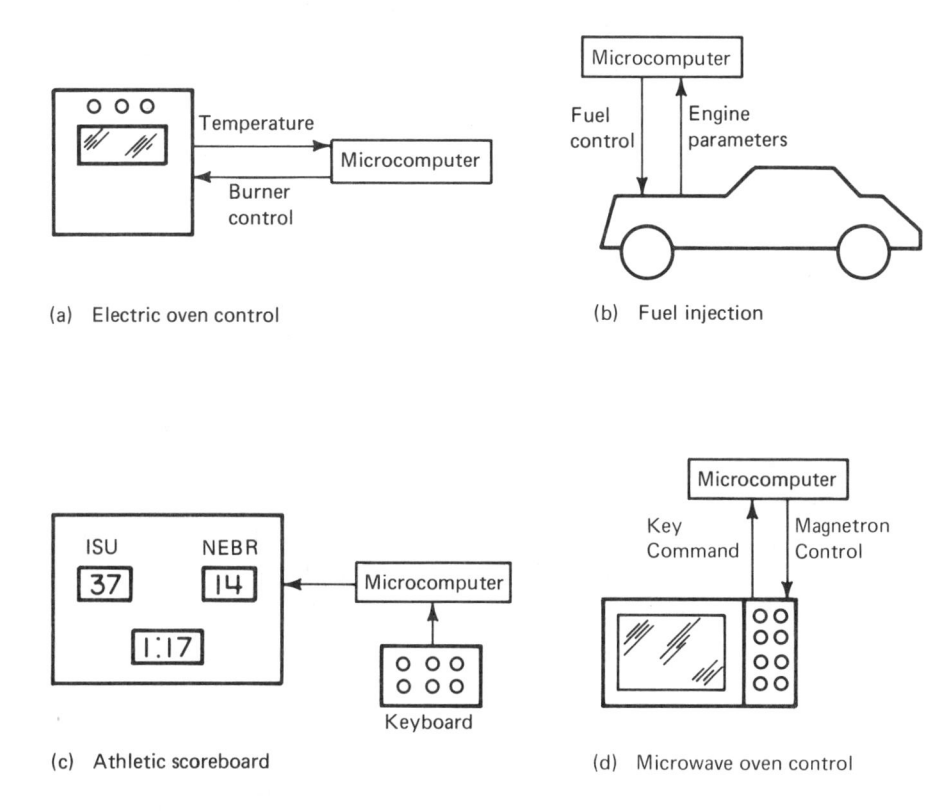

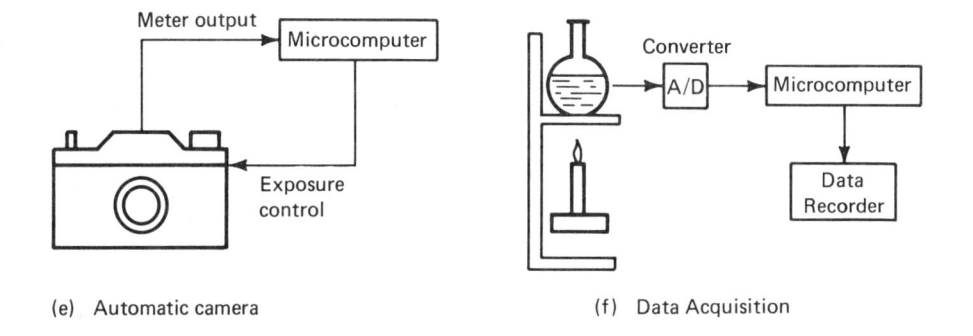

(a) Electric oven control

(b) Fuel injection

(c) Athletic scoreboard

(d) Microwave oven control

(e) Automatic camera

(f) Data Acquisition

Figure 2.3-1 Typical microcomputer-based products

of the microcomputer or of the fact that it is executing programs. The fact is, that in almost every case, the microcomputer is continuously executing some program, and the user presence, from the microcomputer's point of view, is represented by the occurrence of external signals, recognized by the program during its execution. Thus the image of the human operator, or the automobile, or any of the other "users," as exercising primary control, in misleading. The program itself, installed by the system designer, is the primary controlling agency, and it in turn recognizes the presence of system conditions generated by the user or operator.

Thus, even though the microcomputer may be virtually invisible or physically inconsequential in a particular implementation, its characterization as the controller of the system is appropriate. This leads us, as designers of microcomputer-based systems, to describe the typical system as shown in the block diagram of Figure 2.3-2, in which the "outside world" of automobiles, industrial mechanisms, airplanes, jukeboxes, microwave ovens, etc., is represented by the rather innocuous set of terminals connected to the I/O interface. The major components of a microcomputer-based system, as shown in this figure are:

1. The microprocessor, including a system clock.
2. Some amount of read-only memory (ROM) for storage of system programs.
3. Some amount of read/write memory (RWM) for storage of data, including temporary results of processing. This is often random access memory (RAM).
4. An I/O interface permitting connection to the "outside world," as described above.
5. An interconnection system for transmitting signals among the other system components.

2.3.1 The Microprocessor Unit

The microprocessor unit contains registers, flags, interconnections, arithmetic logic, and control logic which can recognize operation codes unique to a particular model and cause execution of internal sequences of logical activity which produce results which correspond to these operation codes. The microprocessor "manages" activity on its external terminals, which, in most conventional systems, are connected to three major buses, as shown in Figure 2.3-2. The *clock* is a source of raw timing signals, often controlled by a crystal oscillator, which is the basic timing reference for all system activity. Some microprocessors have an

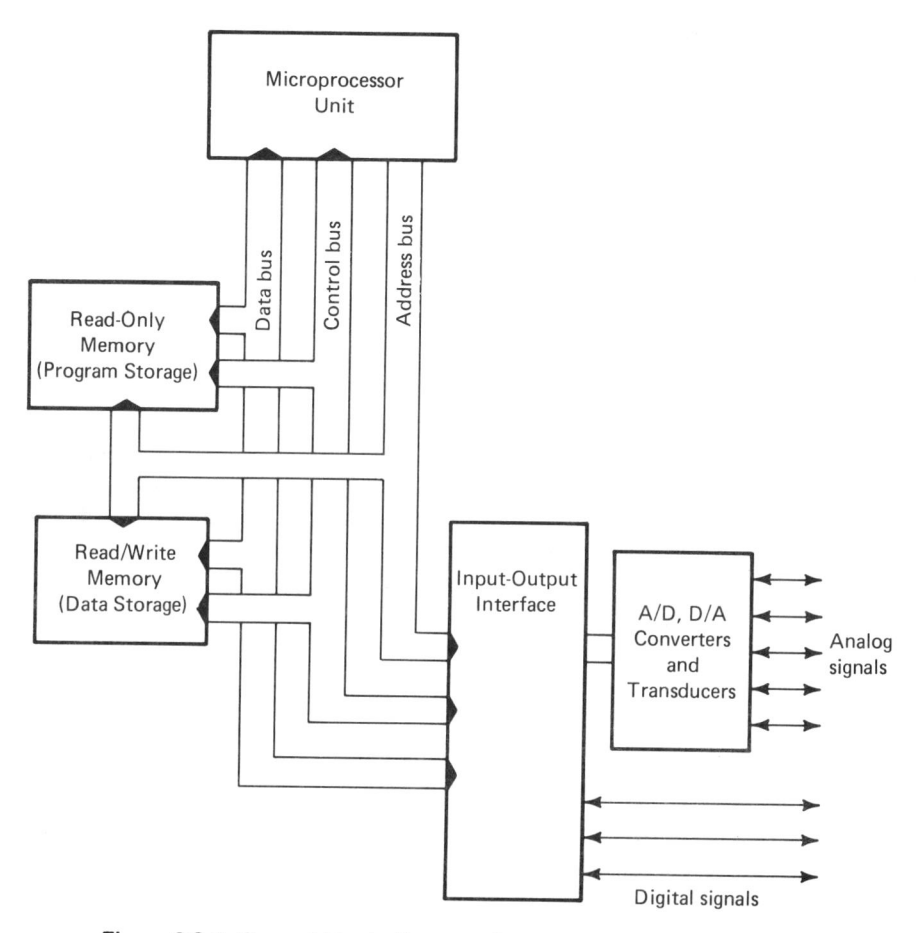

General Aspects of Microprocessor-Based Systems 21

Figure 2.3-2 General block diagram of microcomputer-based system

integral "on-chip" clock circuit, while others require a separate chip to provide this function.

2.3.2 The Read-Only Memory System

This portion of the microcomputer system provides a mechanism for storage of system programs (in coded form, of course). Elements of these programs are fetched from ROM by the microprocessor, which interprets them in its role as system controller. In addition to operation codes, the ROM also stores other information which is to be unmodified by the system such as operand addresses, immediate operands, and interrupt vectors.

The extensive use of read-only memory is one of the distinguishing marks of the microcomputer in contrast to larger systems. It reflects the dedicated or fixed nature of most microcomputers in particular applications, as well as the recognition that semiconductor memory with read/write capability is *volatile* in nature, rendering it incapable of the intrinsic abilty to recover from power-down or power-interrupt situations.

2.3.3 The Read/Write System

This sytem provides a mechanism for storage of information which is capable of modification. Since programs themselves are most often stored in read-only memory, read/write memory is usually used only for temporary storage of data brought into the system, created by the system (by program activity), or to be transmitted from the system.

It should be noted that there is nothing which functionally prevents the storage of program elements in read/write memory. In fact, during the process of program development and debugging, this is commonly done in order to permit convenience of program modification during this design phase. This mode of operation is often encountered in educational laboratories also, but the student should always keep in mind that completion of final design, in the great bulk of systems, requires that debugged programs be stored (either by a special read-only memory programming unit or by direct order from the semiconductor manufacturer) in read-only memory chips.

2.3.4 The I/O Interface

As briefly discussed in Section 2.3, this part of the system represents the connection of the microcomputer to the user or operator elements, and, to that outside agency, is the mechanism via which external control is provided. It is also the mechanism for information transfer to and from the external world. The microprocessor, however, manages the I/O interface in much the same way that memory is managed, i.e., it sends out identification information (in the form of addresses), and control information in the form of read/write and timing signals. Data is then either placed on the data bus by the microprocessor or brought into the microprocessor from the data bus. The former operation is an "output" operation while the latter is an "input" operation.

2.3.4.1 Memory-Mapped Versus Isolated I/O.

In some microprocessor systems, the characterization of I/O operations as memory operations is essentially total, and no effort is made to distinguish between them other than dedicating certain addresses to the I/O function. In other systems I/O operations are separately identified (by control bus signals) and information on the address bus is interpreted as "device number" rather than memory address. This is called *isolated* I/O. Even here, however, the resemblance between memory operations and I/O operations is essentially complete.

2.3.4.2 I/O Device Speed Constraints.

One factor which tends to distinguish between memory and I/O operation in all systems is the relative speed of the two types of operation. Whereas memory operations tend to be relatively fast, capable of accomplishment within a given machine cycle, many I/O operations are not. There are a number of reasons for this difference, most often related to sluggishness of mechanical or electromechanical devices. One way of accommodating such intrinsic speed difficulties is to provide the microprocessor with the capability for waiting until a particularly selected device has either provided or accepted the data involved in the transfer. Such a *ready/wait* control mechanism (implemented via special signals in the control bus group) also permits synchronization with memory devices which may be too slow in response to be used in a clock-synchronous mode. A second means for accommodating the slow response of I/O devices is to provide special *interface adapters* which serve as intermediary units between the microprocessor and the I/O device. Thus, for example, an output operation can consist of sending a byte of data to such an interface adapter in the normal high-speed memory mode, after which the microprocessor returns to its normal mode of program execution. The interface adapter stores the information until the external device can respond and accept it, completing the I/O transfer. Input operations can be similarly accomplished. Typical interface adapters are *programmable*, implying that the microprocessor can, by appropriate transmission of control codes to the adapter, tailor the input/output characteristics of the adapter to a particular collection of I/O device connections. This transmission of control codes is itself, of course, accomplished via execution of an *initialization program* by the microprocessor.

The use of such peripheral interface adapters in microcomputer systems is widespread and it represents an extremely convenient and powerful means of achieving very general I/O connection and, in some cases, the further ability to modify the I/O configuration dynamically during system operation. In the KIM-1 microcomputer, for example, a single peripheral interface adapter is timeshared between a keyboard-monitor input program and a display-management output program.

2.3.4.3 I/O Interface Configuration. The digital I/O interface of Figure 2.3-2 would in most cases consist of a collection of one or more peripheral interface adapters. The remaining element in the interface, the nondigital interface, would be unique to a particular application and, in many cases would represent one of the major design challanges. It might include analog/digital and digital/analog converters, special circuits for converting nonstandard voltage levels to those required by the digital interface elements, or electro-optical couplers to convert high-voltage signals to standard levels while maintaining necessary electrical isolation.

2.3.4.4 Using Interrupts in I/O Management. Because I/O activities are often unsynchronized or unpredictable relative to normal processor activity, the microcomputer's *interrupt-handling system* is frequently brought into play in managing I/O activity. Such a system permits orderly handling of such external events without time-consuming program execution devoted to external device interrogation (polling). In some cases both interrupt and polling techniques are combined. For example, if multiple devices are present, an interrupt request may result in execution of a routine which successively polls these devices to determine which one should receive service. When this determination is made, a branch to an appropriate service routine associated with the device can then be made.

2.3.5 The Interconnection System

This portion of the microcomputer system is not really a separate entity, of course, but the method by which the system is packaged and by which appropriate interconnections are provided. It does represent an important design element. The most common mechanization of the interconnection system is in the form of a single printed-circuit board, typically about the size of a standard printed page. Some contemporary systems have much more sophisticated packaging. The exposure control unit in the Canon AE-1 camera, for example, is microprocessor-based and fits well within a conventional pentaprism viewer such as is found on regular single-lens reflex cameras.

In those systems configured as a single board, space is ordinarily provided for a few thousand bytes of memory (divided between ROM and

RWM), some number of peripheral interface adapters, and, perhaps, buffering logic which provides the system with enhanced drive capability and therefore the potential for controlling a significant number of peripheral boards. For applications requiring expanded memory capability, companion boards comprising this capability are commonly available.

2.4 INFORMATION FLOW IN MICROCOMPUTERS

There are three major classifications of information encountered in the microcomputer. The first classification is the operation code or op-code. This information element, often stored in read-only memory, is brought into the microprocessor and placed in its internal instruction register during the process of normal program flow. The content of this register is then decoded by special logic circuitry built into the microprocessor. The decoded outputs are combined with timing signals (generated by the system clock circuit) to provide control signals in proper sequence to generate the result desired by the programmer. Upon completion of such a sequence of activity, the microprocessor returns to read-only memory for the *next* operation code, upon whose receipt the process is repeated. The microprocessor is thus said to alternate between two principal modes of operation, the *Fetch* mode during which operation codes are brought into the instruction register, and the *Execute* mode during which the operation is interpreted and its goals attained. Note that the detailed operations which are performed during the Fetch cycle would be fixed (since the processor must treat all *a priori* operation codes in identical fashion) while those operations which constitute the Execute cycle could, and most often do, vary quite widely from one op-code to another.

The second major classification of information is called *Address*. An element of address information discloses the *location* of other information in the microcomputer system. The address may identify a unique memory location, a unique processor register, a particular I/O device or device register, or some other entity capable of storing and delivering information. The important thing to remember about an address is that it tells the microprocessor *where to go to find another element of information*. The element of information sought could be: an operation code as described in the previous paragraph; another address; or an *operand (data element)*. The word "operand" implies that the information element is to be operated on, presumably by the microprocessor during execution of a particular operation code. An operand is the third major classification of information.

Sometimes the distinction between address information and data information is a bit blurred. For example, addresses are sometimes operated on arithmetically, by being incremented, decremented, augmented by some value contained in an index register, or some other operation. Obviously addresses in such cases play the role of operands, in that they are the object of arithmetic operations.

Having classified types of information in a fairly general way, let us examine the flow of information in a conventional microcomputer system. Since we must start someplace, we will assume that we have somehow managed to store a collection of information elements which collectively comprise our program in read-only memory, and that we have further contrived to load the microprocessor's *Program Counter* (see Sec. 2.5.7) with an address corresponding to the read-only memory location containing the first operation code we wish to have executed. The microprocessor begins its Fetch cycle, which mainly consists of placing the Program Counter (PC) contents on the address bus and generating control signals via the control bus requesting that a memory read operation be performed. The desired operation code is thus routed via the data bus to the microprocessor, where, as described earlier, it is placed in the instruction register. As a final housekeeping step in the Fetch process, the PC is incremented so that, upon the subsequent Fetch, the next instruction in the stored program sequence will be obtained (assuming that execution of the current operation code does not itself cause modification of the PC's contents). Now the microprocessor reverts to the Execute mode. No general characterization of this mode is possible because of the range of varied possibilities, but in general the Execute cycle will involve fetching of address information from read-only memory, fetching the operand or operands corresponding to the addresses, transforming these operations into new information via arithmetic or logical operations, modifying the PC contents to accommodate jump or branch operations, testing and setting system condition flag flip-flops, etc. It is important to remember that, whether a modification of program sequence via jump or branch instructions is desired or not, the value in the PC must be properly managed so that, when the microprocessor finally reverts to the Fetch mode, this value is the address of the next operation code.

2.5 CENTRAL PROCESSOR HARDWARE ELEMENTS

The microprocessor itself is the central processing unit (CPU) in a microcomputer system, and its characteristics obviously dictate the

General Aspects of Microprocessor-Based Systems 27

general features of the system. There are many criteria which distinguish the various microprocessor types, including instruction sets, speed characteristics, presence or absence of specialized control features like interrupt-handling and tri-state bus connections, and the hardware register set, arithmetic/logic unit and other specialized hardware features. Microprocessors differ rather widely in the sets of hardware elements provided within them, and an understanding of the rationale for including or omitting some of them in comparative units is important in making comparisons or in selecting a unit most suitable for a particular application.

2.5.1 Accumulator Registers

Most contemporary systems include as a principal hardware element one or more *accumulators* or *A-registers*. Such a unit, as its name implies, stores operands before an arithmetic/logic processing step and the result of the operation following its execution. The unit thus "accumulates" the results of successive additions or other such operations.

Some microprocessors have no accumulator, requiring that the destination of the result produced by an arithmetic/logic step be specified by an address associated with the instruction. Some processors have more than one accumulator. The Motorola 6800, for example, has two, called Accumulator A and Accumulator B.

2.5.2 Status Flags

Because the result of arithmetic processing resides in the accumulator, its state is naturally reflected in the states of the various *flag flip-flops* which contain the special results (zero, negative, positive, carry, overflow, parity, etc.) produced by an arithmetic/logic operation. The particular set of flag flip-flops provided in a given design comprise the *status register* or *condition-code register* of that system. The states of these flags are used in determining the program flow sequence via the use of conditional jump or branch operations (see Section 2.7.1.2.4).

2.5.3 Register Files

A number of microprocessors have a so-called *register file*, sometimes referred to as a *general purpose register set*. This unit provides local high-speed memory within the microprocessor itself. The registers typically are of sufficient size to store memory addresses, providing a means whereby short instructions (which need only designate one of a few register locations) can address operands in a much larger memory space (since the register can contain a full-size address). Obviously other instructions are needed to store the addresses in the registers in the first place.

2.5.4 Index Registers

In some systems the general-purpose registers of Section 2.5.3 are referred to as *index registers* in that, by successively incrementing them, one may effectively move a pointer (another name for an address) successively through a list of operand values stored contiguously in memory. The word *index* is used to allude to the similarity of this process to that achieved by referring to successive vector or array elements by subscripts called index values. *True index registers*, however, provide this capability in a somewhat more convenient way. The value stored in such a register represents an offset or displacement from some base address value associated with a particular instruction. Thus, as before, stepping through a set of data elements whose first member is stored at a location specified by this base value can be accomplished by adding the value stored in an index register to this base address. A program using this technique would most typically contain a loop, or repeated execution, involving incrementing the index register each time around the loop and checking the value contained in the index register until the desired number of passes has been made. In many cases it is more convenient to preload the index register with the desired value and decrement it each time around the loop, checking for zero to determine if an exit from the loop is to be made.

This latter use of index registers, for program loop control, is often applied when the primary function is not address modification. In systems using index registers, a varied set of special instructions is usually provided for loading, incrementing, and testing their contents. Most microprocessors have some form of index register or registers. Generally a variety of simple transfers between the index registers and other main system registers and memory are implemented as part of the instruction set.

2.5.5 Stack Pointer

In those microprocessors which implement a system stack for subroutine and interrupt return addresses (see Section 2.11.3), a *stack pointer register* is provided. This register contains an address designating the current position of the top of the stack. The stack itself is, in such a

General Aspects of Microprocessor-Based Systems 29

case, contained in read/write memory. Sometimes the stack pointer is of sufficient capacity to store a full-length address, making it possible to build very large stacks or multiple stacks; sometimes a more limited stack pointer register is provided, limiting the amount of storage available for stack maintenance.

2.5.6 Arithmetic/Logic Unit

The Arithmetic/Logic unit (ALU) in a particular microprocessor provides a mechanism whereby two operands can be combined into one via one of a number of processes, including addition, subtraction, addition with carry, subtraction with borrow, incrementing, decrementing, ANDing, ORing, etc. The particular process to be invoked depends on the current operation code. Usually subtraction is performed using 2's complement arithmetic, using the high-order bit of each operand as sign bits. In systems with accumulators, the output of the ALU is routed to the selected accumulator, which also serves as the source of one of the operands. A feature present in many microprocessors is *decimal adjust logic*. This logic senses the state of the accumulator following an arithmetic operation and, if invoked, corrects the value found there to proper binary-coded decimal (BCD) representation. (See Section 2.10.3.) Thus, in an eight-bit microprocessor, BCD values may be packed into a succession of contiguous locations in memory, two digits to a byte, and decimal addition performed by streaming these digits from memory (incidently using indexing to select the consecutive bytes) where they can be added and corrected via the decimal adjust logic. Digit-to-digit carries are automatically handled by carry flag values and Add-With-Carry operation codes.

2.5.7 Program Counter

A program, stored in contiguous locations in memory, consists of a string of information units made up of operation codes, address bytes, and immediate operands. If proper control of program sequence is to be maintained, it is necessary to maintain a pointer which designates the current position in memory from which the next program element is to be obtained upon completion of the current operation. The *program counter* is a processor register dedicated to this function. When a program element is to be fetched, the program counter contents are sent to the system address bus and a memory fetch operation is initiated. Upon completion of this fetch, the program counter contents are automatically incremented so that the pointer is prepared for the next fetch cycle.

The execution of branch or jump operations is accomplished by the simple step of replacing the current program counter contents with the jump address. In the case of relative jumps (see Section 2.7.1.2.6) program counter contents are augmented arithmetically by the offset value provided by the program itself.

As discussed in Section 2.11.7.3, the program counter contents are a primary element in the composite *program state*, and considerable effort is expended in system design to assure that program counter contents are properly tucked away for future recall when such events as subroutine calls and interrupts occur.

2.5.8 Internal Control Logic

Probably the most sophisticated single logic system in any microprocessor chip is its collection of internal control logic. When an operation code is fetched from memory, it is placed in an instruction register whose outputs are interpreted by a system of decoders. The decoder outputs, combined with timing signals from the system clock, generate a sequence of control signals which effect register transfers, shift operations, arithmetic/logic operations, set and clear operations, and a number of other such primitive logical operations. Such a sequence, which in some cases is many clock intervals in duration, has as its goal the accomplishment of the ends of the machine instruction corresponding to the operation code. Upon completion of the instruction execution sequence, the internal control system generates the sequence of primitive control signals which constitute the instruction fetch cycle.

In most contemporary MOS microprocessor systems, the internal control logic is "hard-wired", i.e., configured as a set of gates and flip-flops properly connected to provide the control functions. In some cases, however, the sequence of control operations is controlled by information elements stored in a control memory, and the generation of a control sequence involves deriving gating signals from words sequentially fetched from this memory. Since, in such a case, the operation code serves principally as an entry point into this control memory, following which the sequence of control is handled by the control memory fetch sequence, it is natural to think of such a sequence as a program. Since such a program is composed of primitive "microoperations", it is called a *microprogram*, and the information elements stored in control memory are called *microinstructions*.

In most contemporary bipolar microprocessors, as discussed in Section 2.12.3, a bit-slice configuration is used, and the control function is separated from the processor function. The control function is

General Aspects of Microprocessor-Based Systems 31

provided as a separately connected logical entity. In such cases, it is common to implement the control function as a microprogrammed system, permitting the designer the capability for tailoring his instruction set to individual applications. Special LSI elements for conveniently configuring microprogrammed control are often provided in such cases.

2.6 ADDRESSING MODES

In discussing the different types of information to be handled in a microcomputer system, we classified these types into *operation codes*, *addresses*, and *operands* or *data values*. An address was defined as an element of information telling *where to go in the system to find another element of information*, which could in turn be an operation code, an address, or an operand.

Nearly every machine language instruction in a program and stored in read-only memory has one or more addresses associated with it, since it is necessary for such an instruction to specify not only the operation to be performed but also the data element or elements (operands) to be the object of the operation. It is common in contemporary microprocessors for operand locations to be specified in one of several ways, by use of a variety of so-called *addressing modes*.

2.6.1 General Considerations in Addressing

The longer the address, the greater the number of unique memory locations it can specify. Since the operand address is part of the instruction, however, the longer it is the more memory space it requires for program storage. Similarly, if a two-operand instruction is written, and both operand addresses are to be uniquely specified, a great penalty in program storage requirement is the result.

The fewer memory operations required to obtain an operand, the more quickly the execution of an instruction can be accomplished. Thus, if speed of execution is important, one should avoid addressing modes which require extra memory accesses. In register-file systems, ability to store operands in the register file, where the ALU has most rapid access to them, can result in enhanced speed of execution.

Finally, the very presence of multiple addressing modes implies the necessity for specification of the mode to be used in a particular case. This mode specification requires some number of bits of representation in the instruction code (the more modes, the more bits required) and therefore occupies some part of read-only memory space.

2.6.2 Addressing Mode Types

The following listing describes the more common addressing modes found in contemporary microprocessor systems. No single unit has all these modes, but it is common for each to have at least three or four of them.

2.6.2.1 Immediate Addressing. This addressing mode specifies that the operand is contained in the instruction itself as it lies in read-only memory. Since, when the operation code which discloses the addressing mode is interrupted, the program counter points at the memory location immediately following the last-accessed location which contained the operation code itself, this next adjacent location is the natural one for the immediate operand. Thus a memory fetch from the program counter location, followed by an incrementing of the program counter (so that it points to the next successive program element), is sufficient to fetch the immediate operand. In some cases, particularly where the operand is an address, more than one byte may be fetched as an immediate operand. Once again appropriate program counter incrementing must be done.

2.6.2.2 Direct or Absolute Addressing. If interpretation of the operation code indicates a direct addressing mode, the subsequent byte or bytes of the instruction are fetched and used as a pointer to the operand, which is then fetched from memory. This is probably the most commonly used mode for transferring data between the microprocessor and read/write memory.

2.6.2.3 Indirect or Deferred Addressing. If an indirect addressing mode is specified, the address contained in the machine language instruction is once again used as a pointer to the operand. (As before, the actual fetching of the operand address from memory may involve multiple-byte operations.) Indirect addressing permits a short limited-range address (see zero page addressing, Section 2.6.2.7, for example) to be converted to a full-size address and thereby, in a sense, to expand addressing capability. Also, if the original address specifies a read/write memory location, that location can be modified under program control, permitting manipulation of data pointers under program control.

In some minicomputers, indirect addressing can be implemented to an arbitrary number of levels, i.e., each new address fetched contains a flag bit which indicates whether another memory fetch is to be

General Aspects of Microprocessor-Based Systems 33

performed using the current pointer. Such a mechanism could be implemented in a microprocessor if it were desirable to do so.

2.6.2.4 Implied Addressing. This is, in a sense, a somewhat degenerate addressing mode in that no address at all is included with the instruction. The operand location is implied by the nature of the operation to be performed. An example of an instruction which uses implied addressing is Decrement Index Register X (DEX) used in the MOS Technology 6502. Since the operand is the value stored in the index register, it need not be specified by a separate address.

2.6.2.5 Relative Addressing. In this mode, the address of the operand is obtained by adding the contents of the associated address field to the current program counter value. The advantage of relative addressing is that a short (one-byte, typically) offset value can produce a full-size address. The disadvantage is the limited range associated with short address fields, coupled with the fact that only pointers into memory space occupied by program elements can be generated by its use. Relative addressing is often used in Branch instructions, where pointers to adjacent program space are often quite useful.

2.6.2.6 Indexed Addressing. A discussion of the role of index registers is given in Section 2.5.4. If indexed addressing is specified, the address field accompanying the operation code is added to the contents of the specified index register to form a pointer to the operand itself. As discussed in Section 2.5.4, this can be a very useful technique for stepping through lists of arrays of data values stored in contiguous memory locations. Another related operation is fetching of data from tables stored in memory. In that case, the base address points to the beginning of the table, and the index register contains a displacement value (previously generated by the program) which displaces the effective address to the desired location in the table.

2.6.2.7 Paged Addressing. In this mode, memory is considered to consist of relatively small divisions called pages, and the address associated with the operation code is sufficiently long to specify only a unique location within a page. The most common version of this mode found in microprocessors is *Zero Page Addressing*, which appends zeros to the high-order section of the specified address to form the effective address. The advantage once again is that short addresses with correspondingly low storage requirements can be used. The disadvantage is that, once all zero page locations have been used by the program, one must revert to another mode.

The PDP-8 minicomputer uses *Current Page Addressing* (along with Zero Page Addressing) as an addressing mode. Once again instruction addresses only need specify a location within the relatively small span of one page, but in this case the remaining address bits are provided by a special pointer maintained within the processor and specifying a Current Page Address which will become the high-order portion of the effective address, the low-order portion being the specified operand address field. If programs are properly structured so that a single value in the current page address register can be held for a significantly long interval of processing, such a technique can be quite efficient. If not, there is considerable overhead associated with modifying the contents of the current address register.

2.6.2.8 Indexed Indirect Addressing. In this combined addressing mode, the specified address value accompanying the operation code is augmented by the value in the specified index register, as in regular index mode, but in this case the fetched value is in turn used as a pointer to the actual operand. This permits stepping through an array of addresses which contain the desired operands. Since these addresses need not be contiguous, a more general form of indexing is provided.

2.6.2.9 Indirect Indexed Addressing. In this combined addressing mode, the specified address value accompanying the operation code is used as a pointer to memory. The value at that location is fetched, added to the contents of the specified index register, and the resulting effective address is used as a pointer to the desired operand. This permits establishment of a table of pointers, contiguously located in memory, and selectable by index register value.

2.6.2.10 Other Combined Modes. It is possible to define other address modes which combine those described in still other ways, and in fact one may find such other combinations in different units. The definitions given should, however, permit one to unambiguously interpret such combinations so long as the same descriptive labels are used. For example, zero page indexed mode would imply that a single-byte operand address (implicitly a page zero address) would be added to the contents of a specified index register to form the effective address of the operand.

2.7 MICROPROCESSOR INSTRUCTION SETS

The machine language instruction set provided with each microprocessor (except those designed for microprogrammed control) is often considered one of its principal features, forming one of the essential bases of comparison with other units. This degree of importance is probably somewhat exaggerated since each instruction set does provide at least some form of solution for the great bulk of programming problems, and ratings are sometimes dependent more on individual programmer experience and prejudice rather than on valid objective criteria. Also, a particular instruction set may be advantageous for certain classes of problems, and yet suffer when applied to other classes.

Regardless of the arguments as to the relative merits of the different instruction sets, it is probably true that the characteristics of such an instruction set and the ability to program in that language (machine or assembly language) is more important in the microprocessor realm than in minicomputers or larger systems. This is because many of the desired operations in a typical microprocessor application are very primitive in nature, involving testing particular bit values, manipulating individual input/output line signals, and so forth. Thus, the machine-directed nature of the machine language make it, in many cases, the most useful one for many problems. This situation will probably change as the development of new high level languages designed for microprocessor-oriented problems proceeds.

2.7.1 Characteristics of Instruction Sets

There is, of course, no instruction set that is absolutely typical, just as there is no typical microprocessor. One may, however, examine the different classes of instructions which are found in the majority of contemporary systems. As we perform this examination, we will attempt to comment on the role of each of these classes in program execution, at least in a cursory way.

2.7.1.1 The Programming Model. Before enumerating the different classes of machine language instructions, let us introduce the concept of the *programming model*. This entity, unique to a particular microprocessor, consists of those hardware elements (principally registers) which are directly referred to by elements of the instruction set. Examples of programming model constituents are accumulators, index registers, stack pointers, condition code flags, etc. Figure 2.7-1 is a diagram of

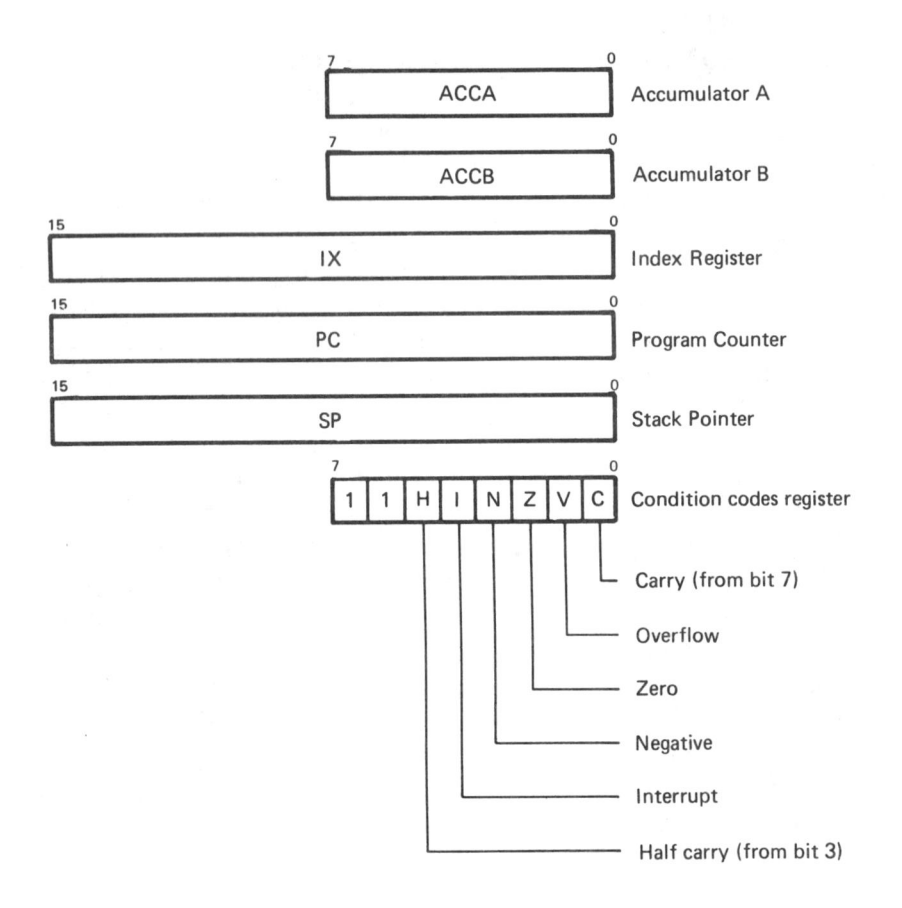

Figure 2.7-1 Motorola 6800 programming model
(Courtesy Motorola Semiconductor Products)

the programming model of the Motorola 6800 microprocessor. It is helpful for the machine language programmer to keep this diagram in mind, since it represents to him his "options" as he characterizes his algorithmic development in machine language form.

2.7.1.2 Classification of Operation Codes. The various types of instructions provided in microcomputers can be catagorized into the following groups:

1. Data Movement
2. Arithmetic
3. Logical
4. Shift/Rotate
5. Status-testing
6. Jumps and Branches

2.7.1.2.1 *Data Movement Instructions*:   This instruction type represents probably the most numerous group, both in terms of instruction type and instruction usage. Included are *Load, Store* and *Move* operations which typically specify memory locations and registers which are the source of data and the destination of data. These instructions result in copying or duplicating the data value, i.e., they leave the source value unchanged. In a few systems one may find *Load Negative* or *Load Absolute* instructions which modify data as it is moved. *Push* and *Pop* instructions are also data movement instructions which refer to transfer of data to and from the system stack.

2.7.1.2.2 *Arithmetic Instructions*:   These instructions cause the development of an arithmetic result. Typical operations include *Add, Subtract, Increment*, and *Decrement*. In some cases separate instructions involving carry and borrow values that have been derived from previous operations are implemented, e.g., *Add With Carry, Subtract With Borrow*. Since these operations imply the manipulation of signed numbers, there is typically an implied form of negative representation, e.g., 2's complement with high-order sign bit.

Contemporary microprocessors do not implement more complex arithmetic instructions such as multiply, divide, etc. These operations can, of course be accomplished via the use of subroutines. As bigger and faster LSI units are developed, it is possible that units with the capability for performing these more complex operations in machine language form might appear.

2.7.1.2.3 *Logical Instructions*:   This group of operations is often classified with the arithmetic operations, since they both involve the transformation of two operands into a single result according to some transformation rule. They differ, however, in that the result is produced on a bit-independent basis, with no carry or borrow propagation. Typical operations include *And, Or, Exclusive Or (EXOR)*, and *Complement* (a one-operand operation). Note the difference between the Complement operation, which produces the bit-by-bit logical complement of the operand, and Negate, an arithmetic operation which produces the negative of the operand, which in many cases would be its 2's complement.

Logical instructions are very powerful tools for bit, byte, and character manipulation. Masking, for example, is performed by ANDing the contents of the accumulator (or any other selected register or memory location) with a selected one-zero pattern, typically supplied as an immediate operand. The result is that any bit or combination of bits within the word to be examined can be extracted by this means. For example, by comparing (via use of the EXOR) an eight-bit value to an appropriately chosen bit pattern provided by the program, the pattern identity (in ASCII code, for example) can be found. Many other types of bit manipulation are commonly used.

2.7.1.2.4 *Shift/Rotate Instructions*: A *Shift* instruction causes the selected bit pattern to be displaced one bit position (either right or left). A *Rotate* operation causes the bit pattern to be circularly permuted one bit position (either clockwise or counter-clockwise). In most Shift operations a zero value is inserted in the end bit from which the shift is performed, but in some cases arithmetic shifts are provided. In this latter case, the inserted value is chosen to make the shift correspond to division by two (arithmetic right shift) or multiplication by two (arithmetic left shift). The proper value depends on the sign of the operand to be shifted.

An important feature of many contemporary microprocessor shift/rotate instructions is their ability to involve other elements such as the carry flip-flop. In some cases the carry flip-flop is in the rotation path; in others, it simply receives the shifted value in parallel with the flip-flop at the other end of the register. This type of operation can be useful, for example, in serial-parallel or parallel-serial data conversions. A simple way to transfer the rightmost bit of Register A to Register B is to perform a *Right Shift With Carry* of Register A, followed by a *Left Shift With Carry* of Register B.

Shift instructions also permit transfer of isolated bits into sign and carry flags to facilitate testing of individual bit values. Microprocessors vary as to the variety of Shift/Rotate operations provided, and the absence of certain particular ones can be a significant inconvenience in certain cases.

2.7.1.2.5 *Status-Testing Instructions*: All microprocessors contain flip-flops which are variously called status flags, condition code flip-flops, or simple "flags". The function of these elements is to provide a mechanism for recording the "state" of the system (or of the program under execution). Examples of the most common flags include *Zero*(Z), *Negative* (N), *Carry* (C), and *Overflow* (V). Others frequently encountered include *Auxiliary Carry* (AC), *Breakpoint* (B), *Decimal* (D), *Interrupt Enable* (I), and *Parity* (P). After each instruction execution, it is possible (and often desirable) to determine the state of one or more of these flags, and to base subsequent program activity on this state. There are two classes of instructions which directly involve controlling the states of these flip-flops. Many instructions affect the flag states as they are executed. For example, an Add instruction which results in a carry from the most significant bit position will set the carry flag. One class of instructions function simply to set or clear particular flag flip-flops, e.g., *Set Carry* (SC), *Clear Carry* (CC). An example of a somewhat more subtle type of status-setting instruction is the *Bit Test* (BIT) instruction. When executed, it is essentially a normal AND instruction, causing the flags to be set according to the value produced by such an instruction. The BIT instruction does not, however, actually produce a new logical result, but leaves the original operand value in the accumulator unchanged. This may appear to be a rather useless operation to perform until one realizes that it is almost invariably followed by a conditional test to determine the subsequent program instruction flow. Thus the BIT instruction makes it possible to perform such a test without modifying a particular operand value. The *Compare* (CMP) instruction operates similarly, except that subtraction rather than ANDing is performed.

2.7.1.2.6 *Jumps and Branches*: This class of instruction is an extremely important one, and the particular forms it takes in a given system may significantly influence that system's performance in a given application. The words *Jump* and *Branch* are used somewhat interchangably in various manufacturers' literature. They both refer to an instruction execution which, by reloading the program counter, causes the normal sequential program flow to be modified.

An *unconditional* jump is an instruction which, when it is encountered during program execution, simply causes the program counter to be loaded with a value specified by the address portion of the instruction (see below for a discussion of absolute and relative jumps, both of which can be either conditional or unconditional). A *conditional* jump will result in such a program counter modification only if a condition or set of conditions (as represented by the state of the system flags) is met. Thus we find *Branch Plus* (BPL), *Branch If Not Equal To Zero* (BNE), and *Branch If Equal To Zero* (BEQ) operation codes. In some systems instructions of this type will often be preceded by a Bit Test (BIT) or Compare (CMP) instruction as described in Section 2.7.1.2.5.

An *absolute* jump (or branch) is one which uniquely specifies the address to be loaded into the program counter when the jump is to be made (also *if* it is to be made in the case of a conditional jump). In most contemporary 8-bit microprocessors which have a 16-bit address space, this requires two bytes of memory space in which to store the jump address. To conserve such space, it is common to provide capability for *relative* jumps (or branches). In the MOS Technology 6502 system, for example, all conditional jumps (called *branches* by that manufacturer) contain an 8-bit address quantity. This quantity is an offset which is said to be added to the current program counter value (as a signed number) to produce the location of the next instruction. Thus branches in that system are limited to a 256-address range centered on the current value of the program counter. Because it is sometimes (but not often) most inconvenient to be limited to such a narrow range for program branching, that system also provides an absolute unconditional jump (called Jump by that manufacturer) for those cases where it is needed.

One sometimes finds implementation of still other addressing modes in the set of jump instructions. A *Jump Indirect* instruction, for example, will cause the program counter to be loaded with the address field of the instruction, and the result found at that address will in turn be placed in the program counter and will therefore point to the desired entry point to the program being executed.

A special jump instruction, the *Subroutine Jump*, is also found in the microprocessor reportoire. It is like other jumps in that it results in program counter loading, in this case with the location of the first instruction in the desired subroutine (see Section 2.11), but it also implements the necessary activity associated with achieving subroutine linkage. This, in systems which have a system stack, involves pushing the "old" program counter contents on the stack before loading it with its new value. After the subroutine is executed, the program counter contents is popped off the stack, incremented and placed back in the program counter. Both conditional and unconditional subroutine jumps are found in the various systems.

2.8 MICROPROCESSOR WORD LENGTH

Computer word length has for many years been one of the criteria of comparison betwen competing systems. In simple terms, the longer the basic computer word, the more precise its fundamental data representation, the greater its addressing capability, the more flexible its instruction set, and so forth. Longer words, however, require larger registers, more signal paths, larger memories, and so forth.

General Aspects of Microprocessor-Based Systems   41

In the microprocessor arena, as would be expected, the shorter word lengths came first, and, as larger chips with higher element density became feasible, the word length increased. Four-bit systems, such as the Intel 4004 and 4040, were the first microprocessors. The four-bit data unit lent itself to convenient representation and manipulation of binary-coded (BCD) digits, and such applications as point-of-sale terminals were exploited. Eight-bit systems, such as Intel's 8080, Motorola's 6800, MOS Technology's 6500 series, Fairchild's F-8, Rockwell's PPS-8, and many others, have proliferated in recent years. Their byte-oriented structure lends itself to both BCD and alphanumeric character representation and manipulation, as well as a great variety of control applications. We presently see the appearance of several 12 and 16 bit systems. These would appear to be direct competitors in computational ability to many contemporary minicomputers, and can probably be expected to fulfill the traditional computational and control functions of those systems.

This book will emphasize the 8-bit microprocessor in its examples, because this would appear to be the arena in which the lion's share of applications will exist for some time to come.

2.9 SYMBOLISM IN DIGITAL COMPUTERS

2.9.1 General Discussion

It is very common for us to characterize the principal function of digital computers to be *information-processing.* The result of this activity may of course appear in one of many forms, e.g., throwing a switch, printing a paycheck, turning on a traffic light, performing a set of complex calculations, and many others. In each case, however, the role of the computer within the confines of its own physical boundary is that of manipulation and transformation of symbols representing information in some form.

If we consider the variety of ways that information is symbolically represented in digital computers, we find an extremely large number of diverse methods. At the most fundamental level, it is well known that physical elements capable of symbolic representation of information are most plentiful in two-valued manifestations, and we therefore almost invariably choose such elements as our physical building blocks. Thus we speak of high/low voltage levels, open/closed switch contacts, on/off transistors, etc., as carrying information. Other common elements are magnetic (two directions of magnetization), optical (light or no light), paper (hole or no hole), and capacitance (charged or uncharged).

While it is true that two-valued elements proliferate because of the low discrimination requirement (it is much easier to detect whether voltage is merely high or low than to evaluate its nearness to one of 10 values, for example) there is a more fundamental reason to think of symbolic information representation in a two-valued sense. Shannon, in his development of information theory, defined the fundamental unit of information to be the binary digit, abbreviated *bit*. This definition corresponds closely to Boole's assignment of 1 and 0 values to logical propositions in his development of Boolean algebra. The point is that, no matter how complex the coding or other representation of information may become, it can always be reduced to binary form, and the two-valued physical implementations described above generally result in this reduction's being accomplished at the operational level of the machine.

HEX ASCII TABLE

00	NUL	18	CAN	30	0	48	H	60	`	78	x
01	SOH	19	EM	31	1	49	I	61	a	79	y
02	STX	1A	SUB	32	2	4A	J	62	b	7A	z
03	ETX	1B	ESC	33	3	4B	K	63	c	7B	{
04	EOT	1C	FS	34	4	4C	L	64	d	7C	|
05	ENQ	1D	GS	35	5	4D	M	65	e	7D	}
06	ACK	1E	RS	36	6	4E	N	66	f	7E	~
07	BEL	1F	US	37	7	4F	O	67	g	7F	DEL
08	BS	20	SP	38	8	50	P	68	h		(RUB
09	HT	21	!	39	9	51	Q	69	i		OUT)
0A	LF	22	"	3A	:	52	R	6A	j		
0B	VT	23	#	3B	;	53	S	6B	k		
0C	FF	24	$	3C	<	54	T	6C	l		
0D	CR	25	%	3D	=	55	U	6D	m		
0E	SO	26	&	3E	>	56	V	6E	n		
0F	SI	27	'	3F	?	57	W	6F	o		
10	DLE	28	(	40	@	58	X	70	p		
11	DC1 (X-ON)	29	)	41	A	59	Y	71	q		
12	DC2 (TAPE)	2A	*	42	B	5A	Z	72	r		
13	DC3 (X-OFF)	2B	+	43	C	5B	[	73	s		
14	DC4	2C	'	44	D	5C	\	74	t		
15	NAK	2D	−	45	E	5D	]	75	u		
16	SYN	2E	.	46	F	5E	^ (↑)	76	v		
17	ETB	2F	/	47	G	5F	— (←)	77	w		

Figure 2.9-1 American Standard Code for Information Interchange (ASCII) (Courtesy Intel Corporation)

2.9.2 Numeric and Nonnumeric Information

Because we have followed Boole's example of representing the logical value *True* as a "1" and the logical value *False* as a "0", much of our information representation has a numeric look to it even though it is nonnumeric in nature. This leads many people to overemphasize the handling of numeric information, particularly as it is represented in the binary number system. It is important to distinguish between so-called binary numbers and information quantities represented by binary codes, even though both may appear to us as similar strings of 1's and 0's. As a primary example of nonnumeric information representation, see the table of Figure 2.9-1, which shows the American Standard Code For Information Exchange, ASCII (pronounced "ASKEE"). Note that each of the symbols in the ASCII character set is associated with an eight-bit binary code (including one bit for parity, sometimes omitted). The symbol '8', for example, has an ASCII code representation of 00111000. Even though you and I may, by previous conditioning, think of '8' as a numeric quantity, in this context it is simply a symbol, and thought of as nonnumeric in character.

2.9.3 Positional Notation

There is, of course, a considerable amount of numeric processing in most digital computer systems. Once again, at the fundament operational level of the machine, arithmetic operations are performed on binary quantities in most, though not all, cases. Decimal multiplication, for example, could be performed via a decimal multiplication table stored in memory. Even though the values would be stored in some form of binary code, no binary arithmetic would necessarily be involved.

The binary number system, sometimes called "pure" binary, is often used in the representation of numbers. In this system, the decimal value of the number represented by the string of binary digits

$$b_n b_{n-1} b_{n-2} \ldots b_3 b_2 b_1 b_0 . b_{-1} b_{-2} \ldots b_{-m+1} b_{-m} \qquad 2.9.1$$

is given by the equation

$$N = \text{Value} = b_n 2^n + b_{n-1} 2^{n-1} + \ldots + b_1 2^1 + b_0 2^0$$
$$+ b_{-1} 2^{-1} + b_{-2} 2^{-2} + \ldots + b_{-m} 2^{-m} \qquad 2.9.2$$

Using this expression to evaluate the binary number 11011.101, we would arrive at an answer of 27.625. There is, however, a subtlety involved which should be recognized. Note that, in performing this evaluation, we have produced a value represented in *decimal* form. We do, whether we realize it or not, nearly always default to the decimal system in representing the value of a numerical quantity. This is natural because, in performing the operations which produce this value, we call upon not only our familiarity with decimal representation but also our familiarity with the rules for decimal arithmetic (addition and multiplication in the above example).

The form of Equation 2.9.2 for general number systems is

$$\text{Value} = s_n r^n + s_{n-1} r^{-1} + \ldots + s_1 r + s_0$$
$$+ s_{-1} r^{-1} + s_{-2} r^{-2} + \ldots + s_{-m} r^{-m} \qquad 2.9.3$$

where each s represents one of r distinct symbols, r is the *radix* or *base* of the number system and the separating mark '.' in expression 2.9.1 is called the *radix point*. Equation 2.9.3 affords us a means for converting a number represented in nondecimal positional notation to a value represented in decimal form. Such conversions are commonly necessary, as are conversions from decimal value to nondecimal representation. Such conversions will be discussed and demonstrated in Section 2.9.4.4.

2.9.4 Useful Number Systems

Equation 2.9.2 places no restriction on the choice of radix in representing numeric values. There are, in fact, several radices in common use.

2.9.4.1 Decimal and Binary Representation. Decimal, or radix 10, representation is extremely important for the obvious reason that it is the standard system used by people throughout the world for numeric representation. Pure binary, or radix 2, representation is widely used because it is the most efficient system in terms of two-valued representation of numeric quantities. For example, it is possible to represent 4096 distinct memory addresses with a 12-bit binary number. If decimal address representation were to be used, the same 12-bit address space would only be capable of representing 3 decimal digits (or 3 4-bit binary-coded decimal values), or 1000 distinct addresses. Addresses are indeed numeric quantities, since they participate in arithmetic opera-

General Aspects of Microprocessor-Based Systems 45

tions involving incrementing, decrementing, etc. Thus address calculations represent one very important area in which pure binary numeric representational and manipulative capability is desirable.

2.9.4.2 Octal Representation. The Octal, or base 8, system is commonly used. The reason for its popularity lies in the ease of conversion between pure binary and octal representation. Rewriting Equation 2.9.1 as follows:

$$\text{Value} = (2^2 b_n + 2b_{n-1} + b_{n-2})2^{n-2} + \ldots + (2^2 b_5 + 2b_4 + b_3)2^3$$
$$+ (2^2 b_2 + 2b_1 + b_0) + \ldots$$
$$(n = 2, 5, 8, 11, \text{etc.}) \qquad 2.9.4$$

we see that a conversion from binary to octal can be performed by simply grouping the binary digits into groups of three and independently converting each of these three-bit groups into their decimal equivalents, which are the same as their octal equivalents, since the maximum three-bit binary value is 7. Conversion from octal to binary is simply the reverse process. The motivation for using octal representation rather than binary lies in the improvement in use of space and readability when *human interaction* is involved, such as in preparing machine language programs and in generating printer or console displays.

2.9.4.3 Hexadecimal Representation. The *Hexadecimal*, or radix 16, system is also widely used for many of the same reasons as in the case of the octal system. In this case conversion from binary to hexadecimal (or simply "hex") is performed by grouping the binary string into groups of 4 digits and converting each of these groups into individual hex digits independently. A minor difference between this system and the octal system lies in the fact that conventional decimal symbolism is inadequate to handle the required 16 unique hex digit values, so the decimal values 10 through 15 are represented by alphabetic symbols A through F. Thus the binary number 011001111010 would be converted to hex by grouping it 0110 0111 1010 and converting these groups to values 6 7 A. The same number would be converted to octal form by grouping it 011 001 111 010 and converting these individual groups to 3 1 7 2. The dedicated student can confirm (or disprove) that this same binary number has a decimal value of 1658.

We often find, in a particular system, a use of either octal or hexadecimal representation, but not both. Each of these systems offer the above-stated convenience for dealing with human interaction with pure binary numbers. In eight-bit computer systems, the tendency is toward the use of hexadecimal representation rather than octal representation because the division of eight-bit data quantities and 16-bit addresses into groups of 4 is somewhat more systematic than division into groups of 3. Where octal rather than hex representation is used, it is often because of the dislike for the mixed alphabetic-numeric digit symbols necessary in hex.

2.9.4.4 Conversions Between Number Systems. As stated in the previous section, the principal use of octal and hexadecimal representation is because of ease of conversion to and from pure binary representation. There are occasions, however, when other conversions are desirable, particularly conversions to and from decimal and binary, octal, and hex. Conversion from any of the binary-oriented systems to decimal is probably most easily accomplished by use of Equation 2.9.2. For example,

$$1FA_{16} = 1 \times 16^2 + 15 \times 16 + 10 = 521_{10}$$
$$673_8 = 6 \times 8^2 + 7 \times 8 + 3 = 443_{10}$$

2.9.5

Conversions from decimal to one of the other systems is slightly more trouble for most of us. Probably the easiest approach is to apply some form of iterated division by the radix of the desired system, taking the remainder in each case to be the next most significant digit of the result. For example, to convert 673_{10} to octal,

$673/8 = 84$, with a remainder of $\underline{1}$
$84/8 = 10$, with a remainder of $\underline{4}$
$10/8 = 1$, with a remainder of $\underline{2}$
$1/8 = 0$, with a remainder of $\underline{1}$

ANSWER: $673_{10} = 1241_8$

To convert 673_{10} to hexadecimal,

$673/16 = 42$, with a remainder of $\underline{1}$
$42/16 = 2$, with a remainder of $\underline{10}$ (or $\underline{A}$)
$2/16 = 0$, with a remainder of $\underline{2}$

ANSWER: $673_{10} = 2A1_{16}$

General Aspects of Microprocessor-Based Systems 47

2.10 ARITHMETIC OPERATIONS IN MICROCOMPUTERS

When one attempts to characterize the functions of a computer or computer system, there is a tendency to immediately jump into the capabilities for arithmetic manipulations that the system possesses. This can be misleading, especially for microcomputers, which more often than not have such primary objectives as control, character manipulation, or data-monitoring rather than arithmetic or computational tasks. It is true, however, that even such noncomputational tasks as those mentioned here depend significantly on the ability of the microcomputer system to perform a variety of arithmetic operations. Addition and subtraction are the basic operations normally implemented as part of the instruction set, while the more complex (and less often demanded) arithmetic operations such as multiplication, division, and higher order operations are generally, but not always, implemented via software when needed. Because of the orientation toward character-oriented data, including such numeric structures as long BCD strings, ability to handle end conditions such as carries and borrows is important. Several systems include special instructions which make decimal operations particularly convenient (see Section 2.10.2).

In the remainder of this section, we will discuss some of the general aspects of arithmetic as it is accomplished in typical microcomputer systems.

2.10.1 Representation of Signed Numbers

It should be emphasized immediately that there is a large class of important arithmetic operations which include subtraction but which do not involve signed numbers. Memory addresses, for example, are unsigned, but they participate in a variety of arithmetic manipulations involving both addition and subtraction. The results obtained are, however, invariably unsigned numbers (or at least interpreted as such).

2.10.1.1 Sign Bit. It should be obvious that there are many occasions where the ability to conveniently represent both positive and negative numbers is important. In most microcomputers, like most larger systems, a first step toward achieving this ability is in allocating one of the data bits to represent the sign of the number. By convention, this bit is the leftmost or highest order bit (bit 7 in an 8-bit computer). Also by convention, the sign bit is assigned the value 1 for negative numbers and 0 for positive numbers. As shown in the following sections, the sign bit can be managed as a numeric quantity in many situations.

2.10.1.2 Sign-Magnitude Representation. Representation of *magnitude* of signed numbers is a little more complicated than one might initially believe. There are several options available. The most natural approach would be to follow our normal pattern of letting the sign change but the magnitude remain fixed as a number is negated. This form of representation, called *sign-magnitude* representation, is intuitively satisfying but has a *very severe shortcoming*. Addition of numbers of unlike sign (or subtraction of numbers of like sign) requires the capability to actually subtract magnitudes. Since addition of magnitudes is also necessary in other cases, two separate sets of arithmetic logic, one for addition and one for subtraction, must be provided. To simplify this need, a different method of representation, called *complement* representation, is often used.

2.10.1.3 Complement Representation of Negative Numbers. To illustrate the basic principle involved in complement arithmetic, consider the very simple case of addition of two single-digit decimal numbers with opposite sign, +7 and −4. The answer our hardware should produce is obviously +3. Now let us somewhat mysteriously decide to represent the negative number −4, by its *10's complement*, which is defined as the result obtained by subtracting the magnitude of the number from 10, which in this case produces the result +6. Now, if we further the mystery by *adding* this result (the complement of −4) to +7, we obtain an answer of 3, along with a *carry* from the arithmetic hardware. *Ignoring* this carry momentarily, note that the magnitude produced is the correct one.

Now let us go through similar steps, but reverse the signs for the numbers, i.e., add −7 to +4. Once again observing that the answer is −3, let's go through the same steps. Forming the 10's complement of −7, we obtain +3. Adding this to +4, we obtain a magnitude of 7 and *no carry*. Since the answer we seek is −3, perhaps we are momentarily disappointed, until we realize that the number −3 has as its complement representation a magnitude of 7. Thus the answer we have obtained is the correct one if indeed a negative number is to be represented as the 10's complement of its positive equivalent.

Summarizing the adding process for single-digit decimal numbers with opposite signs:

1. Form the 10's complement of the magnitude of the negative number.
2. Form the sum of the two numbers [using the result of (1)].

General Aspects of Microprocessor-Based Systems **49**

3. If no carry results, the magnitude of the result is the 10's complement of the desired result, which in turn is the proper representation of a negative result, at least in terms of magnitude.
4. If a carry results, the magnitude of the result is the correct one and indicates that a positive result was produced.

This admittedly rather loose description of the principles of complement arithmetic will hopefully give the reader an understanding of the essence of the idea. A more complete treatment, such as the one given by Flores [1], would demonstrate the results obtained when adding numbers of like sign, either positive or negative, are properly developed when complement representation of negative numbers is consistently used. In adding numbers of like signs, of course, there is a danger of *overflow* not present when mixed-sign addition is performed. Also, careful handling of sign bits and carries are necessary to the process.

To resummarize the reason for using complement arithmetic, note that, by using complement representation, addition or subtraction of mixed-sign numbers can be performed with complete generality by using hardware designed only for performing addition. As an aside, we might note that complement representation would also permit the full range of arithmetic operations to be performed if only *subtraction* hardware were supplied. This approach has in fact been used in some computers, but not in any microcomputers, at least at this writing.

2.10.1.4 Complement Arithmetic With Binary Numbers. Extending the idea of complement arithmetic to binary numbers is fairly simple. Just as we formed the 10's complement of a single-digit decimal number, we form the *2's complement* of a multiple-digit binary number by subtracting the magnitude of the number from a value one unit larger than the largest magnitude capable of representation (just as 10 was 1 unit larger than 9, the largest magnitude of a single-digit decimal number). This value (10 in our decimal example), called the *modulus* of the representational system, cannot itself be conveniently represented, so the process of complementation is commonly achieved by subtracting the magnitude from the largest possible result (an all 1's value in the binary case) and incrementing the result. Note that the subtraction requires no arithmetic hardware, only the ability to independently (without carries) toggle (complement) all magnitude bits. The increment is an addition process, of course, and may result in carries being generated and propagated.

2.10.1.5 Handling the Sign Bit Arithmetically.
As a final bit of frosting on the cake, if the sign bit is included along with the magnitude bits, so that it participates in the arithmetic process, all of the above procedures are still valid and the proper sign is produced during all arithmetic operations, except when an overflow condition occurs. This condition represents a failure of any representational system of fixed modulus, and it is the responsibility of the programmer to make allowances for its occurrence.

2.10.1.6 Examples of 2's Complement Arithmetic.
To illustrate the principles of 2's complement addition and subtraction, the following examples are given. In each case the decimal equivalent of each binary number is shown, along with the decimal equivalent of the result. Also, each magnitude is considered as an integer value. The extension to fractional or integer-fraction combinations is quite simple, requiring only the insertion of a binary point at appropriate locations. The $_x$ subscript is used as a separation mark between the sign bit and the magnitude bits as a convenience to the reader and is usually omitted.

Mixed Sign Addition

(a) $\quad \begin{array}{l} 0_x 1101 \ (+13) \\ 1_x 1100 \ (-4) \\ \hline \text{carry} \, 0_x 1001 \ (+9) \end{array}$
$\qquad$
(b) $\quad \begin{array}{l} 0_x 1101 \ (+13) \\ 1_x 1001 \ (-7) \\ \hline \text{carry} \, 0_x 0110 \ (+6) \end{array}$

(c) $\quad \begin{array}{l} 1_x 0011 \ (-13) \\ 0_x 0100 \ (+4) \\ \hline 1_x 0111 \ (-9) \end{array}$
$\qquad$
(d) $\quad \begin{array}{l} 1_x 0011 \ (-13) \\ 0_x 0111 \ (+7) \\ \hline 1_x 1010 \ (-6) \end{array}$

(e) $\quad \begin{array}{l} 0_x 0100 \ (+4) \\ 1_x 1001 \ (-7) \\ \hline 1_x 1101 \ (-3) \end{array}$
$\qquad$
(f) $\quad \begin{array}{l} 1_x 1100 \ (-4) \\ 0_x 0111 \ (+7) \\ \hline 0_x 0011 \ (+3) \end{array}$

Like Sign Addition

(g) $\quad \begin{array}{l} 0_x 0100 \ (+4) \\ 0_x 0111 \ (+7) \\ \hline 0_x 1011 \ (+11) \end{array}$
$\qquad$
(h) $\quad \begin{array}{l} 1_x 1100 \ (-4) \\ 1_x 1001 \ (-7) \\ \hline \text{carry} \, 1_x 0101 \ (-11) \end{array}$

General Aspects of Microprocessor-Based Systems

(i) $\begin{array}{r} 0_x 1101 \ (+13) \\ 0_x 0111 \ (+\ 7) \\ \hline 1_x 0100 \ \text{Overflow, Error} \end{array}$

(j) $\begin{array}{r} 1_x 0011 \ (-13) \\ 1_x 1001 \ (-\ 7) \\ \hline {}^{\text{carry}} 0_x 1100 \ \text{Overflow, Error} \end{array}$

2.10.1.7 1's Complement Arithmetic. As a final point of discussion, we should note that another form of complement arithmetic, the so-called *1's complement* form, is sometimes used. It closely resembles 2's complement form, the difference being in the form of the complement, which is obtained in the same manner as the 2's complement except that the final increment of the complemented magnitude is omitted. This simplifies the complementation process, since all that is required is the toggling (complementing) of all bits, but it complicates the arithmetic requirement by requiring that so-called end corrections be made when an arithmetic process produces a carry from the most significant bit position. This correction process is sometimes called an "end-around carry".

Most microprocessors employ the 2's complement representational algorithm rather than the 1's complement form because of a general speed advantage. Another shortcoming of 1's complement representation is that two representations of the value "zero" exist (so-called positive zero and negative zero).

2.10.2 Decimal Arithmetic in Microcomputers

Although the fundamental arithmetic operations in microcomputers, as in most computers, involve basic binary addition and subtraction, the often-desirable ability to conveniently handle decimal numbers has led to the inclusion of special logic in some systems for conveniently performing decimal operations. In such cases, the basic decimal representation is the *binary-coded decimal* (BCD) code, shown in Table 2.10-1. (Note that other forms of BCD code exist.)

To illustrate the algorithmic structure which must be present to handle addition of BCD numbers, consider the possible results of adding two such 4-bit coded numbers using ordinary binary arithmetic.

1. If the result is less than 10 (1010), it is correct. No carry is generated.
2. If the result is greater than 9 but less than 16 (between 1010 and 1111) the result is improper, being an improper BCD representation. No carry is produced.

TABLE 2.10-1. BCD CODE FOR DECIMAL DIGITS

Decimal Digit	BCD Representation
0	0000
1	0001
2	0010
3	0011
4	0100
5	0101
6	0110
7	0111
8	1000
9	1001
	(1010, 1011, 1100, 1101, 1110, and 1111 are illegal BCD forms)

3. If the result is greater than 15 (1111), it will produce a proper BCD character, but one which is deficient by 6 units. A carry is produced.

Considering these results, what must be the nature of a correction algorithm which produces the correct results in all cases? The following steps are sufficient.

1. Test the result to see if it is a proper BCD character. If it is, test for the presence of a carry. If none, the result is correct. If there is a carry, add 6 units to the result, producing the correct result. Retain the carry for adding to the next most significant result digit.
2. If an improper BCD character has been produced, add 6 units to it. This will have the effect of producing the correct BCD digit representation and also of generating the proper carry, which will be retained as before for adding to the next most significant digit.

2.10.3 Mechanization of Decimal Adjust Feature

The mechanism for providing the type of correction described in the previous section is provided in a number of contemporary microprocessors, including the Intel 8080, the Motorola 6800, and the MOS Technology 6502. Since these are all 8-bit systems, they can handle two

General Aspects of Microprocessor-Based Systems

BCD digits at a time. Two carries are captured, one from each 4-bit "nibble", and the decimal correction as well as carry propagation between nibbles are automatically handled when the decimal logic is invoked.

The decimal correction capability is invoked in different ways in the different systems. In the 8080 and the 6800, a *Decimal Adjust* (DAA) instruction is provided. Each time a pair of BCD digits is added, the DAA instruction is executed to provide the correction. In the 6502, a decimal (D) flag flip-flop is provided, along with instructions to control its state. So long as this flag is set, the decimal correction is applied to arithmetic operations automatically. This latter approach has the effect of reducing instruction count and execution cycles when a significant amount of arithmetic is to be performed, but it can lead to problems if extreme care is not taken to control the state of the flag at all times, particulary during transitions between routines, such as occur during subroutine calls and interrupts.

2.11 INTERRUPTS AND SUBROUTINES

The "normal" mode of program execution is one in which the computer fetches instructions sequentially (or nearly so) from memory, managing this sequential flow by appropriately incrementing the program counter as consecutive program elements (op-codes, address bytes, and immediate operands) are fetched. When the program contains branches or jumps, these are simply handled by substituting new values into the program counter to modify this sequential ordering.

2.11.1 Subroutine Basics

The concept of a *subroutine* is associated with the idea that, once having generated a program which produces a useful result of some general potential use, it is often efficient to make this program available for general use by other programs without inserting a full-blown copy into these other programs. Instead, a program wishing to use the subroutine may *pass control* to the subroutine, which in simple terms means that the program counter is set to a value which directs the computer to fetch its next op-code from the starting location of the subroutine. This transfer of control is essentially the same as that which occurs in ordinary jumps. Since the subroutine is written for general use, however, it cannot itself contain specific "return" information which directs the program flow back to the calling program upon subroutine completion. Thus the computer must provide a mechanism for handling *subroutine linkage*. The common approach here is to provide a special type of jump instruction, the *Subroutine Jump* (JSR is a common mnemonic), which, before replacing the contents of the program counter with the intial subroutine location, stores away the previous program counter value in some safe place known to the subroutine. The subroutine itself is then terminated with another specially provided instruction, the *Subroutine Return* (RTS). Its function is simply to go to this safe place, find the old program counter value, and place it in the program counter, effectively transferring control to the calling program.

2.11.2 Stack Management of Subroutine Linkage

In the great majority of contemporary microprocessors, a special data structure called a *stack* is automatically maintained by the system. One of the important functions of this system element is to serve as a repository for program counter values in managing subroutine linkage, i.e., to function as the "safe place" mentioned in the previous section. Before demonstrating how the stack performs this function, we will describe the stack a little more carefully.

2.11.3 Stack Principles

A stack, sometimes called a *pushdown list* or *LIFO* (Last-in, First-out) structure, is a variable-size collection of memory locations. Items may be placed on the stack (*pushed*) and retrieved from the stack (*popped*). The simple rule that governs retrieval of an item from the stack is that the item retrieved is the last previous one pushed. The stack can contain a number of items ranging from zero to some arbitrary value whch reflects physical constraints of the system, but the system maintains no record of this size, contenting itself with monitoring the location of the top of the stack, where items are to be pushed and popped. A special register called a *stack pointer* is provided for this monitoring function. As items are pushed and popped, either automatically by the system or by specially provided *Push* and *Pop* instructions, the stack pointer is appropriately incremented and decremented.

We intuitively like to think of the stack as growing *upward* as items are added to it, and of shrinking *downward* as items are deleted. In particular implementations, however, we may find the stack pointer incremented during pop operations and decremented during push operations, which implies stack growth opposite to our intuitive concept. This should not greatly concern us, however, since it reflects only a somewhat arbitrary decision of the system designer to permit downward stack growth rather than upward stack growth. In some cases this decision reflects a choice relative to a means for detecting stack growth which is excessive, i.e., which encroaches on memory space not properly its domain.

2.11.4 Nested Subroutines

Returning now to the concept of subroutine linkage, the JSR instruction may now be seen to simply perform a Push of program counter contents before jumping to the subroutine. When the RTS instruction is encountered, it must simply perform the Pop operation, returning the old program counter value saved on the stack to the program counter. The stack implementation enables considerably more sophisticated control of program flow to be conveniently and reliably accomplished, because it allows subroutines to call other subroutines, resulting in *subroutine nesting*. If Subroutine 1 calls Subroutine 2, the program counter (PC) value following the JSR instruction in Subroutine 1 is simply pushed onto the stack before exiting to Subroutine 2. At that point at least two PC values lie on the stack, since the call of Subroutine 1 resulted in a previous push of program counter contents. The LIFO rule of the stack, however, ensures that the PC values will be retrieved in proper order to ensure orderly program flow.

2.11.5 Other Stack Features

There are still more sophisticated principles involved in the use of the stack in managing subroutine linkage. For example, a subroutine, if properly written, can be *reentrant*, meaning that it can call itself. Another useful feature of the stack is its ability to store items other than PC values. For example, an important activity which often must be performed is the preservation of so-called *program state* (see Section 2.11.7.3). This is ordinarily not a great problem in managing subroutines, but it does appear in a limited sort of way. Suppose that a subroutine is to develop a result which involves the use of the X Index Register. This register may, when the subroutine is called, contain a value which is of some importance to the ultimate goal of the calling program. The subroutine may be written in such a way as to store away (*save*) the contents of X upon entry, use X in developing the desired result, and, just before return, restore X to its old value. The stack is a very convenient repository for X contents in such a case, requiring only that Push and Pop operations be properly located in the subroutine. A little thought will convince the worrier that the use of the stack for such temporary data storage in no way compromises its conceptual ability to manage nested subroutines, although of course it may require that more space be allocated in memory for stack expansion.

2.11.6 Stack Mechanization

The actual mechanization of the stack varies from system to system. As mentioned in Section 2.11.3, in some cases the stack grows upward in memory space, while in others it grows downward. Another variation is sometimes found in that the stack pointer may point at the top entry in the stack or at the next empty location above this top entry. This simply defines the "rest state" of the stack in one case to be prepared for a push, while in the other case to be prepared for a pop. There is little to choose between the two approaches.

A stack feature which could be important in some cases is the capacity of the stack pointer for movement throughout memory space. As an example, the MOS Technology 6502 microprocessor has an 8-bit stack pointer, which restricts stack storage to a 256-address range (page 1 in that system). Since even extreme usage of nested subroutines would usually not require more stack capacity than this, this limitation is not terribly important in many cases. Other systems using 16-bit stack pointers (Intel 8080, Motorola 6800) do exist, however, and they have as a result considerably expanded capability for managing *multiple* stacks, since the stack pointer can be directed anywhere in memory space.

2.11.7 Interrupt-Handling in Microprocessors

The concept of *program interrupt* is closely related to that of subroutine management, since both involve control of program flow from some program to a separate program (the subroutine or interrupt routine) and back again. There are, however, some very important differences which will be pointed out in this section.

2.11.7.1 General Principles. First, let's try to construct an intuitive image of the basic concept of program interrupt. Suppose we wish to configure a system which will control a display, updating that display once per second as a result of data read during each interval. We could thus prepare a data collection and display control program which could accomplish this result. The question is, how is the control of the

General Aspects of Microprocessor-Based Systems **57**

one-second sampling interval to be accomplished? Certainly there must be some source of timing informatin, or clock, whose current value can be monitored in some sense. Our program could periodically read the contents of this clock, evaluate whether the required one-second interval has elapsed, and return to an appropriate entry point which is dependent on this evaluation. Let us, however, postulate a somewhat different approach to this problem. We will provide the clock system with the capability for supplying a signal to the computer when each one-second interval has elapsed. We wish for the computer to receive this signal, to *interrupt* its activity (display refresh) and to read the data used to update the display. When this updating is accomplished, we wish for the display refresh activity to resume and to continue until the next update interval.

What additional requirements does the desire for this sort of operation place on the computer system?

1. The computer must be able to recognize an external request for service (in this case the signal from the clock), commonly called an *Interrupt Request*.
2. Upon receiving the interrupt request, the computer must have capability for temporarily suspending its previous activity and initiating new activity corresponding to the demands of the requesting device.
3. Upon completion of the requested task, the computer must have capability for restoration of previous program state and resumption of that program's desired activity.

Automatic capability for managing this general type of activity is provided with many contemporary microprocessor systems, forming so-called *interrupt-handling systems*. Before mentioning the details and variations involved in typical cases, we will discuss some of the conceptual requirements of an interrupt-handling system.

2.11.7.2 Comparison of Subroutine and Interrupt Handling. First let us take note of the similarity of the interrupt-handling requirement to the subroutine-handling requirement. In both cases it is desired to temporarily suspend the activity of one program and to initiate the activity of another, retaining the capability for return to the suspended program. This similarity suggests that a similar linkage mechanism can be used, and that is in fact quite true. The system stack can be used to manage both subroutine and interrupt routine linkage. There are, however, at least two important differences between subroutine handling and interrupt handling. First, note that a subroutine is called via a regular machine instruction (JSR), and the transition can be handled in an orderly way, under the synchronized control of the central processor's clock. The interrupt request, since it is externally generated, is unsynchronized with the processor clock and could, if recognized indiscriminately, interfere with detailed execution of the interrupted instruction. Thus, no external interrupt requests will be accepted by the computer during such execution. To accomplish proper synchronization, it is customary for the processor to test its interrupt input after completion of execution of each instruction. If no request has been lodged, an orderly transition of control will be initiated.

A second important difference between interrupt-handling and subroutine-handling results from the fact that, whereas jumps to subroutines occur at predictable points in the calling program, a jump to an interrupt service routine can occur after any instruction, representing a far less predictable situation as far as the state of the suspended program is concerned. Thus, it is common to require that, when an interrupt request is honored, that the entire state of the interrupted program be saved so that a guaranteed resumption of that program can be made.

2.11.7.3 The Concept of Program State. What are the elements which completely define the program state? We are aided by the fact that program interruption is permitted only between instruction execution cycles, since the program state is much more clearly defined at those points. Two important elements which comprise much state information are, as before, the current program counter contents (PC), and the state of the condition flags which contain information relative to the result produced by the program step just completed. This set of flip-flops collectively comprise the *Program Status* (PS) register. Nearly all microprocessors in contemporary use stack the PC and PS values when honoring an interrupt request. Note that a special *Return From Interrupt* (RTI) instruction is needed for terminating interrupt-handling routines. It resembles the RTS instruction except that it unstacks both PC and PS values, placing them in their appropriate registers upon resumption of normal processing.

There is considerably more information which is needed to fully define program state. The contents of all system registers (accumulators, index registers, etc.) must be saved if the interrupted program is to properly resume. In some systems (Motorola 6800, for example) this information is also stacked automatically when an interrupt is received and unstacked automatically when the RTI instruction is executed. In others (MOS 6502 and Intel 8080) this is not done, so that the service routine itself must contain steps which perform this *register-save* and *register-restore* operation if it is to be done. It might appear at first glance that the automatic approach is always to be preferred, but we should note that all that stacking and unstacking is quite time-consuming and is sometimes unnecessary for service routines which are so simple as to result in no modification of system registers. As always, the preferred approach depends on the problem at hand.

2.11.7.4 Interrupt Masking. Going back to our original example of an interrupt-driven system, i.e., the display management system, let's postulate that the display management program has certain portions which, if interrupted, would irretrievably result in subsequent errors. During the intervals that this portion of the main program is running, we wish to *mask* interrupt requests so that they are ignored. Many contemporary systems provide this sort of capability in the form of an *Enable Interrupt* flip-flop which, when set (by a specially provided instruction) permits recognition of interrupts but, when cleared, locks them out. Thus, a program segment not to be interrupted can be bounded by instructions which clear and set the Enable Interrupt flag.

2.11.7.5 Multiple Interrupt Inputs. Some microprocessors provide more than one interrupt input, permitting masking of some requests and no masking of others. A nonmaskable interrupt (NMI) input is used for those requests which are either too important to permit masking, or of a nature which will result in no disturbance of program state if the request is honored. An example of the first type of request is found in the KIM-1 microcomputer. The NMI input is used there to implement both STOP and SINGLE-STEP functions. If the IRQ (normal maskable interrupt) input were used for these functions, they would be inoperative when the program had caused the interrupt system to be locked out. An example of the second type of request is found in the use of so-called *Direct Memory Access* (DMA) techniques for transferring data at high speed from external sources to memory, bypassing the central processor. Since such techniques only require the processor to inhibit its usage of the address and data busses, leaving the processor register states unaffected, it is common to permit such access on a nonmasked basis.

2.11.7.6 Interrupt Priority. The above discussion of maskable and unmaskable interrupt inputs implies one type of priority structure, in that certain devices may have uninhibited access to the processor while others gain such access only on a selective basis. Another type of priority structure is present where multiple devices compete for interrupt service at a common interrupt input. There are a considerable number of rather subtle considerations involving the establishment of a priority policy where such contention exists, and the reader is referred to the literature for a complete description. We will say that most contemporary microprocessors require the addition of significant external logic to manage priority in any sophisticated way. Semiconductor manufacturers have designed special-purpose chips which provide this extended capability.

Still another aspect of interrupt priority lies in the relative ability of a requesting device to obtain service by interrupting a service routine currently serving another device. Note that this is a little different than the management of priority among devices competing for service at a common interrupt input.

2.11.7.7 Interrupt Routine Linkage. We have to this point ignored one of the central features of any interrupt-handling system, which is the mechanism whereby the requested service routine is initiated. Since the response to an interrupt request is only to initiate the execution of a program appropriate to the needs of the requesting device, the problem is one of appropriately setting the program counter, assuming of course that the desired program is in memory.

In typical systems, each of the separate types of interrupts (masked, unmasked, reset, etc.) is associated with a unique service routine. The beginning location of each of these routines is stored at a reserved location in memory and automatically loaded into the program counter when the interrupt is serviced. Since these reserved addresses are pointers to the initial points in the service routines, they are often called *Interrupt Vectors*. Their actual position in memory space varies from processor type to processor type.

In those systems where multiple devices are to be served by a single interrupt input, a common service routine will be entered when any one of these devices gains access via an interrupt request. If the service requirements of the devices are different, this common routine might *poll* or sequentially test the devices in turn to find the one whose request is to be honored, at which time a branch to its routine would be made.

General Aspects of Microprocessor-Based Systems 61

2.12 TECHNOLOGICAL FACTORS IN MICROPROCESSORS

The subject of semiconductor technology is a weighty one indeed, and this book will make no attempt to comprehensively describe all or even a high percentage of the technological principles which apply to the design and fabrication of microprocessors and associated LSI circuitry. There are certain overall considerations which should be at least casually understood by the engineer wishing to employ such elements, and this section represents an attempt to provide some insight into these matters.

2.12.1 General Aspects of LSI Design

The development of LSI technology represents a truly marvelous chapter in the history of the engineering art. From the inception of the point-contact transistor in the 1940's, through the subsequent development of junction transistors, integrated circuits, medium-scale integrated circuits (MSI circuits), to the present LSI units comprised of literally tens of thousands of individual interconnected transistors, the rate of development has been literally staggering. Furthermore, projections of still more dramatic leaps forward within years to come imply that this rate is maintaining its level or even increasing. Throughout this period, certain factors have constrained and influenced development. Among those which have been particularly important are yield, chip size, element density, and partitioning. All these factors are interrelated, and the following sections will discuss them in simple terms and describe their influence on LSI development.

2.12.1.1 Process Yield. The basic economic advantage of the integrated circuit at any level, small, medium, or large, depends on the ability to mass-produce many units in one set of processing steps. Thus a given set of masking, diffusion, and metallization processes will produce a relatively large (perhaps 2 or 3 inches in diameter) wafer on which have been formed some fairly large number of identical circuits. The *yield* of a particular process is defined to be the percentage of those identical units which are found to be functional during subsequent testing.

What value of yield must be attained in a cost-effective process? The only general answer which can be given is that the yield must be greater than zero. For simple circuits, such as single transistors or gates, the yield must be high, perhaps greater than 90%. For LSI units such as microprocessors a yield of 1% might be cause for great celebration in certain cases. The yield will tend to be lower for more complex units than for simple ones, but, generally speaking, not in proportion to the level of complexity. In a well-controlled process, the percentage of faulty units will depend heavily on the size of the final chip, as described in the next section.

2.12.1.2 Chip Size. There is a natural tendency to increase chip size as circuitry complexity increases, but the increase in size is often not in proportion to increase in complexity because of such factors as element density (see next section) and "overhead" which accompanies the necessity for providing rather large bonding areas for external interconnections regardless of circuit complexity. If one considers, however, that a given wafer will embody scattered crystalline defects, which in turn will induce component failures, then it is clear that, on a purely statistical basis, the chip yield produced from such a wafer will be less for large chips than for smaller ones. In the extreme case, for example, a wafer with crystalline defects every 20 mils over its surface may still produce a yield of 50% or so if used in a process for making 10 mil transistor chips, while only one defect per chip is sufficient to produce a yield of 0% if a large LSI circuit using the entire wafer area is to be produced.

As methods for producing larger wafers with fewer defects are developed, the use of larger and larger chips is economically feasible. Present microprocessors are produced on chips with linear dimensions in the 0.1 to 0.5 inch range.

2.12.1.3 Element Density. If chip size represents a fairly rigid constraint on LSI circuit development, designers must move toward packing more elements into a given chip area if circuit complexity is to be increased. It is in this area that many of the dramatic gains in LSI development have been made. Although this reflects the improvement made in such areas as photomasking, control of diffusion processes, development of isolation and insulation techniques, and innovative interconnection schemes, the greatest single step in the move toward higher density has resulted from the substitution of metal oxide-semiconductor (MOS) transistor technology for the earlier bipolar technology. An MOS transistor, because of simpler structure and fewer processing steps, can be manufactured in a considerably smaller size than a bipolar transistor. This, combined with the favorable characteristics of MOS transistors for use in a *dynamic* mode of operation (see Section 2.12.2), makes that technology a much more favorable candidate for use in single-chip microprocessors than bipolar technology. The tradeoff lies in the lower-performance characteristics of MOS elements in the areas of device switching speed and drive and interface capability.

There is a relatively new form of bipolar technology, called *integrated-injection logic* (I^2L), which achieves heretofore unattainable density in the bipolar integrated circuit. This approach promises to offer its own particular set of benefits, which include performance near that of conventional bipolar circuits at density and power levels associated with MOS circuits. This low-power capability in fact is most important in certain applications such as wristwatch and camera units. Also note that a particular type of MOS technology called *complementary* MOS, or CMOS, is often used in such low-power systems.

2.12.1.4 LSI Partitioning. As it becomes feasible to produce relatively complex logical systems, considerations regarding market volume of such units become of great importance. Even though per-unit cost of an LSI unit may be very low in the production environment, initial tooling and setup costs for each unique circuit type are quite considerable, in some cases tens or hundreds of thousands of dollars. Thus if the circuit produced is to achieve a low per-unit cost, it must be in demand on a high-volume basis. The *partitioning* decision thus must reflect some judgment with respect to the market demand for the unit chosen. There are those who only a few years ago saw no future in the single-chip computer element because of their feeling that the prospective market volume could never reach the level required to justify setup costs. Even though they appear to have been short-sighted, it is probably true that the microprocessor element itself, in the typical case, will return less income to the manufacturer than the associated memory chips which the use of the microprocessor necessitate. Memory units are in fact ideal LSI elements, because they represent high-volume usage and the type of logical regularity that lends itself to LSI design technique.

The requirement that an LSI unit be partitioned for high-volume sales is reflected in the character of many elements now available on the market. We find a great tendency toward "programmable" modules which can be configured into many different applications, and which in any single application make use of, in many cases, only a fraction of their total logical capability.

2.12.2 Dynamic Versus Static Systems

In the context of microprocessors and their associated units such as memory chips, etc., a *static* unit is one whose *memory function*, as embodied not only in units specifically designated as memories, but in all registers, flags, etc., is provided by conventional semiconductor flip-flops. Those familiar with flip-flop operation will know that even the simplest ones require at least two transistors for successful implementation, and sometimes, if input and output gating is provided, a much larger number of transistors is used in a single flip-flop. It is true, however, that the physical characteristics of a simple MOS field-effect transistor, which include relatively high gate capacitance and input impedance, make it technically feasible to store information in this gate capacitance for a time interval of a few milliseconds before the charge on the gate leaks off. Thus a single transistor can be held "on" by stored charge for an interval which is fairly long by comparison to clock rate. This single transistor can thus perform the function of a flip-flop, if provision is made to "refresh" its stored information periodically (i.e., to add lost charge). An LSI unit which uses such simple devices for information storage is said to be a *dynamic* device. The advantage of such a device is the capacity for element density and associated logical complexity that comes with the great reduction in transistor count. The disadvantage is of course the refresh requirement, which at first glance appears to be considerable. As usual, however, the LSI designers have come to the rescue. Refresh logic is easily implemented in contemporary microprocessors using dynamic storage, and is essentially invisible to the user. Special refresh systems for handling dynamic memories are also provided by the LSI manufacturers. Some microprocessors, such as the Zilog Z-80, provide a special set of output signals designed for refreshing dynamic memories.

Conventional bipolar technology does not lend itself to dynamic operation, and the effect is seen in the greatly reduced logical complexity currently available in LSI systems using that technology.

2.12.3 Bipolar Microprocessors

The advantages of MOS technology relative to element density and the associated dynamic operating mode make this approach the most attractive one for the bulk of popular microprocessor systems, even though performance (speed) is less than that attained in bipolar systems. There is a class of bipolar LSI units which are configured as bit-slice processors and which have application to higher-performance requirements.

General Aspects of Microprocessor-Based Systems 65

A bit-slice unit typically has 2 or perhaps 4 flip-flops per processor register. All interconnections for information transfer among registers on the chip and laterally to other identical chips (such as carry signals and shifting paths) are also provided. Using such units, it is quite feasible to construct processors which handle long operands, typically 16 or 32 bits in length. This expanded word length capability fits in nicely with the higher-performance application areas where the bit-slice units would be most often used.

In MOS microprocessors it is customary for sophisticated control (as reflected in the instruction set provided) to be integrated on the microprocessor chip. The control function, however, does not lend itself to bit-slice partitioning, and so it is customary to include only very primitive control capability on the bit-slice unit. The more sophisticated level of control represented by the conventional assembler-language instruction set is separately provided by other LSI units, typically in a microprogrammed mode. While the opportunity to "tailor" an instruction set to a particular application is present in those systems which offer microprogramming as a system feature, it also represents a considerable expansion of the system design problem.

2.12.4 The Special Role of TTL Bipolar Logic

While, for reasons given in Section 2.11, bipolar technology is not dominant in the microprocessor domain, there is an important role to be played by bipolar elements, principally in the area of system interfacing. The high-impedance, low-power nature of MOS elements that suits them so well in their role as LSI building blocks, is in fact a limitation in the interface area, where the capability for driving multiple inputs or long lines with significant capacitance must exist.

The particular circuit family which has become entrenched as the dominant one in the small and medium-scale integrated circuit market is known as *Transistor-Transistor Logic* (TTL or T^2L). A diagram of the classic TTL NAND circuit is given in Figure. 2.12-1, which shows the characteristic multiple-emitter input configuration and the "totem-pole" output configuration characteristic of such circuits. This input configuration results in high noise immunity, or ability to withstand electrical interference at the input terminals, while the output configuration provides excellent drive capability at respectable speed. There are several subcategories of logical elements within the TTL family, including low-power TTL (which is somewhat slower than standard TTL), and Schottky TTL (which uses Schottky-barrier diodes to reduce storage-time effects in the transistors).

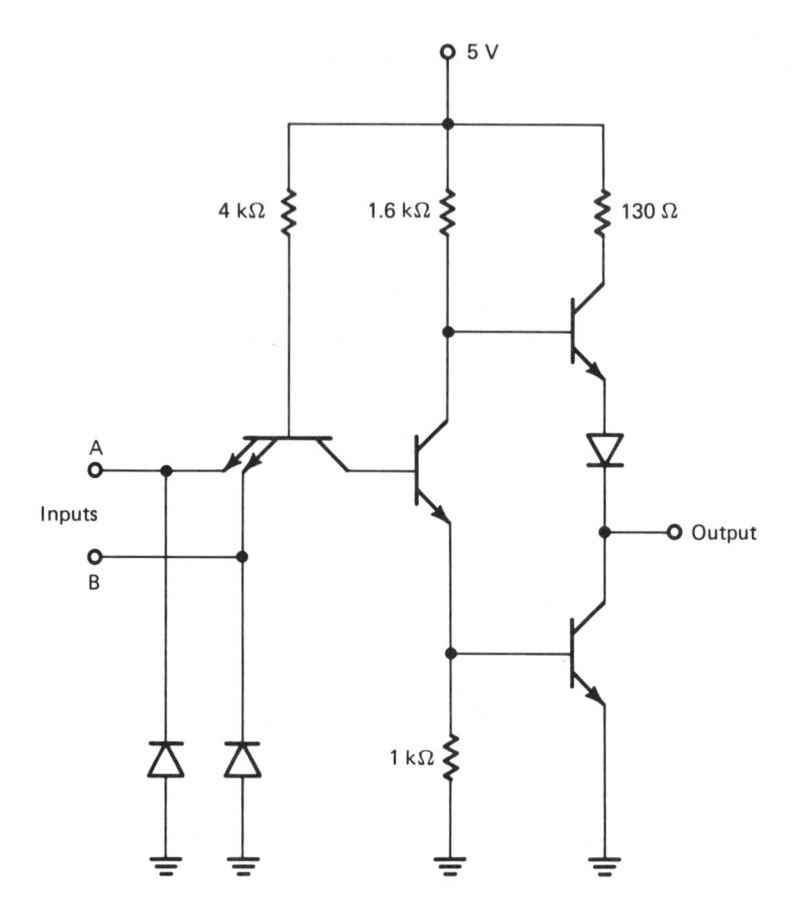

Figure 2.12-1 Standard TTL NAND gate

Because it offers an excellent combination of high speed, modest power consumption, and high noise immunity, the TTL logic family dominates the bipolar logic market. It is natural that, as medium-scale integration (MSI) units have been developed, they have been based on TTL designs. Thus we find such MSI units as counters, buffers, decoders, multiplexers, etc. available in great abundance at low cost, and implemented in TTL form. In a typical microcomputer system it is often necessary to support the microprocessor chip with some amount of external logic, and since TTL offers the best options in the MSI area, considerable effort is spent in making it convenient to interface MOS

LSI units with TTL MSI units. A rundown of a microprocessor manufacturer's catalog of available parts will enumerate a variety of special units specially fabricated to yield this convenience.

The basic incompatability between most MOS units and TTL units lies in the inability of standard TTL to provide adequate drive levels to the standard MOS inputs, and the inadequate current-sinking capability of MOS transistors which limits their capability to drive TTL inputs. Achievement of a proper interface requires either special processing steps during manufacture of the microprocessor chip or special chips designed for interfacing with the microprocessor.

BIBLIOGRAPHY

1. Flores, Ivan, *The Logic of Computer Arithmetic*, Prentice Hall, Englewood Cliffs, New Jersey, 1963.

PROBLEMS

1. Explain why the Microcontroller is likely to require an external control Read Only Memory separate from the microcontroller chip.
2. The Microcontroller is capable of expansion to large word lengths. What factors will establish an upper limit?
3. Make a list of 10 possible applications for microcomputers. Try to think of some which do not yet exist.
4. Make a list of 10 applications which would not be able to use a microcomputer.
5. Take any one of the 10 items you listed in Problem 3 and make a list of 10 product enhancement features which use of a microcomputer would allow.
6. Repeat Problem 5 for a telephone answering machine.
7. Repeat Problem 5 for a wastebasket.
8. Is is possible to amend or alter the microcode of a typical non-bit-slice microcomputer? Be specific (if possible).
9. Make a list of potential advantages and disadvantages of both memory-mapped and isolated I/O.

10. Refer to Section 2.4. In a typical microcomputer would it be possible to operate upon address information as if it were data information? In other words, can we do dynamic address modification of our program?
11. Make a flow diagram of the Fetch-Execute cycle as described in Section 2.4.
12. What alternatives exist to the use of a stack pointer?
13. State in your own words the difference between Jump, Jump to subroutine, and Branch instructions?

    subroutine, and Branch instructions.
14. What are positive logic and negative logic?
15. Prove that a positive logic NAND gate is electrically and logically equivalent to a negative logic NOR gate.
16. List the sequence of hexadecimal numbers which represent your entire name, if ASCII encoded.
17. Express the first eight prime numbers in binary, ternary, octal, decimal, and hexadecimal form.
18. For your pocket calculator write a flow diagram for conversion between binary, octal, decimal, and hecadecimal number representation.
19. Will the following subroutine work?

	JSR	A
A	JSR	B
B	JSR	C
C	RTS	

20. What is the limit for nesting of subroutines in the MOS Technology 6502? Why?
21. List five applications which might involve interrupt handling in a microprocessor.
22. What alternatives exist to DMA data transfer?
23. If an integrated circuit die is known to have 65,536 bits of storage, is 250 mils on each side, and has 15% overhead for drivers and decoders, what is the size of each storage element (assuming square geometry)? Compare this to the thickness of this paper.

3

THE MCS6502 MICROPROCESSOR AND PERIPHERAL PARTS

3.1 INTRODUCTION TO MCS6502

3.1.1 General Characteristics

As discussed in Chapter 1, this book will emphasize the use of the MCS6502 microprocessor. As of mid-year 1978 there are over 30 other microprocessors which could have been chosen, but the availability of the KIM microcomputer, based upon the MCS6502 microprocessor, made it an extremely attractive choice for educational use. This microprocessor is manufactured by MOS Technology and is second-sourced by Synertek and Rockwell. Experience has shown that the transition by the user to other available microprocessors is an easy step.

This chapter will discuss only the microprocessor, although in order to make a functional microcomputer we also need varying amounts of memory and input/output (I/O) parts. The 6502 interacts with these other parts in the three bus configuration mentioned in Section 2.3. Some microprocessor chips reflect the advancement of technology by providing such enhancements as expanded instruction sets or additional on-chip functions such as program memory, data memory, or timer/counter units. Such functions are provided in the case of the MCS6500 family by a separate IC which is called the MCS6530. This part has 1K bytes of ROM, 64 bytes of RWM, two programmable 8-bit I/O ports, and a programmable timer. The combination of these two parts make it possible to fabricate a two-chip microcomputer. Figure 3.1.1-1 is a photograph of an MCS6502 and an MCS 6530.

Figure 3.1.1-1 MOS Technology MCS6502 microprocessor element (bottom) and MCS6530 peripheral interface element (top)

3.1.2 Specifications

The salient characteristics of the MCS6502 microprocessor are summarized as follows:

1. Single 5 volt power supply
2. Byte-oriented structure
3. 151 op codes
4. Decimal or binary arithmetic modes
5. Seven addressing modes
6. True indexing
7. Stack pointer
8. Two interrupt levels
9. 65K address range
10. Integral clock circuit

1. **Single 5 volt supply.** There are several popular fabrication methods for integrated circuits, including N-MOS, P-MOS, C-MOS, and bipolar. Each of these methods of fabrication has variations in forming the elements, such as active devices, resistors, transmission gates, etc. Because of the popularity and availability of TTL bipolar parts (see Section 2.12.4), which use a 5 volt power supply, there is a strong desire to center upon microprocessor parts which use the same supply. At the present time N-MOS fabrication using ion-implant and depletion loads seems to be the developing industry standard.

2. **Byte-oriented structure.** The data bus is 8 bits wide, making it convenient to manipulate data configured as 8-bit bytes.

3. **151 operation codes.** Sections 3.4 and 3.5 discuss the MCS6502 operation codes in detail. Typical operations are logical data operations, register manipulations, comparison, subroutine calls, conditional branches, and unconditional jumps.

4. **Decimal or binary arithmetic modes.** One bit of the Processor Status Register (P Register) is the decimal mode bit. When this bit is set, add and subtract operations involving the Arithmetic Logic Unit (ALU) part of the microprocessor will be adjusted to provide the correct decimal result, assuming binary-coded decimal numeric representation (see Section 2.10). For example, if the accumulator contained $(001\ 1001)_2 = (19)_{16}$ and the immediate value of $(0000\ 0001)_2$ with carry $= \emptyset$ were added, the result would be $(0010\ 0000)_2 = (20)_{16}$. In other words each half of the byte, or nibble, would be treated as a BCD value. It is important to note that Increment and Decrement instructions do not use the ALU and hence are not decimal adjusted. Compared to the previous example, incrementing $(19)_{16}$ would result in $(1A)_{16}$, regardless of the value of the D bit in the P register.

5. **Seven addressing modes.** Among the most important features of any computer is the set of addressing modes possible. We will explore these modes in great detail in Section 3.4. (Also see Section 2.6.) The principal modes of addressing are: Absolute; Immediate; Relative; Zero page; Indirect; Indexed; and Implied. (There are variations and combinations which result in the manufacturer's stated thirteen addressing modes.)

6. True indexing. One of the addressing modes of considerable importance is indexing. Some microprocessors claim to have index registers but do not in fact provide capability for *true* indexing (see Section 2.6.2.6). As noted in Section 2.3.2, the program is usually contained in Read-only memory (ROM), and hence cannot be altered. We often want to manipulate arrays of data in consecutive locations in memory but cannot alter the address part of an instruction stored in ROM. True indexing implies that the contents of an index register and the fixed address part of an instruction are combined to form an effective address. However, neither the index register contents nor the instruction are modified by the operation. Subsequent incrementing or decrementing of the index register allows access to many locations in memory space.

7. Stack pointer. In some of the operations done by the microprocessor some temporary storage is required. For example, when a subroutine is called we need to save the value of the Program Counter (PC) so that we know where to return. The MCS6502, like many other microprocessors, uses an area of Read-Write-Memory (RWM) for this function. This area in RWM is commonly called the *stack* (see Sections 2.5.5 and 2.11.3). A single register on the microprocessor chip designates one location in this area, i.e., it points to a location in the stack and, hence, is called the Stack Pointer (S). An error frequently made by the novice programmer is failure to initialize S so that it points to a region in memory space populated by Read/Write Memory.

8. Two interrupt levels. The concept and specifics of MCS6502 interrupt handling will be expounded upon in Section 3.6 (see also Section 2.1.7 and Appendix B). There are two pins in the 6502 which may cause an interrupt, Interrupt Request ($\overline{IRQ}$), and Nonmaskable Interrupt ($\overline{NMI}$). Since positive logic is assumed throughout, and a low signal level indicates that the interrupt condition exists, the line over each signal name signifies that it is an "active low" signal (i.e., NOT NMI or complement NMI).

9. 65K address range. The MCS6502 has 16 of its 40 pins devoted to address specification. Therefore, without any "tricks" the address range is 2^{16} or 65536. This address range is referred to as representing 65K locations (K = 1024). Many applications do not require this much address range, and since the pinouts cost disproportionately, other related microprocessor chips in 28 pin packages are available in the MCS6500 family. These chips are designated the MCS6503, 4, and 5 and have address ranges of 4K and 8K. Internally, the same die is used, but fewer address lines are bonded out. Although many users cannot afford to fill a full complement of memory space, simple addition of output ports for bank switching facilitates memory expansion to very large address ranges. One 8 bit output port could allow undecoded bank selection of 8 banks of 65K, or decoded bank selection of 256 banks of 65K each.

10. Integral clock circuit. All microprocessors require some type of clock circuit to coordinate the flow of data. Family members MCS6502 through MCS6505 contain necessary clock circuitry, except for one resistor and one capacitor plus an optional crystal. Circuit details of the connections are found in Section 3.6.

3.2 PROGRAMMING MODEL

Figure 3.2-1 gives the programming model of the MCS6502, as well as of the other family members presently in existence and envisioned. A natural evolutionary extension of this family would be a 16-bit unit. It is likely that the manufacturer would attempt to achieve software compatability with the existing units if such a unit were developed.

As discussed in Section 2.7, the programming model contains only those system elements which the programmer can directly control via the use of the instruction set.

3.3 DATA PATHS

Figure 3.3-1 shows the paths which data may take, and the mnemonics of the op codes for each permitted transfer. Memory and Stack are shown separately for simplicity, although the stack is contained in ordinary memory space. Careful handling of the Stack Pointer and memory management is required to prevent overlapping stack and data. Sometimes cleverly organized programs take advantage of the ability to read or write into the stack or pass data via the stack using nonstack operations.

A detailed drawing of the internal architecture of the MCS6502 is shown in Fig. 3.3-2. Note particularly the internal address and data bus, and those components which have access to them.

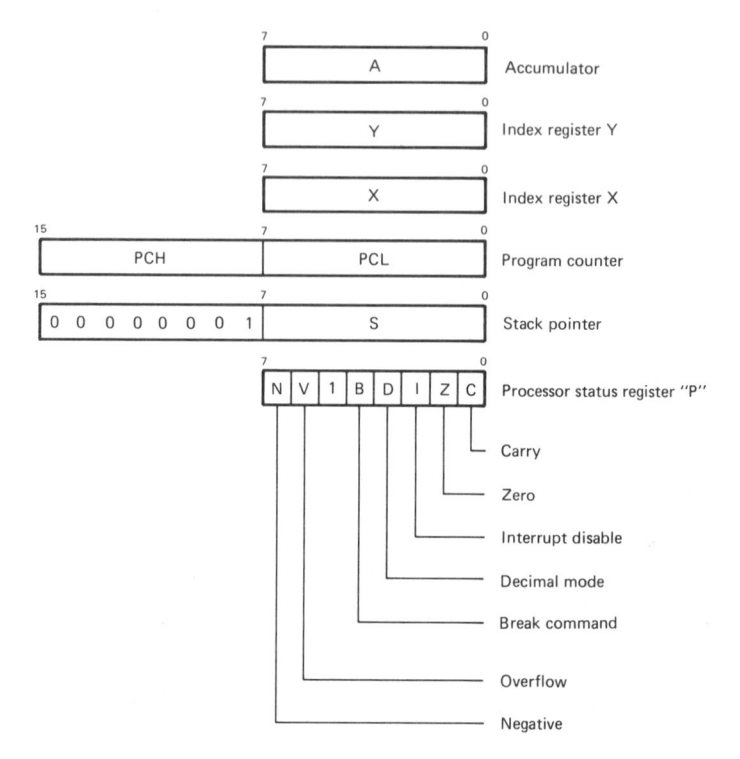

Figure 3.2-1 Programming model MCS6502 (courtesy MOS Technology)

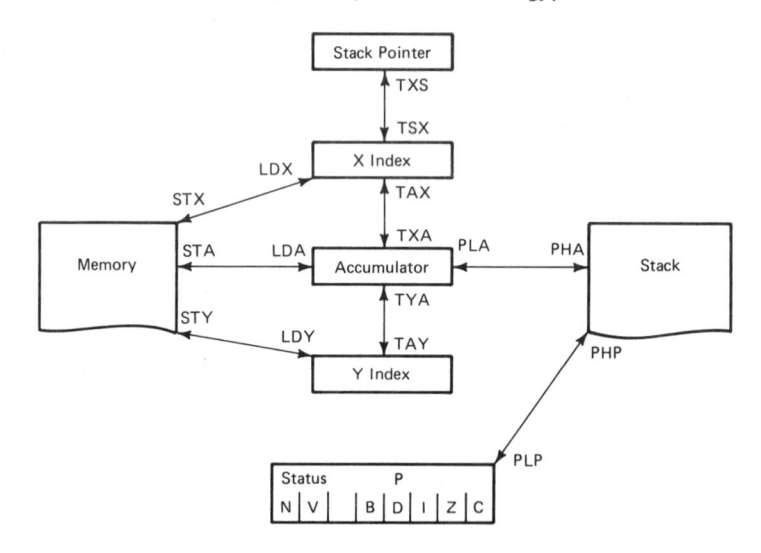

Figure 3.3-1 MCS6502 data paths

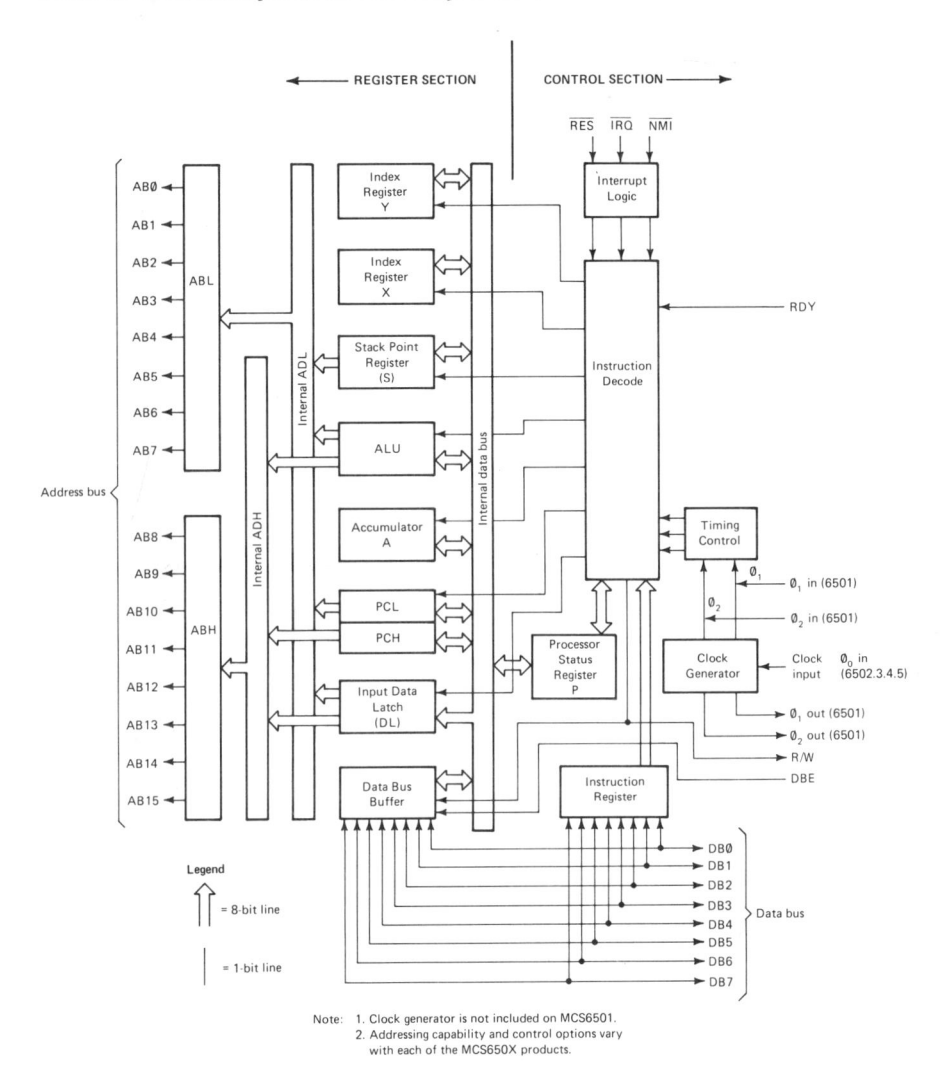

The MCS 6502 Microprocessor and Peripheral Parts   75

Figure 3.3-2 MCS6502 internal architecture
(courtesy MOS Technology)

3.4 CONCEPT OF OPERATION OF MCS6502 INSTRUCTIONS

3.4.1 Instruction Set

Table 3.4-1 is a summary of the MCS6502 Instruction Set in alphabetical order. It is advisable that a serious, thorough inspection of these be made. It is probably unwise to attempt rote memorization, since with use the set will become firmly implanted in the user's mind. Table 3.4-2 is a complete table which lists all 151 possible op codes, including the number of bytes of ROM required for program storage and the number of clock cycles needed for execution.

Table 3.4-2 also indicates which addressing modes (see Section 2.6) are implemented for each instruction. Table 3.4-3 describes all addressing modes used in the MCS6502.

TABLE 3.4-1 MCS6501–MCS6505 MICROPROCESSOR INSTRUCTION SET–ALPHABETIC SEQUENCE (Courtesy MOS Technology)

ADC	Add Memory to Accumulator with Carry	JSR	Jump to New Location Saving Return Address
AND	"AND" Memory with Accumulator		
ASL	Shift Left One Bit (Memory or Accumulator)	LDA	Load Accumulator with Memory
		LDX	Load Index X with Memory
BCC	Branch on Carry Clear	LDY	Load Index Y with Memory
BCS	Branch on Carry Set	LSR	Shift Right One Bit (Memory or Accumulator)
BEQ	Branch on Result Zero		
BIT	Test Bits in Memory with Accumulator	NOP	No Operation
BMI	Branch on Result Minus		
BNE	Branch on Result not Zero	ORA	"OR" Memory with Accumulator
BPL	Branch on Result Plus		
BRK	Force Break	PHA	Push Accumulator on Stack
BVC	Branch on Overflow Clear	PHP	Push Processor Status on Stack
BVS	Branch on Overflow Set	PLA	Pull Accumulator from Stack
		PLP	Pull Processor Status from Stack
CLC	Clear Carry Flag		
CLD	Clear Decimal Mode	ROL	Rotate One Bit Left (Memory or Accumulator)
CLI	Clear Interrupt Disable Bit	ROR	Rotate One Bit Right (Memory or Accumulator)
CLV	Clear Overflow Flag	RTI	Return from Interrupt
CMP	Compare Memory and Accumulator	RTS	Return from Subroutine
CPX	Compare Memory and Index X		
CPY	Compare Memory and Index Y	SBC	Subtract Memory from Accumulator with Borrow
		SEC	Set Carry Flag
		SED	Set Decimal Mode
DEC	Decrement Memory by One	SEI	Set Interrupt Disable Status
DEX	Decrement Index X by One	STA	Store Accumulator in Memory
DEY	Decrement Index Y by One	STX	Store Index X in memory
		STY	Store Index Y in memory
EOR	"Exclusive-Or" Memory with Accumulator		
		TAX	Transfer Accumulator to Index X
INC	Increment Memory by One	TAY	Transfer Accumulator to Index Y
INX	Increment Index X by One	TSX	Transfer Stack Pointer to Index X
INY	Increment Index Y by One	TXA	Transfer Index X to Accumulator
		TXS	Transfer Index X to Stack Pointer
JMP	Jump to New Location	TYA	Transfer Index Y to Accumulator

In the examples to follow, we will use 6502 assembler language conventions (see Section 4.3.3). Careful attention to them at the outset will make the transition to use of the Assembler (conversion from symbolic op codes and addresses to machine code) much easier. Among the more important conventions are the following:

1. All hexadecimal numbers are preceded by $. For example, $16 means 16, which would be equivalent to 22 base 10. If no leading symbol is present, the number is taken to be decimal, or base 10. Note: In all assembly listings the four columns containing Location and Code are always hexadecimal—no $ is shown.
2. Numbers expressed in binary and octal begin with % and @ respectively.
3. The "equate" symbol (=) allows variables to be assigned specific values. It is good programming form to precede all programs with a list of such assignments or symbol definitions and use only symbolic labels, and variables in the program itself. Then, if errors arise only the definition must be changed before reassembling the program.
4. The symbol * is used to designate the location counter value.
5. Immediate data is designated by # preceding the data.

3.4.2 Accumulator and Arithmetic Unit

In many computers, including most microprocessors, one of the most fundamental operations is to load the accumulator with a copy of the contents of a memory location. Complement, Load, and the Store (the inverse of Load) Accumulator instructions serve as the basis for many of the operations that a computer is capable of doing.

The first of these, LoaD Accumulator (LDA), allows transfer to the accumulator of the contents of either a memory location or a peripheral device connected to the data bus. Loading of the accumulator has several addressing mode variations which we will discuss in detail later on. Loading of the accumulator also causes some of the flags in the status register (see Sections 2.5.2 and 3.4.3), to be affected. The fact that given flags are sometimes affected differently by different instructions can be frustrating when programming many computers.

STore the Accumulator (STA) would be used to store the contents of the accumulator in some location in address space. No flags are affected.

TABLE 3.4-2

N ≡ number of execution cycles
\# ≡ number of instruction bytes

MNEMONIC	OPERATION		IMMEDIATE OP N #	ABSOLUTE OP N #	ZERO PAGE OP N #	ACCUM. OP N #	IMPLIED OP N #	(IND, X) OP N #
A D C	A+M+C→A	(1)	69 2 2	6D 4 3	65 3 2			61 6 2
A N D	A M→A	(1)	29 2 2	2D 4 3	25 3 2			21 6 2
A S L	C← $\boxed{7 \quad 0}$ ←0			0E 6 3	06 5 2	0A 2 1		
B C C	BRANCH ON C=0	(2)						
B C S	BRANCH ON C=1	(2)						
B E Q	BRANCH ON Z=1	(2)						
B I T	A∧M			2C 4 3	24 3 2			
B M I	BRANCH ON N=1	(2)						
B N E	BRANCH ON Z=0	(2)						
B P L	BRANCH ON N=0	(2)						
B R K	(See Fig. 1)						00 7 1	
B V C	BRANCH ON V=0	(2)						
B V S	BRANCH ON V=1	(2)						
C L C	0→C						18 2 1	
C L D	0→D						D8 2 1	
C L I	0→I						58 2 1	
C L V	0→V						B8 2 1	
C M P	A−M	(1)	C9 2 2	CD 4 3	C5 3 2			C1 6 2
C P X	X−M		E0 2 2	EC 4 3	E4 3 2			
C P Y	Y−M		C0 2 2	CC 4 3	C4 3 2			
D E C	M−1→M			CE 6 3	C6 5 2			
D E X	X−1→X						CA 2 1	
D E Y	Y−1→Y						88 2 1	
E O R	A⊻M→A	(1)	49 2 2	4D 4 3	45 3 2			41 6 2
I N C	M+1→M			EE 6 3	E6 5 2			
I N X	X+1→X						E8 2 1	
I N Y	Y+1→Y						C8 2 1	
J M P	JUMP TO NEW LOC.			4C 3 3				
J S R	(See Fig. 2) JUMP SUB			20 6 3				
L D A	M→A	(1)	A9 2 2	AD 4 3	A5 3 2			A1 6 2

TABLE 3.4-2 continued

(IND),Y OP N #	Z,PAGE,X OP N #	ABS,X OP N #	ABS,Y OP N #	RELATIVE OP N #	INDIRECT OP N #	Z,PAGE,Y OP N #	N	Z	C	I	D	V
71 5 2	75 4 2	7D 4 3	79 4 3				✓	✓	✓	-	-	✓
31 5 2	35 4 2	3D 4 3	39 4 3				✓	✓	-	-	-	-
	16 6 2	1E 7 3					✓	✓	✓	-	-	-
				90 2 2			-	-	-	-	-	-
				B0 2 2			-	-	-	-	-	-
				F0 2 2			-	-	-	-	-	-
							M_7	✓	-	-	-	M_6
				30 2 2			-	-	-	-	-	-
				D0 2 2			-	-	-	-	-	-
				10 2 2			-	-	-	-	-	-
							-	-	-	1	-	-
				50 2 2			-	-	-	-	-	-
				70 2 2			-	-	-	-	-	-
							-	-	0	-	-	-
							-	-	-	-	0	-
							-	-	-	0	-	-
							-	-	-	-	-	0
D1 5 2	D5 4 2	DD 4 3	D9 4 3				✓	✓	✓	-	-	-
							✓	✓	✓	-	-	-
							✓	✓	✓	-	-	-
	D6 6 2	DE 7 3					✓	✓	-	-	-	-
							✓	✓	-	-	-	-
							✓	✓	-	-	-	-
51 5 2	55 4 2	5D 4 3	59 4 3				✓	✓	-	-	-	-
	F6 6 2	FE 7 3					✓	✓	-	-	-	-
							✓	✓	-	-	-	-
							✓	✓	-	-	-	-
					6C 5 3		-	-	-	-	-	-
							-	-	-	-	-	-
B1 5 2	B5 4 2	BD 4 3	B9 4 3				✓	✓	-	-	-	-

TABLE 3.4-2 continued

MNEMONIC	OPERATION		IMMEDIATE OP N #	ABSOLUTE OP N #	ZERO PAGE OP N #	ACCUM. OP N #	IMPLIED OP N #	(IND, X) OP N #
L D X	M→X	(1)	A2 2 2	AE 4 3	A6 3 2			
L D Y	M→Y	(1)	A0 2 2	AC 4 3	A4 3 2			
L S R	0→[7 0]→C			4E 6 3	46 5 2	4A 2 1		
N O P	NO OPERATION						EA 2 1	
O R A	A V M→A		09 2 2	0D 4 3	05 3 2			01 6 2
P H A	A→Ms S−1→S						48 3 1	
P H P	P→Ms S−1→S						08 3 1	
P L A	S+1→S Ms→A						68 4 1	
P L P	S+1→S Ms→P						28 4 1	
R O L	↱[7 0]←[C]↵			2E 6 3	26 5 2	2A 2 1		
R O R	↳[C]→[7 0]↰			6E 6 3	66 5 2	6A 2 1		
R T I	RTRN. INT.						40 6 1	
R T S	RTRN SUB						60 6 1	
S B C	A−M−C̄ A	(1)	E9 2 2	ED 4 3	E5 3 2			E1 6 2
S E C	1→C						38 2 1	
S E D	1→D						F8 2 1	
S E I	1→I						78 2 1	
S T A	A→M			8D 4 3	85 3 2			81 6 2
S T X	X→M			8E 4 3	86 3 2			
S T Y	Y→M			8C 4 3	84 3 2			
T A X	A→X						AA 2 1	
T A Y	A→Y						A8 2 1	
T S X	S→X						BA 2 1	
T X A	X→A						8A 2 1	
T X S	X→S						9A 2 1	
T Y A	Y→A						98 2 1	

(1) ADD 1 TO "N" IF PAGE BOUNDARY IS CROSSED.
(2) ADD 1 TO "N" IF BRANCH OCCURS TO SAME PAGE.
    ADD 2 TO "N" IF BRANCH OCCURS TO DIFFERENT PAGE.
(3) CARRY NOT = BORROW

\+ ADD
− SUBTRACT
∧ AND
∨ OR

TABLE 3.4-2 continued

(IND),Y	Z,PAGE,X	ABS,X	ABS,Y	RELATIVE	INDIRECT	Z,PAGE,Y	CONDITION CODES					
OP N #	OP N #	OP N #	OP N #	OP N #	OP N #	OP N #	N	Z	C	I	D	V
		BE 4 3				B6 4 2	✓	✓	-	-	-	-
	B4 4 2	BC 4 3					✓	✓	-	-	-	-
	56 6 2	5E 7 3					0	✓	✓	-	-	-
							-	-	-	-	-	-
11 5 2	15 4 2	1D 4 3	19 4 3				✓	✓	-	-	-	-
							-	-	-	-	-	-
							-	-	-	-	-	-
							✓	✓	-	-	-	-
							(RESTORED)					
	36 6 2	3E 7 3					✓	✓	✓	-	-	-
	76 6 2	7E 7 3					V	V	V	-	-	-
							(RESTORED)					
							-	-	-	-	-	-
F1 5 2	F5 4 2	FD 4 3	F9 4 3				✓	✓	(3)	-	-	✓
							-	-	1	-	-	-
							-	-	-	-	1	-
							-	-	-	1	-	-
91 6 2	95 4 2	9D 5 3	99 5 3				-	-	-	-	-	-
						96 4 2	-	-	-	-	-	-
	94 4 2						-	-	-	-	-	-
							✓	✓	-	-	-	-
							✓	✓	-	-	-	-
							✓	✓	-	-	-	-
							✓	✓	-	-	-	-
							-	-	-	-	-	-
							✓	✓	-	-	-	-

```
X  INDEX X                              V  EXCLUSIVE OR
Y  INDEX Y                              ✓  MODIFIED
A  ACCUMULATOR                          -  NOT MODIFIED
M  MEMORY PER EFFECTIVE ADDRESS         M₇ MEMORY BIT 7
Ms MEMORY PER STACK POINTER             M₆ MEMORY BIT 6
```

TABLE 3.4-3. ADDRESSING MODES FOR MCS6502

Immediate	The operand is contained in the second byte of the instruction.
Absolute	The second byte of the instruction contains the 8 low order bits of the effective address. The third byte contains the 8 high order bits of the effective address.
Zero Page	The second byte contains the 8 low order bits of the effective address. The 8 high order bits are forced to be zero.
Accum.	Denotes a one byte instruction operating upon the accumulator.
Z.Page, X Z.Page, Y	Zero page indexed. The second byte of the instruction is added to the contents of the specified index register (carry is dropped) to form the low order 8 bits of the effective address. The 8 high order bits are forced to zero.
Abs, X Abs, Y	Absolute indexed. The second and third bytes of the instruction are added to the contents of the specified index register to form the effective address.
(Ind, X)	Indexed indirect. The second byte of the instruction is added to the contents of the X index register (carry dropped). This result points to a location in zero page which contains the 8 low order bits of the effective address. The next byte contains the 8 high order bits. Also called Pre-indexed.
(Ind), Y	Indirect Indexed. The second byte of the instruction points to a location in zero page. The contents of this location are added to the contents of the Y index register to form the 8 low order bits of the effective address. The carry is propagated and added to the contents of the next zero page location. This forms the 8 high order bits of the effective address. Also called Post-indexed.

The arithmetic unit discussed in Section 2.5.6 is one of the major ingredients of the microprocessor. Generally speaking, the results of most operations that involve the arithmetic unit will have their result left in the accumulator. One of the functions normally associated with the Arithmetic Logic Unit (ALU), is its ability to add two 8-bit numbers or subtract two 8-bit numbers and correctly set or reset the proper flag bits.

3.4.2.1 Input/Output with the MCS6502. The MCS6502 has no input/output (I/O) commands as such (see Section 2.3.4). Any I/O location is treated simply as a location in address space, somewhere between \$0000 and \$FFFF. (I/O locations have capability for manipulation by program steps, the same, therefore, as any RWM location.) The *ports* used to designate and implement I/O are usually 8 bits wide. Therefore, an input port may be read by such instructions as LDA, LDX, LDY, ORA, AND, etc. Likewise, an output operation may take the contents of any register which can write to memory and output its value to an output port. We can also alter a bit pattern sent to an output port by means of ROR, ASL, LSR, INC or DEC.

One I/O implementation, the Peripheral Interface Adapter (PIA), will be described in Section 3.7. One of its important attributes which we should be aware of is the ability for the programmer to designate the direction (input or output) of each bit of the port. Thus an 8-bit port could be initially used as 3 bits in and 5 bits out, and dynamically altered to any other configuration later in the program, if desired. A unit which permits such establishment of I/O configuration by programming steps is said to be a *programmable* interface unit.

3.4.3 Flag and Status Register

In the design of most minicomputers, or larger computers, there are individual one-bit registers distributed throughout the machine whose status is displayed on the operator's front panel. In a microprocessor it is sometimes frustrating that these bits, along with the program accessible registers, are buried inside the microprocessor chip and do not have lights on them to indicate their status. In most microprocessors the collection of such one-bit registers describing status during computation are collected together into a single register. Each of these bits thus makes up one bit of an 8-bit *flag* or *status register* which is accessible by the user under program control. Of the 8 possible bits available in the MCS6502 standard word only 7 are used for status representation. Refer to Figure 3.2-1 for the description of the processor status register (P), and location of each bit within P.

We will now discuss each of these bits individually, starting with the carry bit:

The *Carry* flag (C) is modified as a result of specific operations, or by a SEt Carry or CLear Carry command, SEC or CLC. In the case of Shift and Rotate instructions the carry bit is used as a ninth bit, similar to its use in the arithmetic Add and Subtract operations. Those operations which affect the carry bit are ADC, ASL, CLC, CMP, CPX, CPY, LSR, POP, ROL, ROR, RTI, SBC, or SEC. Notice especially that SEC and CLC should be performed prior to a subtract or an add operation, since the MCS6502 *always* uses the carry value in performing Add and Subtract operations.

The *Zero* flag (Z) is automatically set or reset by the microprocessor during any data movement or calculation operation where the 8 bits of the result are all a logic zero. Therefore, the bit is a logic 1 when the result is all zeros and is at logic zero when any of the bits are not zero. It is not possible to directly set or reset the Z bit as we could Carry. There are instructions which will allow us to test the status of the Z flag. The ability to test for such conditions is the cornerstone of the process which we will call looping (see Section 2.7.1).

The *Interrupt* flag (I) is another bit of importance to the microprocessor programmer. It is very important to observe that this bit, when it is a one, masks the ability to use the interrupt request line (IRQ), not allowing an interrupt to occur. We will discuss the interrupt mask bit further, but for now note that there are two interrupts which the MCS6502 can allow and only one of them can be masked. A request signal on the other line, nonmaskable interrupt (NMI), cannot be ignored. There are two instructions, SEt Interrupt mask-SEI and CLear Interrupt mask-CLI, which allow the programmer to reset or set I depending upon the circumstances. (See Sections 2.11, 3.6, and Appendix B.)

The *Decimal* Mode flag (D) can be set or reset by the instructions SED and CLD. This bit, when set to a one, causes those operations (ADC and SBB) which use the adder to automatically produce a decimally adjusted result. The concept of decimal adjustment is discussed in Section 2.10.3.

The *Break* flag (B) is used by the microprocessor internally in order to denote if entry to an interrupt routine was caused by execution of a

BReak instruction-BRK or an external interrupt request. There are no instructions which can set or reset this bit and it has meaning only during the analysis of a normal interrupt sequence. The principal use of this bit occurs during debugging in which the break command can be inserted to determine the flow of program execution.

The *Overflow* flag (V) is set or cleared as a result of arithmetic operations. It will be affected during add and subtract operations when the least significant 7 bits result in a value (either positive or negative, in a 2's complement sense) which cannot be contained within those 7 bits and would therefore spill over into what we might otherwise consider the sign position. If you are not using signed arithmetic you can obviously ignore this flag during programming. One of the subtle uses of the overflow bit lies in its role in use of the BIt Test (BIT) instruction which is often used for polling of Peripheral Interface Adapters during interrupt servicing. When used in these circumstances the overflow bit has nothing to do with signed arithmetic but is simply another one-bit value which we will be able to test under program control (see Section 3.4.5). Instructions which affect the V bit are ADC, BIT, CLV, PLP, RTI, and SBC. The overflow bit cannot be set by means of an operation code but it can be cleared with the CLV instruction. The V bit may be tested by means of conditional branch instructions (see Section 3.4.4).

The *Negative* flag (N) will contain the value of the sign bit, bit 7, produced by all arithmetic logic unit instructions. We will see later that we are able to test the negative bit with Conditional Branch instructions. The overall applicability of the N bit, however, goes considerably beyond arithmetic instructions and whether the result is in fact negative. We will observe that LDA, as well as many other instructions, affect the N bit. The BIT instruction causes results which affect this bit (see Section 3.4.5). The N bit cannot be set or reset by the programmer and simply represents the status of the last data movement operation. Many instructions affect the flag.

3.4.4 Jump and Branch Instructions

Section 2.4 describes the *Fetch* and *Execute* cycle activity which is common to nearly all computers. The microprocessor in general has internal timing and state control counters which cause us to successively fetch and execute instructions using varying numbers of clock cycles. This counter is precisely controlled by the instruction register decoder. Each time that the microprocessor indicates that a new instruction is needed, the contents of the program counter (PC) is placed on the address bus and the contents of that location are brought back into the MCS6502 and stored in the instruction register. During the fetch cycle the present contents of the program counter will be placed on the address bus and at the very end of every fetch cycle the contents of the program counter will be automatically incremented by one. This occurs regardless of where the next instruction is to be found. Next, during the execution of an instruction, the contents of the PC may need to be changed or modified. Those instructions which cause the program counter to proceed in other than the normal sequential, or counting, mode are the Jump and Branch instructions. Other instructions which may affect the PC are Interrupt and Break. We have already noted that some instructions require more than one byte. When the first byte is brought in during the fetching of an instruction it is immediately inspected to determine if it is a multiple-byte instruction. If so, all of the bytes will be subsequently brought into the microprocessor and routed to the appropriate locations. In the case of the JUMP instruction the second and third bytes have their value placed into the PC, which in the MCS6502 is two bytes long.

Two addressing modes are provided for the JUMP instruction, absolute and indirect. In absolute mode, the second and third bytes of the three byte instruction will be placed into PC. In the indirect mode the second and third bytes of this three byte instruction are sent out onto the address bus and used to fetch a byte to be placed in PCL. Then the next higher address is sent out to fetch a byte to be placed on PCH. These operations are done *without* testing any of the P bits described in the previous section. This instruction therefore is an unconditional JMP to a new location anywhere in address space. These two addressing modes, i.e. JUMP ABSOLUTE and JUMP INDIRECT, are illustrated in Examples 3.4.4-1 and 3.4.4-2 respectively.

The conditional tests and associated branches are provided to permit a program's "normal" consecutive instruction flow to be altered by conditions which arise during the execution of the program. Four flags (C, Z, N, V) can be tested and branching performed on either condition, SET or CLEAR, of each flag. (Some microprocessors, viz., the Motorola 6800, provide capability for branching on combined tests such as equal-to-or-greater-than, etc.)

The 6502 programmer should keep in mind that, when a branch is to be taken, the relative offset is added to the PC value which designates the location of the op code *following* the branch instruction itself. Thus, for example, if it were desired to endlessly repeat a branch instruction,

EXAMPLE 3.4.4-1. JUMP ABSOLUTE EXAMPLE

Address	Byte 1	Byte 2	Byte 3	Label	OpC	Source Code Operand	Comments
					.		
					.		
					.		
∅23∅	4C	3∅	17		JMP	LOC	Note: Least sig-
∅233					.		nificant bit first
					.		
					.		
173∅				LOC	?	?	

EXAMPLE 3.4.4-2. JUMP INDIRECT EXAMPLE

Address	Byte 1	Byte 2	Byte 3	Label	OpC	Source Code Operand	Comments
					.		
					.		
					.		
∅23∅	6C	∅∅	∅5		JMP	(PTR)	
∅233					.		
					.		
					.		
∅5∅∅	3∅	17		PTR	.WORD	$173∅	Note that PTR may be RWM and could be altered
					.		
					.		
					.		
173∅				LOC	?	?	
					.		
					.		
					.		

the offset should be −2($FE, in two's complement form), since the branch instruction is 2 bytes long.

Because the offset is limited to a range of 256 bytes, branches to arbitrary locations in memory space are not possible. The MCS6502 *does* permit branching across page boundaries (1 page = 256 bytes) as long as the desired location is within range of the permitted offset. Assembler programs (see Chapter 4) generally detect such errors as attempts to branch out of range.

EXAMPLE 3.4.4-3. BRANCH INSTRUCTION

Problem: Check the contents of location $0300 to see if it is zero. If it is, go to location $1260 for the next instruction, otherwise "fall through" to location $125A for the next instruction.

Solution:

Address	Byte 1	Byte 2	Byte 3	Label	OpCode	Operand	Comments
					.		
					.		
					.		
1255	AD	00	03		LDA	$300	
1258	F0	06			BEQ	$1260	
125A					.		Loc of next instruction IF ($300) ≠ 0.
					.		
1260							Loc of next instruction IF ($300) = 0. Note that $125A + $06 = $1260

Note that there are eight Branch instructions. The status of Carry, Zero, Sign and Overflow flags can be tested, and Branching on either condition, set or clear, can be performed in each case.

As previously stated, branching is permitted only to locations within the range of −128 to +127 bytes from the present PC value. Since the Branch instruction is always 2 bytes long this means −126 to +129 from the Branch instruction itself. This follows since the PC points at the first byte of the next instruction after Fetch. Under most circumstances we save one storage byte of program and one execution cycle with this method, compared to the JUMP instruction. However, if we need to branch outside this range we must combine the conditional branch and unconditional jump. Example 3.4.4-4 illustrates how a program may test the contents of a memory location and conditionally branch to either of two routines, dependent on the value stored at that location. The "target" routines are both out of normal branch range.

EXAMPLE 3.4.4-4. Extended-range Conditional Branching

Address	Byte 1	Byte 2	Byte 3	Label	OpCode	Operand	Comments
1775	AD	ØØ	Ø3		LDA	$3ØØ	
1778	DØ	Ø3			BNE	NOTZ	
177A	4C	5Ø	12		JMP	FAROUT	
177D	4C	FF	23	NOTZ	JMP	FARIN	Note that $23FF − $177A = 127

The use of the Relative Branch table, Figure 3.4.4-1, will help reduce the errors in determining the correct signed two's complement representation of the backward branch offset. A backward branch as used here means to an address which is less than the present value. As an example let us assume a program section containing 25 bytes plus a conditional branch to the top, which has a symbolic address TOP.

EXAMPLE 3.4.4-5

Address	Byte 1	Byte 2	Byte 3	Label	OpCode	Operand	Comments
125Ø				TOP			
1269	9Ø	E5			BCC	TOP	PC must be −27 from present value or $E5

BACKWARD RELATIVE

	8	9	A	B	C	D	E	F
8 −	128	127	126	125	124	123	122	121	120	119	118	117	116	115	114	113
9 −	112	111	110	109	108	107	106	105	104	103	102	101	100	99	98	97
A −	96	95	94	93	92	91	90	89	88	87	86	85	84	83	82	81
B −	80	79	78	77	76	75	74	73	72	71	70	69	68	67	66	65
C −	64	63	62	61	60	59	58	57	56	55	54	53	52	51	50	49
D −	48	47	46	45	44	43	42	41	40	39	38	37	36	35	34	33
E −	32	31	30	29	28	27	26	25	24	23	22	21	20	19	18	17
F −	16	15	14	13	12	11	10	9	8	7	6	5	4	3	2	1

Most Significant (rows) / Least Significant (columns)

FORWARD RELATIVE

	0	1	2	3	4	5	6	7	8	9	A	B	C	D	E	F
0 −	0	1	2	3	4	5	6	7	8	9	10	11	12	13	14	15
1 −	16	17	18	19	20	21	22	23	24	25	26	27	28	29	30	31
2 −	32	33	34	35	36	37	38	39	40	41	42	43	44	45	46	47
3 −	48	49	50	51	52	53	54	55	56	57	58	59	60	61	62	63
4 −	64	65	66	67	68	69	70	71	72	73	74	75	76	77	78	79
5 −	80	81	82	83	84	85	86	87	88	89	90	91	92	93	94	95
6 −	96	97	98	99	100	101	102	103	104	105	106	107	108	109	110	111
7 −	112	113	114	115	116	117	118	119	120	121	122	123	124	125	126	127

Most Significant (rows) / Least Significant (columns)

Figure 3.4.4-1 RELATIVE BRANCH TABLE: For use with MCS6502 and M6800

The MCS 6502 Microprocessor and Peripheral Parts   91

The offset required is found to be -27. Referring to Figure 3.4.4-1, we find 27 in the "BACKWARD RELATIVE" table and note that the 2's complement of -27 is $E5_{16}$ (most significant character = E; Least significant character = 5).

As a check, note that $+27_{10} = 1B_{16} = 00011011_2$, and therefore -27_{10} in signed two's complement representation is $11100101_2 = E5_{16}$.

As a final comment, note that symbolic labels are used for addresses; an assembler, if available, will perform the branch address offset computation automatically. Also, an assembler will generate an error message if an out-of-range branch is attempted. Such a problem can be remedied with the method shown in Example 3.4.4-4.

The branch instructions are BMI-Branch on result MInus, BPL-Branch on result PLus, BCC-Branch on Carry Clear, BCS-Branch on Carry Set, BEQ-Branch on result EQual zero, BNE-Branch on result Not Equal zero, BVS-Branch on oVerflow Set, and BVC-Branch on oVerflow Clear.

3.4.5 Compare and Bit Test

The CMP-Compare instruction is extremely useful in many situations such as checking to see if the present value of an input port is greater than, equal to, or less than a specified value, and, depending on the result, taking the correct branch to a desired section of program. Another application of the CMP instruction is that of executing a loop program a desired number of times. The basic rule which governs Compare operation is that the ALU is employed to do a subtraction of (A) $-$ (M), setting or resetting N, Z, C (but not V) appropriately, but not saving the result of the subtraction. A simple table, Table 3.4.5-1 below, summarizes the results.

TABLE 3.4.5-1. Status Bit Values Produced by CMP Instruction

STATUS BITS

	N	C	Z	V
(A) < (M)	?	∅	∅	U
(A) = (M)	∅	1	1	U
(A) > (M)	?	1	∅	U

U = Unchanged   ? = Depends upon (+) or ($-$) result

As a first example let us use CMP for executing a loop 35 times.

EXAMPLE 3.4.5-1. Loop Program Using CMP Instruction

```
LINE #   LOC    CODE           LINE
0001     0000                  COUNT = $100
0002     0000                       *=$300
0003     0300   A9 00              LDA    #0        ;INITIALIZE COUNT
0004     0302   8D 00 01           STA    COUNT
0005     0305   EA          LOOP   NOP              ;NONSENSE LOOP TO DEMO
0006     0306   EA                 NOP              ;COMPARE OPCODE
0007     0307   EE 00 01           INC    COUNT     ;COUNT = COUNT + 1
0008     030A   AD 00 01           LDA    COUNT
0009     030D   C9 24              CMP    #36       ;GO THRU LOOP 35(DEC)
0010     030F   90 F4              BCC    LOOP      ;TIMES
0011     0311                      .END
```

The second example program will determine if the number in VALUE is greater than, equal to, or less than 5 and branch accordingly.

EXAMPLE 3.4.5-2. Testing Number Magnitude Using CMP Instruction

	Byte				Source Code		
Address	1	2	3	Label	OpC	Operand	Comments
3C30	A5	C5			LDA	VALUE	Value in $00C5
3C32	C9	05			CMP	#5	
3C34	90	30			BCC	LT	
3C36	F0	7D			BEQ	EQ	
3C38	B0	CF			BCS	GT	Not really needed since it must be >

The BIT-BIt Test instruction is another very useful MCS6502 instruction. It can be used to test bit values on specific lines connected to an input port, for example. In general it can be used to check for any specific bit pattern.

The BIT instruction is similar to the Compare instruction in that the ALU operation AND (rather than subtract in the case of CMP) is performed with N, Z and V affected, but the result not saved. Of considerable importance is the fact that Bits 6 and 7 of the tested location go into the V flag and N flag respectively, no matter what value is in A. This makes it useful for reading bits six and seven (or both) at an I/O port for example. The values read are stored in the V and/or N flags and can therefore be sensed using conditional branch instructions.

3.4.6 Addressing Techniques in the MCS6502

It will be convenient for us to loosely group all addressing group methods into two major categories, those which are *not indexed* and those which are *indexed*.

3.4.6.1 Nonindexed Addressing. There are several varieties of addressing modes which might logically be included under nonindexed addressing modes. As previously discussed, the MCS6502 has three external busses including a 16 bit address bus and an 8 bit bi-directional data bus. The subject of our interest in this section is the generation of the 16 bits which are placed on the address bus. Recall that 16 bits of address information correspond to 65K memory locations containing one byte each. It is convenient to denote this address space as 256 pages, each of which contains 256 bytes. We will attach special significance to the lowest order page, i.e., page zero, both in this section and the next.

An instruction which addresses no operand or an operand which does not require an address for location is said to use an *implied* mode of addressing. Such an instruction might transfer information internally between registers, or it might affect the contents of a single register. An example is LSR, which would cause the contents of the accumulator to be shifted right one position with a zero being placed in bit 7 and the contents of bit ∅ of the Accumulator placed in the carry bit. Another variation in nonindexed addressing is called *absolute addressing*. Absolute addressing in the MCS6502 implies that the second and third bytes of an instruction (following the op code), contain 16 bits of address which allow us to access any location in address space.

Zero page addressing is a limited form of absolute addressing provided by the MCS6502. Instructions which use this mode are two bytes long (op code and 8 bits of address). These instructions are executed faster, but only allow access to information in page zero, the lower 256 locations in address space. Zero page instructions require less code, will operate faster, and require fewer machine cycles for execution.

An MCS6502 feature which is sometimes confusing is that those instructions which include absolute addresses have the low order byte immediately following the op code and the high order byte next. This allows the processor to fetch the least significant byte of an address and modify it before it is placed on the address bus and if a carry is generated, it can be added to the high-order byte without having to move backward in time, as would be required if they were OP-HI-LO.

The designers of the MCS6502 have implemented so-called *pipelining* of instructions. It is this feature which allows a two byte instruction to require only two clock cycles for execution. Its essential feature is that, as as instruction is being executed, the next instruction is simultaneously being fetched and vice versa, even though we may not ultimately use the next fetched instruction (if a branch or jump occurs, for example).

Another of the nonindexed addressing modes is that of relative addressing discussed in Section 3.4.4.

3.4.6.2 Indexed Addressing. The concept of indexed addressing is one which can be understood by looking at the Internal Architecture diagram (Figure 3.3-2) and noting that the internal address busses "can access" the arithmetic/logic unit. This feature permits addition of an address contained in an instruction (in the second, and possibly third, byte(s)), to the contents of one of the index registers, X or Y. In other words, indexed addressing allows the computation of an address, and the results of that computation being placed on the internal address busses. Ultimately the internal address busses are connected to the external address bus.

One of the important reasons why indexed addressing is valuable lies in the technology which makes microcomputers possible. In particular, program storage is often found in Read Only Memory (ROM), and ROM cannot be modified by the microprocessor. Address modification is not possible with a memory which can only be read. This would not be a restriction if we were dealing with instructions stored in RWM. Even in that case, it is usually considered bad programming practice to allow a program to modify itself. Indexed addressing allows modification of a fixed address (part of the instruction) by adding it (through the ALU) to the contents of an indexed register. Several of the operations which the MCS6502 is capable of performing involve absolute addresses modified by either index register X or Y, as well as Zero Page addresses modified by X or Y.

The MCS6502 can directly perform a number of operations on its index registers. They are LDX-LoaD index register X from memory,

The MCS 6502 Microprocessor and Peripheral Parts 95

LDY-LoaD index register Y from memory, STX-STore index register X in memory, STY-STore index register Y in memory, INX-INcrement index register X by one, INY-INcrement index register Y by one, DEX-DEcrement index register X by one, DEY-DEcrement index register Y by one, CPX-ComPare index register X to memory, CPY-ComPare index register Y to memory, TAX-Transfer Accumulator to X, TXA-Transfer index register X to Accumulator, TAY-Transfer Accumulator to index register Y, TYA-Transfer index Y to Accumulator.

Other than loading, storing and transferring of the contents of index registers, probably the most useful operation is that of Incrementing and Decrementing these registers. This mechanism lets us use conditional branches depending upon eventual status of the N or Z Status bits.

The principal use of indexed addressing is to fetch data from locations at some offset value from a base address associated with the op code and as a consequence, be able to operate upon an array of information using a program loop. The most popular method is to go to a value offset from the base address, decrementing X or Y each time through the loop, and then checking to see if the resulting decremented value in X or Y is yet equal to zero. If it is not equal to zero the loop is reentered once more to the new offset position until eventually the index register value results in zero, at which point the program "falls through the loop."

EXAMPLE 3.4.6-1. Example Indexing Program (No.1)

Problem: Copy 32 bytes from $1750 - $176F to $0200 - $021F.

Address	Byte 1	Byte 2	Byte 3	Label	OpC	Source Code Operand	Comments
0320	A2	20			LDX	#$20	
0322	BD	4F	17	LOOP	LDA	FROM-1,X	
0325	9D	FF	01		STA	TO-1,X	
0328	CA				DEX		
0329	D0	F7			BNE	LOOP	
032B				MORE	.		

Note that we are forced to use "one less" in the FROM-1 and TO-1 since our loop is closed with BNE. Also notice that the first-moved location is ($176F) to ($021F).

An alternative formulation which simply moves the "N-1 problem" to the index register is:

EXAMPLE 3.4.6-2. Example Indexing Program (No.2)

Address	Byte 1	2	3	Label	OpC	Source Code Operand	Comments
					.		
					.		
0320	A2	1F			LDX	#$1F	
0322	BD	50	17	LOOP	LDA	FROM,X	
0325	9D	00	02		STA	TO,X	
0328	CA				DEX		
0329	10	F7			BPL	LOOP	
032B				MORE	.		
					.		
					.		

A third method of accomplishing the same result moves the opposite end of the array first, using the Compare instruction to determine when enough elements have been moved. The new program is:

EXAMPLE 3.4.6-3. Example Indexing Program (No.3)

Address	Byte 1	2	3	Label	OpC	Source Code Operand	Comments
					.		
					.		
					LDX	#0	
				LOOP	LDA	FROM,X	
					STA	TO,X	
					INX		
					CPX	#$20	
					BNE	LOOP	
				MORE	.		
					.		

Although the X index register is used in the examples, note that Y could have been used as well.

A limitation encountered in the MCS6502 is that only 256 locations can be moved, compared, scanned, etc. This is an actual result of an 8-bit register augmenting a 16 bit address. Several solutions to this problem are possible, but let us use it as a vehicle to explore indirect addressing, with its several variations.

3.4.6.3 Indirect Addressing. Conceptually, indirect addressing means that the address part of the instruction does not point to data, but to another address which in turn *does* point to the data. Indirect addressing in the MCS6502 assembly language is denoted by writing the pointer location in parentheses. Careful study of the Instruction Table, Table 3.4-2, reveals examples like (IND,X) and (IND),Y. It is important to note that these instructions are two bytes long (including op code), therefore, they are indirect *through zero page*. As an added potential bonus, they can be indexed in two different ways. The most useful of the two mixed modes is called Indirect Indexed, and is denoted by (IND),Y. In this mode an address is found at IND and IND + 1, to which the contents of Y are added to form the effective address. In some minicomputers this has been designated as post-indexing, as contrasted to pre-indexing. Pre-indexing corresponds to the other MCS6502 mixed address mode, indexed indirect (IND,X), where X can be used as a pointer within zero page to find the effective address. Note that only the Y index register can be used in the indirect indexed mode.

Let us develop an example using this addressing mode and the Compare instruction. The object is to develop a subroutine to scan any 256 locations in memory for the pattern in the accumulator A. The calling program must initialize locations START and START + 1 with the low-order and high-order address bytes and put the desired pattern in A. First let us look just at the subroutine, shown in Figure 3.4.6-1, in which several arbitrary choices have been made. Scanning is performed from low to high address values. If a pattern matching the one in A is found, the accumulator contains zero upon return to the calling program. If no match is found, A returns with all-ones. No attempt has been made to save the contents of the Y register which existed before calling the subroutine.

A program which calls the subroutine of Figure. 3.4.6-1 is shown in Fig. 3.4.6-2. The targets for zero ($00) or nonzero ($FF) are again arbitrary. In the interest of simplicity, no use is made of the value returned in Y, which is the offset from START where the match was found.

```
......PAGE ØØØ1
LINE # LOC     CODE        LINE
ØØ18   Ø214                      *=$3ØØ
ØØ19   Ø3ØØ AØ ØØ    FINDR LDY #$ØØ    MUST INITIALIZE TO ZERO
ØØ2Ø   Ø3Ø2 D1 5Ø    FIN1  CMP (START),Y CHECK FOR EQUALITY
ØØ21   Ø3Ø4 FØ Ø7          BEQ FOUND
ØØ22   Ø3Ø6 C8             INY
ØØ23   Ø3Ø7 CØ FF           CPY #$FF    SCAN FROM BOTTOM UP
ØØ24   Ø3Ø9 DØ F7           BNE FIN1
ØØ25   Ø3ØB FØ Ø4           BEQ DONE
ØØ26   Ø3ØD A9 ØØ    FOUND LDA #$ØØ    RETURN WITH A=Ø IF EQUAL
ØØ27   Ø3ØF FØ Ø2          BEQ END
ØØ28   Ø311 A9 FF    DONE  LDA #$FF    RETURN WITH $FF IS NOT Z
ØØ29   Ø313 6Ø       END   RTS
```

Figure 3.4.6-1 Subroutine for indirect indexed address mode example

3.4.7 Use of the Stack

The one remaining register inside the microprocessor which has not been discussed is called the Stack Pointer (S) (see Section 2.11). The stack pointer is a one byte register which is under programmer control. It may be loaded from X or unloaded into the X register. As shown in Fig. 3.3-1 all communications with the stack pointer are via the X index register.

It is important to observe that, in the MCS6502, the stack pointer is only 8 bits long. These 8 bits will be augmented by a fixed high-order byte every time the contents of the stack pointer are to be placed on the address bus. That fixed value is in fact $Ø1 every time it is used. The resulting address will be $Ø1XX where XX is the present value of the stack pointer. Several instructions make use of the stack pointer and in fact may even affect its value. It is normal procedure to initialize S to $FF, allowing the stack to "grow" from $Ø1FF toward $Ø1ØØ.

The basic function of the stack pointer is to point to an area in RWM where variables which relate to processor activity are to be stored. Four of the simplest op codes which use the stack are PusH Accumulator—PHA, PulL Accumulator—PLA, PusH Processor status—PHP and PulL Processor status—PLP. Both of the Push operations cause the contents of the designated register to be written into the address defined by S, and S is then decremented, i.e., S always is left defining the next available memory location. The pull operations first increment S and then read the contents of $Ø1SS into A or P, as designated.

The MCS 6502 Microprocessor and Peripheral Parts

```
......PAGE ØØØ1

LINE    # LOC    CODE           LINE
ØØØ1    ØØØØ                    START  =$5Ø
ØØØ2    ØØØØ                    ADRL   =$ØØ
ØØØ3    ØØØØ                    ADRH   =$Ø4
ØØØ4    ØØØØ                    PATN   =$55
ØØØ5    ØØØØ                    ZERO   =$27Ø
ØØØ6    ØØØØ                    NZER   =$282
ØØØ7    ØØØØ                           *=$2ØØ
ØØØ8    Ø2ØØ  A2 FF      MAIN   LDX #$FF   NORMAL INITIALIZING
ØØØ9    Ø2Ø2  9A                TXS
ØØ1Ø    Ø2Ø3  A9 ØØ             LDA #ADRL  INITIALIZE START VECTOR
ØØ11    Ø2Ø5  85 5Ø             STA START
ØØ12    Ø2Ø7  A9 Ø4             LDA #ADRH
ØØ13    Ø2Ø9  85 51             STA START+1
ØØ14    Ø2ØB  A9 55             LDA #PATN
ØØ15    Ø2ØD  2Ø ØØ Ø3          JSR FINDR
ØØ16    Ø21Ø  FØ 5E             BEQ ZERO   ARBITRARY TARGETS
ØØ17    Ø212  DØ 6E             BNE NZER
ØØ18    Ø214                           *=$3ØØ
ØØ19    Ø3ØØ  AØ ØØ      FINDR  LDY #$ØØ   MUST INITIALIZE Y TO ZERO
ØØ2Ø    Ø3Ø2  D1 5Ø      FIN1   CMP (START),Y CHECK FOR EQUALITY
ØØ21    Ø3Ø4  FØ Ø7             BEQ FOUND
ØØ22    Ø3Ø6  C8                INY
ØØ23    Ø3Ø7  CØ FF             CPY #$FF   SCAN FROM BOTTOM UP
ØØ24    Ø3Ø9  DØ F7             BNE FIN1
ØØ25    Ø3ØB  FØ Ø4             BEQ DONE
ØØ26    Ø3ØD  A9 ØØ      FOUND  LDA #$ØØ   RETURN WITH A=Ø IF EQUAL
ØØ27    Ø3ØF  FØ Ø2             BEQ END
ØØ28    Ø311  A9 FF      DONE   LDA #$FF   RETURN WITH @$FF IF NOT Z
ØØ29    Ø313  6Ø         END    RTS
ØØ3Ø    Ø314                    .END

ERRORS = ØØØØ  WARNINGS = ØØØØ


SYMBOL TABLE

  SYMBOL  VALUE

START   ØØ5Ø
ADRL    ØØØØ
ADRH    ØØØ4
PATN    ØØ55
ZERO    Ø27Ø
NZER    Ø282
MAIN    Ø2ØØ
FINDR   Ø3ØØ
FIN1    Ø3Ø2
FOUND   Ø3ØD
DONE    Ø311
END     Ø313
END OF ASSEMBLY
```

Figure 3.4.6-2 Indirect indexed address mode example program

Another use of S is to save the value of PC during a Jump to Subroutine. A Return from Subroutine will remove from the stack a copy of the saved program counter and place it in the PC so that execution can be resumed at that location following that of the subroutine call. A third use of the stack is to save the contents of both the program counter and P when an interrupt is serviced. The programmer may also find it advantageous to use the stack pointer in communicating variables between a main program and a subroutine.

It should be reemphasized that the stack, pointed to by S, is simply a section of read/write memory and as such has potential for interference or overlapping by nonstack memory operation. It is therefore the programmer's responsibility to ensure that such overlaps do not occur, or if they do, are managed correctly under programmer control.

3.4.8 Shift and Memory Modification Instructions

Those operations that allow shifting and rotating of the contents of various registers, as well as memory locations are very important in the application of microprocessors. For example, it is very common to find information arriving at a microprocessor input port in serial form. One simple but almost universal example is the acquisition of data from a Teletype® or other form of terminal. That information is both bit serial and character serial, requiring a way to convert the serial information into parallel form. Shifting and rotating instructions provide such a mechanism. The shift instruction will take a register, like the accumulator, and move all of its bits one bit to the right and one bit to the left. To be specific: in the event of a ROtate Left instruction – ROL, all of the bits will be rotated one bit left and furthermore, the most significant bit will be placed in C and the previous carry bit value will be placed in bit zero. A shift instruction on the other hand will generally insert zeros on "the far end" with the bit being shifted out going into the carry bit. The three rotates and shifts are logical shift, arithmetic shift, and rotate. Some MCS6502 chips also have ROtate Right – ROR.

The LSR – Logical Shift Right instruction – shifts zero into bit 7 with bit 0 being shifted into the carry flag. It is possible to interact with a location in memory space with this instruction, shifting the high or low-order bit value into the carry appropriately without affecting the accumulator. This can be a very useful means of single-bit transfer in the MCS6502. In the execution of the LSR the N flag is always reset, the Z flag will be appropriately set or reset, and the carry bit will take on the value of the original low-order operand bit.

The ASL — Arithmetic Shift Left instruction — is the counterpart of the logical shift right, inserting zero into bit 0 and shifting the high order bit into the carry bit. The ROtate Left instruction — ROL puts the high order bit in the carry bit and what was in the carry bit will go into the least significant bit. The ROtate Right goes in the opposite direction.

The following example is a combination of instructions which illustrates an equivalent ROtate Right capability for those MCS6502 units which do not provide this instruction explicitly.

EXAMPLE 3.4.8-1. Rotate Right Operation

Address	Byte 1	Byte 2	Byte 3	Label	OpC	Operand	Comments
					.		
					.		
					.		
Ø27Ø	BØ	Ø5			BCS	OK	
Ø272	4E	3Ø	17		LSR	WORD	
Ø275	1Ø	Ø5			BPL	DONE	
Ø277	4E	3Ø	17	OK	LSR	WORD	
Ø27A	Ø9	8Ø			ORA	#$8Ø	
Ø27C				DONE	.		

The last two MCS6502 instructions to be described provide the ability to INCrement (INC) and DECrement (DEC) a single memory location anywhere in memory space. This capability allows us to generate counters anywhere in memory space, which extend the type of capability present in the index registers previously discussed. Figure 3.4.8-1 is a listing of a general looping program which repeats $17F times. Figure 3.4.8-2 is another program of the same type.

```
CARD #   LOC     CODE        CARD 1Ø       2Ø         3Ø          4Ø             5Ø
   1     ØØØØ
   2     ØØØØ
   3     ØØØØ
   4     ØØØØ
   5     ØØØØ                   ∷=$4ØØ
   6     Ø4ØØ              LSB    =       $5Ø
   7     Ø4ØØ              MSB    =       $51
   8     Ø4ØØ  A9 7F              LDA     #$7F
   9     Ø4Ø2  85 5Ø              STA     LSB
  1Ø     Ø4Ø4  A9 Ø1              LDA     #1
  11     Ø4Ø6  85 51              STA     MSB
  12     Ø4Ø8  EA         LOOP    NOP                             GENERAL LOOP
  13     Ø4Ø9  EA                 NOP
  14     Ø4ØA  EA                 NOP
  15     Ø4ØB  C6 5Ø              DEC     LSB
  16     Ø4ØD  A5 5Ø              LDA     LSB
  17     Ø4ØF  C9 FF              CMP     #$FF                    HAS LEAST SIGNIFICANT
  18     Ø411  DØ F5              BNE     LOOP                    BIT ROLLED AROUND YET?
  19     Ø413  A5 51              LDA     MSB
  2Ø     Ø415  FØ Ø5              BEQ     DONE
  21     Ø417  C6 51              DEC     MSB
  22     Ø419  4C Ø8 Ø4           JMP     LOOP
  23     Ø41C  EA         DONE    NOP
  24     Ø41D                     .END
```

END OF MOS/TECHNOLOGY 65ØX ASSEMBLY VERSION 5
NUMBER OF ERRORS = Ø, NUMBER OF WARNINGS = Ø

```
         SYMBOL TABLE

SYMBOL   VALUE   LINE DEFINED        CROSS REFERENCES

DONE     Ø41C        23    2Ø
LOOP     Ø4Ø8        12    18    22
LSB      ØØ5Ø         6     9    15    16
MSB      ØØ51         7    11    19    21
```

Figure 3.4.8-1 MCS6502 program showing use of memory-based counter

3.5 COMPLETE DESCRIPTION OF OPERATION CODES (Courtesy MOS Technology)

The following notation applies to this summary:

   A Accumulator
   X, Y Index Registers
   M Memory
   P Processor Status Register
   S Stack Register

The MCS 6502 Microprocessor and Peripheral Parts

```
......PAGE ØØØ1

LINE    # LOC    CODE            LINE
ØØØ1    ØØØØ                     ∷=$4ØØ
ØØØ2    Ø4ØØ            LSB     = $5Ø
ØØØ3    Ø4ØØ            MSB     = $51
ØØØ4    Ø4ØØ  A9 7F             LDA #$7F
ØØØ5    Ø4Ø2  85 5Ø              STA LSB
ØØØ6    Ø4Ø4  A9 Ø1              LDA #1
ØØØ7    Ø4Ø6  85 51              STA MSB
ØØØ8    Ø4Ø8  EA      LOOP       NOP    GENERAL LOOP
ØØØ9    Ø4Ø9  EA                 NOP
ØØ1Ø    Ø4Ø8  EA                 NOP
ØØ11    Ø4ØB  DB                 CLD
ØØ12    Ø4ØC  38                 SEC
ØØ13    Ø4ØD  A5 5Ø              LDA LSB
ØØ14    Ø4ØF  E9 Ø1              SBC #1
ØØ15    Ø411  85 5Ø              STA LSB
ØØ16    Ø413  A5 51              LDA MSB
ØØ17    Ø415  E9 ØØ              SBC #Ø
ØØ18    Ø417  85 51              STA MSB
ØØ19    Ø419  Ø5 5Ø              ORA LSB
ØØ2Ø    Ø418  DØ EB              BNE LOOP
ØØ21    Ø41D  EA      DONE       NOP
ØØ22    Ø41E                     .END

ERRORS = ØØØØ
```

Figure 3.4.8-2 Variation of memory-based counter example

√	Change
–	No Change
+	Add
∧	Logical AND
−	Subtract
∀	Logical Exclusive Or
↑	Transfer from Stack
↓	Transfer to Stack
→	Transfer to
←	Transfer to
V	Logical OR
PC	Program Counter
PCH	Program Counter High
PLC	Program Counter Low
OPER	Operand
#	IMMEDIATE ADDRESSING MODE

ADC   Add memory to accumulator with carry

Operation: A + M + C → A,C

N Z C I D V
√ √ √ − − √

Addressing Mode	Assembly Language Form	OP CODE	No. Bytes	No. Cycles
Immediate	ADC # Oper	69	2	2
Zero Page	ADC Oper	65	2	3
Zero Page, X	ADC Oper, X	75	2	4
Absolute	ADC Oper	6D	3	4
Absolute, X	ADC Oper, X	7D	3	4*
Absolute, Y	ADC Oper, Y	79	3	4*
(Indirect, X)	ADC (Oper, X)	61	2	6
(Indirect), Y	ADC (Oper), Y	71	2	5*

* Add 1 if page boundary is crossed.

AND   "AND" memory with accumulator
Logical AND to the accumulator
Operation: A ∧ M → A

N Z C I D V
√ √ − − − −

Addressing Mode	Assembly Language Form	OP CODE	No. Bytes	No. Cycles
Immediate	AND # Oper	29	2	2
Zero Page	AND Oper	25	2	3
Zero Page, X	AND Oper, X	35	2	4
Absolute	AND Oper	2D	3	4
Absolute, X	AND Oper, X	3D	3	4*
Absolute, Y	AND Oper, Y	39	3	4*
(Indirect, X)	AND (Oper, X)	21	2	6
(Indirect), Y	AND (Oper), Y	31	2	5

* Add 1 if page boundary is crossed.

The MCS 6502 Microprocessor and Peripheral Parts **105**

ASL ASL Shift Left One Bit (Memory or Accumulator)

Operation: C ← [7][6][5][4][3][2][1][0] ← 0   N Z C I D V
                                                   √ √ √ − − −

Addressing Mode	Assembly Language Form	OP CODE	No. Bytes	No. Cycles
Accumulator	ASL A	0A	1	2
Zero Page	ASL Oper	06	2	5
Zero Page, X	ASL Oper, X	16	2	6
Absolute	ASL Oper	0E	3	6
Absolute, X	ASL Oper, X	1E	3	7

BCC BCC Branch on Carry Clear

Operation: Branch on C = 0   N Z C I D V
                                  − − − − − −

Addressing Mode	Assembly Language Form	OP CODE	No. Bytes	No. Cycles
Relative	BCC Oper	90	2	2*

* Add 1 if branch occurs to same page.
* Add 2 if branch occurs to different page.

BCS BCS Branch on Carry Set

Operation: Branch on C = 1   N Z C I D V
                                  − − − − − −

Addresssing Mode	Assembly Language Form	OP CODE	No. Bytes	No. Cycles
Relative	BCS Oper	B0	2	2*

* Add 1 if branch occurs to same page.
* Add 2 if branch occurs to next page.

BEQ   BEQ Branch on Result Zero

Operation: Branch on $Z = 1$ N $\bcancel{Z}$ C I D V

                                                    — — — — —

Addressing Mode	Assembly Language Form	OP CODE	No. Bytes	No. Cycles
Relative	BEQ Oper	F0	2	2*

* Add 1 if branch occurs to same page.
* Add 2 if branch occurs to next page.

BIT   BIT Test Bits in Memory with Accumulator

Operation: $A \wedge M$, $M_7 \rightarrow N$, $M_6 \rightarrow V$ N $\bcancel{Z}$ C I D V

                                                            $M_7 \checkmark$ — — — M_6

Bits 6 and 7 are transferred to the status register. If the result of $A \wedge M$ is zero then $Z = 1$, otherwise $Z = 0$.

Addressing Mode	Assembly Language Form	OP CODE	No. Bytes	No. Cycles
Zero Page	BIT Oper	24	2	3
Absolute	BIT Oper	2C	3	4

BMI   BMI Branch on Result Minus

Operation: Branch on $N = 1$ N $\bcancel{Z}$ C I D V

                                                    — — — — — —

Addressing Mode	Assembly Language Form	OP CODE	No. Bytes	No. Cycles
Relative	BMI Oper	30	2	2*

* Add 1 if branch occurs to same page.
* Add 2 if branch occurs to different page.

The MCS 6502 Microprocessor and Peripheral Parts

BNE BNE Branch on Result Not Zero

Operation: Branch on Z = 0 N Z̶ C I D V

— — — — — —

Addressing Mode	Assembly Language Form	OP CODE	No. Bytes	No. Cycles
Relative	BNE Oper	D∅	2	2*

* Add 1 if branch occurs to same page.
* Add 2 if branch occurs to different page.

BPL BPL Branch on Result Plus

Operation: Branch on N = ∅ N Z̶ C I D V

— — — — — —

Addressing Mode	Assembly Language Form	OP CODE	No. Bytes	No. Cycles
Relative	BPL Oper	1∅	2	2*

* Add 1 if branch occurs to same page.
* Add 2 if branch occurs to different page.

BRK BRK Force Break

Operation: Forced Interrupt PC ↓ P ↓ N Z̶ C I D V

— — — 1 — —

Addressing Mode	Assembly Language Form	OP CODE	No. Bytes	No. Cycles
Implied	BRK	∅∅	1	7

1. A BRK command cannot be masked by setting I.

BVC BVC Branch on Overflow Clear

Operation: Branch on V = 0

N Z C I D V
— — — — — —

Addressing Mode	Assembly Language Form	OP CODE	No. Bytes	No. Cycles
Relative	BVC Oper	5∅	2	2*

* Add 1 if branch occurs to same page.
* Add 2 if branch occurs to different page.

BVS BVS Branch on Overflow Set

Operation: Branch on V = 1

N Z C I D V
— — — — — —

Addressing Mode	Assembly Language Form	OP CODE	No. Bytes	No. Cycles
Relative	BVS Oper	7∅	2	2*

* Add 1 if branch occurs to same page.
* Add 2 if branch occurs to different page.

CLC CLC Clear Carry Flag

Operation: ∅ → C

N Z C I D V
— — ∅ — — —

Addressing Mode	Assembly Language Form	OP CODE	No. Bytes	No. Cycles
Implied	CLC	18	1	2

CLD
CLD Clear Decimal Mode

Operation: $\emptyset \to D$

N	Z	C	I	D	V
—	—	—	—	$\emptyset$	—

Addressing Mode	Assembly Language Form	OP CODE	No. Bytes	No. Cycles
Implied	CLD	D8	1	2

CLI
CLI Clear Interrupt Disable Bit

Operation: $\emptyset \to I$

N	Z	C	I	D	V
—	—	—	$\emptyset$	—	—

Addressing Mode	Assembly Language Form	OP CODE	No. Bytes	No. Cycles
Implied	CLI	58	1	2

CLV
CLV Clear Overflow Flag

Operation: $\emptyset \to V$

N	Z	C	I	D	V
—	—	—	—	—	$\emptyset$

Addressing Mode	Assembly Language Form	OP CODE	No. Bytes	No. Cycles
Implied	CLV	B8	1	2

CMP   CMP Compare Memory and Accumulator

Operation: A - M   N Z C I D V
                                   √ √ √ — — —

Addressing Mode	Assembly Language Form	OP CODE	No. Bytes	No. Cycles
Immediate	CMP # Oper	C9	2	2
Zero Page	CMP Oper	C5	2	3
Zero Page, X	CMP Oper, X	D5	2	4
Absolute	CMP Oper	CD	3	4
Absolute, X	CMP Oper, X	DD	3	4*
Absolute, Y	CMP Oper, Y	D9	3	4*
(Indirect, X)	CMP (Oper, X)	C1	2	6
(Indirect), Y	CMP (Oper), Y	D1	2	5*

* Add 1 if page boundary is crossed.

CPX   CPX Compare Memory and Index X

Operation: X - M   N Z C I D V
                                   √ √ √ — — —

Addressing Mode	Assembly Language Form	OP CODE	No. Bytes	No. Cycles
Immediate	CPX # Oper	E0	2	2
Zero Page	CPX Oper	E4	2	3
Absolute	CPX Oper	EC	3	4

CPY — CPY Compare Memory and Index Y

Operation: Y − M

N Z C I D V
√ √ √ − − −

Addressing Mode	Assembly Language Form	OP CODE	No. Bytes	No. Cycles
Immediate	CPY # Oper	C0	2	2
Zero Page	CPY Oper	C4	2	3
Absolute	CPY Oper	CC	3	4

DEC — DEC Decrement Memory by One

Operation: M − 1 → M

N Z C I D V
√ √ − − − −

Addressing Mode	Assembly Language Form	OP CODE	No. Bytes	No. Cycles
Zero Page	DEC Oper	C6	2	5
Zero Page, X	DEC Oper, X	D6	2	6
Absolute	DEC Oper	CE	3	6
Absolute, X	DEC Oper, X	DE	3	7

DEX — DEX Decrement Index X by One

Operation: X − 1 → X

N Z C I D V
√ √ − − − −

Addressing Mode	Assembly Language Form	OP CODE	No. Bytes	No. Cycles
Implied	DEX	CA	1	2

DEY DEY Decrement Index Y by One

Operation: Y − 1 → Y

N Z C I D V
√ √ − − − −

Addressing Mode	Assembly Language Form	OP CODE	No. Bytes	No. Cycles
Implied	DEY	88	1	2

EOR EOR "Exclusive−Or" Memory with Accumulator

Operation: A ⊻ M → A

N Z C I D V
√ √ − − − −

Addressing Mode	Assembly Language Form	OP CODE	No. Bytes	No. Cycles
Immediate	EOR # Oper	49	2	2
Zero Page	EOR Oper	45	2	3
Zero Page, X	EOR Oper, X	55	2	4
Absolute	EOR Oper	4D	3	4
Absolute, X	EOR Oper, X	5D	3	4*
Absolute, Y	EOR Oper, Y	59	3	4*
(Indirect, X)	EOR (Oper, X)	41	2	6
(Indirect), Y	EOR (Oper), Y	51	2	5*

* Add 1 if page boundary is crossed.

INC

INC Increment Memory by One

Operation: M + 1 → M

N Z C I D V
√ √ — — — —

Addressing Mode	Assembly Language Form		OP CODE	No. Bytes	No. Cycles
Zero page	INC	Oper	E6	2	5
Zero Page, X	INC	Oper, X	F6	2	6
Absolute	INC	Oper	EE	3	6
Absolute, X	INC	Oper, X	FE	3	7

INX

INX Increment Index X by One

Operation: X + 1 → X

N Z C I D V
√ √ — — — —

Addressing Mode	Assembly Language Form	OP CODE	No. Bytes	No. Cycles
Implied	INX	E8	1	2

INY

INY Increment Index Y by One

Operation: Y + 1 → Y

N Z C I D V
√ √ — — — —

Addressing Mode	Assembly Language Form	OP CODE	No. Bytes	No. Cycles
Implied	INY	C8	1	2

JMP JMP Jump to New Location

Operation: (PC + 1) → PCL   N Z C I D V
         (PC + 2) → PCH   — — — — — —

Addressing Mode	Assembly Language Form	OP CODE	No. Bytes	No. Cycles
Absolute	JMP Oper	4C	3	3
Indirect	JMP (Oper)	6C	3	5

JSR JSR Jump to New Location Saving Return Address

Operation: PC + 2 ↓, (PC + 1) → PCL   N Z C I D V
         (PC + 2) → PCH   — — — — — —

Addressing Mode	Assembly Language Form	OP CODE	No. Bytes	No. Cycles
Absolute	JSR Oper	20	3	6

LDA LDA Load Accumulator with Memory

Operation: M → A   N Z C I D V
                                    √ √ — — — —

Addressing Mode	Assembly Language Form	OP CODE	No. Bytes	No. Cycles
Immediate	LDA # Oper	A9	2	2
Zero Page	LDA Oper	A5	2	3
Zero Page, X	LDA Oper, X	B5	2	4
Absolute	LDA Oper	AD	3	4
Absolute, X	LDA Oper, X	BD	3	4*
Absolute, Y	LDA Oper, Y	B9	3	4*
(Indirect, X)	LDA (Oper, X)	A1	2	6
(Indirect), Y	LDA (Oper), Y	B1	2	5*

* Add 1 if page boundary is crossed.

The MCS 6502 Microprocessor and Peripheral Parts **115**

LDX   LDX Load Index X with Memory

Operation: M → X   N Z C I D V
                                        √ √ — — — —

Addressing Mode	Assembly Language Form	OP CODE	No. Bytes	No. Cycles
Immediate	LDX # Oper	A2	2	2
Zero Page	LDX Oper	A6	2	3
Zero Page, Y	LDX Oper, Y	B6	2	4
Absolute	LDX Oper	AE	3	4
Absolute, Y	LDX Oper, Y	BE	3	4*

* Add 1 when page boundary is crossed.

LDY   LDY Load Index Y with Memory

Operation: M → Y   N Z C I D V
                                        √ √ — — — —

Addressing Mode	Assembly Language Form	OP CODE	No. Bytes	No. Cycles
Immediate	LDY # Oper	A0	2	2
Zero Page	LDY Oper	A4	2	3
Zero Page, X	LDY Oper, X	B4	2	4
Absolute	LDY Oper	AC	3	4
Absolute, X	LDY Oper, X	BC	3	4*

* Add 1 when page boundary is crossed.

LSR LSR Shift Right One Bit (Memory or Accumulator)

Operation: $0 \rightarrow \boxed{7\,6\,5\,4\,3\,2\,1\,0} \rightarrow C$

N Z C I D V
0 √ √ — — —

Addressing Mode	Assembly Language Form		OP CODE	No. Bytes	No. Cycles
Accumulator	LSR	A	4A	1	2
Zero Page	LSR	Oper	46	2	5
Zero Page, X	LSR	Oper, X	56	2	6
Absolute	LSR	Oper	4E	3	6
Absolute, X	LSR	Oper, X	5E	3	7

NOP NOP No Operation

Operation: No Operation (2 cycles)

N Z C I D V
— — — — — —

Addressing Mode	Assembly Language Form	OP CODE	No. Bytes	No. Cycles
Implied	NOP	EA	1	2

ORA ORA "OR" Memory with Accumulator

Operation A V M → A

N Z C I D V
√ √ — — — —

Addressing Mode	Assembly Language Form	OP CODE	No. Bytes	No. Cycles
Immediate	ORA # Oper	Ø9	2	2
Zero Page	ORA Oper	Ø5	2	3
Zero Page, X	ORA Oper, X	15	2	4
Absolute	ORA Oper	ØD	3	4
Absolute, X	ORA Oper, X	1D	3	4*
Absolute, Y	ORA Oper, Y	19	3	4*
(Indirect, X)	ORA (Oper, X)	Ø1	2	6
(Indirect), Y	ORA (Oper), Y	11	2	5

* Add 1 on page crossing

PHA PHA Push Accumulator on Stack

Operation: A ↓

N Z C I D V
— — — — — —

Addressing Mode	Assembly Language Form	OP CODE	No. Bytes	No. Cycles
Implied	PHA	48	1	3

PHP PHP Push Processor Status on Stack

Operation: P ↓

N Z C I D V
— — — — — —

Addressing Mode	Assembly Language Form	OP CODE	No. Bytes	No. Cycles
Implied	PHP	Ø8	1	3

PLA

PLA Pull Accumulator from Stack

Operation: A ↑

N Z C I D V
√ √ — — — —

Addressing Mode	Assembly Language Form	OP CODE	No. Bytes	No. Cycles
Implied	PLA	68	1	4

PLP

PLP Pull Processor Status from Stack

Operation: P ↑

N Z C I D V
From Stack

Addressing Mode	Assembly Language Form	OP CODE	No. Bytes	No. Cycles
Implied	PLP	28	1	4

ROL

ROL Rotate One Bit Left (Memory or Accumulator)

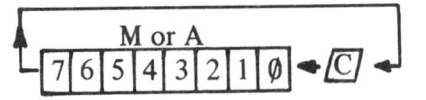

Operation: ⟵ [7 6 5 4 3 2 1 0] ⟵ [C] ⟵
            M or A

N Z C I D V
√ √ √ — — —

Addressing Mode	Assembly Language Form		OP CODE	No. Bytes	No. Cycles
Accumulator	ROL	A	2A	1	2
Zero Page	ROL	Oper	26	2	5
Zero Page, X	ROL	Oper, X	36	2	6
Absolute	ROL	Oper	2E	3	6
Absolute, X	ROL	Oper, X	3E	3	7

ROR   ROR Rotate One Bit Right (Memory or Accumulator)

Operation: →[C]→[7][6][5][4][3][2][1][0]┘

N Z C I D V
√ √ √ — — —

Addressing Mode	Assembly Language Form		OP CODE	No. Bytes	No. Cycles
Accumulator	ROR	A	6A	1	2
Zero Page	ROR	Oper	66	2	5
Zero Page, X	ROR	Oper, X	76	2	6
Absolute	ROR	Oper	6E	3	6
Absolute, X	ROR	Oper, X	7E	3	7

RTI   RTI Return From Interrupt

Operation: P↑ PC↑

N Z C I D V
From Stack

Addressing Mode	Assembly Language Form	OP CODE	No. Bytes	No. Cycles
Implied	RTI	40	1	6

RTS   RTS Return From Subroutine

Operation: PC↑, PC + 1 → PC

N Z C I D V
— — — — — —

Addressing Mode	Assembly Language Form	OP CODE	No. Bytes	No. Cycles
Implied	RTS	60	1	6

SBC   SBC Subtract Memory from Accumulator with Borrow

Operation: $A - M - \overline{C} \rightarrow A$ N Z C I D V

Note: $\overline{C}$ = Borrow   √ √ √ − − √

Addressing Mode	Assembly Language Form	OP CODE	No. Bytes	No. Cycles
Immediate	SBC # Oper	E9	2	2
Zero Page	SBC Oper	E5	2	3
Zero Page, X	SBC Oper, X	F5	2	4
Absolute	SBC Oper	ED	3	4
Absolute, X	SBC Oper, X	FD	3	4*
Absolute, Y	SBC Oper, Y	F9	3	4*
(Indirect, X)	SBC (Oper, X)	E1	2	6
(Indirect), Y	SBC (Oper), Y	F1	2	5*

* Add 1 when page boundary is crossed.

SEC   SEC Set Carry Flag

Operation: $1 \rightarrow C$ N Z C I D V

− − 1 − − −

Addressing Mode	Assembly Language Form	OP CODE	No. Bytes	No. Cycles
Implied	SEC	38	1	2

SED   SED Set Decimal Mode

Operation: $1 \rightarrow D$ N Z C I D V

− − − − 1 −

Addressing Mode	Assembly Language Form	OP CODE	No. Bytes	No. Cycles
Implied	SED	F8	1	2

SEI

SEI Set Interrupt Disable Status

Operation: 1 → I

N Z C I D V
− − − 1 − −

Addressing Mode	Assembly Language Form	OP CODE	No. Bytes	No. Cycles
Implied	SEI	78	1	2

STA

STA Store Accumulator in Memory

Operation: A → M

N Z C I D V
− − − − − −

Addressing Mode	Assembly Language Form	OP CODE	No. Bytes	No. Cycles
Zero Page	STA Oper	85	2	3
Zero Page, X	STA Oper, X	95	2	4
Absolute	STA Oper	8D	3	4
Absolute, X	STA Oper, X	9D	3	5
Absolute, Y	STA Oper, Y	99	3	5
(Indirect, X)	STA (Oper, X)	81	2	6
(Indirect), Y	STA (Oper), Y	91	2	6

STX

STX Store Index X in Memory

Operation: X → M

N Z C I D V
− − − − − −

Addressing Mode	Assembly Language Form	OP CODE	No. Bytes	No. Cycles
Zero Page	STX Oper	86	2	3
Zero Page, Y	STX Oper, Y	96	2	4
Absolute	STX Oper	8E	3	4

STY   STY Store Index Y in Memory

Operation: Y → M   N Z C I D V
                                    – – – – –

Addressing Mode	Assembly Language Form	OP CODE	No. Bytes	No. Cycles
Zero Page	STY Oper	84	2	3
Zero Page	STY Oper, X	94	2	4
Absolute	STY Oper	8C	3	4

TAX   TAX Transfer Accumulator to Index X

Operation: A → X   N Z C I D V
                                    √ √ – – – –

Addressing Mode	Assembly Language Form	OP CODE	No. Bytes	No. Cycles
Implied	TAX	AA	1	2

TAY   TAY Transfer Accumulator to Index Y

Operation: A → Y   N Z C I D V
                                    √ √ – – – –

Addressing Mode	Assembly Language Form	OP CODE	No. Bytes	No. Cycles
Implied	TAY	A8	1	2

TSX   TSX Transfer Stack Pointer to Index X

Operation: S → X

N Z C I D V
√ √ — — — —

Addressing Mode	Assembly Language Form	OP CODE	No. Bytes	No. Cycles
Implied	TSX	BA	1	2

TXA   TXA Transfer Index X to Accumulator

Operation: X → A

N Z C I D V
√ √ — — — —

Addressing Mode	Assembly Language Form	OP CODE	No. Bytes	No. Cycles
Implied	TXA	8A	1	2

TXS   TXS Transfer Index X to Stack Pointer

Operation: X → S

N Z C I D V
— — — — — —

Addressing Mode	Assembly Language Form	OP CODE	No. Bytes	No. Cycles
Implied	TXS	9A	1	2

TYA   TYA Transfer Index Y to Accumulator

Operation: Y → A   N Z C I D V
                                                      √ √ − − − −

Addressing Mode	Assembly Language Form	OP CODE	No. Bytes	No. Cycles
Implied	TYA	98	1	2

3.6 MCS6502 SPECIFICATIONS

3.6.1 External Connections (Pinouts)

See Figure 3.6-1 for package pin numbers corresponding to the following signal descriptions.

V_{CC}, V_{SS} — Supply voltages for the MCS6502

The supply voltage (V_{CC}), pin 8, must be 5 volts DC ± 5%. The absolute maximum value on V_{CC} is 7 volts dc. V_{SS}, pins 1 and 21 are ground, or equivalently, 0 volts.

1. AB0-AB 15 — Address Bus. The Address bus signals on the MCS6502 microprocessor are provided by push-pull drivers capable of driving at least one standard TTL load and 130 picofarads of capacitance. As we will see in Section 3.6.2 the address bus provides, at all times, a valid memory address. (Refer to the latest manufacturers' data sheets for specific information.) The present microprocessor chips are designed so that the address bus will have settled to a correct new value no later than 300 nanoseconds into $\phi 1$ (phase 1) clock pulse interval, and will remain stable at that value until the next rising edge of the $\phi 1$ pulse. The manufacturer is likely to improve these characteristics with continued development.

2. DB0-DB7 — Data Bus. Pins 26 though 33 are connected to the bidirectional data bus. Each of these pins is connected to both an input and an output buffer. The output buffer is in three-state high impedance (isolated) condition, except when it is desired to transfer data out to an external support chip. All data transfers take place

The MCS 6502 Microprocessor and Peripheral Parts **125**

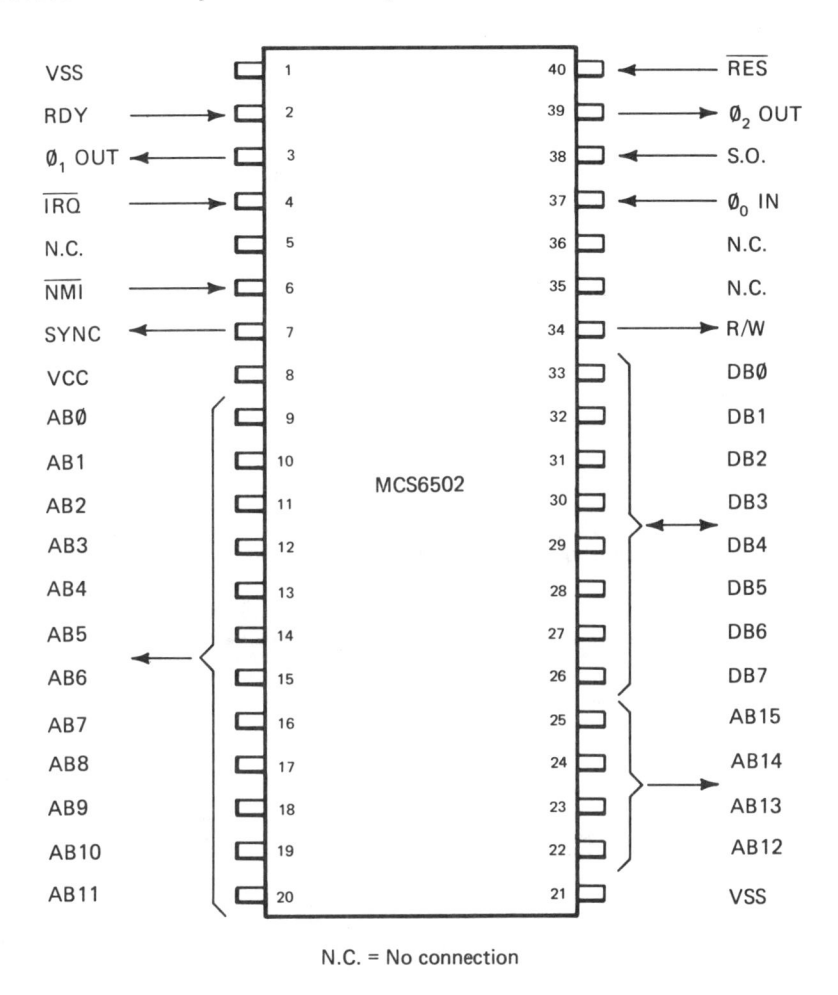

```
VSS      ──┤ 1        40 ├──◄──── RES
RDY ────►──┤ 2        39 ├────►── ∅₂ OUT
∅₁ OUT ◄───┤ 3        38 ├──◄──── S.O.
IRQ ────►──┤ 4        37 ├──◄──── ∅₀ IN
N.C.    ───┤ 5        36 ├─────── N.C.
NMI ────►──┤ 6        35 ├─────── N.C.
SYNC ◄─────┤ 7        34 ├────►── R/W
VCC     ───┤ 8        33 ├─────── DB0
AB0     ───┤ 9        32 ├─────── DB1
AB1     ───┤ 10       31 ├─────── DB2
AB2     ───┤ 11  MCS  30 ├─────── DB3
AB3     ───┤ 12  6502 29 ├─────── DB4
AB4     ───┤ 13       28 ├─────── DB5
AB5     ───┤ 14       27 ├─────── DB6
AB6     ───┤ 15       26 ├─────── DB7
AB7     ───┤ 16       25 ├─────── AB15
AB8     ───┤ 17       24 ├─────── AB14
AB9     ───┤ 18       23 ├─────── AB13
AB10    ───┤ 19       22 ├─────── AB12
AB11    ───┤ 20       21 ├─────── VSS
```

N.C. = No connection

Figure 3.6-1 MCS6502 pinout designation
(courtesy MOS Technology)

during the phase 2 ($\phi 2$) clock pulse. During $\phi 1$ the data bus is in the three state high-impedance condition. The data bus output buffer is a push-pull driver, like the address bus driver, and is capable of driving one TTL load and 130 picofarad of capacitance. The data on this bus from external support chips must be stable prior to the end of the $\phi 2$ pulse. On the present data sheets the data must be stable at least 100 nanoseconds before the end of $\phi 2$. These characteristics are shown graphically in Figure 3.6-2.

Figure 3.6-2 Basic MCS6502 timing

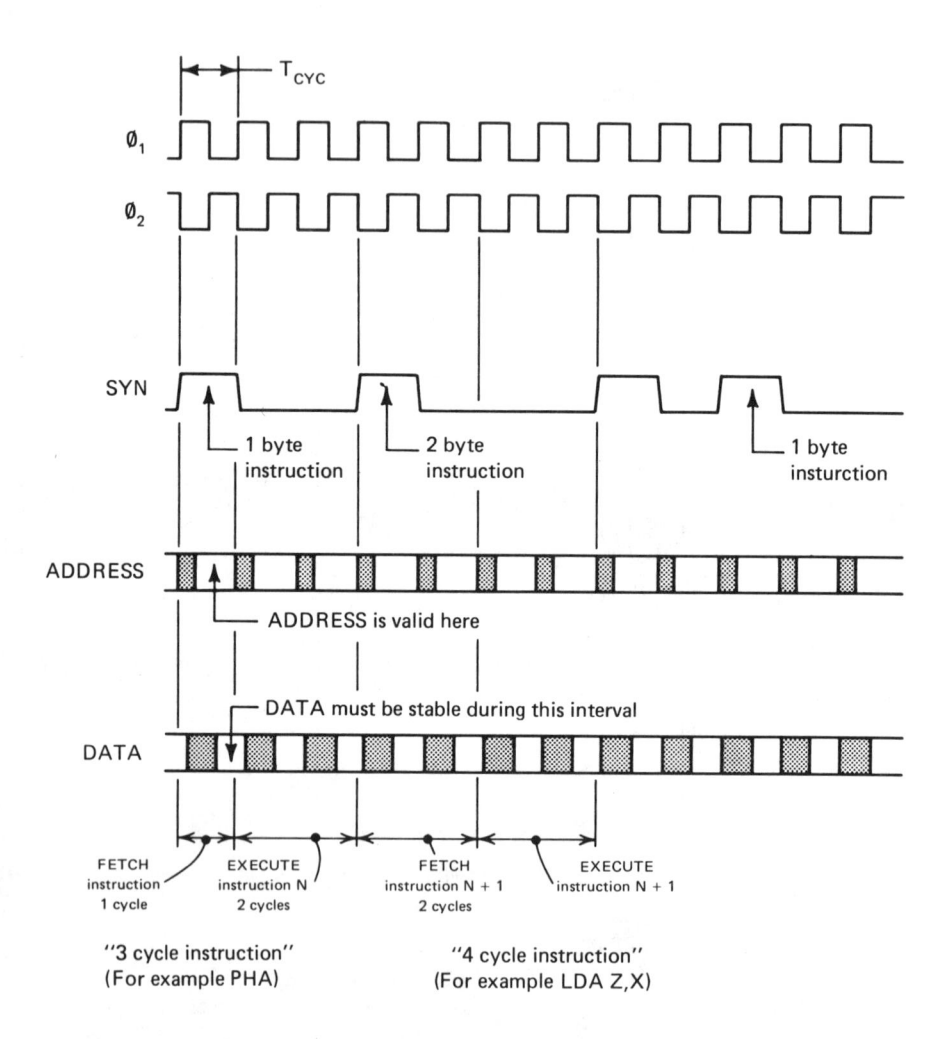

Notes:
1. SYNC is high during FETCH.
2. DATA is read at approximately falling edge of $\emptyset_2$. It must be stable *both* before and after falling edge.
3. For V_{CC} = 5 volts, T_A = 25 °C, T_{CYC} = 1 μs an associated memory must have access time ≤500 μs.
4. Refer to manufacturers latest literature for specific information.

3. R/$\overline{\text{W}}$ – Read/Write.   The R/$\overline{\text{W}}$ line allows the microprocessor to control the direction of data transfer among system components. When the voltage level is high the R/$\overline{\text{W}}$ line is reading from the data bus into the microprocessor. When the voltage level is low it is commanding an external device to write the present contents of the data bus into a peripheral support chip or memory.

All transitions on this line occur during $\phi 1$, which allows control of data transfers during $\phi 2$.

4. RDY – Ready.   The RDY input permits delay of execution of any machine cycle during which RDY is low. This line should be synchronized for operation with slow external devices, i.e., slow RWM or external input sources. Synchronizing constraints require that this line change during $\phi 1$. This change will be recognized during the next $\phi 2$, enabling or disabling the execution of the current internal machine cycle, which normally occurs during the next $\phi 1$ clock cycle. If the ready line goes from high to low during a write cycle the processor will execute that cycle and will then stop in the next read cycle.

Without the RDY line our only alternative would be to slow the system clock to match the slowest functioning component. This alternative, however, is not feasible below a lower limit, since the dynamic MCS6502 registers must be refreshed often (at a rate of roughly 100 Khz or greater).

5. SYNC – The Synchronizing Signal.   The SYNC signal is an output signal produced when the microprocessor is fetching an op code. This line goes high during $\phi 1$, and stays high for the remainder of that cycle. If the RDY line is pulled low during $\phi 1$ of a SYNC high cycle, single-step operation of the MCS6502 can be achieved. Circuits are available from the manufacturer detailing this operation.

6. SO – Set Overflow.   The SO line is an output line whose only function is to set the overflow bit in the status register. Specifically the overflow bit will be set to a logic one on a high to low transition on this pin. Although the manufacturer cautions that this pin is intended for use as a future input/output port, and thus its functions may be changed, it is a very useful systems line, particularly when the microprocessor is connected to very high speed external devices. The ability in a program to test the high to low transition of this pin allows service to external devices no less than 4 cycles after a change takes place. When operating at a 1 megahertz clockrate, this means a maximum delay of 4 microseconds.

7. Integral Clock Circuitry. The MCS6502 requires an external oscillator capacitor plus an optional crystal if extreme clock accuracy is needed. Figures 3.6-3, 4, and 5 show several alternative external timing configurations.

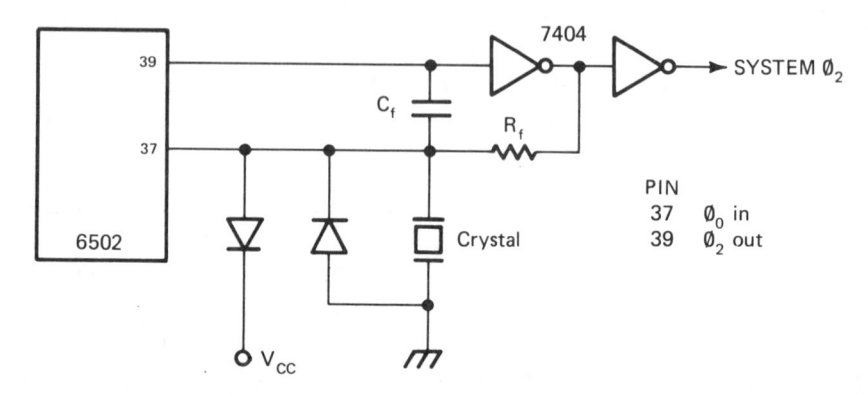

Figure 3.6-3 MCS6502 Parallel Mode Crystal Controlled Oscillator (ROM) (Courtesy MOS Technology)

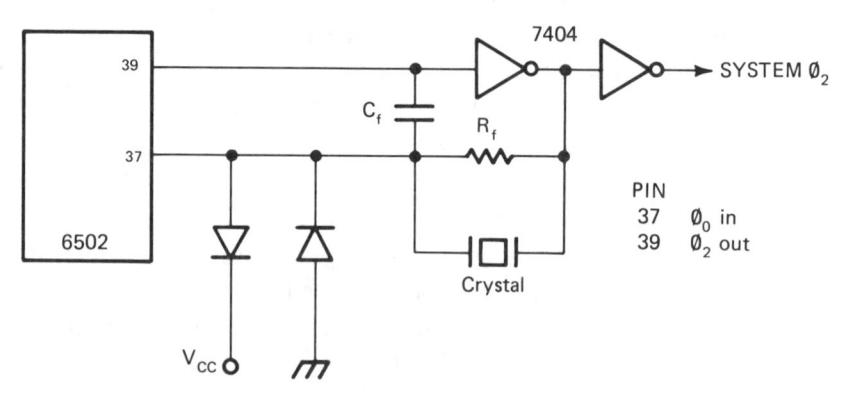

Figure 3.6-4 MCS6502 Series Model Crystal Controlled Oscillator (ROM) (Courtesy MOS Technology)

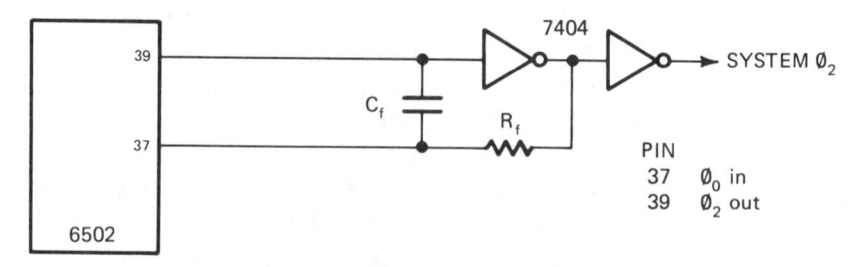

Figure 3.6-5 MCS6502 time base generator — RC network (Courtesy MOS Technology)

The MCS 6502 Microprocessor and Peripheral Parts   **129**

8. $\overline{\text{RES}}$ – **Reset**. The Not Reset line is usually used to initialize the microprocessor during power up. As the power supply is turned on the Reset line must be held low, which will reset certain internal registers. When the line goes high the microprocessor will delay six $\phi 1$ - $\phi 2$ cycles and will then start its Reset sequence. the MCS6502 requires that a reserved pair of memory locations ($FFFC, $FFFD) be preloaded with the starting location of the Reset program (see Appendix B). It is the system designer's responsibility to make sure that the contents of those two locations contain the *location* of the first instruction to be fetched. In common jargon, $FFFC and $FFFD are said to contain a *vector* to the first instruction. It is also imperative that an interval of time be allowed during which the microprocessor can execute several clock cycles before the Reset line goes high.

Many times during execution of a program, especially during debugging, we might like to pull Reset low which will then reinitialize the program as if it had just been turned on. Proper handling of this line is of considerable importance to a systems designer and may be particularly troublesome, since the circuitry which drives it will set its supply voltage from the same line as pin 8 of the microprocessor, V_{CC}. As an aside, many monostable integrated circuits will start in a high condition and then fall low as power is stabilized, making them useless in generating automatic power-up reset signals.

9. $\overline{\text{NMI}}$ – **Nonmaskable Interrupt.** The Not NonMaskable Interrupt input always interrupts the processor after it has completed the instruction being executed when $\overline{\text{NMI}}$ is pulled low. This interrupt cannot be masked by the microprocessor and hence, it has no way to prevent recognition of this interrupt. The MCS6502 responds to a high-to-low transition at the $\overline{\text{NMI}}$ input, after which $\overline{\text{NMI}}$ may stay low indefinitely without affecting the microprocessor or causing another nonmaskable interrupt. The microprocessor will thus not detect another $\overline{\text{NMI}}$ until this line has gone high and then once again goes low. The $\overline{\text{NMI}}$ signal must be low for at least two clock cycles in order to be recognized, at which point the following NMI sequence of events take place. First, the program counter and processor status register will be pushed onto the stack into three successive locations determined by the value of the stack pointer at the time $\overline{\text{NMI}}$ is detected. Specifically the high byte of the program counter (PCH) will be placed in the location pointed to by the stack pointer. The S register will then be decremented and the low program counter byte (PCL) will be written. S will again be decremented, and the processor status register (P), will be pushed. Like Reset sequence activity, a pair of fixed addresses ($FFFA) and ($FFFB)

will be sequentially placed on the address bus and from those two locations data (the NMI vector) will be read and placed in the program counter. The microprocessor will then revert to normal fetch activity and the desired NMI service routine will be executed. This routine should be terminated with an RTI-ReTurn from Interrupt instruction. The RTI instruction will return the previous program counter and status registers to their original condition by reloading these three bytes from the stack, allowing a return to the state which existed prior to the time NMI was detected. Notice especially that only P, among the set of microprocessor registers, has been automatically saved. If the NMI software service routine requires use of A, X, or Y then those registers' contents must be saved before usage, and returned to their proper values prior to RTI. The only other thing which is done during acknowledgement of NMI is that the interrupt mask in the processor status register will be set to a one, thereby disallowing a maskable interrupt. The I bit will be returned to its original condition by RTI since P is restored.

10. IRQ—Interrupt ReQuest. The IRQ request input is very similar to NMI. Its function, however, can be controlled by means of the interrupt mask bit (I), which is bit 2 of the P register. If this bit is a logic one, signals on the IRQ input pin will be disregarded by the microprocessor. Unlike NMI, the IRQ line is level-sensitive, not edge-sensitive. Thus, the microprocessor will be interrupted as long as the flag bit I is low *and* IRQ is low. IRQ must be held low until recognized and the microprocessor begins IRQ servicing. Like NMI requests, IRQ requests are ignored until the instruction being executed when the request is made has been completed. Then, if I = 0, a sequence of operations very much like NMI sequence will take place. The PC and P registers are pushed on the stack, and I set. Vector locations $FFFE and $FFFF will be sequentially placed on the address bus and the contents read from these locations will be placed in program counter low (PCL) and program counter high (PCH), respectively. The MCS6502 will then begin instruction fetch. The terminating instruction for this activity is also RTI.

As we shall see in Section 3.7, which discusses the input/output characteristics and interrupt servicing features of the Peripheral Interface Adapter (MCS6520), there are lines allowing direct connection to IRQ such that the very act of reading I/O ports will reset a latched interrupt request input.

3.6.2 Electrical Characteristics of the MCS6502

Tables 3.6.2-1 and 3.6.2-2 give absolute maximum electrical ratings and recommended electrical operating conditions for the MCS6502 microprocessor.

TABLE 3.6.2-1 MAXIMUM RATINGS FOR MCS6502 MICROPROCESSOR

Maximum Ratings

Supply Voltage	V_{CC}	−0.3 to 7.0	volts
Input Voltage	V_{IN}	−0.3 to 7.0	volts
Operating Temperature	T_A	0 to 70	°C
Storage Temperature	T_{STC}	−55 to 125	°C

3.6.3 Interrupt Applications

One of the important tasks the microcomputer system designer must perform is the management of interrupts in the proposed system. Once it has been decided to use an interrupt-driven system, subsequent tabulations of those signals allowed to cause interrupts and functions to be controlled in response to interrupts must follow. The decision to "go interrupt" must not be taken lightly. The complexities of the attendant software require meticulous attention to detail at every level. Some hardware/software tradeoffs must be faced, as well as determination of specific worst-case frequency of interrupts, length of time allowed for interrupt service, etc. The following examples illustrate the use of interrupt capability in two applications.

3.6.3.1 **A Fully-Decoded Keyboard.** The problem of data entry is solved in many systems by a keyboard. In small systems, development of the binary code associated with each key by detection of simple switch enclosure can be determined by the processor. However, in large data terminals, the keyboard usually includes an encoder which generates a unique code corresponding to each key. When a key is closed, the corresponding code is sent from the encoder output pins and a *strobe signal* is generated to indicate that a key has been pressed.

TABLE 3.6.2-2 OPERATING CHARACTERISTICS OF MCS6502 MICROPROCESSOR

$V_{CC} = 5V \pm 5\%$ $V_{SS} = 0V$ $T_A = 25°\,C$		MIN	TYP	MAX	
Input High Voltage	V_{IH}			5.25	volts
Input Low Voltage	V_{IL}	−0.3			volts
Input High Threshold *	V_{IHT}	2.0			volts
Input Low Threshold *	V_{ILT}			0.8	volts
Input Leakage Current	I_{IN}			2.5	μA
Output High Voltage ($I_{LOAD} = -100\,\mu$A)	V_{OH} DATA, ADDRESS	2.4			volts
Output Low Voltage ($I_{LOAD} = 1.6$ MA)	V_{OL} DATA, ADDRESS			0.4	volts
Power Dissipation	P_D		250	700	MW
Capacitance DATA, ADDRESS, R/W, SYNC	C_{OUT}			15	pF
OTHERS	C_{IN}			10	pF

* Applies to $\overline{RES}$, $\overline{NMI}$, RDY, $\overline{IRQ}$, Data, SO

Such a keyboard represents an excellent candidate for interrupt-driven operation. Interrupts occur relatively infrequently and the operation to be performed is relatively simple. The keyboard strobe line is connected directly to an interrupt input on a peripheral interface device. Each time a strobe signal is generated, an interrupt occurs, the processor reads the data on the peripheral port into memory, analyzes this data and then returns to the program that was in process. If no keys are pressed, the processor spends no time at all in servicing the keyboard.

The MCS 6502 Microprocessor and Peripheral Parts **133**

Without interrupts, the processor would have to read the keyboard data into memory periodically in order to detect an active key. This operation would necessarily be performed about every fifty to one hundred milliseconds. In addition to detecting an active key, the processor must make sure that each separate activation of a key is detected once and only once. This requires much more complex software than the simple interrupt routine. Another drawback of noninterrupt processing is that the processor is required to devote a periodic portion of its time to keyboard activity regardless of usage level of the keyboard. In many systems, this is not a problem, but in large terminals, etc., the time spent checking for keyboard strobes could be more profitably spent in other operations. The designer must therefore determine whether the system under development can tolerate this "overhead" due to the keyboard strobe checking function while still completing its other tasks.

3.6.3.2 A Scanned Display Example. Although time is a major factor in determining the necessity of interrupts, the interrupt technique can also be extremely useful when performing parallel operations. A good example of this can be found in a system which contains a digital display and/or printer.

A digital display is often "scanned" such that each digit is driven for a short period of time in sequence. The display must be scanned in a manner which is undetectable to the eye. This could require the processor's timing of loops to assure that scanning occurs at a proper rate. It is very difficult for the processor to calculate repetitive time intervals while performing its normal system program routines. The processor should run the system program without consideration for the display time intervals, only executing the display software when it is required.

A solution to this problem is the generation of processor interrupts at fixed intervals using an external counter or clock. Each time an interrupt occurs, the data for the next digit in the display is placed on an output port. The processor then returns to the program it had been executing.

A specific example of a 24 hour clock display on the KIM microcomputer is given in the Example programs of Section 3.8. This application uses the built-in timer in the MCD6530 to interrupt the display routine on a regular basis and update the displayed value. Note that, in this case, the normal processor activity is display scan, while interrupt service is display update.

Both of the examples described above represent solutions to system problems. Events which happen very infrequently and events which must be performed in parallel with other events or in parallel with the main system program should be seriously considered as candidates for interrupts. Additional considerations are described in other chapters of this book. It is important to note that a typical system may be capable of interruption by several independent sources, each of which may require a unique response to its interrupt requests.

3.6.4 Interrupt Priority Management

After a careful analysis of the total system and a determination of all the sources of interrupts, the designer must ask himself, "What happens if more than one interrupt source requires attention at one time?" If this can occur, priorities must be established for the various interrupt sources. A high-speed data transfer device (a disk, for example) may need quick response to interrupt requests and may therefore be given high priority. Display management or memory refresh may have noncritical timing requirements and therefore may be given low priority.

A MCS6502 based system can employ several hardware methods of determining the highest priority active interrupt. These can involve using a special "priority encoder" which allows the processor to go directly to the software which services the highest priority interrupt. After this service is completed, software to service the next higher priority task can be executed. However, a less expensive approach to interrupt priority, the "polled" interrupt is often used. With this technique, each time one or more active interrupt sources is detected, the processor executes an interrupt polling program that interrogates the highest priority interrupt device, then the next highest, and so on until an active interrupt is located. The program services that interrupt and then returns to the interrupt polling program and continues to interrogate the next highest priority interrupt until all have been interrogated or clears the interrupt disable to allow nested interrupts. (See Section 2.11.7.5.) The interrupt polling program is always executed when an interrupt occurs so that all interrupts that occur concurrently will be serviced in order of priority level.

3.6.5 System Interconnect for Interrupts

In the simple "polled" interrupt technique for establishing priority, the interrupt software actually determines the highest priority active interrupt. The $\overline{\text{IRQ}}$ or $\overline{\text{NMI}}$ interrupt request signals simply cause the processor to jump to the polling software.

For this reason, it is possible to "OR" the various interrupt signals together to form the signal for the processor. Any active interrupt source will then cause the processor to do the interrupt polling and servicing operation. Provision for generation of this OR function is provided in the MCS6500 family peripheral interface devices. (See Section 3.7.) Devices request interrupt service via requests sent to their particular interface adapters, which in turn provide interrupt outputs to be sent to the processor. These interrupt outputs can be "WIRE-OR'd" by connecting them all together and then connecting this single line to the processor. This input should then be pulled to +5V with a resistor. Any one of the interrupt outputs on the peripheral adaptors can then pull this interrupt low. This simple configuration is shown in Figure 3.6.5-1.

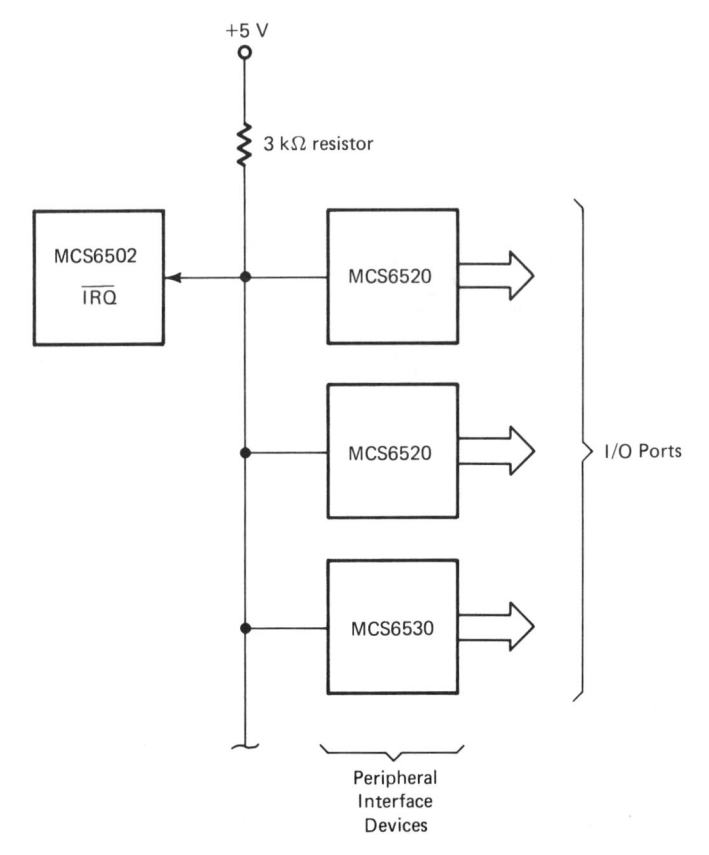

Figure 3.6.5-1 Interrupt wire OR'd hardware configuration from peripheral interface devices to microprocessor

3.7 PERIPHERAL INTERFACE CHIPS

3.7.1 The MCS6530

The MCS6530 is a multiple function component designed for use with the MCS6502 microprocessor. Like the MCS6502 it is second-sourced by Synertek and Rockwell. Its general description was given in Section 3.1.1, and a photograph of it is shown in Figure. 3.7.1-1. It is intended to serve applications requiring 1024 bytes of program, 64 bytes of RWM and 2 I/O ports.

Figure 3.7.1-1 MCS6530 multifunction peripheral element

3.7.1.1 Specifications. The following list summarizes the principal characteristics of the MCS6530:

1. Single 5 Volt supply
2. Byte Oriented
3. 1024 Byte ROM
4. 64 Byte RWM
5. Two 8-bit Bidirectional I/O Ports
6. Programmable Interval Timer
7. Interrupt Generation Capability

1. Single 5 volt supply: Like the MCS6502, the MCS6530 is based on ion-implant, depletion load technology. This fabrication method permits use of a single 5 volt supply.

The MCS 6502 Microprocessor and Peripheral Parts

2. Byte oriented: The MCS6530 attaches directly to the data bus. Its I/O ports may be a full 8 bits wide. ROM and RWM word lengths are also 8 bits.

3. 1024 byte ROM: The ROM is mask-programmed. By judicious choice of two chip select lines the addressing can allow up to 7168 contiguous bytes of ROM without an additional decoder.

4. 64 byte RWM: This RWM can also be "placed" in address space contiguous with other such RWM. The use of 7 MCS6530s with 7168 bytes of ROM would give simultaneously 448 bytes of RWM. This RWM is static, and does not require refreshing.

5. Two 8-bit bidirectional I/O ports: The MCS6530 has potentially 16 pins available for I/O. Three of these pins can be used instead for other purposes, if so masked during manufacture. These three pins can be I/O, two chip selects, or IRQ, in any combination. The two ports, commonly referred to as the A side or B side, are software programmable both in direction (input or output) and data value. A one byte register called the Data Direction Register is accessible by the microcomputer and each bit which is a zero defines the same bit position on the associated port to be input. A logic one defines that pin to be output.

6. Programmable interval timer: The built-in programmable timer allows division of time into intervals varying from 1 to 262,144 clock intervals. The clock signal generated by the MCS6502 is connected to the MCS6530 to synchronize access to the Data Bus, and is also used to drive this timer. This timer can have many applications in MCS6502/6530-based systems.

7. Interrupt generation capability: At the time that the MCS6530 mask is made (during manufacture), pin 17 can be connected internally to IRQ generated by the programmable interval timer or B-side I/O bit 7 (PB7). If connected to the timer IRQ output then it can be in turn routed to pin 4, IRQ, of the MCS6502. If so connected and software enabled, then when the timer count reaches zero the microprocessor will be interrupted if its I (interrupt mask bit) has been cleared. A specific KIM example has been included in the MCS6502 example programs (see Section 3.8).

3.7.1.2 MCS6530 Internal Architecture. A block diagram of the MCS6530 internal architecture is shown in Figure 3.7.1-2. The MCS6530 is divided into four basic sections, RWM, ROM, I/O and TIMER. The

138   Microcomputer Systems Principles

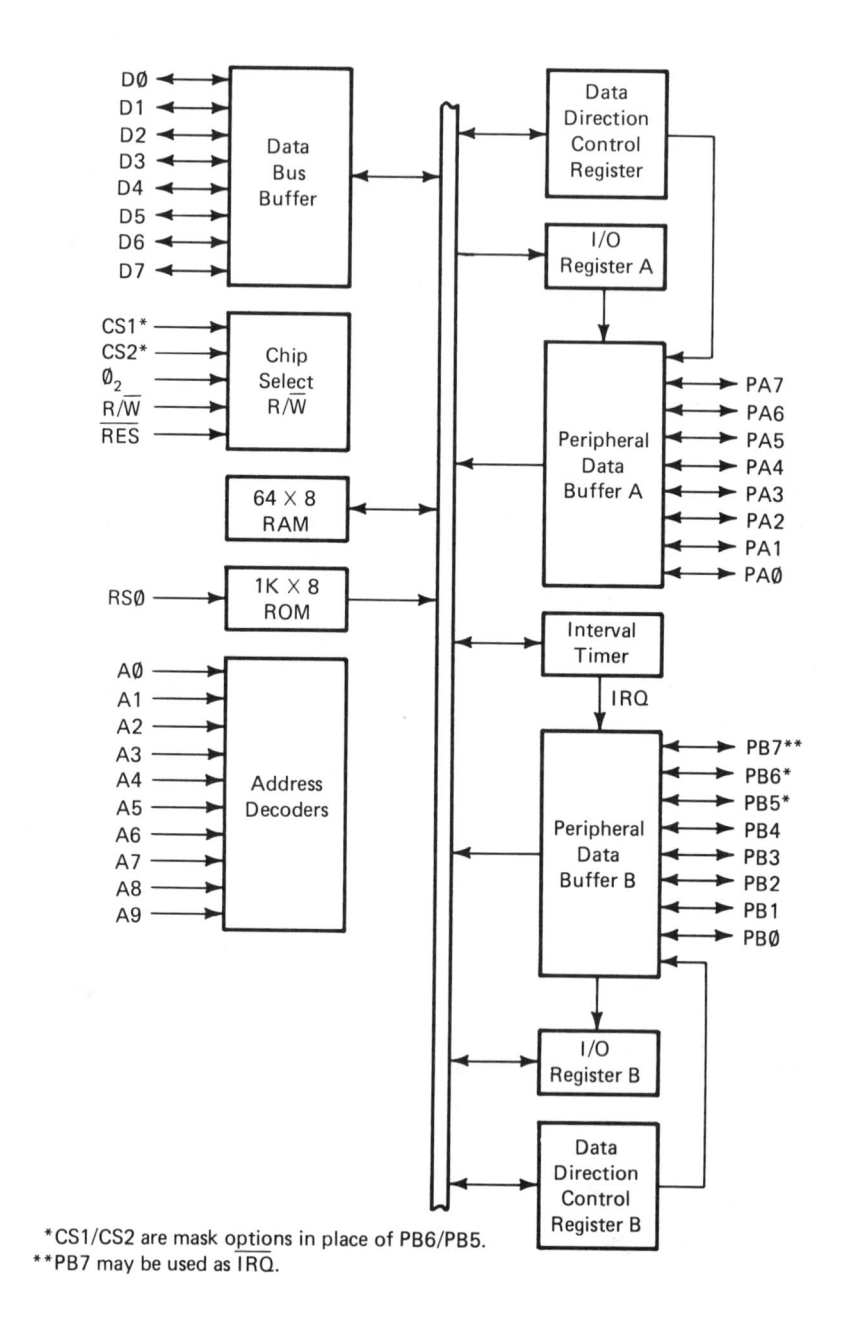

*CS1/CS2 are mask options in place of PB6/PB5.
**PB7 may be used as IRQ.

Figure 3.7.1-2 MCS6530 internal architecture
(Courtesy MOS Technology)

RWM and ROM interface directly with the microprocessor through the system data bus and address lines. The I/O section consists of 2 8-bit halves. Each half contains a Data Direction Register (DDR) and an I/O Register. The DDR controls the peripheral output buffers, as discussed below.

The ROM is in a 1024 × 8 configuration. Address lines A0-A9, as well as RS0 (ROM select) are used to address the entire ROM. With the addition of chip selects CS1 and CS2, up to seven MCS6530s may be addressed, giving 7168 × 8 bits of continuous ROM.

A 64 × 8 static RWM is contained on the MCS6530. It is addressed by A0-A5 (byte select), RS0, A6, A7, A8, A9 and, depending on the number of chips in the system, CS1 and CS2.

There are four internal registers, including two data direction registers and two peripheral I/O data registers. The two data direction registers (A side and B side) control the direction of data into and out of the peripheral pins as discussed earlier. For example, a "1" loaded into data direction register A, position 3 sets up peripheral pin PA3 as an output. If a "0" had been loaded instead, PA3 would be configured as an input. The two data I/O registers are used to latch data from the data bus during a Write operation until the peripheral device can read the data supplied by the microprocessor unit. Although during a Read operation the microprocessor unit reads the peripheral pin, the address is the same as the register. For those pins programmed as outputs by the data direction registers, the data on the pins will be the same as that in the I/O register.

It should be noted that the microprocessor, when reading data from a port, is in fact reading the Peripheral Port Pins and not the I/O register itself. The only way the I/O register data can be changed is by a microprocessor Write operation (such as STA or STX). The I/O register contents are not affected by the data on the Peripheral Pin.

The timer section of the MCS 6530 contains three basic parts; preliminary divide-down register or scaler, a programmable 8-bit "time" register, and interrupt logic. These are illustrated in Figure. 3.7.1-3.

The interval timer can be programmed to count up to 256 time intervals, each having a value of 1T, 8T, 64T or 1024T increments, where T is the system clock period. When a full count is reached (by decrementing through "0"), an interrupt flag is set to a logic "1." After the interrupt flag is set the internal clock begins counting down to a maximum of -255T. Thus, after the interrupt flag is set, a Read of the timer will tell how long since the flag was set up to a maximum of 255T.

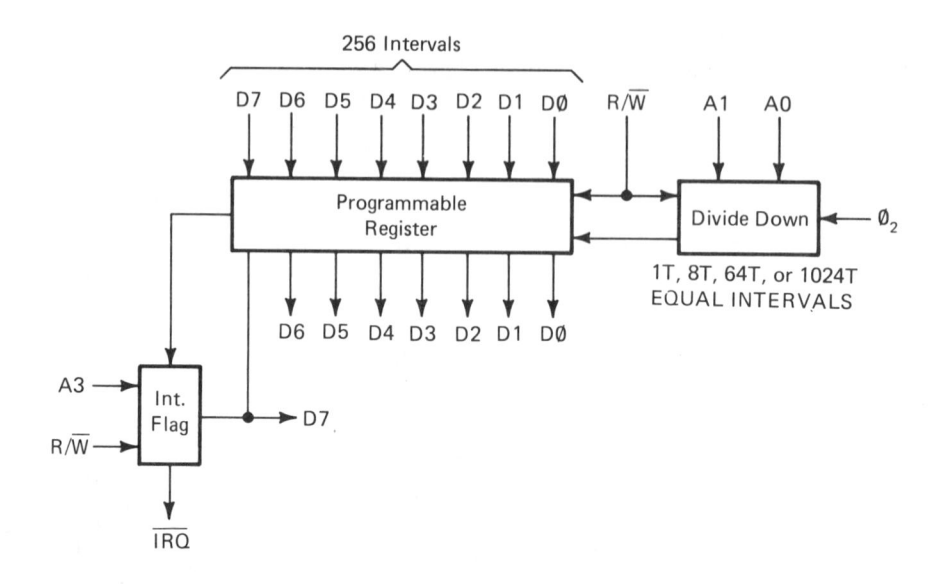

Figure 3.7.1-3 Basic elements of interval timer

When writing to the timer, the high order 8 bits of the timer are loaded from the system data bus. If a count of 52 time intervals were to be counted, for example, 0 0 1 1 0 1 0 0 would be written into the timer section. The scale factor of 1, 8, 64 or 1024T is decoded from address lines A0 and A1 at this same time. Address line A3, if high during this write operation, enables the interrupt flag onto pin PB7. PB7 should be programmed as an input if it is to be used as an interrupt pin. PB7 goes low when an interrupt occurs. When the timer is read (by LDA or LDX, for example), prior to the interrupt flag's being set, the number of time intervals remaining will be read, i.e., 51, 51, 49, etc.

Should the timer be read during the exact clock cycle when interrupt occurs, the value read would be 1 1 1 1 1 1 1 1. After interrupt, the timer register decrements at a divide by "1" rate of the system clock. If after interrupt, the timer is read and a value of 1 1 1 0 0 1 0 0 is read, the time since interrupt is 28T. The value read is in two's complement, and may be checked as follows:

$$
\begin{aligned}
\text{Value read} &= 1\,1\,1\,0\,0\,1\,0\,0 \\
\text{Complement} &= 0\,0\,0\,1\,1\,0\,1\,1 \\
\text{Add 1} &= 0\,0\,0\,1\,1\,1\,0\,0 = 28
\end{aligned}
$$

Thus, to arrive at the total elapsed time, the program may add this value to the original time written into the timer. Thus, again assuming initial time is 0 0 1 1 0 1 0 0 (= 52), with a scale factor of 8, total time to interrupt is (52 × 8) + 1 = 417T. Total elapsed time would thus be 416T + 28T = 444T, assuming the value read after interrupt was 1 1 1 0 0 1 0 0.

After interrupt, whenever the timer is written or read, the interrupt is reset. However, the reading or writing of the timer at the same time interrupt occurs will not reset the interrupt flag.

When reading the timer after an interrupt, A3 would be low so as to disable the $\overline{IRQ}$ pin. This is done to prevent future interrupts until after another Write timer operation.

3.7.1.3 Pinouts for MCS6530. Figure 3.7.1-4 shows the external connections to the MCS6530. Their functions are summarized below:

1. Reset $(\overline{RES})$ - (pin 16): During system initialization a logic "0" on the $\overline{RES}$ input will cause all of the I/O registers to be cleared. This in turn will cause all I/O port connections to act as inputs, thus protecting external components from possible damage and erroneous data while the system is being initially configured under software control. The Data Bus Buffers are put into an OFF state during Reset. Interrupt is disabled when reset. The $\overline{RES}$ signal must be held low for at least one clock period when reset is required.

2. Input Clock - (pin 3): The input clock is a system Phase Two clock, normally provided by the MCS6502, which can be either a low level clock ($V_{IL} < 0.4$, $V_{IH} > 2.4$) or high level clock ($V_{IL} < 0.2$ $V_{IH} = V_{CC} {}^{+.3}_{-.2}$).

3. Read/Write $(R/\overline{W})$ (pin 9): The $R/\overline{W}$ signal is supplied by the microprocessor unit and is used to control the transfer of data to and from the microprocessor unit and the MCS6530. A high on the $R/\overline{W}$ pin allows the processor to read (with proper addressing) the data supplied by the MCS6530. A low on the $R/\overline{W}$ pin allows a write (with proper addressing) to the MCS6530.

4. Interrupt Request $(\overline{IRQ})$ (pin 17): The $\overline{IRQ}$ pin is an interrupt pin from the interval timer. This same pin, if not used as an interrupt, can be used as a peripheral I/O pin (PB7). When used as an interrupt, the pin should be set up as an *input* by the data direction register. The pin will be normally high with a low indicating an interrupt from the MCS6530. Although an internal pull-up resistor is provided on standard chips, it may be omitted by mask modification during manufacture. This permits WIRED-OR connection of multiple parts.

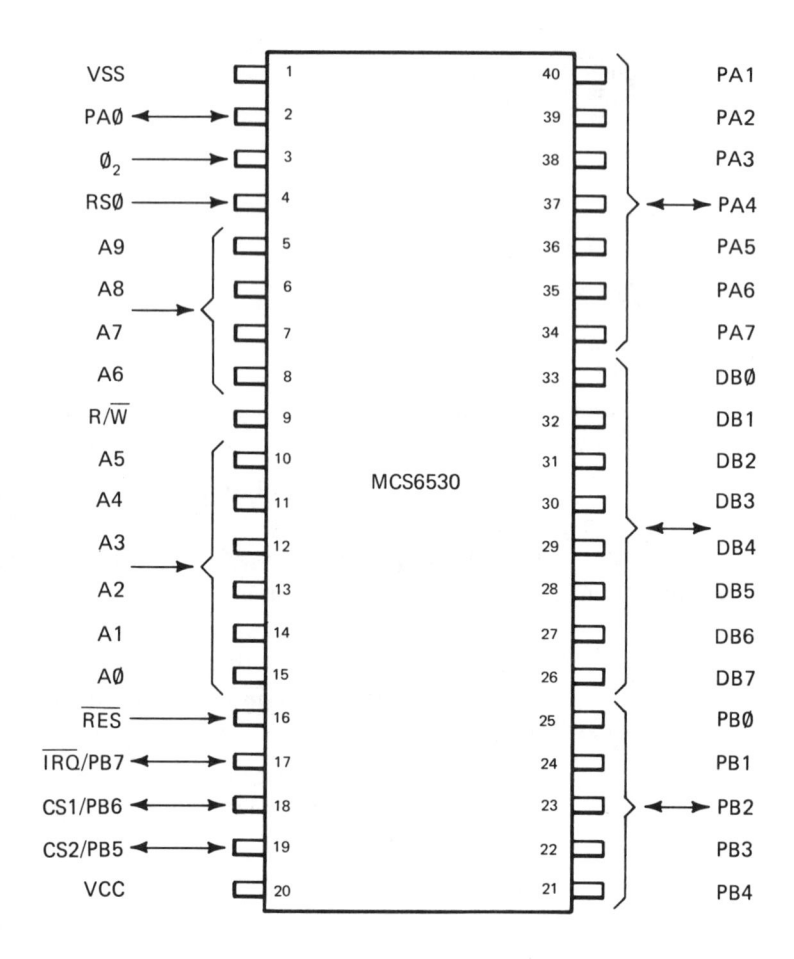

```
         VSS  ──┤ 1         40 ├──  PA1
         PA0 ←─┤ 2         39 ├──  PA2
          Ø2 ─→┤ 3         38 ├──  PA3
         RS0 ─→┤ 4         37 ├──  PA4
          A9  ─┤ 5         36 ├──  PA5
          A8  ─┤ 6         35 ├──  PA6
          A7  ─┤ 7         34 ├──  PA7
          A6  ─┤ 8         33 ├──  DB0
         R/W ─┤ 9         32 ├──  DB1
          A5  ─┤ 10  MCS6530  31 ├──  DB2
          A4  ─┤ 11        30 ├──  DB3
          A3  ─┤ 12        29 ├──  DB4
          A2  ─┤ 13        28 ├──  DB5
          A1  ─┤ 14        27 ├──  DB6
          A0  ─┤ 15        26 ├──  DB7
         RES ─→┤ 16        25 ├──  PB0
      IRQ/PB7 ←┤ 17        24 ├──  PB1
      CS1/PB6 ←┤ 18        23 ├──  PB2
      CS2/PB5 ←┤ 19        22 ├──  PB3
         VCC  ─┤ 20        21 ├──  PB4
```

Figure 3.7.1-4 MCS6530 pinout designation
(courtesy MOS Technology)

5. Data Bus (D0-D7) (pins 33-26): The MCS6530 has eight bi-directional data pins (D0-D7). These pins connect to the system's data lines and allow transfer of data to and from the microprocessor unit. The output buffers which drive these pins remain in the off state except when a Read operation occurs.

6. Peripheral Data Ports (pins 2, 40-34 and pins 25-21, 19-17): The MCS6530 has 16 pins available for peripheral I/O operations. Each pin is individually software programmable to act as either an input or an output (see Section 3.7.1.1). The 16 pins are divided into 2 8-bit ports, PA0-PA7 and PB0-PB7. PB5, PB6 and PB7 also have other potential uses (see items 1 and 7 on this list). The microprocessor will read correct I/O information if the peripheral lines are greater than 2.0 volts for a "1" and less than 0.8 volts for a "0," i.e., the peripheral pins are all TTL compatible. Pins PA0 and PB0 are also capable of sourcing 3mA at 1.5 V, making them capable of Darlington drive.

7. Address Lines (A0-A9) (pins 15-10, 8-5): There are 10 address pins and the ROM SELECT pin. A0-A9 and ROM SELECT are always used as addressing pins. There are 2 additional pins which are mask-programmable and can be used either individually or together as chip Selects. They are pins PB5 and PB6. When used as peripheral data pins they cannot be used as chip selects.

3.7.1.5 Example Programs using the MCS6530. As noted in the previous three sections, the ROM, RWM, TIMER, and I/O ports can be placed in a variety of places in address space. For the sake of simplicity and continuity, let us assume the KIM MCS6530-008 addresses. These addresses are summarized in Table 3.7.1-1 (see Chapter 8 for detailed KIM addressing).

For a first simple example let us configure the A-side I/O port such that pins 0, 1 and 4 are outputs, and the remaining pins are inputs. To be an output the direction register must have a logic 1 in bit positions 0, 1, and 4.

EXAMPLE 3.7.1-1. Configure A-side I/O direction program

```
        SADD  = $1701  (SADD is "Side A Data
                                Direction" Register)
        ACONF = %00010011
        LDA     #ACONF
        STA     SADD
```

It is important to note that an initializing signal on the reset line ($\overline{RES}$) to the MCS6530 forces all I/O lines to be inputs. For this reason all peripherals to be connected to the MCS6530 must not be self-destructive if their inputs are open circuited, which is the condition of the MCS6530 I/O ports on reset.

As a second example, consider a program to produce output pulses from bits 0 and 2 of port B. The program must configure the port and then pulse it. Programs for achieving this result will be written as subroutines.

TABLE 3.7.1-1 KIM MCS6530-003 ADDRESS ASSIGNMENTS

Function	Address	Read	Write
ROM	1800 - 1BFF	X	
RWM	1780 - 17BF	X	X
I/O A-Side Data Register	1700	X	X
I/O A-Side Data Direction Register	1701	X	X
I/O B-Side Data Register	1702	X	X
I/O B-Side Data Direction Register	1703	X	X
TIMER ÷ 1 $\overline{IRQ}$ DISABLED	1704		X
$\overline{IRQ}$ ENABLE	170C		X
TIMER ÷ 8 $\overline{IRQ}$ DISABLED	1705		X
$\overline{IRQ}$ ENABLE	170D		X
TIMER ÷ 64 $\overline{IRQ}$ DISABLED	1706		X
$\overline{IRQ}$ ENABLE	170E		X
TIMER ÷ 1024 IRQ DISABLED	1707		X
ENABLE	170F		X
TIMER $\overline{IRQ}$ DISABLED	1704	X	
$\overline{IRQ}$ ENABLED	170C		
INTERRUPT FLAG (BIT 7 <u>ONLY</u>)	1705	X	

EXAMPLE 3.7.1-2. Configure B-side I/O and pulse

```
        SBDD  = $1703      Define direction address
        SBD   = $1702      Define data address
        BCONF = %00000101
              .
              .
              .
        JSR     CONFIG
              .
              .
```

The MCS 6502 Microprocessor and Peripheral Parts **145**

```
                JSR     PULSE
                  .
                  .
                  .
CONFIG  LDA     #BCONF    Define directions
        STA     SBDD
        LDA     #0        Set all output bits low
        STA     SBD       SBD is "Side B Data" Register
        RTS
PULSE   LDA     #$FF      Assume low initially
        STA     SBD       Inputs not affected
        LDA     #0
        STA     SBD
        RTS
```

Another program which will produce the same result is shown in the following example.

EXAMPLE 3.7.1-3. Variation on EXAMPLE 3.7.1-2

```
        SBDD   = $1703    Define direction address
        SBD    = $1702    Define data address
        BCONF  = %00000101
                  .
                  .
                  .
        JSR     CONFIG
                  .
                  .
                  .
        JSR     PULSE
                  .
                  .
                  .
CONFIG  LDA     #BCONF    Define directions
        STA     SBDD
        LDA     #0        Set all output bits low
        STA     SBD
        RTS
```

```
PULSE   LDA   #$FF          Assume low initially
        STA   SBD
        INC   SBD
        RTS
```

As a final example, the timer will be used to generate a 9.091 millisecond time delay. Assume that the system clock is running at 1 MHz. The routine will achieve the desired delay without using the timer's interrupt capability. First observe that 9.091 ms = 9091 microseconds. This time can be approximated in the timer by 1024 * 8 + 64 * 14 = 9088. This particular time delay is one which would be useful in handling a 10 character per second, 11 bit code hard-copy mechanism like the Teletype® or similar terminal (see Section 5.4.1). Note that, even though the interrupt mechanism of MCS6502 is not being used, the internal interrupt flag of the MCS6530 timer is interrogated by the program to determine when "time out" has occurred. This flag is read as bit 7 of the specified location.

EXAMPLE 3.7.1-4. Time delay using internal timer

```
    DIV64  = $17Ø6    Timer Address w/scale factor of 64
    INTFLG = $17Ø5    Address at which interrupt flag can be read
    NUMDEL = 142

    DELAY   LDA   #NUMDEL    Get number of delays
            STA   DIV64      Store in ÷ IRQ disabled

    DELA1   BIT   INTFLG     Check to see if timed out
            BMI   DELA1      If not then loop
            RTS
```

One of the important things to note is that the accuracy is extremely good, since it is driven by a crystal oscillator with stability greater than 1 part in 1000. Careful adjustment of a variable capacitor on the board against a frequency standard may bring it to 1 part in 100,000.

One of the example programs (see Section 3.8) shows a 24 hour interrupt driven clock using the KIM. The internal timer has its IRQ output connected to the MCS6502 IRQ and is "fine-tuned" to account for the additional delays of jumping to the interrupt software, return, etc.

3.7.2 The MCS6520

The MCS6520 (Figure 3.7.2-1) is a versatile I/O chip originally designed by Motorola for the M6800 family (the Motorola version is designated 6820). It is second-sourced by all MOS Technology and Motorola second sources. The MCS6520 is called a Peripheral Interface Adapter, or PIA. It has two 8-bit programmable I/O ports and two control bits for each port, making a total of 10 pins (lines) per port, 20 in all. The two control lines for each port are often used to accomplish "handshaking" during the exchange of data on the 8 data lines. On the side of the PIA which faces the microprocessor is an 8-bit bidirectional data bus, two $\overline{IRQ}$ lines, $\overline{RES}$ (for Reset), clock ($\emptyset$2), R/$\overline{W}$, and three chip select lines. There are also two Register Select lines to select among four software programmable locations. These four locations allow access to 6 registers which are used to configure the PIA, as well as to accomplish data transfer. This part has greater I/O versatility than the MCS6530, but is similar in general philosophy and usage.

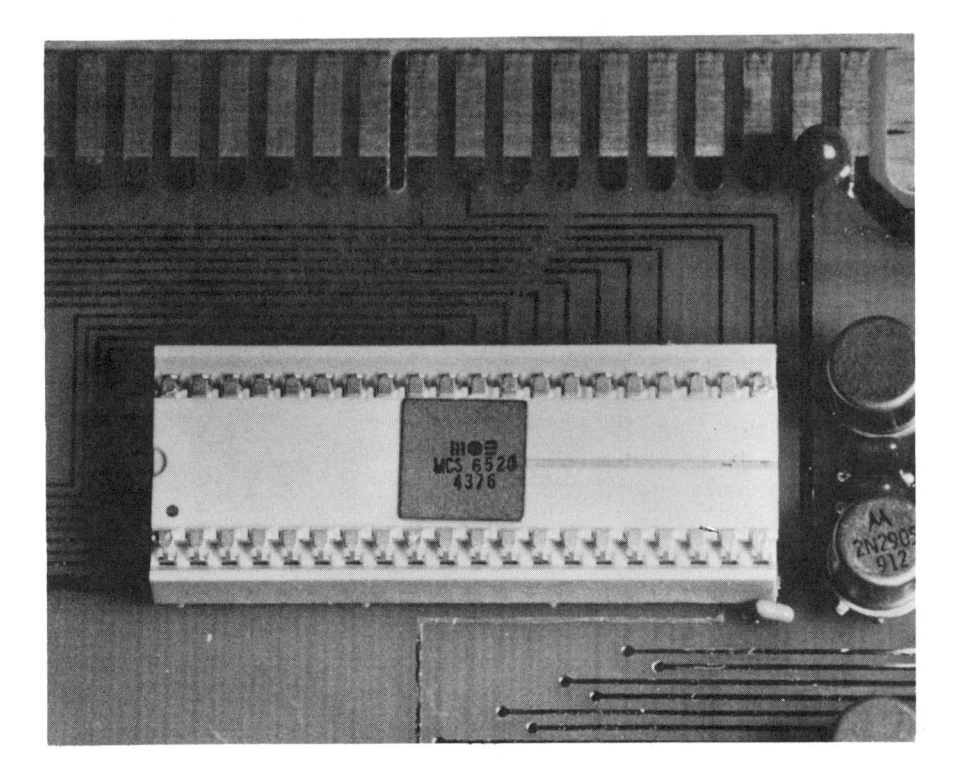

Figure 3.7.2-1 MOS Technology MCS6520 peripheral interface adaptor

3.7.2.1 Specifications. The principal characteristics of the MCS6520 are given by the following list:

1. Single 5 Volt Supply
2. Byte Oriented
3. Two 8-bit Bidirectional I/O Ports
4. Interrupt Generation Capability
5. Automatic Handshaking on Data Transfer

1. Single 5 Volt Supply: Like the MCS6502, the MCS6520 is based on N-MOS, ion-transplant, depletion load technology. This fabrication method allows for a single 5 volt supply.

2. Byte Oriented: This part attaches directly to the Data Bus, and part of the Address and Control busses. Its data transactions always involve transfer of 8-bit bytes.

3. Two 8-bit Bidirectional I/O Ports: The MCS6520 has two 8-bit bidirectional ports with attendant Data Direction registers, like the MCS6530. The usual notation refers to an A-side and a B-side. The two sides are almost identical in function, except that the B-side has greater current-sourcing capability and interacts with its two companion control pins, CB1 and CB2, to provide a "handshake on write." The A-side control pins, CA1 and CA2, provide "handshake on read." (See item 5 on this list.)

4. Interrupt Generation Capability: The MCS6520 can generate an interrupt output from either Side A ($\overline{\text{IRQA}}$) or Side B ($\overline{\text{IRQB}}$). These interrupts are generated by signals received at control inputs CA1, CA2, CB1, and CB2. A rather extensive set of options, including choice of interrupt signal level and capability for masked interrupt operations, may be implemented by appropriate programming of control registers A and B (see Section 3.7.2.5).

5. Automatic Handshaking on Data Transfer: The term "handshaking" refers to the implementation of control lines which, for example, permit a sending device to send out a *strobe* signal to signify to a receiving device that data is available to it, and to receive verification from the receiver (in the form of an *acknowledge* signal) that the transmission has been accomplished. If the MCS6520 is the sender and a peripheral device the receiver, this operation would be called "handshake on write." Handshake on *read* would involve the MCS6520's issuing a request signifying readiness to receive data and receiving a strobe denoting presence of valid data in response to this request.

3.7.2.2 MCS6520 Internal Architecture.

Figure 3.7.2.2 shows that the MCS6520 is organized into two independent sections called the A-side and the B-side. Each of these sides has an output register, a data direction register and a control register. There also exists a Peripheral Interface Buffer and an interrupt status and control mechanism to control the attendant Interrupt Request lines. The right side of Figure 3.7.2-2 includes all I/O components, and the left side includes all components which connect to MPU address, Data, and Control busses. The three Chip Select lines and two Register Select lines will be used to select the chip itself and the registers within it.

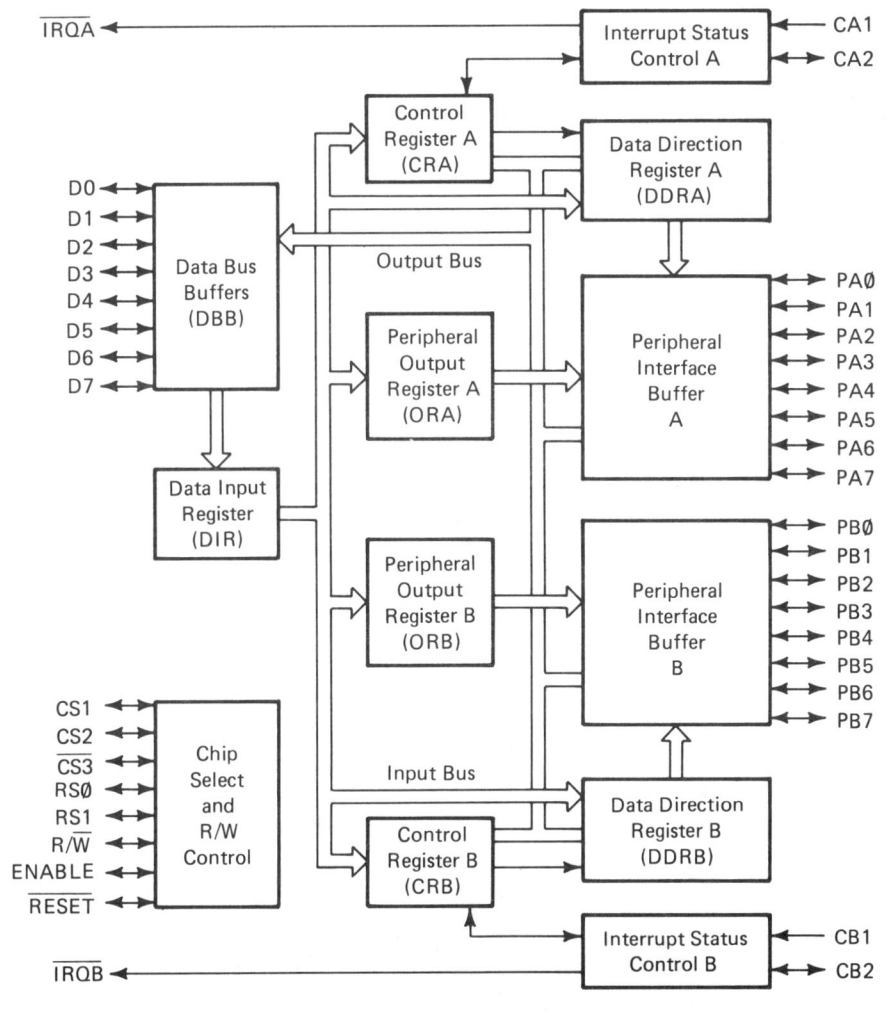

Figure 3.7.2-2 MCS6520 internal architecture (courtesy MOS Technology)

The data input register is used to latch information from the data bus during the phase 2 clock pulse so that, on the trailing edge of phase 2, there will exist a transition without "glitches."

The Control Registers, CRA and CRB, allow control of a number of functions for the MCS6520. Tables 3.7.2-2 – 3.7.2-6 in Section 3.7.2-4, explain the detailed operation of these control registers. In general they allow specification as to whether the CA1, CA2, CB1 and CB2 control lines are to reflect rising edge-triggered or falling edge-triggered interrupt operations, or to serve as input, output, or handshaking lines. The control registers also are used for enabling or disabling of interrupts. Their other function is to select either Data Direction Register or Peripheral Output Register during addressing. The control register can also be read in order to determine the status of the interrupt lines, whether interrupt has been enabled or not. This is a very common procedure in interrupt servicing in order to determine which part has caused the interrupt (see Section 3.6.3).

The Data Direction registers are very similar in function to those in the MCS6530, in that a zero in each bit position in the data direction register causes the corresponding I/O line to act as an input. Conversely a one causes it to act as an output.

The Output registers, ORA and ORB, store the data to be placed on a peripheral I/O port. A zero written into a bit of ORA causes the corresponding output line on the A-side port to go to a logic zero. A logic one will cause the corresponding output line on the A-side to go high.

There are 4 interrupt control lines CA1, CA2, CB1 and CB2. The control register will determine whether CA1 and CB1 are to cause an interrupt on either rising edge or falling edge of a signal. CA2 and CB2 may be programmed to be either input or output, or rising or falling edge triggered. If configured for output we can determine whether or not the output will be high or low. In the final condition, a read from Peripheral Register A is performed and CA2 will be reset. This function is called handshake on read. Conversely, CB2 may be reset by a Write function to the Peripheral Register B.

The peripheral interface buffers and data bus buffers provide the necessary electrical interface to permit interaction with a variety of common microcomputer-based system components.

3.7.2.3. MCS6520 External Connections.
The external connections (pinouts) of the MCS6520 are described in the following sections. Figure 3.7.2-3 shows the mechanical configuration of the output pins.

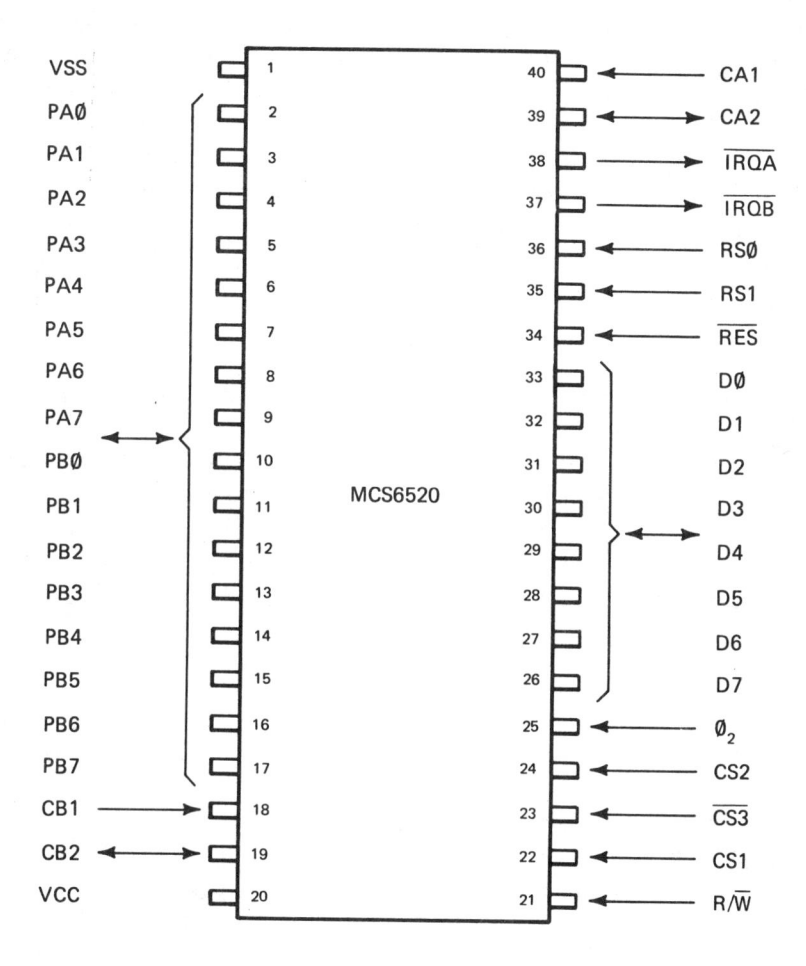

The MCS 6502 Microprocessor and Peripheral Parts 151

Figure 3.7.2-3 MCS6520 pinout designations peripheral interface adaptor

1. V_{SS} (pin 1), V_{CC} (pin 20): V_{CC} is the +5 volt DC supply, V_{SS} is ground.

2. Peripheral Ports (pins 2-17): These I/O lines are TTL compatible. When programmed as outputs the B-side pins are capable of sourcing 1 milliampere at 1.5 volts. This is much greater current (×10) than TTL requires, and is useful for Darlington transistor configurations. A single Darlington pair connected to the B-side should be capable of sinking at least 5 amperes.

Input levels to the MCS6520 are *not* latched, so that the external device must maintain them until the device is read by the MPU. On input the A-side pins have built-in pull-up resistors, while the B-side pins are floating.

The system designer should know that the output register, ORA or ORB, may be written into even if its associated port is configured as an input. If the direction is then reversed to allow output, such previously written values are placed on the pins.

3. Phase Two (pin 25): This signal is the $\phi 2$ clock signal generated at the microprocessor. It is used to synchronize operations using the Data bus.

4. Reset, $\overline{RES}$ (pin 34): A logic zero on this pin resets all MCS6520 registers to zero. Of special importance is that both Data Direction Registers become zero, or input-configured, and interrupt lines (pins 37 and 38) are disabled.

5. Interrupt Requests, $\overline{IRQA}$ and $\overline{IRQB}$ (pins 37, 38): These lines may connect to the microprocessor $\overline{IRQ}$ pin to provide interrupt requests. They are open-collector in nature so that several of them can be connected together to the same $\overline{IRQ}$ input. In use, the MCS6502 must determine which input-output port caused the interrupt. On each side either or both of the two control lines CA1 or CA2, *may* cause an interrupt. If CA2 is configured as an input, then either CA1 or CA2 may cause bits 7 or 6, respectively, of the control register A (CRA in Figure 3.7.2-2 to be set to a logic one. If bits 0 or 3 respectively are set to a logic one, then the interrupt is enabled at the PIA and $\overline{IRQA}$ will go low, causing an interrupt *to* the microprocessor. The microprocessor may then read the control register to determine the source of interrupt. Of course, it (the MCS6502) must also have been enabled by a CLI, Clear Interrupt mask, instruction, in order to permit recognition of interrupts.

6. Read/$\overline{Write}$, R/$\overline{W}$ (pin 21): This line is high for a Read operation and goes low (< 0.4 volts) for Write. R/$\overline{W}$, together with $\phi 2$, RS, and CS control the operation of the MCS6520. Of particular note in KIM applications (see Chapter 8) is that, if a MCS6520 unit is to be used in KIM expansion, R/$\overline{W}$ (Expansion pin B) must be used, rather then RAM-R/$\overline{W}$ (Expansion pin Z). If a write operation is to be performed then pin 21 must go low at least 130 nanoseconds before pin 25, $\phi 2$, goes high.

7. Chip Selects, CS1, CS2, $\overline{CS3}$ (pins 22, 24, 23): Pins 22 and 24 must be high *and* pin 23 low in order to select this chip. In fairly simple systems they will probably be connected directly to address lines. If

The MCS 6502 Microprocessor and Peripheral Parts 153

the system memory space is significantly populated, a separate decoder may be required.

If address connections to these chip select pins are properly made, PIA addresses may be placed in zero page, permitting use of shorter and faster instructions for I/O operations.

8. Register Selects, RS0, RS1 (pins 35, 36): The two Register Select lines, along with bit 2 of the Control Register and $R/\overline{W}$, determine the data path and function. Selection combinations are shown in Table 3.7.2-1.

TABLE 3.7.2-1 PIA Register Selection and Function

$RS0$	$RS1$	$R/\overline{W}$	$CRA2$	$CRB2$	*Function*
0	0	X	0	X	Read *or* Write. DDRA
0	0	0	1	X	Write into ORA
0	0	1	1	X	Read from A-side input pins
0	1	X	X	X	Read *or* Write CRA
1	0	X	X	0	Read *or* Write DDRB
1	0	0	X	1	Write into ORB
1	0	1	X	1	Read from B-side input pins
1	1	X	X	X	Read *or* Write CRB

X = don't care

3.7.2.4 Control Register Definitions. Tables 3.7.2-2 through 3.7.2-6 specify the functions of control register bits.

TABLE 3.7.2-2 Control Register Bit Designations

	7	6	5 4 3	2	1 0
CRA	IRQA1	IRQA2	CA2 Control	DDRA Access	CA1 Control
CRB	IRQB1	IRQB2	CB2 Control	DDRB Access	CB2 Control

TABLE 3.7.2-3 Control of Interrupt Inputs CA1, CB1

CRA (CRB) Bit 1	Bit 0	Active Transition of Input Signal*	$\overline{IRQA}$ ($\overline{IRQB}$) Interrupt Outputs
0	0	negative	Disable — remain high
0	1	negative	Enabled — goes low when bit 7 in CRA (CRB) is set by active transition of signal on CA1 (CB1)
1	0	positive	Disable — remain high
1	1	positive	Enable — as explained above

*Note 1: Bit 7 of CRA (CRB) will be set to a logic 1 by an active transition of the CA1 (CB1) signal. This is independent of the state of bit 0 in CRA (CRB).

TABLE 3.7.2-4 Control of CA2 (CB2) as Interrupt Inputs (Bit 5—"0")

CRA (CRB) Bit 5	Bit 4	Bit 3	Active Transition of Input Signal*	$\overline{IRQA}$ ($\overline{IRQB}$) Interrupt Output
0	0	0	negative	Disable — remains high
0	0	1	negative	Enabled — goes low when bit 6 in CRA (CRB) is set by active transition of signal on CA2 (CB2)
0	1	0	positive	Disable — remains high
0	1	1	positive	Enable — as explained above

*Note: Bit 6 of CRA (CRB) will be set to a logic 1 by an active transition of the CA2 (CB2) signal. This is independent of the state of Bit 3 in CRA (CRB).

The MCS 6502 Microprocessor and Peripheral Parts **155**

TABLE 3.7.2-5 Control of CA2 Output Modes

Bit 5	CRA Bit 4	Bit 3	Mode	Description
1	0	0	"Handshake" on Read	CA2 is set high on an active transition of the CA1 interrupt input signal and set low by a microprocessor "Read A Data" operation. This allows positive control of data transfers from the peripheral device to the microprocessor.
1	0	1	Pulse Output	CA2 goes low for one cycle after a "Read A Data" operation. This pulse can be used to signal the peripheral device that data was taken.
1	1	0	Manual Output	CA2 set low
1	1	1	Manual Output	CA2 set high

3.7.2.5 PIA Example using KIM. Figure 3.7.2-4 shows one possible connection of an MCS6520 to the KIM microcomputer (see Chapter 8). For this connection the four addresses to be used are $0400 through $0403. Each of these four addresses will have several "images," i.e., reading from $0401 will yield the same byte as reading from $0405 etc. The topic of images in address space is covered in greater detail in Chapter 5. In particular:

> $0400   DDRA or PRA (depends on CRA 2)
> $0401   CRA
> $0402   DDRB or PRB (depends on CRB 2)
> $0403   CRB

Using the assumed configuration of Figure 3.7.2-4, a program to generate a square wave from PA0 will be written. It will continue indefinitely until the system is reset.

TABLE 3.7.2-6 Control of CB2 Output Modes

CRB Bit 5	*Bit 4*	*Bit 3*	*Mode*	*Description*
1	0	0	"Handshake" on Write	CB2 is set low on microprocessor "Write B Data" operation and is set high by an active transition of the CB1 interrupt input signal. This allows positive control of data transfers from the microprocessor to the peripheral device.
1	0	1	Pulse Output	CB2 goes low for one cycle after a microprocessor "Write B Data" operation. This can be used to signal the peripheral device that data is available.
1	1	0	Manual Output	CB2 is set low
1	1	1	Manual Output	CB2 set high

EXAMPLE 3.7.2-1. Square Wave Generation Program No. 1

```
            DDRA   = $0400
            PRA    = $0400
            CRA    = $0401
            DIREC  = %00000001   Only PA0 set to output
            CTRLWD = %00000100   CA1 and CA2 disabled
                                 CRA2 set for PRA access
              *    = $200

  CONFIG    LDA    #0            Reset does it - just insurance
            STA    CRA           Clear CRA2 for DDRA access
            LDA    #DIREC
            STA    DDRA          Point DDRA:PA0 out=0 now
            LDA    #CTRLWD
```

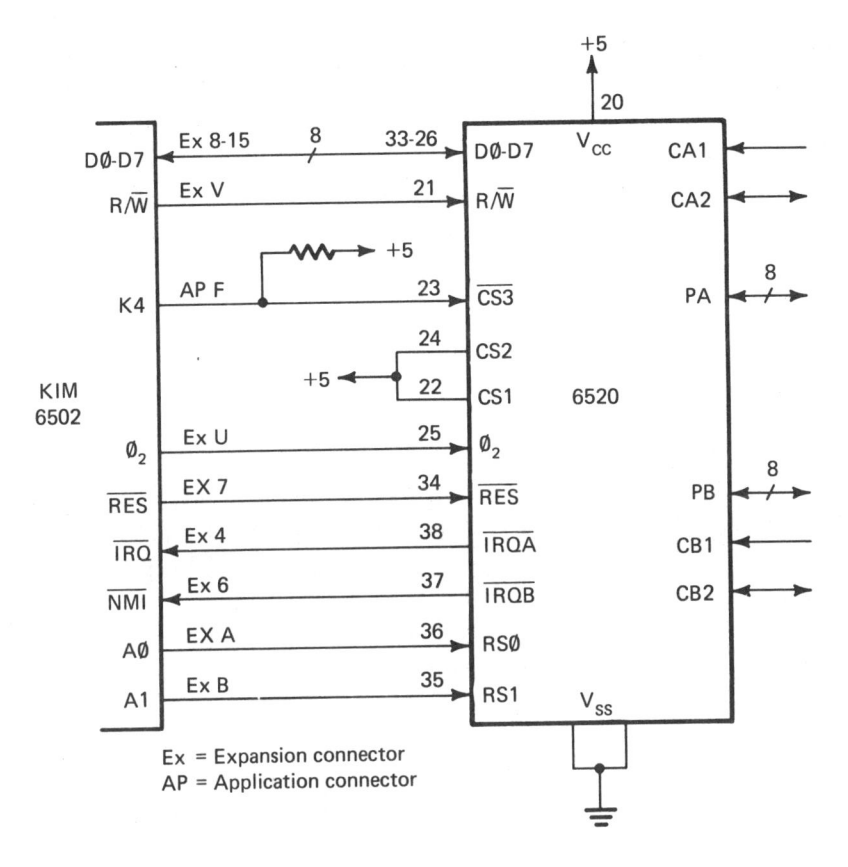

The MCS 6502 Microprocessor and Peripheral Parts 157

Figure 3.7.2-4 Example connection of PIA to KIM

```
         STA   CRA        Point to PRA
         LDA   #0         These two are really not needed
         STA   PRA
LOOP     LDA   PRA        Get port
         EOR   #1         Invert PA0
         STA   PRA        Output it again
         JMP   LOOP
         .END
```

A second example program outputs a rectangular wave on CA2, rather than PA0.

EXAMPLE 3.7.2-2 Square Wave Generation Program No. 2

```
             CRA    = $0401
             CA2ON  = % 00111000
             CA2OFF = % 00110000

               *    = $200

CA2PLS       LDA    #CA2ON
             STA    CRA
             LDA    #CA2OFF
             STA    CRA
             JMP    CA2PLS
```

A third example is a subroutine to force CA2 from its present state to a high then back low without changing any other control register bit values.

EXAMPLE 3.7.2-3. CA2 Output Control Subroutine

```
             CRA    = $0401
             CA2ON  = % 00111000    Manual Mode - 1 out
             CA2MSK = % 00001000    Manual Mode - 0 out mask
               *    = $3D0
PLSCA2       LDA    CRA             Get copy of present CRA
             ORA    #CA2ON          Force CA2 high
             STA    CRA
             EOR    #CA2MSK         Same Mode:Force Low
             STA    ORA
             RTS
```

As a fourth example consider use of the A-side port as an 8-bit parallel input port from a high-speed paper tape reader. Assume that the necessary electronics are available to provide TTL level signals from all eight data bits (positive logic) and the sprocket hole (positive logic). The eight data bits are connected to PA0-7 and the sprocket hole to CA1. The function of CA1 is to tell the microprocessor that the next byte is available and CA2 will reply to the tape reader that the data has been read. The CA2 line will go high with the rising edge of CA1, and will automatically go low when PRA is finally read. If falling edge-triggered operation were desired, a change of one bit (CRA1) would accomplish the desired result. We also note that CA1 is *edge* triggered.

The MCS 6502 Microprocessor and Peripheral Parts **159**

Thus, in this example if data is read at PRA while the sprocket hole is still present it will not be read again. The triggering input to CA1 must fall and then provide another rising edge to activate CRA7.

It is a fairly simple extension to handshake on write using the B-side interrupt-driven data transfer by enabling and connecting the $\overline{\text{IRQA}}$ or $\overline{\text{IRQB}}$ lines to $\overline{\text{IRQ}}$ on the MCS6502. As noted earlier, CA2 can be simultaneously used as an interrupting input. Such details are shown in the tables.

EXAMPLE 3.7.2-4. Read Handshake with MCS6502

; READ HANDSHAKE EXAMPLE WITH MCS6502

```
                CRA   = $0401
                PRA   = $0400
                DDRA  = $0400
                CRHDSK = %00100110   Read Handshake, PRA ACCESS
                                       Rising Edge
                ALL1N = $00          Trigger, Interrupt
                *     = $200         Disabled.

MAIN     JSR    CONFIG
          .
          .
          .
         JSR    READ          Data comes back in A
          .                   Rest of program stores data
          .                      Checks to see if end of
          .                      Block etc. Probably loops
                                  Back to Here.

                *     = $3A0
CONFIG   LDA    #0
         STA    CRA           Get DDRA Access
         LDA    #ALL1N
         STA    DDRA          Want all 8 bits input
         LDA    #CRHDSH       Handshake control word
         RTS
READ     BIT    CRA           N ← CRA7
         BPL    READ          Orbit unit 1 Rising Edge
         LDA    PRA           Get data byte, CA2
         RTS                     goes low
```

3.8 EXAMPLE PROGRAMS

This section consists of a number of MCS6502 example programs, written specifically for execution on a KIM-1 Microcomputer. These programs were written using the RT-11 text editor (see Chapter 4) on a DEC PDP/11-34 minicomputer. Assembly was performed by the MINMIC cross-assembler running on the same machine.

```
                                                          PAGE    1
CARD #  LOC     CODE      CARD   10       20       30       40       50       60       70
   1    0000
   2    0000
   3    0000
   4    0000       .      ; THIS IS A BENCHMARK MULTI-BYTE ADD PROGRAM
   5    0000              ; WHICH MIGHT BE USED IN EVALUATING
   6    0000              ; ONE MICROPROCESSOR (6502) VERSUS
   7    0000              ; SOME OTHER.
   8    0000              ;
   9    0000              ;
  10    0000              NRBYT     =        $00
  11    0000              FIRST     =        $01
  12    0000              SECOND    =        $02
  13    0000              THIRD     =        $03
  14    0000                       *=$0200
  15    0200
  16    0200
  17    0200   A2 00      SUM       LDX      #NRBYT        NUMBER OF BYTES.
  18    0202   18                   CLC                    MUST CLEAR CARRY FOR FIRST TIME THRU.
  19    0203   F8                   SED                    AUTOMATIC DECIMAL ADJUST MODE.
  20    0204              ; IF BINARY MODE IS DESIRED THEN USE CLD (CLEAR DECIMAL MODE)
  21    0204              ; INSTEAD OF SED (SET DECIMAL MODE).
  22    0204   B5 00      LOOP      LDA      FIRST-1,X     GET A DIGIT.
  23    0206   75 01                ADC      SECOND-1,X    ADD SECOND DIGIT + CARRY.
  24    0208   95 02                STA      THIRD-1,X     PUT IN RESULT AREA.
  25    020A   CA                   DEX                    DECREMENT NUMBER OF BYTES PROCESSED.
  26    020B   D0 F7                BNE      LOOP          IF NOT ZERO THEN LOOP.
  27    020D                        .END


END OF MOS/TECHNOLOGY 650X ASSEMBLY VERSION 5
NUMBER OF ERRORS =    0.  NUMBER OF WARNINGS =    0



            SYMBOL TABLE

SYMBOL     VALUE   LINE DEFINED      CROSS-REFERENCES

FIRST      0001        11     22
LOOP       0204        22     26
NRBYT      0000        10     17
SECOND     0002        12     23
SUM        0200        17    ****
THIRD      0003        13     24




CARD #  LOC     CODE      CARD   10       20       30       40       50       60       70
   1    0000
   2    0000
   3    0000
   4    0000              ; THIS IS AN EXAMPLE PROGRAM FOR THE KIM TO
   5    0000              ; EFFECT HEXADECIMAL TO DECIMAL AND DECIMAL TO
   6    0000              ; HEXADECIMAL CONVERSION.
   7    0000              ; IT WILL DISPLAY THE ORIGINAL BRIEFLY THEN CONVERT
   8    0000              ; AND DISPLAY THE RESULT UNTIL STOPPED.
   9    0000              ; IF LOCATION $100 HAS ZERO IN IT THEN   DECIMAL -> HEX
  10    0000              ; IF LOCATION $100 HAS $FF IN IT THEN    HEX -> DECIMAL
  11    0000              ; IF $100 IS NEITHER 00 NOR FF THEN GO TO THE MONITOR.
```

The MCS 6502 Microprocessor and Peripheral Parts

```
CARD #  LOC       CODE         CARD   10          20           ·30           40           50           60          70
  12    0000
  13    0000                   SCAND    =         $1F1F
  14    0000                   TEMP     =         0
  15    0000                   RES      =         $120
  16    0000                   SRC      =         $101
  17    0000                   CONV     =         $100
  18    0000                            *=$200
  19    0200   A2 FF            START   LDX       #$FF         INITIALIZE STACK
  20    0202   9A                       TXS
  21    0203   20 48 02                 JSR       CLRES        CLEAR RESULT AREA.
  22    0206   20 57 02                 JSR       SRCCHK       IF SOURCE (3 BYTES) = 0
  23    0209   F0 2B                    BEQ       EXIT         THEN GO TO EXIT.
  24    020B   20 7F 02                 JSR       SHOW         SHOW SOURCE ON DISPLAY.
  25    020E   AD 00 01         TEST    LDA       CONV
  26    0211   F0 16                    BEQ       DH           IF $100 = 00 THEN DEC -> HEX.
  27    0213   49 FF                    EOR       #$FF
  28    0215   F0 03                    BEQ       HD           IF $100 = $FF THEN HEX -> DECIMAL.
  29    0217   4C 4F 1C                 JMP       $1C4F        IF NEITHER THEN GO TO MONITOR.
  30    021A   F8               HD      SED                    HEX TO DECIMAL ROUTINE
  31    021B   20 61 02                 JSR       UP
  32    021E   D8                       CLD
  33    021F   20 70 02                 JSR       DOWN
  34    0222   20 57 02                 JSR       SRCCHK
  35    0225   D0 F3                    BNE       HD
  36    0227   F0 0D                    BEQ       EXIT
  37    0229   D8               DH      CLD                    DECIMAL TO HEX ROUTINE.
  38    022A   20 61 02                 JSR       UP
  39    022D   F8                       SED
  40    022E   20 70 02                 JSR       DOWN
  41    0231   20 57 02                 JSR       SRCCHK
  42    0234   D0 F3                    BNE       DH
  43    0236   AD 20 01         EXIT    LDA       RES          DISPLAY RESULT FOREVER
  44    0239   85 FA                    STA       $FA          ON SEVEN SEGMENT DISPLAY
  45    023B   AD 21 01                 LDA       RES+1
  46    023E   85 FB                    STA       $FB
  47    0240   AD 22 01                 LDA       RES+2
  48    0243   85 F9                    STA       $F9
  49    0245   20 1F 1F         EXT1    JSR       SCAND
  50    0248   4C 45 02                 JMP       EXT1
  51    024B   A9 00            CLRES   LDA       #0           CLEAR RESULT AREA.
  52    024D   8D 20 01                 STA       RES
  53    0250   8D 21 01                 STA       RES+1
  54    0253   8D 22 01                 STA       RES+2
  55    0256   60                       RTS
  56    0257   AD 01 01         SRCCHK  LDA       SRC          CHECK 3 BYTE SOURCE = 0.
  57    025A   0D 02 01                 ORA       SRC+1
  58    025D   0D 03 01                 ORA       SRC+2
  59    0260   60                       RTS
  60    0261   38               UP      SEC                    INCREASE RESULT AREA:
  61    0262   A6 03                    LDX       #3           EITHER HEX OR DECIMAL DEPENDING
  62    0264   BD 1F 01         UP1     LDA       RES-1,X      UPON SED OR CLD BEFORE CALLING.
  63    0267   69 00                    ADC       #0
  64    0269   9D 1F 01                 STA       RES-1,X
  65    026C   CA                       DEX
  66    026D   D0 F5                    BNE       UP1
  67    026F   60                       RTS
  68    0270   18               DOWN    CLC
  69    0271   A2 03                    LDX       #3
  70    0273   BD 00 01         DOWN1   LDA       SRC-1,X
  71    0276   E9 00                    SBC       #0
  72    0278   9D 00 01                 STA       SRC-1,X
  73    027B   CA                       DEX
  74    027C   D0 F5                    BNE       DOWN1
  75    027E   60                       RTS
  76    027F   A9 10            SHOW    LDA       #$10
  77    0281   85 00                    STA       TEMP
  78    0283   85 01                    STA       TEMP+1
  79    0285   AD 01 01                 LDA       SRC
  80    0288   85 FB                    STA       $FB
  81    028A   AD 02 01                 LDA       SRC+1
  82    028D   85 FA                    STA       $FA
  83    028F   AD 03 01                 LDA       SRC+2
  84    0292   85 F9                    STA       $F9
  85    0294   20 1F 1F         SHO1    JSR       SCAND
  86    0297   C6 01                    DEC       TEMP+1
  87    0299   D0 F9                    BNE       SHO1
  88    029B   C6 00                    DEC       TEMP
  89    029D   D0 F5                    BNE       SHO1
  90    029F   60                       RTS
  91    02A0                            .END
```

```
END OF MOS/TECHNOLOGY 650X ASSEMBLY VERSION 5
NUMBER OF ERRORS =   0.  NUMBER OF WARNINGS =    0
```

```
                SYMBOL TABLE

    SYMBOL    VALUE   LINE DEFINED        CROSS-REFERENCES

    CLRES     024B        51      21
    CONV      0100        17      25
    DH        0229        37      26      42
    DOWN      0270        68      33      40
    DOWN1     0273        70      74
    EXIT      0236        43      23      36
    EXT1      0245        49      50
    HD        021A        30      28      35
    RES       0120        15      43      45      47      52      53      54      62      64
    SCAND     1F1F        13      49      85
    SHOW      027F        76      24
    SH01      0294        85      87      89
    SRC       0101        16      56      57      58      70      72      79      81      83
    SRCCHK    0257        56      22      34      41
    START     0200        19      ****
    TEMP      0000        14      77      78      86      88
    TEST      020E        25      ****
    UP        0261        60      31      38
    UP1       0264        62      66


CARD #  LOC     CODE        CARD    10          20          30          40          50          60          70
   1    0000
   2    0000
   3    0000
   4    0000                ; THIS PROGRAM MULTIPLIES TWO 3 BYTE VALUES TOGETHER TO FORM
   5    0000                ; A 12 DIGIT RESULT -- IN 6 BYTES MSB TO LSB IN ASCENDING NUMBER LOCATIONS.
   6    0000
   7    0000                NDGTS   =       3
   8    0000                MCND    =       $101
   9    0000                MLPR    =       $104
  10    0000                RESUL   =       $107
  11    0000                        *=$200
  12    0200  A0 03         MLPLY   LDY     #NDGTS
  13    0202  F8                    SED
  14    0203  18                    CLC
  15    0204  BE 00 01      MLPL1   LDX     MCND-1,Y
  16    0207  F0 2C         MLPL2   BEQ     ZEROM
  17    0209  AD 06 01              LDA     MLPR+2
  18    020C  79 09 01              ADC     RESUL+2,Y
  19    020F  99 09 01              STA     RESUL+2,Y
  20    0212  AD 05 01              LDA     MLPR+1
  21    0215  79 08 01              ADC     RESUL+1,Y
  22    0218  99 08 01              STA     RESUL+1,Y
  23    021B  AD 04 01              LDA     MLPR
  24    021E  79 07 01              ADC     RESUL,Y
  25    0221  99 07 01              STA     RESUL,Y
  26    0224  A9 00                 LDA     #0
  27    0226  79 06 01              ADC     RESUL-1,Y
  28    0229  99 06 01              STA     RESUL-1,Y
  29    022C  8A                    TXA
  30    022D  38                    SEC
  31    022E  E9 01                 SBC     #1
  32    0230  18                    CLC
  33    0231  AA                    TAX
  34    0232  4C 07 02              JMP     MLPL2
  35    0235  88            ZEROM   DEY
  36    0236  D0 CC                 BNE     MLPL1
  37    0238  60                    RTS
  38    0239                        .END


END OF MOS/TECHNOLOGY 650X ASSEMBLY VERSION 5
NUMBER OF ERRORS =    0.   NUMBER OF WARNINGS =     0




                SYMBOL TABLE

    SYMBOL    VALUE   LINE DEFINED        CROSS-REFERENCES

    MCND      0101         8      15
    MLPLY     0200        12      ****
    MLPL1     0204        15      36
    MLPL2     0207        16      34
    MLPR      0104         9      17      20      23
    NDGTS     0003         7      12
    RESUL     0107        10      18      19      21      22      24      25      27      28
    ZEROM     0235        35      16
```

The MCS 6502 Microprocessor and Peripheral Parts   163

```
CARD #  LOC     CODE         CARD  10       20          30          40          50          60        70
     1  0000
     2  0000
     3  0000
     4  0000
     5  0000                   ; THIS IS AN EXTREMELY SIMPLE PROGRAM TO DISPLAY ' E E' IN THE
     6  0000                   ; FIRST TWO POSITIONS OF THE DISPLAY.
     7  0000                   ;
     8  0000                   ; IT IS ENDLESS SO YOU MUST PRESS STOP TO EXIT.
     9  0000                   ;
    10  0000
    11  0000   A9 7F    DISPL    LDA    #$7F
    12  0002   8D 41 17          STA    $1741       SPECIFY OUTPUT BITS ON PIA.
    13  0005   A9 1E             LDA    #$1E
    14  0007   8D 43 17          STA    $1743       SPECIFY I/O BITS.
    15  000A   A9 79             LDA    #$79
    16  000C   8D 40 17          STA    $1740       DEFINE E'S.
    17  000F   A9 08    AGAIN    LDA    #$8         SPECIFY DISPLAY
    18  0011   8D 42 17          STA    $1742
    19  0014   A9 0A             LDA    #$0A        SPECIFY DISPLAY
    20  0016   8D 42 17          STA    $1742
    21  0019   4C 0F 00          JMP    AGAIN
    22  001C                     .END

END OF MOS/TECHNOLOGY 650X ASSEMBLY VERSION 5
NUMBER OF ERRORS =   0.  NUMBER OF WARNINGS =   0

             SYMBOL TABLE

    SYMBOL   VALUE  LINE DEFINED         CROSS-REFERENCES

    AGAIN    000F      17     21
    DISPL    0000      11    ****


CARD #  LOC     CODE         CARD  10       20          30          40          50          60        70
     1  0000
     2  0000
     3  0000
     4  0000                   ; THIS PROGRAM USES THE FIXED SIX DIGIT DISPLAY
     5  0000                   ; PROGRAM MODIFIED TO BE A SUBROUTINE TO MAKE A MOVING
     6  0000                   ; BROADWAY TYPE DISPLAY.
     7  0000                   ;
     8  0000                   ANY    =    $10
     9  0000                   NRDGT  =    13
    10  0000                   TEMP   =    $FC
    11  0000                   TEMP1  =    $30
    12  0000                   PADD   =    $1741
    13  0000                   SAD    =    $1740
    14  0000                   SBD    =    $1742
    15  0000                   PBDD   =    $1743
    16  0000
    17  0000                   *=$200
    18  0200
    19  0200   A2 55    START    LDX    #$55
    20  0202   86 30             STX    TEMP1       COUNTER
    21  0204   20 2E 02 STAR1    JSR    BEGIN
    22  0207   E6 30             INC    TEMP1
    23  0209   D0 F9             BNE    STAR1
    24  020B   A2 06             LDX    #6          NUMBER OF DIGITS
    25  020D   8E 42 17          STX    SBD         BLANK DISPLAY
    26  0210   A2 55             LDX    #$55
    27  0212   86 30             STX    TEMP1
    28  0214   86 31    STAR3    STX    TEMP1+1
    29  0216   E6 31    STAR2    INC    TEMP1+1
    30  0218   D0 FC             BNE    STAR2
    31  021A   E6 30             INC    TEMP1
    32  021C   D0 F6             BNE    STAR3
    33  021E   A2 0D             LDX    #NRDGT      DISPLAY 13 LOCATIONS
    34  0220   85 10             LDA    ANY,X
    35  0222   85 10             STA    ANY
    36  0224   B5 0F    STAR4    LDA    ANY-1,X
    37  0226   95 10             STA    ANY,X       MOVE IT OVER
    38  0228   CA                DEX
    39  0229   D0 F9             BNE    STAR4
    40  022B   4C 00 02          JMP    START
    41  022E
    42  022E   A9 7F    BEGIN    LDA    #$7F        SET A TO OUTPUT = SEGMENTS
    43  0230   8D 41 17          STA    PADD
    44  0233   8D 43 17          STA    PBDD        SET B TO OUTPUT = DIGITS.
    45  0236   A2 08             LDX    #8          DIGIT 1 SELECT.
    46  0238   A0 06             LDY    #$06        NUMBER OF DIGITS.
    47  023A   B9 10 00 MORE     LDA    ANY,Y       DISPLAY LOCATIONS 11,12,13....
    48  023D   8D 40 17          STA    SAD
    49  0240   8E 42 17          STX    SBD         DIGIT SELECT.
    50  0243   86 FC             STX    TEMP        SAVE IN TEMP.
```

```
CARD # LOC       CODE        CARD   10      20        30      40      50      60       70
  51   0245   A2 7F                 LDX     #$7F      500 MICROSECOND DELAY APPROX.
  52   0247   CA          DECR      DEX
  53   0248   D0 FD                 BNE     DECR
  54   024A   A6 FC                 LDX     TEMP      RECALL X FROM TEMP
  55   024C   E8                    INX               MOVE DISPLAY OVER
  56   024D   E8                    INX               TO NEXT DIGIT.
  57   024E   88                    DEY
  58   024F   D0 E9                 BNE     MORE      ALL 6 DIGITS ?
  59   0251   60                    RTS
  60   0252                         .END


END OF MOS/TECHNOLOGY 650X ASSEMBLY VERSION 5
NUMBER OF ERRORS =   0.  NUMBER OF WARNINGS =   0



           SYMBOL TABLE

   SYMBOL    VALUE   LINE DEFINED      CROSS-REFERENCES

   ANY       0010       8    34     35    36    37    47
   BEGIN     022E      42    21
   DECR      0247      52    53
   MORE      023A      47    58
   NRDGT     000D       9    33
   PADD      1741      12    43
   PBDD      1743      15    44
   SAD       1740      13    48
   SBD       1742      14    25     49
   START     0200      19    40
   STAR1     0204      21    23
   STAR2     0216      29    30
   STAR3     0214      28    32
   STAR4     0224      36    39
   TEMP      00FC      10    50     54
   TEMP1     0030      11    20     22    27    28    29    31


CARD # LOC      CODE        CARD    10      20       30      40      50      60       70
   1   0000
   2   0000
   3   0000
   4   0000               ; THIS PROGRAM READS A KIM FORMATTED PAPER TAPE ON THE
   5   0000               ; TELETYPE AND COMPARES IT TO MEMORY.
   6   0000               ; IF IT IS OK THE PROGRAM WILL TYPE 'KIM' AND THEN TURN
   7   0000               ; OFF THE PAPER TAPE READER WITH AN X-OFF.
   8   0000               ; IF IT IS NOT OK, IT WILL PRINT OUT WHERE THE COMPARE
   9   0000               ; FAILURE WAS LOCATED.  THIS PROGRAM DOES NOT LOAD THE ERROR
  10   0000               ; IN AS THE LOAD FUNCTION OF THE MONITOR WOULD.
  11   0000               ;
  12   0000               GETCH    =    $1E5A         SEVERAL KIM MONITOR ROUTINES USED.
  13   0000               GETBYT   =    $1F9D
  14   0000               POINTH   =    $FB
  15   0000               POINTL   =    $FA
  16   0000               INCPT    =    $1F63
  17   0000               CRLF     =    $1E2F
  18   0000               PRTPNT   =    $1E1E
  19   0000               OUTSP    =    $1E9E
  20   0000               PRTBYT   =    $1E3B
  21   0000               LOAD7    =    $1D2E
  22   0000
  23   0000                        *=$1780
  24   1780   20 5A 1E   CMPAR     JSR     GETCH
  25   1783   C9 3B                CMP     #';           CHECK FOR START OF RECORD.
  26   1785   D0 F9                BNE     CMPAR
  27   1787   20 9D 1F             JSR     GETBYT        GET BLOCK LENGTH
  28   178A   AA                   TAX
  29   178B   20 9D 1F             JSR     GETBYT        GET STARTING ADDRESS.
  30   178E   85 FB                STA     POINTH
  31   1790   20 9D 1F             JSR     GETBYT
  32   1793   85 FA                STA     POINTL
  33   1795   8A                   TXA                   BLOCK LENGTH = ZERO ?
  34   1796   F0 26                BEQ     DONE
  35   1798   20 9D 1F   CMPA2     JSR     GETBYT        TAPE = MEMORY ?
  36   179B   D1 FA                CMP     (POINTL),Y
  37   179D   D0 09                BNE     CMPERR
  38   179F   20 63 1F   CMPA4     JSR     INCPT
  39   17A2   CA                   DEX
  40   17A3   D0 F3                BNE     CMPA2
  41   17A5   4C 80 17             JMP     CMPAR
```

```
42  17A8  20 2F 1E  CMPERR  JSR   CRLF
43  17AB  20 1E 1E          JSR   PRTPNT
44  17AE  20 9E 1E          JSR   OUTSP
45  17B1  A0 00             LDY   #0
46  17B3  B1 FA             LDA   (POINTL),Y
47  17B5  20 3B 1E          JSR   PRTBYT
48  17B8  20 2F 1E          JSR   CRLF
49  17BB  4C 9F 17          JMP   CMPA4
50  17BE  4C 2E 1D  DONE    JMP   LOAD7       TYPE "KIM" AND X-OFF
51  17C1                    .END
```

SYMBOL TABLE

SYMBOL	VALUE	LINE DEFINED	CROSS-REFERENCES
CMPAR	1780	24	26	41
CMPA2	1798	35	40
CMPA4	179F	38	49
CMPERR	17A8	42	37
CRLF	1E2F	17	42	48
DONE	17BE	50	34
GETBYT	1F9D	13	27	29	31	35
GETCH	1E5A	12	24
INCPT	1F63	16	38
LOAD7	1D2E	21	50
OUTSP	1E9E	19	44
POINTH	00FB	14	30
POINTL	00FA	15	32	36	46
PRTBYT	1E3B	20	47
PRTPNT	1E1E	18	43

```
CARD # LOC    CODE       CARD   10        20        30        40        50        60        70
   1  0000
   2  0000
   3  0000
   4  0000               ; THIS PROGRAM WILL PRINT OUT THE ALPHABET ON THE
   5  0000               ; TELETYPE.  MANY VARIATIONS ARE POSSIBLE.
   6  0000               ; FOR EXAMPLE, A SLEW PRINT FOR THE TESTING OF
   7  0000               ; A PRINTER OR TELETYPE.
   8  0000
   9  0000               CRLF    =         $1E2F
  10  0000               OUTCH   =         $1EA0
  11  0000
  12  0000                       *=$200
  13  0200
  14  0200  A2 3F        TOP     LDX       #$3F           ALPHABET IS HEX 41-5A
  15  0202  A2 20                LDX       #$20
  16  0204  85 00                STA       0
  17  0206  A5 00        MORE    LDA       0
  18  0208  20 A0 1E             JSR       OUTCH
  19  020B  E6 00                INC       0
  20  020D  CA                   DEX
  21  020E  D0 F6                BNE       MORE
  22  0210  20 2F 1E             JSR       CRLF
  23  0213  4C 00 02             JMP       TOP
  24  0216                       .END
```

END OF MOS/TECHNOLOGY 650X ASSEMBLY VERSION 5
NUMBER OF ERRORS = 0, NUMBER OF WARNINGS = 0

SYMBOL TABLE

SYMBOL	VALUE	LINE DEFINED	CROSS-REFERENCES
CRLF	1E2F	9	22
MORE	0206	17	21
OUTCH	1EA0	10	18
TOP	0200	14	23

166 *Microcomputer Systems Principles*

```
CARD # LOC      CODE        CARD  10        20           30          40          50          60          70
   1   0000
   2   0000
   3   0000
   4   0000                  ;USING KIM-1 AS 24 HOUR INTERRUPT DRIVEN CLOCK.
   5   0000                  ; A. CONNECT PIA(B7) TO IRQ (A15-E4)
   6   0000                  ; B. IRQ VECTOR (17FE<--$20, 17FF<--00)
   7   0000                          *=00
   8   0000   F8                     SED
   9   0001   58                     CLI                    ENABLE INTERRUPTS.
  10   0002   A2 00                  LDX     #0
  11   0004   86 F8                  STX     $F8            DISPLAY DATA CLEARED.
  12   0006   86 F9                  STX     $F9
  13   0008   86 FA                  STX     $FA
  14   000A   86 FB                  STX     $FB
  15   000C   A9 F4                  LDA     #244
  16   000E   8D 0F 17               STA     $170F          DIVIDE BY 1024<--244
  17   0011   20 1F 1F    SHOW       JSR     $1F1F          ORBIT UNTIL IRQ
  18   0014   4C 11 00               JMP     SHOW
  19   0017                          *=$20
  20   0020   48                     PHA                    IRQ FIX
  21   0021   E6 F8                  INC     $F8
  22   0023   A9 04                  LDA     #$4
  23   0025   C5 F8                  CMP     $F8
  24   0027   D0 31                  BNE     END            1/4 SECOND
  25   0029   A9 00                  LDA     #0
  26   002B   85 F8                  STA     $F8
  27   002D   18                     CLC
  28   002E   A5 F9                  LDA     $F9            INSURE DECIMAL RESULT
  29   0030   69 01                  ADC     #1
  30   0032   85 F9                  STA     $F9
  31   0034   C9 60                  CMP     #$60
  32   0036   D0 22                  BNE     END
  33   0038   A9 00                  LDA     #0
  34   003A   85 F9                  STA     $F9
  35   003C   18                     CLC
  36   003D   A5 FA                  LDA     $FA
  37   003F   69 01                  ADC     #1
  38   0041   85 FA                  STA     $FA
  39   0043   C9 60                  CMP     #$60
  40   0045   D0 13                  BNE     END            1 HOUR
  41   0047   A9 00                  LDA     #0
  42   0049   85 FA                  STA     $FA
  43   004B   18                     CLC
  44   004C   A5 FB                  LDA     $FB
  45   004E   69 01                  ADC     #1
  46   0050   85 FB                  STA     $FB
  47   0052   C9 24                  CMP     #$24
  48   0054   D0 04                  BNE     END            24 HOURS
  49   0056   A9 00                  LDA     #0
  50   0058   85 FB                  STA     $FB
  51   005A   A9 F4       END        LDA     #244
  52   005C   8D 0F 17               STA     $170F
  53   005F   68                     PLA
  54   0060   40                     RTI
  55   0061                          .END

NUMBER OF ERRORS =    0.  NUMBER OF WARNINGS =    0

        SYMBOL TABLE

SYMBOL      VALUE   LINE DEFINED         CROSS-REFERENCES
END         005A         51      24      32      40      48
SHOW        0011         17      18


CARD # LOC      CODE        CARD  10        20           30          40          50          60          70
   1   0000
   2   0000
   3   0000
   4   0000                  ; THIS IS A FORMATTED HEXADECIMAL DUMP FOR THE KIM
   5   0000                  ; THAT IS- THERE IS A HEX CODE PRINTED IN THE CORRECT
   6   0000                  ; ONE, TWO OR THREE BYTE FORM DEPENDING UPON THE CODE
   7   0000                  ; BEING DUMPED.  IT IS THE START OF A DISASSEMBLER.
   8   0000                  ; THE WHOLE THING SITS IN "HIGH" RWM AND SHOULD NOT
   9   0000                  ; INTERFERE WITH "NORMAL" PROGRAMS.
  10   0000                  ;
  11   0000                  ; THE FOLLOWING ARE ALL KIM I/O ADDRESSES AND MONITOR ROUTINES.
  12   0000                  SAL     =       $17F5
  13   0000                  SAH     =       $17F6
  14   0000                  PCINTL  =       $FA
```

The MCS 6502 Microprocessor and Peripheral Parts

```
CARD #  LOC     CODE         CARD 10       20         30         40         50         60         70
  15    0000                 POINTH   =    $FB
  16    0000                 EAL      =    $17F7
  17    0000                 EAH      =    $17F8
  18    0000                 CRLF     =    $1E2F
  19    0000                 CLEAR    =    $1C64
  20    0000                 PRTBYT   =    $1E3B
  21    0000                 PRTPNT   =    $1E1E
  22    0000                 OUTSP    =    $1E9E
  23    0000                 INCPT    =    $1F63
  24    0000
  25    0000                          *=$1780
  26    1780   20 2F 1E  DUMP     JSR     CRLF          NOTE -- YOU MUST SET UP STARTING ADDRESS
  27    1783   AD F5 17           LDA     SAL           SAL,SAH AND ENDING ADDRESS EAL, EAH
  28    1786   85 FA              STA     POINTL        BEFORE INVOKING BY A JSR DUMP.
  29    1788   AD F6 17           LDA     SAH
  30    178B   85 FB              STA     POINTH
  31    178D   20 2F 1E  DUMP1    JSR     CRLF
  32    1790   A5 FA              LDA     POINTL
  33    1792   CD F7 17           CMP     EAL
  34    1795   A5 FB              LDA     POINTH
  35    1797   ED F8 17           SBC     EAH
  36    179A   90 03              BCC     DUMP2         ARE WE DONE? POINT = EA ?
  37    179C   4C 64 1C           JMP     CLEAR
  38    179F   20 1E 1E  DUMP2    JSR     PRTPNT        PRINT ADDRESS OF OPCODE.
  39    17A2   20 9E 1E           JSR     OUTSP
  40    17A5   A0 00              LDY     #0
  41    17A7   B1 FA              LDA     (POINTL),Y    GET OPCODE
  42    17A9   C9 20              CMP     #$20          FILTER OUT A FEW WILD CARDS
  43    17AB   F0 1D              BEQ     THREE         THREE BYTE INSTRUCTIONS, ETC.
  44    17AD   C9 40              CMP     #$40
  45    17AF   F0 1F              BEQ     ONE
  46    17B1   C9 60              CMP     #$60
  47    17B3   F0 1B              BEQ     ONE
  48    17B5   29 0F              AND     #$0F
  49    17B7   C9 08              CMP     #8
  50    17B9   F0 15              BEQ     ONE
  51    17BB   C9 0A              CMP     #$0A
  52    17BD   F0 11              BEQ     ONE
  53    17BF   10 09              BPL     THREE
  54    17C1   B1 FA              LDA     (POINTL),Y
  55    17C3   4A                 LSR     A
  56    17C4   29 0F              AND     #$0F
  57    17C6   C9 0C              CMP     #$0C
  58    17C8   D0 03              BNE     TWO
  59    17CA   20 D6 17  THREE    JSR     PRINT
  60    17CD   20 D6 17  TWO      JSR     PRINT
  61    17D0   20 D6 17  ONE      JSR     PRINT
  62    17D3   4C 8D 17           JMP     DUMP1
  63    17D6   A0 00     PRINT    LDY     #0
  64    17D8   B1 FA              LDA     (POINTL),Y
  65    17DA   20 9E 1E           JSR     OUTSP
  66    17DD   20 63 1F           JSR     INCPT
  67    17E0   60                 RTS
  68    17E1   60                 RTS                   MIGHT REPLACE WITH BRK IF WE
  69    17E2                                            WANT TO RETURN TO HTE MONITOR.
  70    17E2                      .END
```

```
END OF MOS/TECHNOLOGY 650X ASSEMBLY VERSION 5
NUMBER OF ERRORS =   0.  NUMBER OF WARNINGS =    0


             SYMBOL TABLE

   SYMBOL   VALUE   LINE DEFINED       CROSS-REFERENCES

   CLEAR    1C64       19    37
   CRLF     1E2F       18    26   31
   DUMP     1780       26   ****
   DUMP1    178D       31    62
   DUMP2    179F       38    36
   EAH      17F8       17    35
   EAL      17F7       16    33
   INCPT    1F63       23    66
   ONE      17D0       61    45   47   50   52
   OUTSP    1E9E       22    39   65
   POINTH   00FB       15    30   34
   POINTL   00FA       14    28   32   41   54   64
   PRINT    17D6       63    59   60   61
   PRTBYT   1E3B       20   ****
   PRTPNT   1E1E       21    38
   SAH      17F6       13    29
   SAL      17F5       12    27
   THREE    17CA       59    43   53
   TWO      17CD       60    58
```

168 *Microcomputer Systems Principles*

```
CARD #  LOC     CODE        CARD    10          20          30          40          50          60          70
    1   0000
    2   0000
    3   0000
    4   0000                ; TRIANGULAR WAVE GENERATOR USING KIM
    5   0000                ; AND MOTOROLA MC1406 A/D CONVERTER.
    6   0000                ;
    7   0000                ADAT    =           $1700       KIM I/O PORT DEFINITION.
    8   0000                ADIR    =           $1701
    9   0000
   10   0000                        *=$200
   11   0200
   12   0200   A2 FF        TGEN    LDX         #$FF
   13   0202   8E 01 17             STX         ADIR        SET A-SIDE TO OUTPUT.
   14   0205   A0 3F        LOOP1   LDY         #$3F
   15   0207   8C 00 17     LOOP2   STY         ADAT        A/D CONVERTER COMPLEMENTS
   16   020A   20 1E 02             JSR         DLA         THE $3F OUTPUT TO ZERO VOLTS.
   17   020D   88                   DEY
   18   020E   D0 F7                BNE         LOOP2
   19   0210   8C 00 17     LOOP3   STY         ADAT        RUN COUNT BACK UP.
   20   0213   C8                   INY
   21   0214   20 1E 02             JSR         DLA
   22   0217   C0 3F                CPY         #$3F
   23   0219   D0 F5                BNE         LOOP3
   24   021B   4C 07 02             JMP         LOOP2
   25   021E   A2 FF        DLA     LDX         #$FF        DETERMINED FREQUENCY OF THE WAVE.
   26   0220   CA           DLA1    DEX                     COULD VARY DYNAMICALLY TO
   27   0221   D0 FD                BNE         DLA1        FM OR SWEEP, ETC.
   28   0223   60                   RTS
   29   0224                        .END


END OF MOS/TECHNOLOGY 650X ASSEMBLY VERSION 5
NUMBER OF ERRORS =   0.  NUMBER OF WARNINGS =    0



             SYMBOL TABLE

SYMBOL     VALUE   LINE DEFINED        CROSS-REFERENCES

ADAT       1700       7     15     19
ADIR       1701       8     13
DLA        021E      25     16     21
DLA1       0220      26     27
LOOP1      0205      14     ****
LOOP2      0207      15     18     24
LOOP3      0210      19     23
TGEN       0200      12     ****

                                                                            PAGE    1

CARD #  LOC     CODE        CARD    10          20          30          40          50          60          70
    1   0000
    2   0000
    3   0000
    4   0000                ; THIS EXAMPLE PROGRAM IS TO EXTEND
    5   0000                ; THE ' E E ' DISPLAY TO ALSO FLASH
    6   0000                ; THAT IS - BLINK AT A RATE DETERMINED
    7   0000                ; BY THE CLOCK IN THE MCS6530. (ENDLESS PROGRAM)
    8   0000                ;
    9   0000                SAD     =           $1740       KIM I/O DEFINITIONS
   10   0000                PADD    =           $1741          "
   11   0000                SBD     =           $1742          "
   12   0000                PBDD    =           $1743          "
   13   0000                CLKRDI  =           $1747          "
   14   0000                CLKKT   =           $1747          "
   15   0000                DGT1    =           $8          DIGIT SELECTION FOR DECODER
   16   0000                DGT2    =           $0A
   17   0000
   18   0000                        *=$200
   19   0200
   20   0200   A9 7F        FLASH   LDA         #$7F
   21   0202   8D 41 17             STA         PADD        SET A-SIDE TO OUTPUT=SEGMENTS.
   22   0205   A9 1E                LDA         #$1E
   23   0207   8D 43 17             STA         PBDD        SET B-SIDE DIRECTION=DIGITS.
   24   020A   A9 79        TOP     LDA         #$79        SEVEN SEGMENT VALUE FOR 'E'
   25   020C   8D 40 17             STA         SAD
   26   020F   A9 7F                LDA         #$7F        START DIVIDE BY 1024 CLOCK.
   27   0211   8D 47 17             STA         CLKKT
   28   0214   A9 08        AGAIN   LDA         #DGT1       PICK FIRST DISPLAY DIGIT.
```

The MCS 6502 Microprocessor and Peripheral Parts

```
29   0216   8D 42 17            STA   SBD
30   0219   A9 0A               LDA   #DGT2           OTHER DIGIT - SEGMENTS STILL = E.
31   021B   8D 42 17            STA   SBD
32   021E   AD 47 17            LDA   CLKRDI          CHECK CLOCK TIMEOUT.
33   0221   10 F1               BPL   AGAIN
34   0223   A9 7F               LDA   #$7F            START CLOCK AGAIN FOR BLANKED INTERVAL.
35   0225   8D 47 17            STA   CLKKT
36   0228   A9 00               LDA   #0
37   022A   8D 40 17            STA   SAD
38   022D   A9 08      LOOP     LDA   #DGT1           BLANK THEM OUT AND LOOP
39   022F   8D 42 17            STA   SBD                UNTIL CLOCK TIMEOUT.
40   0232   A9 0A               LDA   #DGT2
41   0234   8D 42 17            STA   SBD
42   0237   AD 47 17            LDA   CLKRDI
43   023A   10 F1               BPL   LOOP
44   023C   4C 0A 02            JMP   TOP
45   023F                       .END

END OF MOS/TECHNOLOGY 650X ASSEMBLY VERSION 5
NUMBER OF ERRORS =   0.   NUMBER OF WARNINGS =    0

            SYMBOL TABLE

SYMBOL      VALUE    LINE DEFINED      CROSS-REFERENCES

AGAIN       0214        28   33
CLKKT       1747        14   27   35
CLKRDI      1747        13   32   42
DGT1        0008        15   28   38
DGT2        000A        16   30   40
FLASH       0200        20   ****
LOOP        022D        38   43
PADD        1741        10   21
PBDD        1743        12   23
SAD         1740         9   25   37
SBD         1742        11   29   31   39   41
TOP         020A        24   44


CARD #  LOC      CODE         CARD  10        20        30        40        50        60        70
   1    0000
   2    0000
   3    0000
   4    0000
   5    0000                  ; 6530 RWM CHECKERBOARD TESTER FOR READ-WRITE MEMORY
   6    0000                  ; BETWEEN $1780 AND $17EF IN THE KIM.
   7    0000                  ;
   8    0000
   9    0000                  POINTL   =       $FA
  10    0000                  POINTH   =       $FB
  11    0000                  INCPT    =       $1F63         A KIM MONITOR SUBROUTINE.
  12    0000                  START    =       $1C4F         START OF KIM MONITOR.
  13    0000                  PRTPNT   =       $1E1E         KIM ROUTINE TO PRINT MONITOR VALUES.
  14    0000                  CRLF     =       $1E2F         KIM ROUTINE TO PRINT CARRIAGE RETURN.
  15    0000                           *=$10
  16    0010   A9 80          LDA      #$80                  INITIALIZE INDIRECT BASE PAGE POINTER
  17    0012   85 FA          STA      POINTL
  18    0014   A9 17          LDA      #$17
  19    0016   85 FB          STA      POINTH
  20    0018   A2 6F          LDX      #$6F
  21    001A   A0 00   LOOP   LDY      #0
  22    001C   A9 55          LDA      #$55                  FIRST PATTERN = %01010101
  23    001E   91 FA          STA      (POINTL),Y            STORE AND CHECK.
  24    0020   D1 FA          CMP      (POINTL),Y
  25    0022   D0 11          BNE      ERROR                 ERROR EXIT
  26    0024   A9 AA          LDA      #$AA                  COMPLEMENTED PATTERN.
  27    0026   91 FA          STA      (POINTL),Y
  28    0028   D1 FA          CMP      (POINTL),Y            KIM MONITOR INCREMENTS ($FA,$FB)
  29    002A   D0 09          BNE      ERROR
  30    002C   20 63 1F       JSR      INCPT
  31    002F   CA             DEX
  32    0030   D0 E8          BNE      LOOP
  33    0032   4C 4F 1C       JMP      START                 EXIT WHEN DONE.
  34    0035   20 2F 1E ERROR JSR      CRLF
  35    0038   20 1E 1E       JSR      PRTPNT
  36    003B   20 2F 1E       JSR      CRLF
  37    003E   00             BRK
  38    003F                  .END

END OF MOS/TECHNOLOGY 650X ASSEMBLY VERSION 5
NUMBER OF ERRORS =   0.   NUMBER OF WARNINGS =    0
```

```
                SYMBOL TABLE
SYMBOL    VALUE   LINE DEFINED        CROSS-REFERENCES
CRLF      1E2F         14     34    36
ERROR     0035         34     25    29
INCPT     1F63         11     30
LOOP      001A         21     32
POINTH    00FB         10     19
POINTL    00FA          9     17    23    24    27    28
PRTPNT    1E1E         13     35
START     1C4F         12     33
```

PROBLEMS

1. What is the difference between Op Codes and Instructions? Verify that the MCS6502 has 151 Op Codes. How many instructions does it have?

2. Make your own Instruction Table like Table 3.4.2. Combine all mutually exclusive columns and omit entries for number of execution cycles (N) and bytes of code required (#).

3. Complete the table below at the completion of each instruction indicated.

OP	ADDR	P	A
CLD		2C	2C
SBC	#$∅F		

4. Repeat Problem 3 with SBC #$7A.

5. In Problems 3 and 4 replace A = $C5 and repeat.

6. In Problems 3 and 4 replace P = $2D and repeat.

7. Will the program steps below convert the number in A to its decimal equivalent?

    SED
    ADC   #∅

8. Give a brief example of usage of the two addressing modes: Indexed Indirect and Indirect Indexed.

9. How many instructions affect the N bit in the P register?

10. Critically compare the Reset sequence of events and results with JMP ($FFFC).

11. Prove the statement that Branches may span only -126_{10} to 129_{10} from LABEL.

       LABEL BEQ TO

12. Fill in the two bytes of the instruction below.

           TOP = \$CF$\emptyset$5

    \$CF5A ____ ____ BVC TOP

13. Write assembly language instructions to implement:

      IF A = B THEN GO TO LABEL;
      IF A < B THEN GO TO LABEL;
      IF A > B THEN GO TO LABEL;
      IF A − 5 > B THEN B ← $\emptyset$;

14. Itemize those registers which can force their value on to the Address pins.

15. Complete the table below.

	PC	A	X	Y	S	P
	$\emptyset$2$\emptyset$$\emptyset$	F1	22	33	FF	61
$\emptyset$2$\emptyset$$\emptyset$ CMP #\$55	___	___	___	___	___	___

16. Write an Assembly language subroutine, beginning at location \$2$\emptyset$$\emptyset$, labeled JOGGLE, which moves a 256_{10} element array beginning at \$4$\emptyset$$\emptyset$ down 1 location. ($\emptyset$4$\emptyset$$\emptyset$) → ($\emptyset$3FF), ($\emptyset$4$\emptyset$1) → ($\emptyset$4$\emptyset$$\emptyset$), etc.

17. Repeat 16 except that the array has 512_{10} elements.

18. Repeat 16 except move *up* 1 location.

19. Repeat 17 except move *up* 1 location.

20. If (A) = \$8$\emptyset$ and (M) = \$7F, \$8$\emptyset$ or \$81, complete Table 3.4.5.1 for N.

21. It is our desire to pass 5 one-byte variables to a subroutine via the stack area. Explain exactly how you can accomplish this.

22. Write a general subroutine to pulse Bit $\emptyset$ of Side B of the KIM high for a variable time. When this subroutine is called, A contains a binary value equal to the number of milliseconds duration of the pulse width.

23. We have designed a working microcomputer using MCS6502, MCS6520, ROM, RWM etc. Use the connections below and write a program to initialize the B side of the MCS6520 to be output and low.

ADDRESS		MCS6520
A∅	–	PIN 36
A1	–	PIN 35
A13	–	PIN 22
A14	–	PIN 23
A15	–	PIN 24

24. Explain how CB2 Pulse Output can be used to drive an external circuit. Draw a system diagram and attendant software driver.

25. Write a program to accomplish multiplication by Table-look up.

4

SOFTWARE AIDS

4.1 INTRODUCTION

It takes very little time for the beginner in microprocessor-based system design to discover that development of programs or "software" for his system occupies a great deal of his time and effort. It often surprises people that, even in large computation centers where multi-million dollar computers are found, programming costs are very often greater then hardware costs, often considerably so. It should come as no surprise, then, that the cost of a microprocessor or microcomputer can become almost negligible relative to the costs of developing programs for it.

In the high-volume product situation, of course, it may be possible to expend great sums of money for program development, since the per-unit amortized cost may be small. Where ones, tens, hundreds, or even thousands of units represent the production goal, however, the programming costs will be significant or even dominant.

Because of the high cost of software development, manufacturers have provided a wide range of tools to be used to make the program development process more efficient. Some of these tools, like programming languages, assemblers, simulators, compilers, etc., are traditional in concept, having evolved long before the microprocessor. Others, like in-circuit emulators, PROM programmers, and dedicated support systems with file-handling capability, have been specifically developed to respond to the needs of the microcomputer engineer.

This chapter will discuss a number of these software aids. A general description of each will be given, along with examples of detailed operation of representative systems.

4.2 THE SOFTWARE DESIGN PROCESS

4.2.1 Top-down and Modular Programming

It is impossible to generate general deterministic rules for software design since, like any design process, it demands elements of creativity not subject to such rules. It is possible, however, to suggest overall principles which tend to minimize the pain and/or cost associated with creating reliable programs.

The designation "top-down" design implies one set of such principles. Such an approach requires the programmer to begin his design by generating a concise but logically consistent statement of the design problem. The problem is then subdivided into a collection of subtasks which can be independently characterized. Each of these subtasks is then further subdivided, the process continuing until the individual low-level tasks are sufficiently simple to permit straightforward implementation as individual programs. As each of these individual programs are developed, they are integrated into higher-level modules corresponding to the original subdivision scheme. The final step is integration of all submodules into an operating program which satisfies the needs stated in the original problem.

The modular approach to programming dictated by the above process is one *every* programmer should consider for even fairly modest problems. Figure 4.2-1 is a block diagram which represents the operation of the entire monitor program for the KIM-1 microcomputer. Each program module is identified by function and is describable in very simple terms. Each of these modules is capable of independent development and exahustive testing of module reliability is possible. For example, the "GET KEY" routine, which is intended to sense keyboard keystrokes and generate codes corresponding to each key, can be written and tested with resulting assurance that it is fully reliable. Similarly, the "EXECUTE KEY" routine can be developed and tested to demonstrate that, given a proper keycode input, the appropriate output path is reliably achieved. If one attempted to develop a single program module which combined both the GET KEY and EXECUTE KEY functions, bugs would be much more difficult to isolate than if they were known to exist in one of the two simpler modules.

Another positive aspect of modular programming lies in its adaptation to division of programming effort. This means not only that a large programming problem can be divided among several programmers, but that modules, once developed, can be filed away in a "library" for

Software Aids

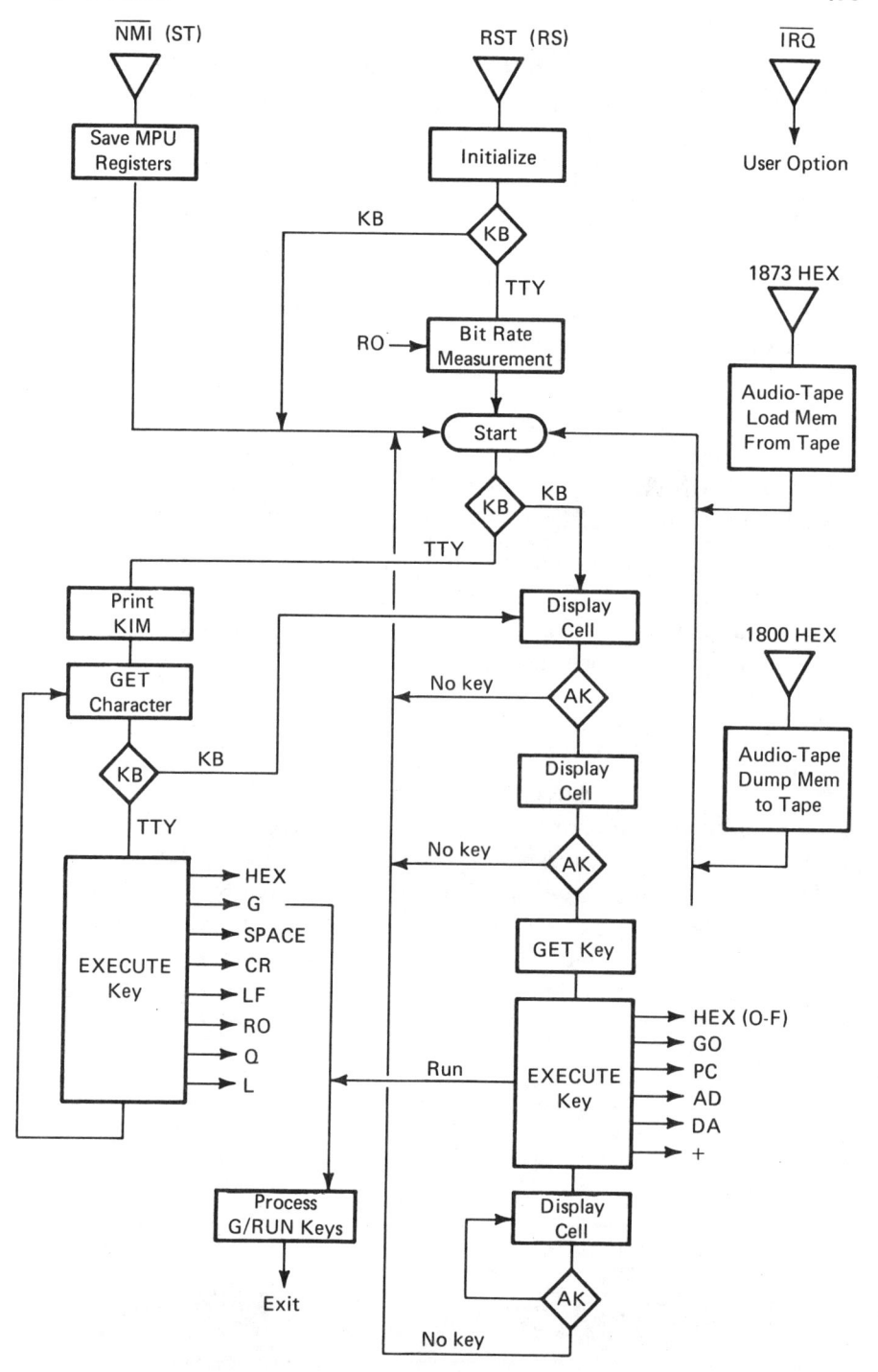

Figure 4.2-1 Flow chart of KIM-1 monitor program

use in other applications, somewhat analogously to the creation of standard logic hardware modules capable of a variety of specific applications.

4.2.2 Structured Programming

A technique related to modular programming is known as "structured programming." The ideas of top-down design and hierarchical modularity are both part of this programming concept. According to Keith (see reference 1), the following code rules are common to most discussions of structured programming:

1. Use simple straightforward code sequences.
2. Use IF–THEN–ELSE logic.
3. Implement a loop control ability such as DO–WHILE or DO–UNTIL.
4. Avoid the use of GO TO statements.

Assembly-language programming doesn't provide the constructs implied by rules 2, 3, and 4 so, strictly speaking, a fully structured programming approach may not be possible in such a language. The motivation for the rules, however, which is to simplify programs and make them more readable and understandable, is well-founded.

Figures 4.2-2, 4.2-3, and 4.2-4, taken from Keith's article, illustrate his approach to top-down structured design of a game program called SHOOTING STARS. These figures illustrate the repeated subdivision of the program into simpler and simpler modules. They also show a numeric left-to-right hierarchical coding which implies sequence of activity, i.e., REPLAY follows PLAY which follows INITIALIZE. Note that these hierarchy diagrams describe the *function* rather than the *logic*. A flow chart (Figure 4.2-1, for example) describes program logic. Keith suggests that complete program documentation might best be accomplished by hierarchy diagrams and accompanying flow charts for nontrivial routines.

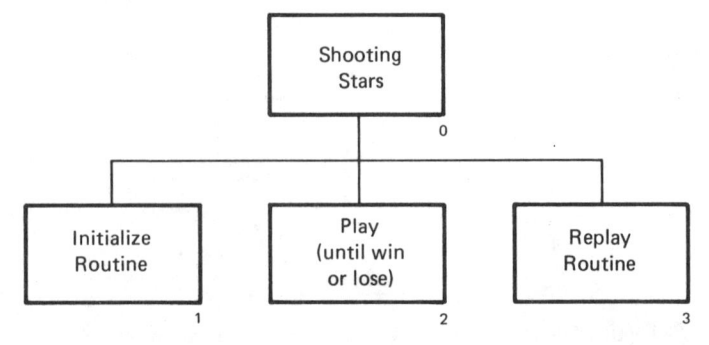

Figure 4.2-2 Program hierarchy diagram - first and second levels

Software Aids

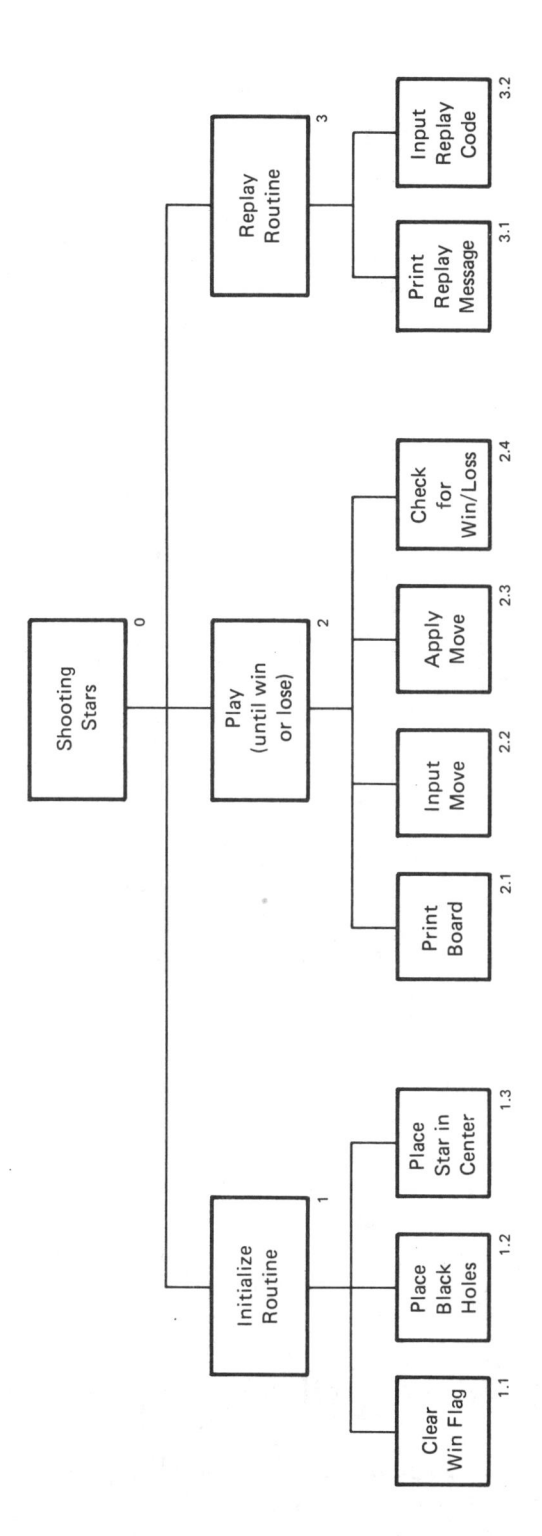

Figure 4.2-3 Program heirarchy diagram - third level

Figure 4.2-4 Program hierarchy diagram - fourth and fifth levels - total development

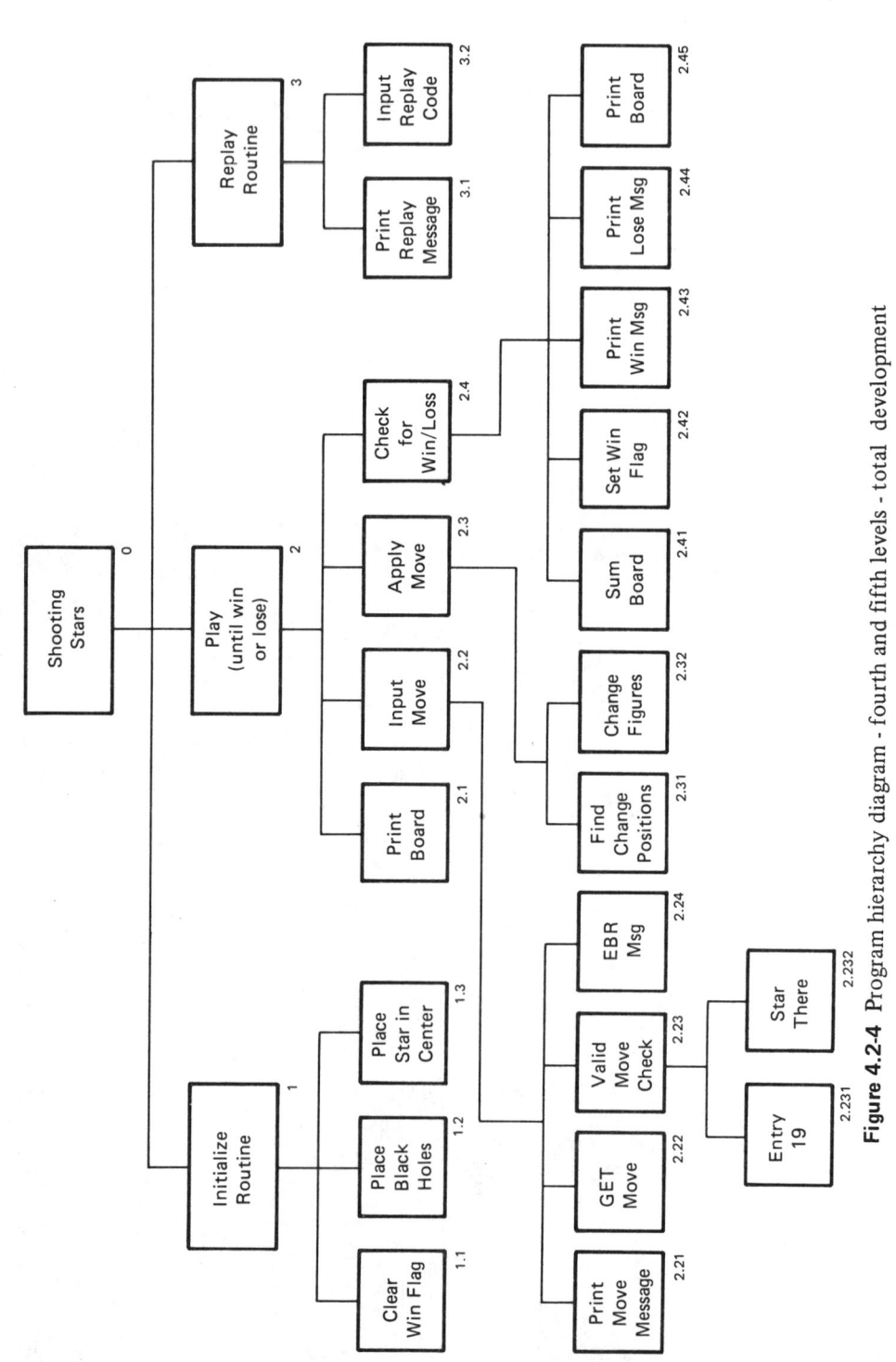

Software Aids 179

4.2.3 Software Design Tools

The specification for a program and the algorithmic structure developed for satisfying that specification largely requires a mental, paper-and-pencil effort. Once this design and planning function is completed, the remaining steps of formal coding and test of the program remains. Figure 4.2-5 is a flow chart showing the elements which comprise this sequence of activity in a typical situation. This diagram implies the use of a microprocessor development system like Intel's MDS-800, Motorola's EXORCISOR or Rockwell's SYSTEM 65.

In a typical situation, the programmer will sit down to a CRT terminal and by typing system commands, invoke a *text editor*. The editor provides the capability for creating, modifying, rearranging, and otherwise manipulating ordinary alphanumeric text. Initially the text desired is the assembly language or higher level language program itself. The programmer codes such a program, following the syntactic rules of the language in use, and terminates the editing session by creating a *source file* on floppy disk (or other secondary storage medium). He then initiates the translation process by invoking the assembler (or compiler). For example, typing the command

ASM80 :F1:SORT.SRC   XREF

will invoke the Intel 8080/8085 assembler program (which itself is stored as a file on floppy disk) to assemble a source program whose file name is SORT.SRC and which resides on floppy disk number 1. The control word XREF asks that the assembly listing file include a cross reference table (see Section 4.3.3.7). The assembler program may take from 5 minutes to a significantly longer time to produce its output, which is manifested as two new files, in the case of our example called SORT.OBJ and SORT.LST. SORT.OBJ contains an object (machine language) program, properly formatted for transfer to a remote system by paper tape or similar medium. SORT.LST is the listing file, which contains a comprehensive record of both the source program and the object program, along with error messages, a symbol table, a cross-reference symbol table (as requested by XREF) and other useful information. If the programmer wishes to see his listing, he may type the command

COPY :F1: SORT.LST TO :LP:

which will produce a copy of the listing on a line printer. If syntax errors are flagged, the programmer may recall his source file for pro-

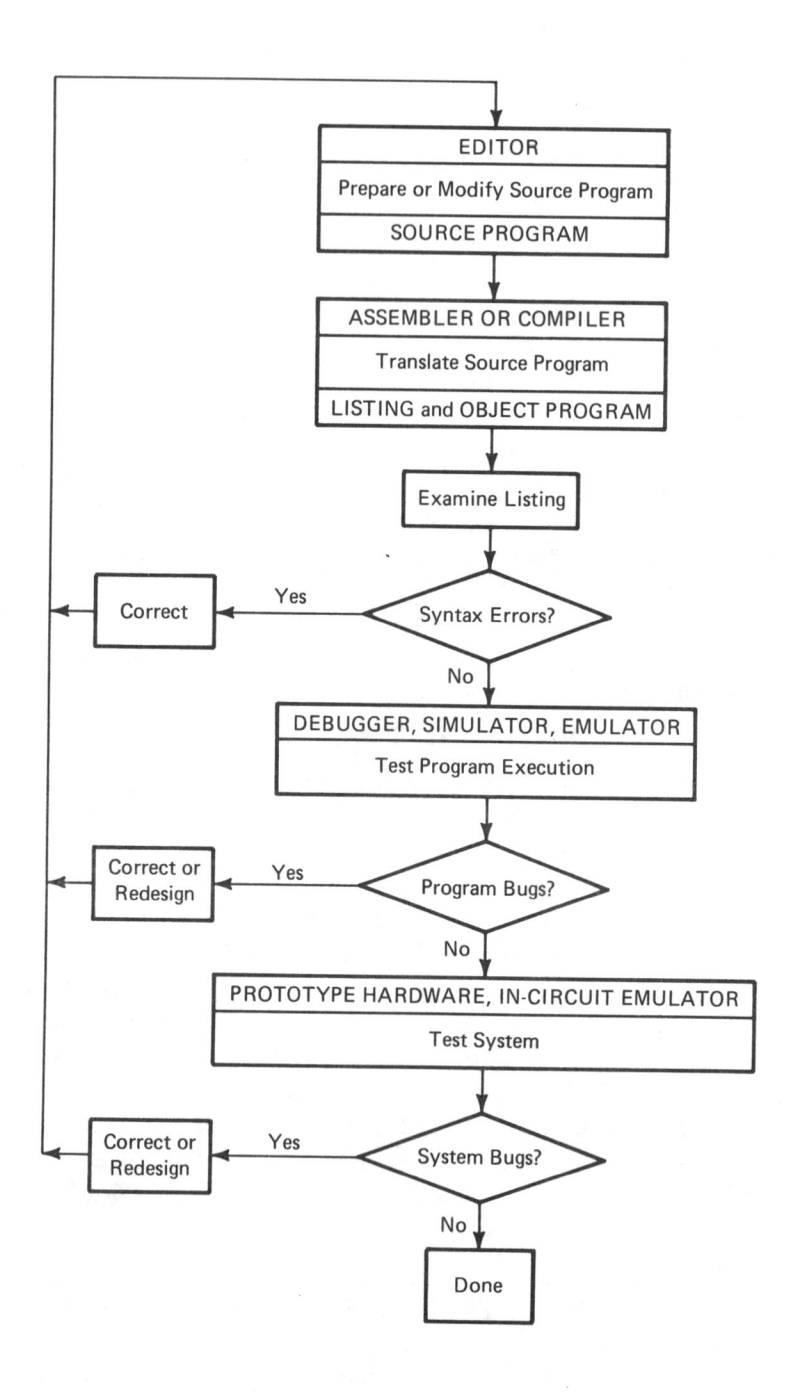

Figure 4.2-5 Flow chart of program development activity

Software Aids 181

cessing by the text editor. Using INSERT, KILL, SEARCH, SUBSTITUTE, and similar editor commands he modifies his source program and creates a new source file. He then can reassemble and repeat the process until his program is syntactically correct. The commands discussed here are for a specific editor. However, most editors will have similar commands.

The program debug phase is usually the most difficult and frustrating part of the development process. If the development system uses the target processor as its own CPU, it is possible to load the object program directly into the system memory and transfer system control to it. In the MDS-800, this could be accomplished by typing the command

DEBUG :F1: SORT.OBJ

followed by (assuming a starting location of 1000 hex)

G 1000

This "GO" command transfers control to the program which begins at location 1000, presumably our program.

The program debug phase is iterative, i.e., as the designer discovers problems or "bugs" he will introduce modifications to his original program and retranslate the new version, continuing the debug cycle until he has corrected problems. Once having generated a program which operates properly in its own right, the final hurdle, software/hardware integration, must be cleared. Special dedicated systems such as in-circuit emulators (see Section 4.8) or logic state analyzers (see Section 4.9) are invaluable at this stage, usually the most difficult step of all.

4.3 ELEMENTS OF PROGRAM TRANSLATION

4.3.1 Translation Levels

We are fond of saying things like "The computer only understands 1's and 0's" but, if we reflect for a moment, the "1" and "0" are symbolic references to physical phenomena such as voltage levels, current levels, punched hole patterns, activated light sources and detectors, and countless other manifestations. Thus even binary machine language is a symbolic language. There are of course, many levels of symbolic language associated with computers, and, in each case, there is an accompanying problem of *translation* of some symbolic information message (normally a program) into some more primitive symbolic information message more nearly suited to direct acceptance by the computer.

Tanenbaum (see reference 2) characterizes the general problem of language translation in terms of a multiplicity of language levels. Level 1 comprises the actual electronic hardware language, capable of direct acceptance by the circuit logic elements. This level is often called the *microprogramming* level, and is characterized by its primitive nature. Examples of instructions at this level would be "Transfer (A) to (X)," "Shift (A) right one place, " and "Clear Sign Bit."

Tanenbaum's Level 2 is the conventional machine language level. Typical instructions at this level might be "Move the contents of location 1 to location 2," "Add the contents of memory location 345 to the accumulator," and "Output a byte to port 45."

Level 3 is the operating system machine level. Typical instructions at this level might be "Print a line of text on the line printer," "Translate FORTRAN program X into machine language," and "Calculate terminal charges for User Y."

Level 4 is the Assembly Language level. In simple terms, this language provides the programmer with the convenience of symbolic statements in a form rather easily readable by him, instead of the numeric symbolism of Level 2, the conventional machine language level. There is, however, a very close correlation between statements in assembly language and statements in numeric machine code. Assembly language also can provide a number of other conveniences in the form of *pseudoinstructions* or *assembler directives* which permit the programmer to direct a variety of activities such as memory allocation, program location, printer listings, and management of symbolic names for data values. Section 4.3.3 provides a detailed discussion of assembly language principles.

Level 5 is loosely defined as the problem-oriented language level. In common usage, Level 5 languages are called *high-level* languages. ALGOL, BASIC, FORTRAN, PL/1, and SNOBOL are high-level languages. Examples of microprocessor-oriented high-level languages include PL/M (Intel), MPL (Motorola) and CSL (MOS Technology, Commodore, and Rockwell). The distinguishing characteristic of instructions written in high-level languages is that they compactly denote operations which can constitute complex data-processing operations without the necessity for concern about detailed machine activity which produces the desired result. For example, the statement "C = SQRT(ARGUMENT)" defines a desired operation, namely, the assignment to variable C the value of the square root of variable ARGUMENT. In machine code or in assembly code, a program achieving this result might require 20 or 30 statements, and would be obscured by detailed

Software Aids 183

attention to machine registers, memory locations, and other hardware elements which might be brought into play to achieve the desired result.

Tanenbaum defines level 6 and above as consisting of collections of programs designed to provide machines that are tailored to specific applications, and contain large amounts of information about that application.

The presence of these language levels and the obvious necessity for converting any program written in any language into code acceptable to the computer naturally leads to the requirement for *translator programs*. These programs, themselves written in some language, accept input in the form of programs written in some language (the *source* language) and produce output in the form of programs written in some other language (the *target* language). It is important to note that the only function of the translation process is to produce a program in another language. The use of a translator does not imply that any execution of the original source program has taken place upon completion of translation.

A translator which converts a program written in assembly language into numerical machine code is called, naturally enough, an *assembler*. A program which converts a program written in high-level language into a lower-level language, perhaps machine language or assembly language, is called a *compiler*.

A process related to language translation is that of *interpretation*. An interpreter program accepts a single statement in the source language, converts it to a machine language, and causes it to be executed before proceeding to the next succeeding source statement. The interpreter has the advantage (relative to the compiler) that it has modest storage requirements since the entire source and target programs need not be treated as entities. Its principal disadvantage is that it can be exceedingly slow, since a given statement must be totally translated each time encountered, rather than only once as during the compilation process.

4.3.2 Economic Factors

A few years ago, before the appearance of microprocessors, it was accepted truth in the computer field that the only type of programming language to be considered was some type of high-level language. Assembly-language programming was a lost art, to be endured only during a small segment of one's educational program. As the microcomputer came rushing into the scene, however, interest in machine-level and assembly-language programming was rekindled with a vengeance. For one thing, no high-level languages devoted to microprocessors existed for a significant period. Such languages exist even today for only a few microprocessor types.

The economic environment of the microprocessor is so significantly different from that of the traditional data processor that it is sometimes unclear whether the proven advantages of high-level languages are as profound in the newer arena. The hobbyist, for example, is typically short on the cash available to procure programming support in the form of high-level language, but is willing to spend abundant time, at no cost to himself, tediously debugging his assembly-language programs. There are significant numbers of such hobbyists who spurn the use of even an assembler.

Another argument in favor of assembly-language programming lies in its demonstrated superiority in terms of efficiency. Such efficiency is measured in terms of amount of memory required to store the program and amount of time required to execute the program. These two parameters are obviously related. Good assembly-language programmers can typically, given time, write programs which are perhaps 20% to 50% shorter than those produced by high-level languages. In those applications where memory space and/or operational speed are paramount, the expenditure of programmer effort may be worth the cost, but this is probably a rare situation for most microcomputer-based systems.

A final argument for the use of assembly language lies in the fact that it is syntactically directed toward management of the hardware elements (registers, I/O ports, stack, etc.) of the processor and, in many cases, the application sought is couched in terms of manipulation of these and associated elements. Thus, one of the traditional advantages of the high-level language, e.g., its machine-independent nature, may be disadvantageous in those cases where the hardware characterization of the machine is a natural part of the problem being solved.

In spite of these arguments for assembly language as a principal tool in microcomputer-based system design, it seems inevitable that ultimately high-level languages will dominate in this area as well as in traditional systems. The following simplified analysis demonstrates some of the factors leading to this conclusion.

A prediction of trends in any engineering area must necessarily include as its primary factor considerations of *cost-effectiveness*. In a hobbyist environment, cost-effectiveness often means minimization of personal cash outlays but relatively unlimited expenditure of personal

Software Aids

time. In a commercial engineering design environment, "people cost" is very often the item of greatest expense, and a great deal of money may be reasonably spent on design aids which make the designer's job easier and of shorter duration.

Addressing ourselves to the programming problem, we will characterize the cost of programming according to the following very simple assumption:

Each line of code in a debugged and fully documented program represents a fixed cost, *regardless of the translator level used.*

Implicit in this assumption is the fact that high-level languages (which result in fewer lines of code than assembler or machine language for a given programming task) eliminate many tedious and error-inducing tasks associated with low-level language programming. The assumption may seem oversimplistic but seems fairly well accepted among those familiar with costs of software development (see references 3 and 4).

Let us now estimate the costs of producing a digital system according to the hypothetical system characteristics of Table 4.3-1. These costs are based on the following additional assumptions:

1. Hardware cost (without memory) is $500 per unit.
2. Assembler or high-level programming costs $15 per line of source code.
3. Each instruction requires an average of two bytes of program memory.
4. Assembler language is 50% more efficient than high-level language in memory usage.
5. Memory costs 6 cents per byte.
6. Assembler or high-level language support costs $2000 for a program of this size.
7. Straight machine-language programming costs twice as much as assembler-language programming.

These assumptions lead to the following equations for per-unit production costs of N units:

HIGH–LEVEL LANGUAGE

$$C_{SH} = \$500 + 3000 \times 0.06 + \frac{250 \times 15 + 2000}{N}$$

$$= \$680 + \frac{5750}{N} \text{ dollars per unit} \qquad 4.3.2.1$$

TABLE 4.3-1 Programming Example Cost Assumptions

Number of Units	N
Cost per line of code	
Assembler Language	$ 15
High-level Language	15
Machine Language	30
Number of Lines of Code	
Assembly Language	1000
High-level Language	250
Machine Language	1000
Number of bytes per assembler instruction	2
Memory cost	$0.06 per byte
Assembler-compiler access cost	$2000
Hardware cost (without memory)	$ 500

ASSEMBLY LANGUAGE

$$C_{SA} = 500 + 2000 \times 0.06 + \frac{1000 \times 15 + 2000}{N}$$

$$= 620 + \frac{17{,}000}{N} \text{ dollars per unit} \qquad 4.3.2.2$$

MACHINE LANGUAGE

$$C_{SM} = 500 + 2000 \times 0.06 + \frac{1000 \times 30}{N}$$

$$= 620 + \frac{30{,}000}{N} \text{ dollars per unit} \qquad 4.3.2.3$$

Figure 4.3-1 is a plot of these three equations 4.3.2.1, 2, and 3 for various N. Among the conclusions one may draw from this diagram are the following:

1. There is no economic justification at any level of production for machine-language programming.

2. At very high production levels, where incremental memory cost is dominant, assembler language may be economically justified due to its efficiency.

Software Aids

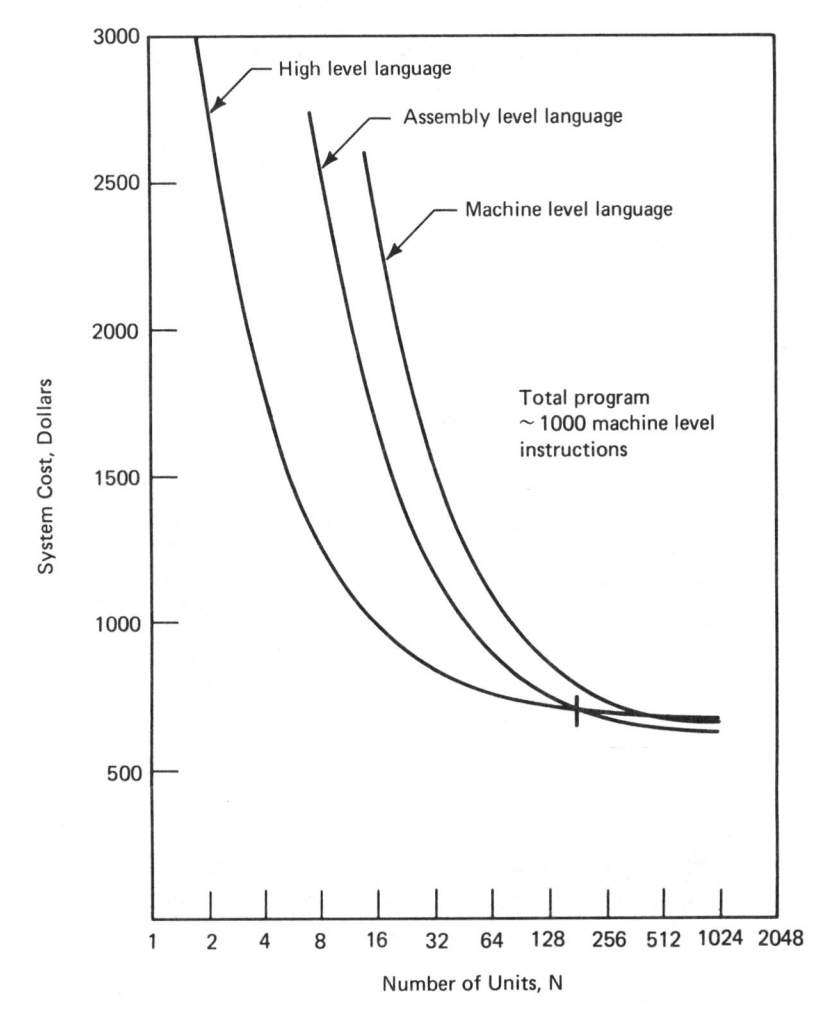

Figure 4.3-1 Digital system cost as a function of production volume for medium-sized program

3. At low or moderate levels of production (up to 200 or so units in our example) high-level language programming is the cost-effective choice.

These conclusions are, of course, a direct result of the assumptions made. To consider a different situation, assume a significantly less complex programming problem requiring only 40 assembly language statements. If we develop the same cost figures as before, we find:

$$C_{SH} = 500 + 120 \times 0.06 + \frac{10 \times 15 + 2000}{N}$$

$$= 507 + \frac{2150}{N} \text{ dollars per unit} \qquad 4.3.2.4$$

$$C_{SA} = 500 + 80 \times 0.06 + \frac{40 \times 15 + 2000}{N}$$

$$= 505 + \frac{2600}{N} \text{ dollars per unit} \qquad 4.3.2.5$$

$$C_{SM} = 500 + 80 \times 0.06 + \frac{40 \times 30}{N}$$

$$= 505 + \frac{1200}{N} \text{ dollars per unit} \qquad 4.3.2.6$$

These equations are reflected in the curves of Figure 4.3-2. Note that in this case machine language is always the most economic approach, principally due to the assumed $2000 software support cost. Note also, however, that programming costs are quite significant in any case. If ten units are produced, for example, programming cost is $120 per unit.

As a final comment, the cost assumptions on which this analysis is based are simply rough estimates which reflect contemporary conditions. In particular cases other assumptions may be appropriate; however, the general analytical approach should be valid for purposes of rough cost estimation.

4.3.3 Assembly-Language Programming

In earlier chapters of this book we have seen many examples of machine language coding of simple programs. We have also found it convenient to use symbolic notation to refer to operation codes, addresses, and operands. An *assembler* is a program which takes as its *source* a program written in such symbolic language and which produces as *object* a machine-language program capable of execution by the *target computer*. An assembler differs from higher-level translator programs in that each assembly-language instruction is converted to a corresponding machine-language instruction (with a few exceptions, as we shall see). An assembler thus may take an instruction of the form:

Software Aids

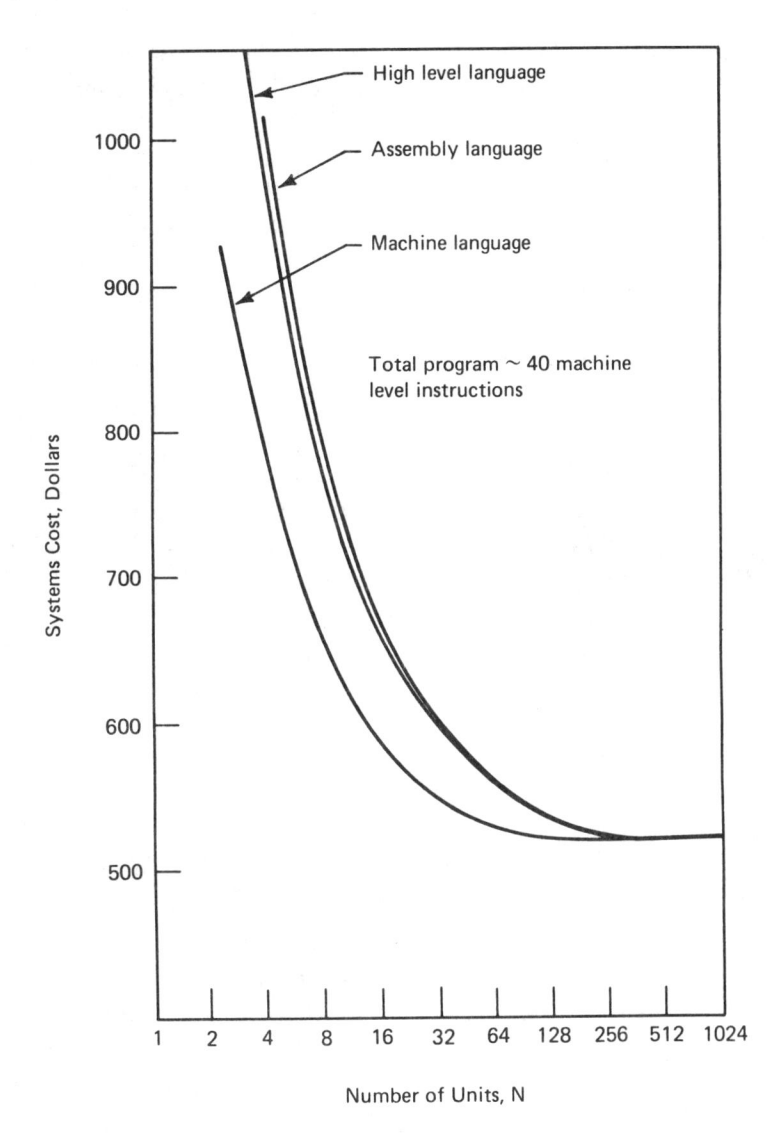

Figure 4.3-2 Digital system cost as a function of production volume for small program

```
LDA   SAD
```

and convert it to a machine language instruction:

```
AD 40 17   (hex)
```

To gain insight into assembler operation, we will create an example program written in assembly language developed for the 6502 microprocessor (see reference 5).

4.3.3.1 Example Problem. Consider two 6-digit decimal numbers stored in memory as contiguous strings of 3 bytes each. Number 1 is stored at locations 0020, 0021, and 0022, while Number 2 is stored at locations 0030, 0031, and 0032. In each case the order is low-to-high digit position. We wish to write a program which will form the decimal sum of these two numbers, placing the result in locations 0040, 0041, and 0043 (if necessary). After the program is executed we wish to return to the KIM monitor via a jump back to the START routine which is a section of that monitor.

We will begin this problem by writing a symbolic program which reflects the algorithmic logic we wish to employ. Thus,

LABEL	OP CODE	ADDRESS	COMMENTS
	LDX	#ZERO	Initialize X and carry
	CLC		
BEGIN	LDA	NUM 1, X	Load 1st digit pair into A
	ADC	NUM 2, X	Add 2nd digit pair
	STA	RESULT, X	Store result digit pair
	INX		Increment X register
	CPX	#N−1	Test for completion
	BNE	BEGIN	Loop back if not done
	BCC	MONITOR	
	INC	RESULT, X	Add 1 to 5th digit if carry
MONITOR	JUMP	START	Jump back to monitor

Notice that this program is almost purely symbolic in that it does not refer to any absolute addresses nor any absolute operand values. Even the number of digits in the two numbers is symbolically referenced as N.

If we submitted this example program to an assembler, we would receive various error messages telling us of certain improprieties and omissions in its construction. Among the various pieces of information which are missing are the following:

1. Locations in memory where the program is to be loaded.
2. Locations in memory where data is to be loaded and held as it is developed by the program.
3. Values for N, the size of NUM 1 and NUM 2.
4. Actual value for START, the monitor entry address.
5. Value for ZERO.

Software Aids

Before trying to take care of these missing items, let us visualize the operation of the assembler program. The source program will be scanned several times. During *PASS 1*, it will scan our program and build a *symbol table* which establishes values for all symbolic names in the program. Then a second pass, *PASS 2*, will be performed. During this scan, as symbolic names or op codes are encountered, the *symbol table* formed during PASS 1 and the *op code table* which is part of the assembler are referenced, and actual values are substituted for the symbolic names in the original program.

To inform the assembler of the desired locations in memory where the program is to be stored, the assembly language includes an *origin directive* which allows the programmer to specify the value of the assembler's location counter. In 6502 language, such a statement could be written

$$* = \$0200$$

This directs the assembler to assemble its next byte of code at the specified location (200 hex, in this case) and to continue the assembly in sequential order from that point until otherwise directed by another origin directive.

To reserve space in memory for data storage or other purposes, the origin statement can be used in a slightly different way. For example:

$$* = * + 6$$

tells the assembler to move its location counter 6 bytes ahead, leaving a 6-byte space for the programmer's use. If the programmer attaches a *label* to such a statement, e.g.,

$$\text{LIST} \quad * = * + 6$$

he may refer symbolically to items in this space as LIST + 1, LIST + 5, etc.

Items 1 and 2 on our list of missing information can now be handled by origin directives. Items 3, 4, and 5 can be handled by means of *equate* directives, written as follows:

$$\text{VAR} = 0065$$

Such a statement simply tells the assembler to create an entry in its symbol table for symbol VAR, giving it a value 65 (decimal, in this case). In our example program, we wish to give values to the names ZERO, N, and START via use of equate directives.

Let's now rewrite our example program using these assembler directives to provide the missing information. Figure 4.3.3-1 shows such

```
                * = $ØØ2Ø
NUM1            * = *+3
                * = $ØØ3Ø
NUM2            * = *+3
                * = $ØØ4Ø
RESULT          * = *+4
                * = $Ø2ØØ          SET PROGRAM LOAD ADDRESS
                N = 3              EQUATES
                ZERO = Ø
                START = $1C4F
BEGIN           LDX #ZERO          INITIALIZE X REGISTER AND CARRY FLAG
                CLC
LOOP            LDA NUM1,X         LOAD FIRST DIGIT PAIR
                ADC NUM2,X         ADD SECOND DIGIT PAIR
                STA RESULT,X       STORE RESULT DIGIT PAIR
                INX                INCREMENT X REGISTER
                CPX #N-1           TEST FOR COMPLETION
                BNE LOOP           LOOP BACK IF NOT DONE
                BCC MONIT          EXIT TO MONITOR
                INC RESULT,X       ADD 1 TO 5TH DIGIT, IF CARRY
MONIT           JMP START          JUMP BACK TO MONITOR
                .END
```

Figure 4.3.3-1 Example program - 6502 assembly language

a program. In addition to the origin and equate directives it includes an .END directive, which is provided so the assember can detect the end of the program.

We have stated that the primary function of an assembler is to convert a symbolic program to a machine-language program. The assembler may also produce a *listing file* or simply a *listing* which provides a record of the original symbolic program, the language program produced during assembly, and the symbol table produced by the assembly process. Most assemblers also generate error messages which inform the programmer of logical or syntactic errors in his program. Some assemblers produce a cross-reference listing which gives a record of the number of occurrences of each symbol in the program.

The *assembly listing* of Figure. 4.3.3-2 was produced by a cross-assembler called MINMIC running on a PDP/11-34 minicomputer. Note that each line of original symbolic code has a corresponding line of machine code produced by the assembler. Those lines containing assembler directives, of course, produce no object code. The symbol table is also part of the listing. A careful examination of this table will confirm that the origin statements in the original program have produced the correct machine code values. Symbols such as MONIT are assigned appropriate values (0212 hex, in this case) even though no

Software Aids

```
0001   0000                   NUM1      * = $0020
0002   0020                             * = *+3
0003   0023                   NUM2      * = $0030
0004   0030                             * = *+3
0005   0033                   RESULT    * = $0040
0006   0040                             * = *+4
0007   0044                             * = $0200     SET PROGRAM LOAD ADDRESS
0008   0200                             N = 3         EQUATES
0009   0200                             ZERO = 0
0010   0200                             START = $1C4F
0011   0200   A2 00           BEGIN     LDX #ZERO     INITIALIZE X REGISTER
                                                      AND CARRY FLAG
0012   0202   18                        CLC
0013   0203   B5 20           LOOP      LDA NUM1,X    LOAD FIRST DIGIT PAIR
0014   0205   75 30                     ADC NUM2,X    ADD SECOND DIGIT PAIR
0015   0207   95 40                     STA RESULT,X  STORE RESULT DIGIT PAIR
0016   0209   E8                        INX           INCREMENT X REGISTER
0017   020A   E0 02                     CPX #N-1      TEST FOR COMPLETION
0018   020C   D0 F5                     BNE LOOP      LOOP BACK IF NOT DONE
0019   020E   90 02                     BCC MONIT     EXIT TO MONITOR
0020   0210   F6 40                     INC RESULT,X  ADD 1 TO 5TH DIGIT,
                                                      IF CARRY
0021   0212   4C 4F 1C        MONIT     JMP START     JUMP BACK TO MONITOR
0022   0215

ERRORS = 0000

SYMBOL TABLE

BEGIN    0200      LOOP    0203      MONIT   0212      N       0003
NUM1     0020      NUM2    0030      RESULT  0040      START   1C4F
ZERO     0000
END OF ASSEMBLY
```

Figure 4.3.3-2 Assembler listing for example program

equate directives are involved. Equates are only necessary when external references, or symbolic names not defined by the program itself, are present in the program.

Another important feature of assembly-language programming is illustrated in Figure 4.3.3-2, i.e., the use of *comments* to describe the operation of the program. The assembler illustrated permits comments to be written to the right of instructions, as shown, or anyplace on a line if preceded by a semicolon. Liberal use of such comments is strongly recommended as good programming practice.

4.3.3.2 Other Assembler Directives.

In addition to the origin directive, the equates, and the .END directive, the 6502 assembler has several other directives, including .BYTE, .WORD, and .OPT.

.BYTE Directive: This directive is used to reserve one byte of memory (like * = *+1) and load it with specified data (unlike * = * + 1). Multiple values may be specified, in which case consecutive locations are reserved and loaded. Examples are:

```
HERE    .BYTE 2
THERE   .BYTE 1, 2, 3, 4
ASCII   .BYTE 'MESSAGE'
```

In case 1, a memory location symbolically named HERE is loaded with value 2. The value of HERE is the address specified by the assembler location counter when the .BYTE directive was encountered by the assembler.

In case 2, 4 bytes are reserved and given values 1, 2, 3, and 4 by the assembler. They may be symbolically referenced as THERE, THERE + 1, THERE + 2, and THERE + 3.

In case 3, 7 bytes are reserved and assigned values equal to the ASCII codes for the symbols M, E, S, S, A, G, E.

Figure 4.3.3.2-1 shows the effect of the three BYTE directives shown.

.WORD Directive: This directive is much like .BYTE except that *two* bytes of data are established per entry. Thus, the directive

```
HERE  .WORD 2
```

creates two bytes of address with value 0002 (stored in memory as 0200). The directive

```
WHERE  .WORD HERE, THERE
```

Software Aids

Case 1

HERE .BYTE 2

MEMORY: 02 — HERE (Address)

Case 2

THERE .BYTE 1, 2, 3, 4

04
03
02
01 — THERE (Address)

Case 3

ASCII .BYTE "MESSAGE"

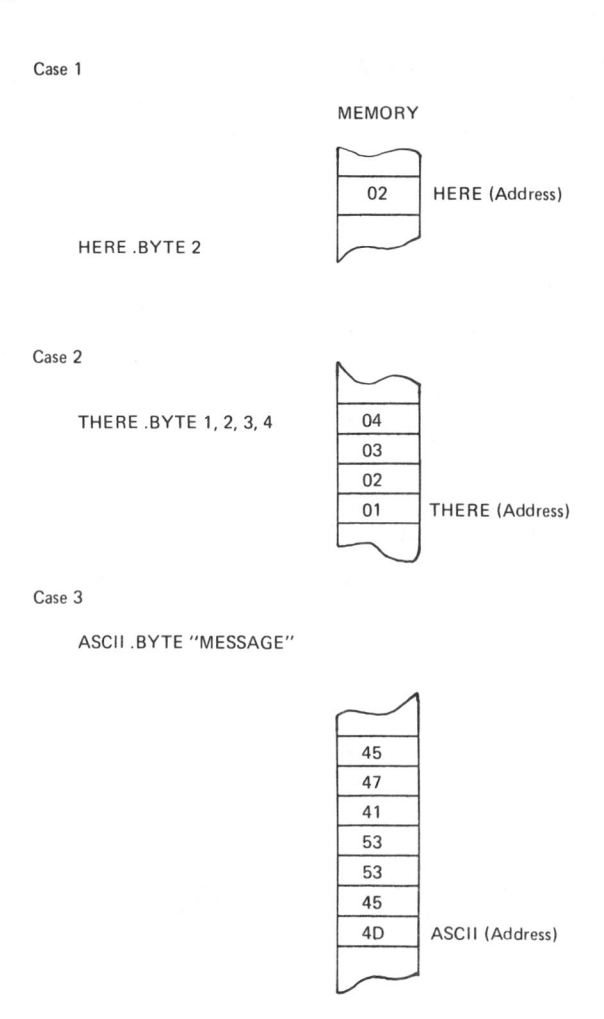

45
47
41
53
53
45
4D — ASCII (Address)

Figure 4.3.3.2-1 Effect of .BYTE directives on memory allocation

stores the two 16-bit values of HERE and THERE at successive locations starting at location WHERE. Since the 6502 fetches addresses from memory in low byte-high byte order, the .WORD directive generates values in this order, i.e.:

THERE .WORD $FF03

would store values 03, FF in ascending order.

.DBYTE Directive: The *double byte* directive, DBYTE is exactly like .WORD except that no high byte-low byte reversal occurs.

.OPT Directive: The *option directive* .OPT allows the programmer to control generation of output fields, listing, and expansion of ASCII strings in .BYTE directives. The options are:

.OPT ERRORS, LIST, SYMBOLS, GENERATE, TAB

.OPT NOERRORS, NOLIST, NOSYMBOLS, NOGENERATE, NOTAB.

Default options are SYM, LIST, ERR, TAB, GENERATE:

1. SYM — print symbol table.
2. ERR — print only errors in assembly listing (when errors corrected, use NOERR to generate full listing).
3. LIST — generate list file.
4. GENERATE — print all ASCII character codes in BYTE directives. (If long text messages are part of program, NOGEN will suppress long listings.)
5. TAB — automatically spaces labels, op codes, and comments. Saves memory space for listing file storage, but may spread listing out too much for CRT display, etc.

4.3.3.3 Representation of Alphanumeric Values. The 6502 assembler, like most assemblers, allows the use of a variety of alphanumeric symbols, and potential ambiguities must be avoided, particularly when various number bases are permitted. This particular assembler has adopted the following alphanumeric symbols:

Decimal Numbers are written with no prefix of any kind, i.e., 100 means 100 (decimal).

Octal Numbers are written with prefix @, i.e., @100 means 64 (decimal).

Hexadecimal Numbers are written with prefix $, i.e., $100 means 256 (decimal).

Binary Numbers are written with prefix %, i.e., %100 means 4 (decimal).

ASCII Characters are enclosed by single quotes, i.e.,
 'A' means 41 hex,
 'APPLE' represents the hex string 41, 50, 50, 4C, 45,
 '12' represents the hex string 31, 32.

4.3.3.4 Addressing Modes. The 6502 has, as we have seen, a variety of addressing modes. The mode of a particular instruction is often

Software Aids

implied by the instruction itself (all branches are relative mode, for example) but in many cases some symbolism is needed to specify address mode; 6502 conventions are as follows:

Immediate mode is indicated by # preceding the operand, e.g.,

LDA # 22

specifies a load accumulator with immediate operand 22 (decimal) or 16 (hex). Thus the assembler would produce an instruction A9 16 if this symbolic instruction were encountered.

Indexed mode is indicated by a comma following the operand address, followed by an X or Y to indicate which index register is involved. Thus,

LDA HERE, X

indicates that the operand to be loaded into A is to be found at address HERE (whose value the assembler gets from the symbol table) added to the contents of X. If HERE had value 1CFF (hex), the instruction would be assembled as

BD FF 1C

If HERE had value 0066 (hex), a ZERO page address, the instruction would be assembled as

B5 66

Indirect mode is indicated by parentheses surrounding the operand address, e.g.,

JMP (JAD)

indicates that the first byte of the jump address is to be found at address JAD (and the second byte at address JAD + 1).

Indexed Indirect and Indirect Indexed modes are, of course, represented by combinations of the above symbolism. Thus:

LDA (HERE), X is indirect indexed;

while

LDA(HERE,X) is indexed indirect.

Absolute mode is simply indicated by the absence of any symbolism other than that of the address itself, i.e.,

LDA NAME

indicates that A is to be loaded with the *contents* of address NAME. Once again, if NAME is an address in page ZERO, the assembler will produce a ZERO page op code and only one byte of address. For example,

        LDA NAME   AD FF02 if NAME = 02FF;

and

        LDA NAME   A5 FF if NAME = 00FF.

In some assemblers, absolute addressing is referred to as *direct* addressing.

4.3.3.5 Expressions. Most assemblers, including the 6502 assembler, permit the use of algebraic *expressions* to represent addresses. For example, an instruction of the form

        LDA TABLE + 3

will be assembled with an address value found by adding to the value of the variable name TABLE the constant 3. If TABLE has value 1000, for example, the above instruction would be assembled as

        AD 03 10

In 6502 assembly language, expressions can use the operators +, −, *, and / (add, subtract, multiply, and divide). Some assemblers (the Intel 8080 assembler, for example) permit a variety of nonarithmetic operators (shift, logical, compare, etc.) to be used in expressions. In all cases expressions are evaluated at assembly time and should not be confused with operations performed at program execution time.

4.3.3.6 Other Assemblers. The architecture of the various microprocessors is reflected in the assemblers which support them. Such factors as differing instruction sets, register complements, interrupt structures, and input-output philosophies require differing assembler style. It is somewhat unfortunate, however, that even though the basic function of assembler directives is common to nearly all systems one can think of, the various manufacturers have developed differing nomenclature and syntax which require familiarization by the programmer who must switch around among various systems.

    Table 4.3.3.6-1 is an abbreviated listing of assembler directives for 6502, 8080, and 6800 assemblers available from MOS Technology, Intel, and Motorola, respectively. The functions provided for the 8080 and the 6800 are essentially the same as those previously discussed for the 6502. (See references 6 and 7.)

    Figure 4.3.3.6-1 is a listing of a portion of an 8080 program which illustrates the use of some of the directives of Table 4.3.3.6-1. A careful

TABLE 4.3.3.6-1 Some Assembler Directives Used in 6502, 8080, and 6800 Assembly Language

FUNCTION	SYMBOLISM		
	6502	8080	6800
ORIGIN STATEMENT			
Set location counter to specified value	* = (value or expression)	ORG (value or expression)	ORG (value or expression)
EQUATE STATEMENT			
Creates symbol table entry (SET directive allows reestablishment of symbol value in different parts of program)	(symbol) = (value or expression)	(symbol) EQU (value or expression) (symbol) SET (value or expression)	(symbol) EQU (value or expression)
DATA DEFINITION			
Generate string of 8-bit values stored sequentially at current location counter. Label is optional.	.BYTE (string of values)	DB (string of values)	FCB (string of values)
Generate 16-bit data values (like above) stored in least-to-most significant order. Label optional.	.WORD (string of values)	DW (string of values)	
Generate 16-bit data values (like above) stored in most-to-least significant order. Label optional.	.DBYTE (string of values)		FDB (string of values)
RESERVE MEMORY SPACE			
Augments location counter by specified value. Label optional.	* = * + (value or expression)	DS (value or expression)	RMB (value or expression)
TERMINATE PROGRAM			
Designate end of program to be assembled.	.END	END	END

(symbol) means any symbolic name satisfying the constraints of the assembler.
(value or expression) means any 8-bit value or expression which evaluates to an 8-bit value.

examination of this program will disclose the effect of the DB, DS, DW, ORG, and EQU directives. Also, notice the use of expressions in lines 15-18. Another point worth noticing is the use of labels on some of the directives to permit symbolic reference to the constants and storage locations created by the directives.

4.3.3.7 Listing Controls. Since the program listing produced by the assembler is of such great importance to the programmer in understanding, recalling, and documenting his program, it is common for a number of special features to be included in the assembler to allow control of the listing. Section 4.3.2.2 describes the .OPT or *option directive*

```
ASM80 :F1:SMAY.ASM PRINT(:LP:) NOOBJECT XREF SYMBOLS TITLE('EXPRESSIONS ALLOWABLE IN 8080 SOURCE TEXT'
ISIS-II 8080/8085 MACRO ASSEMBLER, V2.0          MODULE      PAGE    1
EXPRESSIONS ALLOWABLE IN 8080 SOURCE TEXT

LOC      OBJ        SEQ     SOURCE STATEMENT

3C00                 1
                     2              ORG     3C00H
                     3
3C00                 4      DATA1:  DS      40          ; RESERVE 40 BYTES FOR DATA AREA 1
3C28                 5      DATA2:  DS      20          ; RESERVE 20 BYTES FOR DATA AREA 2
3C3C    004C         6      ADDR:   DW      4C00H
3C3E    204C         7      SUBR:   DW      4C20H
3C40                 8      STK:    DS      40          ; STACK BEGINNING
3C68                 9      STKEND  EQU     $           ; STACK END
000D                10      CR      EQU     0DH         ; CARRIAGE RETURN
000A                11      LF      EQU     0AH         ; LINE FEED
3C68                12      MSG1:   DB      CR,LF,'ENTER TODAYS DATE  -'
3C69    0D
3C6A    454E5445
3C6E    5220544F
3C72    44415953
3C76    20444154
3C7A    4520D20
0016                13      LMSG1   EQU     $-MSG1 ; LENGTH OF MSG1
                    14      ;
3C7E    3E01        15              MVI     A,(11 MOD 2)
3C80    06FF        16              MVI     B,NOT (10-5*2)
3C82    0EAA        17              MVI     C,(10101010B OR 10100000B)
3C84    1632        18              MVI     D,(36 + 40H)/2
                    19      ;
                    20      ;
                    21      ;
                    22              END
```

Figure 4.3.3.6-1 Example listing - 8080 assembly language

```
PUBLIC SYMBOLS

EXTERNAL SYMBOLS

USER SYMBOLS
ADDR  A 3C3C   CR      A 000D   DATA1  A 3C00   DATA2  A 3C28   LF   A 000A   LMSG1  A 0016
STK   A 3C40   STKEND  A 3C68   SUBR   A 3C3E

ASSEMBLY COMPLETE, NO ERRORS


ISIS-II ASSEMBLER SYMBOL CROSS REFERENCE, V2.0

ADDR     6#
CR      10#      12
DATA1    4#
DATA2    5#
LF      11#      12
LMSG1   13#
MSG1    12#      13
STK      8#
STKEND   9#
SUBR     7#

CROSS REFERENCE COMPLETE
```

Figure 4.3.3.6-1 Continued

provided by the 6502 assembler to permit the programmer to choose among various listing options. Other versions of the 6502 assembler give the programmer his choice of the following listing options:

1. XREF (or NOXREF) controls whether a full cross-reference listing will be produced. A cross-reference listing shows every symbol used in the program and tabulates every usage (by line number) of the symbol in the program.
2. ERRORS (or NOERRORS) controls the creation of a separate error file. During early stages of programming, it is often convenient to list only errors. The creation of a full listing is postponed until errors are eliminated.
3. LIST (or NOLIST) controls generation of full listing, including symbol table. If only errors are to be listed, as described in (2) above, the directive would be

.OPT ERRORS, NOLIST

4. COUNT (or NOCOUNT) generates a count of the number of times an instruction is used in a program.
5. GENERATE (or NOGENERATE) is used to control listing of ASCII strings in the .BYTE directive. If long alphanumeric ASCII messages are part of the program data, this option can eliminate the waste associated with printing many lines of machine code in the listing.

Intel has taken a slightly different approach in their provision for listing control. Rather than providing a set of directives for this purpose, they provide controls which may be specified when the assembler is invoked (rather than when the assembly-language program is written). Among the extensive controls provided are the following:

1. OBJECT (or NOOBJECT) − controls generation of machine-language object file.
2. DEBUG (or NODEBUG) − includes symbol table with object file for convenient use with in-current emulator (see Section 4.8).
3. PRINT (or NOPRINT) − controls assembly listing (like NOLIST in 6502 assembler).
4. SYMBOLS (or NOSYMBOLS) − controls symbol table creation in listing.
5. XREF (or NOXREF) − controls generation of cross-listing file (like 6502).
6. PAGELENGTH (n) − allows control of page length for adaptation to printer.

Software Aids 203

7. PAGEWIDTH (n) — allows control of page width for adaptation to printer.
8. PAGING (or NOPAGING) — allows program listing to be divided into pages.
9. LIST (or NOLIST) — allows printing of errors only (via NOLIST option) like ERRORS option of 6502 assembler.
10. GEN (or NOGEN) — controls suppression of macro source text. (See Section 4.3.3.8.)
11. TITLE ('String') — allows specification of 64-character program title to be printed on each page.

If an 8080 programmer desires to provide listing controls in his source program, like the directives available to the 6502 programmer, he can include a command

$$\text{\$ control list}$$

in his program. The string of options following the dollar sign will then be applied to his listing. For example, if you have a title you wish to write in your program and have restated at the beginning of each page of the program listing, you may write in your program the statement

$$\text{\$ TITLE ('THIS IS MY PROGRAM TITLE')}$$

and achieve the desired result.

4.3.3.8 Macros. *Macro* capability is provided by Intel and Motorola assemblers, among others. The concept of a macro arises from the desire to call upon a given program segment multiple times within a program, or even perhaps within some number of different programs. A *macro call* is a request that a copy of an assembly-language program (which is the macro) be inserted into the body of the calling program, there to be assembled along with the rest of the program. This concept shares with the *subroutine call* the obvious advantage of multiple use of a separately-defined routine, but it is important to note the important differences between the two types of calls. Subroutine calls occur during program execution, and transfer control from the calling program to the subroutine. Macro calls occur during the assembly operation and, once assembly is complete, the machine-language object program is essentially that produced if you simply copy the macro's assembly language statements every time a macro call is made. Thus many copies of a macro expansion may be present in a program, while only one copy of a subroutine will be used even though many calls may be made to it.

An important facet of usage of macro capability lies in the convenience of establishment of *macro libraries* to which a programmer or group of programmers may refer in generating user programs. Such a library can provide a source of well-documented and debugged routines which can form the foundation for very efficient programming. Management of such a library can be accomplished if the software development system provides appropriate file-handling mechanisms.

The Intel MDS-800 development system assembler provides a sophisticated macro capability and macro library management features. Interested readers should consult references 7 and 8. As one would expect, a number of assembler directives and controls are provided to permit convenient management of macro capability.

4.3.3.9 Program Relocatability and Linkage. The concept of modular design has great virtue for programs as well as for hardware systems. If one segments his programming problem with the intent to adopt this concept, however, he must accept potential inconveniences, among which are the following:

1. Any given program module should be debugged prior to any attempt to integrate it into the total design. If this debugging is performed by running it on a host machine such as a standalone development system, the memory space allocations of this system may conflict with those of the system under design (see Section 4.7).
2. Early in the design phase, the programmer, in developing a given module, must assume certain characteristics such as starting locations for as-yet undesigned modules. If his estimates are not well-founded, he may find himself in an iterative design situation.
3. Since each program module will contain its own set of symbols, and since it is likely that intermodule references will be common, the problem of symbol/name management may be significant.
4. If memory-space gaps between program modules are to be avoided, it is likely that a final reassembly will be necessary to "pack" the modules together. Such gaps may exist not only between segments of code but also between structures containing both fixed and variable data, such as tables and input/output buffers.

For these and other reasons, an assembler that produces "relocatable" code is a very desirable tool. Such code, once assembled, is capable of being placed anywhere in memory space with a simple

Software Aids

"locate" operation. Furthermore, if the assembler also has *linking* capability (typically the case), a collection of program modules can be linked and then located, resulting in efficient and flexible program handling.

An excellent example of an assembler that provides the type of capability described here is the Intel 8080/8085 assembler provided with the MDS-800 microcomputer development system as part of its ISIS-II operating system.

Among the features of this assembler are the following:

1. The programmer can separately place program elements corresponding to object code, data (both variable and fixed), and stack by use of *three* separate assembler location counters. When several modules are combined (using the LINK operation). these three types of program elements can be separately managed.
2. A LINK program permits convenient combining of program modules into a composite relocatable module.
3. A LOCATE program converts a relocatable program to one absolutely located in memory in areas specified by the programmer.
4. Extensive library-management features permit the programmer to build library files from which he can selectively select program modules ultimately to be combined (via LINK) and converted (via LOCATE) to an absolute user program.
5. Overall management of symbol names to permit external references from any module to a list of "public" names and designation of names within a module to be placed on such a list. Note that this permits convenient use of common names (like START, LOOP, etc.) within many modules without causing so-called "scope" problems due to multiple definition of names.

Tools such as the ISIS-II assembler are very powerful aids to modular programming at the assembler level. Those interested in details of relocation and linkage in ISIS-II should consult references 8 and 9.

4.3.4 Examples of High-Level Microcomputer Languages

The present state of high-level language development is extremely dynamic. The advantages of high-level languages (see Section 4.3.2) are persuasively stated, but the extremely rapid pace of hardware development has seemingly prevented development of high-level language support from "catching up," at least for the great number of systems.

Leach (reference 10) gives an excellent discussion of the principles of high-level language design for microprocessors in which he discusses four such languages (PL/M, PLuS, MPL, and SYCLOPS). In this paper he cautions against adoption of standards in this area until the rapid pace of innovation in both CPU architecture and in system applications has stabilized to some extent.

In this section we will be content to show two example languages applied to a simple programming problem. The uninitiated reader will find it necessary to infer certain language properties by reading the programs, but in a sense, this is a fairly valid test of a language. If syntax and construction follow natural language rules with which we are familiar, the language has met one of its more important goals.

4.3.4.1 Example Problem.* The program to be designed is to be entered when a variable called OK (or OK TO RUN) becomes true. Upon initiation, the program is to do the following:

1. Read ASCII characters from a console port (Address ODC hex), storing the characters in a memory buffer established by the program. This process is to continue until either (a) more than 20 characters have been read, or (b) a carriage return is received.
2. If the string to be read is greater than 20 characters in length, an error message "INPUT STRING IS TOO LONG" is to be generated and the program reinitiated.
3. If a carriage return is received before the 20 character limit is reached, the received string is to be "echoed" back to the console, after which the program is reinitiated.
4. An exit from the program is to occur if the first character received is a carriage return.

Figure 4.3.4-1 is a flow chart representing an algorithm for the desired program.

4.3.4.2 PL/M-80 Solution. Figure 4.3.4-2 is a listing of a PL/M-80 program of solution for the example program. This particular listing was produced by the ISIS-II PL/M-80 Compiler provided by Intel as a resident resource on their MDS-800 system.

No detailed description of all facets of this PL/M-80 example will be given, but the reader should identify and note at least the following elements:

---

*The example problem and accompanying programming solutions were provided by James A. Davis of the Iowa State University Computation Center.

Software Aids

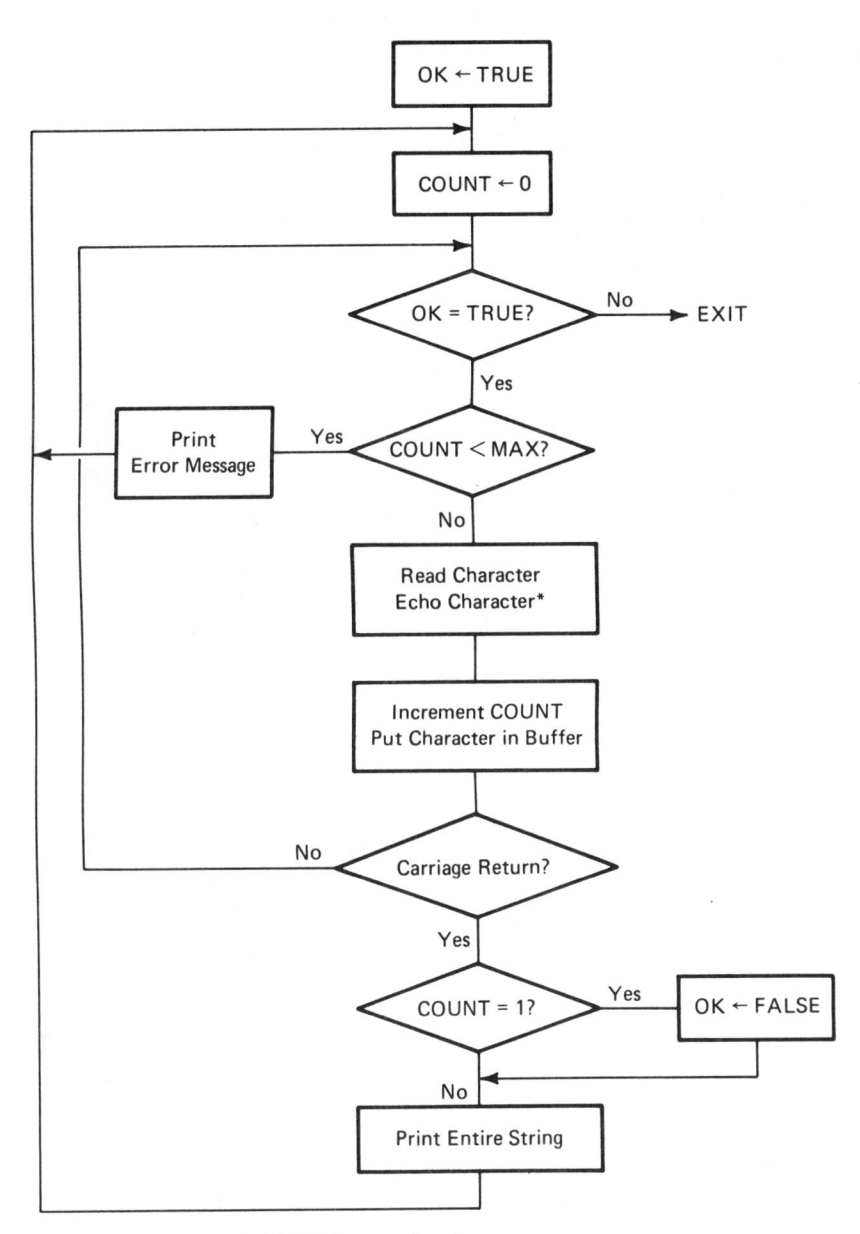

*This step is included in PASCAL example only.

Figure 4.3.4-1 Flow chart for example problem

1. Declaration of variables and constants.
2. Declaration of procedures (READ, WRITE, and WRITE STRING).
3. The program itself. PL/M is a block-structured language, and the block level of each line is denoted both by line indentation and by a numeric designation in the second column from the left.
4. A listing showing the compiler output, in both assembly language and machine language. Each line of the high-level program is shown along with the code it produces.
5. A symbol table. This may be provided to ICE-80 (see Section 4.8) to allow program debugging with symbolic references. Consult references 11 and 12 for detailed information on PL/M.

```
ISIS-II PL/M-80 V3.0 COMPILATION OF MODULE EXAMPLE
OBJECT MODULE PLACED IN :F1:SMAY.OBJ
COMPILER INVOKED BY:   PLM80 :F1:SMAY.PLM PRINT(:LP:) DATE(1-30-78) TITLE('PL/M EXAMPLE PROGRAM')

  1            EXAMPLE: DO;
  2    1          DECLARE
                      CONSOLE$DATA$PORT      LITERALLY '0DCH',
                      CONSOLE$STATUS$PORT    LITERALLY '0DDH',
                      CR                     LITERALLY '0DH',
                      LF                     LITERALLY '0AH',
                      TRUE                   LITERALLY '0FFH',
                      FALSE                  LITERALLY '00H',
                      BUFFER(20)             BYTE,
                      CHAR$COUNT             BYTE,
                      CHAR                   BYTE,
                      OK$TO$RUN              BYTE;
  3    1          READ:
                     PROCEDURE BYTE;
  4    2             DO WHILE ( (INPUT(CONSOLE$STATUS$PORT) AND 2) = 0 ); END;
  6    2             RETURN( INPUT(CONSOLE$DATA$PORT) AND 7FH);
  7    2          END READ;
  8    1          WRITE:
                     PROCEDURE(CHAR);
  9    2             DECLARE CHAR BYTE;
 10    2             DO WHILE( (INPUT(CONSOLE$STATUS$PORT) AND 1) = 0 ); END;
 12    2             OUTPUT(CONSOLE$DATA$PORT) = CHAR;
 13    2          END WRITE;
 14    1          WRITE$STRING:
                     PROCEDURE(STRING$ADDRESS,STRING$SIZE);
 15    2             DECLARE STRING$ADDRESS  ADDRESS,
                             STRING$SIZE     BYTE,
                             (COUNT,I)       BYTE,
                             (STRING BASED  STRING$ADDRESS) (1) BYTE;
 16    2             DO I = 0 TO STRING$SIZE;
 17    3                CALL WRITE(STRING(I));
 18    3             END;
 19    2          END WRITE$STRING;
 20    1          OK$TO$RUN = TRUE;
 21    1          DO WHILE OK$TO$RUN=TRUE;
 22    2             CHAR$COUNT = 0;
 23    2             DO WHILE ((CHAR$COUNT <= LENGTH(BUFFER)) AND (OK$TO$RUN=TRUE));
 24    3                CHAR = READ;
 25    3                BUFFER(CHAR$COUNT) = CHAR;
 26    3                CHAR$COUNT = CHAR$COUNT + 1;
 27    3                IF CHAR = CR
                           THEN DO;
 29    4                      IF CHAR$COUNT=1 THEN OK$TO$RUN = FALSE;
 31    4                      CALL WRITE$STRING(.BUFFER,CHAR$COUNT);
 32    4                      CALL WRITE$STRING(.(CR,LF),2);
 33    4                      CHAR$COUNT = 0;
 34    4                   END;
 35    3             END;
 36    2             IF  OF$TO$RUN THEN CALL WRITE$STRING(.(CR,LF,'INPUT STRING IS TOO LONG',CR,LF),30);
 38    2          END;
 39    1          HALT;
 40    1       END EXAMPLE;
MODULE INFORMATION

        CODE AREA SIZE       = 00FCH     252D
        VARIABLE AREA SIZE   = 001DH      29D
```

Software Aids

```
        MAXIMUM STACK SIZE = ØØØ4H      4D
        71 LINES READ
        Ø PROGRAM ERROR(S)

END OF PL/M-8Ø COMPILATION


ISIS-II PL/M-8Ø V3.Ø COMPILATION OF MODULE EXAMPLE
OBJECT MODULE PLACED IN :F1:SMAY.OBJ
COMPILER INVOKED BY PLM8Ø :F1:SMAY.PLM PRINT(:LP:) CODE SYMBOLS DATE(1-3Ø-78)

1              EXAMPLE: DO;
2     1          DECLARE
                   CONSOLE$DATA$PORT      LITERALLY 'ØDCH',
                   CONSOLE$STATUS$PORT    LITERALLY 'ØDDH',
                   CR                     LITERALLY 'ØDH',
                   LF                     LITERALLY 'ØAH',
                   TRUE                   LITERALLY 'ØFFH',
                   FALSE                  LITERALLY 'ØØH',
                   BUFFER(2Ø)             BYTE,
                   CHAR$COUNT             BYTE,
                   CHAR                   BYTE,
                   OK$TO$RUN              BYTE;
3     1          READ:
                                                    ; STATEMENT # 3
                       ; PROC  READ
                 PROCEDURE BYTE;
4     2            DO WHILE ( (INPUT(CONSOLE$STATUS$PORT) AND 2) = Ø ); END;
                                                    ; STATEMENT # 4
                      @4:
     ØØA8 DBDD              IN        ØDDH
     ØØAA E6Ø2              ANI       2H
     ØØAC FEØØ              CPI       ØH
     ØØAE C2B4ØØ            JNZ       @5
                                                    ; STATEMENT # 5
     ØØB1 C3A8ØØ            JMP       @4
                      @5:
6     2            RETURN( INPUT(CONSOLE$DATA$PORT) AND 7FH );
                                                    ; STATEMENT # 6
     ØØB4 DBDC              IN        ØDCH
     ØØB6 E67F              ANI       7FH
     ØØB8 C9                RET
7     2          END READ;
                                                    ; STATEMENT # 7
8     1          WRITE:
                                                    ; STATEMENT # 8
                       ; PROC    WRITE
     ØØB9 2117ØØ            LXI       H,CHAR
     ØØBC 71                MOV       M,C
                 PROCEDURE(CHAR);
9     2            DECLARE CHAR BYTE;
1Ø    2            DO WHILE( (INPUT(CONSOLE$STATUS$PORT) AND 1) = Ø ); END;
                                                    ; STATEMENT # 1Ø
                      @6:
     ØØBD DBDD              IN        ØDDH
     ØØBF E6Ø1              ANI       1H
     ØØC1 FEØØ              CPI       ØH
     ØØC3 C2C9ØØ            JNZ       @7
                                                    ; STATEMENT # 11
     ØØC6 C3BDØØ            JMP       @6
                      @7:
12    2            OUTPUT(CONSOLE$DATA$PORT) = CHAR;
                                                    ; STATEMENT # 12
     ØØC9 3A17ØØ            LDA       CHAR
     ØØCC D3DC              OUT       ØDCH
13    2          END WRITE;
                                                    ; STATEMENT # 13
     ØØCE C9                RET
14    1          WRITE$STRING:
                                                    ; STATEMENT # 14
                       ; PROC  WRITESTRING
     ØØCF 211AØØ            LXI       H,STRINGSIZE
     ØØD2 73                MOV       M,E
     ØØD3 2B                DCX       H
     ØØD4 7Ø                MOV       M,B
     ØØD5 2B                DCX       H
     ØØD6 71                MOV       M,C
                 PROCEDURE(STRING$ADDRESS,STRING$SIZE);
15    2            DECLARE STRING$ADDRESS  ADDRESS,
                           STRING$SIZE     BYTE,
                           (COUNT,I)       BYTE,
                           (STRING BASED   STRING$ADDRESS) (1) BYTE;
16    2            DO I = Ø TO STRING$SIZE;
                                                    ; STATEMENT # 16
     ØØD7 211CØØ            LXI       H,I
     ØØDA 36ØØ              MVI       M,ØH
                      @8:
```

```
         ØØDC  3A1AØØ          LDA    STRINGSIZE
         ØØDF  211CØØ          LXI    H,I
         ØØE2  BE              CMP    M
         ØØE3  DAFBØØ          JC     @9
17   3           CALL WRITE(STRING(I));
                                            ; STATEMENT # 17
         ØØE6  2A1CØØ          LHLD   I
         ØØE9  26ØØ            MVI    H,Ø
         OOEB  EB              XCHG
         ØØEC  2A18ØØ          LHLD   STRINGADDRESS
         ØØEF  19              DAD    D
         ØØFØ  4E              MOV    C,M
         ØØF1  CDB9ØØ          CALL   WRITE
18   3           END;
                                            ; STATEMENT # 18
         ØØF4  211CØØ          LXI    H,I
         ØØF7  34              INR    M
         ØØF8  C2DCØØ          JNZ    @8
               @9:
19   2       END WRITE$STRING;
                                            ; STATEMENT # 19
         ØØFB  C9              RET
2Ø   1     OK$TO$RUN = TRUE;
                                            ; STATEMENT # 2Ø
         ØØ2Ø  31ØØØØ          LXI    SP,@STACK$ORIGIN
         ØØ23  2116ØØ          LXI    H,OKTORUN
         ØØ26  36FF            MVI    M,OFFH
21   1     DO WHILE OK$TO$RUN=TRUE;
                                            ; STATEMENT # 21
               @1Ø:
         ØØ28  3A16ØØ          LDA    OKTORUN
         ØØ2B  FEFF            CPI    ØFFH
         ØØ2D  C2A4ØØ          JNZ    @11
22   2       CHAR$COUNT = Ø;
                                            ; STATEMENT # 22
         ØØ3Ø  2114ØØ          LXI    H,CHARCOUNT
         ØØ33  36ØØ            MVI    M,ØH
23   2       DO WHILE ((CHAR$COUNT <= LENGTH(BUFFER)) AND (OK$TO$RUN=TRUE));
                                            ; STATEMENT # 23
               @12:
         ØØ35  3E14            MVI    A,14H
         ØØ37  2114ØØ          LXI    H,CHARCOUNT
         ØØ3A  96              SUB    M
         ØØ3B  9F              SBB    A
         ØØ3C  2F              CMA
         ØØ3D  F5              PUSH   PSW      ; 1
         ØØ3E  3A16ØØ          LDA    OKTORUN
         ØØ41  D6FF            SUI    ØFFH
         ØØ43  D6Ø1            SUI    1
         ØØ45  9F              SBB    A
         ØØ46  C1              POP    B        ; 1
         ØØ47  48              MOV    C,B
         ØØ48  A1              ANA    C
         ØØ49  1F              RAR
         ØØ4A  D292ØØ          JNC    @13
24   3         CHAR = READ;
                                            ; STATEMENT # 24
         ØØ4D  CDA8ØØ          CALL   READ
         ØØ5Ø  3215ØØ          STA    CHAR
25   3         BUFFER(CHAR$COUNT) = CHAR'
                                            ; STATEMENT # 25
         ØØ53  2A14ØØ          LHLD   CHARCOUNT
         ØØ56  26ØØ            MVI    H,Ø
         ØØ58  Ø1ØØØØ          LXI    B,BUFFER
         ØØ5B  Ø9              DAD    B
         ØØ5C  3A15ØØ          LDA    CHAR
         ØØ5F  77              MOV    M,A
26   3         CHAR$COUNT = CHAR$COUNT +1;
                                            ; STATEMENT # 26
         ØØ6Ø  2114ØØ          LXI    H,CHARCOUNT

         ØØ63  34              INR    M
27   3         IF CHAR = CR
                                            ; STATEMENT # 27
         ØØ64  23              INX    H
         ØØ65  7E              MOV    A,M
         ØØ66  FEØD            CPI    ØDH
         ØØ68  C28FØØ          JNZ    @1
                 THEN DO;
29   4           IF CHAR$COUNT=1 THEN OK$TO$RUN = FALSE;
                                            ; STATEMENT # 29
         ØØ6B  3A14ØØ          LDA    CHARCOUNT
         ØØ6E  FEØ1            CPI    1H
         ØØ7Ø  C278ØØ          JNZ    @2
                                            ; STATEMENT # 3Ø
         ØØ73  2116ØØ          LXI    H,OKTORUN
         ØØ76  36ØØ            MVI    M,ØH
               @2:
31·  4           CALL WRITE$STRING(.BUFFER,CHAR$COUNT);
                                            ; STATEMENT # 31
```

Software Aids

```
              0078  2A1400          LHLD   CHARCOUNT
              007B  EB              XCHG
              007C  010000          LXI    B,BUFFER
              007F  CDCF00          CALL   WRITESTRING
32    4                     CALL WRITE$STRING(.(CR,LF),2);
                                                 ; STATEMENT # 32
              0082  1E02            MVI    E,2H
              0084  010000          LXI    B,$-84H
              0087  CDCF00          CALL   WRITESTRING
33    4                     CHAR$COUNT = 0;
                                                 ; STATEMENT # 33
              008A  211400          LXI    H,CHARCOUNT
              008D  3600            MVI    M,0H
34    4                     END;
                                                 ; STATEMENT # 34
                          @1:
35    3                     END;
                                                 ; STATEMENT # 35
              008F  C33500          JMP    @12
                          @13:
36    2               IF OK$TO$RUN THEN CALL WRITE$STRING(.(CR,LF,'INPUT STRING IS TOO LONG',CR,LF),30);
                                                 ; STATEMENT # 36
              0092  3A1600          LDA    OKTORUN
              0095  1F              RAR
              0096  D2A100          JNC    @3
                                                 ; STATEMENT # 37
              0099  1E1E            MVI    E,1EH
              009B  010200          LXI    B,$-99H
              009E  CDCF00          CALL   WRITESTRING
                          @3:
38    2                     END;
                                                 ; STATEMENT # 38
              00A1  C32800          JMP    @10
                          @11:
39    1               HALT;
                                                 ; STATEMENT # 39
              00A4  FB              EI
              00A5  76              HLT
40    1               END EXAMPLE;
                                                 ; STATEMENT # 40
              00A6  FB              EI
              00A7  76              HLT
```

SYMBOL LISTING

DEFN	ADDR	SIZE	NAME,	ATTRIBUTES, AND REFERENCES
2	0000H	20	BUFFER	BYTE ARRAY(20)
8	0017H	1	CHAR	BYTE PARAMETER
2	0015H	1	CHAR	BYTE
2	0014H	1	CHARCOUNT	BYTE
2			CONSOLEDATAPORT	LITERALLY
2			CONSOLESTATUSPORT	LITERALLY
15	001BH	1	COUNT	BYTE
2			CR	LITERALLY
1	0020H	136	EXAMPLE	PROCEDURE STACK=0004H
2			FALSE	LITERALLY
15	001CH	1	I	BYTE
2			LF	LITERALLY
	0000H		MEMORY	BYTE ARRAY(0)
2	0016H	1	OKTORUN	BYTE
3	00A8H	17	READ	PROCEDURE BYTE STACK=0000H
15	0000H	1	STRING	BYTE BASED(STRING ADDRESS) ARRAY(1)
14	0018H	2	STRINGADDRESS	ADDRESS PARAMETER
14	001AH	1	STRINGSIZE	BYTE PARAMETER
2			TRUE	LITERALLY
8	00B9H	22	WRITE	PROCEDURE STACK=0000H
14	00CFH	45	WRITESTRING	PROCEDURE STACK=0002H

```
MODULE INFORMATION:
    CODE AREA SIZE     = 00FCH    252D
    VARIABLE AREA SIZE = 001DH    29D
    MAXIMUM STACK SIZE = 0004H    4D
    71 LINES READ
    0 PROGRAM ERROR(S)

END OF PL/M-80 COMPILATION
```

Figure 4.3.4-2 PL/M-80 example program

4.3.4.3 PASCAL Example. The popularity of PASCAL (see reference 14) as a language for small computing systems is increasing at a very high rate. One implementation of this language is available to members of the Intel INSITE 8080 user's group. (See reference 13.) Figure 4.3.4-3 is a listing of a PASCAL solution to our example problem using this implementation of PASCAL. Since this PASCAL translator is an *interpreter* (see Section 4.3.1), no compiler output listing is produced.

Once again no detailed examination of this program will be made, but the following items may be of interest:

1. No declaration of READ or WRITE procedures is made because they are internally defined by this particular PASCAL implementation.
2. PASCAL is seen to be block-structured like PL/M, but certain constructs (REPEAT, for example) are quite different from corresponding PL/M constructs.
3. Literal constant representation is a bit awkward (see line 8, which declares "CR" to be literally the ASCII code for carriage return, which is OD hex, or 13 decimal).
4. This program varies slightly from the PL/M example in that it echoes the individual characters as received in addition to echoing the entire received string when a carriage return is sent.

Consult Reference 14 for a complete discussion of PASCAL.

4.4 TEXT EDITORS

A text editor is a string-processing program which allows convenient manipulation of written test, manifested as a string of ASCII characters. Although editors vary somewhat in their modes of operation and in their command teminology, they tend to be fundamentally similar in concept and operation.

Most editors have rather general applicability, i.e., they can be used to edit text of unspecified nature. In the context of software development, however, they find their most common use in the preparation and modification of source programs written in assembler or higher-level language. Because of this rather special use, some editors emphasize commands which are line-oriented and which allow convenient manipulation of the rather stylized text characteristic of source programs.

Software Aids

```
0001    PROCEDURE READ(VAR C: CHAR);
0002    PROCEDURE WRITE(C: CHAR);
0003
0004
0005    PROGRAM EXAMPLE;
0006
0007    CONST
0008       CR      = '(:13:)';
0009       MAXSIZE = 20;
0010
0011    TYPE
0012       STRING = ARRAY[1..MAXSIZE] OF CHAR;
0013
0014    VAR
0015       BUFFER:       STRING;
0016       OK_TO_RUN:    BOOLEAN;
0017       CHAR_COUNT:   INTEGER;
0018       INPUT_CHAR:   CHAR;
0019
0020
0021
0022
0023    PROCEDURE WRITE_STRING(TEXT: STRING; LENGTH: INTEGER);
0024    VAR
0025       I: INTEGER;
0026    BEGIN
0027       FOR I := 1 TO LENGTH DO WRITE( TEXT[I] );
0028    END;
0029
0030
0031
0032    BEGIN
0033       OK_TO_RUN := TRUE;
0034
0035       REPEAT
0036          CHAR_COUNT := 0;
0037
0038          WHILE (CHAR_COUNT < MAXSIZE) AND OK_TO_RUN DO
0039             BEGIN
0040                READ(INPUT_CHAR);
0041                WRITE(INPUT_CHAR);
0042                CHAR_COUNT := CHAR_COUNT +1;
0043                BUFFER[CHAR_COUNT] := INPUT_CHAR;
0044                IF INPUT_CHAR = CR
0045                   THEN BEGIN
0046                      IF CHAR_COUNT = 1 THEN OK_TO_RUN := FALSE;
0047                      WRITE_STRING(BUFFER,CHAR_COUNT);
0048                      WRITE_STRING('(:13:)(:10:)(:10:)(:10:)',4);
0049                      CHAR_COUNT := 0;
0050                   END;
0051             END; "END OF WHILE STATEMENT"
0052
0053          IF OK_TO_RUN THEN WRITE_STRING('(:13:)(:10:)INPUT TOO LONG(:10:)(:13:)',18);
0054       UNTIL NOT OK_TO_RUN;
0055    END.
```

Figure 4.3.4-3 PASCAL example program

4.4.1 Editor Commands

Because there is no common command syntax among the various available editors, no attempt will be made to give an exhaustive description of their individual characteristics. Instead, a short listing of the most popular command types will be given along with a description of the function of each. (Appendix A includes a detailed discussion of the test editor commands provided by the MDT-650 development system.) Where examples are given, they illustrate the Intel MDS-800 ISIS editor commands and the Digital Equipment Corporation editor provided as a feature of their RT-11 operating system. (See references 9 and 15.)

Before discussing detailed editor commands, let us visualize the editing process in a somewhat general way. The system in which the editor is resident must provide a region of read/write memory for storage of the text string as it is developed. The visualization of a text block as a single one-dimensional string of characters is probably the most useful one, even though our more common visualization is two-dimensional (lines and columns). Carriage return and line feed characters imbedded in the text string render the two dimensional format, of course.

Figure 4.4.1-1 is a simplified block diagram which illustrates the mode of operation of most editors. A file to be edited (the input file) is addressed by the editor and a segment of it is brought into a *text buffer* established in the development system's read/write memory. This segment is edited and sent to the output file, the process repeating until the editing is completed. If a new file is being created, no input file is necessary, of course.

One small detail of editor operation should be explained to make the discussion which follows somewhat easier to follow. For many interactive tasks conducted from a terminal it seems most natural to terminate commands with a carriage return. When using an editor, however, this is often inconvenient, since the carriage return is, in a real

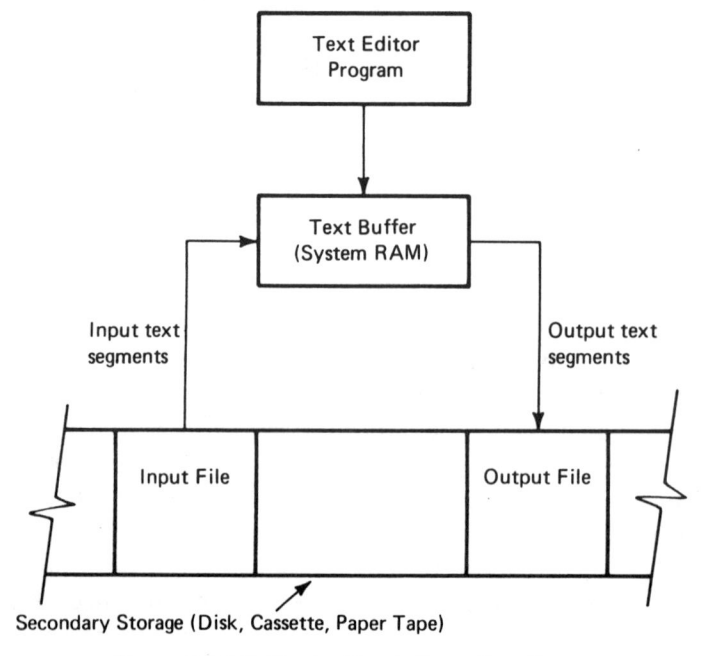

Figure 4.4.1-1 Text editor information flow

Software Aids

sense, simply another character in the string being manipulated. Thus, in the editors discussed here, editor commands are terminated by striking the ESCAPE key on the terminal. As may be seen in the example of Figure. 4.4.2-1, ESCAPE is echoed to the console as a dollar sign ($).

Another small detail one may observe in Figure. 4.4.2-1 is that, while a single ESCAPE terminates a command, a second ESCAPE must be struck to cause command execution. Thus, an ISIS command string

AA$ISTRING$B$10T$$

will not be executed until the $$ occurs at the end of the line, at which time two APPENDS, one INSERT, one B pointer movement, and 10 lines of text printing will occur in rapid succession.

A common sequence of operations when using the editor consists of the following steps.:

1. *Invoke the Editor program:* In ISIS this is done by typing

    EDIT filename.

    In the DEC RT-11 editor the editor is invoked by

    .R EDIT

    which means "Run the Editor."

2. *Establish the source of the text to be edited:* In the case of ISIS, the editor call of step (1) established (via the filename) the source of text. In the case of the DEC RT-11 editor one must type

    *ER filename

    which means "Edit Read filename," i.e., open the file with specified name to permit transfer of text from it into the text buffer.

    If a new text file is being created, the MDS-800 editor call establishes a name for it. In the RT-11 editor this name is established by an "Edit Write" operation (see step 1).

3. *Bring in text to be edited:* This step is only necessary if an existing file is to be edited. In ISIS 50 lines (or the entire file, if less than 50 lines) are loaded into the text buffer by an "A" (append) command. In the RT-11 editor, one page of text is brought in by an "R" (read) command.

4. *Locate the text to be modified:* Editors typically provide a number of commands for this function. One of the most impor-

tant concepts involved here is that of the *text pointer*. It is a conceptual marker which designates at which character position the modification operation specified by a given command will be performed. Certain commands do nothing more than move this text pointer, i.e., (for ISIS)

*B$$

moves the text pointer to the beginning of the text buffer and

*Z$$

moves it to the end of the text buffer.

*nC$$

advances the pointer n characters (n can be negative, which of course "advances" the pointer backwards).

*nL$$

advances the pointer n lines.

As a somewhat more exotic example, the MDS-800 command

*Fstring$$

moves the pointer forward until an exact match with the specified string is found, at which point the text pointer is left pointing to the character following this string. If the string is not found, the pointer moves to the end of the current buffer. (The RT-11 editor also has an F (find) command but it operates somewhat more drastically. If the string is not found, the editor brings in another page of text and continues the search, repeating the process until either the string is found or the end of the file is found.) The G (Get) command in RT-11 is functionally like the F command in the MDS-800 editor.

5. *Modify the Text:* Once again a number of commands are typically provided. Both MDS-800 and RT-11 editors provide an INSERT command, invoked by

*Istring$$

which inserts the specified string into the buffer beginning at the text pointer location. If a new file is being created, the I command is used to insert the entire body of text into the "null" buffer.

Another modification command is the SUBSTITUTE command. In the ISIS editor the command

Software Aids

$$*Sstring1\$string2\$\$$$

will search the text for string 1 and having found it, will substitute string 2. The two strings need not be of the same length.

To perform this substitution function in the RT-11 editor, the somewhat cryptic command string

$$* Gstring1\$ = Cstring2\$\$$$

is typed. This tells the editor to

(a) "get" string1 (move the text pointer to string1) and,
(b) "change" that string to string2.

Another type of editor command provided by both ISIS and RT-11 is text deletion. For example

$$nD\$\$$$

has the same effect in both ISIS and RT-11, viz., to delete n characters following the text pointer. Similarly,

$$nK\$\$$$

will delete (or "kill") n lines of text in either system.

6. *Verify the Text:* Editors provide TYPE or LIST commands which allow the user to view the results of his editing commands. For example,

$$*nL\$\$ (RT-11)$$

$$*nT\$\$ (ISIS)$$

both have the effect of causing the n lines following the text pointer to be printed on the console device. Once again, n can be negative. It is important to note that these commands *do not move the text pointer.*

A variation of the LIST command is (in RT-11)

$$/L\$\$$$

which lists the contents of the entire text buffer following the text pointer.

The RT-11 editor provides a very useful command in the form of the VERIFY command. If one types V$$, the line containing the current text pointer will be printed. It is thus convenient to check a line produced by a series of editing commands.

7. *Store the edited text:* Once the operator is satisfied with his edited text, he probably wishes to store it in a file on floppy

disk, paper tape, or other second-level storage media. In RT-11, he prepares to do this with the command

*EW filename$$

or EDIT WRITE to filename. This does not guarantee the desired file but rather simply opens a file of specified name for output. If the operator then types

*EX$$

he will exit from the editor mode and transfer the contents of the text buffer to the specified file.

In ISIS, the user need not specify the output file at this time since he did so upon invoking the editor (see step 1). Thus, if he types

*E$$

he will create the desired output file.

In some cases (for example, when the user is frustrated with the editor or is simply familiarizing himself with its operation) a user may wish to abort an editing session without creating an output file. He may thus type Q (in ISIS) to "quit" the editor. In RT-11, he may obtain the same result by omitting the EDIT WRITE (EW) operation before invoking the exit from the editor.

Tables 4.4.1-1 and 4.4.1-2 summarize the editor commands of both ISIS and RT-11.

4.4.2 Editing Example

Let us illustrate the operation of the RT-11 editor by a simple example. Figure 4.4.2-1 is a printer listing resulting from activity during an actual editing session. In this particular case, no input file was specified since a new program is being created.

Study the example to observe operation of the various editor commands. The function of each such command is described by a script note in the printout (added by the author, of course).

Note finally that the editing session did not produce an output file, because even though an EDIT WRITE (EW) command designated an output filename, no WRITE (W) command was used, so no text was sent to that file.

Software Aids **219**

TABLE 4.4.1-1 Summary of ISIS Editor Commands

Commands		*Meaning*
File Management Commands		
A	APPEND	bring in 50 lines of text from the specified input file
nW	WRITE	write n lines of text following text pointer to output file.
E	END	empty text buffer to output file, copy remaining input file to output file, and reinitialize editor.
Pointer Movement Commands		
B	BEGINNING	move text pointer to start of text buffer.
Z	END	move text pointer to end of text buffer.
nC	ADVANCE BY CHARACTER	move text pointer n characters forward.
nL	ADVANCE BY LINE	move text pointer n lines forward.
Search Commands		
Fstring	FIND	move text pointer to end of first occurrence of "string."
Modification Commands		
Istring	INSERT	insert "string" into text buffer following text pointer.
Sstring1$string2	SUBSTITUTE	search text for first occurrence of string 1 and replace it with string 2.
nD	DELETE	delete n characters following the text pointer.
nK	KILL	delete n lines following the text pointer.
Print Commands		
nT	TYPE	print the n lines following the text pointer. *The pointer itself is not affected*.
Others		
Q	QUIT	ABORT EDIT IN PROGRESS
n <command string>	REPEAT	repeat editor command string in brackets n times.

TABLE 4.4.1-2 Summary of RT-11 Editor Commands

Command		Meaning
File Management Commands		
ER filename	EDIT READ	establish a file to serve as source of editor input text
EW filename	EDIT WRITE	establish a file to serve as destination of editor output text
EB filename	EDIT BACK	establish an input file and also create a copy for backup
R	READ	input a page of text from the input file
W	WRITE	output a page of text to output file
Listing Commands		
nL	LIST	print the n lines of text following the text pointer
V	VERIFY	print the line of text containing the text pointer
Pointer Movement Commands		
B	BEGINNING	move the text pointer to the start of the text buffer
nJ	JUMP	move the text pointer n characters to the right
nA	ADVANCE	move the text pointer n lines ahead
Search Commands		
nG string	GET	move the text pointer until it is located just following the nth occurrence of "string" in the text buffer
nFstring	FIND	like GET, except that the entire file is searched, with searched pages moving to the output file as they are exhausted
nPstring	POSITION	like FIND, except exhausted pages are discarded rather than being sent to output file
Text Modification Commands		
Istring	INSERT	insert specified string following text pointer
nD	DELETE	delete n characters following text pointer

Software Aids

nK	KILL	delete n lines following text pointer
nCstring	CHANGE	replace n character following text pointer with specified string
nXstring	EXCHANGE	replace lines following text pointer with specified string

Utility Commands

nS	SAVE	copy n lines into special "save buffer"
U	UNSAVE	unload save buffer into text following text pointer

```
.R EDIT           Invoke RT-11 Editor
::I                  Insert string that follows
         ::=$0020
NUM1     ::=#+3
::=$0030
NUM2     ::=::+3
         ::=$0040
RESULT   ::=::+4
Z::=$0200
         N=3
         ZERO=0
         START=$1C4F
LDX #ZERO        INITIALIZE X REGISTER AND CARRY GFLAG
         CLC
LOOP     LDA NUM1,X     LOAD FIRST DIGIT PAIR
         ADC NUM2,X     ADD SECOND DIGIT PAIR
         INX            INCREMENT X REGISTER
         CPX #N-1       TEST FOR COMPLETION
         BNE LOOP       LOOP BACK IF NOT DONE
         BCC MONIT      EXIT TO MONITOR
         INC RESULT,X   ADD 1 TO 5TH DIGIT, IF CARRY
MONIT    JUMP START     JUMP BACK TO MONITOR
         .ENDB$/L$$     Terminate INSERT command
::B$/L$$        Move Pointer to start of buffer. List Buffer contents
         ::=$0020
NUM1     ::=#+3
::=$0030
NUM2     ::=::+3
         ::=$0040
RESULT   ::=::+4
Z::=$0200
         N=3
         ZERO=0
         START=$1C4F
LDX #ZERO        INITIALIZE X REGISTER AND CARRY GFLAG
         CLC
LOOP     LDA NUM1,X     LOAD FIRST DIGIT PAIR
         ADC NUM2,X     ADD SECOND DIGIT PAIR
         INX            INCREMENT X REGISTER
         CPX #N-1       TEST FOR COMPLETION
         BNE LOOP LOOP BACK IF NOT DONE
         BCC MONIT      EXIT TO MONITOR
         INC RESULT,X   ADD 1 TO 5TH DIGIT, IF CARRY
MONIT    JUMP START     JUMP BACK TO MONITOR
         .ENDB::G#$=C$$V$$     Change first '#' to '$' and verify new line
NUM1     ::=$+3
::1A$V$$        Advance pointer 1 line and verify position
::=$0030
::I      $V$$     Insert 'TAB' character and verify
         ::=$0030
::4A$V$$        Advance pointer 4 lines and verify
Z::=$0200
::1D$V$$        Delete unwanted "Z" and verify
::=$0200
```

```
::I        V/V/$V$$   Insert 'TAB' and verify (note mistyped 'V' and
                      deletion of same)
              ::=$0200
::GLDX$V$$         Search for 'LDX' and verify
           LDX #ZERO        INITIALIZE X REGISTER AND CARRY GFLAG
::0A$IBEGIN        $V$$ Move pointer to beginning of line (with 0A) and
                         insert 'BEGIN', 'TAB'. Verify
BEGIN      LDX #ZERO        INITIALIZE X REGISTER AND CARRY GFLAG
::GGFLAG$=CFLAG$V$$    Replace 'GFLAG' with 'FLAG'. Verify.
BEGIN      LDX #ZERO        INITIALIZE X REGISTER AND CARRY FLAG
::GINX$V$$         Search for 'INX'. Verify.
           INX              INCREMENT X REGISTER
::0A$GINX$=CINX    $V$$ Move pointer to start of line. Replace 'INX' with
                         'INX, TAB'. Verify
           INX              INCREMENT X REGISTER
::GJUMP$=CJMP$V$$  Replace 'JUMP' with 'JMP'. Verify.
MONIT      JMP START        JUMP BACK TO MONITOR
::GENDB$=CEND
$V$$
::-1A$V$$  Move pointer back one line to verify.
              .END
::

$$
::B$/L$$   Move pointer to beginning of text buffer. List contents.
              ::=$0020
NUM1          ::=$+3
              ::=$0030
NUM2          ::=::+3
              ::=$0040
RESULT        ::=::+4
              ::=$0200
              N=3
              ZERO=0
              START=1C4F
BEGIN      LDX #ZERO        INITIALIZE X REGISTER AND CARRY FLAG
           CLC
LOOP       LDA NUM1,X       LOAD FIRST DIGIT PAIR
           ADC NUM2,X       ADD SECOND DIGIT PAIR
           INX              INCREMENT X REGISTER
           CPX #N-1         TEST FOR COMPLETION
           BNE LOOP         LOOP BACK IF NOT DONE
           BCC MONIT        EXIT TO MONITOR
           INC RESULT,X     ADD 1 TO 5TH DIGIT, IF CARRY
MONIT      JMP START        JUMP BACK TO MONITOR
              .END
::EWDX1:EXAMP.SRC$$
```

Figure 4.4.2-1 Example of editor session activity

4.5 SIMULATORS

A simulator is a program written to run on one computer and, by analyzing the steps (instructions) of a program written for another computer, can produce results which are equivalent to those of the second computer. Thus, the logical correctness of the program can be verified even though the second computer is not available for testing.

Simulators suffer from the primary handicap of slow execution, i.e., each original program step may take a number of simulator pro-

Software Aids

gram steps to accurately portray the desired logical activity. Also, many simulators provide some program analysis and error-checking capability, which makes real-time execution even slower. Reference 16 discusses simulators for microcomputers.

4.6 SPECIAL PROGRAM DEBUG FEATURES

A number of software development systems provide so-called "debug" capability for programs written for the development system's host CPU. The Intel MDS-800, for example, provides such capability for 8080 programs. Among the features provided by the DEBUG package provided with the MDS-800 are the following:

1. A mechanism for loading object programs into system memory;
2. A mechanism for transferring control to the program to be tested; and
3. A mechanism for detecting "breakpoints" as the program under test is executed. A breakpoint is a specified address which, if encountered during program execution, causes control to pass back to the system's monitor program, at which time analysis of the results of program execution can be performed by examination of register and memory contents.

In the MDS-800, a program can be executed via DEBUG by typing the command

DEBUG filename

where 'filename' denotes a diskette file which presumably contains an object program. This command loads the program into system memory, at which time the operator can type the command

GAddress 1, −Address 2, −Address 3.

This directs the system to begin execution at Address 1, presumably the starting location of the program to be tested, and to examine each memory operation during program execution to determine if either Address 2 or Address 3 is involved, denoting that a breakpoint condition has been found.

A debugging system like the one described here is of somewhat limited usefulness. One primary problem lies in the fact that there are often conflicting memory requirements. For example, if the program under test is ultimately to be used on a separately configured system (in other words, not the MDS-800 itself), it is very likely that the memory required by the MD-800 operating system will infringe on the memory allocated to the program under test in the prototype system. Thus, the program cannot be tested unless its memory addressing is modified to fit into available MDS space.

A second fundamental limitation of this type of debugging system lies in the fact that only one processor is used. Thus, while the program under test is running, no additional resources exist for tracing or analyzing the program in any significant way. This is in contrast to systems with in-circuit evaluation capability (see Section 4.7). See reference 9 for a discussion of ISIS-II debug features.

4.7 IN–CIRCUIT EMULATION

4.7.1 General Features

A very powerful aid to microcomputer system development is the in-circuit emulator (ICE), whose conceptual development is as recent as the microprocessor itself. In essence, the ICE concept allows the designer of a microcomputer-based prototype system to begin software/hardware system integration at a very early point in the design cycle. This is possible because the ICE unit forms a link between the prototype, which may exist initially in very primitive form, and the development system. The resources of the development system are thereby made available to the prototype so that it may be operated in its intended system environment with full access to the memory and I/O capability of the development system. Additionally, sophisticated trace, trap, and display functions permit the operator to quickly locate both program and hardware bugs.

Figure 4.7.1-1 is a simple block diagram of Intel's ICE-80 system which supports 8080 based system development. The *Processor Module* contains an 8080 which serves as a "surrogate" for the prototype's 8080. The processor module therefore plugs into the 8080 socket vacated by removing that chip from the prototype. One of the important functions of the processor module is to manage address mapping, a fundamentally important feature of ICE-80.

The *Trace Module* is the link between the MDS-80 system and the Processor Module. The MDS-80 treats this board as a peripheral unit. The trace board monitors the address bus of the processor module, checking for occurrence of events (address and/or data values) which the operator has designated as triggering events for the trace function. The Trace module also contains a timer which supports extensive timekeeping, permitting measurement of system execution speed even while operating in a nonreal-time mode.

Software Aids   **225**

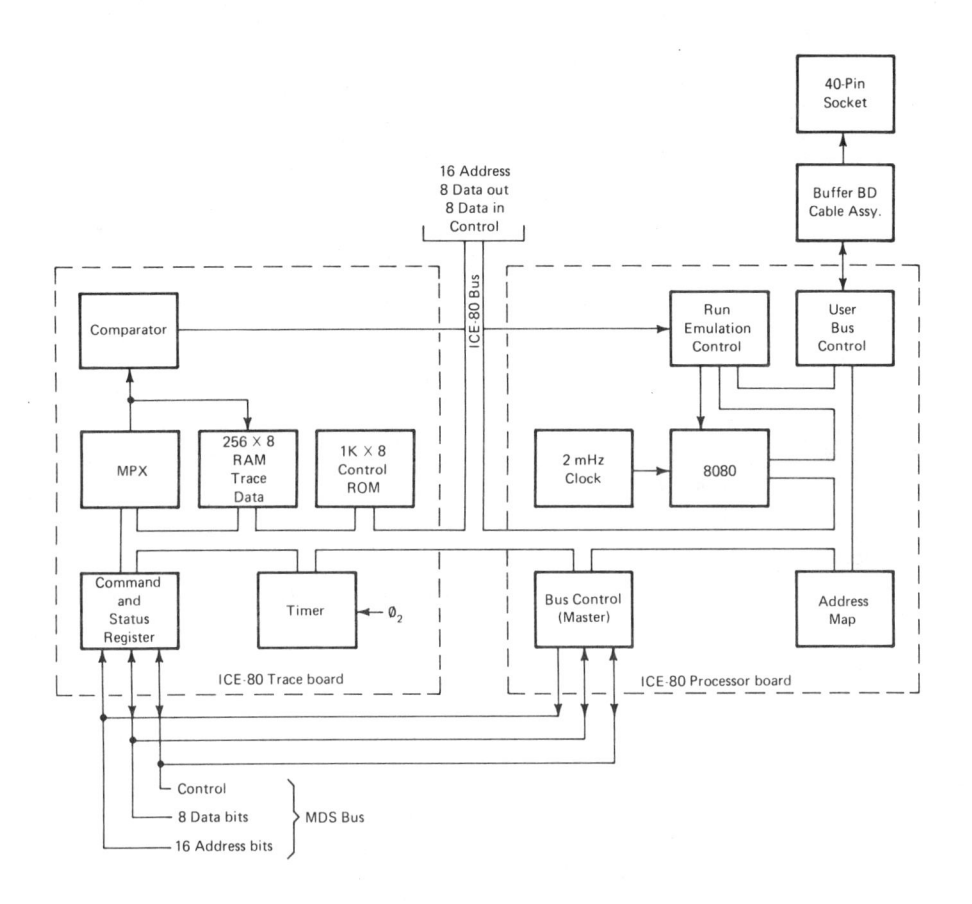

Figure 4.7.1-1 ICE-80 block diagram

Some of the features provided by ICE-80 are enumerated below.

1. *Very flexible memory mapping.* Using appropriate set-up commands, the prototype system can be given access to sections of memory comprised of (a) its own on-board memory, (b) MDS memory "mapped" into prototype memory space at selected blocks, and (c) MDS memory containing MDS code to be used by the prototype. The mapping of (b) avoids the memory conflicts discussed in Section 4.6. Item (c) permits the prototype access to monitor routines and other MDS program resources. Finally, sections of memory can be "guarded," permitting detection of attempts by the prototype to access memory not defined for its use.

2. *Similar mapping capability for I/O ports.* This gives the prototype access to MDS I/O devices and, using the mapping feature if 1 (c), the software for management of these devices.
3. *File-handling capability.* The operator can load programs from secondary storage, save programs by transferring them to secondary storage, and generate an ICE trace listing to a secondary storage or nonconsole I/O device (like a line printer).
4. *Direct memory management.* The operator can fill a memory block with a specified value and also move the contents of one region of memory to another.
5. *Operation in symbolic mode.* The operator can, by providing a symbol table with his program or specifically entering symbol-value correspondences via the ICE EQUATE command, use symbolic names rather than numeric addresses in this interactive activity.
6. *Very sophisticated trace capability.* This includes a mechanism for specifying *trigger* conditions which, when detected by the trace module, initiate storage of system activity. A variety of *trace* options, specifying exactly what information is to be stored when triggering occurs, also are offered. The trigger and trace capability is not specifically identified as such but is intrinsically included in the structure of GO and STEP commands (see Section 4.7.3).

4.7.2 Memory and I/O Mapping

ICE-80 divides the 65K 8080 memory into 16 blocks of 4K bytes each, and the 256-port I/O space into 16 blocks of 16 ports each. The basic idea underlying the mapping function is that a *logical memory* block that is going to be referenced by prototype or user program can be mapped into a *physical memory* block located within the MDS-800. Thus, the command

XFORM MEMORY 3 INTO 15

maps block 3 (addresses 3000-3FFF hex) of prototype memory space into block 15 (F000-FFFF), of actual MDS memory. When subsequent references by the user program to addresses in the 3XXX range are made, the mapping will redirect these references to the FXXX range in the MDS to the program. This mapping is invisible to the prototype, of course. If the prototype system has some on-board memory which the user program needs access to, the operator may issue the command

XFORM MEMORY 0 UNGUARDED

which tells ICE-80 that references to block 0 (addresses 0000-0FFF hex) are to be permitted and are to prototype rather than MDS memory. If the operator wishes to know memory status, he may issue the command (for example)

XFORM MEMORY 0 TO 4

and ICE-80 might respond

$$0H = G, 0H$$
$$1H = G, 1H$$
$$2H = U, 2H$$
$$3H = M, FH$$
$$4H = M, 4H$$

This tells the operator that blocks 0 and 1 are guarded (physically nonexistent to the prototype system), block 2 is unguarded (resident in the prototype system), and blocks 3 and 4 are mapped from MDS blocks 15 and 4, respectively.

Note the distinction between the commands XFORM MEMORY 0 TO 4 and XFORM MEMORY 0 INTO 4. The first is simply a status request, while the second is an actual mapping command.

I/O mapping in ICE-80 is similar to memory mapping except that the prototype port numbers and MDS port numbers must be the same, i.e., the command

XFORM IO number 1 INTO number 2

is in error unless number 1 and number 2 are equal.

4.7.3 Emulation and Trace Capability in ICE-80

There are two basic emulation commands in ICE-80. The GO command transfers control to the prototype program, which will run at real-time speed until a breakpoint (trigger) condition is met. The STEP command directs the program to run until the specified step condition has been satisfied.

Examples of the GO command are

```
GO FROM BEGIN UNTIL 200H READ
GO UNTIL LOOP EXECUTED THEN DUMP
GO UNTIL 10 INPUT OR 20 OUTPUT THEN DUMP &
CONTINUE FOREVER
```

Note that symbolic references (BEGIN and LOOP) are permitted, particular operations such as instruction execution or memory reads can be specified as trigger conditions, and that resumption of emulation can be specified following handling of breakpoints. DUMP specifies that a listing of all 8080 register contents be generated at the time of the breakpoint condition.

STEP THEN DUMP
STEP BY 4 INSTRUCTIONS FROM BEGIN THEN DUMP & CONTINUE FOREVER
STEP BY 1 CALL THEN DUMP CONTINUE 6

The first example implicitly asks that one instruction be executed before the DUMP and return to ICE-80. The third example asks that the program be run until one subroutine call has been executed, at which point a DUMP will occur, the process repeating 6 times.

These examples give only a glimpse of the extremely flexible trigger/trace capability of ICE-80. For a complete description see references 17 and 18.

4.7.4 ICE-80 Example

This section is a fairly lengthy example of ICE-80 usage to debug an 8080 program. It is reproduced from Chapter 8 of the Intel ICE-80 Operator's Manual, Publication 98.185C, with the kind permission of Intel Corporation.

SAMPLE ICE–80 DEBUGGING SESSION

The purpose of this example is to illustrate as many features of MDS ICE80SD as possible in an actual debugging situation. Use of ISIS ICE80SD can be extrapolated easily from this example. An undebugged, untested program is used; it has been assembled by the 8080 cross or resident assembler, and is ready to be checked out. The program accepts an input 'N' following its '=' prompt, $0 \leq N < 10$, and outputs '1' if N is a prime number and '0' if it is not prime. The algorithm is as follows:

1. Input N.
2. Set PRIME to false.
3. If $N < 4$, set PRIME to true, and go to step 11.
4. If N is even, it is not a prime. Go to step 11.
5. Set K, a possible factor of N, to 3.

Software Aids

6. Divide N by K producing quotient Q and remainder R.
7. If R = 0, N is not a prime. Go to step 11.
8. Increment K by 2.
9. If K ≤ Q, then not yet done. Go to step 6.
10. Set PRIME to true.
11. If PRIME is true, output 1, otherwise output 0.
12. Go to step 1.

Step 11 is simple if the true value of the logical variable PRIME is 1 and the false value is 0. Then the value of PRIME itself may be output. An assembly language listing of a program corresponding to this algorithm is shown below.

```
8080 MACRO ASSEMBLER, VER 2.3   ERRORS = 0
                ;   TEST A NUMBER < 10 TO SEE IF IT IS PRIME
000D            CR        EQU  0DH
000A            LF        EQU  0AH
0001            Q         EQU  C
0000            R         EQU  B
0003            N         EQU  E
0002            K         EQU  D
03E8            TOS       EQU  1000       ;TOP OF STACK
F809            CO        EQU  0F809H     ;CONSOLE OUTPUT
F803            CI        EQU  0F803H     ;CONSOLE INPUT
0190                      ORG  400
0190  31E803    START:    LXI  SP,TOS     ;INITIALIZE THE STACK POINTER
0193  0E0D      INPUT:    MVI  C,CR       ;TYPE A CARRIAGE RETURN
0195  CD09F8              CALL CO
0198  0E0A                MVI  C,LF       ;TYPE A LINE FEED
019A  CD09F8              CALL CO
019D  3A0602              LDA  EQUAL      ;TYPE OUT REQUEST FOR DATA
01A0  4F                  MOV  C,A
01A1  CD09F8              CALL CO
01A4  CD03F8              CALL CI         ;INPUT N
01A7  E67F                ANI  7FH        ;MASK OFF PARITY
01A9  4F                  MOV  C,A
01AA  3E00                MVI  A,0
01AC  320502              STA  PRIME      ;INITIALIZE PRIME TO FALSE
01AF  CD09F8              CALL CO         ;ECHO INPUT
01B2  79                  MOV  A,C
01B3  DE30                SBI  '0'        ;CONVERT INPUT ASCII TO BINARY
01B5  5F                  MOV  N,A
01B6  FE04                CPI  4          ;IF N < 4 THEN IT IS PRIME
01B8  D2C201              JNC  MAYBE
01BB  210502              LXI  H,PRIME    ;MARK PRIME TRUE
01BE  34                  INR  M
01BF  C3EB01              JMP  PREND      ;QUIT
                ;   CHECK TO SEE IF N IS EVEN; IF SO CAN QUIT, SINCE N
                ;   IS NOT PRIME
01C2  E6FE      MAYBE:    ANI  0FEH       ;CLEAR RIGHTMOST BIT
01C4  BB                  CMP  N          ;IF (N/2)*2=N, THEN N IS EVEN
01C5  CAEB01              JZ   PREND
                ;   SINCE WE MAY HAVE A PRIME NUMBER, START DIVIDING
                ;   N BY POSSIBLE FACTOR K. WHEN DIVISOR K IS GREATER
                ;   THAN QUOTIENT Q, WE KNOW THAT N MUST BE PRIME.
                ;   HOWEVER, IF BEFORE THIS POINT A REMAINDER R IS
                ;   PRODUCED WHICH IS ZERO, THEN N IS NOT PRIME.
```

```
Ø1C8  16Ø3              MVI  K,3         ;START FACTOR K OFF AT 3
Ø1CA  Ø6ØØ     REDIV:   MVI  B,Ø         ;ZERO UPPER PART OF DIVIDEND
Ø1CC  4B                MOV  C,N         ;N INTO LOWER PART OF DIVIDEND
Ø1CD  CDØ7Ø2            CALL DIV         ;N/K INTO QUOTIENT Q AND
Ø1DØ  78                MOV  A,R         ;REMAINDER R
Ø1D1  FEØØ              CPI  Ø           ;CHECK TO SEE IF R=Ø
Ø1D3  CAEBØ1            JZ   PREND       ;QUIT IF R=Ø, N IS NOT PRIME
Ø1D6  7A                MOV  A,K
Ø1D7  C6Ø2              ADI  2           ;INCREMENT K, KEEP IT ODD
Ø1D9  B9                CMP  Q           ;IF Q>K THEN QUIT, N IS PRIME
Ø1DA  D2E7Ø1            JNC  AGAIN       ;K<=Q, GO LOOP AGAIN
Ø1DD  C2E7Ø1            JNZ  AGAIN
Ø1EØ  21Ø5Ø2            LXI  H,PRIME
Ø1E3  34                INR  M           ;MARK PRIME TRUE
Ø1E4  C3EBØ1            JMP  PREND       ;QUIT
Ø1E7  7A       AGAIN:   MOV  A,K
Ø1E8  C3CAØ1            JMP  REDIV
Ø1EB  21Ø5Ø2   PREND:   LXI  H,PRIME
Ø1EE  34                INR  M
Ø1EF  ØEØD              MVI  C,CR        ;TYPE A CARRIAGE RETURN
Ø1F1  CDØ9F8            CALL CO
Ø1F4  ØEØA              MVI  C,LF        ;TYPE A LINE FEED
Ø1F6  CDØ9F8            CALL CO
Ø1F9  3AØ5Ø2            LDA  PRIME
Ø1FC  F63Ø              ORI  'Ø'         ;CONVERT TO ASCII
Ø1FE  4F                MOV  C,A
Ø1FF  CDØ9F8            CALL CO          ;OUTPUT 1 IF PRIME, Ø IF NOT
Ø2Ø2  C393Ø1            JMP  INPUT       ;GET ANOTHER N
Ø2Ø5  ØØ       PRIME:   DB   Ø
Ø2Ø6  3D       EQUAL:   DB   '='
                  ;   DIVIDE ROUTINE: DIVIDEND IN BC, DIVISOR IN D,
                  ;   QUOTIENT IN C, REMAINDER IN B.
Ø2Ø7  F5       DIV:     PUSH PSW         ;SAVE CALLER'S REGISTERS
Ø2Ø8  D5                PUSH D
Ø2Ø9  E5                PUSH H
Ø2ØA  1EØ9              MVI  E,9         ;INITIALIZE LOOP COUNTER
Ø2ØC  78                MOV  A,B
Ø2ØD  47       DIVØ:    MOV  B,A
Ø2ØE  79                MOV  A,C         ;ROTATE CARRY INTO C REG, ROT
Ø2ØF  17                RAL              ; NEXT MOST SIG BIT TO CARRY
Ø21Ø  4F                MOV  C,A
Ø211  1D                DCR  E
Ø212  CA1FØ2            JZ   DIV1
Ø215  78                MOV  A,B         ;ROTATE MOST SIG BIT TO HIGH
Ø216  17                RAL              ; ORDER QUOTIENT
Ø217  92                SUB  D           ;SUBTRACT DIVISOR. IF < HIGH
Ø218  D2ØDØ2            JNC  DIVØ        ; ORDER QUOT, GO TO DIVØ
Ø21B  82                ADD  D           ;OTHERWISE ADD DIVISOR BACK
Ø21C  C3ØDØ2            JMP  DIVØ
Ø21F  17       DIV1:    RAL
Ø22Ø  5F                MOV  E,A
Ø221  3EFF              MVI  A,ØFFH      ;COMPLEMENT THE QUOTIENT
Ø223  A9                XRA  C
Ø224  4F                MOV  C,A
Ø225  7B                MOV  A,E
Ø226  1F                RAR
Ø227  E1                POP  H           ;RESTORE CALLER'S REGISTERS
Ø228  D1                POP  D
Ø229  F1                POP  PSW
Ø22A  C9                RET
                        END
NO PROGRAM ERRORS
```

Software Aids

SYMBOL TABLE

```
* Ø1
A       ØØØ7    AGAIN   Ø1E7    B       ØØØØ    C       ØØØ1
CI      F8Ø3    CO      F8Ø9    CR      ØØØD    D       ØØØ2
DIV     Ø2Ø7    DIVØ    Ø2ØD    DIV1    Ø21F    E       ØØØ3
EQUAL   Ø2Ø6    H       ØØØ4    INPUT   Ø193    K       ØØØ2
L       ØØØ5    LF      ØØØA    M       ØØØ6    MAYBE   Ø1C2
N       ØØØ3    PREND   Ø1EB    PRIME   Ø2Ø5    PSW     ØØØ6
Q       ØØØ1    R       ØØØØ    REDIV   Ø1CA    SP      ØØØ6
START   Ø19Ø*   TOS     Ø3E8
```

The first step in checking out the program is to load the code into the MDS memory or your prototype system's memory. Assume that the prototype is not yet available and the code is to be debugged in the MDS. Assume also that memory addresses 12K to 16K in the MDS are unused. Thus the first 4K addresses in the sample program should be mapped into the fourth 4K block of addresses in the MDS (locations 3ØØØ - 3FFFH). Also, since the program uses monitor calls for I/O, you should map the high end of your memory into the high end of the MDS memory.

```
MDS ICE-8Ø, V1.Ø
*XFORM MEM Ø INTO 3
*XFORM MEM 15 INTO 15
```

Now establish the same console device for both the sample program and for MDS ICE8ØSD.

```
*XFORM IO 15 INTO 15
```

The program and symbol table can now be loaded, memory locations required by the MDS monitor moved, and the output display mode set to hexadecimal as follows.

```
*LOAD
*MOVE MDSMEM Ø TO 15 INTO MEMORY Ø
*BASE HEX
```

You may now wish to look at the symbol table and the hexadecimal representation of the sample program code.

```
*DISPLAY ALL SYMBOLS
```

And the system responds with the values of all symbols.

```
BLOCKØØ1 ØØØØH
A ØØØ7H
AGAIN Ø1E7H
B ØØØØH
C ØØØ1H
CI F8Ø3H
```

```
CO    F8Ø9H
CR    ØØØDH
D     ØØØ2H
DIV   Ø2Ø7H
DIVØ  Ø2ØDH
DIV1  Ø21FH
E     ØØØ3H
EQUAL Ø2Ø6H
H     ØØ-4H
INPUT Ø193H
K     ØØØ2H
L     ØØØ5H
LF    ØØØAH
M     ØØØ6H
MAYBE Ø1C2H
N     ØØØ3H
PREND Ø1EBH
PRIME Ø2Ø5H
PSW   ØØØ6H
Q     ØØØ1H
R     ØØØØH
REDIV Ø1CAH
SP    ØØØ6H
START Ø19ØH
TOS   Ø3E8H

*DISPLAY MEMORY 19ØH TO 22AH
```

And the system types the hexadecimal representation of the program's code.

```
Ø19ØH=31H E8H Ø3H ØEH ØDH CDH Ø9H F8H ØEH ØAH CDH Ø9H F8H 3AH Ø6H Ø2H
Ø1AØH=4FH CDH Ø9H F8H CDH Ø3H F8H E6H 7FH 4FH 3EH ØØH 32H Ø5H Ø2H CDH
Ø1BØH=Ø9H F8H 79H DEH 3ØH 5FH FEH Ø4H D2H C2H Ø1H 21H Ø5H Ø2H 34H C3H
Ø1CØH=EBH Ø1H E6H FEH BBH CAH EBH Ø1H 16H Ø3H Ø6H ØØH 4BH CDH Ø7H Ø2H
Ø1DØH=78H FEH ØØH CAH EBH Ø1H 7AH C6H Ø2H B9H D2H E7H Ø1H C2H E7H Ø1H
Ø1EØH=21H Ø5H Ø2H 34H C3H EBH Ø1H 7AH C3H CAH Ø1H 21H Ø5H Ø2H 34H ØEH
Ø1FØH=ØDH CDH Ø9H F8H ØEH ØAH CDH Ø9H F8H 3AH Ø5H Ø2H F6H 3ØH 4FH CDH
Ø2ØØH=Ø9H F8H C3H 93H Ø1H ØØH 3DH F5H D5H E5H 1EH Ø9H 78H 47H 79H 17H
Ø21ØH=4FH 1DH CAH 1FH Ø2H 78H 17H 92H D2H ØDH Ø2H 82H C3H ØDH Ø2H 17H
Ø22ØH=5FH 3EH FFH A9H 4FH 7BH 1FH E1H D1H F1H C9H
```

Now the program can be checked piece by piece. First check the code which tests whether N < 4, and if so outputs 1. For the sake of example, jump in blindly without setting any break condition.

```
*GO FROM START
EMULATION BEGUN
```

The system is running and the program will print out the character '=' whenever it requests input. The numbers following the '=' represent input to the program.

```
=3
2
=$              (MDS switch pressed for interrupt level 4)
PROCESSING ABORTED
EMULATION TERMINATED AT FCAEH
```

Software Aids

The emulation was aborted because an error was detected. The sample program is typing back '2' when it should be responding with '1'. Check now to be sure the '2' typed out came from PRIME.

```
*DISPLAY MEM PRIME
```

and the response is

```
0205=02H
```

Apparently, the branch for N < 4 works. But PRIME is evidently being incremented in two places. Setting a break condition whenever the address PRIME is changed should locate the problem.

```
*GO FROM " UNTIL PRIME WRITTEN
EMULATION BEGUN

=EMULATION TERMINATED AT 01ACH
```

This is the initialization of PRIME; continue processing. Note that in this case a digit '3' was entered in response to the equal sign prompt, but emulation terminated before it was echoed. The '3' is echoed below, when emulation resumes.

```
*CONTINUE
EMULATION BEGUN
3EMULATION TERMINATED AT 01BEH
```

This is where it should be set. Maybe we can save time by going until PRIME becomes 2 and not be told about any other changes to PRIME.

```
*GO UNTIL " CONTINUE WHILE MEMORY PRIME <> 2
EMULATION BEGUN
EMULATION TERMINATED AT 01EEH
```

Eureka! This is the unwanted incrementing of PRIME. These addresses can be changed to no-ops for now and corrected in the source program later.

```
*EQUATE NOP = 00
*FILL MEMORY PREND TO PREND+3 WITH NOP
```

Now try again!

```
*GO FROM START
EMULATIN BEGUN

=3
1
=$         (MDS switch pressed for interrupt level 4)
PROCESSING ABORTED
EMULATION TERMINATED AT FCAAH
```

This segment of our program works now. Next, the branch which eliminates even numbers can be checked.

```
*GO FROM "
EMULATION BEGUN

=4
Ø
=$           (MDS switch pressed for interrupt level 4)
PROCESSING ABORTED
EMULATION TERMINATED AT FCACH
```

This branch works. Now a number like 5, which is the smallest integer that gets into the divide loop, should be tried.

```
*GO FROM "
EMULATIN BEGUN

=5
```

This seems to be an endless loop. The debugging session should be performed with dump and break conditions. At this point, put a register dump into the divide loop and try again. To obtain a dump after each instruction, repeated single step mode must be used.

```
=5$          (MDS switch pressed for interrupt level 4)
PROCESSING ABORTED
EMULATION TERMINATED AT Ø2ØFH
```

Using the RANGE command, the amount of information dumped can be limited.

```
*RANGE REDIV TO PREND
*STEP FROM " THEN DUMP CONTINUE FOREVER
EMULATION BEGUN
=5B=ØØH C=35H D=Ø3H E=Ø5H H=Ø2H L=Ø5H F=87H A=Ø4H P=Ø1CCH *=Ø1CAH S=Ø3E8H
B=ØØH C=Ø5H D=Ø3H E=Ø5H H=Ø2H L=Ø5H F=87H A=Ø4H P=Ø1CDH *=Ø1CCH S=Ø3E8H
B=Ø5H C=Ø5H D=Ø3H E=Ø5H H=Ø2H L=Ø5H F=87H A=Ø4H P=Ø2Ø7H *=Ø1CCH S=Ø3E6H
B=Ø2H C=Ø1H D=Ø3H E=Ø5H H=Ø2H L=Ø5H F=87H A=Ø2H P=Ø1D1H *=Ø1DØH S=Ø3E8H
B=Ø2H C=Ø1H D=Ø3H E=Ø5H H=Ø2H L=Ø5H F=12H A=Ø2H P=Ø1D3H *=Ø1D1H S=Ø3E8H
B=Ø2H C=Ø1H D=Ø3H E=Ø5H H=Ø2H L=Ø5H F=12H A=Ø2H P=Ø1D6H *=Ø1D3H S=Ø3E8H
B=Ø2H C=Ø1H D=Ø3H E=Ø5H H=Ø2H L=Ø5H F=12H A=Ø3H P=Ø1D7H *=Ø1D6H S=Ø3E8H
B=Ø2H C=Ø1H D=Ø3H E=Ø5H H=Ø2H L=Ø5H F=Ø6H A=Ø5H P=Ø1D9H *=Ø1D7H S=Ø3E8H
B=Ø2H C=Ø1H D=Ø3H E=Ø5H H=Ø2H L=Ø5H F=12H A=Ø5H P=Ø1DAH *=Ø1D9H S=Ø3E8H
B=Ø2H C=Ø1H D=Ø3H E=Ø5H H=Ø2H L=Ø5H F=12H A=Ø5H P=Ø1E7H *=Ø1DAH S=Ø3E8H
B=Ø2H C=Ø1H D=Ø3H E=Ø5H H=Ø2H L=Ø5H F=12H A=Ø3H P=Ø1E8H *=Ø1E7H S=Ø3E8H
B=Ø2H C=Ø1H D=Ø3H E=Ø5H H=Ø2H L=Ø5H F=12H A=Ø3H P=Ø1CAH *=Ø1E8H S=Ø3E8H
B=ØØH C=Ø1H D=Ø3H E=Ø5H H=Ø2H L=Ø5H F=12H A=Ø3H P=Ø1CCH *=Ø1CAH S=Ø3E8H
B=ØØH C=Ø5H D=Ø3H E=Ø5H H=Ø2H L=Ø5H F=12H A=Ø3H P=Ø1CDH *=Ø1CCH S=Ø3E8H
B=ØØH C=Ø5H D=Ø3H E=Ø5H H=Ø2H L=Ø5H F=12H A=Ø3H P=Ø2Ø7H *=Ø1CDH S=Ø3E6H
B=Ø2H C=Ø1H D=Ø3H E=Ø5$
```
(MDS switch pressed for interrupt level 4)
```
   PROCESSING ABORTED
```

By examining the dump, we can see that K (register D), the divisor, was not being incremented. It is supposed to be incremented in the accumulator and moved back to register D. The MOVE instruction at the bottom of the loop is backwards, since it moves K into A instead of A into

Software Aids 235

K after incrementing. Changing this instruction from a MOV A,K to MOVE K,A should solve the problem.

```
*CHANGE MEMORY 1E7H =57H
```

Now try again.

```
*GO FROM "
EMULATION BEGUN

=5
Ø
=$          (MDS switch pressed for interrupt level 4)
PROCESSING ABORTED
EMULATION TERMINATED AT FCAEH
```

Five is a prime number, so something is wrong. Time to dump again. . .

```
*STEP FROM " THEN DUMP CONTINUE FOREVER
EMULATION BEGUN

=5B=ØØH C=35H D=Ø3H E=Ø5H H=Ø2H L=Ø5H F=87H A=Ø4H P=Ø1CCH *=Ø1CAH S=Ø3E8H
 B=ØØH C=Ø5H D=Ø3H E=Ø5H H=Ø2H L=Ø5H F=87H A=Ø4H P=Ø1CDH *=Ø1CCH S=Ø3E8H
 B=ØØH C=Ø5H D=Ø3H E=Ø5H H=Ø2H L=Ø5H F=87H A=Ø4H P=Ø2Ø7H *=Ø1CDH S=Ø3E6H
 B=Ø2H C=Ø1H D=Ø3H E=Ø5H H=Ø2H L=Ø5H F=87H A=Ø2H P=Ø1D1H *=Ø1DØH S=Ø3E8H
 B=Ø2H C=Ø1H D=Ø3H E=Ø5H H=Ø2H L=Ø5H F=12H A=Ø2H P=Ø1D3H *=Ø1D1H S=Ø3E8H
 B=Ø2H C=Ø1H D=Ø3H E=Ø5H H=Ø2H L=Ø5H F=12H A=Ø2H P=Ø1D6H *=Ø1D3H S=Ø3E8H
 B=Ø2H C=Ø1H D=Ø3H E=Ø5H H=Ø2H L=Ø5H F=12H A=Ø3H P=Ø1D7H *=Ø1D6H S=Ø3E8H
 B=Ø2H C=Ø1H D=Ø3H E=Ø5H H=Ø2H L=Ø5H F=Ø6H A=Ø5H P=Ø1D9H *=Ø1D7H S=Ø3E8H
 B=Ø2H C=Ø1H D=Ø3H E=Ø5H H=Ø2H L=Ø5H F=12H A=Ø5H P=Ø1DAH *=Ø1D9H S=Ø3E8H
 B=Ø2H C=Ø1H D=Ø3H E=Ø5H H=Ø2H L=Ø5H F=12H A=Ø5H P=Ø1E7H *=Ø1DAH S=Ø3E8H
 B=Ø2H C=Ø1H D=Ø5H E=Ø5H H=Ø2H L=Ø5H F=12H A=Ø5H P=Ø1E8H *=Ø1E7H S=Ø3E8H
 B=Ø2H C=Ø1H D=Ø5H E=Ø5H H=Ø2H L=Ø5H F=12H A=Ø5H P=Ø1CAH *=Ø1E8H S=Ø3E8H
 B=ØØH C=Ø1H D=Ø5H E=Ø5H H=Ø2H L=Ø5H F=12H A=Ø5H P=Ø1CCH *=Ø1CAH S=Ø3E8H
 B=Ø$
```

(MDS switch pressed for interrupt level 4)
```
PROCESSING ABORTED
```

Examining the dump shows that the 5 entered was divided by 3, then by 5. It should have quit at 3, since at that point Q (5/3 = 1) is less than K (1 < 3). Apparently the condition checking at the bottom of the divide loop is not correct.

Try setting break conditions when the two jump instructions at the bottom of the divide loop are executed. Then, when a break occurs, the CPU state and the results of the compare can be examined.

```
*GO FROM " UNTIL 1DAH EXECUTED OR 1DDH EXECUTED
EMULATION BEGUN

=5EMULATION TERMINATED AT Ø1DAH
```

Examine the state of the processor now.

```
*DISPLAY ALL REGISTERS
B=Ø2H C=Ø1H D=Ø3H E=Ø5H H=Ø2H L=Ø5H F=12H A=Ø5H P=Ø1E7H *=Ø1DAH S=Ø3E8H
```

Perhaps this data should be displayed using symbolic names just to make sure it's what is expected.

```
*DISPLAY REG Q
Ø1H
*DISPLAY REG R
Ø2H
*DISPLAY REG N
Ø5H
*DISPLAY REG K
Ø3H
```

N = 5 has been divided by K = 3, and a quotient Q = 1 has been left in register C. At this point, the program wants to fall through the loop (Q < K). Therefore, the jump sense of the JNC and JNZ instructions must be reversed; they should be replaced with JC and JZ instructions. This will mean that for K ≤ Q, control will stay in the divide loop, which is the desired result.

```
*CHANGE MEMORY 1DAH = ØDAH, ØE7H, Ø1H, ØCAH
```

And once again. . .

```
*GO FROM "
EMULATION BEGUN

=5
1
=$        (MDS switch pressed for interrupt level 4)
PROCESSING ABORTED
EMULATION TERMINATED AT FCAAH
```

Everything appears to work now, although more exhaustive testing may be needed at a later session. Nothing remains now but to save the debugged program and exit gracefully.

```
*SAVE Ø TO 3ØØH
*EXIT
*FFFF
```

4.8 LOGIC STATE ANALYZERS

One class of hardware/software debugging aids is represented by the *logic state analyzer*, an instrument capable of monitoring logical activity at the external terminals of a digital system. No attempt will be made here to expound on the variations available in this class of instrument, but it should be mentioned that they are very powerful system analysis tools which can play an important role in system development and debugging.

Figure 4.8-1 is a photograph of a particular logic analyzer, the Hewlett-Packard 1611A, which offers the capability for disassembling the program stream measured at the address and data busses of an microprocessor. An example of disassembled code can be observed on the screen of the instrument.

Software Aids **237**

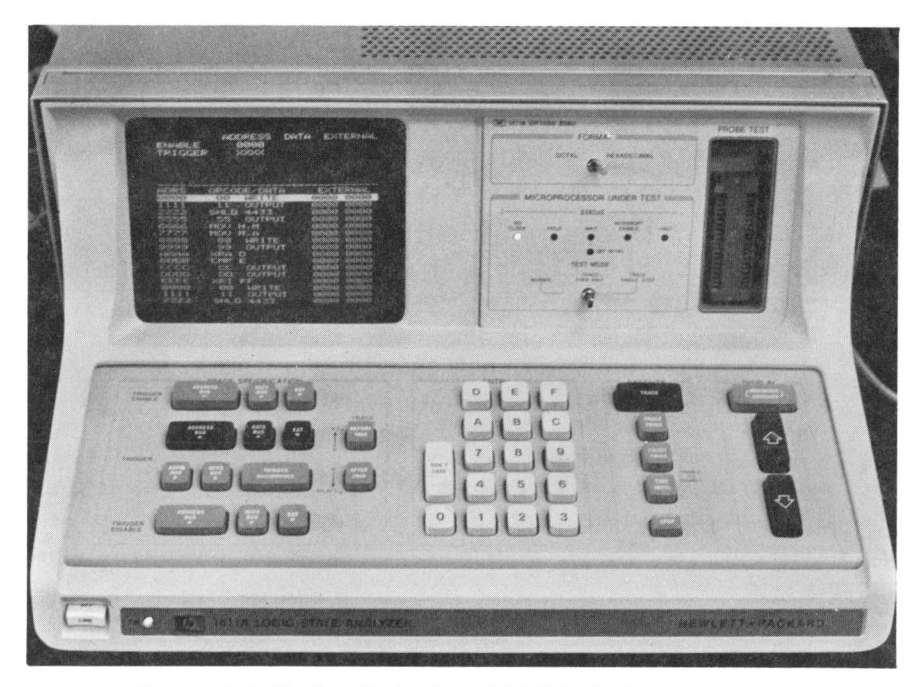

Figure 4.8-1 Hewlett Packard model 1611A logic state analyzer
(note mnemonic program trace on screen)

4.9 PROM PROGRAMMERS

The use of ROMs (read-only memory) and PROMs (programmable read-only memories) became widespread with the use of microcomputer systems having the combined qualities of dedicated use and volatile read/write memory. In dedicated systems it is often possible to use fixed programs which are never modified during the entire system lifetime. Volatile read/write memory is unsuitable for program storage in many systems where operation without program reloading is desired after power-down activity.

In large volume applications, mask-programmed ROMs can be obtained from the manufacturer, but, during system development, field-programmable units are needed for quick turnaround during debugging. Also, the extensive set-up costs associated with mask-programmed ROMs make them unsuitable for low-volume systems. Thus, a system for programming PROMs is an important element of most system development facilities.

Figure 4.9-1 is a photograph of the Intel UPM (Universal PROM Mapper) unit supplied as an accessory to the MDS-800 system. It contains interface circuitry which permits transfer of selected MDS memory contents to a PROM installed in one of the two sockets shown. The ISIS software provided for management of the device includes the following functions:

1. Transferring MDS memory contents to a PROM.
2. Transferring PROM contents to MDS memory for modification, reproduction, or file backup.
3. Comparing PROM contents with MDS contents.
4. Extensively controlling MDS memory format during programming to permit diverse memory arrays (1024 × 8, 512 × 4, 4096 × 1, etc.) to be conveniently programmed.

Adaptation of the UPM unit to different PROM types is accomplished via insertion of so-called "personality modules." These modules are special interface boards which adapt the programmer to various memory types.

4.11 BIBLIOGRAPHY

1. Keith, Ed. "Assembly Language Structured Programming," *Interface Age*, Vol. 2, No. 1, October 1977, pp. 156-158.

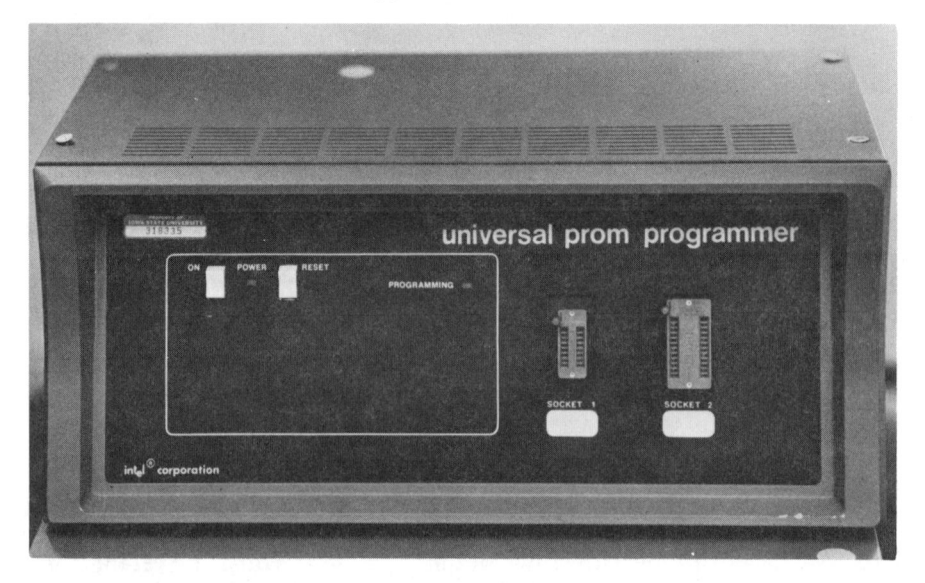

Figure 4.9-1 Intel Universal PROM programmer (UPM)

Software Aids

2. Tanenbaum, Andrew S., *Structured Computer Organization*, Prentice-Hall, Englewood Cliffs, New Jersey, 1976.
3. Stearns, S. K., "Experience with Centralized Maintenance of a Large Application System," *Digest of Papers*, COMPCON 75, February 1975, p. 281.
4. Brantley, C. L., and Osajima, Y. R., "Continuing Development of Centrally Developed and Maintained Software Systems," *Digest of Papers*, COMPCON 75, February 1975, p. 285.
5. *MCS6500 Cross Assembler Manual*, MDS Technology, Inc., August 1975.
6. *M6800 Microprocessor Programming Manual*, Motorola, 1975.
7. *8080/8085 Assembly Language Programming Manual*, Intel Corporation Publication No. 98-301A, 1977.
8. *ISIS-II 8080/8085 Macro Assembler Operator's Manual*, Intel Corporation Publication No. 98-292A, 1977.
9. *ISIS-II System User's Guide*, Intel Corporation Publication No. 98-306 A, 1976.
10. Leach, Geoffrey, C., "Microprocessor Language Design," *DISE Proceedings*, Electrical Engineering Department, University of Pittsburgh, 1976.
11. *PL/M-80 Programming Manual*, Intel Corporation Publication No. 98-268, 1976.
12. Blakeslee, Thomas R., *Digital Design with Standard MSI and LSI*, Wiley, 1975.
13. Rolander, Thomas A., PAS80 Sequential PASCAL Compiler, INSITE User's Group, Ref. No. F13, Intel Corporation.
14. Jensen, Kathleen, and Wurth, Niklaus, *PASCAL USER MANUAL and REPORT*, Springer-Verlag, 1974.
15. *RT-11 System Reference Manual*, Digital Equipment Corporation, DEC-11-ORUGA-C-D, DN1, DN2, January 1976.
16. Mueller, Robert A., and Johnson, Gearold R., "A Generator for Microprocessor Assemblers and Simulators," *Microprocessors: Fundamentals and Applications* (reprinted from June 1976 Proc. IEEE), IEEE Press, 1976, pp. 167-177.
17. *ICE-80 Operator's Manual*, Intel Corportation Publication No. 98-185C, 1976.
18. Kline, Barbara; Maerz, Michael; and Rosenfeld, Paul, "The In-Circuit Approach to the Developement of Microcomputer-Based Products," *Microprocessors: Fundamentals and Applications* (reprinted from June 1976 Proc. IEEE), IEEE Press, 1976.
19. *Universal PROM Mapper Operator's Manual*, Intel Corporation Publication No. 98-236A, 1976.

PROBLEMS

1. Consider the problem of writing a program which is to control the heating and air conditioning system in a home. Develop program hierarchy diagrams (Section 4.2.2) which describe such a program.
2. Repeat 1 for a program designed to implement a tic-tac-toe game.
3. Repeat 1 for a text editor program.
4. Repeat 1 for an assembler program.
5. Does the concept of an *object program* have any validity when one considers an interpretive translator? Explain.
6. Differentiate among the following items: assembler, translator, compiler, interpreter.
7. A microcomputer-based fuel-injection unit is to be designed. Its production cost is estimated to be 20 dollars, half of which is memory cost. Two million units are to be produced, and assembly-language programming yields a potential 10 percent saving in memory cost relative to high-level language programming. Approximately how many man-years of programming effort can be cost-effectively spent to achieve this increase in efficiency?
8. Repeat problem 7 for a home heating/air conditioning controller costing $500, with a manufacturing volume of 1000 units.
9. Modify the program of Section 4.3.3.1 to handle 10-digit decimal numbers.
10. Modify the program of Section 4.3.3.1 so that it *subtracts* rather than adds the two numbers.
11. Consider the program segment (in 6502 assembly language)

    ```
    * = $0200
    * = * + 15
    STUFF        .BYTE        'NONSENSE'
    ```

    (a) Draw a memory map showing the effect of this program segment.
    (b) If LDA STUFF+6 is executed, what will the accumulator contain?
12. Describe the differences between the .BYTE, .WORD, .DWORD, .DBYTE, DS, FCB, and RMB assembler directives.

Software Aids **241**

13. Write an assembler program segment (in 6502 language) which creates a table called PRIME, located in page 3, which contains the first 10 prime numbers.

14. Explain the differences between *macros* and *subroutines*.

15. Consider the example program of Figure 4.3.3.6-1. Verify that the assembler directive on line 12 of this program properly generates the code shown in the listing.

16. In the example program of Figure. 4.3.3.6-1, tabulate all uses of expressions and verify that the code produced is consistent with these expressions.

17. In the example program of Fig. 4.3.3.6-1, how did the programmer get the statement "EXPRESSIONS ALLOWABLE IN 8080 SOURCE TEXT" printed at the top of the listing?

18. In the example program of Figure. 4.3.3.6-1, interpret the information supplied in the cross-reference portion of the listing. Refer to the monitor listing at the end of Appendix B and compare the nature of the cross-reference table in that listing to that of the example.

19. In the example of Figure. 4.3.3.6-1, explain the meaning of the statement on line 9.

20. List the special features an assembler must have if it is to produce relocatable code.

21. Speculate on the operations that the LINK program of Intel's ISIS-II system must perform.

22. Write an 8080 assembly language program which performs the function of the PL/M program of Section 4.3.4.2.

23. Using your solution to 22, calculate the efficiency of the PL/M compiler in this particular case.

24. Why is an assembler or machine-language program listing not provided with the example of Section 4.3.4.3?

5

MICROCOMPUTER INTERFACING AND SYSTEM DESIGN

5.1 INTRODUCTION

A major activity in the process of microcomputer-based "hardware" design is that of establishing the interface between the microcomputer and the other system components. Design of this interface can involve both digital and nondigital considerations. Level-shifting, buffering, bus interconnection, serial-to-parallel conversion, parallel-to-serial conversion, and synchronization are examples of digital interfacing problems. Transducer selection, amplifier design, signal conditioning, analog-to-digital conversion, and digital-to-analog conversion are examples of nondigital interfacing problems.

Interfacing and software development are generally the two most time consuming (and therefore most expensive) aspects of microcomputer-based system design. Chapter 4 discusses the software development process in some detail, and this chapter will give examples of interfacing problems and methods for solving them. This chapter will also discuss the overall problem of system design, which includes software and hardware development.

5.2 GUIDELINES FOR SYSTEM DESIGN

The word "design" implies creative and innovative activity and, like most such efforts, cannot be easily characterized by deterministic rules and procedures. However, even though individual approaches to design may vary widely, it is possible to formulate general guidelines which contribute to cost-effective design. It should be emphasized that the guidelines developed herein apply equally to both *hardware* and *software* development.

5.2.1 Identification of Design Constraints

This activity could also be termed "problem specification." Typical factors to be considered in formulating a detailed problem statement are time, speed, cost, power dissipation, and environmental resistance. Detailed design goals which reflect the priority assigned to each of these factors should be formulated at the outset of the design process. These goals should be periodically reviewed throughout the design period, in order to verify that the priorities and constraints intially established are properly maintained. Such reviews can reveal areas where goals are not being met, and which therefore require additional resources of respecification. Equally important is the determination of areas of "overdesign," reflecting expenditure of resources to achieve results in excess of those required by the problem at hand. A common failing of engineering-dominated projects is the endless process of design improvement well beyond the required level of performance, resulting in costly and behind-schedule system completion.

5.2.2 Use of Top-Down Design Methods

A problem of even moderate complexity requires the system designer to segment it into manageable sections, capable of individual design. In a *top-down* design, this segmentation is rather rigidly ordered, its first step being that of the previous section, i.e., careful problem specification. The next level involves dividing this specification into its major subtasks. Succeeding levels of segmentation divide these subtasks into further simplified subtasks, the process repeating until the entire problem is divided into modules simple enough to be designed and debugged as individual entities. Such low-level modules are capable of being intensively stressed, tested, and perfected, so that their integration into higher-level modules can be achieved with minimum difficulty and maximum reliability.

A "pure" top-down design approach is quite rare. Often the designer, in formulating his problem specification, will be aware of low-level design factors which constrain high higher-level decisions. For example, the characteristics of existing, standardized, low-level hardware and software modules may profoundly influence higher-level decisions.

The experience factor is usually reflected in individual approaches to system design. In a top-down design, the level at which subtasks become "manageable" may be higher for the experienced designer than for the beginner. More often, however, the influence of the experienced designer is manifested by careful attention to details, special cases, marginal testing, and, above all, careful planning of the problem solution.

A final aspect of modular design is that of system "partitioning," which involves choosing modules whose functions are repeated a number of times in the system (or perhaps in many systems). LSI chips, even the microprocessors themselves, derive their existence from clever partitioning decisions which lead to their economically necessary high volume of production. All functions provided by a given LSI unit are seldom used in a single application.

This general idea can sometimes be adapted to design of a particular microcomputer-based system. The hardware layout may contain units of similar function, such that a printed-circuit assembly can be designed to embrace all occurrences of such similarity. Likewise, a software module, such as a subroutine, may be "generalized" by modest extension of its capability, thereby making it useful in more than one system role. The designer should always be aware of the danger that this attempt at economy may backfire, since the increased complexity of extended software modules carries with it the potential hazard of lack of debugging and diagnostic simplicity.

5.2.3 Awareness of Hardware/Software Tradeoffs

A common failing among microcomputer systems designers is an inability to recognize that the characteristics that contribute to good hardware design correspond closely to those characteristics that contribute to good software design.

One of the foremost principles in systems design is to recognize that both hardware and software should be done in *modular* form. For example, in the design of hardware it is foolish to design one large circuit which either works or does not work. Hardware, whether in modular form or not, will very likely break down sometime during its lifetime. A large complex circuit, if not modular, is almost impossible to debug. Thus, any circuit should be capable of being isolated into component modules either by means of modifying jumper connections, or by removing a few integrated circuits. Test signals can then be applied and expected results can be measured for the isolated module, and its integrity thereby verified.

Essentially the same modular approach should be taken in software design. Software should be written in small segments (subroutines or procedures), which can be individually tested. As in hardware design, isolation of software modules may be used to detect bugs which are frequently present even after the system has been committed to production. Software modularity is a basic element in top-down design. As an added benefit, it permits software design tasks to be parcelled out to a number of programmers to achieve rapid development when appropriate.

The term *firmware* is used in microcomputer design to describe software which has been permanently stored in ROM (read-only memory). During the debugging phase it is common to store programs in RWM where they can be executed, tested, and modified if necessary. At some point in the systems development cycle this code will have been extensively tested and debugged until it performs properly and without error, or at least without error detectable by tests performed up to that point. At this point it may be committed to a ROM implementation, making the transition from software to firmware.

Another aspect of microcomputer system design is the consideration of tradeoffs between hardware and software. This means that a given function can often be implemented in either a hardware connection of parts, and little or no software, or software with little or no special hardware. With decreasing cost of very sophisticated integrated circuits as well as larger memories, the choice in a particular case may not be obvious. Some examples of such tradeoffs are:

1. Pulse generation
    a. Hardware: A large variety of monostable multivibrators are found in all logic families. In TTL the old reliables 74121, 74122, and 74123 may be used while in CMOS 14528, 14538 and others may be used. Such circuits can be used to either stretch or shorten pulse widths.
    b. Software: One bit of one port can be used, with the attendant software to provide a pulse for a known duration (see Example 3.7.2-3).
    c. Typical tradeoff considerations are: How wide must a pulse be? If it must be 20 nanoseconds wide an MOS processor is just too slow. How accurate must it be? If extreme accuracy is required, the software solution uses a crystal oscillator time base, and hence is extremely accurate. If there are no available I/O pins without adding another I/O chip then the hardware solution looks best. Would it be desirable to have a pulse width which could be varied depending upon certain conditions? In other words, for one set of conditions a very

short pulse is generated, while for another set a very long pulse is generated.
   2. Flip-Flops and Latches
      a. Hardware: In TTL we find a number of 1, 2, 4, 6, and 8 bit devices, including reset-set, JK, D, T, latches, addressable latches, register files, etc. Similar components are readily available in other logic families.
      b. Software: The design examples in Chapters 3 and 4 demonstrate our ability to set or clear any bit in any location in RWM. This can, of course, be done conditionally, i.e., reset-set with several conditions ANDed together.
      c. Some of the tradeoffs here are speed, available RWM, and insertion cost of another IC.
   3. Decoders
      a. Hardware: Hardware decoders can decode BCD to seven-segment, one-of-ten, one-of-sixteen, Baudot to ASCII, etc.
      b. Software: All decoding may be computed, if indeed there is a conversion algorithm, or by look-up table in either ROM or RWM.
      c. Tradeoffs most likely to affect this choice are speed, size, standard patterns available or need for dynamic modification.

Some other candidates for tradeoffs are serial-parallel conversion, counting events, speed conversions where buffer storage is required, and any operations involving arithmetic or logic operations. As a specific case, a single EOR #$FF is identically equal to $1 1/3$ 7404 TTL integrated circuits if 8-bit complementation is the desired function.

Many tradeoffs between hardware and software reduce to a choice between external hardware and ROM for program storage. Since either choice requires integrated circuits, the best one is often not obvious. In many cases there is little to choose and either choice is satisfactory. A typical factor that must be taken into account is that, in the latter phases of a project, adding five more bytes of code, rather than a separate decoder chip, might require an additional ROM, making the decoder the obvious choice. This choice, however, is perhaps not as obvious as it may seem at first glance, since future product enhancements may require additional code in upgraded systems.

5.2.4 Limiting-Case Testing

As discussed in Section 5.2.2, the influence of the experienced designer is often reflected in attention to extensive testing of hardware and software. It is traumatic indeed to see one's prototype unit, whose successful operation has been achieved through many hours of intense work, subjected to low temperature, high temperature, shock, vibration, salt-spray, and other stress tests. Without adequate tests and redesign to correct for failure, however, it is extremely likely that the product under design will be at best a marginal performer, and at worst a totally unsatisfactory performer.

Software must also be stress-tested as completely as possible. Clock speed-up, high interrupt-request rates, million-fold subroutine repetition, and testing of marginal I/O timing situations represent software tests of this type. All possible parameter values, however unlikely, must be examined for possible deleterious system performance.

As an example, one of the authors recently was asked to test the performance of a system which, among other things, prompted the user to state (via keyboard) the interval (in seconds) he wished to specify between system report on temperature conditions in a home. If the response "0" were typed, representing an unrealistic but *possible* parameter value, the system software became inoperative. The programmer must be alert to the possibility of such nonsense actions by system users.

5.2.5 Matching Available Skills to the Problem

The approach taken in a particular design situation may be strongly influenced by the background skills of the designers. An engineer skilled in electronics design but new to the computer field will take a different approach than one whose expertise is in programming rather than in electronics.

The educational benefits derived from experience in microcomputer-based design should not be overlooked. While a microcomputer-based design executed by inexperienced personnel may not appear cost-effective in some cases, the invaluable experience gained by those participating in the design may represent a significant return in terms of future products. Thus, the company who chooses to "farm out" its microcomputer development to consultants rather than suffer with the inexperience of its own design personnel may find this a short-sighted approach.

5.2.6 Choosing Levels of Implementation

Almost every microcomputer systems design project manager must at some point face squarely up to the problem of deciding whether to build or buy. This decision may exist at several levels, including that of the microcomputer itself. Options here include the following:

1. Roll-your-own
2. Board System Kits
3. Prefabricated Board System
4. Development Microcomputer Kits
5. Prefabricated Microcomputer Development System

Although these five choices may seem fairly clear-cut, there are shades of grey between them. The decision between these levels of implementation, in terms of build or buy, will typically rest upon the volume of the resulting product. High volume applications, or specific design configurations, may dictate building, from scratch, a microcomputer to accomplish the desired function. Medium volume production, perhaps even 50 or more units, might still be best done using a prefabricated board system as a base.

The development microcomputer may be used to do many different things. It would not be too far-fetched to include the KIM, for example, under the category of primitive development system. With added memory, it will control a set of peripherals to do all of those items discussed in Chapter 4, including editing and assembly. In another role, such a development microcomputer may become an integral part of the system being designed. It is reasonable to estimate that, by virtue of sheer volume, if enough development microcomputers of a particular type are made, the price may go down to the point where that particular microcomputer might become an integral part of a business computer system. This has certainly been true in the case of minicomputer systems.

5.2.7 Inclusion of Diagnostic Techniques

One should never be so naive as to think that every unit of a given product will function perfectly from the time it is manufactured, until the time it reaches obsolesence. The predelivery diagnostic phase expense is one which must be borne by the manufacturer, and he passes it on to the consumer. The cost of maintenance, on the other hand, is one which must be ultimately borne by the purchaser. This represents an indirect cost which is often hidden, and as a result often overlooked by a person looking for a "best buy." It nonetheless can represent a significant cost over the lifetime of that product and should be considered. The sum of initial cost and maintenance is best described as "cost of ownership."

A person familiar with doing electronic hardware troubleshooting and diagnostic analysis will almost reflexively reach for a signal generator which will provide a repetitive input so that a repetitive, presumably known or calculable, result can be checked. The same concept applies to using software. Let us take for an example the attachment of a printer to a microcomputer. A good programmer will have written the software which drives this printer as a subroutine. The troubleshooter can thus write a short calling program which will repetitively load the print area, which holds a pattern to be printed, with a test pattern, and then call the print subroutines. This has the same general effect as repetitively exercising electronic equipment. In a sense this could be referred to as software waveform generation.

In the process of troubleshooting a system it is very important to select from the set of peripherals, in a rank order, those items which can themselves be used in troubleshooting. For example, in our example above, once the printer works, we can write a program which scans a keyboard and then prints keyboard values on the printer. This ensures that both the keyboard and its associated software and the printer and its associated software work correctly. Once these two devices work, we could continue to verify that an attached analog-to-digital converter also works correctly. One of the fortunate capabilities of the microprocessor-based system is the ability to exchange, by means of toggle switches, selected ROM chips. An alternative, of course, is to have all ICs socketed, and merely unplug the set of production ROMs and insert a set of diagnostic ROMs. Attention to this sort of diagnostic capability often tends to be overlooked in the development of the microcomputer-based system, and a typical beginner often feels that it is only necessary during the system design phase. As a result, a good diagnostic system is often not provided in the finished product.

5.2.8 Concern for System Maintainability

Development of a system maintenance concept should be an integral part of system design. Fortunately the concepts of modular design and concern for diagnostic capability lend support to this area. Test points, diagnostic software routines, simulated data patterns, switch-selectable self-testing modes, etc., are features which represent marginal cost if considered at design time. Adding such features "after the fact" would be extremely expensive if not impossible.

Many microcomputer-based products will be used in environments (home, automobile, office, etc.) where skilled maintenance personnel will be unavailable. Thus a comprehensive maintenance philosophy is absolutely necessary in many cases. Factors to consider in such a philosophy include module replacement, designation of throwaway and repairable units, provision for warranty and maintenance contracts, and establishment of repair/service centers.

5.3 MISCELLANEOUS ADVICE ON SYSTEM DESIGN

The previous section details guidelines which apply to the majority of design situations. This section will address a few additional areas of concern to the system designer.

5.3.1 System Interconnection

The designer should realize the special role of system interconnection methods in determining system reliability. Faulty connectors, corrosion-prone printed-circuit contacts, faulty printed-circuit plating, and similar problems account for the majority of system reliability difficulties.

5.3.2 Choice of LSI Components

Even though the system designer has a virtually unlimited set of choices in the component area, there are a number of common-sense factors he should consider to limit the field to some extent.

First, he should look beyond the detailed performance characteristics of a particular microprocessor or peripheral chip. While these characteristics may occasionally dictate a choice, such factors as available software support, quick availability, industry acceptance, and other manufacturer-related considerations are often of predominant importance. This does not necessarily mean that the largest manufacturer should always be chosen. Indeed, the low-volume user sometimes obtains better support from smaller suppliers. The point is, marketing factors are often of more importance than technical characteristics.

A related factor is that of multiple-sourcing. Most manufacturers will not consider the use of a microcomputer component unless it is available from at least two independent sources. This constraint exists partially, of course, because of the lower costs which result from competitive production. Of equal or greater importance, however, is the reluctance to commit development of a product whose critical components may become unavailable if a single supplier elects or is forced to terminate their manufacture.

At the product design level, the designer should not let the high cost of a newly-introduced component deter him from using it. Production often lags design by 1 to 2 years, and recent history has shown that circuit cost often drops 5 or 10 times over such an interval. The I8080 or the M6800, for example, cost $360 when introduced, and now cost 10 to 20 dollars. New units which contribute to enhanced system performance can be expected to achieve similar cost levels, since this performance enhancement will lead to their use in high volume.

5.3.3 Getting Started in Microcomputer-Based Design

For those who are just becoming acquainted with microprocessors and microcomputers, there is a cardinal rule, viz., *redo an old system design if at all possible*. It is helpful in learning new concepts to attempt to develop one new skill at a time. If, for example, our design involves a system for controlling or sensing peripheral devices, previous experience in using these devices will make the designer aware of their characteristics and idiosyncracies. He may thus be capable of recognizing system problems which he might otherwise mistakenly attribute to his lack of digital systems background.

This philosophy of taking one step at a time has been found to be a very effective design process. After the original design is complete and the initial prototype implementation has been put together, the trial software should be run from RWM, implementing one new feature at a time, if at all possible. In other words, begin with a basic design as stripped down as it is possible to get, and progressively modify the software to add one new feature at a time. In some cases many of the subroutines can be simply modified so that they do little or nothing except ultimately accomplish a return from subroutine, perhaps returning the value 0 or the value $FF, anything to indicate that it did get called and did return to the main program. There are certainly situations in which this will not work, but if it is at all possible, it allows solving one new problem at a time rather than many problems in parallel.

5.4 INTERFACING EXAMPLES

5.4.1 Interfacing to the Teletype*

A widely used piece of peripheral equipment in microcomputer systems design projects is the Teletype. It has been said that the Tele-

---
*Trademark of Teletype Corporation

Microcomputer Interfacing and System Design 253

type has three important characteristics: it is cheap, it is cheap and it is cheap. It is for this reason that almost every development lab has one or more Teletypes readily available. The Teletype can be considered in very elementary fashion as a mechanical encoding and decoding matrix having serial-to-parallel and parallel-to-serial conversion capability. The Teletype comes in many models, with many variations referred to by the manufacturer as options.

One of the most common peices of Teletype equipment is called the Model 33ASR (Figure 5.4.1-1), where ASR stands for Automatic Send Receive. This piece of equipment has a keyboard for data entry, a printer to produce hard copy, a paper tape reader, and a paper tape punch. These options are modular, and may therefore not be present in all Teletypes. Figures 5.4.1-2 enumerates the principal Teletype functions. One of the characteristics observed in item c is that the transmitter and the receiver must run at the same rotational rate. This is accomplished by driving both the transmitter and the receiver with synchronous motors that are excited from the 60 Hz line. Figure 5.4.1-3 shows a typical transmission pattern for transmitting information between two Teletype-compatible units. The 8 data bits following the start bit could be encoded in a variety of ways, but standard contemporary units use the American Standard Code for Information Inter-

Figure 5.4.1-1 Model 33ASR Teletype

TELETYPE INTRODUCTION — (Model 33)

FUNCTIONS:
a. EACH KEY MECHANICALLY ENCODED. 128 CHARACTERS = 7 BITS PLUS 1 PARITY BIT (OPTIONAL).
b. CODE APPLIED TO INSULATED SECTORS OF TRANSMITTING DISTRIBUTOR (TD) WHICH IS RELEASED TO MAKE ONE ROTATION. A BRUSH MAKES CONTACT WITH EACH SECTOR, WHICH ALLOWS CURRENT TO BE APPLIED TO THE LINE. ELEVEN BITS ARE SENT.
c. AT THE RECEIVER A CURRENT DROP BELOW THRESHHOLD ALLOWS ONE REVOLUTION AT SAME RPM AS THE TRANSMITTER.
d. CURRENT IN EACH TIME SLOT AT RECEIVER ACTIVATES THE SELECTOR MAGNET DRIVER (SMD) WHICH SETS CODE BARS CORRESPONDING TO TRANSMITTED CHARACTER.

Figure 5.4.1-2 Teletype functions

A serial character (Typical of an ASCII character)

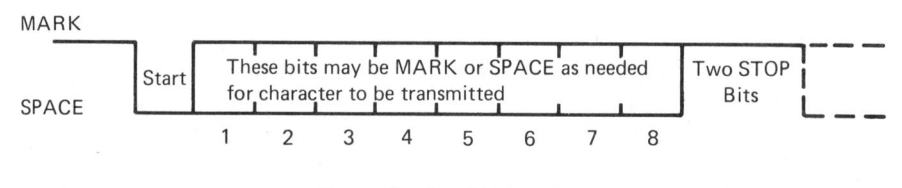

MARK

SPACE

| Start | These bits may be MARK or SPACE as needed for character to be transmitted | Two STOP Bits |

1 2 3 4 5 6 7 8

One cycle of an 11-bit code

Figure 5.4.1-3 Typical Teletype serial data transmission

change, ASCII. Table 5.4.1-1 contains the ASCII encoding definitions. As an example, the letter Capital A is found to be hexadecimal $41, while the numeral 1 is $31. The definitions of SOH, EOT, etc. are given in Table 5.4.1-2. This table also tells how to generate these Control codes on a model 33 or 35 Teletype. For example, to generate ESC, or Escape, one should simultaneously depress the Shift, Control, and K keys.

The serial data transmission represented by Figure 5.4.1-3 is of great importance. It represents the basic concept used in many systems for which asynchronous serial data transmission is required. The line condition between transmitter and receiver is normally held (not trans-

Microcomputer Interfacing and System Design

TABLE 5.4.1-1 UNITED STATES OF AMERICA STANDARD CODE FOR INFORMATION INTERCHANGE

Bits $b_7 b_6 b_5$					0 0 0	0 0 1	0 1 0	0 1 1	1 0 0	1 0 1	1 1 0	1 1 1
$b_4 b_3 b_2 b_1$				Column / Row	0	1	2	3	4	5	6	7
0	0	0	0	0	NUL	DLE	SP	0	@	P		p
0	0	0	1	1	SOH	DC1	!	1	A	Q	a	q
0	0	1	0	2	STX	DC2	"	2	B	R	b	r
0	0	1	1	3	ETX	DC3	#	3	C	S	c	s
0	1	0	0	4	EOT	DC4	$	4	D	T	d	t
0	1	0	1	5	ENQ	NAK	%	5	E	U	e	u
0	1	1	0	6	ACK	SYN	&	6	F	V	f	v
0	1	1	1	7	BEL	ETB	'	7	G	W	g	w
1	0	0	0	8	BS	CAN	(	8	H	X	h	x
1	0	0	1	9	HT	EM	)	9	I	Y	i	y
1	0	1	0	10	LF	SUB	*	:	J	Z	j	z
1	0	1	1	11	VT	ESC	+	;	K	[	k	{
1	1	0	0	12	FF	FS	,	<	L	\	l	¦
1	1	0	1	13	CR	GS	-	=	M	]	m	}
1	1	1	0	14	SO	RS	.	>	N	^	n	~
1	1	1	1	15	SI	US	/	?	O	_	o	DEL

mitting) in the closed-circuit condition. This choice is made so that if the transmission path is broken, an immediately detectable open circuit would result. This closed-circuit condition is normally referred to as the *Marking* condition. A logic-zero definition for Mark is often used. An important event in the asynchronous-serial data transmission system is the Mark to Space (open-circuit) transition, followed by a stable spacing condition for one well-defined time interval. This is referred to as the *Start bit* time. The 8 bits following the Start bit represent the encoded information, as stated earlier, typically encoded in ASCII, least significant bit first. These 9 bits, Start plus data, are usually followed by two time intervals in which the mark condition is guaranteed to exist. Other transmission equipment using this same general format may

TABLE 5.4.1-2 USASCII CONTROL CODE IDENTIFICATION AND GENERATION[1]

Code	Identity	Generation[2]		
		S	C	L
ACK	Acknowledge		*	F
BEL	Bell		*	G
BS	Backspace		*	H
CAN	Cancel		*	X
CR	Carriage Return		*	M
DC_1	Device Control		*	Q
DC_2	Device Control		*	R
DC_3	Device Control		*	S
DC_4	Device Control (Stop)		*	T
DEL	Delete		Rub-Out	
DLE	Data Link Escape		*	P
EM	End of Medium		*	Y
ENQ	Enquiry		*	E
EOT	End of Transmission		*	D
ESC	Escape	*	*	K
ETB	End of Transmission Block		*	W
ETX	End of Text		*	C
FF	Form Feed		*	L
FS	File Separator	*	*	L
GS	Group Separator	*	*	M
HT	Horizontal Tab		*	I
LF	Line Feed		*	J
NAK	Negative Acknowledge		*	U
NUL	Null	*	*	P
RS	Record Separator	*	*	N
SI	Shift In		*	O
SO	Shift Out		*	N
SOH	Start of Heading		*	A
STX	Start of Text		*	B
SUB	Substitute		*	Z

Microcomputer Interfacing and System Design 257

SYN	Synchronous Idle		*	V
US	Unit Separator	*	*	O
VT	Vertical Tab		*	K

(1) These control codes are presently generated and interpreted by Models 33 and 35 Teletype equipment.

(2) Control character generation, in most cases, is performed by simultaneously depressing the Control (C) key and the appropriate letter (L) key; the Shift (S) key must be depressed in addition to the control and letter keys where specified. Separate keys are also provided for Carriage Return, Escape, and Line Feed codes.

---

use only one stop bit, and some use 1.5 stop bits. A very clever feature of this asynchronous transmission concept lies in the capability for a receiver to draw into synchronism with a transmitter, even if the receiver comes on line in the middle of a transmission sequence. The concept is that the receiver will, upon sensing space transition, delay for roughly 1.5 time intervals, or until the center of the first data bit, sample the 8 mark or space time intervals containing data, and then wait for *less* than the remaining 2.5 time intervals. After this time out period, i.e., the two stop bits, the receiver will again start to look for a mark to space transition. In other words the receiver looks for a mark to space transition, will strobe the 8 individual time intervals, wait for approximately 1.5 mark intervals, and then begin again, looking for the mark-to-space transition. In the worst case the receiver should draw into synchronism within a space of no more than 11 characters. In the case of the Teletype it is within the two-stop interval that the character is imprinted on the paper. If the line were continually open a receiving Teletype would just chatter away, or "run open," assuming that a mark-to-space condition just took place.

Figure 5.4.1-4 shows examples of specific ASCII encoded data, including Carriage Return (CR), A, 5 and Sync, (SYN). Note that the least significant bit is transmitted first, right after the Start bit.

An annoying characteristic of the Teletype is that it cannot mechanically return from the right hand edge of the page back to the left hand edge during one 11-bit time interval period. A Teletype running at 100 words per minute (WPM) requires that the carriage

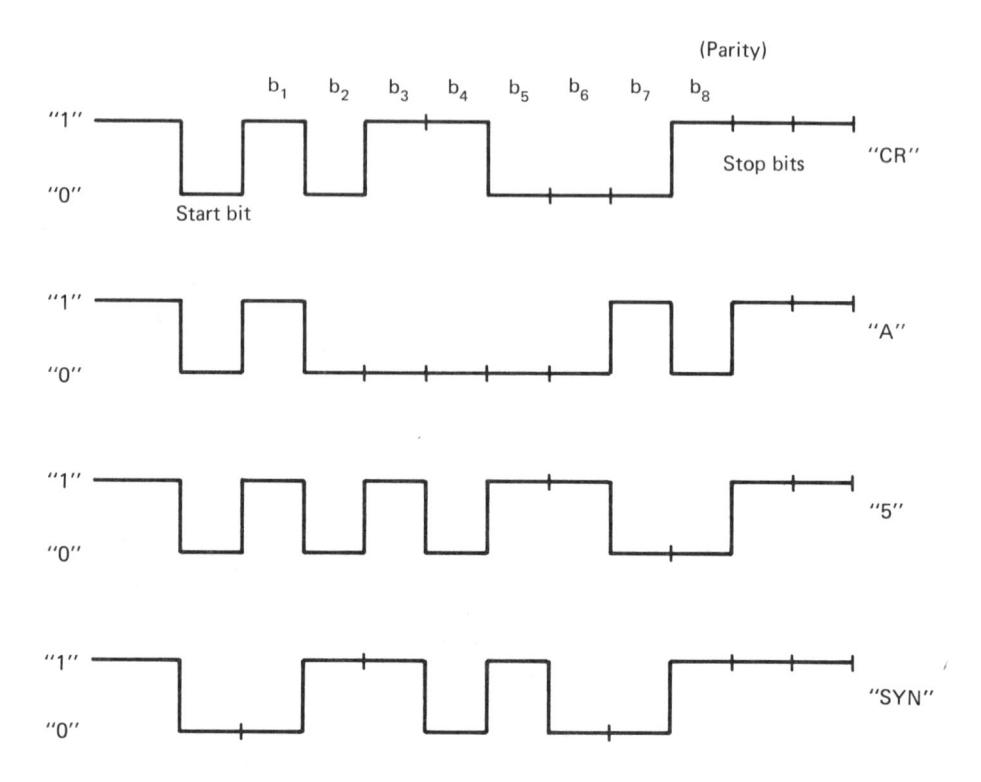

Figure 5.4.1-4 Specific serial data streams using ASCII (even parity, 11 bit code)

return must take place in less than 100 milliseconds, or one-tenth of a second, which it cannot do. Other Teletype-like devices running at 100 WPM have been fabricated which do not require this mechanical retrace, and for them this problem is not important. Figure 5.4.1-5 shows some typical rates for Teletype operation. Probably the most widely used rate is that of an 11-bit code, like that demonstrated in Figure 5.4.1-5 running at 100 WPM. Thinking of this in microprocessor terms each character will require 100,000 microseconds for its transmission. For many microprocessors, an instruction can be executed in roughly 4 microseconds; therefore, during the transmission of one character, the microprocessor is capable of carrying out 25,000 instructions.

Figure 5.4.1-6 shows a symbolic electrical connection between two Teletypes. As described in Figure. 5.4.1-6 the parallel-to-serial conversion is done by the Transmitting Distributor (TD) while the reverse serial-to-parallel conversion is done by the Selector Magnet and Selector Cam assembly represented by the solenoid coil labeled RD.

Microcomputer Interfacing and System Design

TIMING

FOR AN 11 BIT CODE:			
WORDS/MIN.	CHAR./SEC.	BITS/SEC.	MS/BIT
100	10	110	9.091
*150	15	165	6.061
FOR A 10 BIT CODE:			
150	15	150	6.67
300	30	300	3.33

* Seldom used

Figure 5.4.1-5 Typical Teletype times

ELECTRICAL

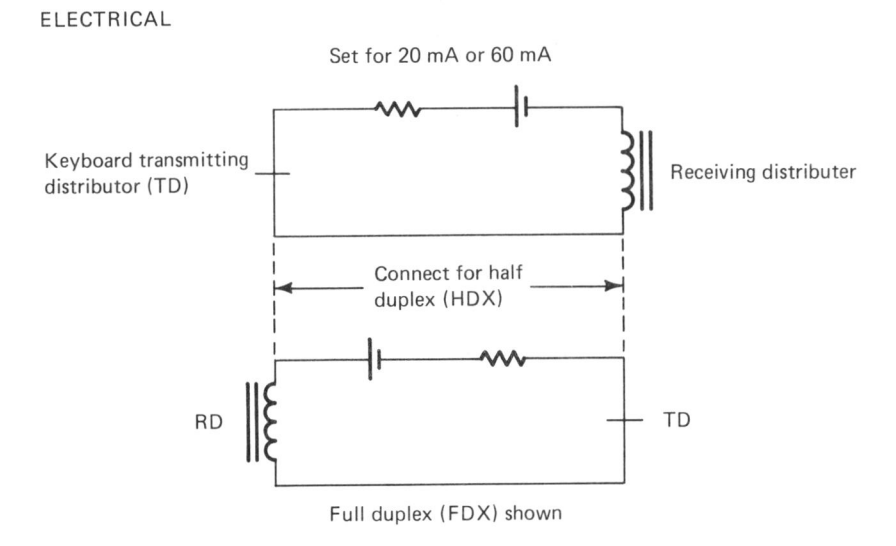

Figure 5.4.1-6 Symbolic electrical connection

When a key is pressed a mechanical encoding to 8 bits is done by a complex apparatus below the keyboard. This byte is transmitted as current levels to sectors of the TD. In a well-adjusted Teletype the mechanical sector contacts are made before the TD is allowed to begin rotating. By this means a serialized, encoded, character is placed on the output line. The receiver, when a space condition is detected, begins rotation, and in each of the 8 time intervals will throw the appropriate "code bar" if a mark condition exists in that time interval. During the stop bits interval the "type box" or "print wheel" is positioned as determined by the code bars and driven forward onto the ribbon and then the paper.

In Figure 5.4.1-6, each Teletype is characterized as having a TD and an RD. Two separate loops can be provided so that while one keyboard talks to the printer at the other end, simultaneously, the keyboard at the other end may talk to the local printer, representing a *full duplex* connection, in which each unit can be transmitting simultaneously and independently to the printer at the opposite end. The mark condition will generally be denoted by current flowing through a closed loop. Typical currents are 20 milliamperes and 60 milliamperes. Most Teletypes allow either current option to be selected by internal wiring jumpers. An alternative connection is shown by the dotted lines in Figure 5.4.1-6, which simply connects both TDs and both RDs in series, and requires only one current loop. This connection is called the half duplex connection and either keyboard, when struck, will type the same character at both ends, unless both ends are inadvertently simultaneously keyed. Most microcomputer interconnections utilize a full duplex connection. When the keyboard is struck a character is received by the computer, which in turn retransmits it back to the printer RD. This provides what is called an echo check, to provide a check that the computer is receiving and retransmitting the correct value. It is a very fundamental type of error check.

Not all Teletypes are of the 11-bit code variety. A large number of very reliable older machine use a 5-level code. This 5-level code is called *Baudot* code. Table 5.4.1-3 gives the Baudot encoding scheme.

5.4.2 RS-232 Interface Standards

The Electric Industries Association (EIA) has defined a widely used interface standard known as the RS232 standard. This standard has undergone two revisions and is now known as RS232C. It is very important to understand exactly what this definition applies to and, by exclusion, what is does *not* apply to. The RS232C standard is applicable specifically to the interconnection of Data Terminal Equipment (DTE), and Data Communications Equipment (DCE), which exchange serial binary data. This interconnection would apply to the connection between a data terminal, as many microcomputer output ports and

Microcomputer Interfacing and System Design **261**

TABLE 5.4.1-3 BAUDOT CODE (CCITT #2)

LETTER SHIFT	FIGURE SHIFT	BAUDOT ENCODING
A	-	11000
B	?	10011
C	:	01110
D	$	10010
E	3	10000
F	!	10110
G	&	01011
H	#	00101
I	8	01100
J	'	11010 *
K	(	11110
L	)	01001
M	.	00111
N	,	00110
O	9	00011
P	0	01101
Q	1	11101
R	4	01010
S	BELL	10100 *
T	5	00001
U	7	11100
V	;	01111
W	2	11001
X	/	10111
Y	6	10101
Z	"	10001
LETTER SHIFT		11111
FIGURE SHIFT		11011
SPACE		00100
CARRIAGE RET.		00010
LINE FEED		01000

The *one* in the chart indicates that a current pulse (MARK) is generated in that position in the code. A *zero* indicates no current (SPACE). Twenty-six letters + 15 characters + 10 numbers + 6 control characters = 57 characters are possible.

* Variations are possible.

input ports might be, and modulator-demodulator, or *modem* units. Many of these definitions are useful for connections between two pieces of DTE or other compatible equipment, but the definition for RS232C applies only to that between DTE and DCE for serial binary data, below a data rate of 20,000 per second.

The RS232 standard applies to the following items:

1. Electrical signal characteristics - The definitions for the electrical characteristics of the interchange signals and the associated circuitry.
2. Interface mechanical characteristics - The definition of a 25-pin connector between these two interconnected devices (see Figure 5.4.2-1).
3. Functional description of interchange circuits - The specific description of the data timing and control circuits for use at this interface.
4. Standard interfaces for selected communications systems configurations.

The RS232C standard includes 13 specific interface configurations intended to meet the needs of 15 defined system applications. These configurations are identified and labeled with alphabetic characters A through M. There is an addition, a type Z, which has been left for undefined usage for cases which have not been covered, i.e., "none of the above." Figure 5.4.2-2 details these definitions.

Figure 5.4.2-1 RS 232 connector

Data Transmission Configuration	Interface Type
Transmit Only	A
Transmit Only*	B
Receive Only	C
Half Duplex	D
Duplex*	D
Duplex	E
Primary Channel Transmit Only*/Secondary Channel Receive Only	F
Primary Channel Transmit Only/Secondary Channel Receive Only	H
Primary Channel Receive Only/Secondary Channel Transmit Only*	G
Primary Channel Receive Only/Secondary Channel Transmit Only	I
Primary Channel Transmit Only*/Half Duplex Secondary Channel	J
Prinmary Channel Receive Only/Half Duplex Secondary Channel	K
Half Duplex Primary Channel/Half Duplex Secondary Channel	L
Duplex Primary Channel*/Duplex Secondary Channel*	L
Duplex Primary Channel/Duplex Secondary Channel	M
Special (Circuits specified by Supplier)	Z

NOTE: Data Transmission Configurations identified with an asterisk (*) indicate the inclusion of Circuit CA (Request to Send) in a One Way Only (Transmit) or Duplex Configuration where it might ordinarily not be expected, but where it might be used to indicate a non-transmit mode to the data communication equipment to permit it to remove a line signal or to send synchronizing or training signals as required.

Figure 5.4.2-2 Interface types for data transmission configurations

The RC232C standard applies only to those systems which have signaling rates in the range from 0 to 20,000 bits per second. It is applicable only to electronic equipment which has a single ground that can be connected at the interface, i.e., it does *not* apply to circuits in which electrical isolation between equipment on opposite sides of the interface is required. It applies to both synchronous and asynchronous serial binary data communications.

In its most elementary form this standard applies to interconnecting a transmitter and a receiver via two wires, and pertains to the voltage and current and impedance of these devices at that connection. It guarantees short circuit protection.

The transmitter or receiver must be capable of withstanding any input signal of 25 volts or less.

A signal is defined as being in the marking condition when the voltage at the interface is more negative than -3 volts with respect to ground and to be in the spacing condition when the voltage is more positive than 3 volts with respect to ground. The area between -3 volts and $+3$ volts is defined as the transition region, i.e., there is no definition at 0 volts, unlike TTL. This standard also uses a negative logic definition. In other words, the marking condition, -3 volts, is defined as a logic one. The spacing condition, greater than $+3$ volts, is defined as a logic zero.

The receiver is to have a DC input resistance of not less than 3,000 ohms or more than 7,000 ohms. The shunt capacitance at the receiver must not exceed 2,500 picofarads. The reactive component of the load must not be inductive. The open circuit receiver voltage must not exceed 2 volts and the source impedance of the transmitter must not be less than 300 ohms.

The following five conditions are required of all signals, data, control and timing at the interface between the modem and DCE.

1. All interchange signals entering into the transition region shall proceed through the transition region to the opposite signal state and not reenter the transition region until the next significant change of signal condition.
2. The signals must not reverse their direction of change while in the transition region.
3. For control signals the time for the signal to pass through the transition region must be less than 1 millisecond.
4. For data and timing signals the time required for the signal to pass through the transition region must not exceed 1 milli-

Microcomputer Interfacing and System Design **265**

second or 4% of the nominal duration of a signal element in that interchange circuit, whichever is less.
5. The maximum instantaneous rate of voltage change shall not exceed 30 volts per microsecond.

Among the things specifically called out in the RS232C standard are the pin definitions for the interconnecting cable between the DTE and the DCE, with the specific function on each pin. By common usage a particular 25 pin connector has come to be called the 232C connector. (See Figure 5.4.2-1.) The intention is, of course, to provide a connector which is universal in nature which the separate manufacturers of each piece of such equipment can always interconnect. Figure 5.4.2-3 defines the 25 pins giving their specific usages. Figure 5.4.2-4 uses those letter definitions of Figure 5.4.2-2 to indicate which of the pins are active for each of the configurations defined.

5.4.3 RS334 and IEEE 488 Interface Standards

Another interface standard in wide usage is the RS334 standard which applies to signal quality between the same DTE and DCE defined by RS232. Many other standards will undoubtedly evolve and be of importance to the microcomputer designer as time goes on. These standards are of considerable importance and may be generated by people other than EIA. One of potential importance is an IEEE standard called the IEEE Standard 488, also called the Hewlett-Packard Interface Bus (HPIB). This standard applies to byte-serial, bit-parallel, data transmission among instruments, terminals, and data processing equipment. It has limited use in data communications but is intended for defining the interface over bus-interconnected data-handling equipment. An important application area of microcomputers is likely to be process control, in which one microcomputer senses and controls several pieces of equipment, DVMs, motors, power supplies, etc. Bus interconnection of such systems is very likely to be used, and the IEEE 488 standard may be helpful in accommodating equipment from several manufacturers in one integrated system. Figure 5.4.3-1 shows an IEEE 488 interface connector provided with the Commodore PET 2001 microcomputer system as a peripheral interface.

5.4.4 Transportability of Programs and Data

A recurrent problem in microcomputer-based system design is the general one of carrying programs and/or data from one computer to

Pin Number	Circuit Symbol	Description
1	AA	Protective Ground
2	BA	Transmitted Data
3	BB	Received Data
4	CA	Request to Send
5	CB	Clear to Send
6	CC	Data Set Ready
7	AB	Signal Ground (Common Return)
8	CF	Received Line Signal Detector
9	—	(Reserved for Data Set Testing)
10	—	(Reserved for Data Set Testing)
11		Unassigned
12	SCF	Secondary Received Line Signal Detector
13	SCB	Secondary Clear to Send
14	SBA	Secondary Transmitted Data
15	DB	Transmission Signal Element Timing (DCE Source)
16	SBB	Secondary Received Data
17	DD	Receiver Signal Element Timing (DCE Source)
18		Unassigned
19	SCA	Secondary Request to Send
20	CD	Data Terminal Ready
21	CG	Signal Quality Detector
22	CD	Ring Indicator
23	CH/CI	Data Signal Rate Selector (DTE/DCE Source)
24	DA	Transmit Signal Element Timing (DTE Source)
25		Unassigned

Figure 5.4.2-3 RS232C interface connector pin assignments

Interchange Circuit		A	B	C	D	E	F	G	H	I	J	K	L	M	Z
AA	Protective Ground	–	–	–	–	–	–	–	–	–	–	–	–	–	–
AB	Signal Ground	X	X	X	X	X	X	X	X	X	X	X	X	X	X
BA	Transmitted Data	X	X			X	X	X		X	X		X	X	o
BB	Received Data			X	X	X	X		X		X		X	X	o
CA	Request to Send		X	X	X	X	X	X	X	X	X	X	X	X	o
CB	Clear to Send	X	X	X	X	X	X	X	X	X	X	X	X	X	o
CC	Data Set Ready	X	X	S	S	S	S	S	S	S	S	S	S	S	o
CD	Data Terminal Ready	S	S			S	S	S	S	S	S	S	S	S	o
CE	Ring Indicator	S	S			S	S	S	S	S	S	S	S	S	o
CF	Received Line Signal Detector			X	X	X	S	S	S	S	S	S	S	X	o
CG	Signal quality Detector														o
CH/CI	Data Signalling Rate Selector (DTE)/(DCE)														o
DA/DB	Transmitter Signal Element Timing (DTE)/(DCE)	t	t	t	t	t	t	t	t	t	t	t	t	t	
DD	Receiver Signal Element Timing (DCE)			t	t	t	t	t	t	t	t	t	t	t	
SBA	Secondary Transmitted Data							X		X	X	X	X	X	o
SBB	Secondary Received Data						X		X						o
SCA	Secondary Request to Send							X		X	X	X	X	X	o
SCB	Secondary Clear to Send							X	X	X	X	X	X	X	o
SCF	Secondary Received Line Signal Detector						X		X		X	X	X	X	o

Legend:
- – To be specified by the supplier
- – – optional
- S – Additional Interchange Circuits required for Switched Service
- t – Additional Interchange circuits required for Synchronous Channel
- X – Basic Interchange Circuits, All Systems

Figure 5.4.2-4 Standard interfaces for selected communication systems configurations

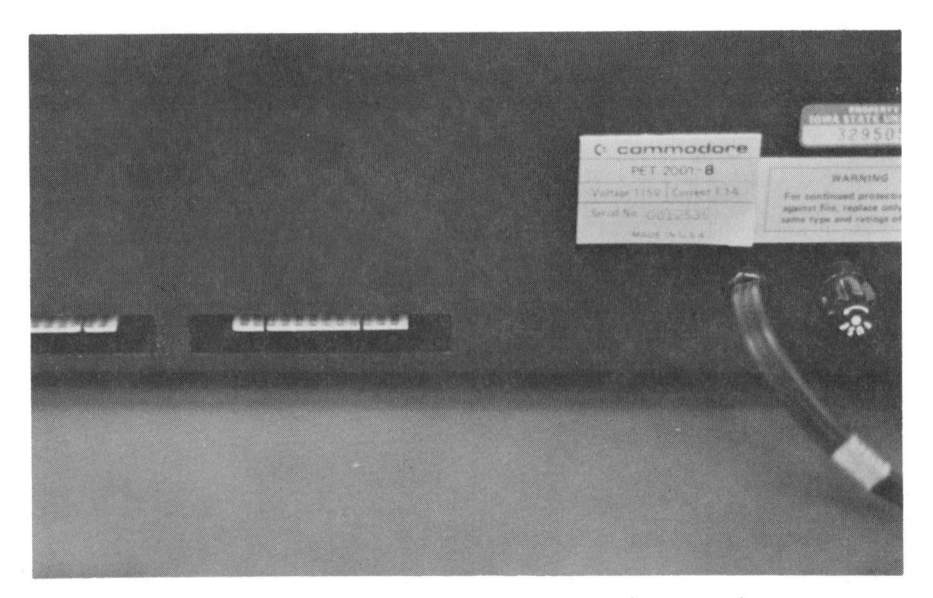

Figure 5.4.3-1 IEEE 488 interface connector (left center) on Commodore Pet 2001 computer

another. Although we can take as a specific example one medium, like paper tape, some general concepts are applicable to almost all media. Since the KIM is generally thought of as paper-tape and magnetic cassette-based, let us consider examples reflecting the use of paper tape.

Some general attributes which make data capable of convenient transport are the following:

1. The data is blocked into records.
2. Specific memory locations for ultimate storage are specified.
3. Different record types may be represented.
4. Records may be of varying length.
5. Data is expressed in common code like hex.
6. Simple error-checking, like check sum value, is provided.

The information as it is transmitted is usually blocked by records as indicated in 1, and it is most common that the first character in a record be a unique start-of-record mark (like a colon, semi-colon, etc.). This allows a heading to be included which may provide descriptive material about the data, but which the loader would ignore if it preceded this mark. In the case of paper tape associated with the KIM, there should be at least the program name and date on such a header. The only absolute requirement, of course, is that the descriptive material *not* contain the character or symbol which indicates the beginning of a record. In the case of the KIM, a semicolon is used as a start-of-record mark, while most M6800 or I8080 based systems use a colon. The device which is loading this information, scans until a start-of-record mark character is found, ignoring everything preceding the mark. Once the start-of-record mark is found, subsequent information is contained in a record whose length may vary. A common convention, based on the KIM, is that the length of this block or record be the first recorded item after the start-of-record mark. At that point the loader program knows how much information is to be read from the input device, and can react accordingly. (An alternative to this is to have two different symbols, one for beginning of record and another for end of record.) It is very common to require that information be stored starting at a specific starting location, with successive bytes of information stored in successive higher numbered locations in memory space. This starting location may be the next value in the record.

It is often found that a given system must handle different record types. Such types might be one including only heading information, or perhaps containing only an overall check sum. A unique record type is sometimes used to indicate that the information to be stored is a set of instructions which are to be located in *relocatable* format, i.e., the loader must be capable of identifying instructions for which the address could be relocated and an offset value provided. Many variations on record types can be found. In the case of the KIM, there is only a single paper tape record type (see Chapter 8 for a detailed discussion).

Many types of data representation exist; however, hexadecimal is the most common. Each data byte is divided into two nibbles, each of which is represented by an ASCII encoded symbol, 0 through F (note that this requires *two bytes* in the record to represent *one byte* of data).

Most of today's microprocessors use positive logic conventions to describe signal levels. This has not always been the case, and it is thus sometimes necessary to define the contents of a storage location containing $FF in terms of high voltage or low voltage levels. The BPNF code can be used in such situations. It uses 10 ASCII characters to represent each 8-bit value in one storage location. These 10 characters are "B" to indicate the *beginning* of the definition of these 8 bits, "N" or "P" to represent *negative* or *positive* voltage levels, followed by an "F" to indicate the *final* character.

A useful feature in carrying programs or data from one computer to another is the *check sum*, usually found at the end of each record. This check sum can be generated in many ways but is most commonly found by simply adding together, after conversion from hexadecimal into binary value, all data bytes on the record, including block length, starting address and data. This check sum is appended to the record. If the check sum computed during loading and the check sum read from the tepe do not compare, then there has been a check sum error. This is an example of a reliable error-checking method which should be followed in any communications procedure. In multi-microcomputer applications it is very wise to include such a check sum in communication between the processors. Such codes can be made single error correcting if the 8th bit of each byte is included as parity, and the check sum will allow detection of a single error. Error correction permits records to be corrected without requiring retransmission of the record. In large computers such methods are often implemented in reading data from main memory. Some large machines have been disassembled and the memory found to have missing cores, which have gone undetected for years. Such schemes can in principle allow detection of multiple errors.

5.5 INPUT/OUTPUT – TTL, SPEED, BITS, SERIAL/PARALLEL CONVERSIONS

The interface standards discussed in Section 5.4 are generally adopted on a voluntary basis, i.e., those who do not use or abide by them reduce their sales base. Another de facto standard is represented by the wide acceptance of Transistor-Transistor logic (TTL). As noted in Chapter 2, even though most microprocessors are fabricated from MOS processes, rather than bipolar like TTL, their terminal characteristics are often specified in TTL terms. This TTL designation is usually given in terms of normalized unit TTL loads. Table 5.5-1 details this definition of voltages and currents. A unit TTL load is seen to be 40 μA in High state and 1.6 mA in the Low state. Any microprocessor part which claims to be TTL compatible must be capable of sourcing and sinking these currents at 2.4 volts and 0.4 volts, respectively. A standard TTL gate is capable of driving 10 such unit loads.

There are several families of TTL circuits. The one which we have been discussing is called Standard TTL. There are also, Schottky, High speed, Low power, and Low power Schottky TTL. Table 5.5-2 shows their relative drive capabilities and loading characteristics. Each of these families also has different signal propagation delays. Table 5.5-3 shows nominal gate propagation delays for each type.

TABLE 5.5-1 Standard TTL Characteristics (For worst-case supply voltage, full temperature range, positive logic)

Parameter		Min	Range Typ	Max	Note
V_{IH}:	Lowest "1" Input	2.0 v			
V_{IL}:	Maximum "0" Input			0.8 v	
V_{OH}:	Lowest "1" Output	2.4 v	3.3 v		
V_{OL}:	Maximum "0" Output		0.2 v	0.4 v	
I_{IL}:	Input Current For Low Input (0.4 volts)		1.0 MA	1.6 MA	Out of input pin Requires current sink
I_{IH}:	Input Current For High Input (2.4 volts)			40 μA	Into input pin Requires current source
I_{OL}:	Output Current in Low State (Sinking)	20 MA		55 MA	
I_{OH}:	Output Current in High State (Source)	800 μA			

TABLE 5.5-2 Unit Load and Drive for TTL Families (Normalized to Normal Unit Values)

Designation	Type	Input High	Input Low	Output High	Output Low
74	Normal	1	1	20	10
74S	Schottky	1.25	1.25	25	12.5
74H	High Speed	1.25	1.25	25	12.5
74L	Low Power	0.5	0.25	10	2.5
74LS	Low Power Schottky	0.5	0.25	10	5

TABLE 5.5-3 Typical Gate Propagation Delays

Designation	Type	Typical Delay (ns)
74	Normal	10
74S	Schottky	3
74H	High Speed	6
74L	Low Power	20
74LS	Low Power Schottky	10

5.6 ADDRESS MAPS AND ORGANIZATION

One of the characteristics which the microcomputer designer will have to confront very early in any project is placement of ROM, RWM, and I/O sections in address space. In Chapter 3, we found that certain constraints (page zero, stack, interrupt vectors, etc.), constrain these decisions somewhat. Separate ROM and RWM allocation is fairly unique to microprocessor-based systems. In many mini-computers and larger scale computers central memory is achieved via magnetic core storage, which can be used for both ROM and RWM functions. In microcomputer systems design the building blocks are ROM and RWM and, for the MCS6502 the stack area *must* be in the second 256 byte page, page 1. It is necessary, then, that this area in address space be RWM. It is necessary very early for the computer systems designer to decide how much RWM will be required for storage of variables in the computational process. Often the ROM requirement need not be exactly determined until system software has been developed and production decisions such as future expansion have been made.

Once an approximate idea of the number of bytes of data storage has been decided for an application, an address map should be started. Figure 5.6-1 shows an initial address map, using the MCS6502 system as an example. This figure reflects the requirement that RWM exist in the address range $0100 to $01FF. There is a trivial case in which no subroutines are called, no interrupts are handled, and no Push or Pull instructions are used so that no stack area (denoted by RWM-S) would

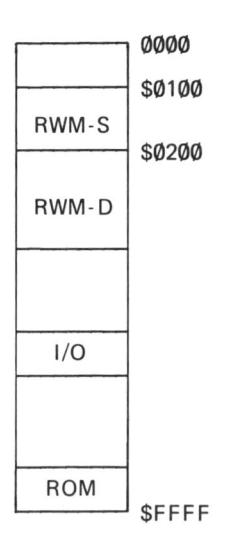

Microcomputer Interfacing and System Design 273

```
┌─────────┐ 0000
│         │
│  RWM-S  │ $0100
├─────────┤
│         │ $0200
│  RWM-D  │
│         │
├─────────┤
│         │
│         │
│   I/O   │
│         │
├─────────┤
│         │
│   ROM   │
└─────────┘ $FFFF
```

Figure 5.6-1 Initial MCS6502 based microcomputer address map

be required. This can be dismissed as an impractical situation for the majority of applications. The Data RWM area could extend from 0000 on up through the stack area, so that, if the stack area is small it could be moved adjacent to $00FF. Some typical stack area sizes are 32, 64, 128, and 256 bytes. This is governed as much as anything by available ICs and system needs. Some ROM must appear in the opposite address extreme (near $FFFF) due to the vectored reset and interrupt mechanism. Input/Output can be anywhere in between, as needs dictate. Although not shown there, the I/O could be in page zero, 0000 to $00FF. Using Zero Page op codes would allow us to speed up I/O-bound systems. Clever handling of interrupting inputs with such a system could allow externally variable vectored interrupts. Such cleverness is unfortunately often accompanied by extremely tedious debugging. Not shown on this map are times, memory-mapped A/D converters, etc.

The next design task is to allocate the RWM to be used for data storage. There is no basic pattern here except that usually arrays of data and their associated names and sizes should be catalogued for future reference. If some variables are not used at the same time as others, perhaps they can be overlayed, i.e., brought in from secondary storage only when needed. Another hardware-saving technique is to use RWM ICs arranged in a 4-bit nibble configuration. For example a single 1024 × 4 package can be used with software separation of high order bytes into every other memory location.

5.7 MEMORY AND I/O SELECTION

Once a particular microprocessor has been selected, amounts of RWM for data and stack have been estimated, and the number of I/O ports resolved, the problem is: How is address selection to be performed? If we are not careful we could have more than one part selected by a single address. As a worst case we could have a RWM and I/O port both attempting to place data on the same System Data Bus. Most MOS microprocessors and family parts are fairly forgiving when this happens, i.e., nothing blows up or smokes. Improper system activity will occur, of course, or worse yet, invalid data will appear *some* of the time. A most useful design tool for avoiding such problems is the Tabular Form Address Table.

First consider some typical microcomputer system elements. The microprocessor will have 16 address lines which must be decoded so that one and only one part is selected at a time. Some ROM parts have up to 4 chip-select inputs which can be chosen as active-low or active-high at the time the fabrication mask is made. Other ROM parts have fusible-link programming capabilities and 4 chip-selects: two inverting and two noninverting. Present UV erasable ROM units have only active-low chip-select. Typical RWM ICs may have one to six chip-selects, while the MCS6502 family I/O parts have one to three chip selects in various inverting and noninverting patterns.

The underlying problem, then, is to select among these parts using the desired address bus pattern using a minimum (zero?) of extra integrated circuits.

To illustrate, let us assume that we are using:

Part Type	Number of Chip Selects	Size	Destination
ROM	4	512 × 8	CS$\emptyset$, CS1, $\overline{CS2}$, $\overline{CS3}$
RWM	6	128 × 8	CS$\emptyset$, CS1, $\overline{CS2}$, $\overline{CS3}$, CS4, CS5
I/O	3	2 ports	CS$\emptyset$, CS1, $\overline{CS2}$

The desired system will use the MCS6502 with vectored reset and a stack in page one. A suitable memory map would thus be that of Figure 5.7-1. The placement of ROM is inflexible since there must be vectors in $FFF8 through $FFFF, and the ROM is 512 × 8. RWM could be anywhere in page one (or page zero actually, if AB8 were not decoded). The I/O part could be placed in a variety of locations, requring only that enough address space for all its registers be provided. The address range shown in Fig. 5.7-1 is thus somewhat arbitrary.

Microcomputer Interfacing and System Design

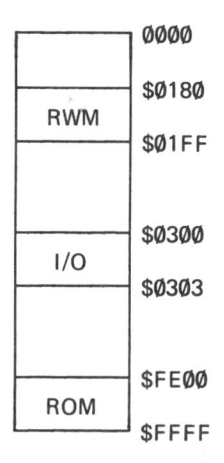

```
        ┌──────┐ 0000
        │      │
        │      │ $0180
        │ RWM  │
        │      │ $01FF
        │      │
        │      │
        │      │ $0300
        │ I/O  │
        │      │ $0303
        │      │
        │      │
        │      │ $FE00
        │ ROM  │
        └──────┘ $FFFF
```

Figure 5.7-1 Example address map

The choices of Figure 5.7-1 will now be represented in tabular form. ROM requirements are shown in Figure 5.7-2a. The high-order ones in address bits 9-15 will be put out by the microprocessor whether

| Address Bits | Part | Address Range |
15 14 13 12 11 10 9 8 7 6 5 4 3 2 1 0		
1 1 1 1 1 1 1 x x x x x x x x x	ROM	$FE00 – $FFFF

Figure 5.7-2a Tabular form address table for ROM only

we choose to decode them or not. In fact, we have only 4 chip-selects, and since two of them are active-low, they are useless in the chip-select decoding process if we wish to directly use high-order address bits as chip select inputs. We will simply wire them to ground and connect AB9 and AB10 to the two noninverting chip-selects. Our table thus becomes as shown in Figure 5.7-2b. The X indicates that the corresponding address line is connected to the similarly-designated address line on the part. For example, AB0 on the MCS6502 connects to AB0

| Address bits | Part | Address Range |
15 14 13 12 11 10 9 8 7 6 5 4 3 2 1 0		
(1)(1)(1)(1)(1) 1 1 x x x x x x x x x	ROM	$FE00 – $FFFF

Figure 5.7-2b Tabular form address table for ROM only

on the part. The parentheses around AB11-AB15 indicates that the microprocessor will send out these values, but that they will not actually be decoded in the part selection process. The two 1's under AB9 and AB10 mean that they are connected and the part will respond via the two CS connections to this address.

It is important to note that 5 address lines are not decoded. There are, therefore, 2^5, or 32, "images" of this part. In other words if the microprocessor did a Fetch from $FE00 the same instruction would be read via the data bus as if it were fetched from $960∅, or one of the other 30 addresses.

Figure 5.7-2c shows Figure 5.7-2 augmented to include RWM and I/O. The remaining symbol used in the address table is the dash to indicate that the corresponding value on the address bus is arbitrary. The microprocessor will not automatically generate it (unlike vectors and stack pointers) and nothing decodes it. A choice of zero for such bits

Address bits																Part	Address Range
15	14	13	12	11	10	9	8	7	6	5	4	3	2	1	0		
(1)	(1)	(1)	(1)	(1)	1	1	x	x	x	x	x	x	x	x	x	ROM	$FE00 – $FFFF
(0)	(0)	(0)	0	0	0	0	1	1	x	x	x	x	x	x	x	RWM	$0180 – $01FF
–	–	–	–	–	0	1	1	–	–	–	–	–	–	x	x	I/O	$0300 – $0303

Figure 5-7-2c Completed example tabular form address table

has been arbitrarily chosen to allow designation of address range for I/O. In computer parlance the dash is a "don't care."

In large systems it might be necessary to add one or more extra decoders connected to the address lines in order to select among a larger number of parts. Decoders would clearly be needed if ROMs with single active-low chip-selects were used.

5.8 SYSTEM DESIGN EXAMPLES

5.8.1 Example 1: A Simple Microcomputer Function Generator

This example illustrates the design of an entire microcomputer. The intended function of the microcomputer is to detect the closure of a push-button switch to ground. When closure is sensed it is to generate a 1 kHz rectangular wave of 33.3% duty cycle. It will recheck for switch closure after each complete cycle of this waveform.

Microcomputer Interfacing and System Design **277**

System components include an MOS Technology MCS 6502 Microprocessor, a Motorola MC 6820 PIA, and an Intel I1702 PROM. No RWM is needed.

The data lines of the three principal elements are bussed together as shown in the detailed system diagram of Figure 5.8-1. No buffers were used because of the light electrical loading.

Since, upon Reset, the MSC6502 address bus successively outputs addresses $FFFC and $FFFD, the 1702A PROM must respond to them. A 7404 TTL gate is used to invert address line A8 to select the I1702. The 6820 PIA has been connected to respond to locations $0000 through $0003. Figure 5.8-2 shows a memory map for the system.

The A-side PIA port is used as an input, while the B-side is an output. Obviously there are many other combinations which would work just as well for this simple case. As seen in Figure 5.8-1 the switch to be sensed (SW1) is connected to PA7. In this configuration when the MPU samples the A-side data register, the sign bit of the accumulator is either set or reset depending upon whether PA7 is high (SW1 open) or low (SW1 closed). A simple branch BPL or BMI can then be used to detect switch closure. PA0 is held high so that when SW1 is closed the accumulator is loaded with a logic "1," which can then be written into the B-side port, PB. This will produce a logic "1" at PB0, which will represent the high portion of the rectangular wave that is generated when switch closure is detected.

Resistor R1 and capacitor C1 form the external circuitry for the microprocessor clock. Although the 1702 PROM and the MCS 6502 μP both have specified 1MHz upper frequency operating limits, a careful examination of the relevant specifications shows that the address-out to data-valid time for a read of the PROM is

$$T_{ACC} + T_{ADS} + T_{DSU} = (1 + 0.3 + 0.1)\,\mu s = 1.4\,\mu s$$

This constitutes an upper bound on the clock frequency, i.e.,

$$f_{max} = (1.4\,\mu s)^{-1} = 714286\ Hz$$

Since the minimum clock frequency required for adequate refreshing of the CPU registers is roughly 100 kHz, the clock frequency for this design was chosen to be 700 kHz. To achieve this frequency, values for R1 and C1 were chosen to be 33 kΩ and 7 pF, respectively. The actual measured clock frequency was found to be about 710 kHz.

If automatic power-up RESET is desired, the RESET line must be held low for two clock cycles after V_{CC} reaches 4.75 volts. The R2, C2

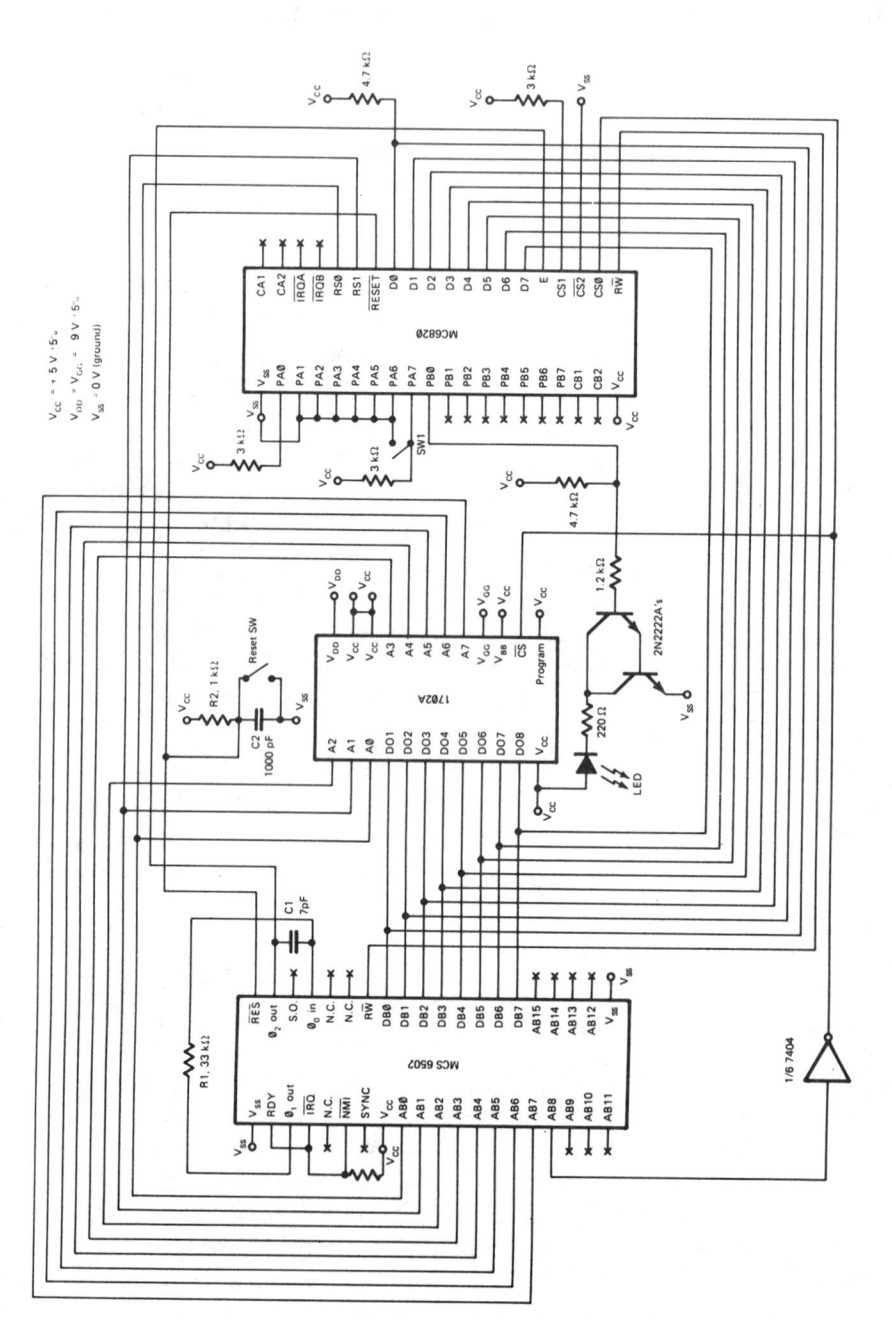

Figure 5.8-1 System diagram

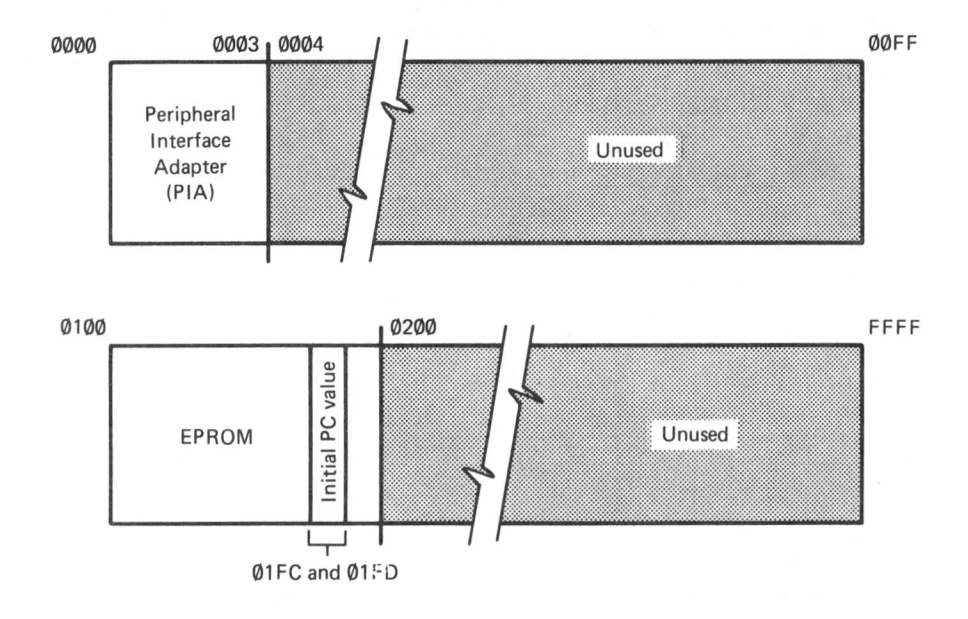

Figure 5.8-2 Memory Map for Example 1

network provides this function in the following way. On power-up the voltage across C2 equals $\emptyset$ volts and $\overline{\text{RESET}}$ is low. The threshold at which $\overline{\text{RESET}}$ is considered to be high is 2.4 volts. Therefore, the voltage across C2 should be much less than 2.4 volts for at least 2.8 μs (2 cycles at 1.4 μs per cycle). For worst case assume V_{CC} = 5 volts instantaneously. Then

$$5[1 - \text{EXP}(2.8 \times 10^{-6}/(R2)(C2))] = 4.75 \text{ volts}$$

or

$$(R2)(C2) = (9.35)(10^{-7}) \text{ seconds}$$

If C2 = 1$\emptyset\emptyset\emptyset$ pF then R2 = 935 Ω, or about 1 kΩ.

The microprocessor and PIA R/W lines are tied together and unused inputs are tied high or low as required. Power supply values are

$$V_{CC} = V_{BB} = +5 \text{ volts} \pm 5\%$$

$$V_{SS} = \emptyset \text{ volts (Ground)}$$

$$V_{DD} = V_{GG} = -9 \text{ volts} \pm 5\%$$

For convenience a manual reset switch is also provided for backup. A program listing for the function generator is shown in Figure 5.8-3. The proper timing for the output waveform on PB∅ is obtained from LOOP 1 (∅.33 ms delay) and LOOP 2 (∅.67 ms delay). Switch sensing is done by the POLL loop.

Switch bounce was not extensively considered in this design. Bounce in the reset switch was not a problem since the manual operation of the switch takes approximately 6 ms minimum, and RESET has to be stable at a low value for only 2.8 μs. Bounce is SW1 likewise should cause no problems. The POLL loop will continue to sense SW1 (through PA7) and will eventually "see" the closure. In some applications switch bounce could cause delay problems at PA7. In those cases, a debouncing circuit using two cross-coupled NAND gates (74∅∅ or similar) and a single-pole, double-throw switch can be used in place of SW1.

```
           ON
           PASS1
           PASS2

              ......PAGE ∅∅1

           LINE # LOC    CODE        LINE

           ∅∅∅1   ∅∅∅∅                   *=$1∅∅
           ∅∅∅2   ∅1∅∅ A9 27   RESET LDA #%∅∅1∅∅111   CONTROL SETTINGS
           ∅∅∅3   ∅1∅2 85 ∅1         STA $∅∅1        STORE IN CRA
           ∅∅∅4   ∅1∅4 A∅ FF         LDY #$FF        SET B FOR OUTPUT
           ∅∅∅5   ∅1∅6 84 ∅2         STY $2
           ∅∅∅6   ∅1∅8 85 ∅3         STA $3          STORE CONTROL IN CRB
           ∅∅∅7   ∅1∅A A2 ∅∅         LDX #$∅∅        PUT ZERO IN OUTPUT
           ∅∅∅8   ∅1∅C 86 ∅2         STX $∅2
           ∅∅∅9   ∅1∅E A5 ∅∅   POLL  LDA   $∅∅       SAMPLE INPUT
           ∅∅1∅   ∅11∅ 3∅ FC         BMI POLL
           ∅∅11   ∅112 85 ∅2         STA $∅2         PUT 1 ON OUTPUT
           ∅∅12   ∅114 A2 3A         LDX #$3A        ∅.33 MS DELAY
           ∅∅13   ∅116 CA      LOOP1 DEX
           ∅∅14   ∅117 D∅ FD         BNE LOOP1
           ∅∅15   ∅119 86 ∅2         S-X $∅2         PUT ∅ ON OUTPUT
           ∅∅16   ∅11B A2 74         LDX #$74        ∅.67 MS DELAY
           ∅∅17   ∅11D CA      LOOP2 DEX
           ∅∅18   ∅11E D∅ FD         BNE LOOP2
           ∅∅19   ∅12∅ F∅ EC         BEQ POLL        SAMPLE AGAIN
           ∅∅2∅   ∅122                   *=$FFFC
           ∅∅21   FFFC ∅∅ ∅1   VECT  .DBYTE $∅∅1
           ∅∅21   FFFE

           ERRORS = ∅∅∅∅ WARNINGS = ∅∅∅∅


           SYMBOL TABLE

              SYMBOL  VALUE
              RESET   ∅1∅∅
              POLL    ∅1∅E
              LOOP1   ∅116
              LOOP2   ∅11D
              VECT    FFFC
           END OF ASSEMBLY
```

Figure 5.8-3 Program listing for example 1

Microcomputer Interfacing and System Design **281**

After the system was constructed it was discovered that pull-up resistors were needed on two bits of the PIA: at bit PBØ because of its tri-state configuration and at bit DØ because of loading and timing problems. A visual indication of the operation of the system was provided by a Darlington transistor pair driving a light-emitting diode on the output at PBØ.

5.8.2 Example 2: An Extended Simple Microcomputer

For those applications which require a limited amount of Read/Write Memory the system of Section 5.8.1 can be augmented with an MCM6810 (128 X 8 RWM).

The address selection pattern has been modified to that shown in Table 5.8.1 below.

TABLE 5.8.1 Address Selection for Extended Microcomputer

Part \ Address bit	15	14	13	12	11	10	9	8	7	6	5	4	3	2	1	Ø
ROM	(1)	(1)	(1)	(1)	(1)	(1)	1	1	X	X	X	X	X	X	X	X
RWM	(Ø)	(Ø)	(Ø)	(Ø)	(Ø)	(Ø)	Ø	1	(Ø)	X	X	X	X	X	X	X
PIA	(Ø)	(Ø)	(Ø)	(Ø)	(Ø)	(Ø)	Ø	Ø	(Ø)	(Ø)	(Ø)	(Ø)	(Ø)	(Ø)	X	X

Ø or 1: value for which the part will be selected
X: connected to like address line on port
( ): a possible address designating this part but not physically connected, other values in these positions represent image addresses.

Since the overall pattern is so similar to that of 5.8.1 we show only that part of the circuit which pertains to chip selection in Figure 5.8-4. With these connections addresses will be

$$\begin{aligned}
\text{ROM} &\quad \$\emptyset 3\emptyset\emptyset - \$\emptyset 3\text{FF} \\
\text{RWM} &\quad \$\emptyset 1\emptyset\emptyset - \$\emptyset 17\text{F} \\
\text{PIA} &\quad \$\emptyset\emptyset\emptyset\emptyset - \$\emptyset\emptyset\emptyset 3
\end{aligned}$$

The only other detail is to connect the R/W line to the 6810. There are *many* "images" of each of these parts, and we are taking advantage of one of them. On Reset we vector through absolute locations $FFFC and $FFFD to get the PC value for our first fetch. We must be extremely careful to decode these two addresses into acceptable locations in ROM. This should help explain the necessity of the parentheses in Table 5.8.1.

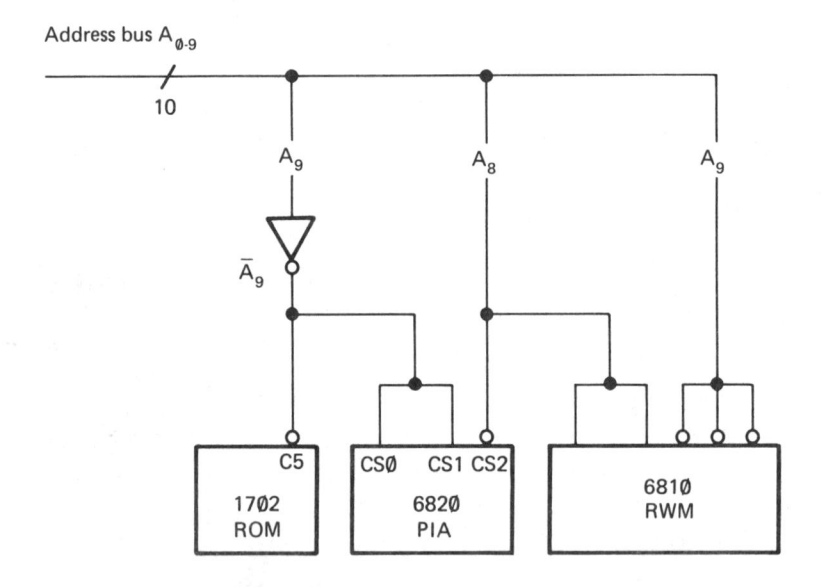

Figure 5.8-4 Chip selection scheme for the extended microcomputer

5.8.3 Example 3: Interfacing to a Keyboard

An important application area encountered in system design is interaction with keyboards, arrays of switches, contact arrays, etc. A preferred approach is to use a separate Keyboard Encoder integrated circuit. Such a chip will encode a large switch matrix, providing a 9-bit code. It can also provide 2-key (or even N-key) rollover, repeat, and key bounce masking. If this were the only job a microprocessor-based system needed to perform, the encoder would probably be the lowest-cost option. If, however, a microprocessor is already needed, then the incremental cost to add keyboard encoding is, in many cases, quite small.

Microcomputer Interfacing and System Design **283**

The basic keyboard configuration to be considered is shown in the simple schematic diagram of Figure. 5.8.5. The basic design objective is to detect if one or more switches that are depressed are making contact. One solution is to apply a desired logic level on one column and scan the rows for that same logic level.

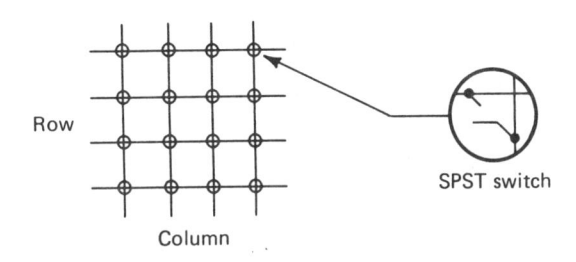

Figure 5.8-5 Switch matrix

The basic design will be demonstrated using the KIM microcomputer. There is a keyboard much like that of Figure. 5.8-5 built into the KIM, and support software and hardware are included as part of the KIM monitor program. An external keyboard will be interfaced through the KIM application port at $1700 - $1703. Once this 16 key pad problem is understood, the serious student may delve into the KIM hardware and software (see Appendix B).

By way of review let us consider the A-side Application port. There are two registers, one for Data Direction and another for Data. For programming purposes these have been labeled ADD and AD respectively, corresponding to addresses $1701 and $1700. The port will be divided into two sets of lines, four for output and four for input. A partial system diagram is shown in Figure. 5.8-6.

The first part of an operating program for the keyboard should initialize the A-side Data Direction register to the configuration shown in Figure 5.8-6. Specifically, location $1701 (ADD) must be set to $0F.

It is also necessary to establish some arbitrary conventions for the operating program. First, if no key is found to be depressed, the program will send a value $C0 to the Accumulator. If a key *is* depressed, its value (0 through F) will be flashed in a KIM display element N + 1 times. Since open inputs look like logic "1," the program will scan for zero levels (corresponding to key closure). A temporary storage location (TEMP) will be incremented as scanning occurs to generate the key value. A SCAN subroutine which accomplishes those tasks is given in

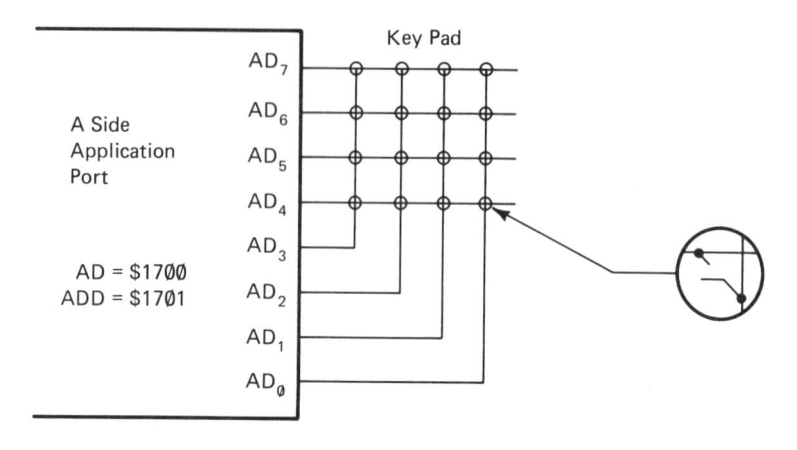

Figure 5.8-6 External key pad connection

Figure 5.8-7. The following observations may be helpful in understanding the operation of the SCAN subroutine:

TEMP is initialized to 1, i.e., N+1, as stated.
Y is used as the X-axis count.
X is used as the Y-axis count.
$C\emptyset$ is loaded into A if no key is pressed.

It might be a good idea to review the BIT and ASL instructions (see Chapter 3), and understand their exact usage here. Also make sure that the use of BEQ in line #37, rather than BNE, is fully understood. Once a key depression is found, the key value +1 is in TEMP ($\emptyset 1 \emptyset \emptyset$).

```
LINE #  LOC    CODE          LINE
 ØØ29   Ø327  A9 Ø1    SCAN  LDA #1
 ØØ3Ø   Ø329  8D ØØ Ø1       STA TEMP
 ØØ31   Ø32C  AØ Ø4          LDY #4
 ØØ32   Ø32E  A9 ØE          LDA #$ØE
 ØØ33   Ø33Ø  8D ØØ 17       STA AD
 ØØ34   Ø333  A2 Ø4    SCA1  LDX #4
 ØØ35   Ø335  A9 1Ø          LDA #$1Ø
 ØØ36   Ø337  2C ØØ 17 SCA2  BIT AD
 ØØ37   Ø33A  FØ 12          BEQ FOUND
 ØØ38   Ø33C  EE ØØ Ø1       INC TEMP
 ØØ39   Ø33F  ØA             ASL A
 ØØ4Ø   Ø34Ø  CA             DEX
 ØØ41   Ø341  DØ F4          BNE SCA2
 ØØ42   Ø343  ØE ØØ 17       ASL AD
 ØØ43   Ø346  EE ØØ 17       INC AD
 ØØ44   Ø349  88             DEY
 ØØ45   Ø34A  DØ E7          BNE SCA1
 ØØ46   Ø34C  A9 CØ    FAIL  DLA #$CØ
 ØØ47   Ø34E  6Ø       FOUND RTS
```

Figure 5.8-7 Key pad scan subroutine

Microcomputer Interfacing and System Design

Figure 5.8-8 gives assembly-language variable equate statements, standard stack pointer and decimal mode setup, an initializing subroutine, and the rather brief main program which consists principally of subroutine calls.

```
......PAGE ØØØ1
LINE #  LOC       CODE           LINE
ØØØ1    ØØØØ                     AD      = $17ØØ  ;THIS IS A STANDARD
ØØØ2    ØØØØ                     ADD     = $17Ø1  ;LEADER FOR ALL
ØØØ3    ØØØØ                     BD      = $17Ø2  ;PROGRAM TAPES
ØØØ4    ØØØØ                     BDD     = $17Ø3
ØØØ5    ØØØØ                     TEMP    = $1ØØ
ØØØ6    ØØØØ                     TABLE   = $1FE7
ØØØ7    ØØØØ                     SAD     = $174Ø
ØØØ8    ØØØØ                     SADD    = $1741
ØØØ9    ØØØØ                     SBD     = $1742
ØØ1Ø    ØØØØ                     SBDD    = $1743
ØØ11    ØØØØ                     *=$3ØØ
ØØ12    Ø3ØØ   A2 FF              LDX  #$FF
ØØ13    Ø3Ø2   9A                 TXS
ØØ14    Ø3Ø3   D8                 CLD
ØØ15    Ø3Ø4   2Ø 14 Ø3    MAIN   JSR  INIT
ØØ16    Ø3Ø7   2Ø 27 Ø3    LOOP   JSR  SCAN
ØØ17    Ø3ØA   C9 CØ              CMP  #$CØ
ØØ18    Ø3ØC   FØ F9              BEQ  LOOP
ØØ19    Ø3ØE   2Ø 4F Ø3           JSR  OUTP
ØØ2Ø    Ø311   4C Ø4 Ø3           JMP  MAIN
ØØ21    Ø314   A9 ØF       INIT   LDA  #$ØF
ØØ22    Ø316   8D Ø1 17           STA  ADD
ØØ23    Ø319   A9 7F              LDA  #$7F
ØØ24    Ø31B   8D 41 17           STA  SADD
ØØ25    Ø31E   8D 43 17           STA  SBDD
ØØ26    Ø321   A2 ØØ              LDX  #$Ø
ØØ27    Ø323   8E 4Ø 17           STX  SAD
ØØ28    Ø326   6Ø                 RTS
```

Figure 5.8-8 Main program for key pad scan

Figure 5.8-9 gives the last two subroutines. DELAY establishes a visible blinking period. The constants shown were evolved by trial and error. OUTP uses the KIM display and a table (part of the KIM monitor program) which converts the Ø-F values into the appropriate seven-segment values to be placed on SAD. The digit position is selected by SBD = 9, corresponding to the leftmost display element. The odd numbers $B, $D, $F, $11, and $13 could be used to select any other digit position, or roll it across like a "Times Square" display.

The entire program as assembled on the MDT development terminal is given in Figure 5.8-10.

Extensions of this application are innumerable. As various phases in system start-up are encountered, a completely new set of key definitions can be invoked. For example, many hand calculators have multi-defined keys with gold-functions, blue-functions, etc. Additions for two-key rollover and debouncing are relatively simple.

For larger switch arrays, a single MC682Ø PIA can service up to 81 keys by using the CA2 and CB2 lines as outputs. The use of decoders, encoders, multiplexers and shift registers allow for variations and extensions.

```
LINE #  LOC      CODE          LINE

0048    034F  AC 00 01    OUTP   LDY  TEMP
0049    0352  B9 E6 1F           LDA  TABLE-1,Y
0050    0355  A2 09       OUT1   LDX  #$09
0051    0357  8E 42 17           STX  SBD
0052    035A  8D 40 17           STA  SAD
0053    035D  20 6C 03           JSR  DELAY
0054    0360  8E 40 17           STX  SAD
0055    0363  20 6C 03           JSR  DELAY
0056    0366  CE 00 01           DEC  TEMP
0057    0369  D0 EA              BNE  OUT1
0058    036B  60                 RTS
0059    036C  A2 90       DELAY  LDX  #$90
0060    036E  A0 FF       DEL1   LDY  #$FF
0061    0370  EA          DEL2   NOP
0062    0371  88                 DEY
0063    0372  D0 FC              BNE  DEL2
```

Figure 5.8-9 Output and delay subroutines

```
LINE #  LOC      CODE          LINE

0001    0000                AD   = $1700  ;THIS IS A STANDARD
0002    0000                ADD  = $1701  ;LEADER FOR ALL
0003    0000                BD   = $1702  ;PROGRAM TAPES
0004    0000                BDD  = $1703
0005    0000                TEMP = $100
0006    0000                TABLE = $1FE7
0007    0000                SAD  = $1740
0008    0000                SADD = $1741
0009    0000                SBD  = $1742
0010    0000                SBDD = $1743
0011    0000                *=$300
0012    0300  A2 FF              LDX  #$FF
0013    0302  9A                 TXS
0014    0303  D8                 CLD
0015    0304  20 14 03     MAIN  JSR  INIT
0016    0307  20 27 03     LOOP  JSR  SCAN
0017    030A  C9 C0              CMP  #$C0
0018    030C  F0 F9              BEQ  LOOP
0019    030E  20 4F 03           JSR  OUTP
0020    0311  4C 04 03           JMP  MAIN
0021    0314  A9 0F        INIT  LDA  #$0F
0022    0316  8D 01 17           STA  ADD
0023    0319  A9 7F              LDA  #$7F
0024    031B  8D 41 17           STA  SADD
0025    031E  8D 43 17           STA  SBDD
0026    0321  A2 00              LDX  #$0
0027    0323  8E 40 A7           STX  SAD
0028    0326  60                 RTS
0029    0327  A9 01        SCAN  LDA  #1
0030    0329  8D 00 01           STA  TEMP
0031    032C  A0 04              LDY  #4
0032    032E  A9 0E              LDA  #$0E
0033    0330  8D 00 17           STA  AD
0034    0333  A2 04        SCA1  LDX  #4
0035    0335  A9 10              LDA  #$10
0036    0337  2C 00 17     SCA2  BIT  AD
0037    033A  F0 12              BEQ  FOUND
0038    033C  EE 00 01           INC  TEMP
0039    033F  0A                 ASL  A
0040    0340  CA                 DEX
0041    0341  D0 F4              BNE  SCA2
0042    0343  0E 00 17           ASL  AD
0043    0346  EE 00 17           INC  AD
0044    0349  88                 DEY
0045    034A  D0 E7              BNE  SCA1
0046    034C  A9 C0        FAIL  LDA  #$C0
0047    034E  60           FOUND RTS
0048    034F  AC 00 01     OUTP  LDY  TEMP
0049    0352  B9 E6 1F           LDA  TABLE-1,Y
0050    0355  A2 09        OUT1  LDX  #$09
```

Microcomputer Interfacing and System Design

```
LINE #  LOC     CODE            LINE
ØØ51    Ø357    8E 42 17                STX  SBD
ØØ52    Ø35A    8D 4Ø 17                STA  SAD
ØØ53    Ø35D    2Ø 6C Ø3                JSR  DELAY
ØØ54    Ø36Ø    8E 4Ø 17                STX  SAD
ØØ55    Ø363    2Ø 6C Ø3                JSR  DELAY
ØØ56    Ø366    CE ØØ Ø1                DEC  TEMP
ØØ57    Ø369    DØ EA                   BNE  OUT1
ØØ58    Ø36B    6Ø                      RTS
ØØ59    Ø36C    A2 9Ø           DELAY   LDX  #$9Ø
ØØ6Ø    Ø36E    AØ FF           DEL1    LDY  #$FF
ØØ61    Ø37Ø    EA              DEL2    NOP
ØØ62    Ø371    88                      DEY
ØØ63    Ø372    DØ FC                   BNE  DEL2
ØØ64    Ø374    CA                      DEX
ØØ65    Ø375    DØ F7                   BNE  DEL1
ØØ66    Ø377    6Ø                      RTS
ØØ67    Ø378                            .END

ERRORS = ØØØØ  WARNINGS = ØØØØ

SYMBOL TABLE

SYMBOL  VALUE

AD      17ØØ
ADD     17Ø1
BD      17Ø2
BDD     17Ø3
TEMP    Ø1ØØ
TABLE   1FE7
SAD     174Ø
SADD    1741
SBD     1742
SBDD    1743
MAIN    Ø3Ø4
LOOP    Ø3Ø7
INIT    Ø314
SCAN    Ø327
SCA1    Ø333
SCA2    Ø337
FAIL    Ø34C
FOUND   Ø34E
OUTP    Ø34F
OUT1    Ø355
DELAY   Ø36C
DEL1    Ø36E
DEL2    Ø37Ø
END OF ASSEMBLY
```

Figure 5.8-10 Complete key pad display program

5.8.4 Example 4: Seiko Printer Interface

The Seiko printer described in this section is only one of several printers with similar characteristics. Seiko also has several other models with varying character fonts, voltage ratings, etc. For the sake of specificity we will explore one model connected to the KIM Application port, using only the A side.

The salient characteristics of this printer are:

1. 17 VDC operation;
2. 2.8 lines per second print speed;

3. 21 columns per printed line;
4. 3½ inch wide paper (or cards);
5. inked ribbon;
6. 16 characters in the print set;
7. motor current of 200 mA no-load, 600 mA full-load;
8. the print hammer circuit is highly inductive with a resistance of approximately 80 ohms; and
9. two pickup coils determine character and position of print drum.

The two pickup coils have voltages induced by magnets rotating on the print drum and motor shaft. These voltages are roughly 0.4 volt peak value, and must therefore be amplified to provide TTL compatible input signals to the KIM port. The print hammers require roughly 300 mA so we must also augment the KIM with print hammer driver circuitry.

Figure 5.8-11 shows the basic timing of the printer. The TR pickup signal is generated once during each revolution of the printing drum. There are 16 TL/TM pickup signals per drum revolution, and they define the intervals during which each drum pointer character is properly positioned. That is, during the interval between TM_0 and TL_0, the first character is positioned; during the interval TM_1 to TL_1 the second character is positioned, etc.

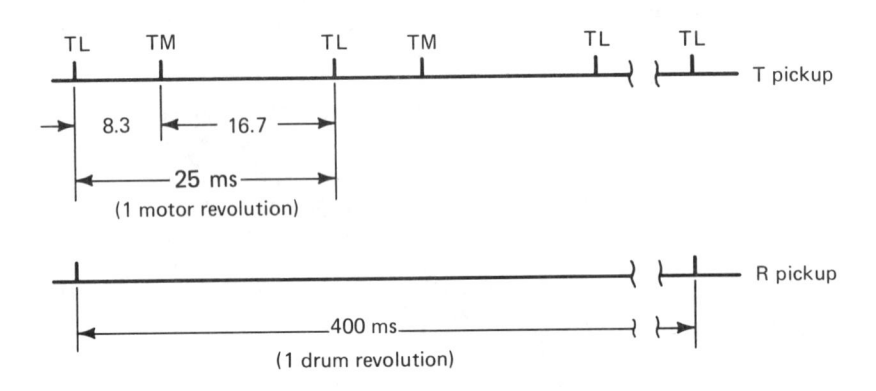

Figure 5.8-11 Basic timing cycle of a Seiko printer

Figure 5.8-12 expands the basic diagram to show the print timing signals for the character "zero." If a zero is to be printed in a character position the print hammer for that position must be driven at 300 mA from TM_0 to TL_0.

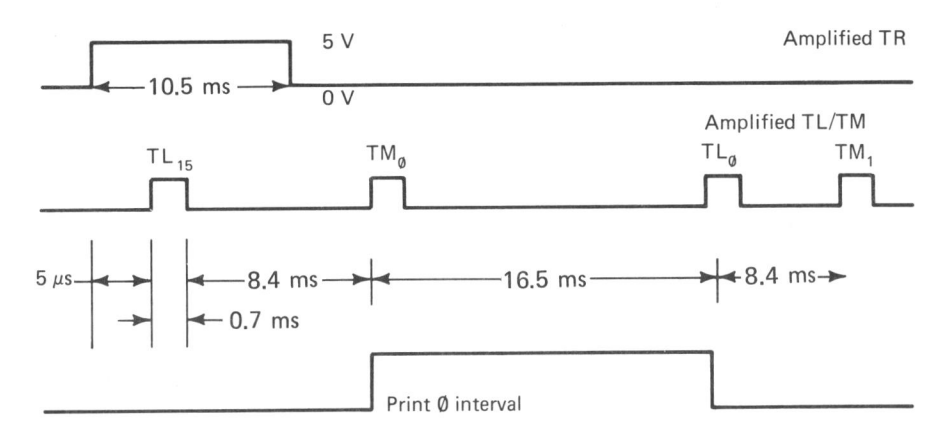

Microcomputer Interfacing and System Design **289**

Figure 5.8-12 Detailed timing showing hammer drive signal for "0" character

The support electronics and KIM connections are shown in Figure 5.8-13. Provision has been made to turn the motor on and off as well as to generate line feeds. In order to conserve I/O port bits, a shift register (74164) is used. In a more sophisticated printer, with a large character set, two or more such shift registers could be cascaded. An inexpensive high current driver (75492) was employed for the print hammer drive circuitry. During loading of the shift register some brief transient drive signals may occur. The mechanical inertia of the hammers effectively filter out such noise.

A main test program and all necessary subroutines are given in Figure 5.8-14. The program will print the contents of memory locations 312 - 319 ($\emptyset$138 - $\emptyset$13E). Subroutine functions are:

- INIT - Initialize the Data Direction Register and clear the print driver Shift Register.
- MTNF - Motor on or off.
- WAIT - Needed to wait out a TL or TM pulse once found. Insures that each TL or TM is counted only once.
- DOIT - The "main part" of the printing function. Finds TR, TL, then TM; loads and clears shift register for all 16 character intervals.
- LF - Causes 1 line feed.
- PFNF - Actual line feed (minus delays).
- DLY - A long delay while motor "revs up."
- TRCHK - Find coincident TR and TL 15. Prevents improper recognition of TL 15 for TM_0.

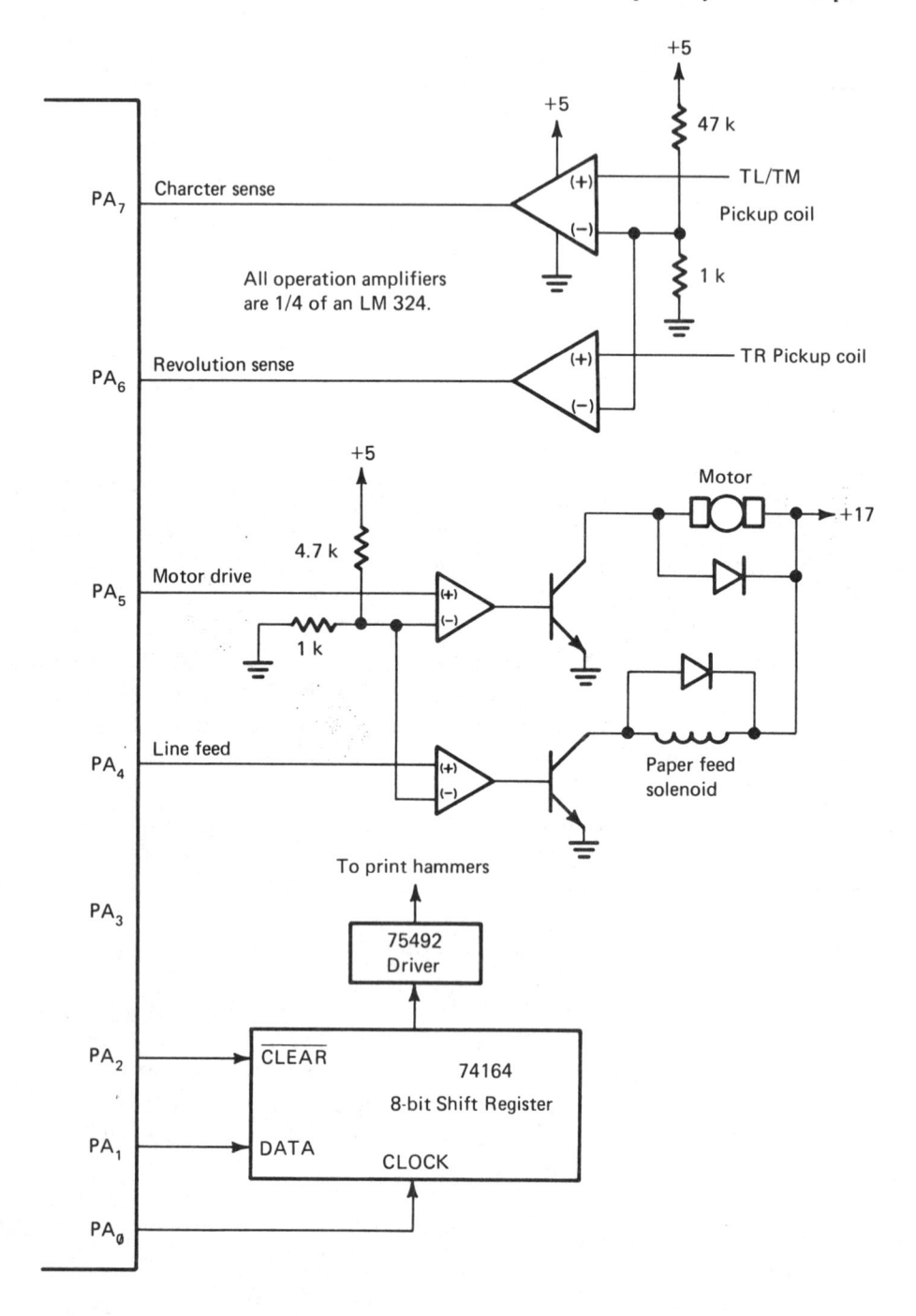

Figure 5.8-13 Printer and KIM system diagram

Microcomputer Interfacing and System Design

TLMCK - Finds TL or TM, whichever is next.
PDCLR - Clears shift register.
PRINT - Decrements each memory location and clocks the appropriate one or zero into the shift register.
ONE - Logic one into shift register.
ZERO - Logic zero into shift register.
CLOCK - Clocks shft register.

In this example the KIM is considered to be dedicated to the printer, and it continuously functions as a printer controller. In a case where the KIM was to be shared with other tasks, this routine could, with little effort, be converted to an interrupt service routine.

```
LINE #  LOC    CODE        LINE

0001    0000               PADD   = $1701
0002    0000               PAD    = $1700
0003    0000               TEMP   = 308
0004    0000               PARS   = 312
0005    0000                      *=$200
0006    0200   A2 FB       MAIN   LDX #$FB
0007    0202   9A                 TXS
0008    0203   20 00 03           JSR INIT
0009    0206   20 10 03           JSR MTNF
0010    3209   20 2F 03           JSR DOIT
0011    020C   20 10 03           JSR MTNF
0012    020F   00                 BRK
0013    0210                      *=$300
0014    0300   A2 37       INIT   LDX #%00110111
0015    0302   8E 01 17           STX PADD
0016    0305   A6 00              LDX 0
0017    0307   8E 00 17           STX PAD
0018    030A   A2 04              LDX #4
0019    030C   8E 00 17           STX PAD
0020    030F   60                 RTS
0021    0310   AD 00 17    MTNF   LDA PAD
0022    0313   49 20              EOR #$20
0023    0315   8D 00 17           STA PAD
0024    0318   A2 FF              LDX #$FF
0025    031A   EA                 NOP
0026    031B   20 22 03    MTN1   JSR WAIT
0027    031E   CA                 DEX
0028    031F   D0 FA              BNE MTN1
0029    0321   60                 RTS
0030    0322   48          WAIT   PHA
0031    0323   A9 FF              LDA #$FF
0032    0325   8D 34 01           STA TEMP
0033    0328   CE 34 01    WAI1   DEC TEMP
0034    032B   D0 FB              BNE WAI1
0035    032D   68                 PLA
0036    032E   60                 RTS
0037    032F   A2 10       DOIT   LDX #16
0038    033'   20 6C 03           JSR TRCHK
0039    0334   20 22 03    AGAIN  JSR WAIT
0040    0337   20 7A 03           JSR TLMCK
0041    033A   20 90 03           JSR PRINT
0042    033D   20 22 03           JSR WAIT
0043    0340   20 7A 03           JSR TLMCK
0044    0343   20 82 03           JSR PDCLR
0045    0346   CA                 DEX
0046    0347   D0 EB              BNE AGAIN
0047    0349   20 4D 03           JSR LF
0048    034C   60                 RTS
0049    034D                      ;
0050    034D   20 5A 03    LF     JSR PFNF
0051    0350   20 63 03           JSR DLY
0052    0353   20 5A 03           JSR PFNF
0053    0356   20 63 03           JSR DLY
0054    0359   60                 RTS
0055    035A                      ;
0056    035A   A9 10       PFNF   LDA #$10
0057    035C   4D 00 17           EOR PAD
```

```
LINE #  LOC    CODE         LINE

0058    035F  8D 00 17           STA  PAD
0059    0362  60                 RTS
0060    0363                     ;
0061    0363  A2 55        DLY   LDX  #$55
0062    0365  20 22 03     DLY1  JSR  WAIT
0063    0368  CA                 DEX
0064    0369  D0 FA              BNE  DLY1
0065    036B  60                 RTS
0066    036C                     ;
0067    036C  A9 40        TRCHK LDA  #$40
0068    036E  2C 00 17     TRC1  BIT  PAD
0069    0371  F0 FB              BEQ  TRC1
0070    0373  0A                 ASL  A
0071    0374  2C 00 17           BIT  PAD
0072    0377  F0 F3              BEQ  TRCHK
0073    0379  60                 RTS
0074    037A                     ;
0075    037A  A9 80        TLMCK LDA  #$80
0076    037C  2C 00 17     TLM1  BIT  PAD
0077    037F  F0 FB              BEQ  TLM1
0078    0381  60                 RTS
0079    0382                     ;
0080    0382  A9 04        PDCLR LDA  #$4
0081    0384  4D 00 17           EOR  PAD
0082    0387  8D 00 17           STA  PAD
0083    038A  49 04              EOR  #$4
0084    038C  8D 00 17           STA  PAD
0085    038F  60                 RTS
0086    0390                     ;
0087    0390  8A           PRINT TXA
0088    0391  48                 PHA
0089    0392  A0 07              LDY  #7
0090    0394  BE 37 01     PRI1  LDX  PARS-1,Y
0091    0397  CA                 DEX
0092    0398  8A                 TXA
0093    0399  99 37 01           STA  PARS-1,Y
0094    039C  E8                 INX
0095    039D  F0 08              BEQ  ONE
0096    039F  D0 19              BNE  ZERO
0097    03A1  88           PRI2  DEY
0098    03A2  D0 F0              BNE  PRI1
0099    03A4  68                 PLA
0100    03A5  AA                 TAX
0101    03A6  60                 RTS
0102    03A7                     ;
0103    03A7  A9 02        ONE   LDA  #$2
0104    03A9  0D 00 17           ORA  PAD
0105    03AC  8D 00 17           STA  PAD
0106    03AF  20 C0 03           JSR  CLOCK
0107    03B2  49 02              EOR  #$2
0108    03B4  8D 00 17           STA  PAD
0109    03B7  4C A1 03           JMP  PRI2
0110    03BA                     ;
0111    03BA  20 C0 03     ZERO  JSR  CLOCK
0112    03BD  4C A1 03           JMP  PRI2
0113    03C0                     ;
0114    03C0  EE 00 17     CLOCK INC  PAD
0115    03C3  CE 00 17           DEC  PAD
0116    03C6  60                 RTS
0117    03C7                     .END

ERRORS = 0000  WARNINGS = 0000

SYMBOL TABLE

  SYMBOL   VALUE

  PADD    1701
  PAD     1700
  TEMP    0134
  PARS    0138
  MAIN    0200
  INIT    0300
  MTNF    0310
  MTN1    031B
  WAIT    0322
  WAI1    0328
  DOIT    032F
  AGAIN   0334
  LF      034D
  PFNF    035A
```

```
DLY      0363
DLY1     0365
TRCHK    036C
TRC1     036E
TLMCK    037A
TLM1     037C
PDCLR    0382
PRINT    0390
PRI1     0394
PRI2     03A1
ONE      03A7
ZERO     03BA
CLOCK    03C0
END OF ASSEMBLY
```

Figure 5.8-14 Seiko printer test program

5.8.5 Example 5: Analog to Digital Conversion

This section will develop the basic concepts of A/D conversion using a microcomputer. Once the concept is understood, the extension to longer word lengths, greater accuracy, faster conversion time, etc., can be explored. The key here is simplicity.

A KIM microcomuter will be used along with an MC 1406 D/A converter and one-half the op-amps of an LM 324 Quad Operational Amplifier. The A-side Application port will be used for interaction with the electronics.

Figure 5.8-15 shows the circuitry involved in this system. The MC 1406 is an integrated D/A converter. Note that the manufacturers' convention makes A1 the most significant bit of input. The required supply voltages are +5, ground, and a negative supply between −5 and −15. −5 volts is chosen for convenience; however, the data sheets indicate that V_{EE} = −6 volts, V_+ = 0 and V_- = −3 volts provides best temperature performance. The resistor network shown provides acceptable voltage and current levels to establish the range of I_O into pin 4 between 0 and 1 mA. The two operational amplifiers Ⓐ and Ⓑ are two of the four on an LM 324 Quad op-amp. Their supply voltages are +5 volts and ground. The Ⓐ op-amp simply converts the current output of the D/A to voltage output. Larger or smaller swings could be generated by altering the feedback resistor. A bipolar output can be generated by the addition of a resistor from pin 2 to the positive supply. The Ⓑ op-amp is used as a comparator. These devices are internally compensated. For more exacting applications, higher performance and higher slew rate op-amp could be used. It would also be wise to use a temperature-compensated zener diode circuit connected

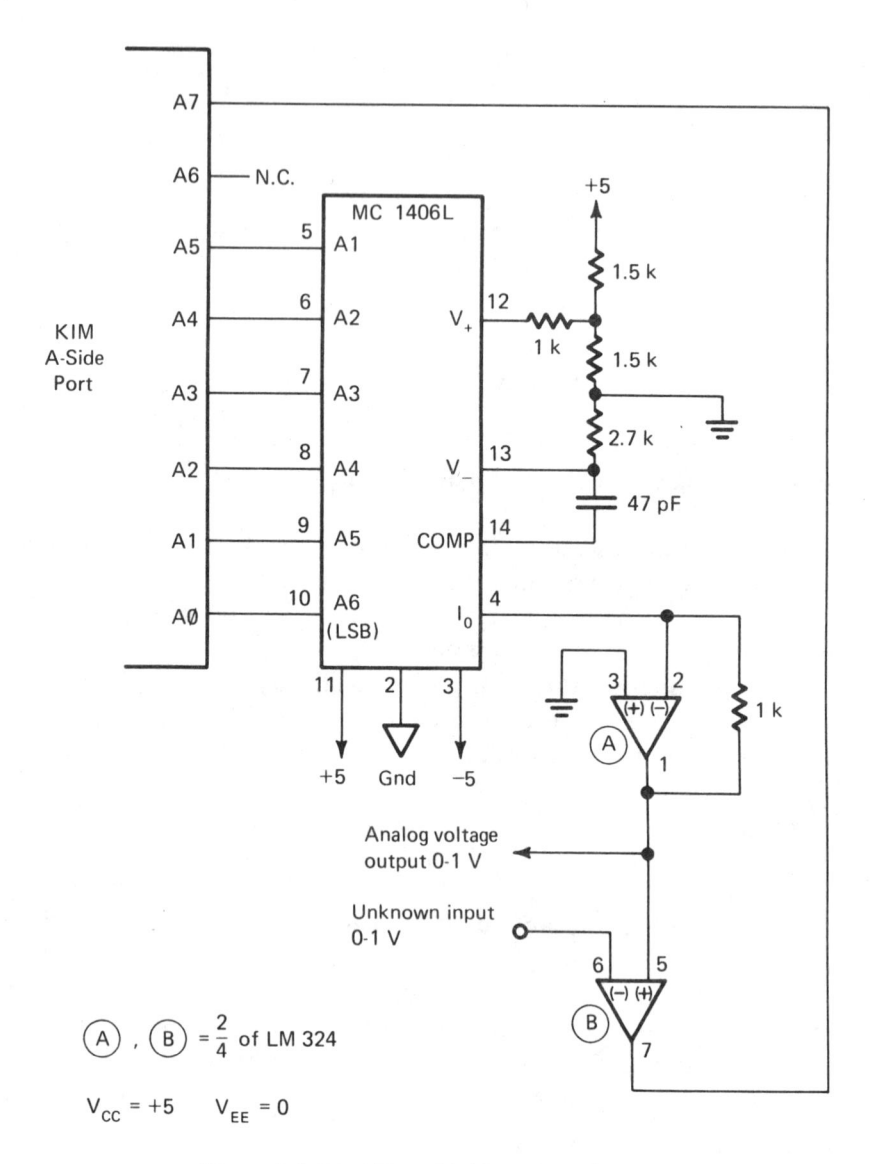

Figure 5.8-15 A/D and D/A system diagram

to pin 12, so that reliance on stability and accuracy of the +5 volt supply is not required. A final note: the D/A inputs are complemented. That is, an input value of \$3F results in ∅ mA for I_O.

Operating software is shown in Figure. 5.8-16. Some portions of the KIM monitor are used. The program starts at address \$1∅1 and, when conversion is completed, the digital value of the analog voltage

Microcomputer Interfacing and System Design

```
LINE #  LOC         CODE        LINE

0001    0000                    POINTL = $FA
0002    0000                    MASK   = $100
0003    0000                    AD     = $1700
0004    0000                    ADD    = $1701
0005    0000                    *=$101
0006    0101  A2 FC             LDX #$FC
0007    0103  9A                TXS
0008    0104  D8                CLD
0009    0105  20 00 02          JSR SAPR
0010    0108  A9 3F             LDA #$3F
0011    010A  2D 00 17          AND AD
0012    010D  49 3F             EOR #$3F
0013    010F  A0 00             LDY #0
0014    0111  91 FA             STA (POINTL),Y
0015    0113  4C 4F 1C          JMP $1C4F
0016    0116                    *=$200
0017    0200  A2 3F      SAPR   LDX #$3F
0018    0202  8E 01 17          STX ADD
0019    0205  A2 06             LDX #6
0020    0207  A9 20             LDA #$20
0021    0209  8D 00 01          STA MASK
0022    020C  49 FF             EOR #$FF
0023    020E  8D 00 17   LOOP   STA AD
0024    0211  20 2E 02          JSR END
0025    0214  20 2E 02          JSR END
0026    0217  2C 00 17          BIT AD
0027    021A  10 06             BPL OK
0028    021C  4D 00 01          EOR MASK
0029    021F  8D 00 17          STA AD
0030    0222  4E 00 01   OK     LSR MASK
0031    0225  AD 00 17          LDA AD
0032    0228  4D 00 01          EOR MASK
0033    022B  CA                DEX
0034    022C  D0 E0             BNE LOOP
0035    022E  60         END    RTS
0036    022F                    .END

ERRORS = 0000  WARNINGS = 0000

SYMBOL TABLE

SYMBOL VALUE

POINTL  00FA
MASK    0100
AD      1700
ADD     1701
SAPR    0200
LOOP    020E
OK      0222
END     022E
END OF ASSEMBLY
```

Figure 5.8-16 A/D KIM software

input will be displayed in the address seven segment display. The subroutine which performs the successive approximation procedure starts in location $200. The first steps are to initialize the A-side Data Direction Register, as well as a mask bit for selectively turning bits on or off, as required. The EOR before LOOP provided inversion to complement the inputs to the MC 1406. The two JSRs after LOOP are simply to provide settling time for the MC 1406 and LM 324. The program then tests a "1" value in each successive bit, restores the partial result if too large, and moves to the next less significant bit. After all six bits have been generated, the correct value is returned.

Other approaches to this same problem could have been used. For example, instead of successive approximation, the input value could be followed or "tracked." In this method, the present digital value is converted to analog form and compared to the input voltage to be converted. The digital value is then incremented or decremented to bring the two analog voltages closer to one another until the resolution of the converter is reached.

Within constraints of quantizing noise, we could use the D/A and (A) op-amp plus software to generate a wide variety of analog waveforms. Another approach is to use one A/D port as we have demonstrated, and transform in software (tables of computation) to be presented on another port D/A. Yet another possiblity is to use a FET switch on the unknown input, selected by another port, for a multiple channel A/D converter. This application would be useful for checking for out-of-limit values in process control, presumably a fairly infrequent operation.

Finally, the configuration of Figure 5.8-15 provides direct capability for D/A conversion as well as A/D conversion. Thus, once the interface shown in this figure is provided, a variety of diverse uses can be implemented via generation of supporting software.

PROBLEMS

1. A system input signal is a pulse one microsecond wide and zero to five volts. Draw the schematic of a circuit using a 74121 to provide a TTL level output one millisecond wide.
2. Do the same thing as 1 except reverse the pulses.
3. What are the practical limits to the circuitry in 1 and 2?
4. For the MCS6502 based system of Figure. 3.7.6 use CA1 as the input and use Side A bit $\emptyset$ as the output. Gererate pulses as in 1 and 3. What are the practical limits? What is the time delay between input and output?
5. Discuss the relative accuracy for the 64121 and microcomputer solutions.
6. Draw the serial data stream of an ASCII encoded *pair* of characters Carriage Return, followed by Line Feed.

7. The MCS6502 Data bus is stated as capable of driving one TTL load and 130 pf. How many 74XX, 74HXX, 74SXX, 74LXX, 74LSXX, and CMOS gates will each drive?

8. In an MCS6502 based microcomputer the partial Tabular Form Address Table below is to be completed.

					Address											Part	Address Range
15	14	13	12	11	10	9	8	7	6	5	4	3	2	1	0		
	1		1	1	x	x	x	x	x	x	x	x	x	x	x	ROM	
			0	1		x	x	x	x	x	x	x	x	x	x	RWM	
	1		0	1										RS1	RS0	PIA	

9. List all "images" of ROM in Problem 8. How many images exist for RWM, PIA?

6
INTRODUCTION TO THE M6800 MICROPROCESSOR

6.1 INTRODUCTION

Chapter 3 discussed the MCS6502 in detail. Because the M6800 is quite similar, it is easy to make the transition to it. The M6800 and its associated family of parts is manufactured by Motorola and second-sourced by both American Microsystems (AMI) and Fairchild, among others.

At some time in the future Motorola will probably include more functions on a single chip, including an on-chip clock circuit and RWM. It is also possible to foresee the emergence of a code-compatible single chip microcomputer containing ROM, RWM, CPU, I/O and a timer of some sort.

6.2 PRINCIPAL CHARACTERISTICS

The following list describes the principal characteristics of the M6800 (Figure 6.2-1).

1. Single 5 volt supply
2. Byte oriented
3. 197 op codes
4. Six addressing modes
5. True indexing
6. Stack pointer
7. Two interrupt levels
8. 65K address range

Figure 6.2-1 Motorola M6800 microprocessor element

1. *Single 5 volt supply:* As we observed in Chapter 3 there are several popular fabrication methods for integrated circuits. The M6800 uses the same technology as the MCS6502, N channel ion implant with depeletion loads. The single 5 volt supply enables the M6800 to be similarly compatible with TTL bipolar parts.

2. *Byte oriented:* As with the MCS6502 the data bus is 8 bits wide, representing a byte-oriented structure.

3. *197 operation codes:* Section 6.2.2 gives a detailed description of all the operation codes for the M6800. Compared to the MCS6502 the M6800 may be seen to have a wider variety of data-handling instructions. For example, it is posssible to clear any location in memory without having to first clear an accumulator and then store. A wider variety of conditional tests is provided, as well as additional shift and rotate operations.

Introduction to the M6800 Microprocessor 301

4. *Six addressing modes:* Unfortunately, the Motorola instruction sheets do not always use the same terminology as used by the MCS6502 manufacturer. In MCS6502 jargon, the six M6800 addressing modes are: Immediate, Zero Page, Absolute, Relative, Zero Page Indexed, and Implied. Indexing can only be done in zero-page mode. Another major deficiency of the M6800 relative to the MCS6502 is its lack of an indirect addressing mode.

5. *True indexing:* The M6800, like the MCS6502, provides true indexing capability, i.e., a reference to a base address offset by an index register is possible. As we observed in Chapters 2 and 3, indexed addressing often permits very compact and flexible programming. The M6800 has a tremendous advantage (relative to the MCS6502) in having a 16-bit register. This larger index value permits operation on a wider range of variables, which can be a significant help in some problems. This advantage is unfortunately somewhat offset by the requirement that all addresses must be zero page indexed. In practice it often seems that it is easier to use what would be considered the zero page address part of an indexed instruction as the offset, while X maintains the base. By comparison with some MCS6502 programs discussed earlier it may be seen that it is more cumbersome with the M6800 to move an array of more than 256 elements from one area to another area displaced by more than 256 decimal locations. In such a case it might be easier to store the index value using zero as the zero page reference and simply have two different values inserted into the X register for each source and destination location.

6. *Stack pointer:* Stack pointer operation in the M6800 is identical to that in the MCS6502 except for one major difference. The stack pointer for the M6800 is 16 bits long and the stack area therefore may be placed anywhere in the 65K of address range. In other words the stack is not constrained to be in page one as it was in the MCS6502. Otherwise, stack operation is the same in handling subroutine jumps, subroutine branches and interrupt handling. The warning given in Chapter 3 must be repeated here, viz., it is mandatory that the stack pointer be set to a specified value as one of the very first operations in initializing the microcomputer upon reset. Failure to do this may cause the first return from subroutine to be to an unknown location, an obviously unacceptable result.

___7. *Two interrupt levels:* The M6800 provides an interrupt request (IRQ) as well as a nonmaskable interrupt request (NMI), which are handled almost like those of the MCS6502.

8. *65K address range:* The M6800 has 16 address lines, like the MCS6502. The resulting address range of 65,536 locations is generally referred to as a 65K (or sometimes, 64K) address range.

6.3 SOME MCS6502 AND M6800 DIFFERENCES

Many of the specific details relating to the M6800 are given in later sections, but first some of the main differences between these two microprocessors will be highlighted.

A principal architectural difference between the two microprocessors is that the M6800 has two 8 bit accumulators, both providing similar capability, e.g., they are both able to operate with the Arithmetic Logic Unit and the input-output interface. As a matter of practical interest, some programmers use accumulator B for a counting function, not unlike that provided by the index registers in the MCS6502. It is initialized to a count, decremented and tested for zero each time through a loop. The stack pointer and index registers are a full 16 bits long, rather than 8 bits as in the MCS6502. Most programmers will find the added length to these two registers to be of material significance.

A major addressing difference is the inability to do Indirect Addressing on the M6800, a deficiency whose importance is often not recognized by the beginning programmer. Another important addressing mode difference is that all indexed operations in the M6800 are the equivalent of zero page indexed in the MCS6502. Perhaps of less importance, the M6800 has six more conditional branches for use after compare and subtract operations. Two of these branches allow testing for unsigned binary representation values and the other four for testing numbers in signed two's complement negative number representation.

Although a relatively minor difference, one that often confronts the individual converting from programming the 6502 to the 6800 is that addresses in the 6800 are in what might be called high-low form, i.e., those instructions that involve a two-byte address will be in the form of op code, high-address byte, followed by low-address byte in ascending numbered memory locations.

Two convenient operations offered by the M6800 are the ability to negate and complement. These two instructions allow the formation of either the signed two's complement or the one's complement of a

Introduction to the M6800 Microprocessor

value in either of the accumulators or in memory. In the MCS6502, it would be necessary to load a number from memory into the accumulator, perform an Exclusive Or with $FF, and then store it back in the memory location in order to get the one's complement in that location. These single-instruction operations are often particularly convenient in dealing with programmable peripheral parts.

A significant loss in the MCS6502 to M6800 conversion is the more limited ability of the 6800 to do decimal mode arithmetic. In order to do decimal arithmetic where binary coded decimal results are stored two per byte, it is necessary to follow each Add operation by a Decimal Adjust Accumulator (DAA) instruction (see Section 2.10.2). It should be noted that, in the M6800, this instruction works correctly only after an Add operation, i.e., a *Subtract* operation does not generate the correct P-register bits to allow a decimal adjust accumulator instruction to give the correct result. The general principle involved in decimal adjusting subtract operations requires: bringing in the first operand; forming its negative; adding the other operand; and then following this with a decimal adjust accumulator. Note that the add operation was done *immediately before the decimal adjust* thereby leaving carry and half carry in their correct state.

The M6800, unlike the MCS6502, does not have an on-chip clock. Although in most cases this is not a severe deficiency, it does mean some additional circuitry is required to generate the clock signals for this microprocessor.

The Ready (RDY) line used for synchronizing the MCS6502 with slow devices is not provided on the M6800. This also limits capability for single-step operation.

Unlike the MCS6502, the M6800 does not always present a so-called "valid" memory address on the address bus. A separate output line, called VMA, is used by the M6800 to signal to peripheral devices when a valid address is present on its address bus.

An important feature of the M6800 is its ability to be placed in a state in which address, data, and read/write lines are essentially open circuited, allowing a convenient direct memory access operation by other controllers connected to these lines. The line which controls this state is called the Tri State Control (TSC) line, whose timing must be synchronized with the clock lines $\phi 1$ and $\phi 2$. TSC, for proper operation, must be brought high, or logic one, during that period in which $\phi 1$ is high and $\phi 2$ is low. When this is done an interval of several microseconds is available for an external processor interact with memory or peripheral units. In other words, during this interval the M6800 completely disconnects itself from the read/write line as well as from all address and all data busses. It is important to note that the M6800 uses dynamic registers and, if held in the Tri State Control condition for an extended period of time *these registers may lose their stored contents.*

An added feature of the M6800, which affects both hardware and software, is preservation of program state during interrupt handling. The interrupt handling mechanism, using vectored addressing, is like the MCS6502. However, unlike the MCS6502 (which saves P and both bytes of PC), the M6800 saves P, PC, X, A, and B automatically upon interrupt.

6.4 M6800 PROGRAMMING

6.4.1 Programming Model

Figure 6.4-1 is the programming model for the M6800. As has been mentioned previously, there are two 8 bit accumulators. Each of these accumulators may be used in arithmetic operations and it is even possible to add the contents of accumulator B to the contents of accumulator A and leave the result in accumulator A. Of special importance is the length of the index register X, which is observed to be 16 bits. The stack pointer is 16 bits long and must be initialized to point to an area which contains RWM. In the M6800 RWM can be placed anywhere in address space by suitable arrangement of the address decoding, and need not be in Page 1, as was required with the 6502. Those which are identical in function to the MCS6502 are Carry, Overflow, Negative, Zero, and Interrupt Mask. The Half Carry bit is new, and has the function of providing carry during an Add operation from the least significant 4-bit nibble into the most significant 4-bit nibble. Two of the bits which are missing, by comparison to the MCS6502, are the Decimal Mode bit and the Break bit.

Figure 6.4-2 shows the data paths provided in the M6800. Once again it is very important to notice that the memory and stack actually represent the same RWM entity. Noticeable by its absence is the ability to push or pull the index register X (to/from the stack). Another type of operation very commonly used in programming the M6800 is that of transferring the contents of X to the stack pointer or vice versa. Information is stored in a memory area defined by the stack pointer by means of Pushes. A call to subroutine is then performed and the value in S is transferred to X. X is now decremented twice which allows us to

Introduction to the M6800 Microprocessor **305**

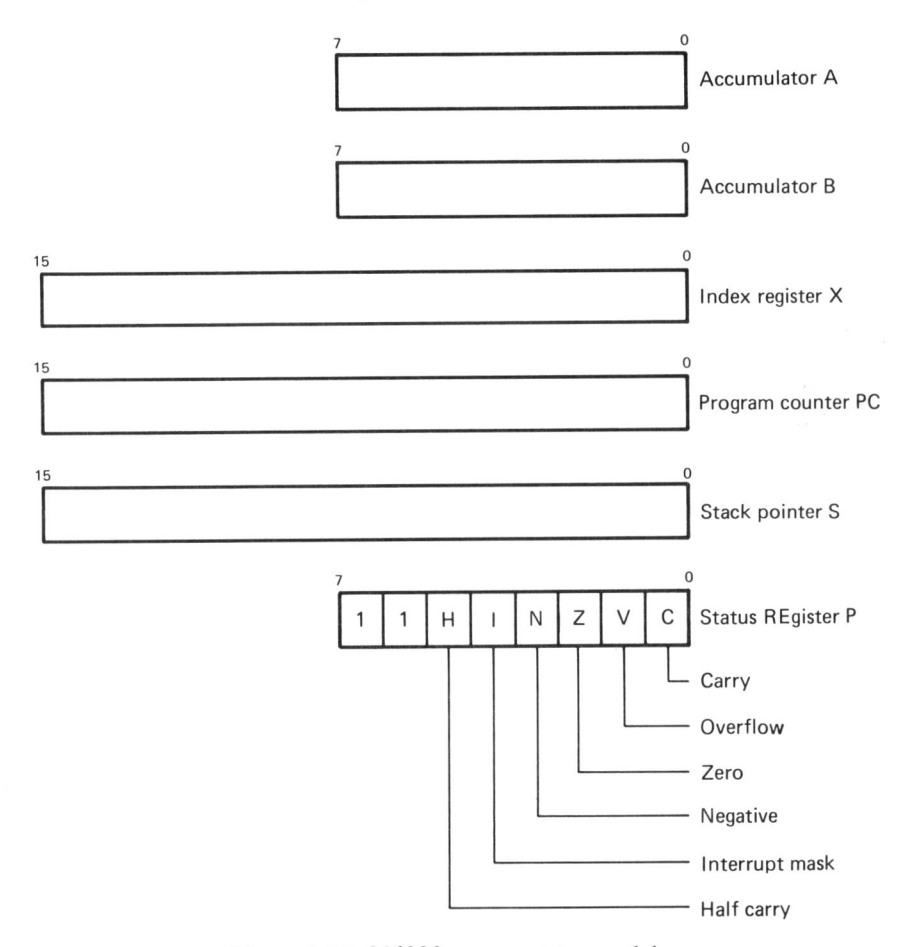

Figure 6.4-1 M6800 programming model

get the variables to be used within the subroutine from the stack area by means of an LDA 0, X and LDA 1, X etc. operations.

Table 6.4-1 is an alphabetic list of all of the M6800 instructions with their word statement equivalents. The details of these instructions are given in Table 6.4-2. Because of the close parallel between the M6800 and the MCS6502, no detailed description of each op code will be given, but some explanation is necessary. First, in referring to Table 6.4-2 notice that some shorthand has been used in this table which did not exist in the similar one for the MCS6502 (Table 3.4-2). In particular, where an operation may be used on either accumulator A or accumulator B they are separated in this table by a slash. For example, Add with Carry Immediate to the A register has a hex 89 op code (in

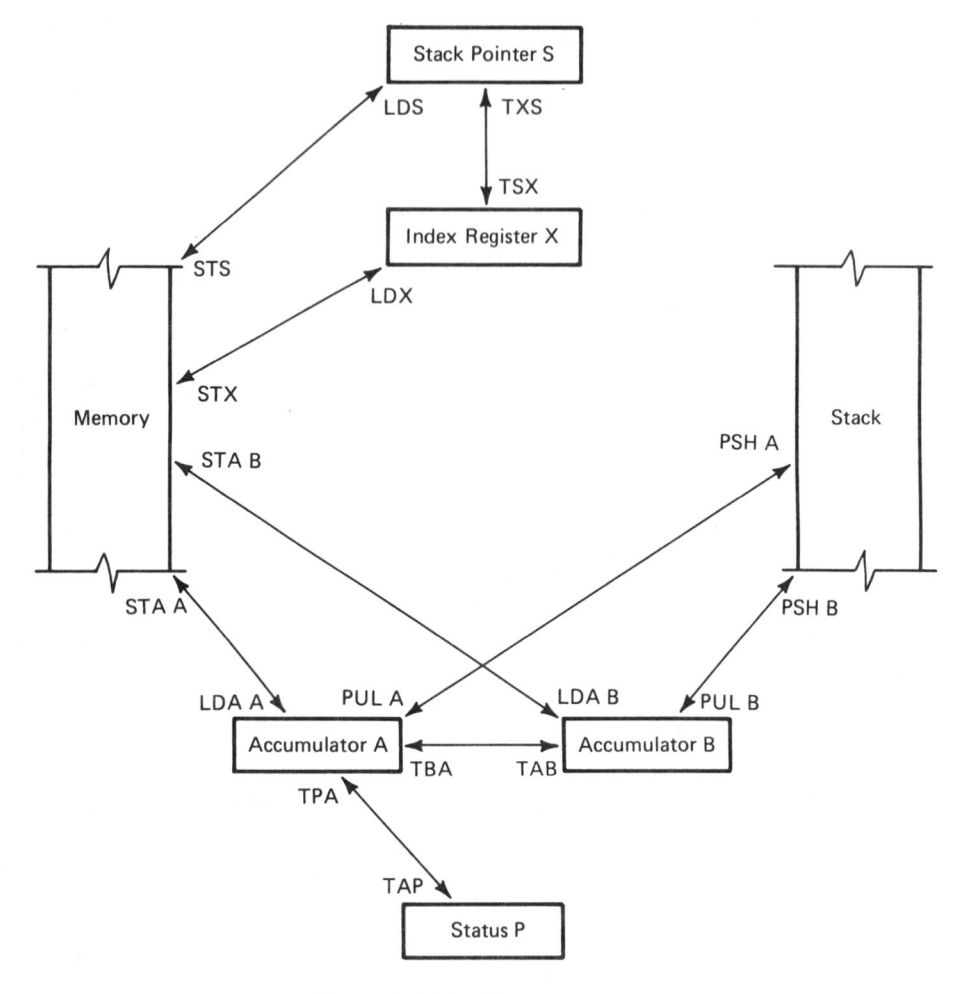

Figure 6.4-2 M6800 data paths

TABLE 6.4-1 M6800 Microprocessor Instruction Set-Alphabetic Sequence (Courtesy Motorola Semiconductor Products)

ABA Add Accumulators
ADC Add with Carry
ADD Add
AND Logical And
ASL Arithmetic Shift Left
ASR Arithmetic Shift Right

BCC Branch if Carry Clear
BCS Branch if Carry Set
BEQ Branch if Equal to Zero
BGE Branch if Greater or
       Equal Zero
BGT Branch if Greater than Zero

Introduction to the M6800 Microprocessor

BHI	Branch if Higher	NEG	Negate
BIT	Bit Test	NOP	No Operation
BLE	Branch if Less or Equal		
BLS	Branch if Lower or Same		
BLT	Branch if Less than Zero	ORA	Inclusive OR Accumulator
BMI	Branch if Minus		
BNE	Branch if Not Equal to Zero	PSH	Push Data
BPL	Branch if Plus	PUL	Pull Data
BRA	Branch Always		
BSR	Branch to Subroutine	ROL	Rotate Left
BVC	Branch if Overflow Clear	ROR	Rotate Right
BVS	Branch if Overflow Set	RTI	Return from Interrupt
		RTS	Return from Subroutine
CBA	Compare Accumulators		
CLC	Clear Carry	SBA	Subtract Accumulators
CLI	Clear Interrupt Mask	SBC	Subtract with Carry
CLR	Clear	SEC	Set Carry
CLV	Clear Overflow	SEI	Set Interrupt Mask
CMP	Compare	SEV	Set Overflow
COM	Complement	STA	Store Accumulator
CPX	Compare Index Register	STS	Store Stack Register
		STX	Store Index Register
DAA	Decimal Adjust	SUB	Subtract
DEC	Decrement	SWI	Software Interrupt
DES	Decrement Stack Pointer		
DEX	Decrement Index Register	TAB	Transfer Accumulators
		TAP	Transfer Accumulators to Condition Code Register
EOR	Exclusive OR		
		TBA	Transfer Accumulators
INC	Increment	TPA	Transfer Condition Code Register to Accumulator
INS	Increment Stack Pointer		
INX	Increment Index Register	TST	Test
		TSX	Transfer Stack Pointer to Index Register
JMP	Jump		
JSR	Jump to Subroutine	TXS	Transfer Index Register to Stack Pointer
LDA	Load Accumulator		
LDS	Load Stack Pointer	WAI	Wait for Interrupt
LDX	Load Index Register		
LSR	Logical Shift Right		

TABLE 6.4-2 M6800 MICROPROCESSOR DETAILED OP CODES

Instructions		Immediate ①			Absolute			Zero Page			Z, Page, X			Relative			Implied			Status
Mnemonic	Operation ②	OP	N # ④		OP	N	#	OP	N	#	OP	N	#	OP	N	#	OP	N	#	HINZVC
ABA	$A \leftarrow B + A$													1B	2	1				v-vvvv
ADC	$R \leftarrow R + M + C$	89/C9	2	2	B9/F9	4	3	99/D9	3	2	A9/E9	5	2							v-vvvv
ADD	$R \leftarrow R + M$	8B/CB	2	2	BB/FB	4	3	9B/DB	3	2	AB/EB	5	2							v-vvvv
AND	$R \leftarrow R \wedge M$	84/C4	2	2	B4/F4	4	3	94/D4	3	2	A4/E4	5	2							--vv∅-
ASL	$C \leftarrow \boxed{R,M} \leftarrow \emptyset$ ③				78	6	3	68	7	2							48/58	2	1	--vvvv
ASR	$\hookrightarrow \boxed{R,M} \rightarrow C$				77	6	3	67	7	2							47/57	2	1	--vvvv
BCC	Branch C = ∅													24	4	2				------
BCS	Branch C = 1													25	4	2				------
BEQ	Branch Z = 1													27	4	2				------
BGE	Branch N ⊻ V = ∅													2C	4	2				------
BGT	Branch ZV(N V V) = ∅													2E	4	2				------
BHI	Branch C V Z = ∅													22	4	2				------
BIT	$R \wedge M$	85/C5	2	2	B5/F5	4	3	95/D5	3	2	A5/E5	5	2							--vvv-
BLE	ZV(N ⊻ V) = 1													2F	4	2				------
BLS	Branch C V Z = 1													23	4	2				------
BLT	Branch N ⊻ V = 1													2D	4	2				------
BMI	Branch N = 1													2B	4	2				------
BNE	Branch Z = ∅													26	4	2				------
BPL	Branch N = ∅													2A	4	2				------
BRA	Branch always													20	4	2				------
BSR	Branch subroutine													8D	8	2				------
BVC	Branch V = ∅													28	4	2				------
BVS	Branch V = 1													29	4	2				------

Introduction to the M6800 Microprocessor

Instructions		Immediate (1)			Absolute			Zero Page			Z, Page, X			Relative			Implied			Status
Mnemonic	Operation (2)	OP	N	#(4)	OP	N	#	OP	N	#	OP	N	#	OP	N	#	OP	N	#	HINZVC
CBA	A − B																11	2	1	--vvvv
CLC	C ← ∅																∅C	2	1	-----∅
CLI	I ← ∅																∅E	2	1	-∅----
CLR	R,M ← ∅				7F	6	3				6F	7	2				4F/5F	2	1	--∅1∅∅
CLV	V ← ∅																∅A	2	1	----/-
CMP	R − M	81/C1	2	2	B1/F1	4	3	91/D1	3	2	A1/E1	5	2							--vvvv
COM	1's complement				73	6	3				63	7	2				43/53	2	1	--vv∅1
CPX	X − M	8C	3	3	BC	5	3	9C	4	2	AC	6	2							--vvv-
DAA	A ← BCD (A)																19	2	1	--vvvv
DEC	R,M ← R,M − 1				7A	6	3				6A	7	2				4A/5A	2	1	--vvv-
DES	S ← S − 1																34	4	1	------
DEX	X ← X − 1																∅9	4	1	---v--
EOR	R ← R ⊻ M	88/C8	2	2	B8/F8	4	3	98/D8	3	2	A8/E8	5	2							--vv∅-
INC	R,M ← R,M + 1				7C	6	3				6C	7	2				4C/5C	2	1	--vvv-
INS	S ← S + 1																31	4	1	------
INX	X ← X + 1																∅8	4	1	---v--
JMP	JUMP				7E	3	3				6E	4	2							------
JSR	JUMP SUBR				BD	9	3				AD	8	2							------
LDA	R ← M	86/C6	2	2	B6/F6	4	3	96/D6	3	2	A6/E6	5	2							--vvv-
LDS	S ← M	8E	3	3	BE	5	3	9E	4	2	AE	6	2							--vv∅-
LDX	X ← M	CE	3	3	FE	5	3	DE	4	2	EE	6	2							--vv∅-
LSR	∅ → R,M → C				74	6	3				64	7	2				44/54	2	1	--∅vvv
NEG	2's complement				70	6	3				60	7	2				40/50	2	1	--vvvv
NOP																	∅1	2	1	------
ORA	R ← R V M	8A/CA	2	2	BA/FA	4	3	9A/DA	3	2	AA/EA	5	2							--vv∅-
PSH																	36/37	4	1	------
PUL																	32/33	4	1	------

TABLE 6.4-2 (Continued)

Instructions		Immediate (1)			Absolute			Zero Page			Z, Page, X			Relative			Implied			Status
Mnemonic	Operation (2)	OP	N #	(4)	OP	N	#	OP	N	#	OP	N	#	OP	N	#	OP	N	#	HINZVC
ROL	R,M ← C				79	6	3				69	7	2				49/59	2	1	--vvvv
ROR	R,M → C				76	6	3				66	7	2				46/56	2	1	--vvvv
RTI																	3B	10	1	vvvvvv
RTS																	39	5	1	------
SBA	A ← B − A																10	2	1	--vvvv
SBC	R ← R − M − C	82/C2	2	2	B2/F2	4	3	92/D2	3	2	A2/E2	5	2							--vvvv
SEC	C ← 1																0D	2	1	-----1
SEI	I ← 1																0F	2	1	-1----
SEV	V ← 1																0B	2	1	----1-
STA	M ← R				B7/F7	5	3	97/D7	4	2	A7/E7	6	2							--vv0-
STS	M ← S				BF	6	3	9F	5	2	AF	7	2							--vv0-
STX	M ← X				FF	6	3	DF	5	2	EF	7	2							--vv0-
SUB	R ← R − M	80/C0	2	2	B0/F0	4	3	90/D0	3	2	A0/E0	5	2							--vvvv
SWI																	3F	12	1	-1----
TAB	B ← A																16	2	1	--vv0-
TAP	P ← A																06	2	1	vvvvvv
TBA	A ← B																17	2	1	--vv0-
TPA	A ← P																07	2	1	------
TST	R,M − 0				7D	6	3				6D	7	2							--vv00
TSX	X ← S																4D/5D	2	1	------
TXS	S ← X																30	4	1	------
WAI																	3E	9	1	-v----

(1) Operation using ACC A/Acc B   (3) R,M means either A or B or Memory   # is number of bytes of code

(2) R means either A or B   (4) N is number of clock cycles to execute

TABLE 6.4-2 (Continued)

Introduction to the M6800 Microprocessor

the third column) whereas in Add with Carry to the B register Immediate is hex C9. In the table, the number of cycles required is designated by N and the number of bytes required for storing the instruction is denoted by #. The letter R in the second column indicates that these instructions will perform their function on either accumulator, i.e., R should be interpreted as either A or B. There are some instructions that can work on accumulator A, accumulator B or on any location in memory depending upon the addressing mode. Those instructions use R, M to mean A, B or memory. As a specific example, the ASL instruction can be used to do an arithmetic shift operation on a memory location defined by an absolute address, or (as in the second column from the right) on either A or B (Inherent addressing mode). In the particular case of arithmetic shift left on memory the contents of both accumulators are unchanged. In the far right column it may be seen that, after the arithmetic shift left operation is performed, the status bits, sign, zero, overflow and carry will have all been affected, while half carry and interrupt mask will not have been affected.

Some liberty has been taken in Table 6.4-2 as well as in the accompanying material to use the same nomenclature for the M6800 as was used for the MCS6502 in Chapter 3. It should be noted that the M6800 manufacturer's literature uses some different terminology. For example, 'Extended" is the manufacturer's designation for what has here been consistently called "Absolute" addressing. Another manufacturer's "Direct" is the exact equivalent of what here has been called "zero page." Also worth noting is the column "Z Page, X." This again reflects the fact that all index operations are referenced to zero page.

As discussed earlier, it is also important to remember that absolute addresses have the address byte in the opposite order to those for the MCS6502, i.e., the byte immediately following the op code is the high order byte.

Table 6.4-3 is a complete detailed instruction set list.

TABLE 6.4-3 Instruction Set for the M6800
  (Courtesy Motorola Semiconductor Products)

Operators

←	= is transferred to
↑	= "is pulled from stack"
↓	= "is pushed into stack"
∧	= Boolean AND

V	= Boolean OR
V̠	= Exclusive OR
–	= Boolean NOT

Registers in the MPU

A	= Accumulator A
B	= Accumulator B
R	= Accumulator A or B
R,M	= Either Accumulator or Memory
CC	= Condition codes register
IX	= Index register, 16 bits
IXH	= Index register, higher order 8 bits
IXL	= Index register, lower order 8 bits
PC	= Program counter, 16 bits
PCH	= Program counter, higher order 8 bits
PCL	= Program counter, lower order 8 bits
SP	= Stack pointer
SPH	= Stack pointer high
SPL	= Stack pointer low

Memory and Addressing

M	= A memory location (one byte)
M + 1	= The byte of memory at ∅∅∅1 plus the address of the memory location indicated by "M"
Rel	= Relative address (i.e., the two's complement number stored in the second byte of machine code corresponding to a branch instruction

---

ABA **Add Accumulator B to Accumulator A**

Operation: A ← B + A   HINZVC
                                                                                              v–vvvv

Description: Adds the contents of B to the contents of A and places the result in A.

Introduction to the M6800 Microprocessor

ADC   **Add with Carry**

Operation: R ← R + M + C   HINZVC
                                                     v-vvvv

Description: Adds the contents of the C bit to the sum of the contents of R and M, and places the result in R.

ADD   **Add without Carry**

Operation: R ← R + M   HINZVC
                                                      v-vvvv

Description: Adds the contents of R and the contents of M and places the result in R.

AND   **Logical AND**

Operation: R ← R ∧ M   HINZVC
                                                      --vv∅-

Description: Performs logical "AND" between the contents of R and the contents of M and places the result in R. (Each bit of R after the operation will be the logical "AND" of the corresponding bits of M and of R before the operation.)

ASL   **Arithmetic Shift Left**

Operation: HINZVC
                  $\boxed{C} \leftarrow \boxed{\ \ \ \ \ \ \ \ } \leftarrow 0$ --vvvv
                     b_7 b_0

Description: Shifts all bits of either R or M one place to the left. Bit ∅ is loaded with a zero. The C bit is loaded from the most significant bit of either R or M.

ASR — Arithmetic Shift Right

Operation:

```
 ┌──────────────┐
 └→[ | | | | | | | | ]→ [C]        HINZVC
    b₇           b₀                --vvvv
```

Description: Shifts all bits of either R or M one place to the right. Bit 7 is held constant. Bit ∅ is loaded into the C bit.

BCC — Branch if Carry Clear

Operation: PC ← PC + ∅∅02 + Rel if C = ∅   HINZVC

Description: Tests the state of the C bit and causes a branch if C is clear.
See BRA instruction for futher details of the execution of the branch.

BCS — Branch if Carry Set

Operation: PC ← PC + ∅∅02 + Rel if C = 1   HINZVC

Description: Tests the state of the C bit and causes a branch if C is set.

BEQ — Branch if Equal

Operation: PC ← PC + ∅∅02 + Rel if Z = 1   HINZVC

Description: Tests the state of the Z bit and causes a branch if the Z bit is set.

Introduction to the M6800 Microprocessor

BGE Branch if Greater than or Equal to Zero

Operation: PC ← PC + 0002 Rel if N ⊻ V = 0   HINZVC
      ------
      i.e., if R ⩾ M
      (Two's complement numbers)

BGT Branch if Greater than Zero

Operation PC ← PC + 0002 + Rel if Z V [N ⊻ V] = 0
      i.e., if R > M   HINZVC
      (Two's complement numbers)   ------

BHI Branch if Higher

Operation: PC ← PC + 0002 + Rel if C V Z = 0 HINZVC
      i.e., if R > M   ------
      (unsigned binary numbers)

Description: Causes a branch if (C is clear) AND (Z is clear)

If the BHI instruction is executed immediately after execution of any of the instructions CBA, CMP, SBA, or SUB, the branch will occur if and only if the *unsigned binary number* represented by the minuend (i.e., R) were greater than the unsigned binary number represented by the subtrahend (i.e., M).

BIT Bit Test

Operation: R ∧ M   HINZVC
                          --vvv-

Description: Performs the logical "AND" of the contents of R and the contents of M and modifies conditin codes accordingly. Neither the contents of R nor M operands are affected. (Each bit of the result of the "AND" would be the logical "AND" of the corresponding bits of M and R.)

BLE   **Branch if Less than or Equal to Zero**

Operation: PC ← PC + ØØØ2 + Rel if Z V [N ⊻ V] = 1
             i.e., if R ≤ M   HINZVC
             (Two's complement numbers)   ------

Description: Causes a branch if [Z is set] OR[(N is set and V is clear) OR (N is clear and V is set)].

If the BLE instruction is executed immediately after execution of any of the instructions CBA, CMP, SBA, or SUB, the branch will occur if and only if the *two's complement number* represented by the minuend (i.e., R) were less than or equal to the *two's complement number* represented by the subtrahend (i.e., M).

BLS   **Branch if Lower or Same**

Operation: PC ← PC + ØØØ2 + Rel if C OR Z = 1   HINZVC
             i.e., if R ≤ M   ------
             (Unsigned binary numbers)

Description: Causes a branch if (C is set) OR (Z is set).

If the BLS instruction is executed immediately after execution of any of the instructions CBA, CMP, SBA, or SUB, the branch will occur if and only if the *unsigned binary number* represented by the minuend (i.e., R) were less than or equal to the *unsigned binary number* represented by the subtrahend (i.e., M).

Introduction to the M6800 Microprocessor 317

BLT   **Branch if Less than Zero**

Operation: PC ← PC + 0002 + Rel if N $\veebar$ V = 1   HINZVC
                 i.e., if R < M   ------
              (Two's complement numbers)

Description: Causes a branch if (N is set and V is clear) OR (N is clear and V is set).

                If the BLT instruction is executed immediately after execution of any of the instructions CBA, CMP, SBA, or SUB, the branch will occur if and only if the *two's complement number* represented by the minuend (i.e., R) were less than the *two's complement number* represented by the subtrahend (i.e., M).

BMI   **Branch if Minus**

Operation: PC ← PC + 0002 + Rel if N = 1   HINZVC

Description: Tests the state of the N bit and causes a branch if N is set.

BNE   **Branch if Not Equal**

Operation: PC ← PC + 0002 + Rel if z = 0 HINZVC

Description: Tests the state of the Z bit and causes a branch if the Z bit is clear.

BPL   **Branch if Plus**

Operation: PC ← PC + 0002 + Rel if N = 0 HINZVC

Description: Tests the state of the N bit and causes a branch if N is clear.

BRA   Branch Always

Operation: PC ← PC + 0002 + Rel   HINZVC

Description: Unconditional branch to the address given by the foregoing formula, in which R is the relative address stored as a two's complement number in the second byte of machine code corresponding to the branch instruction.

BSR   Branch to Subroutine

Operation: PC ← PC + 0002   HINZVC
                ↓   PCL   ------
                S ← S − 0001
                ↓   PCH
                S ← S − 0001
                PC ← PC + REL

Description: The program counter is incremented by 2. The less significant byte of the contents of the program counter is pushed into the stack. The stack pointer is then decremented (by 1). The more significant byte of the contents of the program counter is then pushed into the stack. The stack pointer is again decremented (by 1). A branch then occurs to the location specified by the program.

BVC   Branch if Overflow Clear

Operation: PC ← PC + 0002 + Rel if V = 0   HINZVC

Description: Tests the state of the V bit and causes a branch if the V bit is clear.

Introduction to the M6800 Microprocessor

BVS   **Branch if Overflow Set**

Operation: PC ← PC + ØØØ2 + Rel if V = 1   HINZVC

Description: Tests the state of the V bit and causes a branch if the V bit is set.

CBA   **Compare Accumulators**

Operation: A − B   HINZVC
                                                                        --vvvv

Description: Compares the contents of A and the contents of B and sets the condition codes, which may be used for arithmetic and logical conditional branches. Both operands are unaffected.

CLC   **Clear Carry**

Operation: C ← Ø   HINZVC
                                                                        -----Ø

Description: Clears the carry bit in the processor condition codes register.

CLI   **Clear Interrupt Mask**

Operation: I ← Ø   HINZVC
                                                                        -Ø----

Description: Clears the interrupt mask bit in the processor condition codes register. This enables the microprocessor to service an interrupt from a peripheral device if signalled by a low state of the $\overline{\text{IRQ}}$ control input.

CLR Clear

Operation: R,M ← ∅

```
HINZVC
--0100
```

Description: The contents of R or M are replaced with zero.

CLV Clear Two's Complement Overflow Bit

Operation: V ← ∅

```
HINZVC
----0-
```

Description: Clears the two's complement overflow bit in the processor condition codes register.

CMP Compare

Operation: R − M

```
HINZVC
--vvvv
```

Description: Compares the contents of R and the contents of M and determines the condition codes, which may be used subsequently for controlling conditional branching. Both operands are unaffected.

COM Complement

Operation: R,M ← $\overline{R},\overline{M}$

```
HINZVC
--vv01
```

Description: Replaces the contents of R or M with their one's complement. (Each bit of the contents of R or M is replaced with the complement of that bit.)

CPX Compare Index Register

Operation: X − M

HINZVC
− − v v v −

Description: The more significant byte of the contents of the index register is compared with the contents of the byte of memory at the address specified by the program. The less significant byte of the contents of the index register is compared with the contents of the next byte of memory, at one plus the address specified by the program. The Z bit is set or reset according to the results of these comparisons, and may be used subsequently for conditional branching.

The N and V bits, though determined by this operation, are not intended for conditional branching.

The C bit is not affected by this operation.

DAA Decimal Adjust ACCA

Operation: Adds hexadecimal number ∅∅, ∅6, 6∅, or 66 to ACCA, and may also set the carry bit.

HINZVC
− − v v v v

Description: If the contents of ACCA and the state of the carry-borrow bit C and the half-carry bit H are all the result of applying any of the operations ABA, ADD, or ADC to binary-coded-decimal operands, with or without an intial carry, the DAA operation will function as follows.

Subject to the above condition, the DAA operation will adjust the contents of ACCA and the C bit to represent the correct binary-coded-decimal sum and the correct state of the carry.

DEC   Decrement

Operation: R,M ← R,M − 1   HINZVC
                                                                                                --vvv-

Description: Subtract one from the contents of R or M.

                The N, Z, and V condition codes are set or reset according to the results of this operation.

                The C bit is not affected by the operation.

DES   Decrement Stack Pointer

Operation: S ← S − 1   HINZVC

Description: Subtract one from the stack pointer.

DEX   Decrement Index Register

Operation: X ← X − 1   HINZVC
                                                                                       ---v--

Description: Subtract one from the index register.

                Only the Z bit is set or reset according to the result of this operation.

EOR   Exclusive OR

Operation: R ← R ⊻ M   HINZVC
                                                                                --vv∅-

Description: Perform logical "EXCLUSIVE OR" between the contents of R and the contents of M, and place the result in R. (Each bit of R after the operation will be the logical "EXCLUSIVE OR" of the corresponding bits of M and R before the operation.)

Introduction to the M6800 Microprocessor

INC   **Increment**

Operation: R,M ← R,M + 1   HINZVC
                                                             - - v v - -

Description: Add one to the contents of R or M.

The N, Z, and V condition codes are set or reset according to the result of this operation.

The C bit is not affected by the operation.

INS   **Increment Stack Pointer**

Operation: S ← S + 1   HINZVC
                                                             - - - - - -

Description: Add one to the stack pointer.

INX   **Increment Index Register**

Operation: X ← X + 1   HINZVC
                                                             - - - v - -

Description: Add one to the index register.

Only the Z bit is set or reset according to the result of this operation.

JMP   **Jump**

Operation: PC ← numerical address   HINZVC
                                                             - - - - - -

Description: A jump occurs to the instruction stored at the numerical address. The numerical address is obtained according to the rules for Absolute or Zero Page Indexed addressing.

JSR   **Jump to Subroutine**

Operation: Either: PC ← PC + 3 (for EXTended addressing)
                 or: PC ← PC + 2 (for INDexed addressing)
                Then: ↓ PCL
                          S ← S − 1   HINZVC
                            ↓ PCH   − − − − − −
                          S ← S − 1
                          PC ← numerical address

Description: The program counter is incremented by 3 or by 2, depending on the addressing mode, and is then pushed onto the stack, eight bits at a time. The stack pointer points to the next empty location in the stack. A jump occurs to the instruction stored at the numerical address.

LDA   **Load Accumulator**

Operation: R ← M   HINZVC
                                                         − − v v v −

Description: Loads the contents of memory into the accumulator. The condition codes are set according to the data.

LDS   **Load Stack Pointer**

Operation: S ← M   HINZVC
                                                         − − v v 0 −

Description: Loads the more significant byte of the stack pointer from byte of memory at the address specified by the program, and loads the less significant byte of the stack pointer from the next byte of memory, at one plus the address specified by the program.

Introduction to the M6800 Microprocessor 325

LDX   **Load Index Register**

Operation: $X \leftarrow M$ HINZVC
                                                                                  --vv∅-

Description: Loads the more significant byte of the index register from byte of memory at the address specified by the program, and loads the less significant byte of the index register from the next byte of memory, at one plus the address specified by the program.

LSR   **Logical Shift Right**

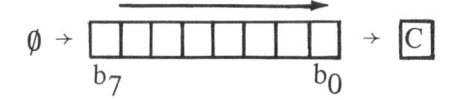

Operation: $0 \rightarrow \boxed{} \rightarrow \boxed{C}$ HINZVC
                              b_7 b_0 --∅vvv

Description: Shifts all bits of R or M one place to the right. Bit 7 is loaded with a zero. The C bit is loaded from the least significant bit of R or M.

NEG   **Negate**

Operation: $R,M \leftarrow 0 - R,M$ HINZVC
                                                                          --vvvv

Description: Replaces the contents of R or M with its two's complement. Note that $80 is left unchanged.

NOP   **No Operation**

Description: This is a single-word instruction which causes only the program counter to be incremented. No other registers are affected.

ORA — Inclusive OR

Operation: R ← R V M   HINZVC
    --vv∅-

Description: Perform logical "OR" between the contents of R and the contents of M and places the result in R. (Each bit of R after the operation will be the logical "OR" of the corresponding bits of M and of R before the operation.)

PSH — Push Data Onto Stack

Operation: ↓ R   HINZVC
S ← S − ∅∅∅1   ------

Description: The contents of R is stored in the stack at the address contained in the stack pointer. The stack pointer is then decremented.

PUL — Pull Data from Stack

Operation: S ← S + 1   HINZVC
↑ R   ------

Description: The stack pointer is incremented. The R is then loaded from the stack, for the address which is contained in the stack pointer.

ROL — Rotate Left

Operation: [C] ← ⬜⬜⬜⬜⬜⬜⬜⬜ ← [C]   HINZVC
    b_7 b_0 --vvvv

Description: Shifts all bits of R or M one place to the left. Bit ∅ is loaded from the C bit. The C bit is loaded from the most significant bit of R or M.

Introduction to the M6800 Microprocessor

ROR   **Rotate Right**

Operation: $\boxed{C} \to \boxed{} \to \boxed{C}$ HINZVC
                 b_7 b_0 --vvvv

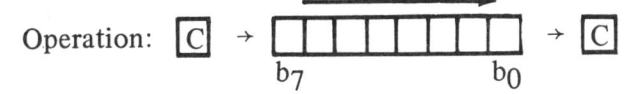

Description: Shifts all bits of R or M one place to the right. Bit 7 is loaded from the C bit. The C bit is loaded from the least significant bit of R or M.

RTI   **Return from Interrupt**

Operation: $S \leftarrow S + 1$, $\uparrow CC$ HINZVC

                 $S \leftarrow S + 1$, $\uparrow ACCB$ vvvvvv

                 $S \leftarrow S + 1$, $\uparrow ACCA$

                 $S \leftarrow S + 1$, $\uparrow IXH$

                 $S \leftarrow S + 1$, $\uparrow IXL$

                 $S \leftarrow S + 1$, $\uparrow PCH$

                 $S \leftarrow S + 1$, $\uparrow PCL$

Description: The condition codes, accumulators B and A, the index register, and the program counter, will be restored to a state pulled from the stack. Note that the interrupt mask bit will be reset if and only if the corresponding bit stored in the stack is zero.

RTS Return from Subroutine

Operation: S ← S + 1   HINZVC
                 ↑ PCH   ------
                 S ← S + 1
                 ↑ PCL

Description: The stack pointer is incremented (by 1). The contents of the byte of memory, at the address now contained in the stack pointer, is loaded into the 8 bits of highest significance in the program counter. The stack pointer is again incremented (by 1). the contents of the byte of memory, at the address now contained in the stack pointer, is loaded into the 8 bits of lowest significance in the program counter.

SBA Subtract Accumulators

Operation: A ← A − B   HINZVC
                                                                    --vvvv

Description: Subtracts the contents of B from the contents of A and places the result in A. The contents of B are not affected.

SBC Subtract with Carry

Operation: R ← R − M − C   HINZVC
                                                                    --vvvv

Description: Subtracts the contents of M and C from the contents of R and places the result in R.

Introduction to the M6800 Microprocessor

SEC   **Set Carry**

Operation: C ← 1   HINZVC
                                                               -----1

Description: Sets the carry bit in the processor condition codes register.

SEI   **Set Interrupt Mask**

Operation: I ← 1   HINZVC
                                                               -1----

Description: Sets the interrupt mask bit in the processor condition codes register. The microprocessor is inhibited from servicing an interrupt from a peripheral device, and will continue with execution of the instructions of the program, until the interrupt mask bit has been cleared.

SEV   **Set Two's Complement Overflow Bit**

Operation: V ← 1   HINZVC
                                                               ----1-

Description: Sets the two's complement overflow bit in the processor condition codes register.

STA   **Store Accumulator**

Operation: M ← R   HINZVC
                                                               --vv∅-

Description: Stores the contents of R in memory. The contents of R remains unchanged.

STS   Store Stack Pointer

Operation: M ← S   HINZVC
                                                    --vv∅-

Description: Stores the more significant byte of the stack pointer in memory at the address specified by the program, and stores the less significant byte of the stack pointer at the next location in memory, at one plus the address specified by the program.

STX   Store Index Register

Operation: M ← X   HINZVC
                                                    --vv∅-

Description: Stores the more significant byte of the index register in memory at the address specified by the program, and stores the less significant byte of the index register at the next location in memory, at one plus the address specified by the program.

SUB   Subtract

Operation: R ← R − M   HINZVC
                                                    --vvvv

Description: Subtracts the contents of M from the contents of R and places the result in R.

Introduction to the M6800 Microprocessor

SWI   **Software Interrupt**

Operation: PC ← (PC) + 0001   HINZVC
↓ (PCL) , S ← S − 1   -1----
↓ (PCH) , S ← S − 1
↓ (IXL)   , S ← S − 1
↓ (IXH) , S ← S − 1
↓ (ACCA) , S ← S − 1
↓ (ACCB) , S ← S − 1
↓ (CC)   , S ← S − 1
I ← 1
PCH ← ($FFFA)
PCL ← ($FFFB)

Description: The program counter is incremented (by 1). The program counter, index register, and accumulator A and B, are pushed into the stack, with condition codes H, I, N, Z, V, and C going respectively into bit positions 5 through 0, and the top two bits (in bit positions 7 and 6) are set (to the 1 state). The stack pointer is decremented (by 1) after each byte of data is stored in the stack.

The interrupt mask bit is then set. The program counter is then loaded with the address stored in the software interrupt pointer at memory locations $FFFA and $FFFB, where n is the address corresponding to a high state on all lines of the address bus.

TAB   **Transfer from Accumulator A to Accumulator B**

Operation: B ← A   HINZVC
                                                                --vv0-

Description: Moves the contents of A to B. The former contents of B are lost. The contents of A are not affected.

TAP   **Transfer from Accumulator A to Processor Condition Codes Register**

Operation: P ← A   HINZVC
                                                               vvvvvv

Bit Positions

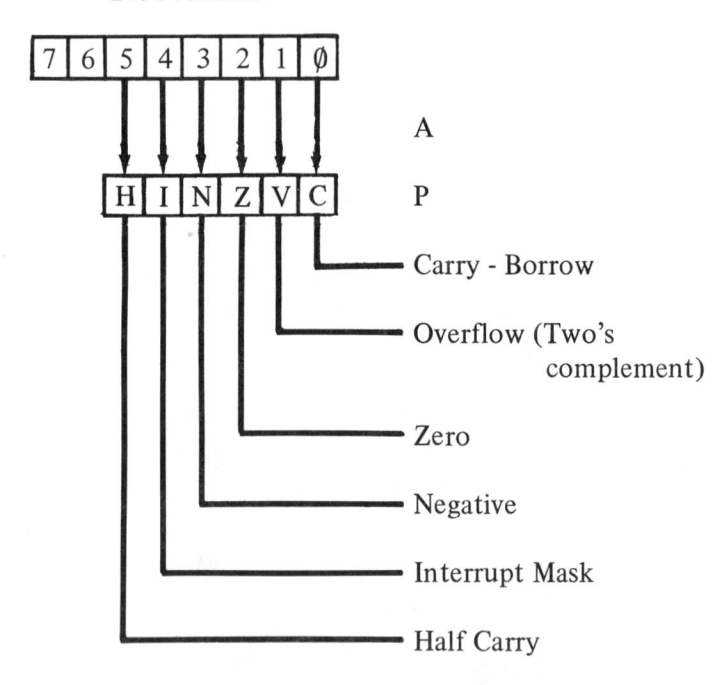

```
┌─┬─┬─┬─┬─┬─┬─┬─┐
│7│6│5│4│3│2│1│0│  A
└─┴─┴─┴─┴─┴─┴─┴─┘
     │ │ │ │ │ │
     ▼ ▼ ▼ ▼ ▼ ▼
    ┌─┬─┬─┬─┬─┬─┐
    │H│I│N│Z│V│C│  P
    └─┴─┴─┴─┴─┴─┘
```

- Carry - Borrow
- Overflow (Two's complement)
- Zero
- Negative
- Interrupt Mask
- Half Carry

Description: Transfers the contents of bit positions 0 though 5 of accumulator A to the corresponding bit positions of the processor condition codes register. The contents of accumulator A remain unchanged.

TBA   **Transfer from Accumulator B to Accumulator A**

Operation: A ← B   HINZVC
                                                               --vv0-

Description: Moves the contents of B to A. The former contents of A are lost. The contents of B are not affected.

Introduction to the M6800 Microprocessor

TPA   **Transfer from Processor Condition Codes Register to Accumulator A**

Operation: A ← P   HINZVC

Bit Positions

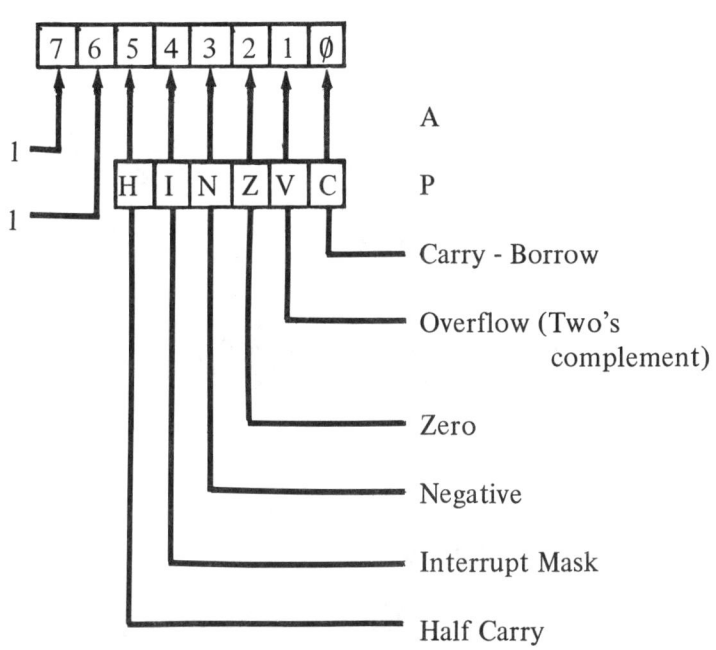

```
 7  6  5  4  3  2  1  0
 ↑  ↑  ↑  ↑  ↑  ↑  ↑  ↑      A
1┘  │  │  │  │  │  │  │
 1──┤ ┌─┬─┬─┬─┬─┐ │  │
    └─┤H│I│N│Z│V│C│       P
      └─┴─┴─┴─┴─┴─┘
                  └── Carry - Borrow
                └──── Overflow (Two's
                                complement)
              └────── Zero
            └──────── Negative
          └────────── Interrupt Mask
        └──────────── Half Carry
```

Description: Transfers the contents of the processor condition codes register to corresponding bit positions 0 through 5 of accumulator A. Bit positions 6 and 7 of accumulator A are set (i.e., go to the "1" state). The processor condition codes register remains unchanged.

TST   **Test**

Operation: R,M ← R,M − 0   HINZVC
                                                          --vv00

Description: Set condition codes N and Z according to the contents of R or M.

TSX   Transfer from Stack Pointer to Index Register

Operation: X ← S + 1   HINZVC

Description: Loads the index register with one plus the contents of the stack pointer. The contents of the stack pointer remains unchanged. Note that S is normally "off by one."

TXS   Transfer from Index Register to Stack Pointer

Operation: S ← X − 1   HINZVC

Description: Loads the stack pointer with the contents of the index register, minus one. The contents of the index register remains unchanged.

WAI   Wait for Interrupt

Operation: PC ← PC + 0001   HINZVC
             ↓ (PCL) , S ← S − 1   -v----
             ↓ (PCH) , S ← S − 1
             ↓ (IXL) , S ← S − 1
             ↓ (IXH) , S ← S − 1
             ↓ (ACCA), S ← S − 1
             ↓ (ACCB), S ← S − 1
             ↓ (CC) , S ← S − 1

Description: The program counter is incremented (by 1). The program counter, index register, and accumulators A and B are pushed into the stack. The condition codes register is then pushed into the stack, with condition codes H, I, N, Z, V and C going respectively into bit positions 5 through 0, and the top two bits (in bit positions 7 and 6) are set (to the 1 state). The stack pointer is decremented (by 1) after each byte of data is stored in the stack.

Introduction to the M6800 Microprocessor 335

Execution of the program is then suspended until an interrupt from a peripheral device is signalled, by the interrupt request control input going to a high state.

When an interrupt is signalled on the interrupt request line, and provided the I bit is clear, execution proceeds as follows. The interrupt mask bit is set. The program counter is then loaded with the address stored in the internal interrupt pointer at memory locations $FFF8 and $FFF9, where n is the address corresponding to a high state on all lines of the address bus.

6.5 ELECTRICAL CHARACTERISTICS OF THE M6800

Figure 6.5-1 shows the mechanical arrangement of the M6800 external connections. This section will briefly describe the function of those signals.

1. V_{ss} *(pins 1 and 21)*, V_{CC} *(pin 8)*: V_{CC} is the +5 volt DC supply relative to V_{ss}, ground.

2. A_0 - A_{15} *Address Bus (pins 9 - 25)*: These pins, like the identical ones of the MCS6502, comprise the address bus. They are driven by three-state bus drivers capable of driving one standard TTL load and 130 pF capacitance. When an output is turned off (by TSC, item 6 on this list), it is essentially an open circuit. This permits the MPU to be used in DMA applications.

3. D_0 - D_7 *Data Bus (pins 26 - 33)*: Again, these are identical to the MCS6502.

4. *R/$\overline{W}$ Read/Write (pin 34)*: This TTL compatible output line signals the peripherals and memory devices whether the MPU is in a Read (high) or Write (low) state. The nonactive state of this signal is Read (high). Three-State Control (TSC) going high will turn Read/Write to the off (high impedance) state. When the processor is halted, it will be in the off state. This output is capable of driving one standard TTL load and 90 pF of capacitance.

5. *$\phi 1$, $\phi 2$ Clock Signals (pins 3 and 37)*: Input to the M6800 from a two-phase nonoverlapping clock generator must generate voltage levels within 0.3 volts of V_{ss} and V_{CC}.

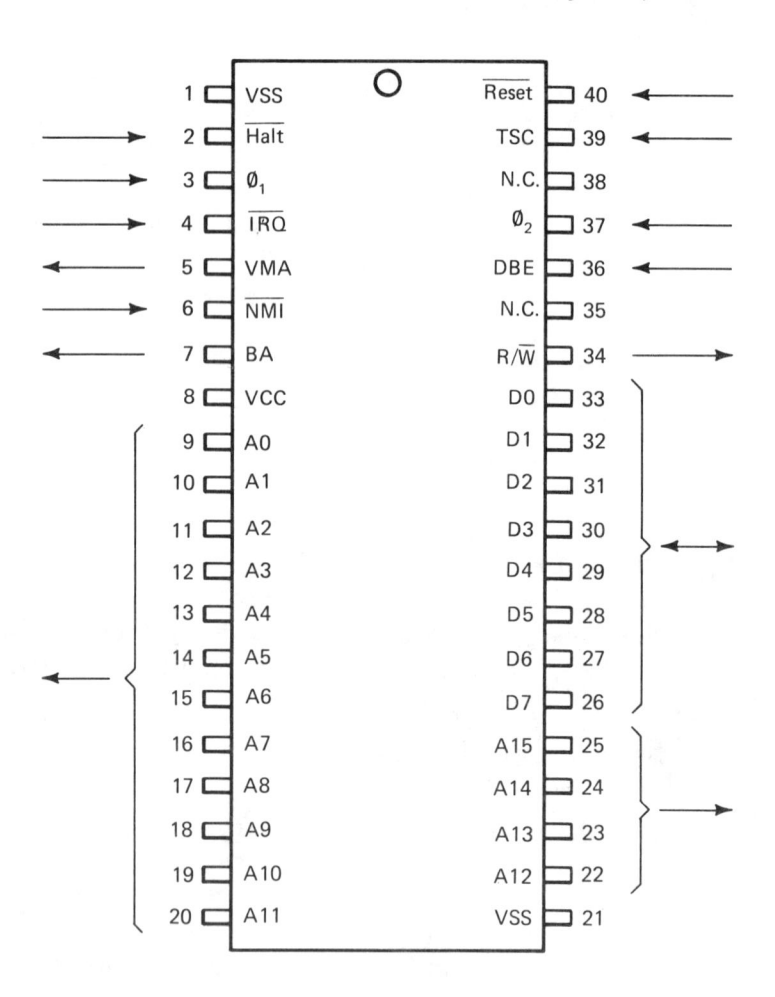

```
         ┌─────────────┐
    1 ─┤ VSS     Reset ├─ 40
    2 ─┤ Halt     TSC  ├─ 39
    3 ─┤ Ø₁      N.C.  ├─ 38
    4 ─┤ IRQ      Ø₂   ├─ 37
    5 ─┤ VMA      DBE  ├─ 36
    6 ─┤ NMI     N.C.  ├─ 35
    7 ─┤ BA      R/W   ├─ 34
    8 ─┤ VCC      D0   ├─ 33
    9 ─┤ A0       D1   ├─ 32
   10 ─┤ A1       D2   ├─ 31
   11 ─┤ A2       D3   ├─ 30
   12 ─┤ A3       D4   ├─ 29
   13 ─┤ A4       D5   ├─ 28
   14 ─┤ A5       D6   ├─ 27
   15 ─┤ A6       D7   ├─ 26
   16 ─┤ A7      A15   ├─ 25
   17 ─┤ A8      A14   ├─ 24
   18 ─┤ A9      A13   ├─ 23
   19 ─┤ A10     A12   ├─ 22
   20 ─┤ A11     VSS   ├─ 21
         └─────────────┘
```

Figure 6.5-1 M6800 pin assignment

6. *Three-State Control (TSC) (pin 39):* This input causes all of the address lines and the Read/Write line to go into high impedance state. This state will occur within 700 ns after TSC = 2.0 volts. The Valid Memory Address and Bus Available signals will be forced low. The data bus is not affected by TSC and has its own enable (Data Bus Enable). In DMA applications, the Three-State Control line should be brought high on the leading edge of the Phase One clock. The $\phi 1$ clock must be held in the high state and the $\phi 2$ in the low state for this function to operate properly. The address bus will then be available for other devices to

Introduction to the M6800 Microprocessor

directly address memory. Since the MPU is a dynamic device, it can be held in this state for only 4.5 μs or loss of data held in internal MPU registers may occur.

7. *Halt (pin 2):* When this input is in the low state, all activity in the machine will be halted. This input is level sensitive. When HALT is invoked, the machine will stop after executing its current instruction. Bus Available will go high, level, Valid Memory Address will go low, and all three-state lines will go into the high-impedance state.

Transition of the Halt line must not occur during the last 250 ns of phase one. To ensure single instruction operation, the Halt line must go high for one Clock cycle.

8. *Interrupt Request (IRQ) (pin 4):* This level-sensitive input requests that an interrupt sequence be generated within the machine. The processor will wait until it completes the current instruction that is being executed before it recognizes the request. At that time, if the interrupt mask bit in the Condition Code (Status) Register is not set, the machine will begin an interrupt sequence. As first steps in this sequence, the Index Register, Program Counter, Accumulators, and Condition Code Register are stored away on the stack. Next the MPU will respond to the interrupt request by setting the interrupt mask bit high so that no further interrupts may occur. As in the MCS6502, two 16-bit addresses (FFF8 and FFF9) are next placed on the address bus, fetching a 16-bit address which, when loaded into PC, causes the MPU to branch to an interrupt routine in memory.

The Halt line must be in the high state for interrupts to be serviced. Interrupts will be latched internally while Halt is low.

The IRQ has a high impedance pullup device internal to the chip; however, a 3 kΩ external resistor to V_{CC} should be used if multiple interrupt sources are connected using a WIRED-OR configuration.

9. *Valid Memory Address (VMA pin 5):* This output indicates to peripheral devices that there is a valid address on the address bus. In normal operation, this signal should be utilized for enabling peripheral interfaces such as the PIA and ACIA (Asynchronous Communication Interface Adapter). This signal is *not* three-state. One standard TTL load and 90 pF may be directly driven by this active-high signal.

10. *NonMaskable Interrupt (NMI pin 6):* A low-going edge on this input requests that a nonmaskable-interrupt sequence be generated within the processor. As with the Interrupt Request signal, the pro-

cessor will complete the current instruction that is being executed before it recognizes the $\overline{\text{NMI}}$ signal. The interrupt mask bit in the Condition Code Register has no effect on $\overline{\text{NMI}}$.

The Index Register, Program Counter, Accumulators, and Condition Code Register are stored away on the stack. The same interrupt sequence described in item 8 above is performed, except that the vector is read from locations FFFC and FFFD in this case.

$\overline{\text{NMI}}$ has a high impedance pullup resistor internal to the chip; however a 3 kΩ external resistor to V_{CC} should be used if multiple interrupt sources are connected via a WIRED-OR connection.

11. *Bus Available (BA pin 7):* The Bus Available signal will normally be in the low state; when activated, it will go to the high state indicating that the microprocessor has stopped and that the address bus is available. This will occur if the $\overline{\text{Halt}}$ line is in the low state or the processor is in the WAIT state as a result of the execution of a WAIT instruction. At such time, all three-state output drivers will go to their off state and other outputs to their normally inactive level. The processor is removed from the WAIT state by the occurrence of either an enabled maskable or a nonmaskable interrupt. This output is capable of driving one standard TTL load and 30 pF.

12. *Data Bus Enable (DBE pin 36):* This input is the three-state control signal for the MPU data bus and will enable the bus drivers when in the high state. This input is TTL compatible; however in normal operation, it would be driven by the phase two clock. During an MPU read cycle, the data bus drivers will be disabled internally. When it is desired that another device control the data bus such as in Direct Memory Access (DMA) applications, DBE should be held low.

13. *$\overline{\text{Reset}}$ ($\overline{\text{RESET}}$ pin 40):* The input is used to reset and start the MPU from a power down condition, resulting from a power failure or an initial start-up of the processor. If a low level is detected on this input, the MPU will begin to reset sequence. This will start execution of a sequence to initialize the processor. This sequence resembles IRQ and NMI sequences, except that no program state is saved on the stack. For the reset, the contents of the last two ($FFFE, $FFFF) locations in

memory will be loaded into the program counter. During the reset routine, the interrupt mask bit is set and must be reset before the MPU can be interrupted by $\overline{IRQ}$.

6.6 M6800 BASED MICROCOMPUTER EXAMPLE

Figure 6.6-1 shows a simple M6800-based microcomputer. Specific details of the clock and control are not shown, but they consist of simple circuits requiring from one to three extra chips, capacitors, resistors and switches. Several characteristics are worth noting. First, since the address lines are not always guaranteed to have a valid address, all ROM, RWM, and PIA parts must be selected, or enabled by VMA. Second, some address lines (A_{13} - A_{15}) are never used, i.e., they are not connected to anything. Since the stack area does not have to be in Page 1 for the M6800, more latitude is possible than with the MCS6502 in memory mapping. However, since zero page address mode is conservative of both time and program ROM, it would likely be used for RWM variable storage. If the microcomputer were heavily I/O bound it might be advisable to place all PIA addresses in zero page, and RWM elsewhere.

Table 6.6-1 shows the tabular form address selection table for the M6800 example microcomputer. As discussed in Chapter 5 the X indicates that an address line is connected, and used for selection within the corresponding part. The 1 or 0 indicates chip selection and (1) or (0) means that it is not connected (thus is a "don't care"). Because the MPU generates address values, whether connected or not, care must be taken that image addresses (which match at the pins which are con-

TABLE 6.6-1 Address Selection Table

ADDRESS LINES																*SELECTED*	*ADDRESS*
15	*14*	*13*	*12*	*11*	*10*	*9*	*8*	*7*	*6*	*5*	*4*	*3*	*2*	*1*	*∅*	*PART*	*RANGE*
(1)	(1)	(1)	1	1	1	X	X	X	X	X	X	X	X	X	X	ROM	1C∅∅–1FFF
			∅	∅	∅			∅	X	X	X	X	X	X	X	RWM	∅∅∅∅–∅∅7F
			1	∅	1									X	X	PIA	14∅∅–14∅3

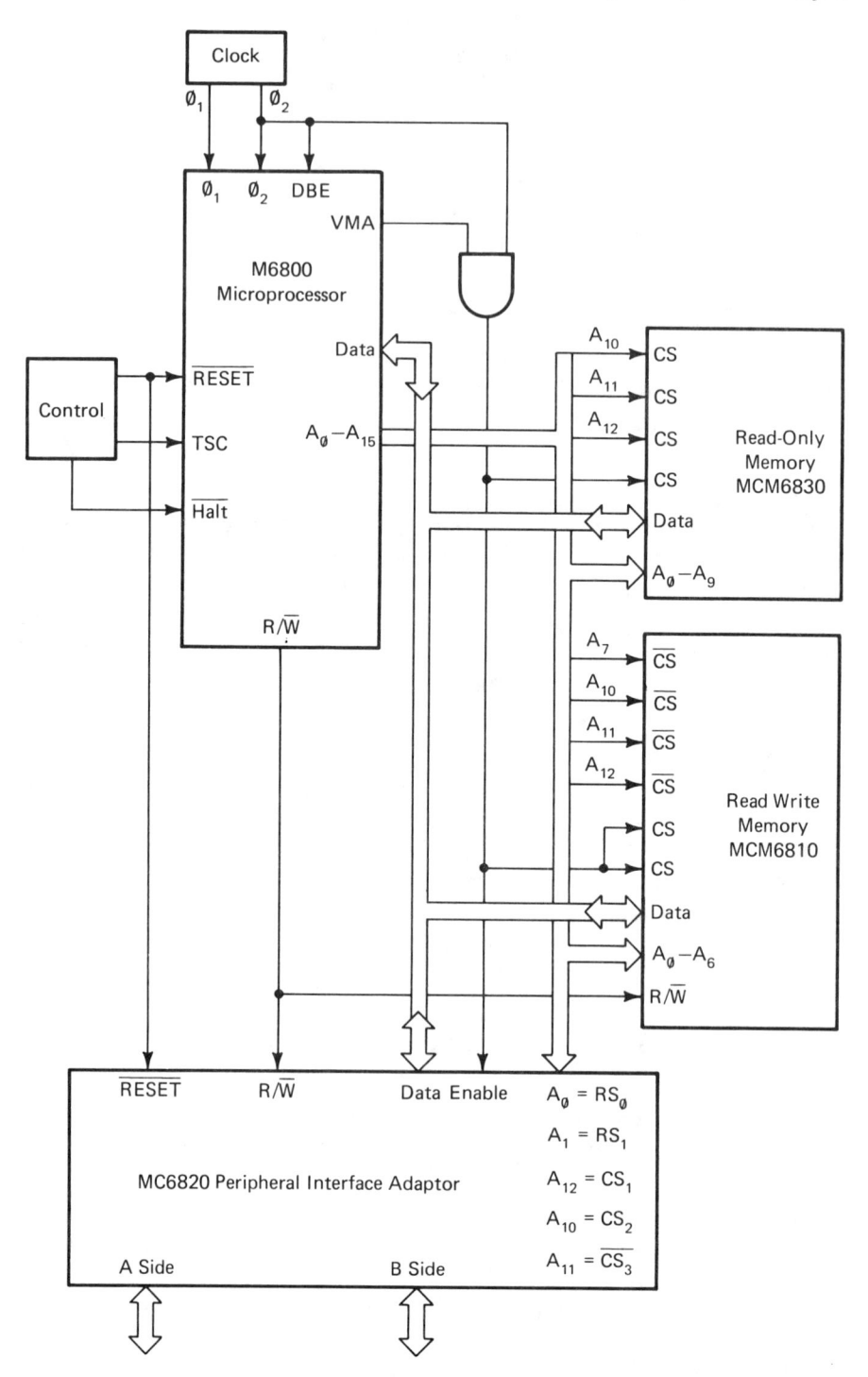

Figure 6.6-1 Example M6800 based microcomputer

Introduction to the M6800 Microprocessor 341

nected) are not assigned to other devices which may be accessed. For example, the same byte in ROM will be selected if the address line contains $1C00, $3C00, $5C00, $7C00, $9C00, $BC00, $DC00 or $FC00. Although it would be natural to use addresses $1C00 to $1FFF in writing code for this system, the M6800 will present $FFFE and $FFFF to the address bus during Reset handling. The vectors to the initial program location upon Reset would most likely be in ROM ($1C00 - $1FFF) and must be placed upon the data bus in response to Reset. Therefore, without these images it would be necessary to decode the additional address bits to guarantee vectoring on $FFFE and $FFFF.

6.7 EXAMPLE PROGRAMS

This section contains listings of a number of example M6800 programs. These listings were produced by the Motorola M68SAM cross-assembler running on an IBM 360/65.

```
                  M68SAM IS THE PROPERTY OF MOTOROLA SPD, INC.
                  COPYRIGHT 1974 BY MOTOROLA INC

                  MOTCROLA M6800 CROSS ASSEMBLER, RELEASE 1.1

00001                          NAM      MULTIPLY
00002                *
00003                ***************************************************
00004                *    PROGRAM #1       8 X 8 BIT MULTIPLY           *
00005                *                     (16 BIT RESULT)              *
00006                *                                                  *
00007                *    UNSIGNED PRODUCT OF (A) * (B)                 *
00008                *    RESULT LEFT IN (A,B)                          *
00009                *                                                  *
00010                ***************************************************
00011                *
00012 0000                     ORG      0
00013                *
00014 0000 36        MULT8     PSH A              SAVE A ON STACK.
00015 0001 86 08               LDA A    #8
00016 0003 36                  PSH A              LOOP COUNT TO TOP OF STACK.
00017 00C4 30                  TSX                INDEX REG POINTS TO TOS.
00018 0005 4F                  CLR A              BOTH A AND C CLEARED.
00019 0006 56                  ROR B              CHECK LSB OF B.
C0020 0007 24 02               BCC      MULT2     IF LSB=0 DO NOT ADD MCND.
00021 0009 AB 01               ADD A    1,X       MCND NEXT ONE UP ON STACK.
00022 000B 46        MULT2     ROR A
00023 000C 56                  ROR B              MOVE A,B PAIR OVER TOGETHER.
00024 000D 6A 00               DEC      0,X       DECREMENT LOOP COUNT.
00025 000F 26 F6               BNE      MULT1     IF N.E. 0 THEN LOOP AGAIN.
00026 0011 31                  INS
00027 0012 31                  INS                CLEAN UP STACK.
00028 0013 39                  RTS                AND RETURN.
00029                          END

SYMBOL TABLE
MULT8   0000    MULT1   0007    MULT2   000B
```

```
                    M68SAM IS THE PROPERTY OF MOTOROLA SPD, INC.
                       COPYRIGHT 1974 BY MOTOROLA INC

                    MOTOROLA M6800 CROSS ASSEMBLER, RELEASE 1.1

00001                           NAM     BLOCK    MOVE
00002                   *
00003                   ***************************************************
00004                   *  PROGRAM   #2    EXTENDED BLOCK MOVE.            *
00005                   *  REGS A, X, P  ALTERED                           *
00006                   *                                                  *
00007                   ***************************************************
00008                   *
00009 0000                      ORG     0
00010 0000 A000 FROM    FDB     $A000
00011 0002 C000 TO      FDB     $C000
00012 0004 0150 LENGTH  FDB     $150
00013 0006 0000 FMSAV   FDB     0
00014 0008 0000 TOSAV   FDB     0
00015 000A 0000 LENSAV  FDB     0
00016 0100                      ORG     $100
00017                   *
00018                   *   SAMPLE CALL
00019                   *
00020 0100 DE 00                LDX     FROM
00021 0102 DF 06                STX     FMSAV
00022 0104 DE 02                LDX     TO
00023 0106 DF 08                STX     TOSAV
00024 0108 DE 04                LDX     LENGTH
00025 010A DF 0A                STX     LENSAVE
00026 010C BD 0110              JSR     BLKMOV
00027 010F 3E                   WAI
00028                   *
00029 0110 DE 06        BLKMOV  LDX     FMSAV
00030 0112 A6 00                LDA A   0,X
00031 0114 08                   INX
00032 0115 DF 06                STX     FMSAV
00033 0117 DE 08                LDX     TOSAV
00034 0119 A7 00                STA A   0,X
00035 011B 08                   INX
00036 011C DF 08                STX     TOSAV
00037 011E DE 0A                LDX     LENSAV
00038 0120 09                   DEX
00039 0121 DF 0A                STX     LENSAV
00040 0123 26 EB                BNE     BLKMOV
00041 0125 39                   RTS
00042                           END


SYMBOL TABLE



BLOCK              MOTOROLA M68SAM CROSS-ASSEMBLER


FROM    0000    TO      0002    LENGTH  0004    FMSAV   0006    TOSAV   0008
LENSAV  000A    BLKMOV  0110
```

Introduction to the M6800 Microprocessor

```
                    M6BSAM IS THE PROPERTY OF MOTOROLA SPD, INC.
                    COPYRIGHT 1974 BY MOTOROLA INC

                MOTOROLA M6800 CROSS ASSEMBLER, RELEASE 1.1

00001                           NAM    MULTIPLE  BYTE ADD
00002                   *****************************************
00003                   *                                       *
00004                   *   PROGRAM  #3  MULTIPLE BYTE ADD      *
00005                   *                                       *
00006                   *****************************************
00007                   *
00008 0000                      ORG    $000
00009 0000 0010         STRNG1  RMB    $10
00010 0010 0010         STRNG2  RMB    $10
00011 0020 0010         RESULT  RMB    $10
00012                   *
00013 0200                      ORG    $200
00014                   *
00015                   *  SAMPLE CALL
00016                   *
00017 0200 CE 0005              LDX    #5        NUMBER OF BYTES = 5
00018 0203 4F                   CLR A
00019 0204 BD 0208              JSR    DECADD
00020 0207 3E                   WAI
00021                   *
00022                   *
00023 0208 A6 FF        DECADD  LDA A  STRNG1-1,X
00024 020A A9 0F                ADC A  STRNG2-1,X
00025 020C 19                   DAA
00026 020D A7 1F                STA A  RESULT-1,X
00027 020F 09                   DEX
00028 0210 26 F6                BNE    DECADD
00029 0212 39                   RTS
00030                   *
00031                   *
00032                           END


SYMBOL TABLE


STRNG1 0000   STRNG2 0010   RESULT 0020   DECADD 0208




   SUBTRA             MOTOROLA M68SAM CROSS-ASSMBLER




SYMBOL TABLE


STRNG1 0000   STRNG2 0010   RESULT 0020   SAVX   0030   DECSUB 0207
DECSB1 0209   DECSB2 0215
```

```
                    M68SA4 IS THE PROPERTY OF MOTOROLA SPD, INC.
                         COPYRIGHT 1974 BY MOTOROLA INC

                    MOTOROLA M6800 CROSS ASSEMBLER, RELEASE 1.1

00001                              NAM     SUBTRACT
00002                    ***********************************************
00003                    *                                              *
00004                    *   PROGRAM  #4  MULTIPLE BYTE DECIMAL SUBTRACT *
00005                    *   RESULT = STRNG1 - STRNG2                   *
00006                    *   IF NEGATIVE RESULT THEN MSB OF RESULT = 9  *
00007                    *                                              *
00008                    ***********************************************
00009                    *
00010 0000                         ORG     $000
00011 0000 0010          STRNG1    RMB     $10
00012 0010 0010          STRNG2    RMB     $10
00013 0020 0010          RESULT    RMB     $10
00014 0030 0002          SAVX      RMB     2
00015                    *
00016                    *
00017                    *   SAMPLE CALL
00018                    *
00019                    *
00020 0200                         ORG     $200
00021 0200 CE 0005                 LDX     #5        NUMBER OF BYTES
00022 0203 BD 0207                 JSR     DECSUB
00023 0206 3E                      WAI
00024                    *
00025                    *
00026                    *
00027 0207 DF 30         DECSUB    STX     SAVX
00028 0209 86 99         DECSB1    LDA A   #$99      FORM 9'S COMPLEMENT OF STRNG2
00029 020B A0 0F                   SUB A   STRNG2-1,X  IN STRNG2 APRAY.
00030 020D A7 0F                   STA A   STRNG2-1,X
00031 020F 09                      DEX
00032 0210 26 F7                   BNE     DECSB1
00033 0212 0D                      SEC               INITIAL+1 FOR 10'S COMPLEMENT
00034 0213 DE 30                   LDX     SAVX      RESULT
00035 0215 A6 FF         DECSB2    LDA A   STRNG1-1,X
00036 0217 A9 0F                   ADC A   STRNG2-1,X
00037 0219 19                      DAA
00038 021A A7 1F                   STA A   RESULT-1,X
00039 021C 09                      DEX
00040 021D 26 F6                   BNE     DECSB2
00041 021F 39                      RTS
00042                    *
00043                    *
00044                              END
```

PROBLEMS

1. How many op codes does the M6800 have? How many instructions?

2. Make a table to show the branch conditions which explore the use of BGT and BHI. Try especially $80 and $7F.

Introduction to the M6800 Microprocessor 345

3. Write a subroutine for the M6800 which gives a 100 μsec delay.

4. Redo 3 for 1 MS delay and 10 second delay.

5. The example microcomputer of Section 6.4 is to sense a rising edge signal on Side B - bit ∅. In response, bit 1 is to provide a 1 MS positive pulse. This is the only function required. How many bytes of code? What is the "jitter" on bit 1?

6. Refer to Figure 6.6-1. Add 3 more MCM6810 chips immediately above the present one. Make a tabular Form Address Table and draw the schematic.

7. In using the example microcomputer the stack pointer was inadverately not initialized. How (and when) would we notice this omission? Compare this to the MCS6502 based microcomputer.

8. In the MCS6502 we make extensive use of the BRK instruction to allow debugging. What is the equivalent instruction for the M6800?

9. Make a table of the vectors of the M6800 with their addresses, and parallel them with those of the MCS6502.

10. Are we limited by Branches of -126_{10} to $+129_{10}$ from LABEL as in the MCS6502?
$$\text{LABEL BRA TO}$$

11. Make a table comparing the M6800 and MCS6502 Branches.

12. Write assembly language instructions to implement:
    IF P = Q THEN GO To LABEL;
    IF P < Q THEN GO To LABEL;
    IF P > Q THEN GO To LABEL;
    IF P - 5 > Q THEN Q ← ∅;

13. Write an assembly language subroutine, beginning at location $200, labeled JOGGLE, which moves 512_{10} elements beginning at $400, down one location, the 16 bit register should be a great help.

14. Repeat 13 except move up.

15. In our example M6800 microcomputer exchange R5∅ and RS1. Make a table of addresses of Control, Data and Data Direction registers and associated addresses. Could we now use LDX as a 16 bit input?

16. Compare Rotate and Shift instructions for the M6800 and the MCS6502.

17. Write a subroutine for the M6800 to convert the 16 bit binary number in A,B to its decimal equivalent, placed in A,B at Return.

7

INTRODUCTION TO I8080 MICROPROCESSOR

7.1 CHARACTERISTICS

7.1.1 Comparison to MCS6502 and M6800

The similarities between the MCS6502 and the I8080 are not as numerous as those between the MCS6502 and the M6800. The I8080 is stack-oriented, having a stack pointer 16 bits long. As with the M6800 this allows the stack to be placed anywhere in memory space. The I8080, like the MCS6502 and the M6800, is byte-oriented, having a word length of 8 bits. The I8080 can also be interrupted via a line labeled INT, but interrupt-handling is quite different. Unlike the MCS6502 and M6800 with vector handling interrupt mechanisms, the I8080 expects an instruction to be "jammed" onto the data bus after interrupt has been acknowledged (see Section 7.4).

The I8080 is a 3 bus microcomputer system processor, like the MCS6502 and the M6800. The I8080 has an input labeled *Wait* which operates in similar fashion to the *Ready* control input of the MCS6502.

The processor status register in the I8080 is labeled F, standing for Flag register. A slightly different set of flag bits are provided in the I8080, including Carry, Zero, Sign, Parity, and Auxiliary Carry.

The I8080, unlike the MCS6502 and the M6800, requires three power supplies with voltages of +12, +5, and −5 volts. It, like the M6800, also requires a separate clock circuit, with specified input levels of 0 and +12 volts, which are not, of course, TTL voltage levels. The specified clock interval is 480 nanoseconds, and instruction execution requires from 4 to 18 of these clock cycles, roughly 2 to 9 microseconds.

I8080 addressing modes are significantly different from those of the MCS6502. Two identical addressing modes are Absolute and Implied. On-chip registers are used to point to locations in memory space, resulting in an addressing mode called Register Indirect, i.e., the contents of a register pair provides a 16 bit pointer to a specific memory location.

Because of its external clock requirement and its need for external control bus signal generation, the I8080 requires more chips to constitute a microcomputer than did either the MCS6502 or M6800.

The I8080, like the M6800, requires a decimal adjust accumulator instruction, DAA, to facilitate decimal mode arithmetic. This DAA instruction will not work correctly except when following an Add or Add With Carry instruction.

The I8080 requires a different approach to allocation of memory space than that used with the MCS6502. In general, an I8080 microcomputer will be found to have the ROM containing the program in lower numbered memory locations (starting at location 0000). This results from the fact that, when this machine is reset, the program counter is cleared to zero. Therefore, the first instruction to be fetched will be in location zero. Another difference lies in input/output, I/O which may be characterized in terms of *ports* separate from regular memory space. Thus, no memory locations are required for input/output allowing the full 65K range to be used as memory space. Up to 256 input/output ports may be specified.

The I8080 contains more on-chip registers than the MCS6502 for temporary storage, as well as for indirect addressing. There are six registers, each one byte long, labeled B, C, D, E, H, and L. These registers can be manipulated singly and in pairs, referred to as BC, DE, or HL. Certain register-pair instructions allow for fairly unsophisticated 16 bit arithmetic logic capability. The ability to add 16 bit quantities is convenient in applications involving greater accuracy than 1 byte will allow.

The Hold input to the I8080 permits convenient DMA handling capabilities. An external input to this pin requests the processor to proceed to a "hold" state at the conclusion of the presently executing instruction. When this state is achieved, an output line from the microprocessor called Hold Acknowledge, HLDA, indiates that the I8080 is in the hold condition. This condition is characterized by the cessation of processor activity and the high-impedance disconnect of address and data busses. The I8080 can remain in this state for an extended period of time because, unlike the M6800, its internal registers are refreshed. The Hold state is terminated by releasing the Hold input.

Introduction to the I8080 Microprocessor

7.1.2 Principal Characteristics

The principal characteristics of the I8080 (Figure 7.1.2-1) are:
1. Three Power Supplies
2. Byte Oriented
3. 244 Op Codes
4. Three Addressing Modes
5. Stack Pointer
6. Interrupt Capability
7. 65K Address Range
8. DMA Hold Capability
9. Six Working Registers
10. Addressed I/O

Figure 7.1.2-1 Intel I8080 microprocessor element

7.2 I8080 ARCHITECTURE AND PROGRAMMING MODEL

Figure 7.2-1 is a block diagram showing the internal architecture of the I8080. The diagram shows that register pairs BC, DE, and HL may be multiplexed internally onto the internal data bus, as well as onto the internal address bus. In Figure 7.2-1 some internal registers which facilitate data transfers are not shown. Refer to Intel documentation for exact details.

Figure 7.2-2 is a programming model of the I8080. It shows the 16 bit stack pointer and the 6 working registers which can be handled

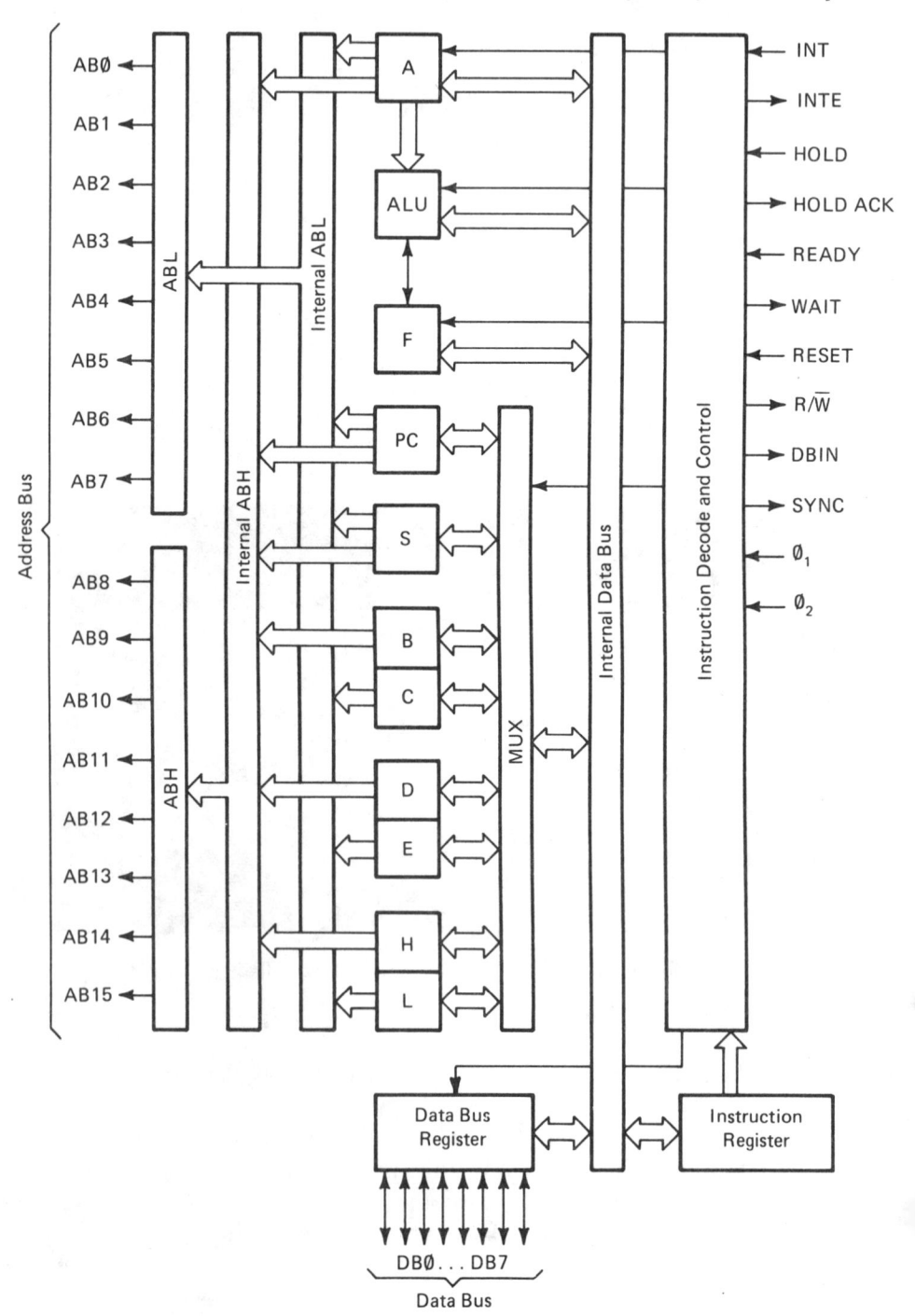

Figure 7.2-1 Approximate internal I8080 architecture

Introduction to the I8080 Microprocessor 351

```
 7              0 7              0
┌────────────────┬────────────────┐
│       B        │       C        │  Working registers
└────────────────┴────────────────┘
 7              0 7              0
┌────────────────┬────────────────┐
│       D        │       E        │  Working registers
└────────────────┴────────────────┘
 7              0 7              0
┌────────────────┬────────────────┐
│       H        │       L        │  Working registers
└────────────────┴────────────────┘
 15                              0
┌─────────────────────────────────┐
│               PC                │  Program counter
└─────────────────────────────────┘
 15                              0
┌─────────────────────────────────┐
│               SP                │  Stack pointer
└─────────────────────────────────┘
                 7              0
                ┌────────────────┐
                │       A        │   Accumulator
                └────────────────┘
```

Flag register: | S | Z | 0 | AC | 0 | P | 1 | C |
— Carry
— Parity
— Auxiliary carry
— Zero
— Sign

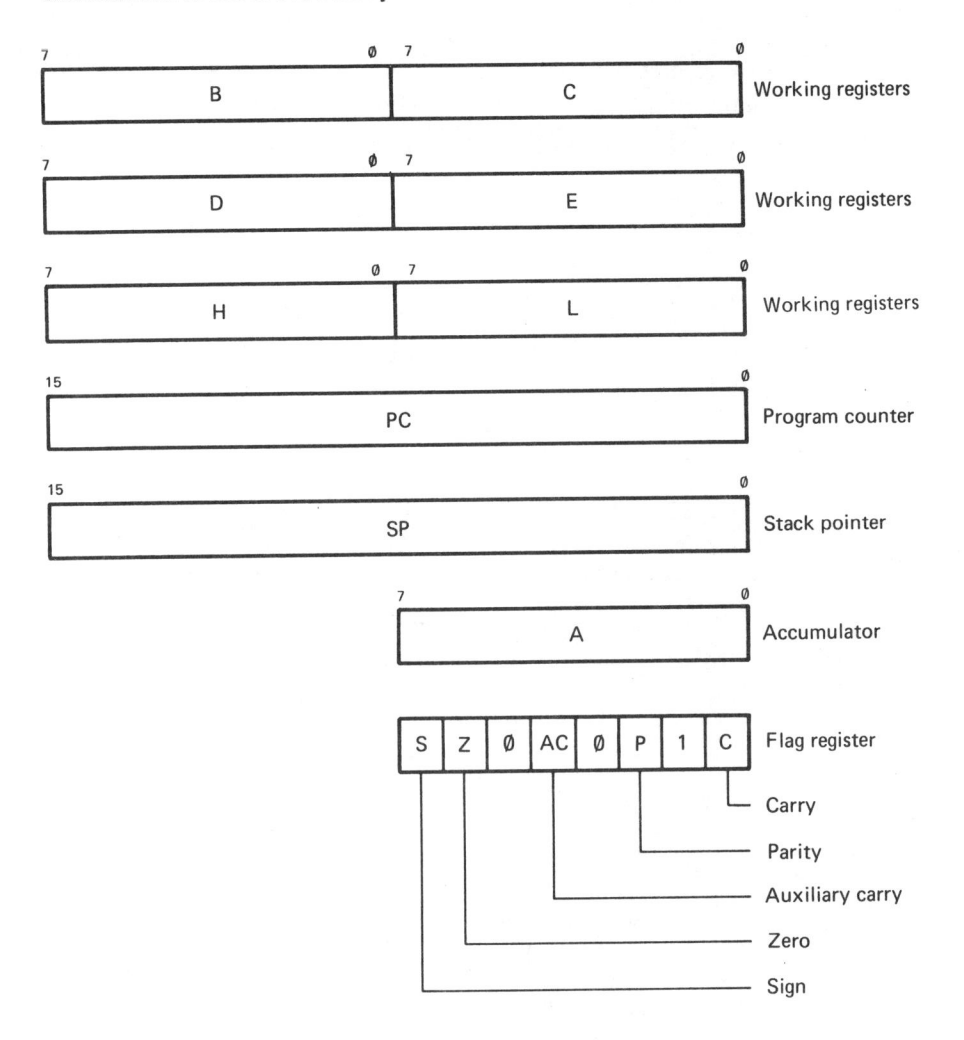

Figure 7.2-2 Programming model I8080

individually or as register pairs. The 8 bit accumulator (A) accumulates the results of arithmetic and logical operations. The flag register F contains the Sign, Zero, Auxiliary Carry, Parity, and Carry bits. The other 3 bits are 0 or 1 as indicated.

The Sign bit is usually found to be the sign bit produced by the last arithmetic or logical instruction. As with the previous microprocessors, a zero indicates positive and a 1 indicates negative. An ALU operation producing a 0 result will generally set the zero flag to 1, although it is possible to generate a $00 value in the accumulator without setting the Z bit in some cases. The Auxiliary Carry bit has the exact same function as the half carry bit (H), in the M6800 (see Section 6.3). The Parity bit is set if the result produced by an arithmetic or logical operation contains an odd number of 1's.

7.3 DATA PATHS

Figure 7.3-1 is a graphical representation of the data paths in the I8080. Note that input and output operations require the use of the accumulator (A). Most registers can be moved onto the stack or re-

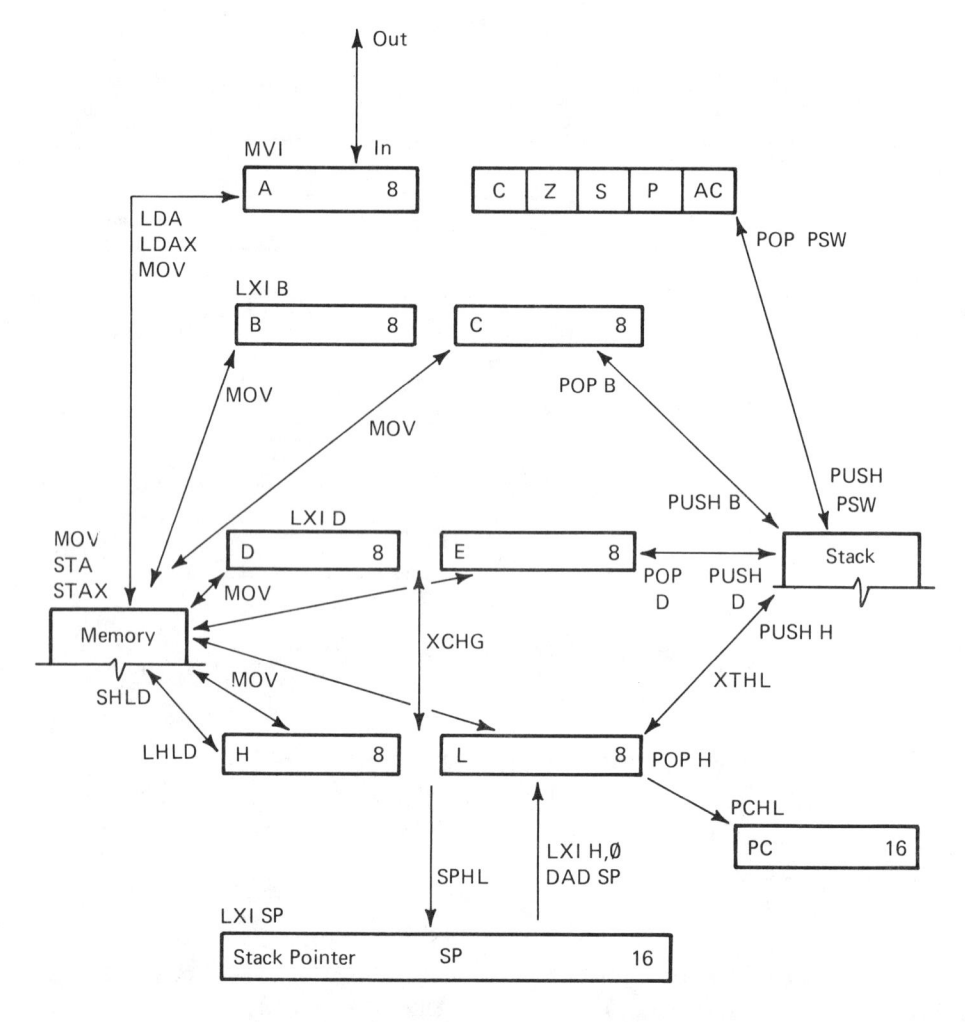

Figure 7.3-1 Data paths for the I8080

moved from the stack by means of Push and Pop instructions. The push and pop operations that involve the AF register pair are labeled Push PSW or Pop PSW, where PSW denotes the *program status word*. The stack pointer can be replaced with the contents of the HL pair, but in order to retrieve the contents of the stack pointer it is necessary to first clear the HL pair, and then add to it the contents of the stack pointer, by means of a 16 bit add, DAD SP. Figure 7.3-1 shows both of these instructions. In order to simplify the diagram, all paths are not shown, e.g., moving B to Memory, Memory to B, etc., are omitted. (An instruction involving "memory" implies that the desired operand is to be fetched from or stored at the location designated by the 16-bit address in the HL register pair.) We can also move any of the working registers or Memory, A, B, C, D, E, H, L, or M to any other. (An exception to this lies in the F register.) If all of these paths were included, Figure 7.3-1 would look very much like a spider's web. These paths nonetheless exist.

7.4   I8080 INSTRUCTION SET

Table 7.4-1 is an alphabetic list of the instructions which the I8080 may execute. Although not specifically shown in the table, Call, Jump and Return instructions can be either Unconditional or Conditional. A call instruction has the same effect as JSR in the MCS6502, i.e., the value of the program counter when the call occurs will be pushed onto the stack. A Return instruction causes two bytes to be transferred from the stack to the program counter (like RTI in the MCS6502). A Jump instruction does not save the PC value.

Call, Jump and Return instructions can be conditionally executed depending on tests of the flag register bits carry, zero, sign, or parity. This feature can be very convenient in managing subroutine entry and exit and in setting up branches which are to result from tests of status bits. Call and Jump are three-byte instructions, using Absolute addressing, and allow transfer to *anywhere* in address space. Return is a one-byte instruction.

Figure 7.4-2 is a detailed listing of the specific op codes for each of these instructions. All 244 district op codes are found in this table. Op codes for instructions which affect *two* working registers are shown between columns. For example, the DAD BC (double add register pair BC to HL0) instruction will add the contents of the BC register pair to the contents of the HL register pair (BC, DE, SP, or HL) and leave the result in HL. The contents of four different register pairs can be added

TABLE 7.4-1 Alphabetic List of Instructions

ACI	Add with carry immediate to accumulator
ADC	Add with carry to accumulator
ADD	Add without carry to accumulator
ADI	Add without carry immediate to accumulator
ANA	And with accumulator
ANI	And with accumulator immediate
CALL	Call subroutine
CMA	Complement (one's) accumulator
CMC	Complement carry bit
CMP	Compare with accumulator
DAA	Decimal adjust accumulator
DAD	16 Bit add register pair to HL pair
DCR	Decrement register
DCX	Decrement register pair by one
DI	Disable interrupt
EI	Enable interrupt
HLT	Halt
IN	Input
INR	Increment register
INX	Increment register pair
JMP	Jump
LDA	Load accumulator absolute
LDAX	Load accumulator via register indirect
LHLD	Load HL pair using absolute address
LXI	Load immediate to register pair
MOV	Move one byte
MVI	Move immediate byte to register
NOP	No operation
ORA	OR with accumulator
ORI	OR with accumulator immediate
OUT	Output
PCHL	Replace program counter with contents of HL
POP	Pop data from stack to register pair
RAL	Rotate accumulator left through carry
RAR	Rotate accumulator right through carry
RET	Return from subroutine
RLC	Rotate accumulator left with MSB to carry
RRC	Rotate accumulator right with LSB to carry

Introduction to the I8080 Microprocessor 355

RST	Restart	
SBB	Subtract from accumulator with borrow	
SBI	Subtract from accumulator immediate	
SHLD	Store HL pair using absolute address	
SPHL	Stack pointer replaced by HL pair	
STA	Store accumulator using absolute address	
STAX	Store accumulator using register indirect	
STC	Set carry	
SUB	Subtract from accumulator without borrow	
SUI	Subtract from accumulator immediate	
XCHG	Exchange DI and HL register pairs	
XRA	Exclusive OR with accumulator	
XRI	Exclusive OR with accumulator immediate	
XTHL	Exchange top two stack bytes and HL pair	
NOTE:	All CALL, JUMP and RETURN instructions can be made conditional upon status of Carry, Zero, Sign or Parity bits	

to the contents of the HL pair. A very handy programming technique is to DAD HL, thereby shifting HL left 1 bit position. This double byte characteristic is also found in the decrement extended (DCS), increment extended (INX), and load A extended (LDAX), which uses the BC or DE register pairs as memory pointers. The Load Extended Immediate (LXI) instruction allows immediate loading of constants into both registers of a register pair with one op code and two bytes of immediate data. Of course Push and Pop affect both registers of the four register pairs AF, BC, DE, and HL. The entry for Restart (RST), does not have a separate heading in Figure. 7-4-2. A restart instruction is, in fact, a one byte subroutine call, often used as a response to an interrupt request (see Section 7.6). After such a request and subsequent acknowledgment, via the INTE line, the I8080 requires an instruction to be externally provided ("jammed") on the data bus. A two-byte or three-byte instruction could be used, but a single byte instruction provides quickest response to the request. Restart instructions provide a subroutine call to every eighth location starting at address 0. Therefore the seven locations 8, 16, 24, 32, 40, 48, 56, and 64 are typically used as the beginning locations for service routines provided to respond to interrupting conditions, and location 0 is reserved for the Reset routine. It is not without some degree of foresight that the op code for RST 7

Instruction		A	F	B	C	D	E	H	L	Stack Pointer	Absolute	Reg. ind. (HL)=M	Uncond.	Zero	$\overline{Zero}$	Carry	$\overline{Carry}$	(+)	(−)	Parity Even	Parity Odd	Implied	Immed.	Status				
Mnemonic	Operation																							S	Z	AC	P	CY
ADC	A ← RMI + A + CY	8F		88	89	8A	8B	8C	8D			8E											CE	v	v	v	v	v
ADD	A ← RMI + A	87		80	81	82	83	84	85			86											C6	v	v	v	v	v
ANA	A ← A ∧ RMI	A7		A0	A1	A2	A3	A4	A5			A6											E6	v	v	v	v	—
CALL	Call Subroutine												CD	CC	C4	DC	D4	F4	FC	EC	E4			—	—	—	—	—
CMA	A ← $\bar{A}$																					2F		—	—	—	—	—
CMC	Cy → $\overline{CY}$																					3F		—	—	—	—	v
CMP	A − RMI	BF		B8	B9	BA	BB	BC	BD			BE											FE	v	v	v	v	v
DAA	Decimal Adj. A																					27		v	v	v	v	v
DAD	HL ← HL + rp			09		19		29		39														—	—	—	—	v
DCR	RM ← RM − 1	3D		05	0D	1D	25	2D				35												v	v	v	v	—
DCX	rp ← rp − 1			0B		1B		2B		3B														—	—	—	—	—
DI	Disable Inter.																					F3		—	—	—	—	—
EI	Enable Inter.																					FB		—	—	—	—	—
HLT	Halt																					76		—	—	—	—	—
IN	A ← Input																					DB		—	—	—	—	—
INR	RM ← RM + 1	3C		04	0C	14	1C	24	2C			34												v	v	v	v	—
INX	rp ← rp + 1			03		13		23		33														—	—	—	—	—
JMP	Jump												C3	CA	C2	DA	D2	F2	FA	EA	E2			—	—	—	—	—
LDA	Load A Absolute										3A													—	—	—	—	—
LDAX	Load A Reg. Ind.			0A		1A																		—	—	—	—	—
LHLD	Load HL Absolute								7E		2A													—	—	—	—	—
LXI	Load rp Immed.			01		11		21		31														—	—	—	—	—
MOV	Move to A	7F		78	79	7A	7B	7C	7D			7E											3E	—	—	—	—	—
MOV	Move to B	47		40	41	42	43	44	45			46											06	—	—	—	—	—
MOV	Move to C	4F		48	49	4A	4B	4C	4D			4E											0E	—	—	—	—	—
MOV	Move to D	57		50	51	52	53	54	55			56											16	—	—	—	—	—
MOV	Move to E	5F		58	59	5A	5B	5C	5D			5E											1E	—	—	—	—	—
MOV	Move to H	67		60	61	62	63	64	65			66											26	—	—	—	—	—
MOV	Move to L	6F		68	69	6A	6B	6C	6D			6E											2E	—	—	—	—	—
MOV	Move to M	77		70	71	72	73	74	75														36	—	—	—	—	—
NOP	No operation																					00		—	—	—	—	—

Figure 7.4-2 Instruction Table

Introduction to the I8080 Microprocessor

Instruction		A	F	B	C	D	E	H	L	Stack Pointer	Absolute	Reg. ind. (HL)=M	Uncond.	Zero	Z̅e̅r̅o̅	Carry	C̅a̅r̅r̅y̅	(+)	(−)	Parity Even	Parity Odd	Implied	Immed.	Status				
Mnemonic	Operation																							S	Z	AC	P	CY
ORA	A←A V RMI	B7		B0	B1	B2	B3	B4	B5			B6											F6	v	v	v	v	v
OUT	Output ← A																					D3		−	−	−	−	−
PCHL	PC ← HL																					E9		−	−	−	−	−
POP	Pop rp, AF	F1	F5	C1	C5	D1	D5	E1	E5															Only AF				
PUSH	Push rp, AF																							−	−	−	−	−
RAL	┌C ← A┐																					17		−	−	−	−	v
RAR	┌C → A┐																					1F		−	−	−	−	v
RET	Return from Subr.												C9	C8	C0	D8	D0	F0	F8	E8	E0			−	−	−	−	−
RLC	┌C ← A┐																					07		−	−	−	−	v
RRC	┌C → A┐																					0F		−	−	−	−	v
RST	Restart is a 1 byte subroutine										Call RST0=C7 RST1=CF RST2=D7 RST3=DF RST4=E7 RST5=EF RST6=F7 RST7=FE													−	−	−	−	−
SBB	A ← A − RMI − CY	9F		98	99	9A	9B	9C	9D			9E											DE	v	v	v	v	v
SUB	A ← A − RMI	97		90	91	92	93	94	95			96											D6	v	v	v	v	v
SHLD	Store HL Absolute										22													−	−	−	−	−
SPHL	SP ← HL																					22		−	−	−	−	−
STA	Store A Absolute										32													−	−	−	−	−
STAX	Store A Reg. Ind.			02		12																		−	−	−	−	−
STC	Cy ← 1																					37		−	−	−	−	1
XCHG	DE ↔ HL																					EB		−	−	−	−	−
XRA	A ← A ∀ RMI	AF		A8	A9	AA	AB	AC	AD		AE												EE	v	v	−	v	−
XTHL	HL ↔ Top of Store																					E3		−	−	−	−	−

R = A, B, C, D, E, H, L
M = Memory Location defined by HL
I = Immediate
rp = Register pair BC, DE, HL, SP
V = Logical AND
V = Logical OR
∀ = Logical Exclusive OR
+ = ADD
− = Subtract
v = Modified
− = Not changed

Figure 7.4-2 Continued

is $FF, since this is the value which would occur automatically if nothing were placed on the data bus (i.e., an open circuit). Therefore, a subroutine call, saving the program counter at time of interrupt, would be made to location 56, or $38, even if no external circuitry were provided for generating the Restart instruction.

Table 7.4-2 gives a detailed description of each individual I8080 instruction.

TABLE 7.4-2 I8080 Instruction Set
(Courtesy Intel Corporation)

Symbols and Abbreviations

Symbols	*Meaning*
Accumulator	Register A
Addr	16-bit address quantity
Data	8-bit data quantity
Data 16	16-bit data quantity
Byte 2	The second byte of the instruction
Byte 3	The third byte of the instruction
Port	8-bit address of an I/O device
r, r1, r2	One of the registers A, B, C, D, E, H, L
DDD, SSS	The bit pattern designating one of the registers A, B, C, D, E, H, L (DDD = destination, SSS = source):

DDD or SSS	Register Name
111	A
∅∅∅	B
∅∅1	C
∅1∅	D
∅11	E
1∅∅	H
1∅1	L

rp   One of the register pairs:

B represents the B, C pair with B as the high-order register and C as the low-order register;

D represents the D, E pair with D as the high-order register and E as the low-order register;

Introduction to the I8080 Microprocessor 359

	H represents the H, L pair with H as the high-order register and L as the low-order register;
	SP represents the 16-bit stack pointer register.
RP	The bit pattern designating one of the register pairs B, D, H, SP:

RP	Register Pair
ØØ	B-C
Ø1	D-E
1Ø	H-L
11	SP

rh	The first (high-order) register of a designated register pair.
rℓ	The second (low-order) register of a designated register pair.
PC	16-bit program counter register (PCH and PCL are used to refer to the high-order and low-order 8 bits respectively).
SP	16-bit stack pointer register (SPH and SPL are used to refer to the high-order and low-order 8 bits respectively).
r_m	Bit m of the register r (bits are numbered 7 through Ø from left to right).
Z, S, P, CY, AC	The condition flags:

                    Zero
                    Sign
                    Parity
                    Carry
                    and Auxiliary Carry, respectively

( )	The contents of the memory location or registers enclosed in the parentheses.

Symbol	Meaning
←	"Is transferred to"
∧	Logical AND
⊻	Exclusive OR
V	Inclusive OR
+	Addition
−	Two's complement subtraction
*	Multiplication
↔	"Is exchanged with"
‾	The one's complement (e.g., $\overline{A}$)
n	The restart number ∅ through 7
NNN	The binary representation ∅∅∅ through 111 for restart number ∅ through 7 respectively.

The two types of branch instructions are unconditional and conditional. Unconditional transfers simply perform the specified operation on register PC (the program counter). Conditional transfers examine the status of one of the four processor flags to determine if the specified branch is to be executed. The conditions that may be specified are as follows:

	Condition	CCC
NZ −	not zero (Z = 0)	∅∅∅
Z −	zero (Z = 1)	∅∅1
NC −	no carry (CY = 0)	∅1∅
C −	carry (CY = 1)	∅11
PO −	parity odd (P = 0)	1∅∅
PE −	parity even (P = 1)	1∅1
P −	plus (S = 0)	11∅
M −	(S = 1)	111

Introduction to the I8080 Microprocessor

ACI   **Add Immediate with Carry**

Operation: (A) ← (A) + (byte 2) + (CY)   S Z AC P CY
                                                v v v v

Description: The content of the second byte of the instruction and the content of the CY flag are added to the contents of the accumulator. The result is placed in the accumulator.

1	1	0	0	1	1	1	0
\multicolumn{8}{c}{Data}

Bytes: 2   States: 7   Addressing: immediate

ADC M   **Add Memory with Carry**

Operation: (A) ← (A) + ((H)(L)) + (CY)   S Z AC P CY
                                                v v v v

Description: The content of the memory location whose address is contained in the H and L registers and the content of the CY flag are added to the accumulator. The result is placed in the accumulator.

1	0	0	0	1	1	1	0

Bytes: 1   States: 7   Addressing: reg. indirect

ADC r   Add Register with Carry

Operation: (A) ← (A) + (r) + (CY)   S Z AC P CY
                                           v v v v v

Description: The content of register r and the content of the carry bit are added to the content of the accumulator. The result is placed in the accumulator.

| 1 | 0 | 0 | 0 | 1 | S | S | S |

Bytes: 1   States: 4   Addressing: register

ADD M   Add Memory

Operation: (A) ← (A) + ((H)(L))   S Z AC P CY
                                           v v v v v

Description: The content of the memory location whose address is contained in the H and L registers is added to the content of the accumulator. The result is placed in the accumulator.

| 1 | 0 | 0 | 0 | 0 | 1 | 1 | 0 |

Bytes: 1   States: 7   Addressing: reg. indirect

ADD r   Add Register

Operation: (A) ← (A) + (r)   S Z AC P CY
                                           v v v v v

Description: The content of register r is added to the content of the accumulator. The result is placed in the accumulator.

| 1 | 0 | 0 | 0 | 0 | S | S | S |

Bytes: 1   States: 4   Addressing: register

Introduction to the I8080 Microprocessor

ADI data   **Add Immediate**

Operation: (A) ← (A) + (byte 2)   S Z AC P CY
                                          v v v v v

Description: The content of the second byte of the instruction is added to the content of the accumulator. The result is placed in the accumulator.

1	1	0	0	0	1	1	0
Data								

Bytes: 2   States: 7   Addressing: immediate

ANA M   **AND Memory**

Operation: (A) ← (A) ∧ ((H)(L))   S Z AC P CY
                                          v v v v 0

Description: The contents of the memory location whose address is contained in the H and L registers is logically ANDed with the content of the accumulator. The result is placed in the accumulator. THE CY FLAG IS CLEARED.

1	0	1	0	0	1	1	0

Bytes: 1   States: 7   Addressing: reg. indirect

ANA r   **AND Register**

Operation: (A) ← (A) ∧ (r)   S Z AC P CY
                                     v v v v 0

Description: The content of register r is logically ANDed with the content of the accumulator. The result is placed in the accumulator. THE CY FLAG IS CLEARED.

$$\boxed{1\,|\,0\,|\,1\,|\,0\,|\,0\,|\,S\,|\,S\,|\,S}$$

Bytes: 1   States: 4   Addressing: register

ANI data   **AND Immediate**

Operation: (A) ← (A) ∧ (byte 2)   S Z AC P CY
                                      v v 0 v 0

Description: The content of the second byte of the instruction is logically ANDed with the contents of the accumulator. The result is placed in the accumulator. THE CY AND AC FLAGS ARE CLEARED.

$$\boxed{\begin{array}{c}1\,|\,1\,|\,1\,|\,0\,|\,0\,|\,1\,|\,1\,|\,0\\ \hline \text{Data}\end{array}}$$

Bytes: 2   States: 7   Addressing: immediate

Introduction to the I8080 Microprocessor 365

CALL addr   Call

Operation: ((SP) − 1) ← (PCH)   S Z AC P CY
             ((SP) − 2) ← (PCL)   - - - - -
             (SP) ← (SP) − 2
             (PC) ← (byte 3)(byte 2)

Description: The high-order eight bits of the next instruction address are moved to the memory location whose address is one less than the content of register SP. The low-order eight bits of the next instruction address are moved to the memory location whose address is two less than the content of register SP. The content of register SP is decremented by 2. Control is transferred to the instruction whose address is specified in byte 3 and byte 2 of the current instruction.

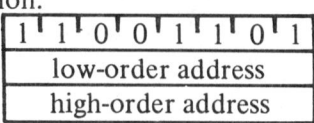

1	1	0	0	1	1	0	1
low-order address							
high-order address							

Byte: 3   States: 17   Addressing: immediate/reg. indirect

C-- addr   Conditional Call

Operation: ((SP) − 1) ← (PCH)   S Z AC P CY
             ((SP) − 2) ← (PCL)   - - - - -
             (SP) ← (SP) − 2
             (PC) ← (byte 3)(byte 2)

Description: Test Carry, Zero, Sign, or Parity bit. (See Symbols and Abbreviations), and if specified condition is true, the actions specified in the CALL instruction (see above) are performed; otherwise, control continues sequentially.

1	1	C	C	C	1	0	0
low-order address							
high-order address							

Bytes: 3   States: 11/17   Addressing: immediate/reg. indirect

CMA   Complement Accumulator

Operation: (A) ← $(\overline{A})$ S Z AC P CY
                                                                  – – – – –

Description: The contents of the accumulator are complemented (zero bits become 1, one bits become 0). NO FLAGS ARE AFFECTED.

0	0	1	0	1	1	1	1

Bytes: 1   States: 4

CMC   Complement Carry

Operation: (CY) ← $(\overline{CY})$ S Z AC P CY
                                                                  – – – – v

Description: The CY flag is complemented. NO OTHER FLAGS ARE AFFECTED.

0	0	1	1	1	1	1	1

Bytes: 1   States: 4

CMP M   Compare Memory

Operation: (A) − ((H) (L))   S Z AC P CY
                                                                  v v v v v

Description: The content of the memory location whose address is contained in the H and L registers is subtracted from the accumulator. The accumulator remains unchanged. The condition flags are set as a result of the subtraction. The Z flag is set to 1 if (A) = ((H) (L)). The CY flag is set to 1 if (A) < ((H) (L)).

1	0	1	1	1	1	1	0

Bytes: 1   States: 7   Addressing: reg. indirect

CMP r **Compare Register**

Operation: (A) − (r) S Z AC P CY
 v v v v v

Description: The content of register r is subtracted from the accumulator. The accumulator remains unchanged. The condition flags are set as a result of the subtraction. THE Z FLAG IS SET TO 1 if (A) = (r). THE CY FLAG IS SET TO 1 if (A) < (r).

| 1 | 0 | 1 | 1 | 1 | S | S | S |

Bytes: 1   States: 4   Addressing: register

CPI data **Compare Immediate**

Operation: (A) − (byte 2) S Z AC P CY
 v v v v v

Description: The content of the second byte of the instruction is subtracted from the accumulator. The condition flags are set by the result of the subtraction. The Z flag is set to 1 if (A) = (byte 2). The CY flag is set to 1 if (A) < (byte 2).

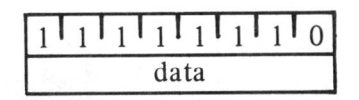

| 1 | 1 | 1 | 1 | 1 | 1 | 1 | 0 |
| data |

Bytes: 2   States: 7   Addressing: immediate

DAA　　　　**Decimal Adjust Accumulator**

Operation:　　　　　　　　　　　　　　　　　　　　　　S Z AC P CY
　　　　　　　　　　　　　　　　　　　　　　　　　　　v v v v v

Description: The eight-bit number in the accumulator is adjusted to form two four-bit Binary-Coded-Decimal digits by the following process:

1. If the value of the least significant 4 bits of the accumulator is greater than 9 or if the AC flag is set, 6 is added to the accumulator.

2. If the value of the most significant 4 bits of the accumulator is not greater than 9, or if the CY flag is set, 6 is added to the most significant 4 bits of the accumulator.

NOTE: All flags are affected.

0	0	1	0	0	1	1	1

Bytes: 1　　　States: 4

DAD rp　　　　**Add Register Pair to H and L**

Operation:　(H)(L) ← (H)(L) + (rh)(rℓ)　　　　　S Z AC P CY
　　　　　　　　　　　　　　　　　　　　　　　　　　　-- - - - v

Description: The content of the register pair rp is added to the content of the register pair H and L. The result is placed in the register pair H and L. NOTE: ONLY THE CY FLAG IS AFFECTED. It is set if there is a carry out of the double precision add; otherwise it is reset.

0	0	R	P	1	0	0	1

Bytes: 1　　　States: 10　　　Addressing: register

Introduction to the I8080 Microprocessor 369

DCR M **Decrement Memory**

Operation: ((H)(L)) ← ((H)(L)) − 1   S Z AC P CY
                                            v v v v

Description: The content of the memory location whose address is contained in the H and L registers is decremented by one. NOTE: all condition flags EXCEPT CY are affected.

$$\boxed{0\,|\,0\,|\,1\,|\,1\,|\,0\,|\,1\,|\,0\,|\,1}$$

Bytes: 1   States: 10   Addressing: reg. indirect

DCR r **Decrement Register**

Operation: (r) ← (r) − 1   S Z AC P CY
                                  v v v v −

Description: The content of register r is decremented by one. NOTE: All condition flags EXCEPT CY are affected.

$$\boxed{0\,|\,0\,|\,D\,|\,D\,|\,D\,|\,1\,|\,0\,|\,1}$$

Bytes: 1   States: 5   Addressing: register

DCX rp **Decrement Register Pair**

Operation: (rh)(rℓ) ← (rh)(rℓ) − 1   S Z AC P CY
                                            − − − − −

Description: The content of the register pair rp is decremented by one. NOTE: NO CONDITION FLAGS ARE AFFECTED.

$$\boxed{0\,|\,0\,|\,R\,|\,P\,|\,1\,|\,0\,|\,1\,|\,1}$$

Bytes: 1   States: 5   Addressing: register

DI   Disable Interrupts

Operation: S Z AC P CY
                                                             – – – – –

Description: The interrupt system is disabled IMMEDIATELY FOL-LOWING THE EXECUTION OF THE DI INSTRUCTION.

1	1	1	1	0	0	1	1

Bytes: 1   States: 4

EI   Enable Interrupts

Operation: S Z AC P CY
                                                            – – – – –

Description: The interrupt system is enabled FOLLOWING THE EXECUTION OF THE NEXT INSTRUCTION.

1	1	1	1	1	0	1	1

Bytes: 1   States: 4

HLT   Halt

Operation: S Z AC P CY
                                                            – – – – –

Description: The processor is stopped. The registers and flags are unaffected.

0	1	1	1	0	1	1	0

Bytes: 1   States: 7

IN port   **Input**

Operation: (A) ← (data)   S Z AC P CY
                                                             – – – – –

Description: The data placed on the eight bit bidirectional data bus by the specified port is moved to register A.

1	1	0	1	1	0	1	1
			port				

Bytes: 2   States: 10   Addressing: Absolute

INR M   **Increment Memory**

Operation: ((H)(L)) ← ((H)(L)) + 1   S Z AC P CY
                                                             v v v v –

Description: The content of the memory location whose address is contained in the H and L registers is incremented by one. NOTE: All condition flags EXCEPT CY are affected.

0	0	1	1	0	1	0	0

Bytes: 1   States: 10   Addressing: reg. indirect

INR r   **Increment Register**

Operation: (r) ← (r) + 1   S Z AC P CY
                                                             v v v v –

Description: The content of register r is incremented by one. NOTE: All condition flags EXCEPT Y are affected.

0	0	D	D	D	1	0	0

Bytes: 1   States: 5   Addressing: register

INX rp   **Increment Register Pair**

Operation: (rh) (rl) ← (rh) (rl) + 1   S Z AC P CY
                                                          ‾‾ ‾ ‾ ‾ ‾

Description: The content of the register pair rp is incremented by one.
             NOTE: NO CONDITION FLAGS ARE AFFECTED.

| 0 | 0 | R | P | 0 | 0 | 1 | 1 |

Bytes: 1   States: 5   Addressing: register

JMP addr   **Jump**

Operation: (PC) ← (byte 3) (byte 2)   S Z AC P CY
                                                          ‾‾ ‾ ‾ ‾ ‾

Description: Control is transferred to the instruction whose address is
             specified in byte 3 and byte 2 of the current instruction.

1	1	0	0	0	0	1	1
low-order addr								
high-order addr								

Bytes: 3   States: 10   Addressing: immediate

Introduction to the I8080 Microprocessor 373

J- - addr   **Conditional Jump**

Operation: (CCC)
                (PC) ← (byte 3) (byte 2)   S Z AC P CY
                                                               - - - - -

Description: Test Carry, Zero, Sign, or Parity bit. (See symbols and abbreviations), and if the specified condition is true, control is transferred to the instruction whose address is specified in byte 3 and byte 2 of the current instruction; otherwise, control continues sequentially.

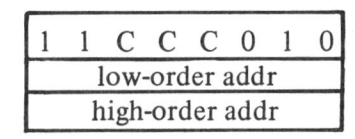

1	1	C	C	C	0	1	0
low-order addr							
high-order addr							

Bytes: 3   States: 10   Addressing: immediate

LDA addr   **Load Accumulator Direct**

Operation: (A) ← ((byte 3) (byte 2))   S Z AC P CY
                                                                 - - - - -

Description: The content of the memory location, whose address is specified in byte 2 and byte 3 of the instruction, is moved to register A.

0	0	1	1	1	0	1	0
low-order addr							
high-order addr							

Bytes: 3   States: 13   Addressing: Absolute

LDAX rp   **Load Accumulator Indirect**

Operation: (A) ← ((rp))   S Z AC P CY

                                                                – – – – –

Description: The content of the memory location, whose address is in the register pair rp, is moved to register A. Note: Only register pairs rp = B (registers B and C) or rp = D (registers D and E) may be specified.

0	0	R	P	1	0	1	0

Bytes: 1   States: 7   Addressing: Register indirect

LHLD addr   **Load H and L Direct**

Operation: (L) ← ((byte 3)(byte 2))   S Z AC P CY
                        (H) ← ((byte 3)(byte 2) + 1)   – – – – –

Description: The content of the memory location, whose address is specified in byte 2 and byte 3 of the instruction, is moved to register L. The content of the memory location at the succeeding address is moved to register H.

0	0	1	0	1	0	1	0
low-order addr								
high-order addr								

Bytes: 3   States: 16   Addressing: Absolute

LXI rp, data 16 Load Register Pair Immediate

Operation: (rh) ← (byte 3)   S Z AC P CY
             (rℓ) ← (byte 2)   − − − − −

Description: Byte 3 of the instruction is moved into the high-order register (rh) of the register pair rp. Byte 2 of the instruction is moved into the low-order register (rℓ) of the register pair rp.

0	0	R	P	0	0	0	1
low-order data							
high-order data							

Bytes: 3   States: 10   Addressing: Immediate

MOV M,r   Move to Memory

Operation: ((H)(L)) ← (r)   S Z AC P CY
                                                 − − − − −

Description: The content of register r is moved to the memory location whose address is in registers H and L.

0	1	1	1	0	S	S	S

Bytes: 1   States: 7   Addressing: Register indirect

MOV r,M   Move from Memory

Operation: (r) ← (H)(L)   S Z AC P CY
                                                 − − − − −

Description: The content of the memory location, whose address is in registers H and L, is moved to register r.

0	1	D	D	D	1	1	0

Bytes: 1   States: 7   Addressing: Register indirect

MOV r1, r2 Move Register

Operation: (r1) ← (r2)   S Z AC P CY
                                                      - - - - -

Description: The content of register r2 is moved to register r1.

0	1	D	D	D	S	S	S

Bytes: 1   States: 5   Addressing: Register

MVI M, data Move to Memory Immediate

Operation: ((H)(L)) ← (Byte)   S Z AC P CY
                                                      - - - - -

Description: The content of byte 2 of the instruction is moved to the memory location whose address is in registers H and L.

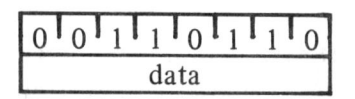

0	0	1	1	0	1	1	0
data							

Bytes: 2   States: 10   Addressing: immed./reg. indirect

MVI r, data Move Immediate

Operation: (r) ← (byte 2)   S Z AC P CY
                                                      - - - - -

Description: The content of byte 2 of the instruction is moved to register r.

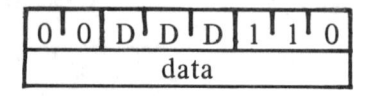

0	0	D	D	D	1	1	0
data							

Bytes: 2   States: 7   Addressing: Immediate

Introduction to the I8080 Microprocessor 377

NOP   **No Operation**

Operation: S Z AC P CY
                                                                      - - - - -

Description: No operation is performed. The registers and flags are unaffected.

| 0 | 0 | 0 | 0 | 0 | 0 | 0 | 0 |

Bytes: 1   States: 4

ORA M   **OR Memory**

Operation: (A) ← (A) V ((H)(L))   S Z AC P CY
                                               v v v v v

Description: The content of the memory location whose address is contained in the H and L registers is inclusive-OR'd with the content of the accumulator. The result is placed in the accumulator. THE CY AND AC FLAGS ARE CLEARED.

| 1 | 0 | 1 | 1 | 0 | 1 | 1 | 0 |

Bytes: 1   States: 7   Addressing: Reg. indirect

ORA r   **OR Register**

Operation: (A) ← (A) V (r)   S Z AC P CY
                                               v v v v v

Description: The content of register r is inclusive-OR'd with the content of the accumulator. The result is placed in the accumulator. THE CY AND AC FLAGS ARE CLEARED.

| 1 | 0 | 1 | 1 | 0 | S | S | S |

Bytes: 1   States: 4   Addressing: Register

ORI data   **OR Immediate**

Operation: (A) ← (A) V (byte 2)   S Z AC P CY
                                                     v v v v

Description: The content of the second byte of the instruction is inclusive-OR'd with the content of the accumulator. The result is placed in the accumulator. THE CY AND AC FLAGS ARE CLEARED.

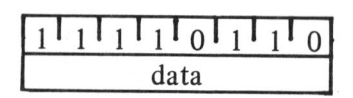

1	1	1	1	0	1	1	0
data							

Bytes: 2   States: 7   Addressing: Immediate

OUT port   **Output**

Operation: (data) ← (A)   S Z AC P CY
                                                     - - - - -

Description: The content of register A is placed on the eight bit bidirectional data bus for transmission to the specified port.

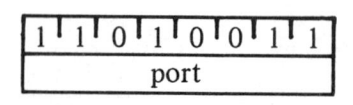

1	1	0	1	0	0	1	1
port							

Bytes: 2   States: 10   Addressing: Absolute

Introduction to the I8080 Microprocessor 379

PCHL Jump H and L Indirect - Move H and L to PC

Operation: (PCH) ← (H)   S Z AC P CY
            (PCL) ← (L)
                                                         – – – – –

Description: The content of register H is moved to the high-order eight bits of register PC. The content of register L is moved to the low-order eight bits of register PC.

| 1 | 1 | 1 | 0 | 1 | 0 | 0 | 1 |

Bytes: 1   States: 5   Addressing: Register

POP rp Pop

Operation: (rℓ) ← ((SP))   S Z AC P CY
            (rh) ← ((SP) + 1)   – – – – –
            (SP) ← (SP) + 2

Description: The content of the memory location, whose address is specified by the content of register SP, is moved to the low-order register of register pair rp. The content of the memory location, whose address is one more than the content of the register SP, is moved to the high-order register of register pair rp. The content of register SP is incremented by 2. NOTE: REGISTER PAIR rp = SP MAY NOT BE SPECIFIED.

| 1 | 1 | R | P | 0 | 0 | 0 | 1 |

Bytes: 1   States: 10   Addressing: Reg. indirect

POP PSW   **Pop Processor Status Word**

Operation: $(CY) \leftarrow ((SP))_0$ S Z AC P CY
               $(P) \leftarrow ((SP))_2$
               $(AC) \leftarrow ((SP))_4$ v v v v v
               $(Z) \leftarrow ((SP))_6$
               $(S) \leftarrow ((SP))_7$
               $(A) \leftarrow ((SP) + 1)$
               $(SP) \leftarrow (SP) + 2$

Description: The content of the memory location whose address is specified by the content of register SP is used to restore the condition flags. The content of the memory location whose address is one more than the content of register SP is moved to register A. The content of register SP is incremented by 2.

1	1	1	1	0	0	0	1

Bytes: 1   States: 10   Addressing: Reg. indirect.

PUSH rp   **Push**

Operation: $((SP) - 1) \leftarrow (rh)$ S Z AC P CY
               $((SP) - 2) \leftarrow (r\ell)$
               $(SP) \leftarrow (SP) - 2$ - - - - -

Description: The content of the high-order register of register pair rp is moved to the memory location whose address is one less then the content of register SP. The content of the low-order register or register pair rp is moved to the memory location whose address is two less than the content of register SP. The content of register SP is decremented by 2. NOTE: REGISTER PAIR rp = SP MAY NOT BE SPECIFIED.

1	1	R	P	0	1	0	1

Bytes: 1   States: 11   Addressing: Reg. indirect

Introduction to the I8080 Microprocessor 381

PUSH PSW   **Push Processor Status Word**

Operation: $((SP) - 1) \leftarrow (A)$ S Z AC P CY
$((SP) - 2)_0 \leftarrow (CY), ((SP) - 2)_1 \leftarrow 1$
$((SP) - 2)_2 \leftarrow (P), ((SP) - 2)_3 \leftarrow 0$ - - - - -
$((SP) - 2)_4 \leftarrow (AC), ((SP) - 2)_5 \leftarrow 0$
$((SP) - 2)_6 \leftarrow (Z), ((SP) - 2)_7 \leftarrow (S)$
$(SP) \leftarrow (SP) - 2$

Description: The content of register A is moved to the memory location whose address is one less than register SP. The contents of the condition flags are assembled into a processor status word and the word is moved to the memory location whose address is two less than the content of register SP. The content of register SP is decremented by two.

$$\boxed{1\ 1\ 1\ 1\ 0\ 1\ 0\ 1}$$

Bytes: 1   States: 11   Addressing: Reg. indirect

RAL   **Rotate Left Through Carry**

Operation: $(A_{n+1}) \leftarrow (A_n) : (CY) \leftarrow (A_7)$ S Z AC P CY
$(A_0) \leftarrow (CY)$ - - - - v

Description: The content of the accumulator is rotated left one position through the CY flag. The low order bit is set equal to the CY flag and the CY flag is set to the value shifted out of the high order bit. ONLY THE CY FLAG IS AFFECTED.

$$\boxed{0\ 0\ 0\ 1\ 0\ 1\ 1\ 1}$$

Bytes: 1   States: 4

RAR   **Rotate Right Through Carry**

Operation: $(A_n) \leftarrow (A_{n+1})$; $(CY) \leftarrow (A_0)$ S Z AC P CY
            $(A_7) \leftarrow (CY)$ $-\ -\ -\ -\ $ v

Description: The content of the accumulator is rotated right one position through the CY flag. The high order bit is set to the CY flag and the CY flag is set to the value shifted out of the low order bit. ONLY THE CY FLAG IS AFFECTED.

0	0	0	1	1	1	1	1

Bytes: 1   States: 4

RET   **Return**

Operation: (PCL) ← ((SP))   S Z AC P CY
            (PCH) ← ((SP) + 1)
            (SP) ← (SP) + 2 $-\ -\ -\ -\ -$

Description: The content of the memory location whose address is specified in register SP is moved to the low-order eight bits of register PC. The content of the memory location whose address is one more than the content of register SP is moved to the high-order eight bits of register PC. The content of register SP is incremented by 2.

1	1	0	0	1	0	0	1

Bytes: 3   States: 10   Addressing: Reg. indirect

Introduction to the I8080 Microprocessor 383

R - - **Conditional Return**

Operation: (CCC)   S Z AC P CY
(PCL) ← ((SP))
(PCH) ← ((SP) + 1)   - - - - -
(SP) ← (SP) + 2

Description: Test Carry, Zero, Sign, or Parity bit. (See symbols and abbreviations), and if the specified condition is true, the actions specified in the RET instruction (see above) are performed; otherwise, control continues sequentially.

1	1	C	C	C	0	0	0

Bytes: 1   States: 5/11   Addressing: Reg. Indirect

RLC   **Rotate Left**

Operation: $(A_{n+1}) \leftarrow (A_n); (A_0) \leftarrow (A_7)$ S Z AC P CY
$(CY) \leftarrow (A_7)$ - - - - v

Description: The content of the accumulator is rotated left one position. The low order bit and the CY flag are both set to the value shifted out of the high order bit position. ONLY THE CY FLAG IS AFFECTED.

0	0	0	0	0	1	1	1

Bytes: 1   States: 4

RRC — Rotate Right

Operation: $(A_n) \leftarrow (A_{n-1}); (A_7) \leftarrow (A_0)$
$(CY) \leftarrow (A_0)$

S Z AC P CY
- - - - - v

Description: The content of the accumulator is rotated right one position. The high order bit and the CY flag are both set to the value shifted out of the low order bit position. ONLY THE CY FLAG IS AFFECTED.

| 0 | 0 | 0 | 0 | 1 | 1 | 1 | 1 |

Bytes: 1   States: 4

RST n — Restart

Operation: $((SP) - 1) \leftarrow (PCH)$
$((SP) - 2) \leftarrow (PCL)$
$(SP) \leftarrow (SP) - 2$
$(PC) \leftarrow 8 * (NNN)$

S Z AC P CY
- - - - -

Description: The high-order eight bits of the next instruction address are moved to the memory location whose address is one less than the content of register SP. The low-order eight bits of the next instruction address are moved to the memory location whose address is two less than the content of register SP. The content of register SP is decremented by two. Control is transferred to the instruction whose address is eight times the content of NNN.

| 1 | 1 | N | N | N | 1 | 1 | 1 |

Bytes: 1   States: 11   Addressing: Reg. Indirect

15	14	13	12	11	10	9	8	7	6	5	4	3	2	1	0
0	0	0	0	0	0	0	0	0	0	N	N	N	0	0	0

Program Counter After Restart

Introduction to the I8080 Microprocessor

SBB M **Subtract Memory with Borrow**

Operation: (A) ← (A) − ((H)(L)) − (CY)   S Z AC P CY
                                             v v v v v

Description: The content of the memory location whose address is contained in the H and L registers and the content of the CY flag are both subtracted from the accumulator. The result is placed in the accumulator.

$$\boxed{1\,|\,0\,|\,0\,|\,1\,|\,1\,|\,1\,|\,1\,|\,0}$$

Bytes: 1   States: 7   Addressing: Reg. indirect

SBB r **Subtract Register with Borrow**

Operation: (A) ← (A) − (r) − (CY)   S Z AC P CY
                                        v v v v v

Description: The content of register r and the content of the CY flag are both subtracted from the accumulator. The result is placed in the accumulator.

$$\boxed{1\,|\,0\,|\,0\,|\,1\,|\,1\,|\,S\,|\,S\,|\,S}$$

Bytes: 1   States: 4   Addressing: register

SBI data **Subtract Immediate with Borrow**

Operatin: (A) ← (A) − (byte 2) − (CY)   S Z AC P CY
                                            v v v v v

Description: The contents of the second byte of the instruction and the contents of the CY flag are both subtracted from the accumulator. The result is placed in the accumulator.

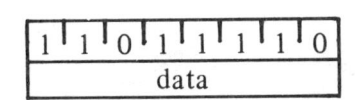

$$\boxed{\begin{array}{c}1\,|\,1\,|\,0\,|\,1\,|\,1\,|\,1\,|\,1\,|\,0\\ \hline data\end{array}}$$

Bytes: 2   States: 7   Addressing: Immediate

SHLD addr   **Store H and L Direct**

Operation: ((byte 3) (byte 2)) ← (L)   S Z AC P CY
((byte 3) (byte 2) + 1) ← (H)   - - - - -

Description: The content of register L is moved to the memory location whose address is specified in byte 2 and byte 3. The content of register H is moved to the succeeding memory location.

0 0 1 0 0 0 1 0
low-order addr
high-order addr

Bytes: 3   States: 16   Addressing: Absolute

SPHL   **Move HL to SP**

Operation: (SP) ← (H) (L)   S Z AC P CY
                                                 - - - - -

Description: The contents of registers H and L (16 bits) are moved to register SP.

1	1	1	1	1	0	0	1

Bytes: 1   States: 5   Addressing: Register

Introduction to the I8080 Microprocessor 387

STA addr   **Store Accumulator Direct**

Operation: ((byte 3) (byte 2)) ← (A)   S Z AC P CY
                                                                                 - - - - -

Description: The content of the accumulator is moved to the memory location whose address is specified in byte 2 and byte 3 of the instruction.

0	0	1	1	0	0	1	0
low-order addr							
high-order addr							

Bytes: 3   States: 13   Addressing: Absolute

STAX rp   **Store Accumulator Indirect**

Operation: ((rp)) ← (A)   S Z AC P CY
                                                            - - - - -

Description: The content of register A is moved to the memory location whose address is in the register pair rp. Note: only register pairs rp = B (registers B and C) or rp = D (registers D and E) may be specified.

0	0	R	P	0	0	1	0

Bytes: 1   States: 7   Addressing: Reg. indirect

STC Set Carry

Operation: (CY) ← 1

S Z AC P CY
- - - - 1

Description: The CY flag is set to 1. NO OTHER FLAGS ARE AFFECTED.

| 0 | 0 | 1 | 1 | 0 | 1 | 1 | 1 |

Bytes: 1   States: 4

SUB M Subtract Memory

Operation: (A) ← (A) − ((H)(L))

S Z AC P CY
v v v v v

Description: The content of the memory location whose address is contained in the H and L registers is subtracted from the content of the accumulator. The result is placed in the accumulator.

| 1 | 0 | 0 | 1 | 0 | 1 | 1 | 0 |

Bytes: 1   States: 7   Addressing: Reg. indirect

SUB r Subtract Register

Operation: (A) ← (A) − (r)

S Z AC P CY
v v v v v

Description: The content of register r is subtracted from the content of the accumulator. The result is placed in the accumulator.

| 1 | 0 | 0 | 1 | 0 | S | S | S |

Bytes: 1   States: 4   Addressing: Register

Introduction to the I8080 Microprocessor

SUI data   **Subtract Immediate**

Operation: (A) ← (S) − (byte 2)   S Z AC P CY
                                                                               v v v v v

Description: The content of the second byte of the instruction is subtracted from the content of the accumulator. The result is placed in the accumulator.

1	1	0	1	0	1	1	0
data							

Bytes: 2   States: 7   Addressing: Immediate

XCHG   **Exchange H and L with D and E**

Operation: (H) ↔ (D)   S Z AC P CY
                 (L) ↔ (E)   − − − − −

Description: The contents of registers H and L are exchanged with the contents of registers D and E.

1	1	1	0	1	0	1	1

Bytes: 1   States: 4   Addressing: Register

XRA M   **Exclusive OR Memory**

Operation: (A) ← (A) ∀ ((H)(L))   S Z AC P CY
                                                                                   v v v v v

Description: The content of the memory location whose address is contained in the H and L registers is exlusive-OR'd with the content of the accumulator. The result is placed in the accumulator. THE CY AND AC FLAGS ARE CLEARED.

1	0	1	0	1	1	1	0

Bytes: 2   States: 7   Addressing: Reg. indirect

XRA r   Exclusive OR Register

Operation: (A) ← (A) ∀ (r)   S Z AC P CY
                                     v v v v v

Description: The content of register r is exclusive-OR'd with the content of the accumulator. The result is placed in the accumulator. THE CY AND AC FLAGS ARE CLEARED.

$$\begin{array}{|c|c|c|c|c|c|c|c|} \hline 1 & 0 & 1 & 0 & 1 & S & S & S \\ \hline \end{array}$$

Bytes: 1   States: 4   Addressing: Register

XRI data   Exclusive OR Immediate

Operation: (A) ← (A) ∀ (byte 2)   S Z AC P CY
                                     v v v v v

Description: The content of the second byte of the instruction is exclusive-OR'd with the content of the accumulator. The result is placed in the accumulator. THE CY AND AC FLAGS ARE CLEARED.

$$\begin{array}{|c|c|c|c|c|c|c|c|} \hline 1 & 1 & 1 & 0 & 1 & 1 & 1 & 0 \\ \hline \multicolumn{8}{|c|}{\text{data}} \\ \hline \end{array}$$

Bytes: 2   States: 7   Addressing: Immediate

Introduction to the I8080 Microprocessor

XTHL   Exhange Stack Top with H and L

Operation: $(L) \leftrightarrow ((SP))$ S Z AC P CY
             $(H) \leftrightarrow ((SP) + 1)$ $-\ -\ -\ -\ -$

Description: The content of the L register is exchanged with the content of the memory location whose address is specified by the content of register SP. The content of the H register is exchanged with the content of the memory location whose address is one more than the content of register SP.

1	1	1	0	0	0	1	1

Bytes: 1   States: 18   Addressing: Reg. indirect

7.5 I8080 EXAMPLE PROGRAM

This section contains several assembly-language programs for the I8080 microprocessor. These programs were prepared using the WYLBUR editor and assembled using an 8080 cross-assembler running on an Intel AS-5 computer.

```
01/04/78   MICRO-RESEARCH GROUP     8080 ASSEMBLER

   ADDR    CODE       SEQ   SOURCE
                       1    ;***********************************************************        8.
                       2    ;*    PROGRAM #1        8 X 8 BIT MULTIPLY (16 BIT RESULT)  *        9.
                       3    ;*                                                          *       10.
                       4    ;*    INPUT:    REG A - MULTIPLIER                          *       11.
                       5    ;*              REG E - MULTIPLICAND                        *       12.
                       6    ;*    OUTPUT:   RESULT IN (H,L)                             *       13.
                       7    ;*                                                          *       14.
                       8    ;***********************************************************       15.
   0000                9              ORG       3C00H                                          16.
                      10    ;                                                                  17.
                      11    ;                                                                  18.
   3C00               12    MULT8:                                                             19.
   3C00  21 0000      13              LXI       H,0000    ; CLEAR RESULT REGISTER              20.
   3C03  06 08        14              MVI       B,8       ; INITIALIZE BIT COUNTER             21.
   3C05  16 00        15              MVI       D,00      ; CLEAR REG. D FOR DAD INSTRUCTION   22.
   3C07               16    LOOP:                                                              23.
   3C07  29           17              DAD       H         ; SHIFT (H,L) LEFT 1 BIT             24.
   3C08  07           18              RLC                 ; MSB OF MULTIPLIER TO CARRY         25.
   3C09  D2 0D3C      19              JNC       DEC       ; IF CARRY IS CLEAR, DO NOT ADD      26.
   3C0C  19           20              DAD       D                                              27.
   3C0D  05           21    DEC:      DCR       B         ; DECREMENT BIT COUNTER              28.
   3C0E  C2 073C      22              JNZ       LOOP      ; CONTINUE UNTIL REG. B = 0          29.
   3C11  C9           23              RET                                                      30.
                      25    ;***********************************************************       32.
                      26    ;*    PROGRAM #2       EXTENDED BLOCK MOVE                   *      33.
                      27    ;*                                                           *      34.
                      28    ;*    INPUT:    REG (B,C) - NUMBER OF BYTES TO BE MOVED      *      35.
                      29    ;*              REG (D,E) - DESTINATION ADDRESS OF MOVE      *      36.
                      30    ;*              REG (H,L) - SOURCE ADDRESS FOR MOVE          *      37.
                      31    ;*    OUTPUT:   NONE                                         *      38.
                      32    ;*                                                           *      39.
                      33    ;***********************************************************       40.
   3C12               34              ORG       3C00H                                          41.
                      35    ;                                                                  42.
                      36    ;                                                                  43.
   3C00               37    FROM:     DS        100                                            44.
   3C64               38    TO:       DS        100                                            45.
   3CC8  6400         39    LENGTH:   DW        100                                            46.
```

```
                            40   ;
                            41   ;
                            42   ;       SAMPLE CALL:
                            43   ;
3CCA   21 063C              44               LXI     H,FROM
3CCD   01 C83C              45               LXI     B,LENGTH
3CD0   11 643C              46               LXI     D,TO
3CD3   CD 0010              47               CALL    BLKMOVE
3CD6   76                   48               HLT
                            49   ;
                            50   ;
                            51   ;
3CD7                        52               ORG     1000H
                            53   ;
1000                        54   BLKMOVE:
1000   78                   55               MOV     A,B         ; IF LENGTH IS ZERO, RETURN
1001   B1                   56               ORA     C
1002   C8                   57               RZ
1003   7E                   58               MOV     A,M         ; GET BYTE AT (H,L)
1004   12                   59               STAX    D           ; AND STORE IT AT (D,E)
1005   23                   60               INX     H
1006   13                   61               INX     D
1007   0B                   62               DCX     B           ; DECREMENT BYTE COUNT
1008   C3 0010              63               JMP     BLKMOVE
                            64
                            65   ;****************************************************
                            66   ;*  PROGRAM #3      16 BIT UNSIGNED COMPARE          *
                            67   ;*                                                   *
                            68   ;*  INPUT:    REGS (H,L), (D,E) - REGISTERS TO BE COMPARED  *
                            69   ;*  OUTPUT:   CARRY SET IF (D,E) >= (H,L)            *
                            70   ;*            CARRY CLEARED IF (D,E) < (H,L)         *
                            71   ;*                                                   *
                            72   ;****************************************************
                            73               ORG     3C00H
                            74   ;
                            75   ;
100B                        76   UCOMP:
3C00   7C                   77               MOV     A,H
3C01   BA                   78               CMP     D
3C02                        79               RNZ
3C03   7D                   80               MOV     A,L         ; H=D, FURTHUR TESTING IS NECESSARY
3C04   BB                   81               CMP     E
3C05   C0                   82               RNZ
3C06   37                   83               STC                 ; (H,L) = (D,E), FORCE CARRY
3C07   C9                   84               RET
                            85
                            86   ;****************************************************
                            87   ;*  PROGRAM #4      16 BIT SIGNED COMPARE            *
                            88   ;*                                                   *
                            89   ;*  INPUT:    REGS (H,L), (D,E) - REGISTERS TO BE COMPARED  *
                            90   ;*  OUTPUT:   CARRY SET IF (D,E) >= (H,L)            *
                            91   ;*            CARRY CLEARED IF (D,E) < (H,L)         *
                            92   ;*                                                   *
                            93   ;****************************************************
3C08                        94               ORG     3C00H
                            95   ;
                            96   ;
3C00                        97   SCOMP:
3C00   7A                   98               MOV     A,D         ; ARE SIGNS THE SAME ?
3C01   AC                   99               XRA     H
3C02   F2 0D3C             100               JP      SCOMP10     ; /YES - NORMAL 16 BIT COMPARE
3C05   7A                  101               MOV     A,D         ; /NO  - SENSE OF CARRY IS REVERSED
3C06   BC                  102               CMP     H
3C07   C0                  103               RNZ
3C08   7B                  104               MOV     A,E         ; D=H, FURTHUR TESTING IS NECESSARY
3C09   BD                  105               CMP     L
3C0A   C0                  106               RNZ
3C0B   37                  107               STC                 ; (D,E) = (H,L), FORCE CARRY
3C0C   C9                  108               RET
                           109   SCOMP10:
3C0D   7C                  110               MOV     A,H         ; SAME SIGNS
3C0E   BA                  111               CMP     D
3C0F   C0                  112               RNZ
3C10   7D                  113               MOV     A,L         ; D=E, FURTHUR TESTING IS NECESSARY
3C11   BB                  114               CMP     E
3C12   C0                  115               RNZ
3C13   37                  116               STC                 ; (H,L) = (D,E), FORCE CARRY
3C14   C9                  117               RET
                           118
                           119   ;****************************************************
                           120   ;*  PROGRAM #5      MULTIPLE BYTE DECIMAL ADD        *
                           121   ;*                                                   *
                           122   ;*  INPUT:    REG A - NUMBER OF BYTES TO BE ADDED    *
                           123   ;*                   ( 2 BCD DIGITS PER BYTE)        *
                           124   ;*            REG (B,C) - ADDRESS OF THE RESULT      *
                           125   ;*            REGS (H,L), (D,E) - ADDRESSES OF DECIMAL STRINGS  *
                           126   ;*                   TO BE ADDED. (MUST BE THE SAME LENGTH)    *
                           127   ;*  OUTPUT:   RESULT LOCATED AT (B,C)                *
                           128   ;*                                                   *
                           129   ;****************************************************
                           130   ;
                           131
3C15                       132   STRING1: DS    10
3C1F                       133   STRING2: DS    10
3C29                       134   RESULT:  DS    10
3C33   00                  135   COUNT:   DB    00              ; TEMPORARY LOCATION USED BY DECADD
                           136   ;
                           137   ;
                           138   ;       SAMPLE CALL
                           139   ;
3C34   01 293C             140               LXI     B,RESULT
3C37   21 153C             141               LXI     H,STRING1
3C3A   11 1F3C             142               LXI     D,STRING2
3C3D   3E 0A               143               MVI     A,10
3C3F   CD 0010             144               CALL    DECADD
3C42   76                  145               HLT
                           146   ;
                           147   ;
3C43                       148               ORG     1000H
                           149   ;
1000                       150   DECADD:
1000   32 333C             151               STA     COUNT       ; SAVE BYTE COUNT
1003   AF                  152               XRA     A           ; CLEAR FLAGS (SPECIFICALLY CARRY)
1004                       153   ADD10:
1004   F5                  154               PUSH    PSW         ; PROTECT FLAGS FROM THE FOLLOWING COMPARE
1005   3A 333C             155               LDA     COUNT       ; RECALL BYTE COUNT
1008   B7                  156               ORA     A           ; IF COUNT IS ZERO, WE ARE FINISHED
1009   CA 1B10             157               JZ      ADD20
100C   3D                  158               DCR     A
100D   32 333C             159               STA     COUNT
1010   F1                  160               POP     PSW         ; RESTORE FLAGS
                           161   ;
```

Introduction to the I8080 Microprocessor

```
1011  1A           162             LDAX    D           ; FETCH OPERANDS              169.
1012  8E           163             ADC     M                                         170.
1013  27           164             DAA                                               171.
1014  02           165             STAX    B                                         172.
1015  23           166             INX     H                                         173.
1016  03           167             INX     B                                         174.
1017  13           168             INX     D                                         175.
1018  C3 0410      169             JMP     ADD10                                     176.
101B               170     ADD20:                                                    177.
101B  F1           171             POP     PSW                                       178.
101C  C9           172             RET                                               179.
                   174     ;***********************************************************  181.
                   175     ;*  PROGRAM #6      MULTIPLE BYTE DECIMAL SUBTRACT        *   182.
                   176     ;*                                                        *   183.
                   177     ;*  INPUT:     REG A - NUMBER OF BYTES TO BE SUBTRACTED   *   184.
                   178     ;*                    ( 2 BCD DIGITS PER BYTE)            *   185.
                   179     ;*             REG (B,C) - ADDRESS OF THE RESULT          *   186.
                   180     ;*             REG (D,E) - ADDRESS OF THE SUBTRAHEND      *   187.
                   181     ;*             (H,L)     - ADDRESS OF THE MINUEND         *   188.
                   182     ;*             (IE. @(B,C) = @(H,L) - @(D,E)  )           *   189.
                   183     ;* RESTRICTION: THE DECIMAL STRINGS TO BE OPERATED ON     *   190.
                   184     ;*              MUST BE THE SAME LENGTH                   *   191.
                   185     ;* OUTPUT: RESULT LOCATED AT (B,C)                        *   192.
                   186     ;*                                                        *   193.
                   187     ;***********************************************************  194.
                   188     ;                                                             195.
                   189     ; SAMPLE STORAGE DECLARATION:                                 196.
                   190     ;                                                             197.
101D               191     OPRND1:  DS     10      ; SUBTRAHEND DECIMAL STRING           198.
1027               192     OPRND2:  DS     10      ; MINUEND DECIMAL STRING              199.
1031               193     RSLT:    DS     10                                            200.
103B  00           194     BCOUNT:  DB     00      ; TEMPORARY LOCATION USED BY SUBADD   201.
                   195     ;                                                             202.
                   196     ;                                                             203.
                   197     ;   SAMPLE CALL                                               204.
                   198     ;                                                             205.
103C  01 3110      199             LXI     B,RSLT                                       206.
103F  11 1D10      200             LXI     D,OPRND1  ; SUBTRAHEND DECIMAL STRING        207.
1042  21 2710      201             LXI     H,OPRND2  ; MINUEND DECIMAL STRING           208.
1045  3E 0A        202             MVI     A,10      ; LENGTH OF DECIMAL STRINGS (#DIGITS) 209.
1047  CD 0010      203             CALL    DECSUB                                       210.
104A  76           204             HLT                                                  211.
                   205     ;                                                             212.
                   206     ;                                                             213.
                   207     ;   DECIMAL SUBTRACTION IN THE FOLLOWING ROUTINE IS ACCOMPLISHED BY  214.
                   208     ;   ADDING THE TENS COMPLEMENT OF THE SUBTRAHEND DIGIT TO THE MINUEND 215.
                   209     ;   DIGIT.  EXAMPLE: TO SUBTRACT 30 FROM 77, WE FIRST FORM THE TENS   216.
                   210     ;   COMPLEMENT OF 30 (99-30=69+1=70) AND ADD IT TO THE MINUEND (70+77=147) 
                   211     ;   BY IGNORING THE CARY OUT OF THE HIGH ORDER DIGIT (47), THE RESULT 218.
                   212     ;   IS CORRECTED.  FOR MULTI-BYTE DECIMAL SUBTRACTION, THE SUBTRAHEND IS 219.
                   213     ;   FORMED BY TENS COMPLEMENT WHEN THERE IS NO BORROW (CARRY SET),    220.
                   214     ;   OR BY NINES COMPLEMENT IF THERE WAS A BORROW (CARRY CLEAR) FROM THE 221.
                   215     ;   LAST SUBTRACTION.                                                 222.
                   216     ;                                                                    223.
104B               217             ORG     1000H                                                224.
                   218     ;                                                                    225.
1000               219     DECSUB:                                                              226.
1000  32 3B10      220             STA     BCOUNT   ; SAVE BYTE COUNT                           227.
1003  37           221             STC              ; SET CARRY TO INDICATE NO BORROW           228.
1004               222     SUB10:                                                               229.
1004  F5           223             PUSH    PSW      ; PROTECT FLAGS FROM THE FOLLOWING COMPARE  230.
1005  3A 3B10      224             LDA     BCOUNT   ; RECALL BYTE COUNT                         231.
1008  B7           225             ORA     A                                                    232.
1009  CA 2310      226             JZ      SUB20    ; IF COUNT IS ZERO, WE ARE FINISHED         233.
100C  3D           227             DCR     A                                                    234.
100D  32 3B10      228             STA     BCOUNT                                               235.
1010  F1           229             POP     PSW      ; RESTORE FLAGS                             236.
                   230     ;                                                                    237.
1011  1A           231             LDAX    D        ; FETCH SUBTRAHEND                          238.
1012  C5           232             PUSH    B                                                    239.
1013  47           233             MOV     B,A      ; SAVE SUBTRAHEND IN REG. B                 240.
1014  3E 99        234             MVI     A,99H                                                241.
1016  CE 00        235             ACI     0                                                    242.
1018  96           236             SUB     M        ; FORM NINES OR TENS COMPLEMENT OF SUBTRAHEND 243.
1019  80           237             ADD     B        ; ADD MINUEND                               244.
101A  27           238             DAA              ; AND DECIMAL ADJUST RESULT                 245.
101B  C1           239             POP     B        ; RESTORE (B,C)                             246.
101C  02           240             STAX    B                                                    247.
101D  23           241             INX     H                                                    248.
101E  03           242             INX     B                                                    249.
101F  13           243             INX     D                                                    250.
1020  C3 0410      244             JMP     SUB10                                                251.
1023               245     SUB20:                                                               252.
1023  F1           246             POP     PSW                                                  253.
1024  C9           247             RET                                                          254.
```

NO ERRORS DECTECTED.

```
SYMBOL      VALUE (HEX)
MULT8       3C00
LOOP        3C07
DEC         3C0D
FROM        3C00
TO          3C64
LENGTH      3CC8
BLKMOVE     1000
UCOMP       3C00
SCOMP       3C00
SCOMP10     3C0D
STRING1     3C15
STRING2     3C1F
RESULT      3C29
COUNT       3C33
DECADD      1000
ADD10       1004
ADD20       101B
OPRND1      101D
OPRND2      1027
RSLT        1031
BCOUNT      103B
DECSUB      1000
SUB10       1004
SUB20       1023
```

7.6 ELECTRICAL CHARACTERISTICS OF THE I8080

7.6.1 External Connections

Figure 7.6-1 contains the pinout designations for the I8080 microprocessor.

1. *Supply Voltages:* Three supplies of ±5% accuracy are required, with typical current requirements as follows:

+12 volts 40 mA (pin 28)
+ 5 volts 60 mA (pin 20)
− 5 volts 10 mA (pin 11)

Pin 2 is ground.

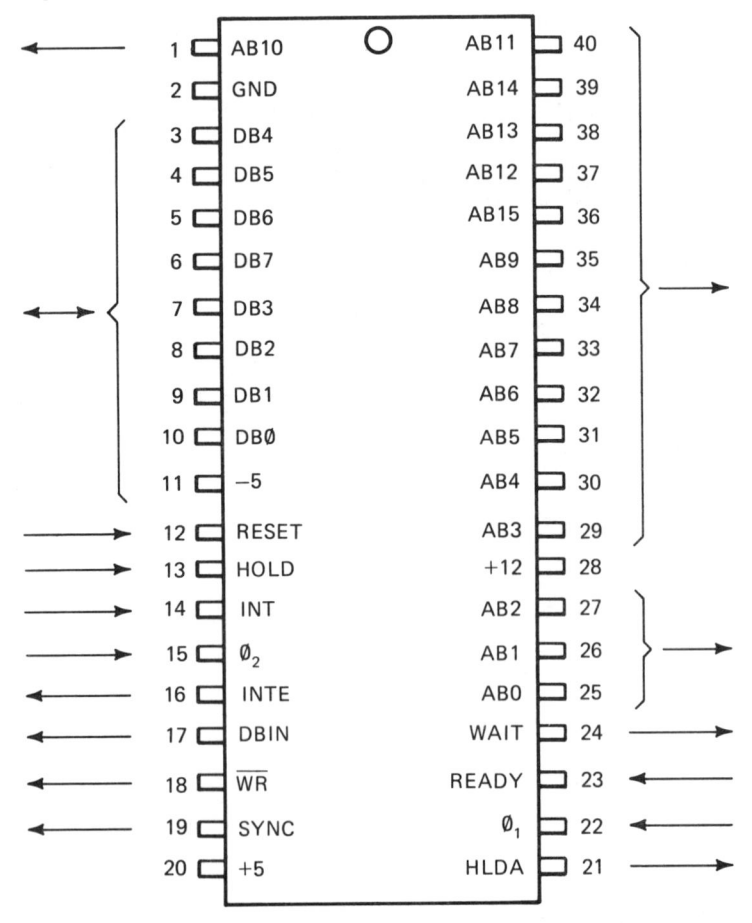

```
 1  AB10        AB11  40
 2  GND         AB14  39
 3  DB4         AB13  38
 4  DB5         AB12  37
 5  DB6         AB15  36
 6  DB7         AB9   35
 7  DB3         AB8   34
 8  DB2         AB7   33
 9  DB1         AB6   32
10  DB0         AB5   31
11  −5          AB4   30
12  RESET       AB3   29
13  HOLD        +12   28
14  INT         AB2   27
15  Ø2          AB1   26
16  INTE        AB0   25
17  DBIN        WAIT  24
18  WR          READY 23
19  SYNC        Ø1    22
20  +5          HLDA  21
```

Figure 7.6-1 I8080 pinout designation

Introduction to the I8080 Microprocessor 395

2. *AB0 − AB15 Address Bus:* The address bus in the I8080 is used for two different functions. The normal function is to provide 16-bit addresses, representing access to 65536 one-byte words of program or data. In its other function, the address bus is used during input/output to denote the port number (sometimes called the device number) for designating up to 256 input and 256 output devices. During IN and OUT instruction executions, this device number is sent out on address lines AB0 - AB7 and repeated on address lines AB8 - AB15. As with the previous microprocessors AB0 denotes the least significant address bit.

The address bus is capable of driving one TTL load and 100 picofarads under rated conditions. Note that these drive levels are similar to those of the MCS6502 and the M6800.

3. *DB0 − DB7 Data Bus:* Pins 3 through 10 are used for the bidirectional data bus. Each of these pins is connected to both an input and an output buffer. The data bus buffer allows bidirectional communication between the microprocessor, memory, and I/O devices, for instructions and data transfer. A unique characteristic of the I8080 bus is the time sharing of the data bus between data and "status" information. During the first clock cycle of every machine cycle the microprocessor puts out a so-called status word on the data bus which is descriptive of the present type of machine cycle which the microprocessor is carrying out. Table 7.6.1-1 lists the status bit definitions for each data bus line, and shows the particular status bit patterns which correspond to the 10 types of *machine cycles* which can occur. The 8228 system controller detects and stores these bit patterns, and subsequently uses this stored information to generate the control signals shown in Figure 7.6.3-1. An 8228 System Controller chip automatically latches and decodes these status bits to generate control signals to memory and I/O devices (see Figure 7.6.3-1). The data bus is capable of being placed in the high impedance condition (for DMA applications) and can drive 100 picofarads plus one TTL load.

4. *RESET Reset (pin 12):* The Reset line is used in the I8080 to reset the microprocessor to a known state of initialization, typically after turning the power on. To be effective, the reset line must be in the high condition for a minimum of 3 clock cycles. At this time the program counter will be forced to zero, causing the processor execution to transfer to that location. It should be noted that the flag register, the accumulator and stack pointer values are unchanged by Reset. Once again, as discussed for the MCS6502, it is incumbent upon the program-

TABLE 7.6.1-1 I8080 Status (Courtesy Intel Corporation)

Instructions for the 8080 require from one to five machine cycles for complete execution. The 8080 sends out 8 bits of status information on the data bus at the beginning of each machine cycle (during SYNC time). The following table defines the status information.

STATUS INFORMATION DEFINITION

Symbols	Data bus Bit	Definition
INTA*	D_0	Acknowledge signal for INTERRUPT request. Signal should be used to gate a restart instruction onto the data bus when DBIN is active.
$\overline{WO}$	D_1	Indicates that the operation in the current machine cycle will be a WRITE memory or OUTPUT function ($\overline{WO}$ = 0). Otherwise, a READ memory or INPUT operation will be executed.
STACK	D_2	Indicates that the address bus holds the push-down stack address from the stack pointer.
HLTA	D_3	Acknowledge signal for HALT instruction.
OUT	D_4	Indicates that the address bus contains the address of an output device and the data bus will contain the output data when $\overline{WR}$ is active.
M_1	D_5	Provides a signal to indicate that the CPU is in the fetch cycle for the first byte of an instruction.

Introduction to the I8080 Microprocessor

INP* D_6 Indicates that the address bus contains the address of an input device and the input data should be placed on the data bus when DBIN is active.

MEMR* D_7 Designates that the data bus will be used for memory read data.

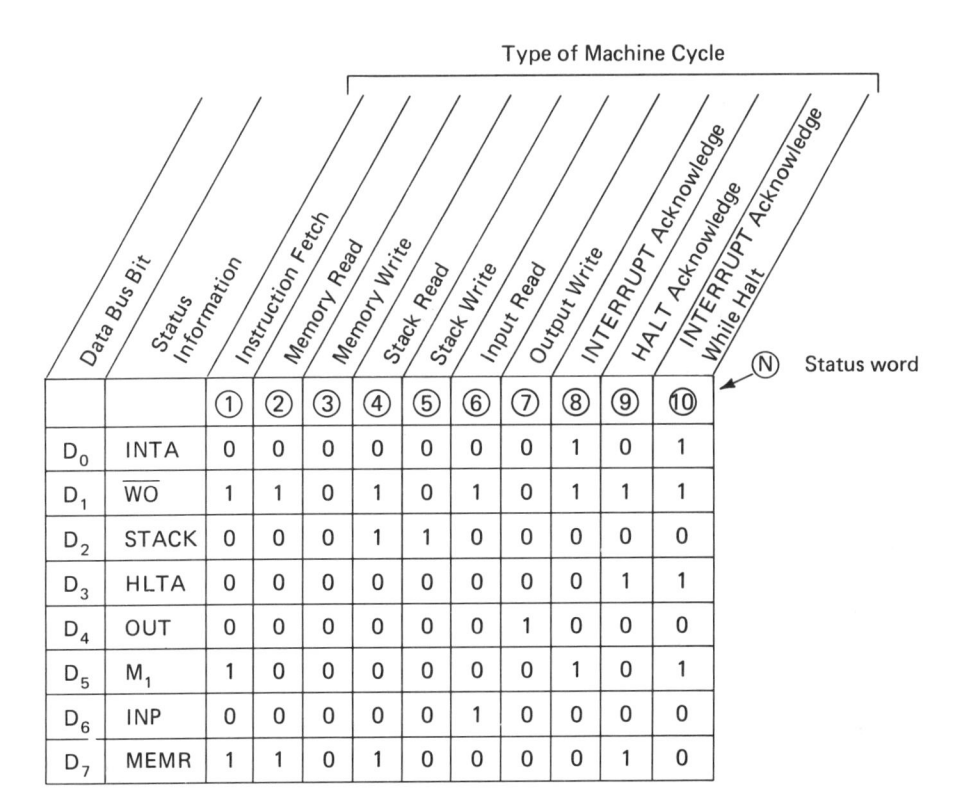

* These three status bits can be used to control the flow of data onto the 8080 data bus.

Type of Machine Cycle:
① Instruction Fetch
② Memory Read
③ Memory Write
④ Stack Read
⑤ Stack Write
⑥ Input Read
⑦ Output Write
⑧ INTERRUPT Acknowledge
⑨ HALT Acknowledge
⑩ INTERRUPT Acknowledge While Halt

Ⓝ Status word

Data Bus Bit	Status Information	①	②	③	④	⑤	⑥	⑦	⑧	⑨	⑩
D_0	INTA	0	0	0	0	0	0	0	1	0	1
D_1	$\overline{WO}$	1	1	0	1	0	1	0	1	1	1
D_2	STACK	0	0	0	1	1	0	0	0	0	0
D_3	HLTA	0	0	0	0	0	0	0	0	1	1
D_4	OUT	0	0	0	0	0	0	1	0	0	0
D_5	M_1	1	0	0	0	0	0	0	1	0	1
D_6	INP	0	0	0	0	0	1	0	0	0	0
D_7	MEMR	1	1	0	1	0	0	0	0	1	0

mer to initialize the stack pointer to an area in read/write memory in which valid read/write actions can be performed.

5. *HOLD, HLDA. Hold (pin 13), Hold Acknowledge (pin 12):* The Hold line requests the microprocessor to enter the hold state. The function of the hold state is to allow an external device to assume control of the address and data bus as soon as the instruction being executed has been completed. Entry into the hold condition will be acknowledged via the hold acknowledge line. HLDA, either if the microprocessor is in the halt state, or if the microprocessor is in the T2 or wait state and the ready signal is high. Once one of these two conditions are met the I8080 address bus and the data bus will be placed in the high impedance state and the hold acknowledge line will go high.

6. *INT, INTE. Interrupt (pin 14), Interrupt Enable (pin 16):* The interrupt line is a line recognized by the microprocessor as an interrupt request. At the end of execution of the current instruction, or if halted, the microprocessor will recognize an interrupt and will signify this condition via the interrupt enable line. In order for an interrupt to occur, it is necessary that the internal interrupt-enable flip-flop have previously been set under software control. The instruction which accomplishes this effect is EI, enable interrupt. After the interrupt enable line has gone high, signifying recognition of an interrupt request, the microprocessor will disable further interrupts, and will subsequently look for an instruction to be jammed onto the data bus in response to this interrupt-enable output.

7. *DBIN. Data Bus In (pin 17):* The Data Bus In line is a signal generated by the microprocessor to convey to external circuits that the data bus is presently in the input mode, i.e., the data bus buffer is set to the input condition. This line is normally used by external parts as a chip enable to gate data onto the data bus from memory or I/O.

8. $\overline{WR}$. *Write if in the low state (pin 18) (sometimes labeled RD for Read or R/$\overline{W}$):* The $\overline{WR}$ line is an active low signal used for memory or input/output control in those cases where a value is to be written from the data bus into the memory or I/O device. Under normal circumstances the data on the data bus is stable during the interval in which $\overline{WR}$ is low. This line is sometimes labeled RD, signifying that if it is high it is in the read condition, and if it is low it is in the read, hence write, condition.

Introduction to the I8080 Microprocessor **399**

9. *SYNC Synchronizing Signal (pin 19):* The SYNC line delivers a signal generated by the microprocessor at the beginning of each memory cycle, and is used by external devices (principally the 8228 System Controller) to detect the status bits, which are placed on the data bus during SYNC. The combination of SYNC and $\phi 2$ is the indication by the microcomputer that the data bus contains the status bits.

10. *READY, WAIT. Ready (pin 23), Wait (pin 24):* The Ready input is a signal which tells the I8080 that valid memory or input data is available on the 8080 data bus. This signal is used to synchronize the microprocessor with slower memory or slower input/output devices. If the microprocessor delivers an address output and does not find a ready line high it will enter what is called the wait state for as long as the ready line is not high. A popular use of Ready is to single-step the microprocessor during systems debugging.

11. *$\phi 1$, $\phi 2$. Clock signals (pins 22 and 15):* The clock inputs are two nonoverlapping, nonTTL compatible signals which must be generated by external circuitry. A special IC part has been developed for this purpose, the 8224. This part also provides several other signals needed by an I8080-based microcomputer.

The two clock signals must not only be nonoverlapping but there must be a specified delay between the falling edge of $\phi 2$ and the rising edge of $\phi 1$. They are also usually asymmetrical, i.e., of unequal duration.

7.6.2 Basic Timing for the I8080

Timing considerations for the I8080 are somewhat different than for the previous microprocessors. For example, the I8080 requires from 4 to 18 states (clock cycles) to fetch and execute each instruction. These states are in turn grouped into what are called *machine cycles*, each of which consists of 1 to 5 states. Each instruction, in turn, may require multiple cycles. Each state for a standard microprocessor part running at rated speed requires approximately one-half microsecond.

An instruction cycle is the largest element of time in this chain and is the time required to fetch and execute an instruction. During Fetch a selected instruction is read from memory and deposited in the I8080 instruction register. During the execution phase this instruction is decoded and multiple machine cycles are used to perform the specific processing activity.

A machine cycle is that interval of time, 3 to 5 machine states, during which one memory or one input/output access is made. The fetch portion of an instruction cycle requires one machine cycle for each byte to be fetched. The duration of the execution portion of the instruction cycle depends upon the kind of instruction that has been fetched. Some instructions require no additional machine cycles for execution, other than that necessary for op code fetch. Other instructions may require additional memory cycles to read or write data to or from memory or input/output devices. The DAD instruction differs from this description, in that it requires two additional memory cycles to complete an *internal* register-pair add, but no actual memory or I/O access is performed.

In summary, each clock interval from the rising edge of $\phi 1$ to the rising edge of the next $\phi 1$ is defined as a state. Three to five states make up one machine cycle and one to five machine cycles constitute an instruction cycle. For typical parts, running at slightly less than rated speed, each instruction will require from 2 to 9 microseconds to fetch and execute.

Figure 7.6.2-1 is the microprocessor state transition diagram for the I8080 microprocessor. This is a very useful diagram indicating the flow of events in which a check is made for Ready, Interrupt, and Hold. The states T_1, T_2, T_3, T_4, and T_5 represent individual machine states during which specific activity is carried out. As an example, during every T_1 cycle, the program counter value will be sent out on the address bus and the status information will be placed on the data bus. A better appreciation for this will be gained in Table 7.6.2-1 which details the flow of activities for each individual op code.

Reference to this table shows that during states T_1 through T_5 the following activities typically take place: during T_1 a memory address (or I/O device number) is placed on the address bus and status information is placed on the data bus. During T_2 the microprocessor will sample the Ready and Hold input lines and check to see if it should halt. T_3 is used for an instruction fetch, a data byte read either from memory or from stack or for a Reset (interrupt-response) instruction to be input from the data bus. Alternatively, during memory write, stack write, or output a data byte may be sent out via the data bus. States T_4 and T_5 are optional and depend on the instruction being executed. They are always used for internal processor operations and do not involve address or data bus.

Table 7.6.2-1 gives the exact operations during each state for all instructions.

Introduction to the I8080 Microprocessor 401

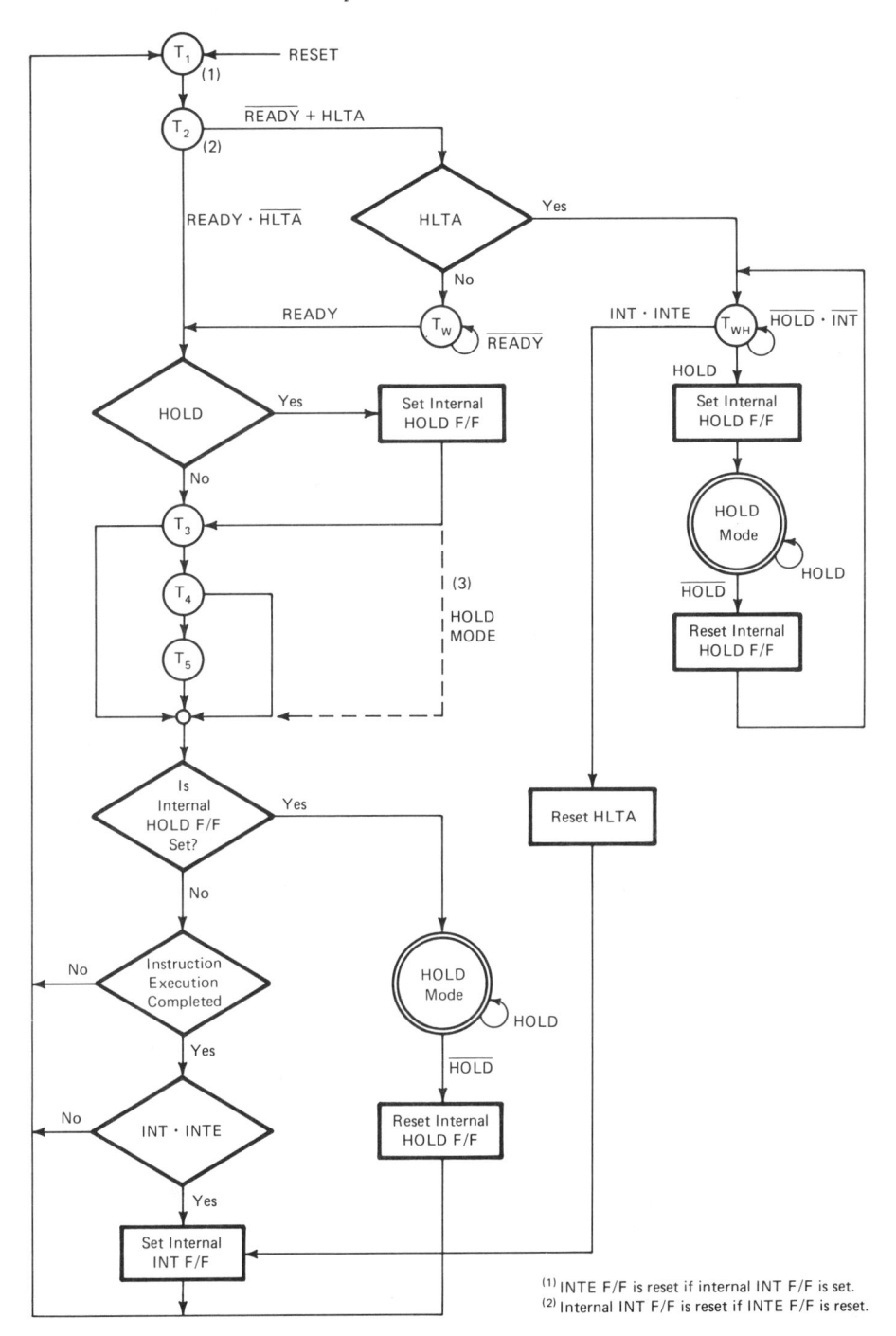

Figure 7.6.2-1 CPU state transition diagram
(courtesy Intel Corporation)

TABLE 7.6.2-1 Detailed State Description

MNEMONIC	OP CODE			M1[1]					M2		
	$D_7 D_6 D_5 D_4$	$D_3 D_2 D_1 D_0$	T1	T2[2]	T3	T4	T5	T1	T2[2]	T3
MOV r1, r2	0 1 D D	D S S S	PC OUT STATUS	PC = PC + 1	INST→TMP/IR	(SSS)→TMP	(TMP)→DDD			
MOV r, M	0 1 D D	D 1 1 0	↑	↑	↑	X[3]		HL OUT STATUS[6]	DATA → DDD	
MOV M, r	0 1 1 1	0 S S S				(SSS)→TMP		HL OUT STATUS[7]	(TMP) → DATA BUS	
SPHL	1 1 1 1	1 0 0 1				(HL) ──── → SP				
MVI r, data	0 0 D D	D 1 1 0				X		PC OUT STATUS[6]	B2 → DDDD	
MVI M, data	0 0 1 1	0 1 1 0				X		↑	B2 → TMP	
LXI rp, data	0 0 R P	0 0 0 1				X			PC = PC + 1 B2 → r1	
LDA addr	0 0 1 1	1 0 1 0				X			PC = PC + 1 B2 → Z	
STA addr	0 0 1 1	0 0 1 0				X			PC = PC + 1 B2 → Z	
LHLD addr	0 0 1 0	1 0 1 0				X			PC = PC + 1 B2 → Z	
SHLD addr	0 0 1 0	0 0 1 0				X		PC OUT STATUS[6]	PC = PC + 1 B2 → Z	
LDAX rp[4]	0 0 R P	1 0 1 0				X		rp OUT STATUS[6]	DATA → A	
STAX rp[4]	0 0 R P	0 0 1 0				X		rp OUT STATUS[7]	(A) → DATA BUS	
XCHG	1 1 1 0	1 0 1 1				(HL)↔(DE)				
ADD r	1 0 0 0	0 S S S				(SSS)→TMP (A)→ACT		[9]	(ACT)+(TMP)→A	
ADD M	1 0 0 0	0 1 1 0				(A)→ACT		HL OUT STATUS[6]	DATA → TMP	
ADI data	1 1 0 0	0 1 1 0				(A)→ACT		PC OUT STATUS[6]	PC = PC + 1 B2 → TMP	
ADC r	1 0 0 0	1 S S S				(SSS)→TMP (A)→ACT		[9]	(ACT)+(TMP)+CY→A	
ADC M	1 0 0 0	1 1 1 0				(A)→ACT		HL OUT STATUS[6]	DATA → TMP	
ACI data	1 1 0 0	1 1 1 0				(A)→ACT		PC OUT STATUS[6]	PC = PC + 1 B2 → TMP	
SUB r	1 0 0 1	0 S S S				(SSS)→TMP (A)→ACT		[9]	(ACT)−(TMP)→A	
SUB M	1 0 0 1	0 1 1 0				(A)→ACT		HL OUT STATUS[6]	DATA → TMP	
SUI data	1 1 0 1	0 1 1 0				(A)→ACT		PC OUT STATUS[6]	PC = PC + 1 B2 → TMP	
SBB r	1 0 0 1	1 S S S				(SSS)→TMP (A)→ACT		[9]	(ACT)−(TMP)−CY→A	
SBB M	1 0 0 1	1 1 1 0				(A)→ACT		HL OUT STATUS[6]	DATA → TMP	
SBI data	1 1 0 1	1 1 1 0				(A)→ACT		PC OUT STATUS[6]	PC = PC + 1 B2 → TMP	
INR r	0 0 D D	D 1 0 0				(DDD)→TMP (TMP)+1→ALU	ALU→DDD			
INR M	0 0 1 1	0 1 0 0				X		HL OUT STATUS[6]	DATA → TMP (TMP)+1 → ALU	
DCR r	0 0 D D	D 1 0 1				(DDD)→TMP (TMP)+1→ALU	ALU→DDD			
DCR M	0 0 1 1	0 1 0 1				X		HL OUT STATUS[6]	DATA → TMP (TMP)−1 → ALU	
INX rp	0 0 R P	0 0 1 1				(RP) + 1 ──── → RP				
DCX rp	0 0 R P	1 0 1 1				(RP) − 1 ──── → RP				
DAD rp [8]	0 0 R P	1 0 0 1				X		(rl)→ACT	(L)→TMP, (ACT)+(TMP)→ALU	ALU→L, CY
DAA	0 0 1 0	0 1 1 1				DAA→A, FLAGS[10]				
ANA r	1 0 1 0	0 S S S	↓	↓	↓	(SSS)→TMP (A)→ACT		[9]	(ACT)+(TMP)→	
ANA M	1 0 1 0	0 1 1 0	PC OUT STATUS	PC = PC + 1	INST→TMP/IR	(A)→ACT		HL OUT STATUS[6]	DATA → TMP	

Introduction to the I8080 Microprocessor

	M3			M4			M5				
	T1	T2[(2)]	T3	T1	T2[(2)]	T3	T1	T2[(2)]	T3	T4	T5
	HL OUT STATUS[(7)]	(TMP) → DATA BUS									
	PC OUT STATUS[(6)]	PC = PC + 1	B3 → rh								
		PC = PC + 1	B3 → W	WZ OUT STATUS[(6)]	DATA → A						
		PC = PC + 1	B3 → W	WZ OUT STATUS[(7)]	(A) → DATA BUS						
		PC = PC + 1	B3 → W	WZ OUT STATUS[(6)]	DATA WZ = WZ + 1	→ L	WZ OUT STATUS[(6)]	DATA → H			
	PC OUT STATUS[(6)]	PC = PC + 1	B3 → W	WZ OUT STATUS[(7)]	(L) WZ = WZ + 1	→ DATA BUS	WZ OUT STATUS[(7)]	(H) → DATA BUS			
		(5)	(ACT)+(TMP)→A								
		(5)	(ACT)+(TMP)→A								
		(5)	(ACT)+(TMP)+CY→A								
		(5)	(ACT)+(TMP)+CY→A								
		(5)	(ACT)−(TMP)→A								
		(5)	(ACT)−(TMP)→A								
		(5)	(ACT)−(TMP)−CY→A								
		(5)	(ACT)−(TMP)−CY→A								
	HL OUT STATUS[(7)]		ALU → DATA BUS								
	HL OUT STATUS[(7)]		ALU → DATA BUS								
	(rh)→ACT	(H)→TMP (ACT)+(TMP)+CY→ALU	ALU→H, CY								
		(5)	(ACT)+(TMP)→A								

TABLE 7.6.2-1 Continued

MNEMONIC	OP CODE $D_7 D_6 D_5 D_4$ $D_3 D_2 D_1 D_0$		M1[1] T1	T2[2]	T3	T4	T5	M2 T1	T2[2]	T3
ANI data	1 1 1 0	0 1 1 0	PC OUT STATUS	PC = PC + 1	INST→TMP/IR	(A)→ACT		PC OUT STATUS[6]	PC = PC + 1	B2→TMP
XRA r	1 0 1 0	1 S S S				(A)→ACT (SSS)→TMP		[9]	(ACT)+(TMP)→A	
XRA M	1 0 1 0	1 1 1 0				(A)→ACT		HL OUT STATUS[6]		DATA→TMP
XRI data	1 1 1 0	1 1 1 0				(A)→ACT		PC OUT STATUS[6]	PC = PC + 1	B2→TMP
ORA r	1 0 1 1	0 S S S				(A)→ACT (SSS)→TMP		[9]	(ACT)+(TMP)→A	
ORA M	1 0 1 1	0 1 1 0				(A)→ACT		HL OUT STATUS[6]		DATA→TMP
ORI data	1 1 1 1	0 1 1 0				(A)→ACT		PC OUT STATUS[6]	PC = PC + 1	B2→TMP
CMP r	1 0 1 1	1 S S S				(A)→ACT (SSS)→TMP		[9]	(ACT)−(TMP), FLAGS	
CMP M	1 0 1 1	1 1 1 0				(A)→ACT		HL OUT STATUS[6]		DATA→TMP
CPI data	1 1 1 1	1 1 1 0				(A)→ACT		PC OUT STATUS[6]	PC = PC + 1	B2→TMP
RLC	0 0 0 0	0 1 1 1				(A)→ALU ROTATE		[9]	ALU→A, CY	
RRC	0 0 0 0	1 1 1 1				(A)→ALU ROTATE		[9]	ALU→A, CY	
RAL	0 0 0 1	0 1 1 1				(A), CY→ALU ROTATE		[9]	ALU→A, CY	
RAR	0 0 0 1	1 1 1 1				(A), CY→ALU ROTATE		[9]	ALU→A, CY	
CMA	0 0 1 0	1 1 1 1				(Ā)→A				
CMC	0 0 1 1	1 1 1 1				C̄Y→CY				
STC	0 0 1 1	0 1 1 1				1→CY				
JMP addr	1 1 0 0	0 0 1 1				X		PC OUT STATUS[6]	PC = PC + 1	B2→Z
J cond addr [17]	1 1 C C	C 0 1 0				JUDGE CONDITION		PC OUT STATUS[6]	PC = PC + 1	B2→Z
CALL addr	1 1 0 0	1 1 0 1				SP = SP − 1		PC OUT STATUS[6]	PC = PC + 1	B2→Z
C cond addr [17]	1 1 C C	C 1 0 0				JUDGE CONDITION IF TRUE, SP = SP − 1		PC OUT STATUS[6]	PC = PC + 1	B2→Z
RET	1 1 0 0	1 0 0 1				X		SP OUT STATUS[15]	SP = SP + 1	DATA→Z
R cond addr [17]	1 1 C C	C 0 0 0			INST→TMP/IR	JUDGE CONDITION[14]		SP OUT STATUS[15]	SP = SP + 1	DATA→Z
RST n	1 1 N N	N 1 1 1			φ→W INST→TMP/IR	SP = SP − 1		SP OUT STATUS[16]	SP = SP − 1	(PCH)→DATA BUS
PCHL	1 1 1 0	1 0 0 1			INST→TMP/IR	(HL)→PC				
PUSH rp	1 1 R P	0 1 0 1				SP = SP − 1		SP OUT STATUS[16]	SP = SP − 1	(rh)→DATA BUS
PUSH PSW	1 1 1 1	0 1 0 1				SP = SP − 1		SP OUT STATUS[16]	SP = SP − 1	(A)→DATA BUS
POP rp	1 1 R P	0 0 0 1				X		SP OUT STATUS[15]	SP = SP + 1	DATA→r1
POP PSW	1 1 1 1	0 0 0 1				X		SP OUT STATUS[15]	SP = SP + 1	DATA→FLAGS
XTHL	1 1 1 0	0 0 1 1				X		SP OUT STATUS[15]	SP = SP + 1	DATA→Z
IN port	1 1 0 1	1 0 1 1				X		PC OUT STATUS[6]	PC = PC + 1	B2→Z, W
OUT port	1 1 0 1	0 0 1 1				X		PC OUT STATUS[6]	PC = PC + 1	B2→Z, W
EI	1 1 1 1	1 0 1 1				SET INTE F/F				
DI	1 1 1 1	0 0 1 1				RESET INTE F/F				
HLT	0 1 1 1	0 1 1 0				X		PC OUT STATUS	HALT MODE[20]	
NOP	0 0 0 0	0 0 0 0	PC OUT STATUS	PC = PC + 1	INST→TMP/IR	X				

Introduction to the I8080 Microprocessor

	M3			M4			M5				
T1	T2(2)	T3	T1	T2(2)	T3	T1	T2(2)	T3	T4	T5
(9)	(ACT)+(TMP)→A									
(9)	(ACT)+(TMP)→A									
(9)	(ACT)+(TMP)→A									
(9)	(ACT)+(TMP)→A									
(9)	(ACT)+(TMP)→A									
(9)	(ACT)−(TMP); FLAGS									
	(ACT)−(TMP); FLAGS									
PC OUT STATUS(6)	PC = PC + 1 B3 → W									WZ OUT STATUS(11)	(WZ) + 1 → PC
PC OUT STATUS(6)	PC = PC + 1 B3 → W									WZ OUT STATUS(11,12)	(WZ) + 1 → PC
PC OUT STATUS(6)	PC = PC + 1 B3 → W		SP OUT STATUS(16)	(PCH) SP = SP − 1	→ DATA BUS	SP OUT STATUS(16)	(PCL)	→ DATA BUS		WZ OUT STATUS(11)	(WZ) + 1 → PC
PC OUT STATUS(6)	PC = PC + 1 B3 → W(13)		SP OUT STATUS(16)	(PCH) SP = SP − 1	→ DATA BUS	SP OUT STATUS(16)	(PCL)	→ DATA BUS		WZ OUT STATUS(11,12)	(WZ) + 1 → PC
SP OUT STATUS(15)	SP = SP + 1 DATA → W									WZ OUT STATUS(11)	(WZ) + 1 → PC
SP OUT STATUS(15)	SP = SP + 1 DATA → W									WZ OUT STATUS(11,12)	(WZ) + 1 → PC
SP OUT STATUS(16)	(TMP = 00NNN000) → Z (PCL) → DATA BUS									WZ OUT STATUS(11)	(WZ) + 1 → PC
SP OUT STATUS(16)	(rl) → DATA BUS										
SP OUT STATUS(16)	FLAGS → DATA BUS										
SP OUT STATUS(15)	SP = SP + 1 DATA → rh										
SP OUT STATUS(15)	SP = SP + 1 DATA → A										
SP OUT STATUS(15)	DATA → W		SP OUT STATUS(16)	(H)	→ DATA BUS	SP OUT STATUS(16)	(L)	→ DATA BUS	(WZ) → HL	
WZ OUT STATUS(18)	DATA → A										
WZ OUT STATUS(18)	(A) → DATA BUS										

TABLE 7.6.2-1 Continued

NOTES:

1. The first memory cycle (M1) is always an instruction fetch; the first (or only) byte, containing the op code, is fetched during this cycle.
2. If the READY input from memory is not high during T2 of each memory cycle, the processor will enter a wait state (TW) until READY is sampled as high.
3. States T4 and T5 are present, as required, for operations which are completely internal to the CPU. The contents of the internal bus during T4 and T5 are available at the data bus; this is designed for testing purposes only. An "X" denotes that the state is present, but is only used for such internal operations as instruction decoding.
4. Only register pairs rp = B (registers B and C) or rp = D (registers D and E) may be specified.
5. These states are skipped.
6. Memory read sub-cycles; an instruction or data word will be read.
7. Memory write sub-cycle.
8. The READY signal is not required during the second and third sub-cycles (M2 and M3). The HOLD signal is accepted during M2 and M3. The SYNC signal is not generated during M2 and M3. During the execution of DAD, M2 and M3 are required for an internal register-pair add; memory is not referenced.
9. The results of these arithmetic, logical or rotate instructions are not moved into the accumulator (A) until state T2 of the next instruction cycle. That is, A is loaded while the next instruction is being fetched; this overlapping of operations allows for faster processing.
10. If the value of the least significant 4-bits of the accumulator is greater than 9 *or* if the auxiliary carry bit is set, 6 is added to the accumulator. If the value of the most significant 4-bits of the accumulator is now greater than 9, *or* if the carry bit is set, 6 is added to the most significant 4-bits of the accumulator.
11. This represents the first sub-cycle (the instruction fetch) of the next instruction cycle.
12. If the condition was met, the contents of the register pair WZ are output on the address lines (A_{0-15}) instead of the contents of the program counter (PC).

Introduction to the I8080 Microprocessor **407**

13. If the condition was not met, sub-cycles M4 and M5 are skipped; the processor instead proceeds immediately to the instruction fetch (M1) of the next instruction cycle.
14. If the condition was not met, sub-cycles M2 and M3 are skipped; the processor instead proceeds immediately to the instruction fetch (M1) of the next instruction cycle.
15. Stack read sub-cycle.
16. Stack write sub-cycle.
17. CONDITION   CCC

$$
\begin{array}{ll}
NZ - \text{not zero } (Z = 0) & 000 \\
Z - \text{zero } (Z = 1) & 001 \\
NC - \text{no carry } (CY = 0) & 010 \\
C - \text{carry } (CY = 1) & 011 \\
PO - \text{parity odd } (P = 0) & 100 \\
PE - \text{parity even } (P = 1) & 101 \\
P - \text{plus } (S = 0) & 110 \\
M - \text{minus } (S = 1) & 111
\end{array}
$$

18. I/O sub-cycle: the I/O port's 8-bit select code is duplicated on address lines 0 - 7 (A_{0-7}) and 8 - 15 (A_{8-15}).
19. Output sub-cycle.
20. The processor will remain idle in the halt state until an interrupt, a reset or a hold is accepted. When a hold request is accepted, the CPU enters the hold mode; after the hold mode is terminated, the processor returns to the halt state. After a reset is accepted, the processor begins execution at memory location zero. After an interrupt is accepted, the processor executes the instruction forced onto the data bus (usually a restart instruction).

SSS or DDD	Value	rp	Value
A	111	B	00
B	000	D	01
C	001	H	10
D	010	SP	11
E	011		
H	100		
L	101		

7.6.3 I8080 Microcomputer System Example

Figure 7.6.3-1 shows an example microcomputer based upon the I8080 microprocessor. The associated Tabular Form Address Table is given in Table 7.6.3-1. As with our previous examples (see Chapter 5) many images exist, for ROM, RWM, and I/O ports. The functions of the 8224 and 8228 chips are illustrated in this figure. $\overline{\text{IOR}}$ and $\overline{\text{IOW}}$ are generated by the 8228 to facilitate I/O handling.

TABLE 7.6.3-1 Tabular Form Address Table for Simple I8080-based Microcomputer

15	14	13	12	11	10	9	8	7	6	5	4	3	2	1	0	Selected Part	Address Range
(∅)	(∅)	(∅)	(∅)	(∅)	∅	x	x	x	x	x	x	x	x	x	x	ROM	∅∅∅∅ - ∅3FF
-	-	-	-	∅	1	-	-	x	x	x	x	x	x	x	x	RWM	∅4∅∅ - ∅4FF
1	-	-	-	-	-	-	-	-	-	-	-	-	-	-	-	I/O	Port Number 8∅

PROBLEMS

1. Write an assembly language program for the I8080 microcomputer in Figure 7.6.3, to add the numbers in ∅3∅∅H and ∅3∅1H and store the result in ∅3∅∅H.

2. Identify the types of machine cycles and describe the function of each. What activity takes place during each?

3. What constraints exist in placement of ROM and RWM in address space? How does this compare to the MCS6502?

4. What is meant by "status" in the I8080? Is this the same as the MCS6502?

5. Make a table with MCS6502, M6800, and I8080 on one axis and Addressing Modes on the other. Put checks at the appropriate intersections.

6. The I8080 manufacturers' literature refers to B, C, D, E, H, and L registers as index registers. Comment on the accuracy of this usage.

Introduction to the I8080 Microprocessor **409**

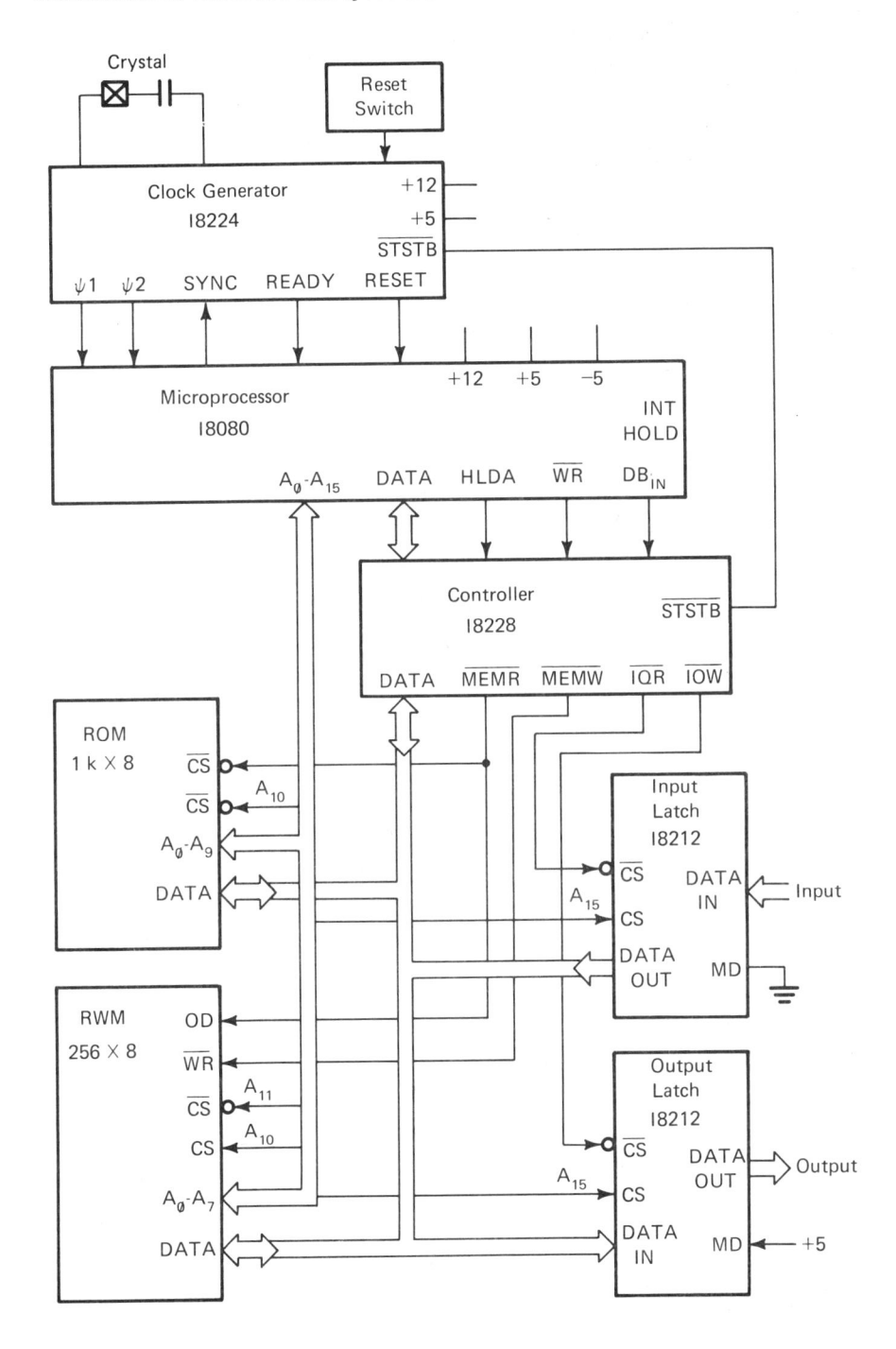

Figure 7.6.3-1 Simple I8080 based microcomputer

7. Describe the difference between Memory-Mapped I/O and Isolated (IN and OUT instructions) I/O. What happens on the Address line?
8. If the instruction OUT 7FH is executed, what is on the Address bus?
9. Develop an algorithm which would describe the DAA operation. Would this also work for the M6800?
10. Comment on the I8080 16 bit arithmetic capability. List all instructions to facilitate this capability.
11. Write a subroutine to give a 24 bit up-counter in RWM. Do it first without and then with the conditional return statements.
12. Give an example which would entail the use of the Conditional Subroutine Call.
13. Describe in your own words the use of Restart N (RST N).
14. Draw as much as possible of a Memory Map showing the Restart routines. How long can these routines be maximum?
15. Restart instructions are usually used in response to Interrupt requests. Can they be used in "normal" programs? Why? How? Give an example.
16. Describe the function of the Hold input to the I8080.
17. Does Halt stop the I8080? What must precede the use of this instruction?
18. How is NMI implemented in the I8080? Be specific.
19. What are Wait states in the I8080? What causes them? What can they be used for?
20. What are the maximum and minimum instruction execution times? Assume that the crystal is 18 MHz in Figure 7.6.3-2. This results in a clock frequency of 2 MHz.
21. In Problem 20 the I8224 uses a basic frequency 9-times the required clock frequency. What is this "overkill" needed? Hint: Consider the $\varphi 1$ and $\varphi 2$ timing constraints.
22. What happens if you Fetch an instruction from nonexistent address location? In other words "nothing" is placed on the Data Bus during Fetch.

8

AN MCS6502-BASED MICROCOMPUTER—THE KIM-1

INTRODUCTION

This chapter is written for persons who need to become acquainted with the KIM-1® microcomputer. This chapter uses the programmed instruction approach. Beginning with a discussion of the actual power supply connections, the chapter then proceeds to discuss the function of each key on the KIM-1 keyboard. The function of each key is highlighted by tables showing keys pressed and the corresponding display. After the keyboard entry of a simple problem is discussed, the use of the Teletype® model ASR33 as an input/output terminal is presented. The use of the Teletype is discussed in detail with reproductions of actual printed outputs and punched paper tapes being provided. Next the use of an audio cassette tape recorder is presented. Examples illustrate the detailed step by step procedure for recording onto magnetic tape from the microcomputer, and vice versa. Simple programming examples are used in all cases so that the reader can focus his attention on the operation of a microcomputer at machine or assembly language levels.

This chapter provides detailed information on the interaction between a user and a microcomputer when assembly level (or machine) language is used. After studying this chapter the reader will be in a position to decide whether this detailed level of interaction is acceptable,

---

® KIM-1 is a registered trademark of the MOS Technology Corporation

or whether he should consider the use of a microcomputer equipped with a higher level language. A higher level language, such as **BASIC**, makes the computer much more transparent to the user. (The reader should be forewarned, however, that there are literally hundreds of different versions of BASIC, so purchase of a microcomputer with a resident BASIC does not solve all of the user's problems.)

8.1 WHAT IS A KIM–1?

A KIM-1 (Keyboard Input Monitor) is a microcomputer built around the 6502 microprocessor presently manufactured by **MOS** Technology and Rockwell. The KIM-1 presently (1977 - 1978) sells for a little over $200 and is a complete microcomputer which includes the following:

* The microprocessor
* 2048 ROM bytes
* 1024 + 128 RAM bytes
* 30 input/output pins
* 2 timers
* Interface for audio cassette
* Interface for a Teletype
* 23 key keyboard
* Display consisting of 6 seven bar characters

The KIM-1 is an example of the so-called single-board microcomputers, because, except for the power supplies, it is fabricated on a single printed circuit board measuring approximately 20 by 28 cm, (8½ by 11 inches). Figure 8.1-1 is a photograph of the KIM-1 and the single 5 volt power supply which is required when using only the keyboard, a Teletype, or other compatible terminal. An additional 12 volt power supply is required if an audio cassette tape recorder is added. The KIM-1 circuit board is shown in Figure 8.1-2.

The KIM-1 is typical of the many microprocessor based microcomputers which are presently being sold. It is the authors' opinion that this chapter will be of more use to the reader if one microcomputer is presented in depth as opposed to discussing several microcomputers in more general terms. Somewhat like learning to drive an automobile, or to ride a bicycle, the carryover from the use of one microcomputer to another is large so the adjustment period in learning to use a different microcomputer is surprisingly short.

MCS 6502 Based Microcomputer — The KIM-1

Figure 8.1-1(a) The KIM-1 microcomputer

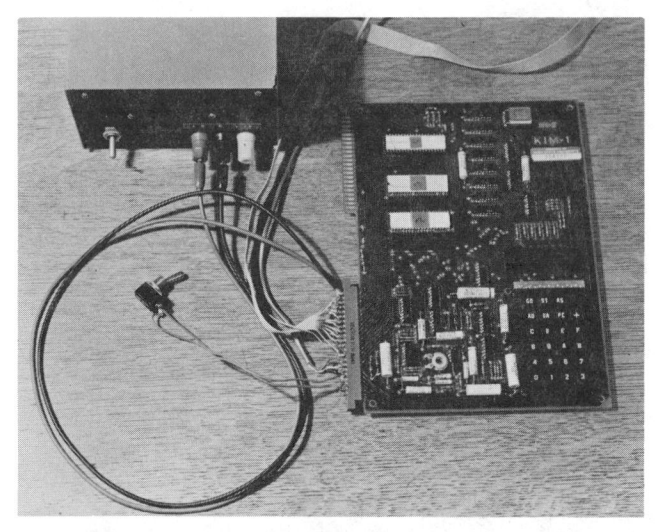

(b) The KIM-1 microcomputer connected to a 5 volt power supply (Note Teletype mode switch.)

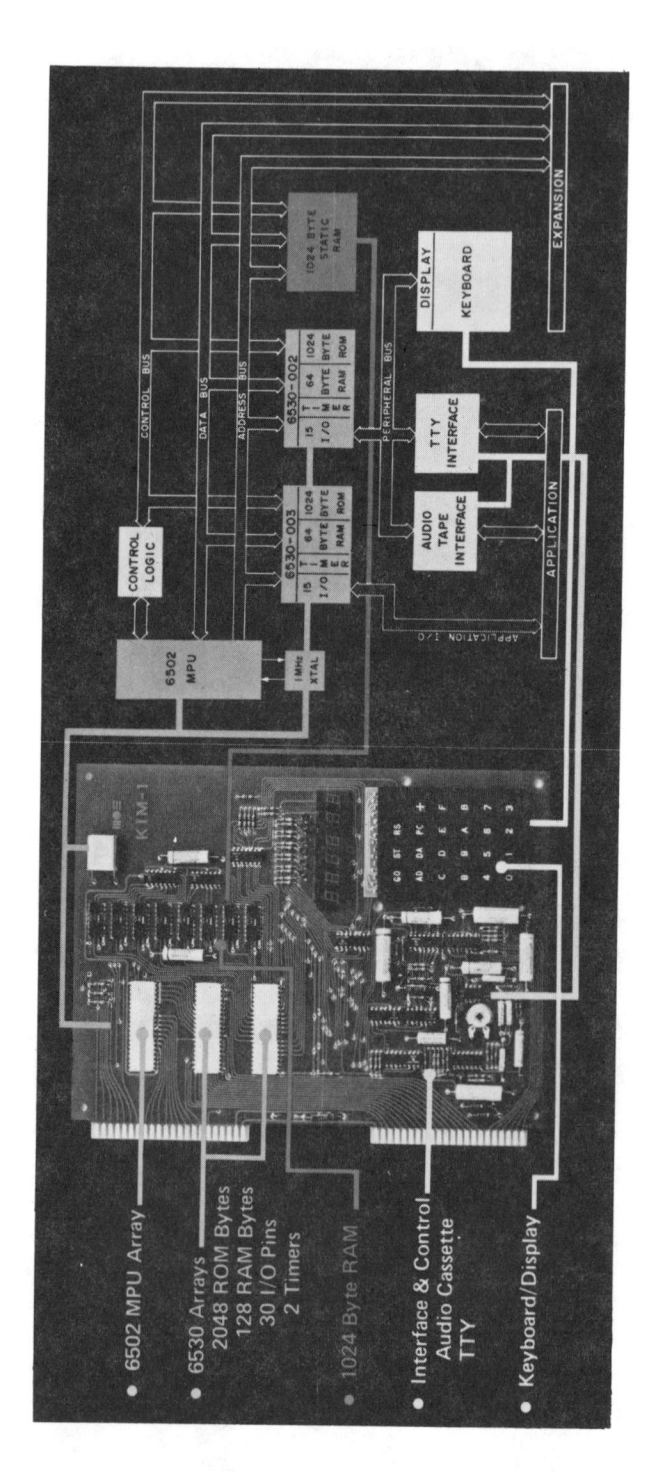

Figure 8.1-2 Identification of the major components on the KIM-1 microcomputer printed circuit board (Courtesy RCC News)

8.2 THE KIM—1 SYSTEM: (A Micro versus a Mini)

A microcomputer system, such as the KIM-1, differs from a minicomputer system in much more than just cost. With a minicomputer, such as the Digital Equipment Corporation PDP-11, the documentation provided by the manufacturer is extensive, diversified, and quite specialized. It is not unusual to find all of the following documents:

1. An Installer's Manual - provides unpacking information and power supply connections for the electrician.
2. An Operator's Manual - provides front panel information for the operator.
3. A Software Manual - provides information for the programmer.
4. A Hardware Manual - provides information about the theory of operation.
5. A Maintenance and Trouble Shooting Manual - provides the technician with schematic diagrams and periodic maintenance requirements, such as air filters which need to be changed or cleaned.

In the case of a microcomputer, the documentation is frequently very limited. (Fortunately, in the case of the KIM-1, rather extensive documentation is provided with three manuals; a Hardware Manual, a Software Manual, and a KIM-1 User's Manual.) Furthermore, in the case of the microcomputer, the installer, electrician, operator, programmer, and technician for maintenance and trouble shooting, are one and the same person.

8.3 AN EXAMPLE PROGRAM (EXAMPLE 8.1)

The purpose of this example program is to serve as a vehicle for illustrating the steps which are involved in going from the statement of a problem to a functioning computer program on the KIM-1 microcomputer. These steps will be the same, in principle, for any microprocessor; only the details will change from one particular microprocessor to another. These steps may be summarized as follows:

* statement of problem
* conversion to assembly language program
* conversion to machine language program
* entry of program into computer
* execution and debugging of program
* modification of program

The following additional steps are sometimes involved:

* entry and execution from a Teletype (includes use of paper tape)
* recording and playing back from an audio cassette tape recorder

Example 8.1. Add two positive numbers located intially in two memory locations and store the sum into a third memory location.

Comments. In order to keep this example as simple as possible:
1. We are considering only positive, one byte numbers.
2. We will not check for a carry out (overflow).

8.3.1 Example 8.1 — Assembly Language Program

The assembly language program for Example 8.1 is given in Table 8.3-1. The assembly language program is also frequently referred to as the "source code" and this designation is used in Table 8.3-1. The reader should note that the lefthand 4 columns are blank. At this time we could also insert the object code for all of the op codes, such as LDA, CLC, STA, etc. This has been done, and is shown in Table 8.3-2.

TABLE 8.3-1 Source Code for Example 8.1.
Note that the object code columns are blank.

	OBJECT CODE				SOURCE CODE		
MEMORY ADDRESS	BYTE 1	BYTE 2	BYTE 3	LABEL	OP CODE	OPERAND	COMMENT
				NUM1			Designate one of the two numbers to be added as NUM 1.
				NUM2			Designate the second of the two numbers to be added as NUM2.
				SUM			Designate the sum of the two numbers to be SUM.
					⋮		
					SED		Set decimal Mode.
					LDA	NUM1	Load the accumulator with the numerical value of NUM1.
					CLC		Clear Carry.
					ADC	NUM2	Add with carry NUM1 + NUM2. (There is no ADD instruction.)
					STA	SUM	Store the sum of two numbers into memory location SUM.
				WAIT	JMP	WAIT	The 6502 microprocessor has no halt or stop command. This is a jump to itself.

TABLE 8.3-2 Source Code but Only Partial Object Code for Example 8.1. The Memory Map is needed in order to complete this table.

	OBJECT CODE			SOURCE CODE		
MEMORY ADDRESS	BYTE 1	BYTE 2	BYTE 3	LABEL	OP CODE	OPERAND	COMMENT
				NUM1			Designate one of the two numbers to be added as NUM1.
				NUM2			Designate the second of the two numbers to be added as NUM2.
				SUM			Designate the sum of the two numbers to be SUM.
					⋮		
	F8				SED		Set Decimal Mode.
	A5	ØØ			LDA	NUM1	Load the accumulator with the numerical value of NUM1.
	18				CLC		Clear carry.
	65	Ø1			ADC	NUM2	Add with carry NUM1 + NUM2. (There is no ADD instruction.)
	85	Ø2			STA	SUM	Store the sum of two numbers into memory location SUM.
	4C			WAIT	JMP	WAIT	The 6502 microprocessor has no halt or stop command. This is a jump to itself.

In order to complete Table 8.3-2, we need to decide where to store the program and where to store (or look for) data (the two numbers to be added and the sum). In other words, we need to know where RAM is located *and* if it is available to the user. Frequently, some bytes of RAM are reserved for use by the Monitor program in the microcomputer. As we shall see later, in the case of the KIM-1, 17 bytes (ØØEF to ØØFF in hex) are reserved for the KIM-1 Monitor program. (The user may still decide to use these reserved memory locations, but with the caution that the Monitor program will store its own data in these memory locations.

We are now ready to proceed to the next section in order to learn more about the KIM-1 hardware. In particular, we are anxious to study the KIM-1 Memory Map, which will tell us how much memory we have, what type it is, and where it is located.

8.4 KIM—1 MEMORY MAP AND TABLE

In order to be able to use any microcomputer (including the KIM-1) at the assembly language (or machine code) level, the user

must know the answers to the following questions:
* How much memory is there?
* What type is it; (ROM, RAM, PROM, etc.)
* Where is it in memory? (i.e., What is its address?)

The answers to these questions are provided in the memory map and the memory table. The memory map for the KIM-1 is shown in Figure 8.4-1. For convenience of notation, memory is divided into pages. Each page is 256_{10} bytes long. For example, page ∅ encompasses ∅ through $FF while page 4 encompasses $4∅∅ through $4FF. We will use decimal page numbers throughout this material. The reader will note that a user generated program may make use of the following areas of memory:
* all of page ∅ except for ∅∅EF to ∅∅FF which are reserved for the KIM-1 Monitor program
* all of page 1 with the caution that the stack will use some of page 1
* all of page 2 and page 3
* in page 23 - all input/output locations from 1700 to 173F
              - all 64 bytes of RAM from 1780 to 17BF
              - an additional 44 bytes of RAM from 17C0 to 17EB

The memory table for the KIM-1 is given in Table 8.4-1. The reader will note that some of the information is the same as that provided in the memory map of Figure 8.4-1, but additional and more detailed address information is also provided. When using the KIM-1 the user will need to refer frequently to both of these memory information sources.

We will now use the information provided by the memory map and the memory table to complete the coding for Example 8.1 so that we may enter the program into the KIM-1 memory. This will be the subject for the next section.

8.5 MACHINE CODE FOR EXAMPLE 8.1

If we now refer back to Table 8.3-2, the reader will note that in order to complete that table, we need to decide where to store the program and where to store the data that will be used by the program in the RAM memory. It is usually a good programming technique to store the numerical data in page ∅ because then we can use the so-called zero page instructions which require only two, rather than three, bytes

MCS 6502 Based Microcomputer — The KIM-1

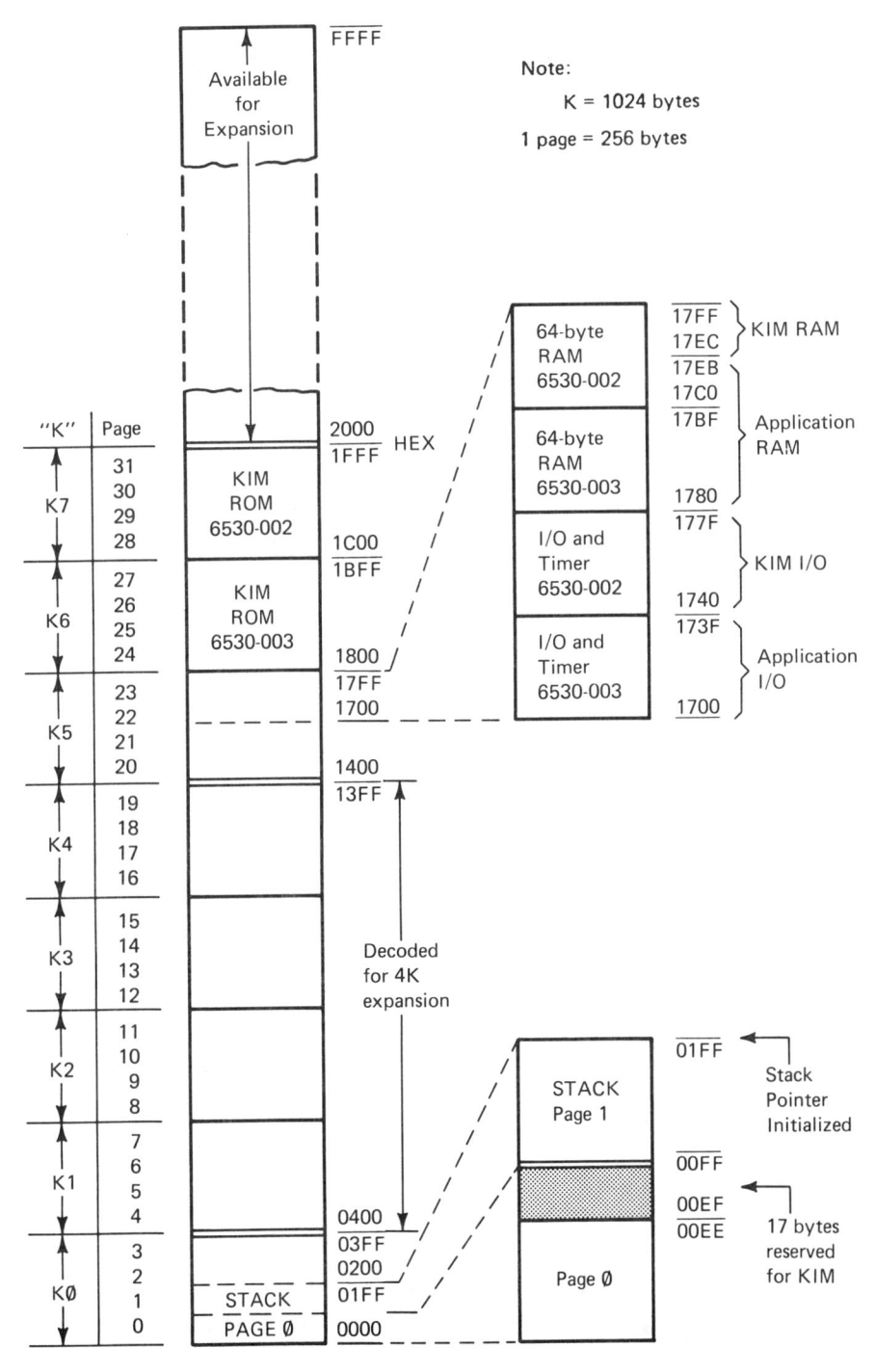

Note:
K = 1024 bytes
1 page = 256 bytes

Figure 8.4-1 Memory map for the KIM-1 microcomputer (MOS Technology)

TABLE 8.4-1 Memory Table for the KIM-1 Microcomputer (Courtesy MOS Technology, Inc.)

ADDRESS	AREA	LABEL	FUNCTION
00EF		PCL	Program Counter - Low Order Byte
00F0		PCH	Program Counter - High Order Byte
00F1	Machine	P	Status Register
00F2	Register	SP	Stack Pointer
00F3	Storage	A	Accumulator
00F4	Buffer	Y	Y-Index Register
00F5		X	X-Index Register
1700		PAD	6530-003 A Data Register
1701	Application	PADD	6530-003 A Data Direction Register
1702	I/O	PBD	6530-003 B Data Register
1703		PBDD	6530-003 B Data Direction Register
1704 ↓ 170F	Interval Timer		6530-003 Interval Timer (see Table 3.7.1-1, page 144)
17F5		SAL	Starting Address - Low Order Byte
17F6	Audio Tape	SAH	Starting Address - High Order Byte
17F7	Load & Dump	EAL	Ending Address - Low Order Byte
17F8		EAH	Ending Address - High Order Byte
17F9		ID	File Identification Number
17FA		NMIL	NMI Vector - Low Order Byte
17FB		NMIH	NMI Vector - High Order Byte
17FC	Interrupt	RSTL	RST Vector - Low Order Byte
17FD	Vectors	RSTH	RST Vector - High Order Byte
17FE		IRQL	IRQ Vector - Low Order Byte
17FF		IRQH	IRQ Vector - High Order Byte
1800	Audio Tape	DUMPT	Start Address - Audio Tape Dump
1873		LOADT	Start Address - Audio Tape Load
1C00	STOP Key + SST		Start Address for NMI using KIM "Save Machine" Routine (Load in 17FA & 17FB)
17F7	Paper Tape	EAL	Ending Address - Low Order Byte
17F8	Dump (Q)	EAH	Ending Address - High Order Byte

MCS 6502 Based Microcomputer – The KIM-1 421

of code, and hence less memory. Also, these two byte, zero page, instructions require less time to execute. We will not use this programming technique here because we require only three bytes of memory for the numerical data and the program itself is so short.

Using the memory map data given in Figure 8.4-1, we decide to:

* store NUM1, NUM2, and the SUM into memory locations ØØØØ, ØØØ1, and ØØØ2 (base 16), respectively
* store the machine code into memory locations beginning with memory location ØØ1Ø (base 16)

As a result of making these memory allocation decisions, the machine code for Example 8.1 may now be completed and it is shown in Table 8.5-1.

We are now ready to load the machine code for Example 8.1 into the KIM-1 memory. This is the subject of the next section.

TABLE 8.5-1 Assembly and Machine Code for Example 8.1

OBJECT CODE				SOURCE CODE			
MEMORY ADDRESS	BYTE 1	BYTE 2	BYTE 3	LABEL	OP CODE	OPERAND	COMMENT
ØØØØ				NUM1			Designate one of the two numbers to be added as NUM1.
ØØØ1				NUM2			Designate the second of the two numbers to be added as NUM2.
ØØØ2				SUM			Designate the sum of the two numbers to be SUM.
				⋮			
ØØ1Ø	F8				SED		Set Decimal Mode.
ØØ11	A5	ØØ			LDA	NUM1	Load the accumulator with the numerical value of NUM1.
ØØ13	18				CLC		Clear Carry.
ØØ14	65	Ø1			ADC	NUM2	Add with carry NUM1+NUM2. (There is no ADD instruction.)
ØØ16	85	Ø2			STA	SUM	Store the sum of two numbers into memory location SUM.
ØØ18	4C	18	ØØ	WAIT	JMP	WAIT	The 6502 microprocessor has no halt or stop command. This is a jump to itself.

Comment 1: We have arbitrarily decided to store NUM1, NUM2, and SUM into memory locations ØØØØ, ØØØ1, and ØØØ2, respectively.

Comment 2: We have also arbitrarily decided to begin storing the object code into memory locations beginning with memory location ØØ1Ø.

8.6 ENTERING EXAMPLE 8.1 CODE INTO KIM—1

We are now ready to enter the machine code for Example 8.1 (as given in Table 8.5-1) into the KIM-1 memory locations we selected in Section 8.4.

The first step is to apply power to the KIM-1 microcomputer printed circuit board. In this case, we need 5 volts, ± 5%, with a current rating of at least 0.75 amperes. The circuit connections are shown in Figure 8.6-1. It is strongly recommended that these connections be checked very carefully each time the KIM-1 is used. Power supply polarity reversals can be catastrophic.

Table 8.6-1 presents a detailed key by key stroke entry of the machine code for Example 8.1 into the KIM-1 memory according to the decisions made and presented in Table 8.5-1. Table 8.6-1 also gives the information that the user will see on the display following the depression of the various keys. Comments are supplied, where necessary.

TABLE 8.6-1 Key by Keystroke Entry of Example 8.1 Code per TABLE 8.5-1 into KIM-1 Memory

Press Keys	See on Display	Comments
	blank	Apply 5 volts, ±5%, 0.75 amp. per Figure 8.6-1. There is no power ON-OFF switch on the KIM-1. The SST-ON switch is for selecting the single-step mode.
[RS]	xxxx xx	x implies an unpredictable display.
[AD]	no change	Puts KIM into address mode.
[0][0][1][0]	0010 xx	Contents of memory location 0010 are displayed.
[DA]	no change	Puts KIM into DATA mode.
[F][8]	0010 F8	Enters F8 code into memory location 0010.
[+]	0011 xx	Increments the memory address displayed by one. This is easier than pressing the four keys for location 0011, which would accomplish the same thing.
[A][5]	0011 A5	Enters A5 code into memory location 0011.
[+][0][0]	0012 00	Enters 00 code into memory location 0012.
[+][1][8]	0013 18	Similarly, enters 18 code into memory location 0013, etc.
[+][6][5]	0014 65	
[+][0][1]	0015 01	
[+][8][5]	0016 85	
[+][0][2]	0017 02	
[+][4][C]	0018 4C	
[+][1][8]	0019 18	
[+][0][0]	001A 00	This completes the loading of the code for Example 8.1. It is suggested that the user go back to memory location 0010, and then, using the [+] key, check sequentially through memory location 001A for possible errors.

MCS 6502 Based Microcomputer – The KIM-1 423

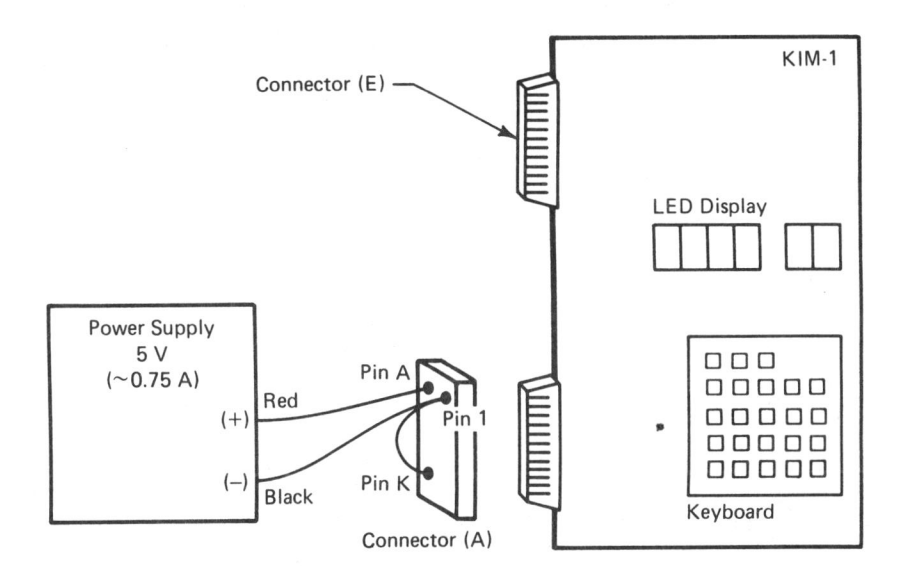

Figure 8.6-1 When used without Teletype, CRT, or audio tape recorder, the KIM-1 requires only one power supply connected as shown

8.7 EXECUTION OF EXAMPLE 8.1 FROM THE KIM–1 KEYBOARD

Table 8.7-1 presents a key by key stroke sequence for entering the numerical values of NUM1 and NUM2 and then executing the program using the |GO| key. We have arbitrarily selected NUM1 = 43 and NUM2 = 25. Again, we have presented the displays which the user will see after depressing the various keys and appended comments, where necessary. The resulting SUM is displayed in the last step of the table and is seen to be equal to 68, which is the correct answer in the decimal mode.

It is suggested that the user modify the program by changing the SED (set decimal mode) op code to CLD (clear decimal mode) and try different numerical values for NUM1 and NUM2 in order to gain a greater understanding of what the decimal and binary modes in the KIM-1 really mean. Problems are provided at the end of this chapter to help guide the user in this endeavor.

8.7.1 Single Step Execution of Example 8.1 Program

Table 8.7-2 presents a key by key stroke sequence for entering the numerical values for NUM1 and NUM2 and then executing the program

TABLE 8.7-1 Execution of the Example 8.1 Program from the KIM-1 Keyboard
NUM1 + NUM2 = SUM where NUM1 = 43; NUM2 = 25

Press Keys	See on Display	Comments
[RS]	xxxx xx	Reset. x implies display is not predictable.
[AD]	no change	Puts KIM-1 into ADDRESS input mode.
[0][0][0][0]	0000 xx	Present contents of memory location 0000 are displayed.
[DA]	no change	Puts KIM-1 into DATA input mode.
[4][3]	0000 43	Enter 43 as the numerical value of NUM1 into location 0000.
[+][2][5]	0001 25	Enter 25 as the numerical value of NUM2 into location 0001.
[+][0][0]	0002 00	Clears memory location 0002 where the SUM will be placed.
[AD][0][0][1][0]	0010 F8	Prepares to run program by loading the beginning address (0010) of our program.
[GO]	blank	Program executes in literally a few microseconds.
[RS]	0010 F8	Reset KIM-1.
[AD][0][0][0][0]	0000 43	NUM1 is still equal to 43.
[+]	0001 25	NUM2 is still equal to 25.
[+]	0002 68	SUM is 68 and is the correct answer in the decimal mode. Recall that we had previously cleared this memory location.

TABLE 8.7-2 Single Step Execution of Example 8.1 Program from the KIM-1 Keyboard
NUM1 + NUM2 = SUM where NUM1 = 43; NUM2 = 25

Press Keys	See on Display	Comments
[RS]	xxxx xx	Reset.
[AD][1][7][F][A]	17FA xx	This sequence of 3 lines must be performed in order to use the [ST] key and/or the single step mode. To be more specific: memory location 1C00 is stored into interrupt vector locations 17FA and 17FB.
[DA][0][0]	17FA 00	
[+][1][C]	17FB 1C	
[AD][0][0][0][0]	0000 xx	Present contents of memory location 0000 are displayed.
[DA][4][3]	0000 43	Enter 43 for NUM1 into location 0001.
[+][2][5]	0001 25	Enter 25 for NUM2 into location 0002.
[+][0][0]	0002 00	Clear location 0002 where SUM will be placed.
[AD][0][0][1][0]	0010 F8	Loads beginning address (0010) of our program.
[GO]	0011 A5	Each time the [GO] key is depressed, a single line of code is executed and the memory address of the next line of code is displayed. A "line of code" is defined in TABLE 8.5-1. Note: The same numbers are missing here as in column 1 of TABLE 8.5-1.
[GO]	0013 18	
[GO]	0014 65	
[GO]	0016 85	
[GO]	0018 4C	
[GO]	no change	
[AD][0][0][0][0]	0000 43	NUM1 is still equal to 43.
[+]	0001 25	NUM2 is still equal to 25.
[+]	0002 68	SUM is 68 again. Recall that we had previously cleared this memory location to zero. Do *not* forget that the SST-ON switch is in the ON position.

MCS 6502 Based Microcomputer — The KIM-1   **425**

for Example 8.1 in the *single step mode*. We have again selected NUM1 = 43 and NUM2 = 25. The usual display information and comments are given.

An important item for the reader to note in Table 8.7-2 is the need to properly initialize the interrupt vector locations 17FA and 17FB. This must always be done if the $\boxed{\text{ST}}$ key and the single step switch mode are to function properly. For more information, please refer to the $\overline{\text{NMI}}$ section of the 6502 microprocessor discussion.

The KIM-1 user will find that the single step mode is used primarily during program debugging.

8.8 DECIMAL OR BINARY CODE

Any system which uses the 6502 microprocessor has the option of operating in either the decimal mode or the binary mode. In the case of the KIM-1, the designers choose not to include a CLD or SED command in the reset programs, so it is not possible to predict whether the KIM-1 will be in the decimal mode or in the binary mode when first energized. (These writers' experiences with about a dozen KIM-1s conform with this observation; about half come up on the binary mode and about half in the decimal mode; unfortunately, it is not always the same half.)

This uncertainty - decimal or binary mode - is responsible for most of the problems encountered by first-time KIM-1 users. These problems appear to the user to be one of the following two major types:

1. The numerical results to arithmetic operations do not appear to be correct.
2. Programs recorded on audio cassette tapes do not load.

Problems of the first type are solved if the user (programmer) develops the habit of preceding each arithmetic operation with a CLD or SED command. (The reader will recall that our solution to Example 8.1 in Table 8.2-1 followed this suggestion.)

Problems of the second type are solved if the user (operator) sets the KIM-1 into the binary or decimal mode immediately after powerup. This may be done by loading all 0s or all 1s into the memory location 00F1. When we press the Go button, the contents of this location will be loaded into the P register. Actually only the decimal bit in the status register needs to be set to a 1 for the decimal mode and set to 0 for the binary mode, but it is much easier for the user to set all 1s or all 0s. (There are 64 different ways to set one bit to a 1 or to a 0 in a byte.)

8.9 KIM-1 KEYBOARD KEY FUNCTIONS

The KIM-1 keyboard key functions are summarized in Figure 8.9-1.

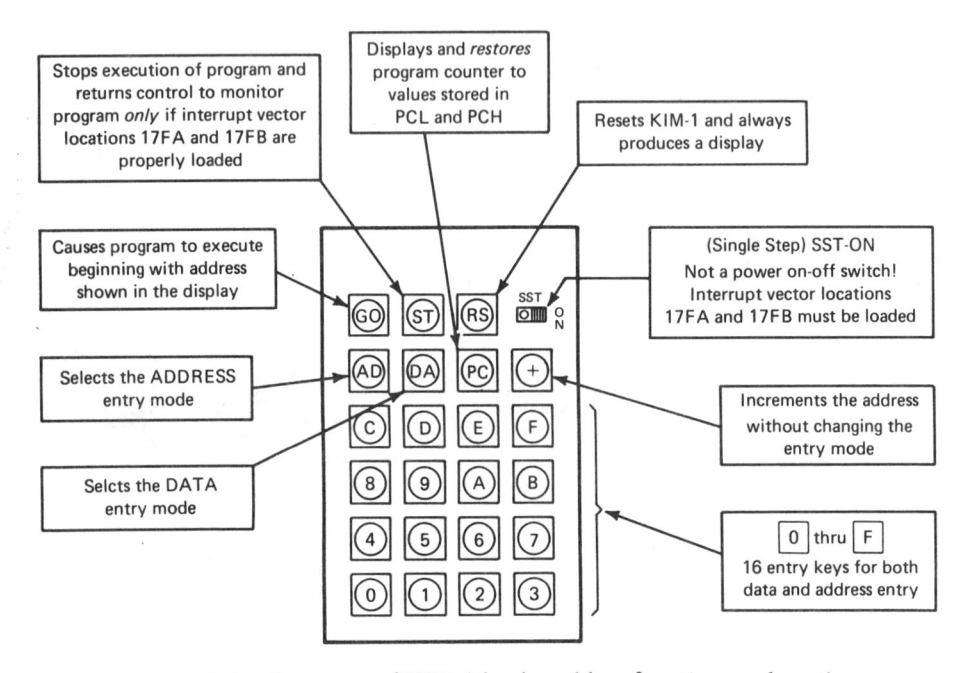

Figure 8.9-1 Summary of KIM-1 keyboard key functions and cautions

8.10 OPERATING THE KIM-1 VIA A TELETYPE

Before energizing a KIM-1 system that is using a serial teleprinter such as the TELETYPE® Model 33ASR (Automatic Send and Receive)* the following items should be verified.

1. The Model 33 is wired for full duplex 20 mA operation.
2. The 5 volt power supply is connected to the KIM-1 application connector as shown in Figure 8.6-1. Be sure a jumper is connected between pins 1 and K.

---

* Models 33KSR or RO can also be used.

MCS 6502 Based Microcomputer — The KIM-1

3. Pins R, U, S, and T of the KIM application connector are connected to the Teletype as follows:

    R   X-7   or   P2-8
    U   X-6   or   P2-7
    S   X-3   or   P2-5
    T   X-4   or   P2-6

    X denotes Terminal Block X and P2 denotes Plug 2. (On the 33ASR Teletype terminal block X can be located by noting the ac line cord connected to X1 and X2. It is the second receptacle from the left on the top row as viewed from the rear of the machine.
4. The toggle switch TTY-KB (keyboard) is in the TTY (TELETYPE) position.

8.10.1 The KIM-1 Prompting Message

If you have checked all of the electrical connections specified in Sec. 8.1, you may now proceed to do the following:

1. Energize the 5 volt power supply.
2. Plug the TELETYPE into a 115 volts, 60 Hz. power outlet and turn the switch marked LINE-OFF-LOCAL to LINE. This switch is located at the right side of the small vertical front panel strip which bears the letters T E L E T Y P E as shown in Figure 8.10.1.

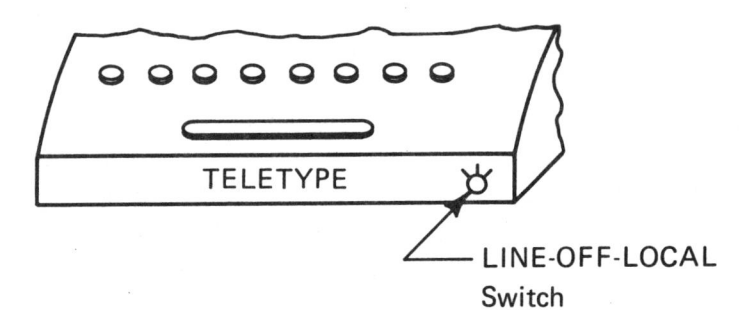

Figure 8.10-1 Closeup view of LINE-OFF-LOCAL switch on model 33ASR TELTEYPE

The following steps are most important because the KIM-1 system adjusts to the bit rate of the serial teleprinter and requires this sequence of key strokes to establish the proper bit rate:

Press KIM key	Press TTY key	See printed
[RS]	(RUB OUT)	KIM xxxx xx

where xxxx xx denotes an arbitrary, unpredictable set of six (6) printed characters. If everything is working properly, you should immediately observe the message KIM xxxx xx being typed in the two line format shown above. This is a prompting message telling you that the TTY is on-line and that the KIM-1 system is ready to accept commands from the TTY keyboard.

If the "KIM" prompting message is not typed, repeat the two key sequence given above; that is, press the [RS] key on the KIM-1 keyboard and the (RUB OUT) key on the TTY. If the "KIM" message is still not typed, recheck all connections and try again. If the problem still persists, obtain assistance.

8.10.2 Possible Input and Output Modes

Immediately after the "KIM" prompting message is typed on the TTY, the KIM-1 system is ready to accept commands from the TTY keyboard. As soon as you decide what type of input and/or output you desire, you may refer to Figure 8.10.2 and determine what sections describe the procedure you must follow.

8.10.3 Another Simple Example (Example 8.2)

The purpose of this simple example is to explain and to illustrate the different possible input and output modes using the TELETYPE Model 33ASR. It also illustrates another way of terminating a program. Rather than just jumping to itself, the program jumps into the Monitor Program and displays the numerical value of the SUM and its memory location.

Example 8.2. Add two positive integers located in two memory locations and store the sum into a third memory location. Output and display the sum and its memory location. It is not necessary to check for overflow. The solution to Example 8.2 is presented in Table 8.10-1.

MCS 6502 Based Microcomputer – The KIM-1   429

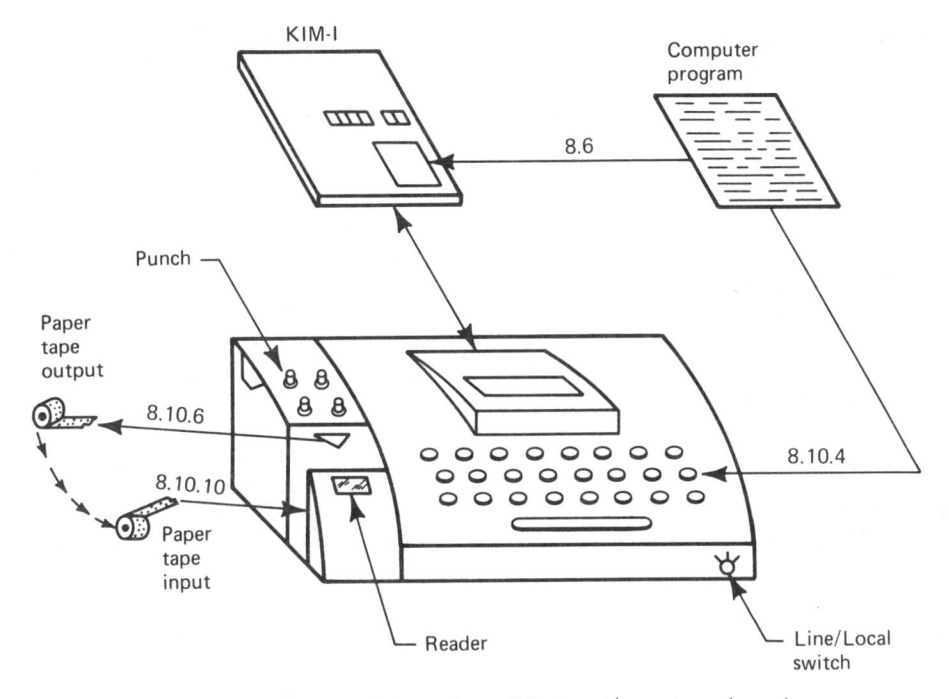

Figure 8.10-2 Pictorial view of possible input/ouput modes using a TELETYPE 33ASR with the KIM-1

TABLE 8.10-1 Source code and machine code for adding two numbers, storing, and displaying the sum. Refer to Example 8.2 for more details.

Memory Map	Byte 1	Byte 2	Byte 3	LABEL	OP CODE	OPERAND
ØØ				NUM1		
Ø1				NUM2		
Ø2				SUM		
Ø3	18			PROGRAM	CLC	
Ø4	F8				SED	
Ø5	A5	ØØ			LDA	NUM1
Ø7	65	Ø1			ADC	NUM2
Ø9	85	Ø2			STA	SUM
ØB	A9	Ø2			LDA	#Ø2
ØD	85	FA			STA	$FA
ØF	A9	ØØ			LDA	#$ØØ
11	85	FB			STA	$FB
13	4C	4F	1C		JMP	1C4F

8.10.4 Using the TELETYPE Keyboard to Enter a Program

While using the TELETYPE keyboard to enter a program, you may perform the following operations:

To Select an Address
    1. Type four hex keys (0 to F) to define the address.
    2. Press the [SPACE] bar.

The TTY will respond by typing the address code selected followed by a two hex digit code corresponding to the data stored at the selected address location.

Example:
Type: 1802   [SPACE]
TTY printer responds: 1802 8D

showing that data 8D is stored at memory location 1802, which is in ROM, so its contents cannot be changed.

Time saving hint: Leading zeros need not be entered.

Examples:
EF [SPACE] selects address 00EF
 A [SPACE] selects address 000A
   [SPACE] selects address 0000

To Modify an Address
    1. Select an address as above. Don't forget to press the [SPACE] bar.
    2. Type two hex characters to define the data to be stored at this address.
    3. Press the TTY period key, hereafter denoted by $\odot$.

Example:
Type: 0234   [SPACE]
TTY printer responds: 0234 xx
Type: 6D $\odot$
TTY printer responds: 0235 xx

MCS 6502 Based Microcomputer — The KIM-1 **431**

Note: The selected address ∅234 has been incremented automatically by one to the next address ∅235 and the contents xx of memory location ∅235 have been displayed.

Time saving hint: Leading zeros need not be entered.

Examples:

A ⊙ enters data ∅A
⊙ enters data ∅∅

(This is a frequent source of errors for even experienced programmers who clear memory locations inadvertently by using this short-cut.)

To Step To Next Address (Without modifying the contents of the current address)

1. Press key (RETURN)

Example:

See printed:	1234 xx	
Type:		(RETURN)
Printer responds:	1235 xx	
Type:		(RETURN)
Printer responds:	1236 xx	
etc.		

To Step to Preceding Address (Without modifying the contents of the current address)

1. Press key (LF)

Example:

See printed:	1234 xx	
Type:		(LF)
Printer responds:	1233 xx	
Type:		(LF)
Printer responds:	1232 xx	
etc.		

To Abort Current Operation

1. Press key (RUB OUT)

Example:

See printed:	1264
Type:	(RUB OUT)
Printer responds:	KIM
	xxxx xx
Type:	1234 [SPACE]
Printer responds:	1234 xx

In this example, the (RUB OUT) key was used to correct an erroneous address selection.

Note: The (RUB OUT) key must be depressed after each depression of the KIM-1 [RST] key in order to allow the operating program to define the serial bit rate for the particular Teletype being used.

8.10.5 Using the TELETYPE Keyboard to Execute a Program

To Execute a Program (From the TTY keyboard)

1. Enter the starting address of the program followed by [SPACE].
2. Type ⓖ .[This is analogous to the [GO] key on the KIM-1 keyboard.]

Example 8.2 may be executed as follows:

Type:	0003 [SPACE]
See printed:	0003 18
Type:	ⓖ (on TELETYPE keyboard!)

Comments: In this example, program execution begins from location 0003 and will continue until memory location 0015 is reached. In other cases, program execution continues until the [ST] or [RS] keys on the KIM-1 keyboard are depressed.

MCS 6502 Based Microcomputer – The KIM-1   **433**

Actual TTY output for Sec. 8.10.3 Example 8.2 stored in the KIM-1 with 8 stored in memory location ∅∅∅∅ and 9 stored in memory location ∅∅∅1. As you may recall, the sum = 17 and is stored in memory location ∅∅∅2. The Teletype output is shown in Figure 8.10.3

			COMMENTS
		∅∅∅3	Program begins in memory location ∅∅∅3.
∅∅∅3	18	G	Note that G is typed on the same line as the
KIM			previous response.
∅∅∅2	17		Sum = 17 and is stored in memory location ∅∅∅2.

Figure 8.10-3 Actual TELETYPE output for Example 8.2
NUM1 + NUM2 = SUM for NUM1 = 8 and NUM2 = 9
SUM = 17

To Execute a Program (Single step from TTY keyboard)

1. Enter the starting address of the program followed by $\boxed{\text{SPACE}}$.
2. Slide switch on KIM-1 keyboard marked SST-ON to ON.
3. Type key Ⓖ once for each step of program you wish to have executed.

Example 8.2 may be executed from the TELETYPE keyboard in the *single-step* mode as follows:

Type:	∅∅∅3 $\boxed{\text{SPACE}}$
See printed:	∅∅∅3 18
Type:	Ⓖ and continue depressing the Ⓖ key until output does not change. See Figure 8.10.4 for the actual output as well as comments.

8.10.6 Using the TELETYPE Keyboard to Punch a Paper Tape

To Punch Paper Tape

1. Load and thread blank paper tape into the punch unit.
2. Decide on the starting address and ending address of the data block to be punched on the paper tape.

A paper tape for *Example 8.2* may be punched as follows:

```
                         COMMENTS
                Ø3       SPACE  key does not print, of course!
ØØØ3    18      G        If you are having problems - - did you load the interrupt
KIM                      vector for proper ST key operation as described in Sec. 1.1.3?
ØØØ4    F8      G
KIM
ØØØ5    A5      G        In the course of single stepping through a program, certain
KIM                      addresses will appear to be skipped. This is normal and to be
ØØØ7    65      G        expected, because all of the bytes involved in the execution
KIM                      of the single instructions are accessed and the program halts
ØØØ9    85      G        only on the first byte of each successive instruction.
KIM
ØØØB    A9      G
KIM
ØØØD    85      G
KIM
ØØØF    A9      G
KIM
ØØ11    85      G
KIM
ØØ13    4C      G
KIM
1C4F    2Ø      G        From here on, this would repeat indefinitely.
KIM
1C4F    2Ø      G
KIM
1C4F    2Ø      G
KIM
1C4F    2Ø
  •
  •
  •
                Ø2
ØØØ2    17               SUM = 17 and is stored in memory location ØØØ2.
```

Figure 8.10-4 Actual TELETYPE output for the execution of Example 8.2 in the *single-step* mode
Numerical values: 8 + 9 = 17

Comments:

a) Load the program's ending address ØØ15 into KIM-1 memory locations 17F7 (EAL) and 17F8 (EAH) where

EAL = Ending Address - Low Order Byte
EAH = Ending Address - High Order Byte

b) A starting address = ØØØØ has been selected. We could have selected a starting address of ØØØ3, if we did not wish to include the numerical values of NUM1, NUM2, and SUM.

c) The key by key stroke sequence for Example 8.2 are:

MCS 6502 Based Microcomputer — The KIM-1   435

Type:	17F7 [SPACE]	
See printed:	17F7 xx	
Type:	15 ⊙	
See printed:	17F8 xx	
Type:	∅∅ ⊙	
See printed:	17F9 xx	Comment: Ignore this memory location because our next step is to specify the starting memory location.
Type:	∅∅∅∅ [SPACE]	
See printed:	∅∅∅∅ xx	Activate punch by depressing button on punch marked ON.
Press key:	Ⓠ	Comment: Watch and listen to the tape being punched!

Please refer to Figure 8.10.5 for the actual printed output corresponding to Example 8.2. Figure 8.10.6 presents the actual punched paper tape for Example 8.2.

```
       Q
;18∅∅∅∅∅8∅91718F8A5∅∅65∅185∅2A9∅285FAA9∅∅85FB4C4F1C22∅4∅812
;∅∅∅∅1∅∅1
```

Figure 8.10-5 Actual printed output for Example 8.2

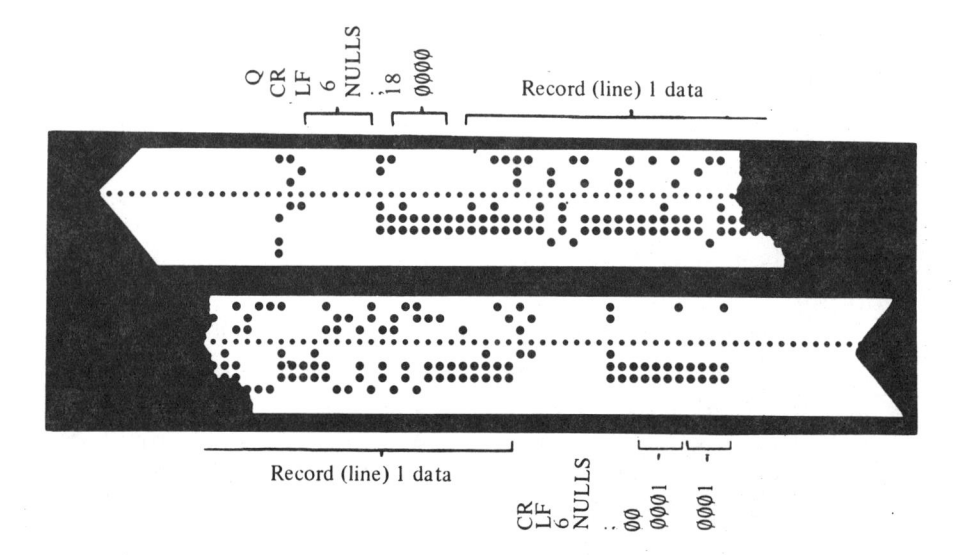

Figure 8.10-6 Actual punched paper tape for Example 8.2

A Handy Hint:

It is convenient to have a leader on each paper tape which has the minimum number of holes punched so that you can write your name, date, and other information. You can do this in three steps:

1. Press keys *in this order and hold down* until about 2 inches of tape extends out of the punch.

   SHIFT → CTRL → REPT → @ P

2. Tear off and discard this paper tape. The "V" cutting bar will form the tip of an arrow so that you will know in what direction the tape is to move. The sprocket holes, which are off-center, will prevent you from placing the tape in up-side-down.
3. Repeat Step 1 until you have the desired amount of leader at the front of your tape.

8.10.7 Using the TELETYPE Keyboard to List a Program

A printed record of the contents of the KIM-1 memory may be typed on the TELETYPE. The procedure is the same as for punching a paper tape *except* that the punch mechanism is not activated. This is assured if you press the OFF button located on top of the punch mechanism.

8.10.8 Using the TELETYPE Keyboard to List KIM-1 Memory

There is no difference between using the TELETYPE keyboard to list the contents of the KIM-1 memory and to list a program as described in Sec. 8.10.7.

8.10.9 KIM-1 Paper Tape Format

The paper tape DUMP and LOAD routines in the KIM-1 Monitor store and retrieve data in a format designed to reduce errors. Each byte of data is converted to two half bytes (nibbles). Each half byte (in hex) is translated to its ASCII equivalent and written out onto paper tape in ASCII form.

Each line of the output begins with a ";" character (ASCII 3B) to indicate the start of a valid record. The next byte (18 in hex) is the number of data bytes in that line. Then the starting address lower order

MCS 6502 Based Microcomputer — The KIM-1

byte (1 byte, 2 characters), starting address higher order byte (1 byte, 2 characters), and then then data (18_{16} bytes, 30_{16} characters) follow. Each record (line) is terminated by its checksum (2 bytes, 4 characters), a carriage return (ASCII $\emptyset$D), line feed (ASCII $\emptyset$A), and six "Null" characters (ASCII $\emptyset\emptyset$).

The last record (line) has zero bytes of data (indicated by ;$\emptyset\emptyset$). The starting address field is replaced by a four digit hex number representing the total number of data records (lines), followed by the checksum. A "XOFF" characters ends the transmission.

During a load, all incoming data is ignored until a ";" character is encountered. The receipt of nonASCII data or a mismatch between the calculated checksum and the checksum read from the tape will cause an error condition and the KIM-1 Monitor Program will cause the message "'KIM ERROR" to be printed. The checksum is calculated by adding all data in each record (line) except the ";" character.

Figure 8.10.7 illustrates and interprets how the above description of the paper tape format applies to the Example 8.2 TELETYPE printed output.

```
      ┌─ Each record (line) begins with a ";"
      │ ┌─ Next byte is the number of data bytes in that line
      │ │ ┌─ Starting address of that record (line)
      │ │ │  ┌─ Data 18₁₆ bytes, 30₁₆ characters whether requested or not
      │ │ │  │   ┌─ Checksum for each record (line) ─────────────┐
      │ │ │  │   │  Carriage return, line feed and six null characters do not print ─┐
      │ │ │  │   │  ┌─ Q prints when Ⓠ key is depressed                               │
      │ │ │  │   │  │  (See 8.1.4 TO PUNCH A PAPER TAPE)                              │
      │ │ │  │   │  Q                                                                 │
      ;18ØØØØØ8Ø91718F8A5ØØ65Ø185Ø2A9Ø285FAA9ØØ85FB4C4F1C22Ø4Ø812
      ;ØØØØ1ØØØ1 KIM
                           These two bytes were not requested ──┘
              └─ Checksum for this record (line)
           └─ 4 digit hex number representing total number of record (lines) replaces
              starting address field
       └─ Zero bytes of data
```

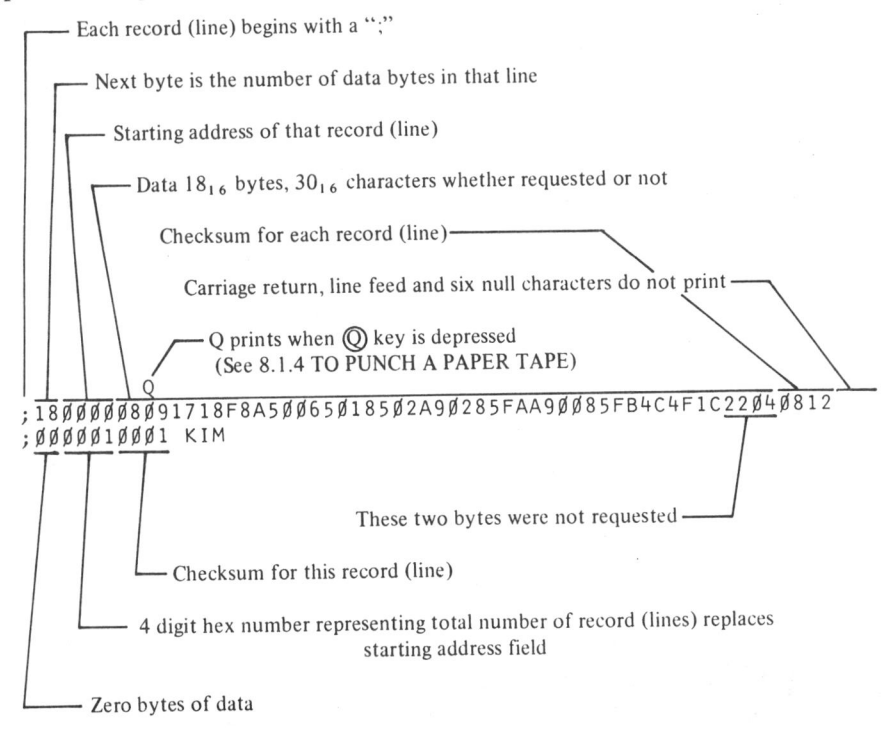

Figure 8.10-7 Illustration and interpretation of the KIM-1 paper tape format as it applies to Example 8.2 output

8.10.10 Reading a Paper Tape into the KIM-1

Paper tapes read into the KIM-1 system must have the format specified in Section 8.10.9. Paper tapes generated by the KIM-1 have, of course, this format. To read a paper tape with the proper format, proceed as follows:

1. Set the Paper Tape Reader switch to FREE.
2. Insert the tape into the tape reader mechanism being careful to align the sprocket holes. Move the tape slightly back and forth to make sure it is free.
3. Press [RS] on the KIM-1 keyboard and (RUB OUT) key on TELETYPE.
4. Type (L) on TELETYPE (mnemonic for Load).
5. Move the tape reader switch to START and remove your hand. Switch will automatically return to its center position, and the reader will begin to read the tape.

Caution: Keep fingers away from the paper tape reading mechanism!

Figure 8.10.8 illustrates the Teletype output corresponding to Example 8.2.

```
       LQ
;18Ø ØØØØ8Ø91718F8A5ØØ65Ø185Ø2A9Ø285FAA9ØØ85FB4C4F1C22Ø4Ø812
;ØØØØ1ØØØ1 KIM

KIM
ØØØ1    Ø9
```

Figure 8.10-8 Actual TELETYPE printed output when paper tape for Example 8.2 is loaded into the KIM-1

8.11 ADDING AN AUDIO TAPE RECORDER TO THE KIM-1

8.11.1 Why Add an Audio Tape Recorder?

There are at least four reasons to add an audio tape recorder to the KIM-1 microcomputer:

1. Programs and data which the user has stored in the KIM-1 RAM may be saved before the power is turned off.
2. An audio tape recorder is much less expensive (as low as $20) compared to a paper tape punch and reader.

3. Computer programs and data which are stored on magnetic tape may be readily duplicated and exchanged with other KIM-1 users.
4. Magnetic audio tape, as compared to paper tape, permits a storage density, a smaller more convenient package to handle, and is reusable.

Although both reel-to-reel and cassette tape recorders may be used, the cassette type is used in almost all KIM-1 applications because of its small size, portability, and cost. The discussion that follows will apply to both reel-to-reel and cassette types. (Other types of tape recorders, such as miniaturized recorders without external jacks, are usually intended primarily for dictating applications and require internal modifications. Recorders requiring internal modifications will not be discussed here.)

8.11.2 The Audio Tape Recorder Connection

The audio tape recorder unit to be used should possess the following features:
1. A jack, usually labeled microphone or input, to permit recording the electrical signal provided by the KIM-1 circuit board onto the magnetic tape.
2. A jack, usually labeled earphone or external speaker, to supply the electrical signal of the appropriate level to the KIM-1 circuit board for loading into the microcomputer memory.
3. The standard control switches for PLAY, RECORD, REWIND, and STOP. Other features, such as FAST FORWARD or FAST REVERSE, are convenient for locating programs when more than one program is stored on a tape side.

With the power off to all of the components, check that all of the cables and jumpers are present as shown in Figure 8.11.1. All wires, except for the shielded wires, should be as short as possible and kept away from other wires which might introduce electrical noise.

The Audio Data Out (LO) at pin M has a level of approximately 15 mv peak. The Audio Data Out (HI) at pin P has a level of approximately 1 volt peak. Pin P is used with some of the more expensive tape recorders which have an input (usually labeled "LINE") that accepts higher voltage input signals. The lower level Audio Data Output at pin M is the one which is used with most small inexpensive audio cassette tape recorders.

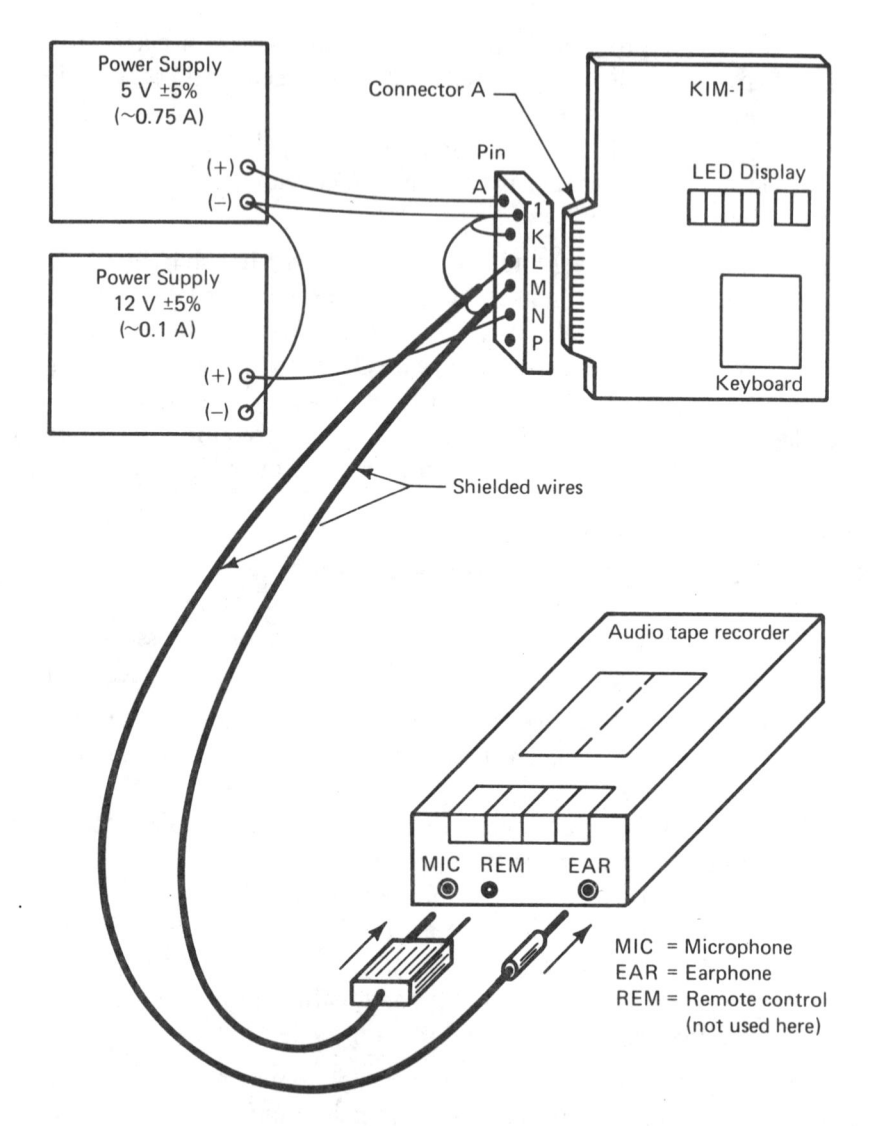

Figure 8.11-1 With an audio tape recorder, the KIM-1 system requires one 5 volt power supply, one 12 volt power supply, one jumper, and two shielded wires connected as shown above

8.11.3 How to Record On an Audio Tape

Before we list the steps to be followed for recording a program and/or data from memory on an audio magnetic tape, let us document the assumptions we are making:

MCS 6502 Based Microcomputer – The KIM-1

a) There is a program and/or data stored in memory with a known starting and a known ending address.

b) The program and data have been thoroughly tested and the program produces known results given specific data. This prevents confusing program errors with recording/playback errors.

c) The special addresses for the Audio Tape Load and Audio Tape Dump subroutines are known or obtained from Figure 8.11.2.

The procedure for recording on an audio magnetic tape from the KIM-1 memory is:

(If not already on, turn on the 5 volt and the 12 volt power supplies and check power to the tape recorder, if it is not battery powered)**

Step 1.* Verify that the 6502 microprocessor is in the binary mode. This may be done by inspecting the contents of memory location $00F1 and recalling that the decimal mode bit (1 = True) is bit three (b3 of b0 - b7) of the processor status word (which is stored in memory location $00F1). Since bit 3 is zero for so many different hexadecimal numbers, it is frequently easier just to *clear* the decimal mode and place into the binary mode by performing the following steps:

Press Keys	*Display*	*Comments*
[AD] [0] [0] [F] [1]	00F1 xx	Selects the address mode and displays the contents of memory location $00F1.
[DA]	[0] [0] 00F1 00	Stores 00 into memory location $00F1.

Step 2. Store the starting address in memory locations 17F5 and 17F6. Be sure the place the low order byte into 17F5 and the high order byte into 17F6.

Step 3. Store the ending address into memory locatins 17F7 and 17F8. Be sure to place the low order byte into 17F7 and the high order byte into 17F8.

The ending address is defined to be one greater than the last actual memory location of our program.

---

* If it were financially acceptable, we could add CLD instructions to the Audio Tape subroutines, manufacture new ROMs, and remove the need for Step 1.

** Some users have reported erratic operation when using the internal batteries in some of the tape recorders and they suggest using 115 volt 60 Hz adaptors instead.

Microcomputer Systems Principles

```
0000


All memory addresses are in HEX
```

Label		Function
17F5	SAL	Starting address—Low order byte
17F6	SAH	Starting address—High order byte
17F7	EAL	Ending address—Low order byte
17F8	EAH	Ending address—High order byte
17F9	ID	File identification number
1800	DUMPT	Starting address—Audio tape dump subroutine
1873	LOADT	Starting address—Audio tape load subroutine

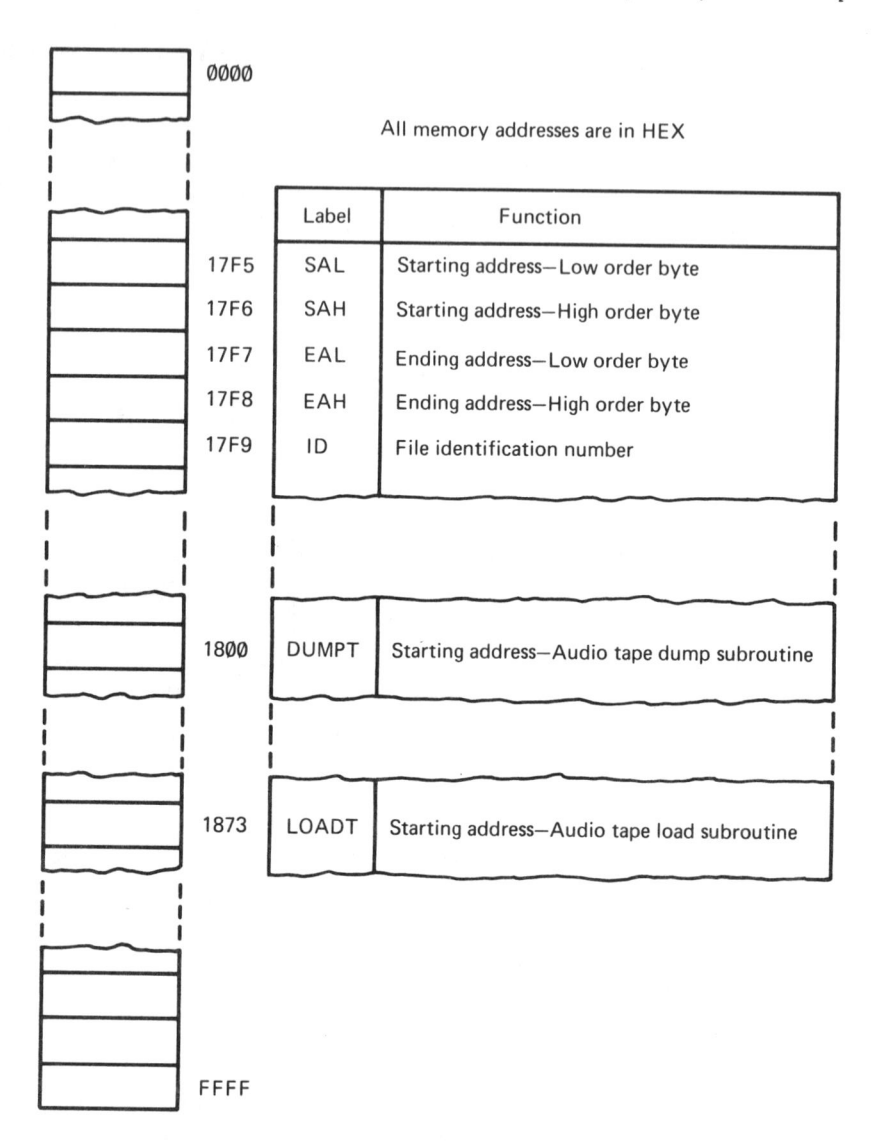

FFFF

Figure 8.11-2 Special memory addresses for Audio Tape Load (1873) and Audio Tape Dump (18ØØ), starting address, ending address, and ID

Step 4. Pick a two digit hexadecimal number as the file identification number (ID) and store into memory location 17F9.

Do *not* choose ID = ØØ or ID = FF.

For an explanation, please refer to Section 8.11.6, Hint #4.

Step 5. Refer to Figure 8.11.2 and note that the starting address for the Audio Tape Dump subroutine is 18∅∅. Load 18∅∅ into the field of the KIM-1. Do not press the [GO] key because the tape is not moving at this time.

Step 6. Select the RECORD mode of the tape recorder and wait a few seconds for the tape to start moving and to attain a constant speed.

Press [GO] key.

Comment: The display will become dark for a time and then the display will light and show

0000 xx   where xx is arbitrary

The amount of time during which the display is dark varies with the length of the program. In our example, which involves only about a dozen memory locations, the display is dark for about 16 seconds.

The recording is complete as soon as the display relights.

Step 7. STOP the tape recorder.

Step 8. (optional) REWIND the tape cassette to its starting position.

Step 9. (optional) Listen to the tape. With experience, you will be able to identify the beginning 100 sync pulses, the program in the middle, and the terminating characters at the end of each record by their distinctive sounds.

8.11.4 How to Read an Audio Tape into the KIM-1

Before we list the steps to be followed for reading from an audio tape into the KIM-1 microcomputer, let us list the assumptions we are making:

a) The file identification number (ID) of the record we wish to transfer into the KIM-1 memory is known.

b) The starting address of the Audio Tape Load (LOADT) subroutine is known to be $1873.

The procedure for transferring information from an audio magnetic tape into the KIM-1 memory is:

(If not already on, turn on all power supplies.)

Step 1.* Verify that the 6502 microprocessor is in the binary mode and not in the decimal mode. Please refer to Section 8.11.3, Step 1, for details on how to do this.

Step 2. Place the cassette into the tape recorder and REWIND the tape, if necessary, so that the tape will start to move and will attain a constant speed about 3 seconds before reaching the spot where the record with the desired ID exists on the tape.

Step 3. Store the known file identification number (ID) into memory location $17F9.

Step 4. Load $1873 (the starting address of the Audio Tape Load subroutine) into the address field of the display.

Step 5. Press the GO key.

Comment: The display will become dark and the KIM-1 will search for a tape input with the specified ID number. The tape is not moving so the search is not successful.

Step 6. Set the volume control on the tape recorder to approximately its midpoint position.

Step 7. Place the tape recorder into the PLAY mode. The tape should begin to move forward.

Comment: As soon as the data record with the specified ID number is located <u>and completely read in</u>, the display will relight and show

        0000 xx   where xx is arbitrary

Step 8. STOP the tape recorder after the display relights.

In reading an audio tape into a KIM-1, three types of problems may be encountered.

Trouble #1. In step 7, the display relights and shows FFFF xx. This means that the record with the specified ID was located but the check sum test failed as a result of either a record or a playback error.

FIX: Repeat the entire recording and playback procedures checking each step carefully. In a short program, step through all of the

---

* If is were financially acceptable, we could add CLD instructions to the Audio Tape subroutines, manufacture new ROMs, and remove the need for Step 1.

memory locations involved and compare with your written program. If the problem still persists, refer to the KIM USERS MANUAL, Appendix C, "In Case of Trouble."

Trouble #2. In step 7, the tape continues to run to the end and the display remains dark. This usually means that the record with the specified ID number was not "found."

FIX: a) Verify that the record was actually on this cassette and on the correct side. (Cassettes have side A and side B recordings.) Repeat the entire recording and playback procedure checking each step carefully.

b) Actually listen to the recording through the speaker or an earphone. With some practice, you will be able to identify the beginning 100 sync pulses, the program in the middle, and the terminating characters at the end of each record by their distinctive sounds.

c) Verify again that the 6502 microprocessor is in the binary mode and not in the decimal mode.

Trouble #3. If you use the tape recorder to erase a tape, you may record a "noise" which seems to be related to a subharmonic of the clock frequency.

FIX: Disconnect the tape recorder from the KIM-1 board while using the tape recorder to erase the tape.

8.11.5 An Example of Record and Playback

The purpose of this example is to illustrate the procedure for recording programs and/or data on audio magnetic tape from the KIM-1 system, and vice versa.

Example 8.11.1. Record and play back into the KIM-1 memory a program which will add two decimal numbers located in two memory locations and will store the sum in a third memory location.

Solution: The source program code and machine code for this example are given in Table 8.11-1. Because the 6502 microprocessor has no stop, wait, or halt instructions, the last instruction in the program is an absolute jump to itself. Pressing the RESET key will cause the KIM-1 system to exit from this infinite loop. In subsequent examples, we will jump to a display subroutine.

TABLE 8.11-1 Source Program Code and Machine Code for Adding Two Numbers and Storing the Sum

Memory Map	Byte 1	Byte 2	Byte 3	LABEL	SOURCE CODE OP CODE	OPERAND	Comments
∅∅				NUM1			First number in location ∅∅.
∅1				NUM2			Second number in ∅1.
∅2				SUM			Sum in location ∅2.
∅3	F8			PROGRAM	SED		Set decimal mode.
∅4	A5	∅∅			LDA	NUM1	Load NUM1 into accumulator.
∅6	18				CLC		Clear carry.
∅7	65	∅1			ADC	NUM2	Add NUM2 to NUM1 with carry.
∅9	85	∅2			STA	SUM	Store SUM into location ∅2.
∅B	4C	∅B	∅∅	HALT	JMP	HALT	Jump to itself over and over again.
∅E							

Using the KIM-1 keyboard, load the program given in Table 8.11-1 into memory locations $∅3 through $∅D. If you do not know how to do this, or have forgotten how, please refer to Section 8.6.

Now thoroughly test and verify that this program is correctly loaded and that it performs as expected. Be sure to load two numbers, run the program, and inspect the contents of memory location $∅2 to see if the correct sum is present there.

To record a program from the KIM-1 on audio tape. Please refer to Section 8.11.3 and note that we have satisfied all of the assumptions stated there and we are ready to proceed with performing Steps 1 through 8. The results are summarized in Table 8.11-2.

To playback the audio tape into the KIM-1. The assumptions which we have made require us to know that:

a) The desired tape record ID is $11;
b) The starting address of the Audio Tape Load subroutine is $1873.

Recall that in this example, we have arbitrarily chosen $11 as the file ID. However, the starting address $1873 is fixed for the KIM-1 Monitor Program and will always have this value.

Please refer to Section 8.11.4 and note that we have satisfied all of the assumptions stated there and we are now ready to proceed with performing Steps 1 through 6. The results are given in Table 8.11-3.

TABLE 8.11-2 Solution to Example 8.1 for the case of recording on an audio tape from the KIM-1 Microcomputer. The step numbers corresond with those given in Section 8.11-3

Press Keys	Display	Comments
[RS]	xxxx xx	Step 1:
[AD][0][0][F][1]	00F1 xx	Places in binary mode by clearing
[DA] [0][0]	00F1 00	decimal mode.
[AD][1][7][F][5]	17F5 xx	Step 2:
[DA] [0][3]	17F5 03	Stores starting address $\emptyset\emptyset03$ into
[+] [0][0]	17F6 00	memory locations 17F5 (low byte) and 17F6 (high byte).
		Step 3:
[+] [0][E]	17F7 0E	Stores ending address $\emptyset\emptyset\emptyset$E into
[+] [0][0]	17F8 00	memory locations 17F7 (low byte) and 17F8 (high byte).
[+] [1][1]	17F9 11	Step 4: Loads ID=11 into location 17F9.
		Step 5:
[AD][1][8][0][0]	1800 A9	Loads the starting address of the subroutine Audio Tape Dump.
On Tape Recorder [RECORD]		
wait about [GO] 3 seconds	dark (about 16 sec.) 0000 xx	Step 6: Program is being recorded. Recording is complete.
On Tape Recorder [STOP]		
	0000 xx	Step 7: Tape recorder is stopped.
	0000 xx	Step 8: (optional) Rewind tape.

TABLE 8.11-3 Solution to Example 8.11.1 for case of reading from an audio tape into the KIM-1 microcomputer memory. The step numbers correspond with those given in Section 8.11.4

Press Keys	Display	Comments
[RS] [AD][0][0][F][1] [DA] [0][0]	xxxx xx 00F1 xx 00F1 00	Step 1: Places KIM-1 into binary mode by clearing the decimal mode.
	00F1 00	Step 2: Place cassette into tape recorder and rewind tape, if necessary.
[AD][1][7][F][9] [DA] [1][1]	17F9 xx 17F9 11	Step 3: Load ID = 11 into memory location $17F9.
[AD][1][8][7][3]	1873 A9	Step 4: Loads the starting address of the subroutine Audio Tape Load.
[GO]	dark	Step 5: KIM-1 is searching for ID = 11.
	dark	Step 6: Set volume control to midpoint.
On tape recorder [PLAY]		
	dark	Step 7: Places recorder into PLAY mode and tape begins to move.
	(about 16 sec.) 0000 xx	Playback is complete.
[STOP]		
		Step 8: Stops tape recorder.

MCS 6502 Based Microcomputer — The KIM-1   449

8.11.6 Some Helpful Tape Hints

The following hints are offered to help you make the most effective use of your cassette tapes without encountering some of the more commonly associated problems:

Hint #1. Voice messages may be added between the record data blocks on the tape. The KIM-1 system will ignore these audio messages when the tape is read back provided the voice messages occur only between record blocks. However, you will have to install an earphone or speaker in parallel with the KIM-1 audio tape data pin in order to hear the voice messages.

Hint #2. If more than one data block is to be recorded per cassette side, proceed as follows:

Case 1. Data blocks are to be recorded in sequence without rewinding between blocks.

You need only to specify the parameters of each new block (ID, SAL, SAH, EAH, EAL) and proceed with recording each block following the standard steps listed in Section 8.11.3. It is best to use unique ID numbers for each block.

Case 2. Tape has been rewound or the location of the end of the last data block has been lost.

You must know the ID number of the last recorded data block. Rewind the tape to well before the anticipated starting point and set up the parameters to read the last data block following the steps given in Section 8.11.3, Step 4.

If the data transfer is successful (as indicated by the display showing 0000 xx), you may proceed to load the next data block. Refer to Section 8.11.3.

Hint #3. Avoid placing a data block between two existing data blocks or in an area of the tape which has previously been used for recorded data. You may recall that data blocks may be of arbitrary length and hence variations in block length and tape speed may result in overlapping of recorded data blocks.

Hint #4. Recall that when *recording* on a magnetic tape, you cannot select ID = ∅∅ or ID = FF. However, when *reading* from a magnetic tape into the KIM-1 memory, we can use these ID numbers as follows:

Case 1. If we select ID = ØØ, the ID number recorded on the tape will be ignored and the system will read the first valid data block encountered on the tape. The data read from the tape will be loaded into memory addresses as specified on the tape.

Comment: This is useful if you forget your ID number or if the ID number was not provided to you. Note that you still need the original starting and ending addresses in order to locate and execute the program.

Case 2. If we select ID = FF, the ID number recorded on the tape will be ignored and the system will read the first valid data block encountered on the tape. In addition, the data block will be loaded into successive memory locations beginning at the address specified in locations 17F5 and 17F6 (starting address low, SAL, starting address high, SAH) instead of the locations specified on the tape.

Comment: This is useful if you forget, or do not know, the ID number and the starting address. Note that you still should know the maximum length of the program so that you don't "write over" and destroy other data stored in memory.

8.12.1 Manipulating the KIM-1 Display (Example 8.12.1)

The KIM-1 display is controlled by the 6530-002 I/O ports. A diagram of the KIM-1 display and 6530 RAM ROM I/O interface is shown in Figure 8.12.1. This diagram is simplified to the point where it does not show any of the drivers, inverters, or pin connections. The primary purpose of Figure 8.12.1 is to help to explain how the KIM-1 six character, 7 segment LED display may be used to display many of the alphabetical characters. In addition, it will be found that it is possible to blink and to shift the characters which are displayed.

The A-side data determines which of the seven segments are illuminated for the character selected by the B-side data. Segments A through G are selected by bits Ø through 6, respectively.

Example 8.12.1. Determine A-side and B-side data which will cause

| E | r | r | o | r |

to be displayed in the first four character positions.

MCS 6502 Based Microcomputer – The KIM-1

Character	A-side data	B-side data
E	79	∅8
r	5∅	∅A
r	5∅	∅C
o	5C	∅E
r	5∅	1∅

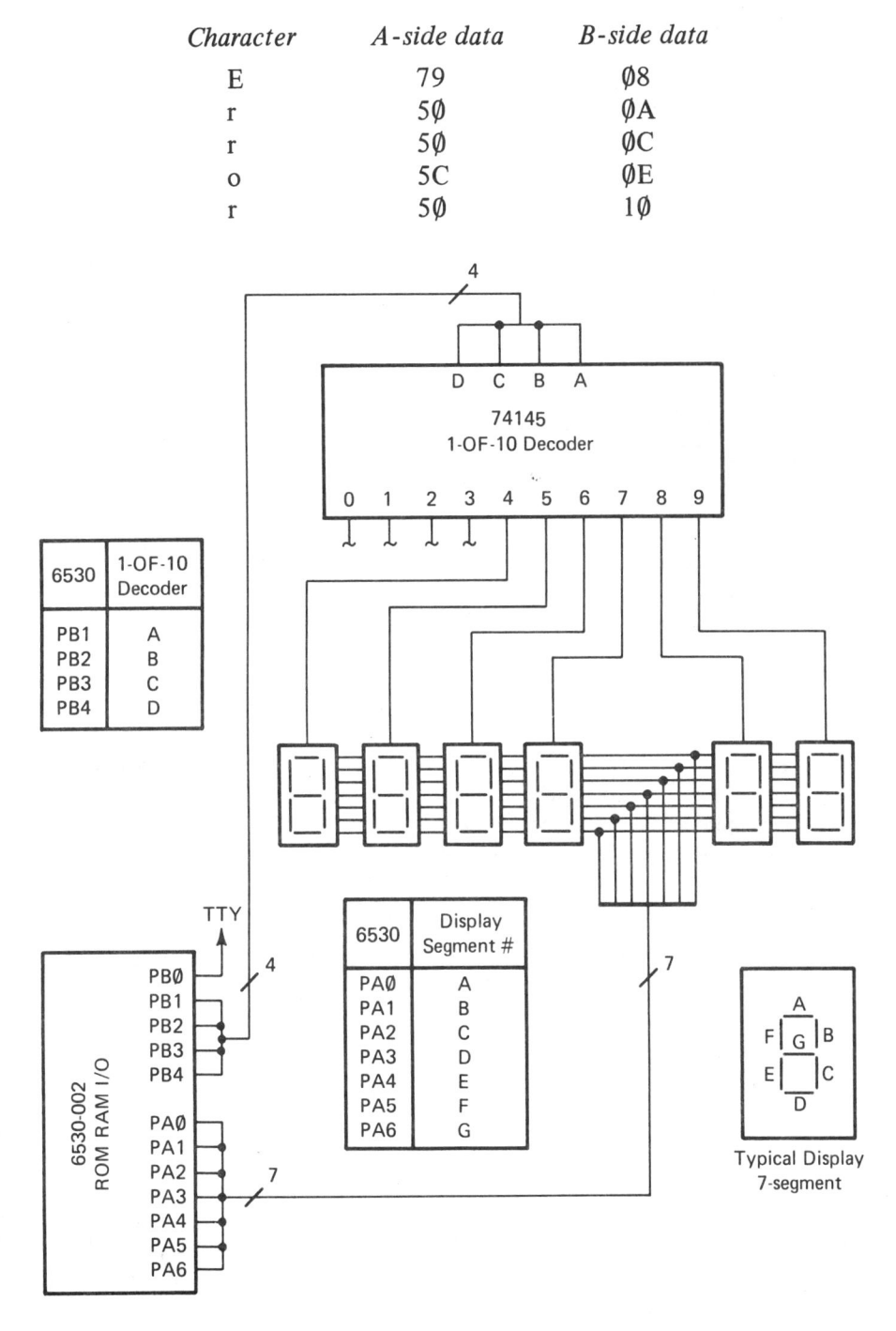

Figure 8.12-1 Simplified diagram of KIM-1 display and control by the 6530-002

Comment 1. A-side data are determined as follows:

	Segments On G F E D C B A	Hex Code
Character E	1 1 1 1 ∅ ∅ 1	79
Character r	1 ∅ 1 ∅ ∅ ∅ ∅	5∅
Character o	1 ∅ 1 1 1 ∅ ∅	5C

Comment 2. Computation of the B-side data may appear to be confusing at first. Because PB1, PB2, PB3, PB4 (instead of the more typical PB∅, PB1, PB2, PB3) are sent to the 1-0F-10 decoder, the decoder supplies an output which is only one-half of the actual input. In other words, we have to supply an input which is twice as large so that character positions ∅4, ∅5, ∅6, ∅7, ∅8, ∅9 actually require as B-side data inputs: ∅8, ∅A, ∅C, 1∅, and 12.

The specific memory addresses associated with the 6530-002 I/O ports are as follows:

174∅	SAD	A-side Data
1741	PADD	A-side Data Direction
1742	SBD	B-side Data
1743	PBDD	B-side Data Direction

A clearer perspective of the relative memory locations may be obtained by referring to Figure 8.12-2 which is Figure 8.4-1 with the above memory locations added. It may be seen that some pins on both data direction registers must be set for output. (Remember 1 = output and ∅ = input.) Just exactly which pins ports A and B are set for input and which pins are set for output is given in Figure 8.12-3.

A program which will load the A and B data direction registers with 7F and 1E respectively, is as follows:

Op Codes	Source Codes
A9 7F	LDA #7F
8D 41 17	STA PADD
A9 1E	LDA #1E
8D 43 17	STA PBDD

Example 8.12.2. Write a program which will display the letters "EE" in the two left-handmost characters of the KIM-1 display. The remaining four characters are to be dark.

The solution to Example 8.12.2 is shown in Table 8.12-1.

MCS 6502 Based Microcomputer — The KIM-1

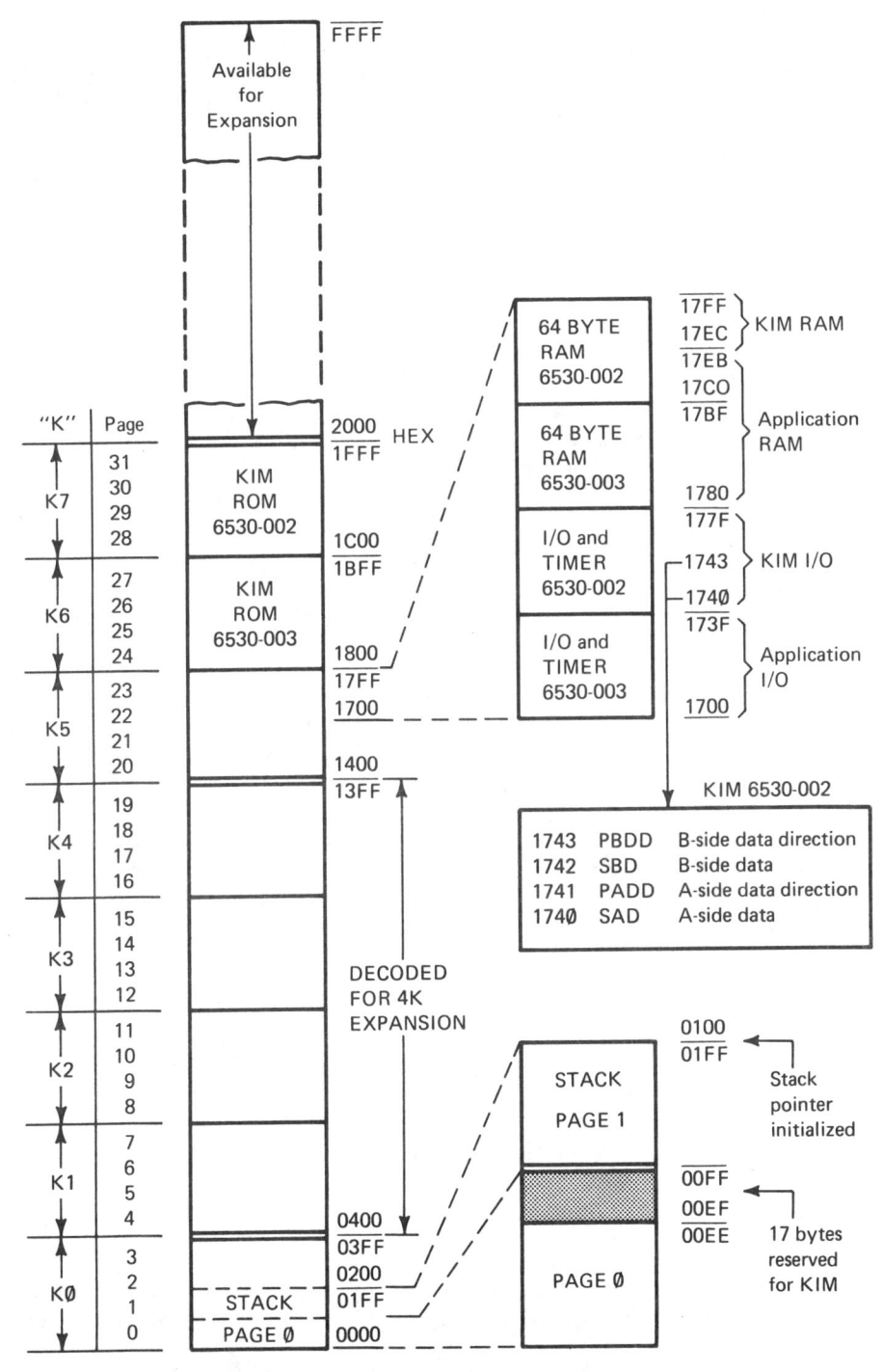

Figure 8.12-2 MEMORY MAP with 6530-002 ports A and B added
(Courtesy MOS Technology)

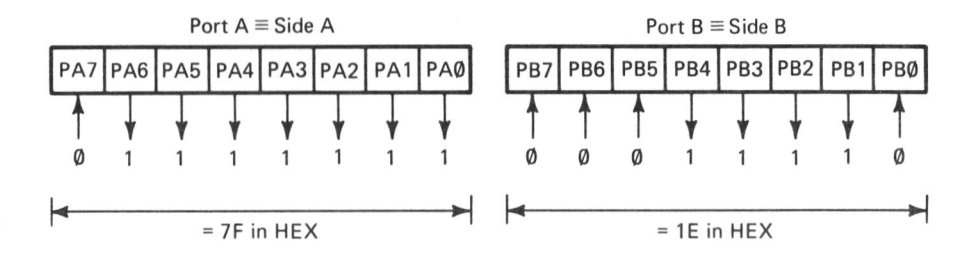

```
                Port A ≡ Side A                              Port B ≡ Side B
        ┌───┬───┬───┬───┬───┬───┬───┐        ┌───┬───┬───┬───┬───┬───┬───┐
        │PA7│PA6│PA5│PA4│PA3│PA2│PA1│PA0│    │PB7│PB6│PB5│PB4│PB3│PB2│PB1│PB0│
        └─↑─┴─↓─┴─↓─┴─↓─┴─↓─┴─↓─┴─↓─┴─↓─┘    └─↑─┴─↑─┴─↑─┴─↓─┴─↓─┴─↓─┴─↓─┴─↑─┘
          0   1   1   1   1   1   1   1        0   0   0   1   1   1   1   0
        |←──────────── = 7F in HEX ──────────→|  |←──────────── = 1E in HEX ──────────→|
```

Figure 8.12-3 Input/Output pin configuration for ports A and B in Example 8.12.1
1 = output; 0 = input

TABLE 8.12-1 Source and Op Codes which display the letters "EE" in the KIM-1 display

Memory Map	Byte 1	Byte 2	Byte 3	LABEL	OP CODE	OPERAND	Remarks
0030	A9	7F			LDA	#7F	Set output pins on
32	8D	41	17		STA	PADD	Port A.
35	A9	1E			LDA	#1E	Set output pins on
37	8D	43	17		STA	PBDD	Port B.
3A	A9	79			LDA	#79	Load the letter E.
3C	8D	40	17		STA	SAD	
3F	A9	08		AGAIN	LDA	#08	Display the letter E
41	8D	42	17		STA	SBD	in the first position.
44	A9	0A			LDA	#0A	Display the letter E
46	8D	42	17		STA	SBD	in the second position.
49	4C	3F	00		JMP	AGAIN	Jump back and display EE again.

8.12.2 Generating a Variable Frequency Square Wave (Example 8.12.3)

The purpose of this example is to illustrate one of the many different ways of defining the Input/Output interface ports of the KIM-1 microcomputer for both input and output. In order to be more specific and practical as well, we will use Example 8.12.3, which may be stated as follows:

MCS 6502 Based Microcomputer — The KIM-1

Example 8.12.3*. Write a computer program for the KIM-1 which will generate a variable frequency square wave with amplitudes of 0 and +5 volts.

As shown in Figure 8.12-4, the eight pins of Port A are programmed such that one pin (PA∅) is the output and the other seven pins (PA1 to and including PA7) are connected to seven switches which serve as the input control to determine the frequency of the square wave.

It is further desired that the switch connected to PA1 is to be the least significant bit (LSB) and the switch connected to PA7 is to be the most significant bit (MSB). We would also like each switch to act as a 1 when closed, and as a 0 when open. If this is done, the status of the switches define binary numbers from zero (all switches open) to 127_{10} (with all switches closed).

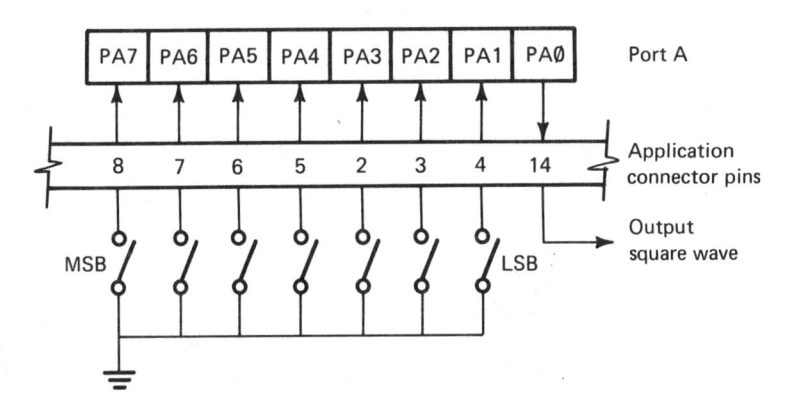

Figure 8.12-4 Input/Output connections for the variable frequency square wave generator (Example 8.12.3)

A Solution to Example 8.12.3. One of the many possible solutions to Example 8.12.3 is given in Figure 8.12-5, which presents in a modified form, both the assembly language program as well as the machine code. It is said to be "modified" form because of the additional column labeled MACHINE CYCLES. This column has been added because of the importance of determining exactly how much time (number of machine cycles) are required to execute each line of code.

---

* Example 8.12.3 is similar to the "Real Application" example given on page 55 of the KIM-1 USER MANUAL. (MOS Technology Inc.)

Memory Map	INSTRUCTION Byte 1	Byte 2	Byte 3	MACHINE CYCLES	LABEL	OP CODE	MACHINE CODE OPERAND	Remarks
0200	A9	01		2	INIT	LDA	#$01	Define I/O. PA0=Output=1. PA1-PA7=Input=0.
0202	8D	01	17	4		STA	PADD	PADD = Port A Data Direction Register
0205	EE	00	17	6	START	INC	PAD	Toggle PA0 pin only on Port A.
0208	AD	00	17	4	READ	LDA	PAD	Read switch settings into accumulator.
020B	49	FF		2		EOR	#$FF	Complement switch value because closed = 1.
020D	4A			2		LSR	A	Shift accumulator one bit to right.
020E	AA			2		TAX		Transfer COUNT into X-Index Register.
020F	CA			2	DELAY	DEX		Loop to delay by amount specified by
0210	10	FD		3,2	BPL	DELAY		COUNT stored in the X-Index Register.
0212	30	F1		3		BMI	START	Go back to START.
					PADD = $1701			Defines absolute address of Port A Data Direction Register.
					PAD = $1700			Defines absolute address of Port A Data Register as specified by the KIM Monitor.

Figure 8.12-5 Assembly language, Machine code, and MACHINE CYCLES for a variable frequency square wave generator (Example 8.12.3)

Execution of Example 8.12.3. Enter the program as usual, but before executing the program, load the NMI vector locations 17FA and 17FB with 00 and 1C respectively, so that the ST key will function properly. The program begins in memory location 0200, so load this memory location, and press the GO key. The display will remain dark and the output square wave will be available at pin 14 of the Applications Connector. This output may now be connected to an audio amplifier to serve as a tone generator; or it may be applied to the horizontal input of an oscilloscope and used to calibrate the horizontal sweep of the oscilloscope.

The Output Square Wave. The square wave output is shown in Figure 8.12-6 along with equations for the frequency and period of the square wave as a function of the switch settings. When numerical values are substituted, the resulting frequencies and periods are:

Input Switch Settings		Frequency $(f = 1/T)$ Hz.	Period $T = 1/f$ μsec.
Binary	Decimal		
000000	0	21,740	46
111111	127_{10}	760	1362

MCS 6502 Based Microcomputer — The KIM-1

Input Switch Settings		Frequency	Period
Binary	Decimal	f = 1/T (Hz)	T = 1/f (μs)
000000	0	21,740	46
111111	127_{10}	760	1,362

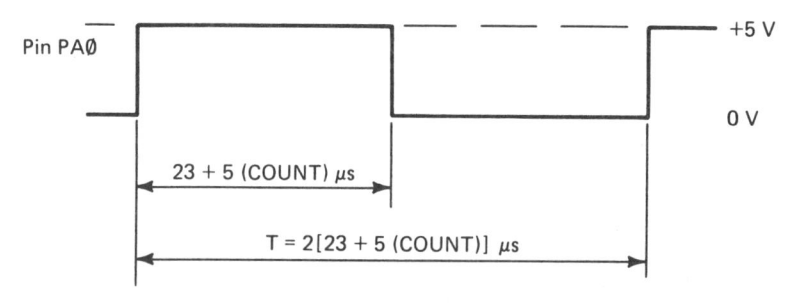

Figure 8.12-6 Output square wave for Example 8.12.3. Note that the period is T, the frequency is 1/T, and COUNT is determined by the input switch setting with $0 \leq COUNT \leq 127_{10}$.

PROBLEMS

1. Use the KIM keyboard and display to inspect the contents of memory locations (in hex) 0000, 0400, 1800, and FFFF. Record the contents as observed. Refer to Figure 8.4.1, the memory map for the KIM-1 microcomputer, and the 6530 Monitor listings to explain your observations.

2. List the contents of the following addresses: 1C00 through 1C0A, 1746, 0000 through 0010, and 1780 through 1790.

3. Sketch and label all MCS6502 μP registers. Briefly describe their functions.

4. List the addresses where the following can be found in KIM: ROM, RWM, TIMERS, and I/O.

5. Use KIM keyboard and data keys to clear memory locations $00EF through $00FE. If this is not possible, explain.

6. Where are the internal registers (A, X, Y, S, P and Z) stored during a single-step operation?

7. Explain why it is necessary to load memory locations 17FA and 17FB before the KIM-1 microcomputer may be used in the single-step mode. Refer to 6530-002 listing between lines 600 and 620 and correlate with the use of the above two memory locations.

8. Refer to Table 8.7-2 which presents the single step execution of Example 8.1 and fill in the table below for each step.

   PC   P   A   X   Y   S

9. Study the program below and understand how it works. (There is at least one error.) The intention of the program is to set the contents of locations $0000 through $00FF to all ones ($FF).

ADDR	CODE		PROGRAM
0200	AE FF		LDX #$FF
0202	18		CLA
0203	95 00	LOOP	STA 0, X
0205	CA		DEX
0206	D0 FB		BNE LOOP
0208	4C 4F 1C		JMP $1C4F

10. If you use the KIM-1 microcomputer in the binary mode, what result would you expect if you added 34 and 27? What would you expect in the decimal mode? Use the solution to Example 8.1 and verify your answers using the KIM-1 microcomputer.

11. Modify the source code for Example 8.1 which is given in Table 8.3-1 so as to check for possible overflow. What would you suggest doing in the event of an overflow?

12. Modify the source code for Example 8.1 which is given in Table 8.3-1 so as to display the sum instead of "jumping to itself" at the end of the program. Display the sum in the four leftmost locations of the display. You will need to study the Monitor Listing for the 6530s in order to do this.

13. Modify the source code for Example 8.1 which is given in Table 8.3-1 for the case where the two positive numbers are each three bytes long. Your program should check for overflow and allow enough memory locations to store the sum. Use the decimal mode. Repeat for binary mode.

14. Write a program for execution on the KIM-1 microcomputer which will output all of the printable ASCII characters to a printer such as the Teletype Model ASR33. In the next line printed, move

MCS 6502 Based Microcomputer — The KIM-1

all of the characters one character to the right and bring the character shifted off to the right back to the leftmost position. (In other words, circular shift right.) Repeat printing new lines until all characters have been printed in all possible positions. (This is a program which printer technicians find very useful when making printer adjustments.)

15. Punch a paper tape for Example 8.2 and compare to the punched paper tape shown in Figure 8.10-6. Explain any differences.

16. Write a program for execution on the KIM-1 which will display the characters as they are "read in" from a magnetic tape recorder. Display the character which has just been read in the leftmost position of the display and then shift the characters to the right to make room for each new character. (The characters will appear at a rate which may be too fast to permit reading every character reliably.)

17. Write a program for execution on the KIM-1 which will generate a very long string of sync characters, an ASCII SYN character ($16). Record approximately five minutes of only sync characters on a magnetic tape and then play them back using the program written in Problem 16. Vary the volume control and tone control (if your recorder has one) and determine the range for which synchronization is maintained. Determine the optimum settings for your tape recorder.

18. Modify the program given in Table 8.12-1 for Example 8.12.2 so that the two characters E E blink on and off at the rate of about once per second. Although the timers in the 6530s might be used, write a program which will accomplish the same thing. (Not all microcomputers have timers.)

19. Modify the program given in Table 8.12-1 for Example 8.12.2 so that six characters (all of which may be different) will be displayed on the KIM-1 display. (Caution: Be sure to turn off a character before proceeding to turn on the next character.) In order to demonstrate that your program works, display the six characters E, R, R, O, R, and a blank.

20. Modify the program given in Table 8.12-1 for Example 8.12.2 so that more than six characters may be displayed at the rate of six at a time and then shifted one character to the right and displayed again in an endless loop.

21. Add steps to your program for Problem 20 so that the display blinks on and off at the rate of about once per seond with on and off times being equal.

22. The solution to Example 8.12.3 in Figure 8.12-5 provides a frequency range from 760 to 21,740 Hz. What changes would be necessary to provide frequencies up to 50,000 Hz? What about for frequencies below 760 Hz?

23. Modify the program given in Figure 8.12-5 for Example 8.12.3 so that the postiive portion of the square wave represents only 10% of the period instead of 50%.

A

USER'S GUIDE TO THE MDT 650

A.1 INTRODUCTION—WHAT'S AN MDT 650?

The Microcomputer Development Terminal (MDT) 650 is a *special purpose* microcomputer which is intended to serve as a software development aid in the design of systems which use the 650X series of microprocessors currently being manufactured by MOS Technology and the Rockwell International Corporation. We will primarily be concerned with the 6502 microprocessor in the 650X series.

In terms of size, shape, and weight, the MDT 650 resembles an electric office typewriter. The keyboard has additional keys for control and there is a single line alphanumeric display consisting of 32 (20_{16}) characters. It is also possible to connect peripheral equipment such as cathode ray tube terminals (CRTs) and teleprinters such as the model 33ASR Teletype with paper tape reader and punch.

For purposes of this discussion, the MDT is much more than just another "piece of hardware." Rather, it is the vehicle for discussing the general area known as microcomputer systems design aids. The reader should ponder (maybe even meditate!) on each of the following:

   a) what functions a software aid can and cannot do for the user.
   b) the relative advantages and disadvantages of including automatic features and defaults in the design of software development aids themselves.
   c) software development aids, like the microcomputer digital computers they really are, do not lessen in any way the need for the

[Software for the MDT650 was done by COMPAS, Computer Applications Corporation, Ames, Iowa. Information relating to the MDT650 software is used with the kind permission of COMPAS.]

user to be meticulously careful about what appears to be an infinite number of "nit picking" details. All digital computers are "impartial" graders, which seldom, if ever, give "partial credit" to the user for work submitted which is only slightly in error.

Figure A.0 presents a functional block diagram of the MDT as viewed by the user. It shows the two primary modes designated as EDITOR and MONITOR; as well as the key stroke sequences to enter each of the five secondary modes: LOAD, EDIT, ASSEMBLE, EXECUTE, and OUTPUT MODES.

A.2 SUMMARY: HOW TO USE THE MDT 650

This entire section of the appendix describes in detail how to use the MDT 650. It may best be summarized by listing and briefly explaining the five modes of operation.

1. LOAD MODE

In the LOAD MODE, TEXT is stored into the MDT 650 memory. TEXT includes the source program, comments, and assembler directives, such as .END statements. It could also be poetry.

TEXT may be entered into the MDT 650 memory via the MDT 650 keyboard, but more efficient use may be made of the MDT 650's special capabilities if off-line peripheral devices are used to prepare paper tape. A considerable number of errors (but not of every possible type) are tolerated on the off-line prepared paper tape since they may be removed easily in the EDIT MODE.

2. EDIT MODE

TEXT currently stored in the MDT 650 memory may be modified and/or corrected by inserting a character, deleting a character, inserting a line, or delating a line.

It is also possible with a single key stroke to display the top line of TEXT or the bottom line of the TEXT.

3. ASSEMBLY MODE

The source program is converted to machine language. The assembler is a two pass assembler and about 23 error code diagnostic messages are available to aid in detecting errors.

User's Guide to the MDT 650

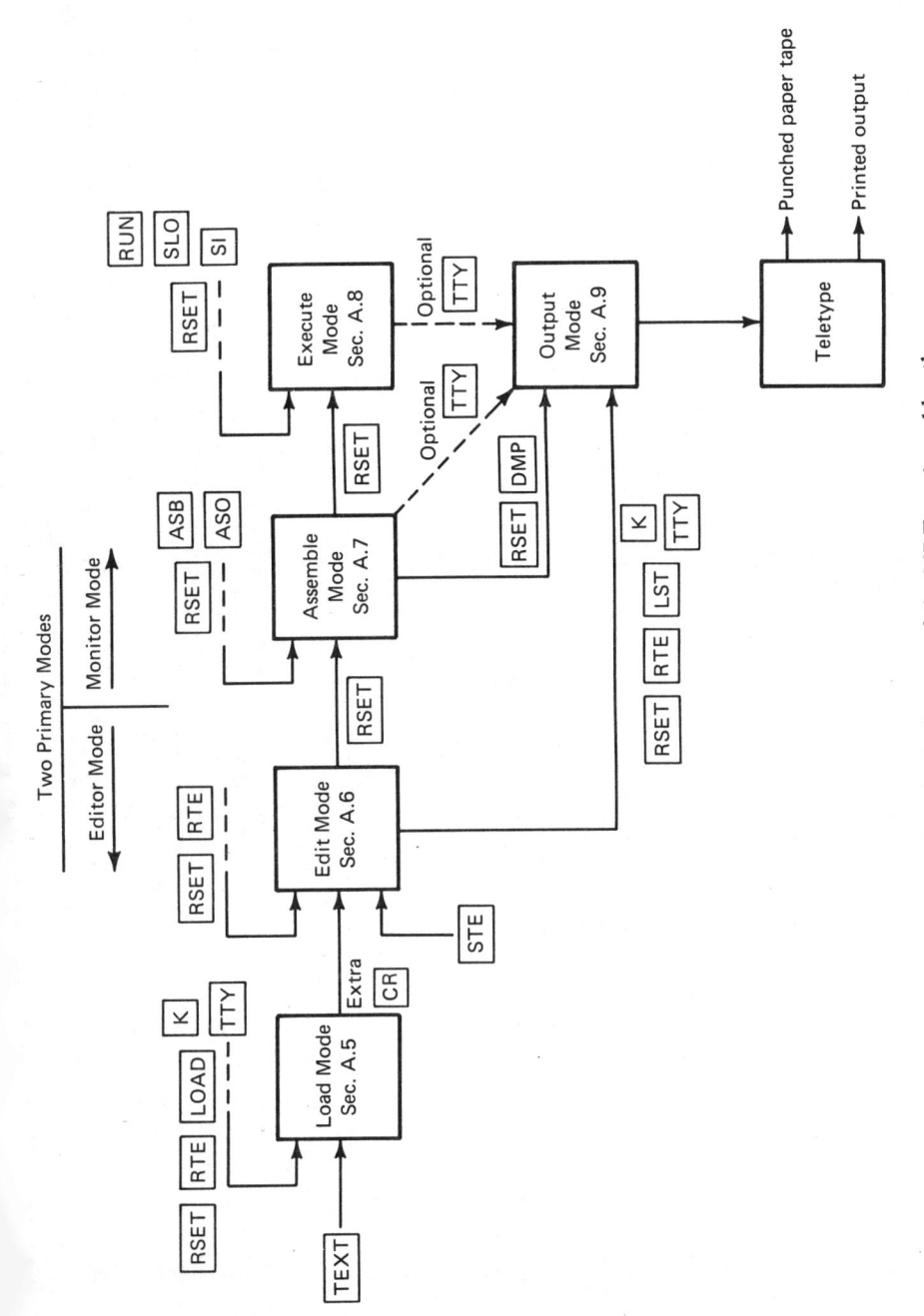

Figure A.0 Functional block diagram of the MDT as viewed by the user

4. EXECUTION MODE

The entire computer program may be executed or the execution can be done one line of code at a time (called single-step). Single-step operation may be controlled manually or it may be automatic with a variable, but selectable, interval of time between the single-steps.

An additional feature, called TRACE, permits the optional display of the contents of all of the microprocessor registers immediately following the execution of each single-step.

Two hardware breakpoints may be implemented to stop the user's microprocessor on any desired address when one of four user selectable conditions are satisfied.

5. OUTPUT MODE

Printed outputs and optional punched paper tapes corresponding to the corrected TEXT and the object code (machine code) are available.

The printed versions of the TEXT have three possible formats: a) exactly as entered, b) "tabbed" for ease of human interpretation, and c) "squished" to reduce the length of each line which reduces printing time and improves the possibility of showing the entire line on the MDT 650 display.

The format of the punched paper tape is correct for reading into some (but not all) 6502 microprocessor based systems such as the KIM-1 microcomputer.

A.3 EXAMPLE A1—A BENCHMARK EXAMPLE

Example A1 is a benchmark example in the usually accepted sense, namely, it serves as a reference point to compare corresponding results, such as the numerical answers, and the amount of work involved in working a problem two or more different ways. Example A1 has intentionally been chosen to be so simple that results obtained with the MDT 650 may be easily compared with those obtained manually. These comparisons include the machine code obtained during assembly, symbol table generation, addition in both binary and decimal modes, and the register contents at the end of each step during program execution.

Example A1. Add two positive numbers of one byte each located in two memory locations and store the sum into a third memory location.

User's Guide to the MDT 650

Comments.

1. We are considering only positive, one byte numbers.
2. In order to obtain the correct numerical results, we will have to consider the possibility of a *carry in* because the 6502 microprocessor has only an add with carry (ADC) and no simple just add (ADD) instruction.
3. We need to determine if a *carry out* occurred if we wish to verify the numerical answers in some cases.

A.4 SOURCE AND OBJECT CODE FOR EXAMPLE A1— MANUAL ASSEMBLY

The source and object code for Example A1 may be written using many different formats. If only one person is involved in writing the source code, and that same person will manually convert it to object code, no special format needs to be followed and no other special restrictions (such as the length of labels being limited to 6 characters beginning with an alphabetical character) exist. However, seldom is only one person involved, and even if that is the case, a formatted, systematic approach is desirable to prevent errors and to make the program easier to read and to understand. The ever present problem of documentation is also partially solved at this point if a systematic, standardized format is followed. We will therefore use the format dictated by the 6502 Assembler Language even though at this point we will do the assembly *manually*.

The source and object codes for Example A1 are shown in Table A.1.

A.5 MDT 650 IN THE LOAD MODE

The primary purpose of the LOAD MODE is to provide a means of transferring and storing the TEXT into the user side of the MDT 650 memory. TEXT includes the source program, comments, and assembler directives, such as .END. We note in passing that the TEXT could consist of cooking recipes or even poems. Hence an unusual application of the MDT 650 might be to modify recipes or compose poetry. We will primarily concern ourselves here with the normal, *intended applications* of the MDT 650, i.e., as a software development aid.

TEXT may be stored into the memory via the MDT 650 keyboard, but a more efficient use of the MDT's special capabilities is made if offline peripheral devices are used to prepare the punched paper tape. The

TABLE A.1 Source and Object Code for Example A1
— Manual Assembly

	OBJECT CODE			SOURCE CODE		
MEMORY ADDRESS	BYTE 1	BYTE 2	BYTE 3	LABEL	OP CODE	OPERAND	COMMENT
0000				NUM1			Designate one of the two numbers to be added as NUM1.
0001				NUM2			Designate the second of the two numbers to be added as NUM2.
0002				SUM			Designate the sum of the two numbers to be SUM.
				⋮			
0010	F8				SED		Set Decimal Mode.
0011	A5	00			LDA	NUM1	Load the accumulator with the numerical value of NUM1.
0013	18				CLC		Clear carry.
0014	65	01			ADC	NUM2	Add with carry NUM1 + NUM2. (There is no ADD instruction.)
0016	85	02			STA	SUM	Store the sum of two numbers into memory location SUM.
0018	4C	18	00	WAIT	JMP	WAIT	The 6502 microprocessor has no halt or stop command. This is a jump to itself.

Comment 1: We have decided to store NUM1, NUM2, and SUM into memory locations 0000, 0001, and 0002, respectively. Refer to Sec. 8.5 for more details.

Comment 2: We have also decided to begin storing the object code into memory locations beginning with memory location 0010.

recommended procedure for preparing punched paper tape on a Model 33ASR Teletype is shown in Table A.2. Please note that errors have *intentionally* been made in the preparation of the paper tape so that we will be able to demonstrate the correcting and modifying capabilities in the EDIT MODE of operation.

Table A.3 presents the detailed key by keystroke sequences for loading the TEXT into the user side memory via a Teletype Model 33ASR paper tape reader. The suggested memory allocation in the user side memory is presented in a conventional format in Figure A.1. This particular memory allocation provides the maximum amount of contiguous (touching) memory for TEXT but at the same time it makes it impossible to utilize the interrupts. Other memory allocations are possible if necessary. Each block of 4K RAM may be moved to any one of 16 different locations by means of switches inside the MDT case.

Figure A.2 is another view of the TEXT as stored in the memory with the requested starting address SSSS and the ending address EEEE. When uisng the MDT in the EDIT MODE, this may be a more useful format than the memory map format shown in Figure A.1.

User's Guide to the MDT 650 **467**

Table A.4 presents the detailed key by key stroke sequences for loading the TEXT via the MDT 650 keyboard. Only consecutive lines of TEXT may be entered and there is *no* editing capability except for the backspace key.

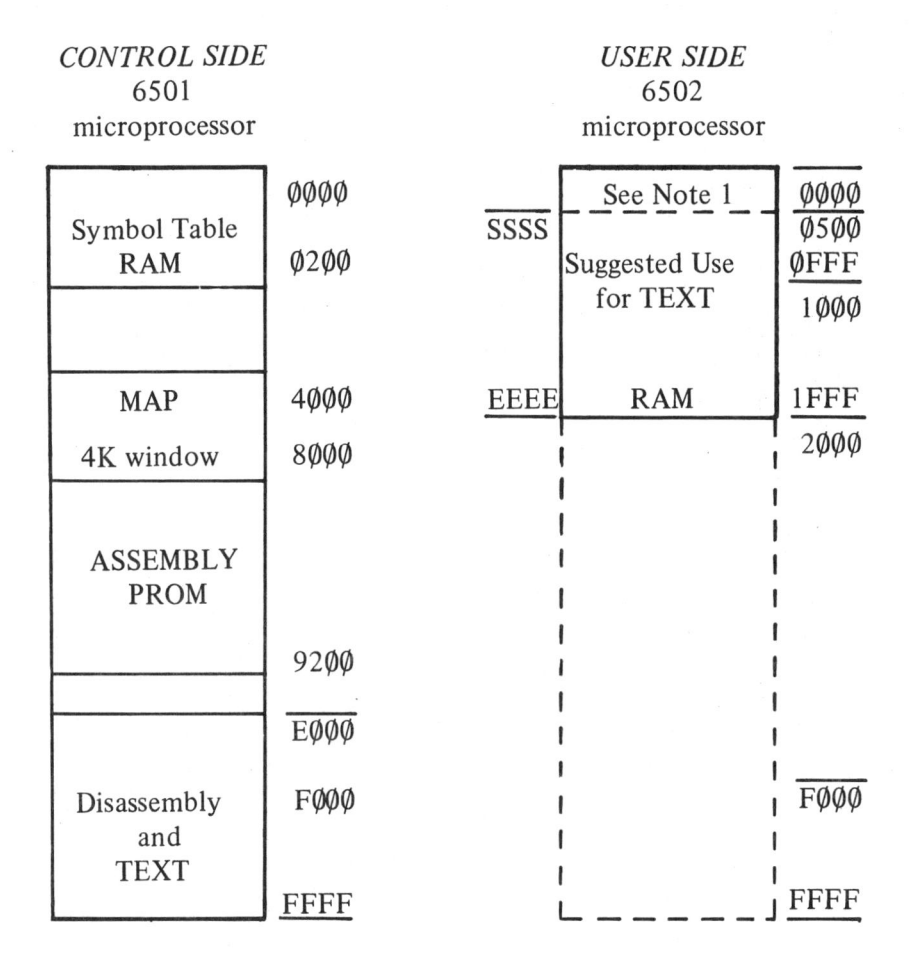

```
   CONTROL SIDE                    USER SIDE
      6501                            6502
   microprocessor                 microprocessor
```

CONTROL SIDE (6501)		USER SIDE (6502)	
Symbol Table RAM	∅∅∅∅	See Note 1	∅∅∅∅
	∅2∅∅	SSSS	∅5∅∅
		Suggested Use for TEXT	∅FFF
			1∅∅∅
MAP 4K window	4∅∅∅	EEEE RAM	1FFF
	8∅∅∅		2∅∅∅
ASSEMBLY PROM			
	92∅∅		
	E∅∅∅		
Disassembly and TEXT	F∅∅∅		F∅∅∅
	FFFF		FFFF

Figure A.1 Memory map of the user and control sides of the MDT 650. Only the user side is available to the user for storage. The control side is shown only for reference purposes and the memory locations are only approximate.

Note 1. These RAM memory locations are suggested for symbols and machine code (object code).

TABLE A.2 Off-Line Preparation of Paper Tape on the TTY Model 33ASR for Subsequent Entering into the MDT 650 Memory. The TTY is operated in the LOCAL mode with no connection to the MDT 650. Example A1 is used to illustrate the procedure.

Step 1: Apply 115 VAC, 60 Hz. to the TTY and turn switch to LOCAL.

Step 2: On the paper tape READER/PUNCH unit, press the ON button.

Step 3: Punch a series of RUBOUTS (all 8 holes punched with even parity). You may press the REPEAT and RUBOUT keys simultaneously to do this.

WARNING: If you punch a leader consisting of characters other than RUBOUTS, you may encounter difficulty later when reading the paper tape into the MDT 650. Even no print characters such as CR (carriage return) and LF (line feed) cause problems. For example, a CR as the first character read will cause an automatic transfer from the LOAD MODE to the EDIT MODE before any data are read in.

To be more specific: The first line encountered in TEXT which contains a CR as its first character will immediately cause an automatic transfer from the LOAD MODE to the EDIT MODE. This is a useful feature most of the time, but is can cause problems.

Step 4: Type your program on the TTY keyboard.

Comments: The input is relatively "free format" and every line of TEXT *may* begin in column 1. About the only format constraint is that a blank must appear between the LABEL (if any), OP CODE, and OPERAND fields. LABELS are limited to a maximum of 6 characters, the first of which must be alphabetical. None of the OP CODES may be chosen to be LABELS.

Step 5: Although not mandatory, it is suggested that that last line of your TEXT have as its first and only character a CR in order to automatically transfer from the LOAD MODE to the EDIT MODE.

Step 6: Punch a series of RUBOUTS to protect the end of your paper tape.

TABLE A.2 (continued) Actual TTY punched paper tape and TTY printed output for the source code of Example A1. Many errors have been deliberately made so that subsequently we will be able to demonstrate the correcting and modifying features of the EDIT MODE of operation.

```
;
;USER,S GIDE TO THE MDT 650
;EXAMPLER A1
;
NUM1=$0000
NUM2=$0001
SUM=$0002
*=$0010
SED
LDA NUM1
ADC NUM2
STA SUM
WAIT JMP WAIT
; THIS IS AN EXTRA LINE
.END
```

1. Missing character - U
2. Extra character - R
3. Missing line - CLC
4. Obviously an extra line

User's Guide to the MDT 650   469

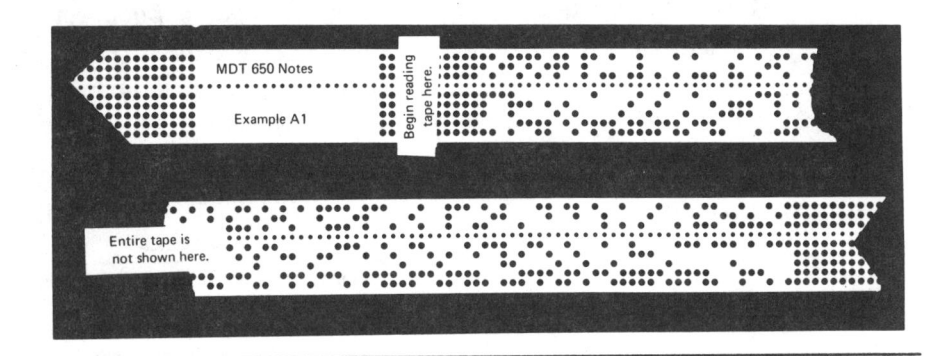

TABLE A.3 Procedure for loading off-line prepared punched paper tape into MDT 650 memory via a Model 33ASR Teletype paper tape reader. The specific data applies to Example A1 as shown in Table A.1.

Press Keys on MDT Keyboard	See Displayed	Comments
COLD START Plug MDT into 115 VAC. Plug fans into 115 VAC. There are no ON/OFF switches.	Blinking ? and S	The MDT is not being used. There is no power ON/OFF switch. Wait about 15 sec. for the display to blink.
[TEXT]	ENTER SSSS EEEE LL ⋮	MDT is asking for Starting Address, Ending Address, and the Line Length of the TEXT.
BATCH PROCESSING		There is a waiting line of users. Previous user has left and the MDT is in an unknown state. 115 VAC, 60 Hz. power is still applied.
[RSET] [TEXT]	ENTER SSSS EEEE LL	MDT is asking for Starting Address, Ending Address, and the Line Length of the TEXT.
[0][5][0][0][1][F][F][F][2][0]		You have just entered the suggested addresses and line length as given in Figure A.1.
Check that TTY is one and switch in LINE position. [LOAD] [TTY] Move lever switch on TTY paper tape reader to START momentarily and release.	Lines of text are displayed, line by line, as they are read in. Miscellaneous characters may appear in the MDT display, but are usually not an indication of a problem.	Don't forget to load the paper tape in such a way that only rubouts are read before the TEXT characters are encountered. No characters, not even nonprint characters such as CR or LF, are permitted before the TEXT.
Any of the EDIT keys. (True only if the automatic transfer to EDIT MODE feature was used. If not, proceed to Table A.5.)		The first time user may wish to check the TEXT completely. This may be done by pressing the [TOP] key and then proceeding through the TEXT, line by line using the [L+1] key. If the TEXT is correct, go to Table A.5, the ASSEMBLER MODE. If not, go to Table A.4, the EDIT MODE.

TABLE A.4 Keystroke sequences for entering the *Source Code* for Example A.1 (as shown in Table A.2) via the MDT keyboard in the *LOAD* mode. Only consecutive lines of text may be entered with *no* editing capability except for the backspace key.

Press Keys on MDT Keyboard	See Displayed	Comments
Plug into 115 VAC 60 Hz. (There is no ON/OFF switch.)	Blinking ? and S	Display is dark for about 15 sec. and then blinks.
[TEXT]	ENTER SSSS EEEE LL	MDT is asking for the Starting Address, Ending Address, and Line Length of the TEXT.
[0][5][0][0][1][F][F][F][2][0]	Blinking + Characters are displayed as entered.	You have just entered the suggested starting and ending addresses given in Figure A.1 for the text and a Line Length of 20 hex.
[LOAD][K]	Blinking +	MDT is now in the LOAD from keyboard mode.
[N][U][M][1][=][$][0][0][0][0] [CR]		Memory location 0000 is assigned to NUM1 [CR] key terminates each line of text from here on.
[N][U][M][2][=][$][0][0][0][1] [CR]		Memory location 0001 is assigned to NUM2.
[S][U][M][=][$][0][0][0][2] [CR]	Characters are displayed as entered. When the [CR] key is pressed, a blinking + is displayed; if a line of text is rejected, a blinking ? is displayed.	Memory location 0002 is assigned to SUM.
[*][=][$][0][0][1][0] [CR]		From here on, memory locations will be assigned consecutively beginning with 0010 hex.
[S][E][D] [CR]		Set the decimal mode.
[C][L][C] [CR]		Clear carry.
[L][D][A][N][U][M][1] [CR]		LOAD into the accumulator the value of NUM1.
[A][D][C][N][U][M][2] [CR]		Add with carry NUM1 + NUM2.
[S][T][A][S][U][M] [CR]		Store the sum into the SUM memory location.
[W][A][I][T][J][U][M][P][W][A][I][T] [CR]		Jump to itself.
[.][E][N][D] [CR]		.END must be the last line of text.
[CR]		A line of text with the first nonblank character being a [CR] puts us into the EDIT mode.

A.6 MDT 650 IN THE EDIT MODE

The purpose of the EDIT MODE is to provide a convenient way for the user to correct and/or to change TEXT which is currently stored in the user side of memory of the MDT 650. In general, the ability to "edit" implies the capability to insert, delete, and change characters within a line without retyping the entire line; to insert, delete, and change entire lines of TEXT; and to locate lines containing key words. The MDT provides all of the above editing capability with the following keys:

User's Guide to the MDT 650

First character of the TOP line is stored in memory location SSSS.

Maximum Line Length LL in HEX

(Top Line) TOP

TEXT

The "bottom" line moves up and down as lines are inserted and deleted.

(Bottom Line) BOT

TEXT

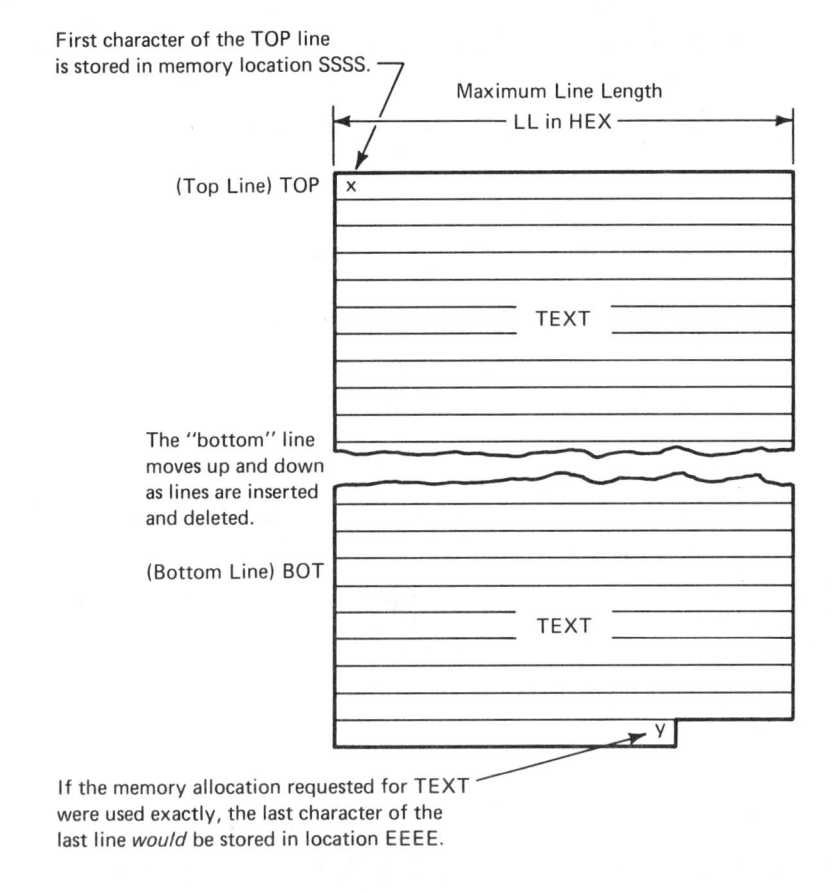

If the memory allocation requested for TEXT were used exactly, the last character of the last line *would* be stored in location EEEE.

Figure A.2 A user's view of the TEXT as stored in memory with the requested starting address SSSS and the ending address EEEE. When using the MDT in the EDIT mode, this may be a more useful viewpoint than the memory map shown in Figure A.1.

TOP	Displays the top line of TEXT.
BOT	Displays the bottom line of TEXT.
FND	Locates and displays a line of TEXT selected by a key word or character string.
L+1	Displays the next line of TEXT.
L−1	Displays the previous line of TEXT.
C+1	Moves the blinking cursor one character position to the right, until it reaches the rightmost position, where it remains.

[C-1]	Moves the blinking cursor one character position to the left, unless it is already in its leftmost position.
[DLL]	Deletes the line being displayed and moves all lines below this line, one line up, respectively.
[INL]	The new line will be inserted *after* the line being displayed. After the [INL] key is depressed, the display will go blank, but it may take several seconds in long TEXTS. Do *not* attempt to insert characters until the display goes blank and a single, blinking + appears on the display. Terminate with [CR].
[BS]	Moves cursor one character position to the left each time it is depressed. The blinking character may be *replaced* by simply pressing the key corresponding to the desired character.
[STE]	Restart Text Editor. Destroys all TEXT currently stored.
[NEXT]	Moves cursor forward to blank or end of line.
[LAST]	Moves cursor backward to blank or start of line.
[DLC]	Delete character located in the cursor position.

Table A.5 presents a detailed key-by-keystroke illustration of the use of the EDIT keys as they apply to Example A1. At this time, the reader may wish to refer back to part 2 of Table A.2 to review the intentional errors which were made at that time.

A.7 MDT 650 IN THE ASSEMBLE MODE

The purpose of the ASSEMBLE MODE is to translate mnemonic or symbolic computer programs into actual machine code. Assemblers, although usually slightly different in detail, are essentially the same in substance. The three parts of the source program (TEXT) are handled as follows:

1. Mnemonics for op codes are mapped, one to one, to the corresponding op codes in machine code, usually hex.
2. Assembler directives are used to reserve storage, to initialize memory locations, and, in general, to direct information to the assembler.
3. User comments are stored, but otherwise ignored by the assembler.

User's Guide to the MDT 650

TABLE A.5 Keystroke sequences for editing TEXT as loaded in user side memory of the MDT 650. Refer to Table A.4 for the TEXT (with errors) currently stored in memory.

Press Keys on MDT Keyboard	See Displayed	Comments
[RSET] [RTE]	Blinking ; and +	Pressing [RSET] and [RTE] is optional if automatic transfer to EDIT MODE was used.
[L+1]	;USER'S GIDE TO THE MDT 650	Second line of TEXT is displayed. ; blinks and alternates with + to indicate position of the cursor.
[C+1] press (9 times)	;USER'S GIDE TO THE MDT 650	I blinks to indicate cursor position.
[U]	;USERS GUIDE TO THE MDT 650	Character U has been inserted as shown.
[L+1]	;EXAMPLER A1	; blinks and alternates with +
[C+1] (8 times)	;EXAMPLER A1	R blinks and alternates with +
[DLC]	;EXAMPLE A1	Space between E and A blinks with + R has been deleted.
[L+1] (7 times)	;LDA NUM1	; blinks and alternates with +
[INL]	Display remains unchanged for a few seconds; then a blinking + appears.	Do *not* attempt to insert characters until display goes blank and a single, blinking + appears. With long TEXTS, this may take several seconds.
[C][L][C]	CLC+ (+ blinks)	Blinking + indicates cursor position.
[CR]	CLC	First C blinks and alternates with +
[L+1] (4 times)	; THIS IS AN EXTRA LINE	Line to be deleted is displayed
[DLL]	.END	. blinks and alternates with a +

Suggestion: As a recheck on the correctness of the TEXT now stored in memory, press the TOP key and then press [L+1] key repeatedly to display all of the TEXT, line by line, consecutively.

TABLE A.6 TEXT after corrections were made in the EDIT MODE. Note the relatively free format which is acceptable.

```
;
;USER'S GUIDE TO THE MDT 65Ø
;EXAMPLE A1
;
NUM1=$ØØØØ
NUM2=ØØØ1
SUM=ØØØ2
*=$ØØ1Ø
SED
LDA NUM1
CLC
ADC NUM2
STA SUM
WAIT JMP WAIT
.END
```

Additional characteristics of the MDT 650 assembler are discussed very briefly below. For further information, as well as numerous examples, please refer to the CROSS ASSEMBLER MANUAL, MOS Technology, Inc.

Instruction Format. The full set of op codes for the 6502 microprocessor is available on the MDT 650 resident assembler. There is a limitation, however, on the type of expressions allowed. At the present time, only addition (+) and subtraction (−) are evaluated in the expressions. Multiplication (*) and division (/) are not implemented.

Assembler Directives. There are 8 assembler directives:

.BYTE   Reserves and loads one or more bytes of memory.

.WORD   Reserves and loads two bytes of data at a time.

.DBYTE   Is exactly like .WORD except that bytes are stored in high byte, low byte, order. Warning: Files generated by .DBYTE *cannot* be used as indirect addresses.

.PAGE   Causes an immediate jump to the top of a page and may also be used to generate or reset the title printed at the top of the page. In the MDT 650, this is not true. Instead, .PAGE causes 4 line feeds plus a new page heading rather than top of form.

.SKIP   Generates blank lines in a listing.

.OPT   Controls generation of output files, listing and expansion of ASCII strings in .BYTE directives. In the MDT 650 the only useful parameters for the .OPT directive is GEN for the generation of ASCII strings in a .BYTE.

=   = is the EQUATE directive and is used to reserve memory locations, reset the program counter, or assign a value to a symbol.

.END   Signals the physical end of the program. When using the MDT 650 assembler, .END *must* be used as the last line of the TEXT. It is optional in the MOS Technology assembler.

User Comments. Begin with a semicolon ; .

Before assembly can take place on the MDT 650, the user must perform several "housekeeping" tasks using the following keys:

User's Guide to the MDT 650 475

[NUL] Inserts null characters after each carriage return to allow time for the 'carriage' to return to the left side of the paper. TTY Model 33ASR requires no nulls; Model 38 requires at least one null. For other devices, the number of nulls may be determined experimentally by observing if, and when, extraneous characters appear on the "retrace." Enter number of nulls, and press [CR].

[TAB] Allows the user to specify the format of the displayed and printed (black key) outputs. The options are:

    ØØ   Prints the source code exactly as entered by the user.
    1Ø   Prints and displays output in discrete columns.
    Ø1   Permits the user to manually step through the assembly by depressing the SPACE bar.

[SYM] Initializes the symbol table. The user must enter *four (4)* hex characters corresponding to at least the maximum number of symbols in the source program. The MDT responds by displaying the number of symbols requested and an approximation of the number of lines of source code which this table should be able to accommodate.

[SRC] The MDT can be instructed to assemble from several sources and devices such as paper tape, cassette, etc. It is a dual pass assembler, so if external devices are used, instead of internal user side memory, the program must be "put through" twice.
If the program is to be assembled directly from user side memory, two options are available:

    [SRC][M] or [SRC][M][TTY] (if printed Teletype
                                     output is desired)

[ASB] Assembles the source program and creates a new symbol table. The assembler assumes that the program is complete and that no reference is made to symbols which are not defined someplace.

[ASO] Assembles the source program, but does not create an entirely new symbol table. During the assembly process, each *new* label encountered will be added to the symbol table. However, all symbols previously defined will remain and can be referenced in the new program.

Table A.7 presents a detailed key by keystroke illustration of the above ASSEMBLE MODE keys as they apply to Example A1.

TABLE A.7 Suggested procedure to be used to ASSEMBLE the correct TEXT located in the user side memory of the MDT 650. The specific data applies to Example A1 as shown in Table A.6.

Press Keys on MDT Keyboard	See Displayed	Comments
	Almost anything	The TEXT is located in user side memory; it seems "correct"; you are ready to ASSEMBLE.
[RSET] [RSET]	MDT V1	With only one [RSET] additional miscellaneous characters *may* appear. Newer versions of the MDT assembler will require only one [RSET].
[NUL]	NULLS = Ø1	Enter desired number of nulls and press [CR]. We are satisfied with 1 null, so just press [CR].
[CR]	S (blinking)	
[TAB] (black key) [1][Ø][CR]	TAB,SQUISH = XX	Enter 1Ø for TAB yes, SQUISH no.
[SYM] (Do not use [CR])	SYMBOLS?	MDT is asking the user for the number of SYMBOLS. User *must enter four (4)* hex characters.
[Ø][Ø][Ø][F]	S ØØØF Ø22A LINES (S blinks)	Displays the number of symbols requested and an approximation of the number of lines of source code which this symbol table should be able to accommodate. ØØØF is a conservative estimate; we really have only 4 symbols.
Check that TTY switch is in LINE and punch is OFF.		
[SRC] [M] [TTY]	ON	Teletype prints ON; if Teletype prints OFF, then press [TTY] key again. If no Teletype printed output is desired, do not press [TTY] key even once.
[ASB]	MDT displays each line of output, line by line, as printed on the TTY.	Teletype prints PASS1 PASS2 The remainder of the Teletype printed output is shown in Tables A.8, A.9, and A.10.

Examples of the assembler output as printed on a Teletype are shown in Tables A.8, A.9, and A.10 for the three TAB,SQUISH options. The fourth option, TAB,SQUISH = 11 (TAB yes, SQUISH yes) is not possible, of course.

The reader will also note that an ERRORS and WARNINGS count is printed. There are 23 possible errors. Two of these (Symbol Table Overflow and Length Table Overflow) are assembly errors which cause the assembly to stop. The remaining errors are caused by invalid assembly coding and do not cause the assembly to stop. When errors occur,

User's Guide to the MDT 650 477

they are printed in the assembly listing and identified by the following numbers:

1. Undefined Symbol
2. Label Previously Defined
3. Illegal or Missing Op Code
4. Address Not Valid
5. Accumulator Mode Not Allowed
6. N/A (Not Available)
7. Ran Off End of Card
8. Label Doesn't Begin with Alphabetic Character
9. Label Greater Than Six Characters
10. Label or Op Code Contains Nonalphanumeric
11. Forward Reference in Equate
12. Invalid Index - Must be X or Y
13. Invalid Expression
14. Undefined Assembler Directive
15. Invalid Operand for Page Zero Mode
16. Invalid Operand for Absolute Mode
17. Relative Branch Out of Range
18. Illegal Operand Type for This Instruction
19. Out of Bounds on Indirect Addressing
20. A, X, Y, S, and P are Reserved Labels
21. Program Counter Negative - Reset to $\emptyset$
22. Symbol Table Overflow   (Assembler stops!)
23. Length Table Overflow   (Assembler stops!)

The assembler output also provides a SYMBOL TABLE which contains a listing of the symbols and corresponding values, but it is not sorted alphabetically, as in the case of the MOS Technology assembler. There is no option for cross-references, error files, or op code count.

It would be instructive for the reader at this point to compare the results of manual assembly for Example A1 as shown in Table A.1, with the results of MDT 650 assembly as shown in Table A.8, A.9, and A.10.

A.8 MDT 650 IN THE EXECUTE MODE

The purpose of the EXECUTE MODE is to provide the user with the means to execute the computer program instructions that modify data, registers, or memory. The entire program may be executed either at clock speed or the execution may be done one line of code at a time

TABLE A.8 Teletype printed output corresponding to Table A.6. Note that TAB,SQUISH = 1∅ (TAB yes, SQUISH no).

```
ON
PASS1
PASS2

. . . . .PAGE ∅∅1

LINE # LOC      CODE           LINE

∅∅∅1   ∅∅∅∅                   ;
∅∅∅2   ∅∅∅∅                   ;USER'S GUIDE TO THE MDT 65∅
∅∅∅3   ∅∅∅∅                   ;EXAMPLE A1
∅∅∅4   ∅∅∅∅                   ;
∅∅∅5   ∅∅∅∅            NUM1=$ ∅∅∅∅
∅∅∅6   ∅∅∅∅            NUM2=$ ∅∅∅1
∅∅∅7   ∅∅∅∅            SUM=$∅ ∅∅2
∅∅∅8   ∅∅∅∅                   *=$∅∅1∅
∅∅∅9   ∅∅1∅ F8                SED
∅∅1∅   ∅∅11 A5  ∅∅             LDA NUM1
∅∅11   ∅∅13 18                CLC
∅∅12   ∅∅14 65  ∅1             ADC NUM2
∅∅13   ∅∅16 85  ∅2             STA SUM
∅∅14   ∅∅18 4C  18  ∅∅ WAIT    JMP WAIT
∅∅15   ∅∅1B                   .END

ERRORS = ∅∅∅∅   WARNINGS = ∅∅∅∅

SYMBOL TABLE

  SYMBOL  VALUE

  NUM1    ∅∅∅∅
  NUM2    ∅∅∅1
  SUM     ∅∅∅2
  WAIT    ∅∅18
END OF ASSEMBLY
```

TABLE A.9 Teletype printed output corresponding to Table A.6 *except* that TAB,SQUISH = ∅1 (TAB no, SQUISH yes)

```
          ON
          PASS1
          PASS2

          . . . . .PAGE ∅∅∅1

          LINE # LOC    CODE LINE

          ∅∅∅1   ∅∅∅∅   ;
          ∅∅∅2   ∅∅∅∅   ;USER'S GUIDE TO THE MDT 65∅
          ∅∅∅3   ∅∅∅∅   EXAMPLE A1
          ∅∅∅4   ∅∅∅∅   ;
          ∅∅∅5   ∅∅∅∅   NUM1=$∅∅∅∅
          ∅∅∅6   ∅∅∅∅   NUM2=$∅∅∅1
          ∅∅∅7   ∅∅∅∅   SUM=$∅∅∅2
          ∅∅∅8   ∅∅∅∅   *=$∅∅1∅
```

User's Guide to the MDT 650

```
            0009    0010    F8            SED
            0010    0011    A5   00       LDA NUM1
            0011    0013    18            CLC
            0012    0014    65   01       ADC NUM2
            0013    0016    85   02       STA SUM
            0014    0018    4C   18   00  WAIT JMP WAIT
            0015    001B    .END

            ERRORS = 0000  WARNINGS = 0000


            SYMBOL TABLE

             SYMBOL VALUE

             NUM1   0000
             NUM2   0001
             SUM    0002
             WAIT   0018
            END OF ASSEMBLY
```

TABLE A.10 Teletype printed output corresponding to Table A.6 *except* that TAB,SQUISH = 00 (Source code is printed as entered)

```
        ON
        PASS1
        PASS2


         . . . . .PAGE 0001

        LINE # LOC      CODE        LINE

        0001   0000                 ;
        0002   0000                 ;USER'S GUIDE TO THE MDT 650
        0003   0000                 ;EXAMPLE A1
        0004   0000                 ;
        0005   0000                 NUM1=$0000
        0006   0000                 NUM2=$0001
        0007   0000                 SUM=$0002
        0008   0000                 *=$0010
        0009   0010    F8           SED
        0010   0011    A5   00      LDA NUM1
        0011   0013    18           CLC
        0012   0014    65   01      ADC NUM2
        0013   0016    85   02      STA SUM
        0014   0018    4C   18   00 WAIT JMP WAIT
        0015   001B                 .END

        ERRORS = 0000   WARNINGS = 0000


        SYMBOL TABLE

         SYMBOL VALUE

         NUM1   0000
         NUM2   0001
         SUM    0002
         WAIT   0018
        END OF ASSEMBLY
```

(called single-step). Single-step operation may be controlled manually, or it may be automatic with a variable, but user selectable, interval of time between the single-steps.

An additional feature, called TRACE, permits the optional display of the contents of all of the microprocessor registers immediately following the exeuction of each single-step.

Two hardware breakpoints may be implemented to stop the user microprocessor on any desired address when one of four user selectable conditions are satisfied.

The user controls the MDT 650 in the EXECUTE MODE by depressing the following keys:

|BRK| Causes the user processor to stop on a desired address when one of four conditions are satisfied. Two break points are available. Immediately after the BRK key is depressed, the MDT displays

BREAKPOINTS=ØØØØ RN ØØØØ RN

The first two fields ØØØØ RN control Breakpoint 1 as follows:

field ØØØØ   corresponds to the breakpoint address
field R   corresponds to the break condition
field N   allows the user to specify if the processor should stop when a breakpoint is encountered.

How to initialize Breakpoint 1. (Breakpoint 2 is similar.)

Press |BRK| key

Enter 4 hex characters; if the control processor cannot identify them as a valid address, a ? will be displayed and the cursor will return to the high order position. Try again. When successful, cursor will move to the first R.

Enter one of the following to specify the condition which will initiate the breakpoint:

A   specified address is encountered for any reason
I   specified address is accessed for an op code fetch (sync = high)
W   user processor *writes* into the specified address
R   user processor *reads* from the specified address

Cursor now moves to the first N position.

Enter one of the following:

Y   user processor will stop when breakpoint is encountered (Yes)

User's Guide to the MDT 650 481

|N| user processor will not stop but a pulse will be provided on the rear BNC connector each time the breakpoint is encountered. This pulse could, for example, be used to trigger an oscilloscope. (No)

|DSP| Format: |DSP||h||h||h||h| where |h| is a hex character.

Displays the contents of memory location hhhh, the three previous bytes, and the next four bytes. Brackets [ ] frame the current byte and the cursor is positioned at the first character of the current byte in preparation for changing its contents. To alter, type in two hex characters and the display will then be automatically updated one memory position in each position and the cursor will be returned to its original position with the brackets [ ].

|GO| (Must always be followed by a four (4) hex character address of the first instruction of the program to be executed.)

The control processor immediately places the 4 hex character address into FFFC and FFFD (reset vector location) of the user processor memory and then activates reset on the user processor along with all input/output devices. The user processor then executes the instruction loaded at the "GO" address and *stops*. This instruction is then disassembled and displayed. The remainder of the program can be executed by depressing the |RUN| key.

|REG| Displays the contents of all of the user microprocessor registers with this format:

*xxxx Axx Yxx Sxx   NV BDIZC

The registers are in the order: Program Counter, Accumulator, X-register, Y-register, Stack Pointer, and Processor Status.

|RUN| Directs the user processor to execute the program starting at the address currently in the Program Counter register.

|SI| (Single-step Instruction) Executes user program one instruction at a time each time the |SI| key is depressed. This instruction is then disassembled by the control processor and displayed.

The |SI| key may be pressed whether the control processor is stopped or running. If it is stopped, a single instruction is executed. If running, the control processor "snap shots" the instruction being executed at the time, i.e., the current instruction

|SLO| Causes the user processor to execute the user program one instruction at a time with an automatic advance to the next instruction. Immediately after the |SLO| key is depressed, the MDT displays

DELAY COUNT=∅∅ I & Y =

with the cursor located in the high order column of the DELAY COUNT field ∅∅. Enter a delay count in the range of 3∅ to F∅. The lower number will cause a rapid execution (about 1 sec/step) and the higher number will cause a *very* slow execution (about 60 sec/step).

After the delay count is entered, a Y will appear to the right of the I & R field. If the user enters a Y (Yes), the MDT will print the contents of the user processor registers after each instruction execution. Entering a N (No) will direct the MDT to print only the instructions (disassembled) but not the register contents.

Warning: The slow run mode does not automatically provide for setting the program counter to the desired starting point.

|TTY| (It is optional to also have the Teletype print all of the output while executing the program in either the single-step |SI| or the slow |SLO| modes.)

The |TTY| key *must* be depressed before depressing the |SLO| key. Execution speed will be determined by the time required by the Teletype to print the results, so it is recommended that a delay count of approximately 1∅ be entered.

The |TTY| key is a "toggle switch" type, that is, press once for ON, press again for OFF, press again for ON, etc.

|STP| "Stops" the user processor. This is one of two ways to stop the execution of programs in the user processor. The other way is to use breakpoints.

Detailed key by keystroke illustrations of the above keys in the EXECUTE MODE are provided in the following Tables:

User's Guide to the MDT 650   483

TABLE A.11   Using the [RUN] key. Also [DSP], [M+1], [M+8], [REG], and [STP] keys.
TABLE A.11a Using the [GO] key.
TABLE A.12   Using the [SI] key.
TABLE A.13   Using the [SLO] key. (With registers displayed)
TABLE A.14   Using the breakpoint [BRK] key.

TABLE A.11   Suggested procedure for executing the program associated with Example A1 in the EXECUTE MODE using the [RUN] key. We are adding 9 + 6 in the decimal mode.

Press Keys on MDT Keyboard	See Displayed	Comments
[RSET]	MDT V1	Source program for Example A1 has been assembled.
[DSP][∅][∅][1][∅]	∅∅1∅ xx xx xx [F8] A5 ∅∅ 18 65	Contents of memory location ∅∅1∅ are shown in [ ] See Sec. A.8 for more detail on the display format. At this point the reader should compare the contents
[M+1]	∅∅11 xx xx F8 [A5] ∅∅ 18 65 ∅1	of memory location ∅∅1∅ through ∅∅1A with Table
[M+8]	∅∅19 85 ∅2 4C [18] ∅∅ xx xx xx	A.8 and verify that the correct op codes are stored.
[CR]	S (blinking)	Terminates this display mode.
[DSP][∅][∅][∅][∅]	∅∅∅∅ xx xx xx [xx] xx xx xx xx	Contents of memory location ∅∅∅∅ are shown in [ ].
[∅][9]	∅∅∅1 xx xx ∅9 [xx] xx xx xx xx	Loaded ∅9 for NUM1 into memory location ∅∅∅∅ and display automatically incremented 1 memory location.
[∅][6]	∅∅∅2 xx ∅9 ∅6 [xx] xx xx xx xx	Loaded ∅6 for NUM2 into memory location ∅∅∅1.
[∅][∅]	∅∅∅3 ∅9 ∅6 ∅∅ [xx] xx xx xx xx	Cleared the SUM memory location to zero.
[CR]	S (blinking)	Terminates this display mode.
[REG]	*xxxx Axx Xxx Yxx Sxx xxxxxx	Displays contents of Program Counter, Accumulator, X-register, Y-register, Stack Pointer, and Status
[∅][∅][1][∅]	*∅∅1∅ Axx Xxx Yxx Sxx xxxxxx	Register, in this order. We have just loaded the starting address ∅∅1∅ of our program into the PC.
[CR]	S (blinking)	Terminates this register display mode.
[RUN]	R (blinking)	Example A1 program is executing.
[STP]	∅∅18 WAIT JMP WAIT	Displays last instruction executed.
[CR]	(S and ? blinking alternately)	Terminates this display mode.
[REG]	*∅∅18 A15 Xxx Yxx Sxx xxxDxx	As expected: Program Counter = ∅∅18 and the contents of the Accumulator are 15 (SUM = 9+6 = 15). D indicates we are in the decimal mode.
[CR]		
[DSP][∅][∅][∅][∅]	∅∅∅∅ xx xx xx [∅9] ∅6 15 xx xx	Contents of NUM1, NUM2, and SUM are displayed corresponding to memory locations ∅∅∅∅, ∅∅∅1, and ∅∅∅2.
[CR]		

TABLE A.11a Procedure for executing the program associated with Example A.1 in the EXECUTE MODE using the [GO] key.

Press Keys on MDT Keyboard	See Displayed on MDT	Comments
	With the memory allocation shown in Figure A.1, the [GO] key can not be used because the control processor immediately places the 4 hex characters into user side memory locations FFFC and FFFD. (Figure A.1 shows FFFC and FFFD in user memory space where no actual hardware RAM memory was allocated.)	
	The user processor then executes the instruction loaded in the [GO] address and "stops." The instruction is then disassembled and displayed.	
	The remainder of the program can be executed by depressing the [RUN] key as in Table A.11.	
	To demonstrate this would require a relocation of memory shown in Figure A.1 and will not be done here because of the similarity with just using the [REG] and [RUN] keys.	

TABLE A.12 Suggested procedure for executing the program associated with Example A1 in the EXECUTE MODE using the [SI] key. Again, we are adding 9 + 6 in the decimal mode. To avoid duplication, we will enter Table A.11 at the [CR] line just above the [RUN] key line and use the [SI] key instead.

Press Keys on MDT Keyboard	See Displayed on MDT (Teletype printed output, optional)			Comments
[CR]	S (blinking)	TOP PORTION OF TABLE A.11		Terminates current display mode.
[RUN]	R (blinking)			Example A1 program is executing.
	⋮			
[SI]	ØØ10.	SED		First line of code was executed, disassembled, and displayed. Refer to Table A.8.
[SI]	ØØ11.	LDA NUM1	Ø9	Same for the second line of code.
[SI]	ØØ13.	CLC		Same for the third line of code.
[SI]	ØØ14.	ADC NUM2	Ø6	Same for the fourth line of code.
[SI]	ØØ16.	STA SUM	15	Same for the fifth line of code.
[SI]	ØØ18. WAIT	JMP WAIT		Same for the sixth line of code.
[SI]	ØØ18. WAIT	JMP WAIT		We are now in the jump to itself loop and will continue to do this each time SI is pressed.
[SI]	ØØ18. WAIT	JMP WAIT		

User's Guide to the MDT 650   485

[SI]	0018. WAIT JMP WAIT	
[CR]	(S and ? blinking alternately)	
[REG]	*0018 A15 Xxx Yxx Sxx xxxDxx	As expected, identical to the corresponding line in Table A.11.
[CR]		
[DSP]	0000 xx xx xx [09] 06 15 xx xx	Again, identical to the corresponding line in Table A.11.
[CR]		Terminates current display mode.

TABLE A.13 Suggested procedure for executing the program associated with Example A1 in the EXECUTE MODE using the SLO key. Again, we are adding 9 + 6 in the decimal mode. To avoid duplication, we will enter Table A.11 at the CR line just above the RUN key and use the SLO key instead of the RUN key.

Press Keys on MDT Keyboard	See Displayed on MDT (Teletype printed output, optional)	Comments
[CR]	S (blinking) TOP PORTION OF TABLE A.11	Terminates current display mode.
~~[RUN]~~	~~R (blinking)~~	~~Example A1 program is executing.~~
	⋮	
[SLO]	DELAY COUNT=00 I&R=	Enter DELAY COUNT in the range of 30 to F0. 30 provides about 1 sec./step; F0 provides about 30 sec./step.
[3][0]	DELAY COUNT=30 I&R=Y (Y blinks)	We wish to display registers; so type [Y] for YES.
[Y]	0010. SED	Be patient; wait for 1 to 30 seconds.
	*0011 A00 Xxx Yxx Sxx xx xDxxx	Accumulator contents are 00; D implies decimal mode. Now, new lines will appear in the display at
	0011. LDA NUM1 09	the rate of approximately 1 sec./line.
	*0013 A09 Xxx Yxx Sxx xx xDxxx	Accumulator loaded with 09.
	0013. CLC	
	*0014 A09 Xxx Yxx Sxx xx xDxxx	Carry flag was not set previously so effect of CLC carry is not apparent.
	0014. ADC NUM2 06	
	*0016 A15 Xxx Yxx Sxx xx xDxxx	Accumulator contents are 15, the sum of 9 + 6.
	0016. STA SUM 15	
	*0018 A15 Xxx Yxx Sxx xx xDxxx	Accumulator contents remain 15.
	0018.WAIT JMP WAIT	
	*0018 A15 Xxx Yxx Sxx xx xDxxx	
	0018.WAIT JMP WAIT	We are now quite obviously in the jump to itself loop.
	*0018 A15 Xxx Yxx Sxx xx xDxxx	
[STP]	0018.WAIT JMP WAIT	Display remains constant.

TABLE A.14 Suggested procedure for adding a breakpoint to Table A.13 so that when a memory location ∅∅18 is encountered for any reason, the user processor will "stop."

Press Keys on MDT Keyboard	See Displayed on MDT (Teletype printed output optional)	Comments
	⋮	
[BRK]	BREAKPOINTS=∅∅∅∅ RN ∅∅∅∅ RN	Breakpoints may be set anytime prior to execution with the [SLO], [SI] or [RUN] keys.
[∅][∅][1][8]	BREAKPOINTS=∅∅18 AN ∅∅∅∅ RN	R blinks asking for condition A, I, W, or R? Enter A for the "any reason" condition.
[A] [CR]	BREAKPOINTS=∅∅18 AN ∅∅∅∅ RN	N blinks asking for Yes or No. Enter [Y] for Yes. Terminates breakpoint entry mode. We did not wish to activate the second breakpoint.
[TTY]	ON	Activates the Teletype.
	⋮	
[SLO]	DELAY COUNT=∅∅ I&R=	Enter DELAY COUNT in the range of 3∅ to F∅. 3∅ provides about 1 sec./step; F∅ provides about 60 sec./step.
[3][∅]	DELAY COUNT=3∅ I&R=Y (Y blinks)	We wish to display registers; so type [Y] for Yes.
[Y]	∅∅1∅. SED	Be patient; wait for 1 to 30 seconds.
	*∅∅11 A∅∅ Xxx Yxx Sxx xx xDxxx	Accumulator contents are ∅∅; D implies decimal; Now, new lines will appear in the display at the rate of approximately 1 sec./line.
	∅∅11. LDA NUM1 ∅9	
	*∅∅13 A∅9 Xxx Yxx Sxx xx xDxxx	Accumulator loaded with ∅9.
	∅∅13. CLC	
	*∅∅14 A∅9 Xxx Yxx Sxx xx xDxxx	Carry flag was not set previously so effect of CLC carry is not apparent.
	∅∅14. ADC NUM2 ∅6	
	*∅∅16. A15 Xxx Yxx Sxx xx xDxxx	Accumulator contents are 15, the sum of 9 + 6.
	∅∅16. STA SUM 15	
	*∅∅18 A15 Xxx Yxx Sxx xx xDxxx	Accumulator contents remain 15.
	∅∅18.WAIT JMP WAIT	User processor "stopped" by the breakpoint.

A.9 MDT 650 IN THE OUTPUT MODE

The MDT 650 is said to be in the OUTPUT MODE when peripheral devices, such as a Teletype or a Cathode Ray Tube (CRT) Terminal, are connected and activated. The primary concern here will be a Teletype with a paper tape punch/reader unit. The punched paper tape copy of the TEXT may be reentered into the MDT at some later time for reassembly and execution. The punched paper tape copy of the object code may be used to program a PROM or be read into a microcomputer memory, such as the KIM-1 microcomputer. It is also possible to obtain a printed copy of the output during single-step and slow modes

User's Guide to the MDT 650   487

of execution, but because of the slow printing speed of the Teletype, this is not done very often.

The punched paper tape copy of the object code cannot be reentered into the MDT, but this is not a disadvantage because the TEXT may be assembled in just a few seconds (provided the Teletype is not energized).

The user controls the MDT 650 by depressing the following keys:

| DMP | Directs the MDT to output the object code with a format to include the number of bytes per record, the number of records, and the checksums. Immediately after the DMP key is depressed, the MDT displays

DUMP SSSS EEEE

The SSSS refers to the starting address of the object code dump. The EEEE refers to the ending address of the object code dump. The Teletype is automatically energized.

| LST | Directs the MDT to output the TEXT (including comments). The Teletype is automatically energized.

Warning: Depress the | TOP | key in the EDIT MODE if a copy of the entire TEXT is desired.

Detailed key by keystroke illustrations of the use of the above keys in the OUTPUT MODE are provided in the following Tables:

TABLES A.15 Using the LST key to output a printed and a and A.15a punched paper tape copy of the TEXT.

TABLE A.16 Using the DMP key to output a printed and a punched paper tape copy of the object code.

TABLE A.15 Suggested procedure to punch source code (TEXT including comments) on a paper tape. This paper tape may be read back into the MDT 650 via a Teletype which has a paper tape reader unit.

Press Keys on MDT Keyboard	*See Displayed*	*Comments*
With the TTY switch in LOCAL prepare a paper tape leader.[1]	Almost anything	The TEXT resides in the MDT 650 memory need not have taken place.
Rotate the TTY switch to LINE; depress the ON punch button.		
|RSET| |RTE|		Reset and return to TEXT editor mode.
|TOP|		Output is to begin at the top of TEXT.

488   *Microcomputer Systems Principles*

[LST][TTY] [2]   MDT displays each line of output, line by line, as printed on the TTY.   The TTY is automatically energized when the [TTY] key is depressed.

The last line of output remains on the MDT display.

Rotate the TTY switch to LOCAL. Punch about 6 rubouts to protect the end of the paper tape.   Both the actual TTY punched paper tape and the TTY printed outputs are shown in Table A.15a.

Footnotes: 1. It is suggested that a suitable paper tape leader be prepared with the usual warnings about extraneous characters (including nonprint characters, such as line feed or carriage returns) appearing at the beginning of the tape. Even a blank leader (only sprocket holes) is not acceptable and is usually indicated by a series of @@@@@@s displayed on the MDT display. For the inexperienced user, the best procedure is to punch a number of rubouts.
2. [LST][K] is another option.

TABLE A.15a Teletype printed output and punch paper tape generated by TABLE A.15 for the TEXT of Example A1.

```
;
;USER'S GUIDE TO THE MDT 650
;EXAMPLE A1
;
NUM1=$0000
NUM2=$0001
SUM=$0002
*=$0010
SED
LDA NUM1
CLC
ADC NUM2
STA SUM
WAIT JMP WAIT
.END
```

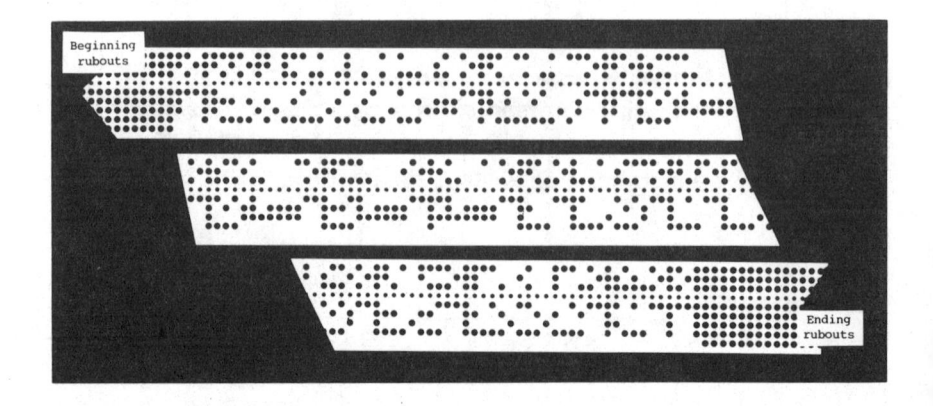

User's Guide to the MDT 650   489

TABLE A.16   Procedure to punch object (machine) code on a paper tape. This paper tape could be used to program a PROM or it could be entered into a microcomputer memory, such as the KIM-1 microcomputer, using a Teletype paper tape reader.

Press Keys on MDT Keyboard	See Displayed	Comments
With the TTY switch in LOCAL prepare a paper tape leader.	Almost anything	The TEXT has been assembled. Execution need not have taken place.
Rotate the TTY switch to LINE; depress the ON punch button.		
[RSET]	MDT V1	
[DMP]	DUMP SSSS EEEE	The MDT is asking for the starting and ending addresses of the object code which the user wishes to punch on paper tape.
[Ø][Ø][1][Ø][Ø][Ø][1][B]	MDT displays each line of output, line by line, as printed on the Teletype.	The starting and ending addresses may be obtained from any of the assembled outputs, such as TABLE A.8. The Teletype is automatically energized when the last character of SSSS EEEE is entered.
	The last line of output remains on the MDT display.	
Teletype Printed Output	;ØBØØ1ØF8A5ØØ1865Ø185Ø24C18ØØØ321 ;ØØØØØ1ØØØ1	

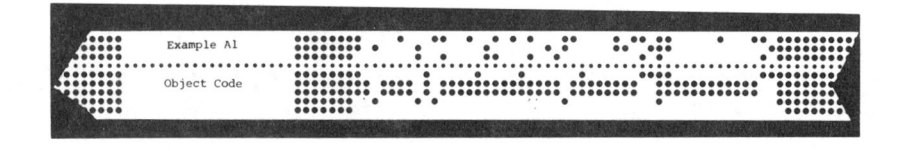

A.10 IN CASE OF DIFFICULTY!

TABLE A.17   A partial list of difficulties which have been noted and may be of some assistance to the user of the MDT 650

SYMPTOMS	WHAT TO DO
TEXT appears to be read in normally from the Teletype but in the EDIT MODE can not be found and appears not to have been stored.	Locate and *&$#@! the last user who relocated the two 4K RAMs from the locations shown on the memory map shown in Figure A.1 and did not tag the MDT to notify other users.

	Each 4K RAM board has a 4 section DIP switch. One board should have all 4 sections *not* OPEN; the other board should have A - OPEN and B, C, D *not* OPEN.
The RSET key on the keyboard is depressed but the display remains blank.	Lift the cover of the MDT and press the super reset *red* button. The black button next to it is essentially the same as the RSET key on the keyboard. Press both, if you wish.
During the initial portion of the LOAD MODE from the Teletype a series of @@@@s are displayed.	An illegal character is punched on the paper tape leader. The most typical error is a nonprinting character such as a carriage return or line feed. Verify the tape contents with the Teletype in LOCAL and print the contents of the paper tape on the Teletype. Do not read sprocket holes.
During the LOAD MODE from Teletype, characters on the MDT display do not correspond with those on the tape, and many are even nonASCII.	Remove the cover of the MDT and note the red *toggle* switch on the top of the rightmost board. For a Teletype, it should be in the forward position (110 baud) and not toward the rear (the 300 baud position).

B

OPERATING PRINCIPLES OF THE KIM-1 MONITOR AND ON-BOARD I/O HARDWARE

B.1 INTRODUCTION

In Chapter 8, detailed methods for operating the KIM-1 system and associated peripheral units are described. This appendix will present some of the principles underlying these methods of operation. There are two principal reasons for such a presentation. First, the KIM-1 is an excellent example of a microprocessor-based system, and the underlying design principles present a useful case study for one who aspires to do such design himself. Second, the KIM-1 user will find an understanding of these principles very helpful in actual operation. For example, the user who wishes to use the on-board peripherals, such as the keyboard and the display for nonmonitor functions, will find an understanding of monitor subroutines an invaluable aid.

Figure 4.2-1 is a flow chart of the KIM-1 monitor program. It will serve as an important reference for most of the discussion in this Appendix.

Another important reference is the KIM-1 monitor listing itself, which is included herein as Section B.8.

B.2 SINGLE STEP OPERATION OF THE KIM MICROCOMPUTER

The normal mode of operation for any digital computer, including the KIM, is that in which instructions are executed sequentially at high speed. Automatic high-speed sequencing accounts for most of the unique capability of such systems. It is often desirable, however, to execute a sequence of instructions at manual speed, either to examine step-by-step program execution and thereby verify program integrity, or to diagnose reasons for program malfunction, i.e., to perform "debugging." The KIM system permits manual sequencing via the keyboard switch labeled SST (single step).

The 6502 CPU chip used in the KIM system has several built-in features which make single-step operation convenient to perform. One such feature is the control output designated as *SYNC*. The 6502 produces a pulse from this terminal during each machine cycle which, if completed, constitutes the fetch of an instruction op code from memory. Since such a cycle signals the end of an instruction execution, the ability to stop the computer when SYNC occurs would accomplish the single-step operation desired (assuming, of course, that the system can be restarted).

One other feature of the 6502 which could be used to accomplish single-step operation is the RDY (READY) control input. If, during the PHASE ONE clock of any machine cycle when a memory read is being performed, the RDY input is pulled low, the completion of the cycle will be inhibited at PHASE TWO clock time. (A memory write cycle will not be inhibited, but the subsequent read cycle will be.) The principal use of the RDY control is in managing transfers between the CPU and slow memory or I/O devices which may not respond to read requests with sufficient speed to keep up with the 6502 clock. Such devices can, by properly energizing the RDY input, force the CPU to wait until it is ready to deliver the requested data. A second use of this input is implemented by inverting and feeding back the SYNC pulse to the RDY input. This will cause the system to stop each time a SYNC pulse occurs. Therefore the system stops after the execution of each instruction. (Actually the SYNC pulse must be stored in a separate flip-flop. The flip-flop will inhibit system operation until it is cleared, at which time the system will fetch and execute the next instruction. Refer to Section 3.1, page 124, of the MOS HARDWARE MANUAL, reference 2, for a detailed description of one mechanization of this scheme.)

The KIM system does not use the RDY control to achieve single-step operation. Recall that one of the principal motivations for establishing single-step operation was to permit a leisurely examination of the result of executing each instruction. The KIM monitor affords a powerful mechanism for performing such an examination because the KIM system implements a procedure whereby, after each step of the program under study is executed, system control is passed back to this

Operating Principles of the KIM-1 Monitor and On-Board I/O Hardware   **493**

monitor. The monitor is then used to examine register contents, data values, etc. To understand the actual mechanization built into the KIM system, refer to Figure B.1. Gate U26, a two-input NAND gate, has as its inputs SYNC from the 6502 and a signal labeled K7. For the time being, assume that K7 is high or at the "1" level. If the single-step switch SST is closed, the occurrence of SYNC will pull the NMI input low, constituting a nonmaskable interrupt input to the 6502. Service of this interrupt is in the form of execution of the monitor routine which lights the display and scans the keyboard. This mode reflects the transfer of control to the monitor as described above. Pushing the GO key on the keyboard will cause other monitor routines (see the discussion of the KIM keyboard below) to be called. These routines will fetch the next user instruction, giving the desired result of stepping through one more step. At this point the process will be repeated.

    The perceptive reader will have detected a logical flaw in the above operation. He will ask, "Since the execution of the monitor program is conceptually identical to the execution of the user program, why doesn't the system halt after the execution of each step in the monitor program?" This is the point where the role of the K7 signal must be considered. Examination of the logic diagram will confirm that the K7 signal is produced when an address in *page 7* (address range 1C∅∅ to 1CFF) is present on the KIM address bus. Since the 74145 decoder which generates K7 produces active-low outputs, when such an address is present, the K7 signal is at a low level. Thus the NAND gate driving the NMI input will not produce its active low output when a page 7 address is on the address bus, even though the SYNC signal denoting completion of instruction execution is generated. Since the keyboard/display monitor is located in page 7, it will be executed in uninterrupted fashion. This also has the effect of preventing one from stepping through any of the monitor routines located in page 7.

    One final point about single-step operation in the KIM should be mentioned. As discussed more fully in Section B.3 on RESET and STOP operation in the KIM, proper execution of the STOP routine in response to an NMI request demands that the user, as a necessary step in system initialization, load the proper interrupt vectors into the system. Since single-step operation depends on this routine, such loading is necessary to properly enable this mode of operation. In plain English, this means that locations 17FA and 17FB must be loaded with address 1C∅∅, the beginning location of the STOP monitor routine.

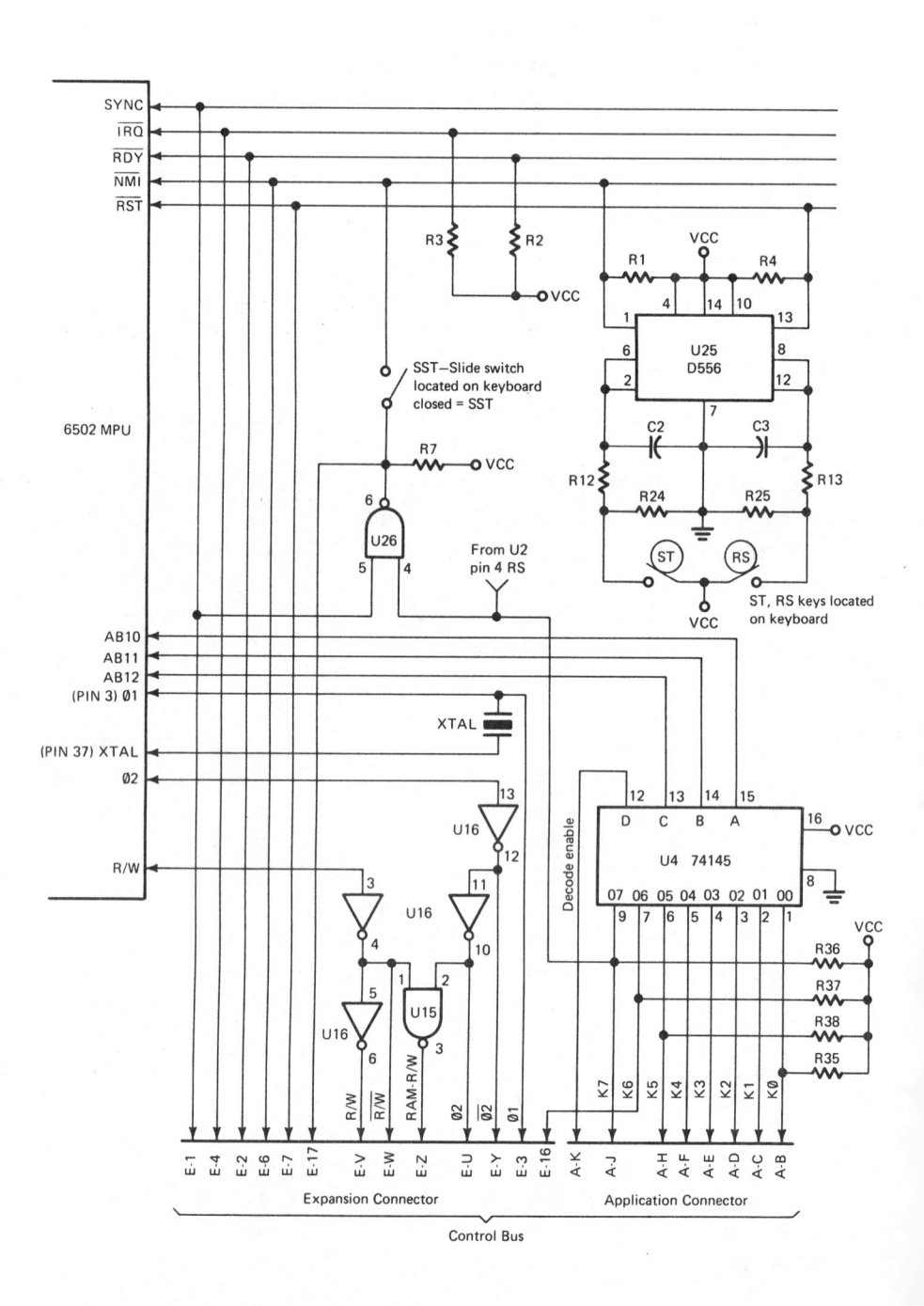

Figure B.1 KIM-1 control and timing circuitry

Operating Principles of the KIM-1 Monitor and On-Board I/O Hardware **495**

B.3 RESET AND STOP OPERATIONS

These two operations bear considerable similarity to one another and will therefore be discussed together. Each of them is initiated by depressing a keyboard key. Referring to the logic diagram of Figure B.1 it may be observed that pushing the ST (STOP) key introduces a positive-going voltage onto pins 2 and 6 of U25, a dual timer. This circuit's characteristics are such that this input will pro$\underline{\text{duc}}$e a negative-going transition at pin 1, which is delivered to the $\overline{\text{NMI}}$ input of the CPU. Before examining the effect of this input, let us digress and point out the principal function of the dual timer circuit. Its characteristics are such that, even if the ST keystroke manifests *switch bounce* (which is typically the case), the timer output will respond only to the *initial positive transition* at its inputs, effectively debouncing the switch.

Let us return now to $\underline{\text{an}}$ examination of the sequence of events which occur when the $\overline{\text{NMI}}$ input is energized. This constitutes a *nonmaskable interrupt* request and results in a somewhat feverish interval of activity by the CPU. The steps which constitute this activity are:

1. When the NMI request arrives, the current contents of the program counter and the status (P) register are pushed onto the system stack. This allows return to the interrupted routine when the interrupt has been serviced.
2. The contents of memory locations 1FFA and 1$\underline{\text{F}}$FB are fetched from memory and placed in the program counter. This is an automatic step performed by the 6502 hardware in response to the NMI request. Locations 1FFA and 1FFB are ROM locations, which collectively contain the address 1C1C. (The actual addresses are FFFA and FFFB, but, in the KIM-1, the high-order three address bits are ignored in an unexpanded system.)
3. Normal processor activity resumes. This activity consists of placing the program counter contents on the address bus and performing a memory read. The contents of location 1C1C are thus fetched as an instruction op code.
4. Location 1C1C, also a ROM location, contains 6C, a *jump indirect* op code. The next two locations, 1C1D and 1C1E, are thus accessed by the CPU, producing address 17FA, also preprogrammed in ROM. The nature of the jump indirect instruction is such that this address (along with the next consecutive location 17FB) contains the actual address of the next instruction to be executed. Since 17FA and 17FB are RAM locations,

they must be previously loaded by the system user with the address of the first step in the NMI service routine he wishes to call. The STOP routine provided with the KIM monitor begins at location 1C∅∅, and, if this is the desired routine, that value should have been loaded into 17FA and 17FB during system initialization.
5. The CPU begins execution of the STOP routine. Its details will not be discussed, but it generally consists of a continuous scan of the keyboard combined with a continuous display of the last memory location referenced by the user program along with the data stored at that location. (See the monitor listing of Section B.8 for details.)

This rather lengthy list of activities can be confusing and some care is necessary to sort out some of the terminology encountered. The various elements of 6502 literature refer to the contents of addresses FFFA and FFFB (which translate into 1FFA and 1FFB in limited address space of the unexpanded KIM) collectively as an *interrupt vector*, since they point into memory toward the requested service routine. In the particular case of the KIM, however, the desire to permit the system user to choose not only the monitor STOP routine but any other routine of his choosing as a response to an NMI request results in several of the extra steps outlined above. Since the 17FA, 17FB locations contain the actual address of the first location of the desired service routine, the contents of these locations are referred to in the KIM literature as the NMI interrupt vectors.

The RST (RESET) key on the KIM results in a sequence of activity which closely resembles that discussed above. The other half of the U25 dual timer debounces the switch, applying a request input to the $\overline{\text{RST}}$ input of the 6502. Once again, a sequence of activity ensues, involving fetching interrupt vectors from locations 1FFC and 1FFD. These locations contain the address 1C22, which, when sent to memory as a request for op code, yields not a jump indirect op code, but the actual first instruction in the RESET routine, which is a system initialization routine.

It is interesting to reflect on the fundamental difference between the NMI and RST responses to service requests. The most obvious difference is that the user has some flexibility in the use of the NMI routine, since by loading interrupt vectors of his choice into the appropriate RAM locations, he can control the response to such requests. It may seem that this flexibility is missing relative to the RST routine because the KIM designers saw no need for substitution of a user-

Operating Principles of the KIM-1 Monitor and On-Board I/O Hardware 497

defined response in place of the one provided by the system monitor. The actual reason for the difference is, however, more fundamental. Note that the resources of the monitor program must be used to load the appropriate interrupt vectors into the NMI locations. In order to call upon these resources, the sytem must enter a state in which a scan of the keyboard is performed. Once this state is entered, the keys can be used to call monitor routines to perform desired activities. Placing the system into this state requires the use of the system initialization routine. If this routine also depended upon the preloading of interrupt vectors, note that, somewhat embarrassingly, there would be no way to perform this preloading. The fixed interrupt vectors for RESET are therefore necessary in order to initiate proper system activity. This general procedure is one of several types most often described as *bootstrap procedures*.

B.4 OPERATION OF THE KIM KEYBOARD AND DISPLAY

Chapter 8 describes in some detail the operational manner in which the user can interact with the KIM system via the keyboard and display units. Beyond considerations of simply being able to operate the KIM system, however, it is of considerable educational value to examine in some detail the methods by which these system elements are interfaced to the KIM system, because they constitute excellent examples of peripheral units and their interface to a microprocessor system.

As the management of the display and keyboard interfaces is discussed, reference will be made to the routines which comprise the KIM operating system. The reader will find it useful to refer to the listing of these programs (included in Section B.8) as the discussion proceeds, not only to understand the actual KIM software mechanization, but also to learn by example how such software is written. The KIM designers achieved considerable efficiency by sharing one I/O port for the dual functions of display output and keyboard input and by sharing keyboard scan routines between manual keyboard and Teletype interfaces. This achievement of efficiency is, unfortunately, at the expense of simplicity of understanding in some cases, particularly to one who is examining such methods for the first time. An attempt will be made in this discussion to avoid some of the detail of the implementation which tends to obscure a basic understanding of the system. For example, in the discussion, the display drive mechanization will be separated from the keyboard scan mechanization.

B.4.1 Display Drive in the KIM System

Figure B.2 shows the principal elements in the display drive system. The diagram is simplified by omitting the electrical interface elements. The logical information flow is correct. The peripheral interface adaptor labeled 6530-002 is the key I/O element in this system. The display itself consists of six seven-segment display elements and, as configured, may conveniently be thought of as a two-dimensional array. Control over which *character* is displayed is provided by the A port of the 6530. Lines PA$\emptyset$ through PA6 are routed (through display drivers not shown in the diagram) to the seven LED segments (A through G, as shown in the figure) of each display unit. The other display selection dimension is activated by a 74145 BCD decoder as shown. The active output of this decoder (active-low) is a function of the four-bit code at the ABCD inputs. Any one of 10 binary codes (regular BCD decoding) produces an output from one of the decoder terminals. Thus, to drive a particular display element, the CPU must place the appropriate four-bit code in the SBD (Side B Data Register) positions 1 through 4. If these 4 bit positions are programmed as outputs (by appropriate loading of the Port B Data Register, PBDD), then this code is present on the PB1 through PB4 lines, and will appropriately drive the display array.

Output positions $\emptyset$ through 3 of the decoder of Figure 4.3 are not used in the display drive. They function as part of the keyboard scan system and as part of the Teletype/keyboard selection control.

Table B.1 indicates the data which must be loaded into the B port Data Register (SBD) to appropriately select any one of the display elements.

TABLE B.1 KIM Display Character Position Selection Codes

To Select Character Position (Left-to-Right)	Active Decoder Output Must Be	Decoder Inputs Must Be D C B A	Port B Data Register Contents Must Be* (In Hex)
1	4	$\emptyset$ 1 $\emptyset$ $\emptyset$	$\emptyset$8
2	5	$\emptyset$ 1 $\emptyset$ 1	$\emptyset$A
3	6	$\emptyset$ 1 1 $\emptyset$	$\emptyset$C
4	7	$\emptyset$ 1 1 1	$\emptyset$E
5	8	1 $\emptyset$ $\emptyset$ $\emptyset$	1$\emptyset$
6	9	1 $\emptyset$ $\emptyset$ 1	12

Operating Principles of the KIM-1 Monitor and On-Board I/O Hardware

*Since only bits 1 through 4 of the Port B data register affect the decoder, there are a number of other hex values which could be used in each of these postions. The only requirement is that bits 1 through 4 must be identical to the pattern for the values shown.

Since only output positions 1 through 4 affect the display, there are a number of redundant combinations which may be used. The hex values shown in the table are those which assume that ∅s are to be used in output positions ∅, 5, 6, and 7. (Actually, the 6530-002 has no PB6 output.) In the KIM, these other outputs are used for other interfacing functions and it may be that in some cases some value other than ∅ might be desired.

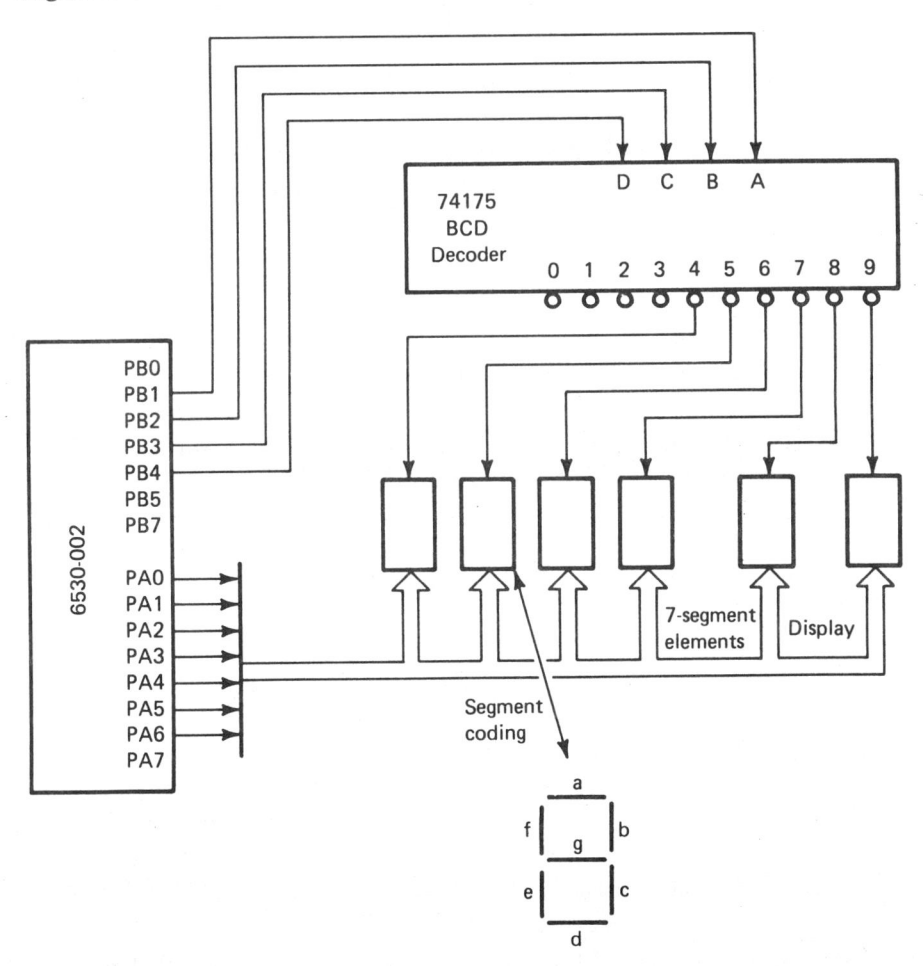

Figure B.2 Simplified block diagram of KIM-1 display drive interface

Table B.2 is a listing of some of the possible 128 characters which can be produced by a seven-segment display. In each case, the ABCDEFG element combination which produces the character is expressed in terms of the hex value which, when produced by the PA∅-6 output bus, will light the appropriate segments. Once again, since the PA7 output does not participate in the display drive, it is assigned the value ∅ in the table. Since this terminal is used by the KIM system as a serial Teletype input port, its actual output assignment is immaterial.

In summary, to display a desired character in one of the display positions, the following steps must be performed:

1. Program the peripheral Data Direction Registers PADD and PBDD to configure PA∅-6 and PB1-4 as outputs.
2. Load the B side Data Register (SBD) with a value appropriate for the selection of the desired display element, as given in Table B.1.
3. Load the A side Data Register (SAD) with a value appropriate to the desired character, as given by Table B.2.

A program for performing the above steps is quite simple to write, but is very limited in application, since only one display position is affected by it. A more complex program is used by the KIM monitor, and is designated as SCAND (for Scan Display).

B.4.2 Scand, The KIM Display Drive Program

This program is written as a subroutine and begins on line 1057, page 25, of the KIM monitor listing (Section B.8). The first three steps of the program fetch a byte (two characters) to be displayed and stored in INH, the location reserved for the high byte of the input buffer. The next two steps program the A side of the 6530 port as an output. Next index register X is loaded with ∅9 to serve as a pointer to the rightmost digit position of the display. Index register Y is loaded with ∅3 preparatory to counting the number of characters to be displayed (6 characters, three bytes). Then routine SCAND1 is entered.

SCAND1 starts by fetching the first byte to be displayed, shifts it right four positions to isolate a single character, and then jumps to subroutine CONVD (Convert Display) which starts at line 1085. CONVD searches a conversion table (line 1202) similar in function to Table B.2. It places the appropriate data value found in the table on the PA∅-6 outputs, moves the preset value of index register X (set to ∅9 previously) to SBD, selecting the rightmost digit position of the display, and exe-

TABLE B.2 KIM Display Character Codes

Character	Symbol Displayed	Segments Lit	Hex Code
1		BC	∅6
2		ABDEG	5B
3		ABCDG	4F
4		BCFG	66
5		ACDGF	6D
6		ACDEFG	7D
7		ABC	∅7
8		ABCDEFG	7F
9		ABCDFG	6F
∅		ABCDEF	3F
A		ABCEFG	77
B		CDEFG	7C
C		ADEF	39
D		BCDEG	5E
E		ADEFG	79
F		AEFG	71
G		?	?
H		BCEFG	76
I		BC	∅6
J		BCDE	1E
K		?	?
L		DEF	38
M		?	?
N		?	?
O		CDEG	5C
P		ABEFG	73
Q		?	?
R		EG	5∅
S		ACDFG	6D
T		EFG	7∅
U		CDE	1C
V		?	?
W		?	?
X		?	?
Y		BEFG	72
Z		?	?

cutes a delay routine which lights the display for 500 instruction cycles. CONVD finally increments index X by 2 (to prepare a pointer to the next leftmost digit position the next time around the loop), restores the value in index register Y, and returns to the calling routine SCAND1. This routine refetches the same byte, masks out the most significant 4 bits to isolate the *other* character in the byte and calls CONVD again to display the second character. Upon return, index Y is decremented, and, if it is not zero, (zero signifies that all characters have been displayed) routine SCAND1 is reentered to display the next two characters.

When all six characters have been displayed, signified by Y having been decremented to ∅, the display is turned off by forcing SBD bits 1 through 4 to ∅, so that no display element is selected. Peripheral port A is next reconfigured as an input and a jump to AK (get any key) is performed, initiating a scan of the keyboard.

B.4.3 Operation of the KIM Keyboard

The keyboard mounted on the KIM circuit board, like the display, is in a very real sense nothing more than a peripheral unit which interacts with the CPU via the 6530-002 peripheral interface unit. The function of the various keys in providing system control will not be discussed here because Chapter 8 covers this in great detail. However, a somewhat detailed examination of the control of this keyboard will be made, to promote understanding of the more general problem of peripheral control, in this case, the control of an input device.

Figure B.3 is a simplified logic diagram which illustrates the principal components which are involved in KIM keyboard interaction. The 74145 decoder is the same one previously discussed relative to display management. In that case the active decoder outputs were those labeled 4 through 9, but, as mentioned there, outputs ∅ through 3 are the important ones in connection with keyboard interaction. Actually, output 3 is reserved for use as an indicator that the Teletype (rather than the KIM keyboard/display) is the selected controlling device, see Section B.6. Outputs ∅ through 2 are connected to rows ∅ through 2 of the KIM keyboard, as shown in Figure B.3. Basic keyboard operation consists of sequentially selecting rows ∅, 1, and 2 of the keyboard via an operating program. Any depressed key in a selected row will couple this active-low selection signal (through the vertical keyboard bus line connected to that key) back into one of the port A inputs (assuming that port A is programmed to serve as an input). After the sequential scan of the three rows is complete, the information gathered from the port by the CPU

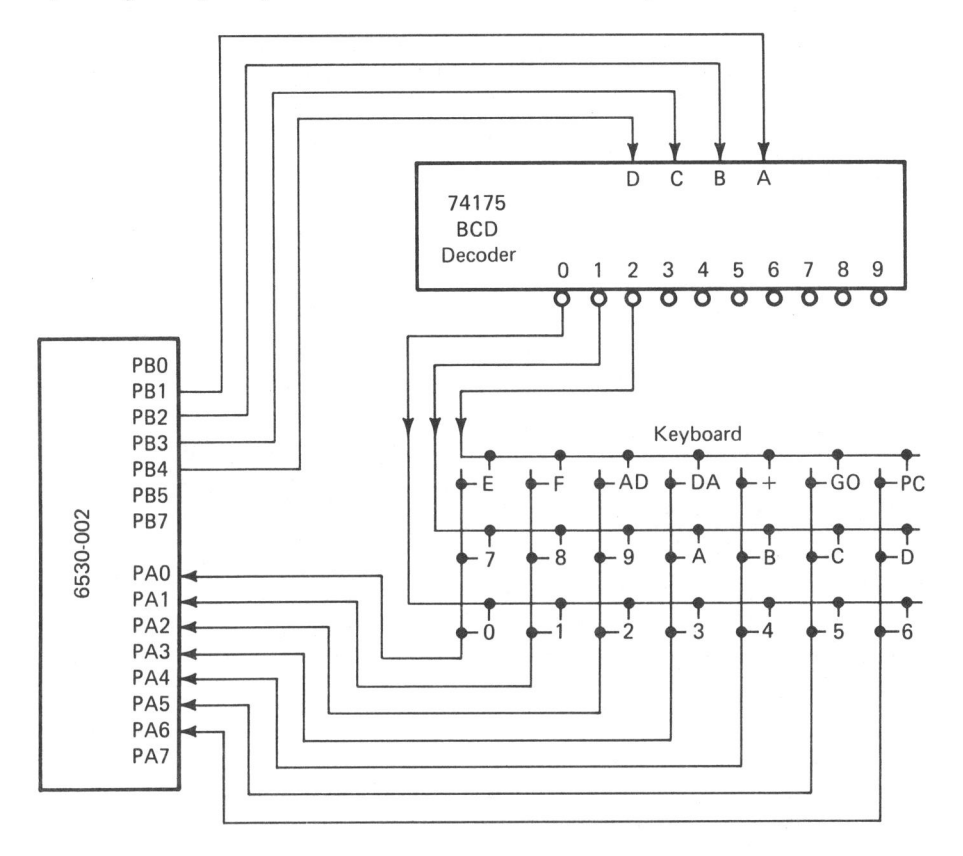

Operating Principles of the KIM-1 Monitor and On-Board I/O Hardware

Figure B.3 Simplified block diagram of KIM-1 keyboard scan system

during the scan can be interpreted and the depressed key identified. The CPU can then branch to a routine designed to service that key. Note that the programmer has complete liberty in assigning each key its role in the system, since the software he provides to service each keystroke is whatever he chooses it to be.

B.4.4 AK (Get Any Key) Keyboard Service Routine

To examine one implementation of a keyboard scan routine, we will examine the principal steps found in the KIM keyboard service routine. Recall that, upon completion of the display management routine (SCANDS) the KIM monitor software, after reconfiguring the port A I/O interface as an input, performs a subroutine jump to a routine called AK (any key), which may be found in the KIM monitor listing beginning on line 1037.

The first pair of steps in AK set index register Y and index register X values to ∅3 and ∅1, respectively. The Y value is used to count through the 3 rows of the display and the X value is used, via the BCD decoder and port B output, to sequentially select the three rows. The accumulator is loaded with all 1s (FF hex), and row ∅ selected by storing the X value in SBD. The X value is then incremented by 2 to prepare for selection of row 2 during the next pass. Any key depressed on row ∅ will send a low-level signal (a "0") back to the corresponding port A input line. Thus, when the next monitor instruction forms the logical AND of SAD contents with the accumulator, the corresponding accumulator bit will become ∅. After this operation, Y is decremented and tested for zero, with a branch back to the scan routine if Y is not zero. Thus three such scans, one for each row will be performed. Any key depression will change the original FF value in the accumulator to some other value.

The next three program steps are included to set up the Teletype selection for potential future use and to take care of the possiblity that the Teletype, even though not being used, may have transferred data to the KIM.

A final EOR (exclusive-or) instruction complements the entire accumulator. Thus, if no keys were depressed during the scan, an all-zero accumulator state will be reached. If one or more keys were depressed, the accumulator will contain a nonzero value.

After the AK routine is finished, a RTS (Return from Subroutine) instruction is executed. This transfers control back to the SCAND routine. Reexamination of this routine, however, discloses that the JSR (Jump to Subroutine) to AK was its last step. However, SCAND, as it turns out, is reached via JSR instructions itself, so the actual return will be to the routine which called SCAND in the first place. There are several such calls in the monitor, all on page 17 of the listing. In particular, note the pair of calls on lines 662 and 664. A return from SCAND the first time with a nonzero accumulator value will result in a second call of SCAND, again followed by a test for zero accumulator. Once again the problem of unreliable logical outputs from mechanical switch contacts is being addressed. The KIM CPU refuses to believe the answer given by just one pass of SCAND, so it calls it one more time just to make sure the key is still depressed during the second scan. If it is, the routine designated GETK (line 667) is entered. This routine has as its function the determination of what key was pressed, information AK does not yield.

B.4.5 GETK and GETKEY Monitor Routines

GETK begins with a jump to subroutine GETKEY, beginning on line 1114 of the monitor listing. GETKEY is a moderately involved routine and its details will not be expounded here. Figure B.4 is a flow chart of GETKEY. Suffice it to say that when it is entered, it scans the KIM keyboard in a manner similar to that done during the AK routine, except that much more processing of the data is performed. The result of this processing is that, when a return from GETKEY occurs, a code is left in the accumulator which uniquely specifies the key that was depressed. Table B.3 shows the association between the keyboard keys and the codes produced by GETKEY. Note that a code with a hex value greater than 15 represents a so-called "illegal" code, and is an indicator that the key was not steadily depressed during the execution of the scan, or that two keys or more were depressed. Such an illegality is rare, because it is extremely difficult to create a keystroke so short as to not appear rather slow to the KIM monitor program. Also, two keys would have to be depressed with near-perfect simultaneity to be detected as an illegal activity by the GETKEY routine.

Returning to the flow of events engendered by the original keystroke, return from GETKEY is back to GETK. The key code having been placed in A, the next few steps of GETK are simply comparisons with code values corresponding to NO KEY, PC, ADDRESS MODE, DATA MODE, STEP (+), and GO key depressions. In each of these cases a jump to a subroutine for handling that particular activity is performed, after which a return to normal keyboard scan will be made. If none of the above codes are found, the code must be a data value held in the lower 4 bit positions of A. In this case, two principal activities must be performed by routine DATA. First, a determination as to whether the keystroke was intended to affect Data or Address portions of the display is made. The routine accomplishes this by examining the MODE value (held at the reserved address ØØFF). If ADDRESS mode is selected, the routine loads the display buffer area with the proper characters, shifts the characters around in such a way as to reflect a right-to-left insertion of new characters to the display, and fetches the data at the resulting memory address. This data is loaded into the display buffer area so that when a return is made to the SCAND routine, the display will indicate the new address and the data stored there. If DATA mode is selected, the address presently held in the display buffer will be used to read memory, shift the low-order data

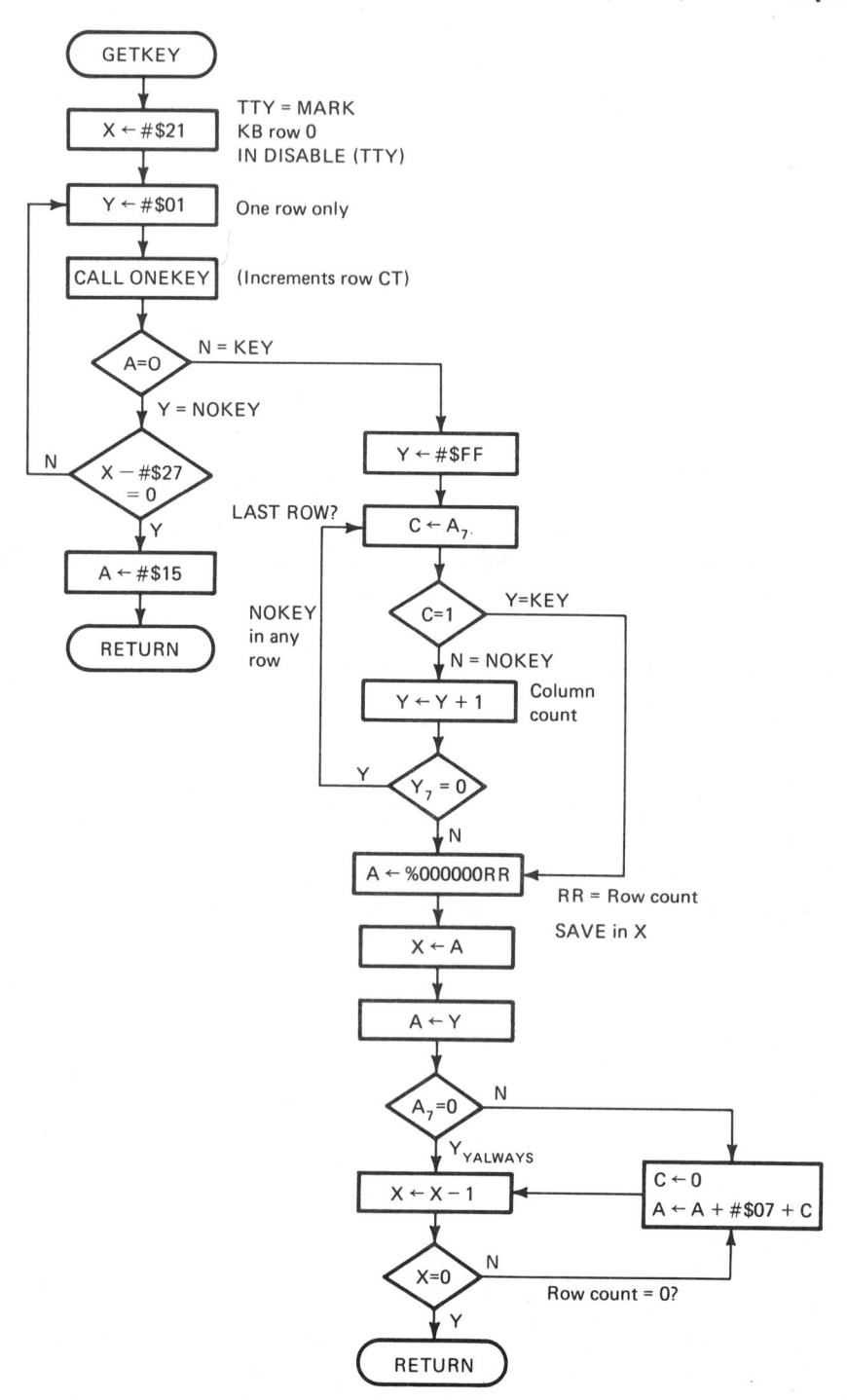

Figure B.4 Flow chart - GETKEY monitor routine

TABLE B.3 KIM Monitor Keystroke Codes

Key Depressed	Code Placed in A by GETKEY (hex)
NONE	15
PC	14
AD	10
DA	11
+	12
GO	13
1	01
2	02
3	03
4	04
5	05
6	06
7	07
8	08
9	09
0	00
A	0A
B	0B
C	0C
D	0D
E	0E
F	0F
Illegal	> 15

character left one hex position and insert the new value (obtained by GETKEY) in the vacated position. The modified value is then rewritten into memory and a return to SCAND (via START, line 636) is performed.

In reading the KIM monitor listing, it is easy to become confused by some program activities which appear to be meaningless or at least obscure. This is a common reaction when trying to obtain an understanding of another programmer's thought processes via a listing of his program. Novice programmers should remember this when writing their own programs, and should try to follow the following two rules:

1. Be very liberal in your use of comments in your programs.

2. Try to avoid being too clever. It may cost a little extra code to to things in a straightforward manner as opposed to developing short but intricate routines. Be forewarned that such "cleverness" will not only be confusing to another worker trying to understand your program listing, but to yourself when you are trying to use or debug the routine a couple of days after having written it.

B.5 USE OF KIM SUBROUTINES

The discussions of the previous sections involved examinations of some of the activity managed by the KIM monitor. In looking over this operation, you may have noticed that much use is made in the KIM monitor of subroutines performing desired operations. This rather fortunate implementation, one which is a good model for programmers in general, makes available to the KIM user a variety of routines for use outside the normal monitor usage. Table B.4 is a listing of those subroutines included in the portion of the KIM monitor provided for management of display, keyboard, and Teletype. The user can call these routines by simply using the JSR instruction and providing the starting location of the desired routine. They may be thought of as a rather limited "library" available to the system user. The only difference between these subroutines and those you might write for yourself lies in their behavior during the single-step operation of the KIM. Since they all lie in page 7 of memory, you cannot step through them. This does *not* mean that you cannot use them, however, in programs you might like to step through. The only effect will be that in stepping through a JSR instruction which calls one of these routines, you will find that the entire subroutine will be executed before the KIM stops and waits for the next instruction in sequence, the one following the JSR. Note that, in such a case, you are using the subroutine for your own purposes, and the KIM monitor is using the same subroutine, without any conflict between the two uses.

This concept of use of a subroutine library is a very important one. You will find in your future use of microcomputers that the establishment of such a library for use by yourself or others will greatly enhance your ability to use your system without the necessity to develop all software "from the ground up" each time a new and different problem or application is to be examined. You will also find the use of subroutines developed by other users to be an important aid.

TABLE B.4 KIM Monitor Subroutines

Subroutine Name	Starting Address	Description	Comments
INITS	1E88	Initializes system, performing the following steps: 1. Set keyboard to address mode. 2. Program 6530 A port terminals as inputs. 3. Program the lower 6 6530 B port terminals as outputs, and the upper bit as an input (for TTY mode). 4. Loads ∅3 into B port data register (setting up test for TTY mode). 5. Clear decimal mode of KIM arithmetic unit.	
INIT1	1E8C	Same as INITS, except does not affect keyboard mode.	
SCAND	1F19	Drives KIM display, displaying 4-character address and data stored in memory at that address. Branches to AK routine at completion to test for occurrence of KIM keyboard depression. Returns to calling program after AK.	Address to be displayed stored at POINTL, POINTH.
SCANDS	1F1F	Identical to SCAND, except simply displays data at POINTL, POINTH, INH.	6 hex digits to be displayed must be stored at POINTL, POINTH, AND INH.
AK	1EFE	Scans KIM keyboard to see if any key is depressed. Loads A with ∅ if no key, with some nonzero number if key.	PA port must be programmed as input.
GETKEY	1F6A	Scans KIM keyboard, producing code (in A) identifying key depressed (see Table B.4).	PA port must be programmed as input.
INCPT	1F63	Increments the 16-bit value in POINTL, POINTH.	

TABLE B.4 (Continued)

Subroutine Name	Starting Address	Description	Comments
OPEN	1FCC	Moves data from INL to POINTL and from INH to POINTH.	
CONVD	1F48	1. Converts hex digit in A to code suitable for driving KIM display element. 2. Selects display element with contents of X (see section on driving KIM display). 3. Drive display element for about 0.5 milliseconds. 4. Increments X by 2, points to next rightmost display element.	Hex digit to be displayed in lower half of A, with upper half cleared. X contains code selecting display element. X will be modified (incremented by 2) by the routine.
GETCH	1E5A	Get one character from Teletype, placing it in A.	X unchanged, Y=FF on return.
GETBYT	1F9D	Get two hex characters from Teletype (as one byte) and pack into INH and INL (See PACK).	X unchanged, Y=∅ on return.
PACK	1FAC	Shift character in A into the INH, INL string. Loses the high-order character of INH. If A does not contain a hex digit, return with no execution.	Clears A on return (if transfer successful).
CHK	1F91	Computes check sum (used with paper tape routine).	
PRTST	1FD5	Prints (via Teletype) a string of ASCII characters from TOP+X to TOP (TOP is a table prestored in ROM).	X must contain pointer into table.
CRLF	1E2F	Prints (via Teletype) a carriage return and line feed.	
OUTCH	1EA∅	Prints (via Teletype) one character (in A).	A contains character to be printed, X unchanged, Y=FF on return.

OUTSP	1E9E	Prints (via Teletype) a space.	X unchanged, Y=FF on return.
PRTPNT	1E1E	Prints (via Teletype) the contents of POINTL and POINTH as 4 hex characters.	
PRTBYT	1E3B	Prints (via Teletype) a byte (in A) as two hex characters.	A contains byte at start and at return.
HEXTA	1E4C	Extracts lower 4 bits of A, prints (via Teletype) as hex character.	
DELAY	1ED4	Delay one Teletype bit time.	Delay depends on baud rate constant (CNTL30, CNTLH30) stored during initialization.
DEHALF	1EEB	Like DELAY, except delays one-half bit time.	

B.6 KIM KEYBOARD/TELETYPE SELECTION CONTROL

The KIM system permits the user to select as his primary I/O device either the integral keyboard/display or a console device such as an ASR33 Teletype. It is instructive to examine the means by which the KIM system goes about implementing the choice of option for I/O.

If one reads only the bare operating procedures for the KIM, he finds that the steps involved in setting up the TTY option include wiring of a connector jumper or a switch which is used to select the option. This may suggest that some wiring of hardware is being accomplished, but in fact the selection is performed almost entirely in software. Refer to Figure B.5 which shows a logic drawing of the 6530-002 peripheral interface unit and the switch wired in to permit implementation of the TTY option. Note that output number ∅3 is tied through this switch to PA∅ of the 6530. PA∅ should be configured as an input. During the initialization program executed during a RESET operation (a small portion of which is shown in both listing and flow chart form in Figure 4.7), the Port B data register (SBD) is loaded with ∅7, producing an active-low output at the ∅3 terminal of the BCD decoder. If the TTY mode switch is closed, this signal will be coupled into the PA∅ input. When the program shown executes a BIT (bit test) instruction, (comparing the contents of PA to ∅1) and then follows this with a BNE (branch on nonzero), the branch will not be taken, since the zero

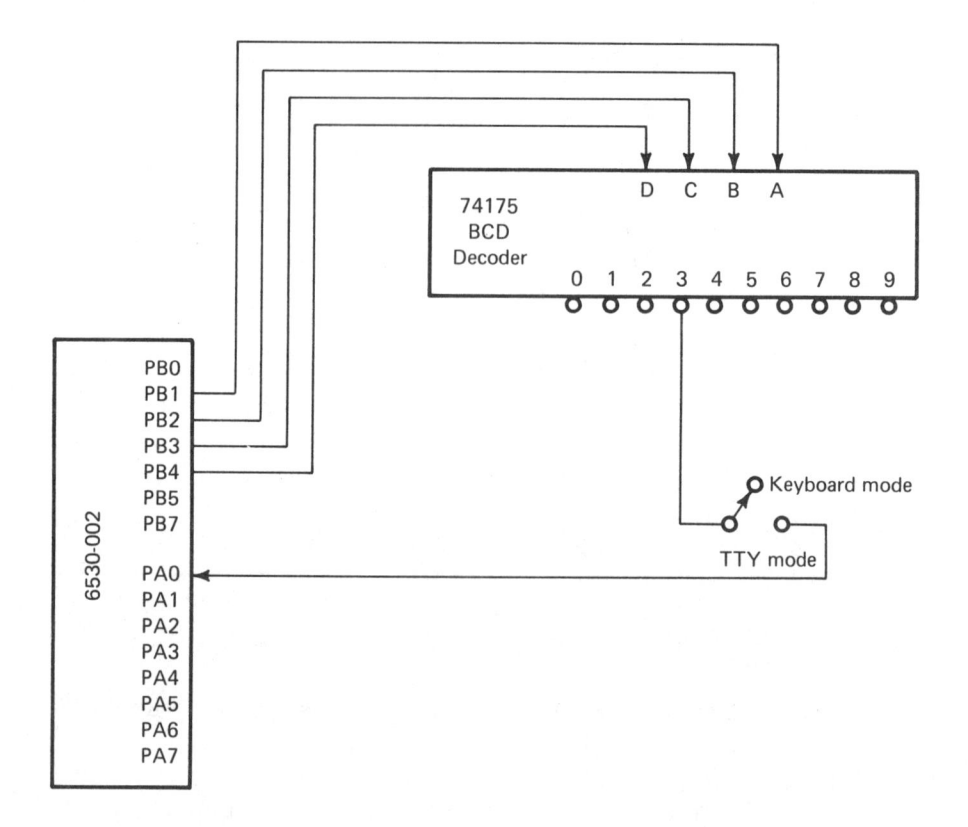

Figure B.5 KIM-1 keyboard/Teletype mode selection circuitry

flag will have been cleared by the bit test operation. Thus the program sequence will not be broken, and the monitor will enter a Teletype handling software mode. If, on the other hand, the BIT, BNE sequence resulted in a zero flag set, indicating that PA∅) was 1, a branch to monitor routine START would result, corresponding to keyboard/display selection. (Note that this means that an unconnected input to PA∅ is interpreted as a high level or a "1").

There are several branch points in the monitor program which require testing for TTY mode. In each case, a procedure similar to the one described is executed by the software. (See, for example, lines 614, 637, and 659 of the KIM monitor listing.)

B.7 TELETYPE I/O INITIALIZATION

Figure B.6 is a diagram which shows the interface circuitry required to properly connect the 6530-002 to a 20-milliampere current-loop

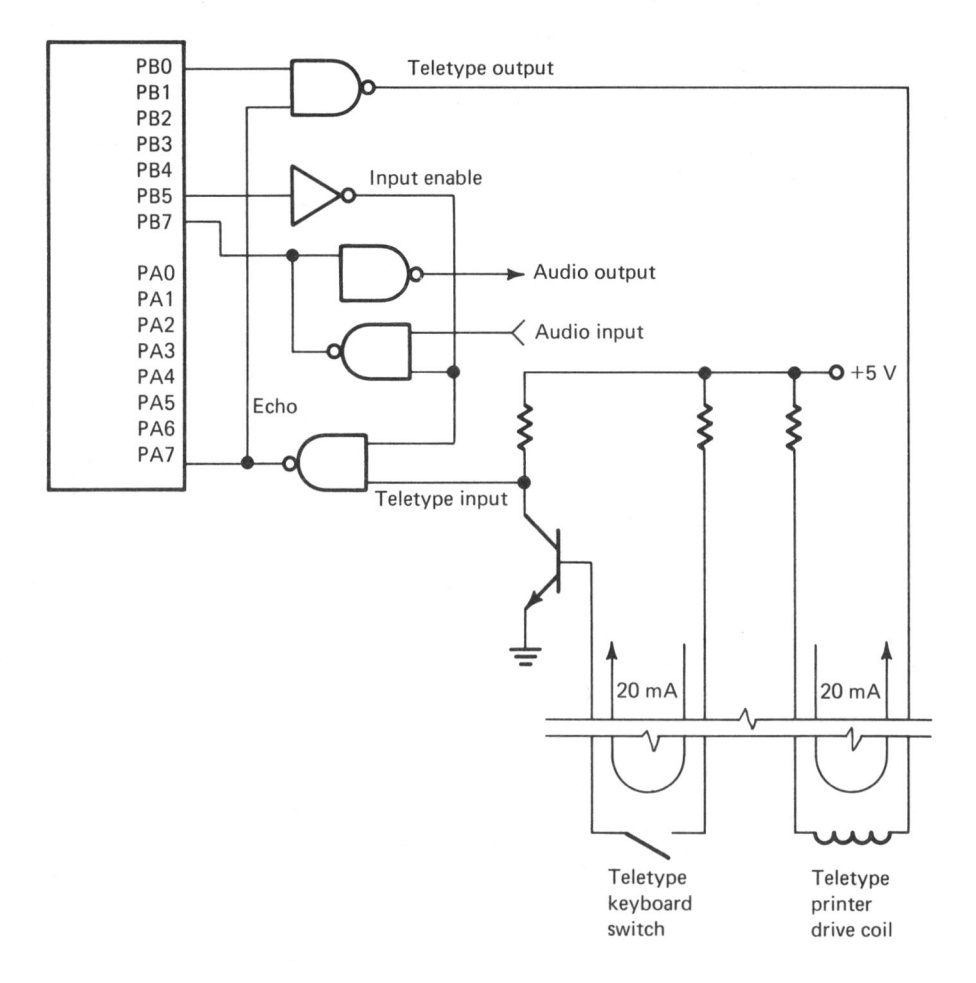

Operating Principles of the KIM-1 Monitor and On-Board I/O Hardware   **513**

Figure B.6 Teletype current-loop interface circuitry

interface such as is found in a standard ASR33 Teletype. (Also shown is a portion of the audio cassette interface, which will not be discussed here.)

Chapter 5 discusses asynchronous communication principles in some detail, so it is assumed that basic Teletype operation is understood. From the diagram it can be seen that 6530 initialization to support this interface requires that:

1. PB∅ be programmed as an output.
2. A high or "1" value be sent to PB∅.
3. PA7 be programmed as an input.
4. PB5 be programmed as an output.

514   *Microcomputer Systems Principles*

    5. PB5 be programmed as an output.
    6. A low or "0" value be sent to PB5.

The KIM-1 monitor established the 6530-002 interface during an initialization sequence called INITS (lines 966-977). The reader should verify that the steps listed here are performed during this routine.

B.8 KIM-1 MONITOR PROGRAM LISTING

This section consists of a reproduction of the KIM-1 Monitor listing, included with permission of MOS Technology, Inc.

```
CARD # LOC      CODE       CARD
    3                        ;       666666    555555    333333    000000
    4                        ;       6         5              3    0    0
    5                        ;       6         5              3    0    0
    6                        ;       666666    555555    333333    0    0
    7                        ;       6    6         5         3    0    0
    8                        ;       6    6         5         3    0    0
    9                        ;       666666    555555    333333    000000
   10                        ;
   11                        ;
   12                        ;
   13                        ;                 000000    000000    333333
   14                        ;                 0    0    0    0         3
   15                        ;       ------    0    0    0    0         3
   16                        ;       ------    0    0    0    0    333333
   17                        ;       ------    0    0    0    0         3
   18                        ;                 0    0    0    0         3
   19                        ;                 000000    000000    333333
   20                        ;
   21                        ;
   22                        ;
   23                        ;
   24                        ;
   25                        ;       COPYRIGHT
   26                        ;       MOS TECHNOLOGY, INC
   27                        ;       DATE OCT 18 1975 REV D
   28                        ;
   29                        ;
   30                        ;
   31                        ;       6530-003 IS AN AUDIO CASSETT TAPE
   32                        ;       RECORDER ENTENSION OF THE BASIC
   33                        ;       KIM MONITOR
   34                        ;
   35                        ;       IT FEATURES TWO BASIC ROUTINES
   36                        ;       LOADT-LOAD MEM FROM AUDIO TAPE
   37                        ;       DUMPT-STOR MEM ONTO AUDIO TAPE
   38                        ;
   39                        ;       LOADT
   40                        ;         ID=00         IGNORE ID
   41                        ;         ID=FF         IGN. ID USE SA FOR START ADDR
   42                        ;         ID=01-FE      IGN. ID USE ADDR ON TAPE
   43                        ;
   44                        ;       DUMPT
   45                        ;         ID=00         SHOULD NOT BE USED
   46                        ;         ID=FF         SHOULD NOT BE USED
   47                        ;         ID=01-FE      NORMAL ID RANGE
   48                        ;         SAL           LSB STARTING ADDRESS
   49                        ;         SAH           MSB
   50                        ;         EAL           LSB ENDING ADDRESS
   51                        ;         EAH           MSB
   52                        ;
```

```
CARD # LOC      CODE        CARD
 54                         ;
 55                         ;       EQUATES
 56                         ;       SET UP FOR 6530-002 I/O
 57                         ;
 58                         SAD     =$1740          6530 A DATA
 59                         PADD    =$1741          6530 A DATA DIRECTION
 60                         SBD     =$1742          6530 B DATA
 61                         PBDD    =$1743          6530 B DATA DIRECTION
 62                         CLK1T   =$1744          DIV BY 1 TIME
 63                         CLK8T   =$1745          DIV BY 8 TIME
 64                         CLK64T  =$1746          DIV BY 64 TIME
 65                         CLKKT   =$1747          DIV BY 1024 TIME
 66                         CLKRDI  =$1747          READ TIME OUT BIT
 67                         CLKRDT  =$1746          READ TIME
 68                         ;
 69     0000                        *=$00EF
 70                         ;       MPU REG. SAVX AREA IN PAGE 0
 71                         ;
 72     00EF                PCL     *=*+1 PROGRAM CNT LOW
 73     00F0                PCH     *=*+1 PROGRAM CNT HI
 74     00F1                PREG    *=*+1 CURRENT STATUS REG.
 75     00F2                SPUSER  *=*+1 CURRENT STACK POINT
 76     00F3                ACC     *=*+1 ACCUMULATOR
 77     00F4                XREG    *=*+1 X INDEX
 78     00F5                YREG    *=*+1 Y INDEX
 79                         ;
 80                         ;       KIM FIXED AREA IN PAGE 0
 81                         ;
 82     00F6                CHKHI   *=*+1
 83     00F7                CHKSUM  *=*+1
 84     00F8                INL     *=*+1 INPUT BUFFER
 85     00F9                INH     *=*+1 INPUT BUFFER
 86     00FA                POINTL  *=*+1 LSB OF OPEN CELL
 87     00FB                POINTH  *=*+1 MSB OF OPEN CELL
 88     00FC                TEMP    *=*+1
 89     00FD                TMPX    *=*+1
 90     00FE                CHAR    *=*+1
 91     00FF                MODE    *=*+1
 92                         ;
 93                         ;       KIM FIXED AREA IN PAGE 23
 94                         ;
 95     0100                        *=$17E7
 96     17E7                CHKL    *=*+1
 97     17E8                CHKH    *=*+1           CHKSUM
 98     17E9                SAVX    *=*+3
 99     17EC                VEB     *=*+6           VOLATILE EXECUTION BLOCK
100     17F2                CNTL30  *=*+1           TTY DELAY
101     17F3                CNTH30  *=*+1           TTY DELAY
102     17F4                TIMH    *=*+1
103     17F5                SAL     *=*+1           LOW STARTING ADDRESS
104     17F6                SAH     *=*+1           HI STARTING ADDRESS
105     17F7                EAL     *=*+1           LOW ENDING ADDRESS
106     17F8                EAH     *=*+1           HI ENDING ADDRESS
107     17F9                ID      *=*+1
108                         ;
109                         ;       INTERRUPT VECTORS
110                         ;
111     17FA                NMIV    *=*+2           STOP VECTOR (STOP=1C00)
112     17FC                RSTV    *=*+2           RST VECTOR
113     17FE                IRQV    *=*+2           IRQ VECTOR (BRK= 1C00)
114                         ;
115     1800                        *=$1800
116                         ;
117                         ;       INIT VOLATILE EXECUTION BLOCK
118                         ;       DUMP MEM TO TAPE
119                         ;
120
121     1800  A9 AD         DUMPT   LDA     #$AD    LOAD ABSOLUTE INST
```

```
CARD # LOC    CODE         CARD
 122   1802  8D EC 17             STA    VEB
 123   1805  20 32 19             JSR    INTVEB
 124                        ;
 125   1808  A9 27                LDA    #$27        TURN OFF DATAIN PB5
 126   180A  8D 42 17             STA    SBD
 127   180D  A9 BF                LDA    #$BF        CONVERT PB7 TO OUTPUT
 128   180F  8D 43 17             STA    PBDD
 129                        ;
 130   1812  A2 64                LDX    #$64        100 CHARS
 131   1814  A9 16        DUMPT1  LDA    #$16        SYN CHAR'S
 132   1816  20 7A 19             JSR    OUTCHT
 133   1819  CA                   DEX
 134   181A  D0 F8                BNE    DUMPT1
 135                        ;
 136                        ;
 137   181C  A9 2A                LDA    #'*         START CHAR
 138   181E  20 7A 19             JSR    OUTCHT
 139                        ;
 140   1821  AD F9 17             LDA    ID          OUTPUT ID
 141   1824  20 61 19             JSR    OUTBT
 142                        ;
 143   1827  AD F5 17             LDA    SAL         OUTPUT STARTING
 144   182A  20 5E 19             JSR    OUTBTC      ADDRESS
 145   182D  AD F6 17             LDA    SAH
 146   1830  20 5E 19             JSR    OUTBTC
 147                        ;
 148   1833  AD ED 17     DUMPT2  LDA    VEB+1       CHECK FOR LAST
 149   1836  CD F7 17             CMP    EAL         DATA BYTE
 150   1839  AD EE 17             LDA    VEB+2
 151   183C  ED F8 17             SBC    EAH
 152   183F  90 24                BCC    DUMPT4
 153                        ;
 154   1841  A9 2F                LDA    #'/         OUTPUT END OF DATA CHR
 155   1843  20 7A 19             JSR    OUTCHT
 156   1846  AD E7 17             LDA    CHKL        LAST BYTE HAS BEEN
 157   1849  20 61 19             JSR    OUTBT       OUT PUT    NOW OUTPUT
 158   184C  AD E8 17             LDA    CHKH        CHKSUM
 159   184F  20 61 19             JSR    OUTBT
 160                        ;
 161                        ;
 162   1852  A2 02                LDX    #$02        2 CHAR'S
 163   1854  A9 04        DUMPT3  LDA    #$04        EOT CHAR
 164   1856  20 7A 19             JSR    OUTCHT
 165   1859  CA                   DEX
 166   185A  D0 F8                BNE    DUMPT3
 167                        ;
 168   185C  A9 00                LDA    #$00        DISPLAY 0000
 169   185E  85 FA                STA    POINTL      FOR NORMAL EXIT
 170   1860  85 FB                STA    POINTH
 171   1862  4C 4F 1C             JMP    START
 172                        ;
 173   1865  20 EC 17     DUMPT4  JSR    VEB         DATA BYTE OUTPUT
 174   1868  20 5E 19             JSR    OUTBTC
 175                        ;
 176   186B  20 EA 19             JSR    INCVEB
 177   186E  4C 33 18             JMP    DUMPT2
 178                        ;
 179                        ;     LOAD MEMORY FROM TAPE
 180                        ;
 181                        ;
 182   1871  0F 19         TAB    .WORD  LOAD12
 183   1873  A9 8D         LOADT  LDA    #$8D        INIT VOLATILE EXECUTION
 184   1875  8D EC 17             STA    VEB         BLOCK WITH STA ABS.
 185   1878  20 32 19             JSR    INTVEB
 186                        ;
```

Operating Principles of the KIM-1 Monitor and On-Board I/O Hardware

```
CARD # LOC    CODE         CARD
 187   187B  A9 4C              LDA   #$4C      JUMP TYPE RTRN
 188   187D  8D EF 17           STA   VEB+3
 189   1880  AD 71 18           LDA   TAB
 190   1883  8D F0 17           STA   VEB+4
 191   1886  AD 72 18           LDA   TAB+1
 192   1889  8D F1 17           STA   VEB+5
 193                       ;
 194   188C  A9 07              LDA   #$07      RESET PB5=0 (DATA IN)
 195   188E  8D 42 17           STA   SBD
 196                       ;
 197   1891  A9 FF       SYNC   LDA   #$FF      CLEAR SAVX FOR SYNC AREA
 198   1893  8D E9 17           STA   SAVX
 199                       ;
 200   1896  20 41 1A    SYNC1  JSR   RDBIT     GET A BIT
 201   1899  4E E9 17           LSR   SAVX      SHIFT BIT INTO CHAR
 202   189C  0D E9 17           ORA   SAVX
 203   189F  8D E9 17           STA   SAVX
 204   18A2  AD E9 17           LDA   SAVX      GET NEW CHAR
 205   18A5  C9 16              CMP   #$16      SYN CHAR
 206   18A7  D0 ED              BNE   SYNC1
 207                       ;
 208   18A9  A2 0A              LDX   #$0A      TEST FOR 10 SYN CHARS
 209   18AB  20 24 1A    SYNC2  JSR   RDCHT
 210   18AE  C9 16              CMP   #$16
 211   18B0  D0 DF              BNE   SYNC      IF NOT 10 CHAR  RE-SYNC
 212   18B2  CA                 DEX
 213   18B3  D0 F6              BNE   SYNC2
 214                       ;
 215                       ;
 216   18B5  20 24 1A    LOADT4 JSR   RDCHT     LOOK FOR START OF
 217   18B8  C9 2A              CMP   #'*       DATA CHAR
 218   18BA  F0 06              BEQ   LOAD11
 219   18BC  C9 16              CMP   #$16      IF NOT * SHOULD BE SYN
 220   18BE  D0 D1              BNE   SYNC
 221   18C0  F0 F3              BEQ   LOADT4
 222                       ;
 223   18C2  20 F3 19    LOAD11 JSR   RDBYT     READ ID FROM TAPE
 224   18C5  CD F9 17           CMP   ID        COMPARE WITH REQUESTED ID
 225   18C8  F0 0D              BEQ   LOADT5
 226   18CA  AD F9 17           LDA   ID        DEFAULT 00 READ RECORD
 227   18CD  C9 00              CMP   #$00      ANYWAY
 228   18CF  F0 06              BEQ   LOADT5
 229   18D1  C9 FF              CMP   #$FF      DEFAULT FF IGNOR SA ON
 230   18D3  F0 17              BEQ   LOADT6    TAPE
 231   18D5  D0 9C              BNE   LOADT
 232                       ;
 233   18D7  20 F3 19    LOADT5 JSR   RDBYT     GET SA FROM TAPE
 234   18DA  20 4C 19           JSR   CHKT
 235   18DD  8D ED 17           STA   VEB+1     SAVX IN VEB+1,2
 236   18E0  20 F3 19           JSR   RDBYT
 237   18E3  20 4C 19           JSR   CHKT
 238   18E6  8D EE 17           STA   VEB+2
 239   18E9  4C F8 18           JMP   LOADT7
 240                       ;
 241   18EC  20 F3 19    LOADT6 JSR   RDBYT     GET SA BUT IGNORE
 242   18EF  20 4C 19           JSR   CHKT
 243   18F2  20 F3 19           JSR   RDBYT
 244   18F5  20 4C 19           JSR   CHKT
 245                       ;
 246                       ;
 247   18F8  A2 02       LOADT7 LDX   #$02      GET 2 CHARS
 248   18FA  20 24 1A    LOAD13 JSR   RDCHT     GET CHAR(X)
 249   18FD  C9 2F              CMP   #'/       LOOK FOR LAST CHAR
 250   18FF  F0 14              BEQ   LOADT8
 251   1901  20 00 1A           JSR   PACKT     CONVERT TO HEX
```

```
CARD # LOC    CODE       CARD
252    1904  D0 23              BNE    LOADT9    Y=1 NON-HEX CHAR
253    1906  CA                 DEX
254    1907  D0 F1              BNE    LOAD13
255                       ;
256    1909  20 4C 19            JSR    CHKT      COMPUTE CHECKSUM
257    190C  4C EC 17            JMP    VEB       SAVX DATA IN MEMORY
258    190F  20 EA 19  LOAD12 JSR  INCVEB    INCREMENT DATA POINTER
259    1912  4C F8 18            JMP    LOADT7
260                       ;
261    1915  20 F3 19  LOADT8 JSR  RDBYT     END OF DATA COMPARE CHKSUM
262    1918  CD E7 17            CMP    CHKL
263    191B  D0 0C               BNE    LOADT9
264    191D  20 F3 19            JSR    RDBYT
265    1920  CD E8 17            CMP    CHKH
266    1923  D0 04               BNE    LOADT9
267    1925  A9 00               LDA    #$00
268    1927  F0 02               BEQ    LOAD10    NORMAL EXIT
269                       ;
270    1929  A9 FF    LOADT9 LDA  #$FF      ERROR EXIT
271    192B  85 FA    LOAD10 STA  POINTL
272    192D  85 FB               STA    POINTH
273    192F  4C 4F 1C            JMP    START
274
276                       ;
277                       ;      SUBROUTINES FOLLOW
278                       ;
279                       ;      SUB TO MOVE SA TO VEB+1,2
280                       ;
281    1932  AD F5 17  INTVEB LDA  SAL
282    1935  8D ED 17            STA    VEB+1
283    1938  AD F6 17            LDA    SAH
284    193B  8D EE 17            STA    VEB+2
285    193E  A9 60               LDA    #$60      RTS INST
286    1940  8D EF 17            STA    VEB+3
287    1943  A9 00               LDA    #$00      CLEAR CHKSUM AREA
288    1945  8D E7 17            STA    CHKL
289    1948  8D E8 17            STA    CHKH
290    194B  60                  RTS
291                       ;
292                       ;      COMPUTE CHKSUM FOR TAPE LOAD
293                       ;      RTN USES Y TO SAVX A
294                       ;
295    194C  A8       CHKT   TAY
296    194D  18              CLC
297    194E  6D E7 17            ADC    CHKL
298    1951  8D E7 17            STA    CHKL
299    1954  AD E8 17            LDA    CHKH
300    1957  69 00               ADC    #$00
301    1959  8D E8 17            STA    CHKH
302    195C  98                  TYA
303    195D  60                  RTS
304                       ;
305                       ;      OUTPUT ONE BYTE USE Y
306                       ;      TO SAVX BYTE
307                       ;
308    195E  20 4C 19  OUTBTC JSR  CHKT      COMP CHKSUM
309    1961  A8       OUTBT  TAY             SAVX DATA BYTE
310    1962  4A              LSR    A        SHIFT OFF LSD
311    1963  4A              LSR    A
312    1964  4A              LSR    A
313    1965  4A              LSR    A
314    1966  20 6F 19            JSR    HEXOUT    OUTPUT MSD
315    1969  98                  TYA
316    196A  20 6F 19            JSR    HEXOUT    OUTPUT LSD
317    196D  98                  TYA
```

```
CARD # LOC    CODE        CARD
 318   196E   60                  RTS
 319                       ;
 320                       ;      CONVERT LSD OF A TO ASCII
 321                       ;      AND OUTPUT TO TAPE
 322                       ;
 323   196F   29 0F        HEXOUT AND    #$0F
 324   1971   C9 0A               CMP    #$0A
 325   1973   18                  CLC
 326   1974   30 02               BMI    HEX1
 327   1976   69 07               ADC    #$07
 328   1978   69 30        HEX1   ADC    #$30
 329                       ;
 330                       ;      OUTPUT TO TAPE ONE ASCII
 331                       ;      CHAR  USE SUB'S ONE + ZRO
 332                       ;
 333   197A   8E E9 17     OUTCHT STX    SAVX
 334   197D   8C EA 17            STY    SAVX+1
 335   1980   A0 08               LDY    #$08         START BIT
 336   1982   20 9E 19     CHT1   JSR    ONE
 337   1985   4A                  LSR    A            GET DATA BIT
 338   1986   B0 06               BCS    CHT2
 339   1988   20 9E 19            JSR    ONE          DATA BIT=1
 340   198B   4C 91 19            JMP    CHT3
 341   198E   20 C4 19     CHT2   JSR    ZRO          DATA BIT=0
 342   1991   20 C4 19     CHT3   JSR    ZRO
 343   1994   88                  DEY
 344   1995   D0 EB               BNE    CHT1
 345   1997   AE E9 17            LDX    SAVX
 346   199A   AC EA 17            LDY    SAVX+1
 347   199D   60                  RTS
 348                       ;
 349                       ;
 350                       ;      OUTPUT 1 TO TAPE
 351                       ;      9 PULSES 138 MICROSEC EACH
 352                       ;
 353   199E   A2 09        ONE    LDX    #$09
 354   19A0   48                  PHA                 SAVX A
 355   19A1   2C 47 17     ONE1   BIT    CLKRDI       WAIT FOR TIME OUT
 356   19A4   10 FB               BPL    ONE1
 357   19A6   A9 7E               LDA    #126
 358   19A8   8D 44 17            STA    CLK1T
 359   19AB   A9 A7               LDA    #$A7
 360   19AD   8D 42 17            STA    SBD          SET  PB7=1
 361   19B0   2C 47 17     ONE2   BIT    CLKRDI
 362   19B3   10 FB               BPL    ONE2
 363   19B5   A9 7E               LDA    #126
 364   19B7   8D 44 17            STA    CLK1T
 365   19BA   A9 27               LDA    #$27
 366   19BC   8D 42 17            STA    SBD          RESET PB7=0
 367   19BF   CA                  DEX
 368   19C0   D0 DF               BNE    ONE1
 369   19C2   68                  PLA
 370   19C3   60                  RTS
 371                       ;
 372                       ;
 373                       ;      OUTPUT 0 TO TAPE
 374                       ;      6 PULSES 207 MICROSEC EACH
 375                       ;
 376   19C4   A2 06        ZRO    LDX    #$06
 377   19C6   48                  PHA                 SAVX A
 378   19C7   2C 47 17     ZRO1   BIT    CLKRDI
 379   19CA   10 FB               BPL    ZRO1
 380   19CC   A9 C3               LDA    #195
 381   19CE   8D 44 17            STA    CLK1T
 382   19D1   A9 A7               LDA    #$A7
```

```
CARD #  LOC     CODE            CARD
 383    1903    8D 42 17        STA     SBD     SET PB7=1
 384    1906    2C 47 17  ZRO2  BIT     CLKRDI
 385    1909    10 FB           BPL     ZRO2
 386    190B    A9 C3           LDA     #195
 387    190D    8D 44 17        STA     CLK1T
 388    1910    A9 27           LDA     #$27
 389    1912    8D 42 17        STA     SBD     RESET PB7=0
 390    1915    CA              DEX
 391    1916    D0 DF           BNE     ZRO1
 392    1918    68              PLA             RESTORE A
 393    1919    60              RTS
 394                            ;
 395                            ;       SUB TO INC VEB+1,2
 396                            ;
 397    19EA    EE ED 17  INCVEB INC    VEB+1
 398    19ED    D0 03           BNE     INCVE1
 399    19EF    EE EE 17        INC     VEB+2
 400    19F2    60        INCVE1 RTS
 401                            ;
 402                            ;       SUB TO READ BYTE FROM TAPE
 403                            ;
 404    19F3    20 24 1A  RDBYT JSR     RDCHT
 405    19F6    20 00 1A        JSR     PACKT
 406    19F9    20 24 1A  RDBYT2 JSR    RDCHT
 407    19FC    20 00 1A        JSR     PACKT
 408    19FF    60              RTS
 409                            ;
 410                            ;       PACK A=ASCII INTO SAVX
 411                            ;       AS HEX DATA
 412                            ;
 413    1A00    C9 30     PACKT CMP     #$30
 414    1A02    30 15           BMI     PACKT3
 415    1A04    C9 47           CMP     #$47
 416    1A06    10 1A           BPL     PACKT3
 417    1A08    C9 40           CMP     #$40
 418    1A0A    30 03           BMI     PACKT1
 419    1A0C    18              CLC
 420    1A0D    69 09           ADC     #$09
 421    1A0F    2A        PACKT1 ROL    A
 422    1A10    2A              ROL     A
 423    1A11    2A              ROL     A
 424    1A12    2A              ROL     A
 425    1A13    A0 04           LDY     #$04
 426    1A15    2A        PACKT2 ROL    A
 427    1A16    2E E9 17        ROL     SAVX
 428    1A19    88              DEY
 429    1A1A    D0 F9           BNE     PACKT2
 430    1A1C    AD E9 17        LDA     SAVX
 431    1A1F    A0 00           LDY     #$00    Y=0 VALID HEX CHAR
 432    1A21    60              RTS             Y=0 VALID HEX
 433    1A22    C8        PACKT3 INY            Y=1 NOT HEX
 434    1A23    60              RTS
 435                            ;
 436                            ;       GET 1 CHAR FROM TAPE AND RETURN
 437                            ;       WITH CHAR IN A  USE SAVX+1 TO ASM CHAR
 438                            ;
 439    1A24    8E EB 17  RDCHT STX     SAVX+2
 440    1A27    A2 08           LDX     #$08    READ 8 BITS
 441    1A29    20 41 19  RDCHT1 JSR    RDBIT   GET NEXT DATA BIT
 442    1A2C    4E EA 17        LSR     SAVX+1  RIGHT SHIFT CHAR
 443    1A2F    0D EA 17        ORA     SAVX+1  OR IN SIGN BIT
 444    1A32    8D EA 17        STA     SAVX+1  REPLACE CHAR
 445    1A35    CA              DEX
 446    1A36    D0 F1           BNE     RDCHT1
 447                            ;
```

Operating Principles of the KIM-1 Monitor and On-Board I/O Hardware

```
CARD # LOC    CODE        CARD
 448   1938   AD 6A 17         LDA   SAVX+1      MOVE CHAR INTO A
 449   193B   2A               ROL   A           SHIFT OFF PARITY
 450   193C   4A               LSR   A
 451   193D   AE 6B 17         LDX   SAVX+2
 452   1940   60               RTS
 453                      ;
 454                      ;    THIS SUB GETS ONE BIT FROM
 455                      ;    TAPE AND RETURNS IT IN SIGN OF A
 456                      ;
 457   1941   2C 42 17    RDBIT BIT  SBD         WAIT FOR END OF START BIT
 458   1944   10 FB             BPL  RDBIT
 459   1946   AD 46 17          LDA  CLKRDT      GET START BIT TIME
 460   1949   A0 FF             LDY  #$FF        A=256-T1
 461   194B   8C 46 17          STY  CLK64T      SET UP TIMER
 462                      ;
 463   194E   A0 14             LDY  #$14
 464   1950   88          RDBIT3 DEY             DELAY 100 MICROSEC
 465   1951   D0 FD             BNE  RDBIT3
 466                      ;
 467   1953   2C 42 17    RDBIT2 BIT SBD
 468   1956   30 FB             BMI  RDBIT2      WAIT FOR NEXT START BIT
 469                      ;
 470   1958   38                SEC
 471   1959   ED 46 17          SBC  CLKRDT      (256-T1)-(256-T2)=T2-T1
 472   195C   A0 FF             LDY  #$FF
 473   195E   8C 46 17          STY  CLK64T      SET UP TIMER FOR NEXT BIT
 474                      ;
 475   1961   A0 07             LDY  #$07
 476   1963   88          RDBIT4 DEY             DELAY 50 MICROSEC
 477   1964   D0 FD             BNE  RDBIT4
 478                      ;
 479   1966   49 FF             EOR  #$FF        COMPLEMENT SIGN OF A
 480   1968   29 80             AND  #$80        MASK ALL EXCEPT SIGN
 481   196A   60                RTS
 482                      ;
 483                      ;    DIAGNOSTICS
 484                      ;       MEMORY
 485                      ;       PLLCAL
 486                      ;
 487                      ;
 488                      ;
 489                      ;
 490                      ;    PLLCAL OUTPUT 166 MICROSEC
 491                      ;    PULSE STRING
 492                      ;
 493   196B   A9 27       PLLCAL LDA #$27
 494   196D   8D 42 17          STA  SBD         TURN OFF DATIN PB5=1
 495   1970   A9 BF             LDA  #$BF        CONVERT PB7 TO OUTPUT
 496   1972   8D 43 17          STA  PBDD
 497                      ;
 498   1975   2C 47 17    PLL1   BIT CLKRDI
 499   1978   10 FB             BPL  PLL1
 500   197A   A9 9A             LDA  #154        WAIT 166 MICRO SEC
 501   197C   8D 44 17          STA  CLK1T
 502   197F   A9 A7             LDA  #$A7        OUTPUT PB7=1
 503   1981   8D 42 17          STA  SBD
 504                      ;
 505   1984   2C 47 17    PLL2   BIT CLKRDI
 506   1987   10 FB             BPL  PLL2
 507   1989   A9 9A             LDA  #154
 508   198B   8D 44 17          STA  CLK1T
 509   198E   A9 27             LDA  #$27        PB7=0
 510   1990   8D 42 17          STA  SBD
 511   1993   4C 75 1A          JMP  PLL1
 512                      ;
 513                      ;
```

```
CARD # LOC    CODE       CARD
  514                    ;        INTERRUPTS PAGE 27
  515                    ;
  516   1A96             ;        *=*+$0164   RESERVED FOR TEST
  517   1BFA  6B 1A      NMIP27 .WORD PLLCAL
  518   1BFC  6B 1A      RSTP27 .WORD PLLCAL
  519   1BFE  6B 1A      IRQP27 .WORD PLLCAL
  520                    ;
  522                    ;
  523                    ;
  524                    ;
  525                    ;
  526                    ;             666666     555555     333333     000000
  527                    ;             6          5               3     0    0
  528                    ;             6          5               3     0    0
  529                    ;             666666     555555     333333     0    0
  530                    ;             6    6          5          3     0    0
  531                    ;             6    6          5          3     0    0
  532                    ;             666666     555555     333333     000000
  533                    ;
  534                    ;
  535                    ;
  536                    ;                        000000     000000     222222
  537                    ;                        0    0     0    0          2
  538                    ;             ------     0    0     0    0          2
  539                    ;             ------     0    0     0    0     222222
  540                    ;             ------     0    0     0    0     2
  541                    ;                        0    0     0    0     2
  542                    ;                        000000     000000     222222
  543                    ;
  545                    ;
  546                    ;
  547                    ;
  548                    ;             COPYRIGHT
  549                    ;             MOS TECHNOLOGY INC.
  550                    ;             DATE  OCT 13 1975      REV E
  551                    ;
  552                    ;        KIM   :TTY INTERFACE
  553                    ;              :KEYBOARD INTERFACE
  554                    ;              :7 SEG 6 DIGIT DISPLAY
  555                    ;
  556                    ;
  557                    ;        TTY CMDS:
  558                    ;              G     GOEXEC
  559                    ;              CR    OPEN NEXT CELL
  560                    ;              LF    OPEN PREV. CELL
  561                    ;              .     MODIFY OPEN CELL
  562                    ;              SP    OPEN NEW CELL
  563                    ;              L     LOAD (OBJECT FORMAT)
  564                    ;              Q     DUMP   FROM OPEN CELL ADDR TO HI L)
  565                    ;              RO    RUB OUT - RETURN TO START (KIM)
  566                    ;                    ((ALL ILLEGAL CHAR ARE IGNORED))
  567                    ;
  568                    ;        KEYBOARD CMDS:
  569                    ;              ADDR  SETS MODE TO MODIFY CELL ADDRESS
  570                    ;              DATA  SETS MODE TO MODIFY DATA IN OPEN
  571                    ;              STEP  INCREMENTS TO NEXT CELL
  572                    ;              RST   SYSTEM RESET
  573                    ;              RUN   GOEXEC
  574                    ;              STOP  $1C00 CAN BE LOADED INTO NMIV TO
  575                    ;                    USE STOP FEATURE
  576                    ;              PC    DISPLAY PC
  577                    ;
  578                    ;        CLOCK IS NOT DISABLED IN SIGMA 1
  579                    ;
  580                    ;
```

Operating Principles of the KIM-1 Monitor and On-Board I/O Hardware   523

```
CARD # LOC      CODE         CARD
  581                         ;
  582                         ;
  584   1C00                          *=$1C00
  585                         ;
  586                         ;
  587   1C00   85 F3         SAVE     STA   ACC      KIM ENTRY VIA STOP (NMI)
  588   1C02   68                     PLA            OR BRK (IRQ)
  589   1C03   85 F1                  STA   PREG
  590   1C05   68            SAVE1    PLA            KIM ENTRY VIA JSR  (A LOST)
  591   1C06   85 EF                  STA   PCL
  592   1C08   85 FA                  STA   POINTL
  593   1C0A   68                     PLA
  594   1C0B   85 F0                  STA   PCH
  595   1C0D   85 FB                  STA   POINTH
  596   1C0F   84 F5         SAVE2    STY   YREG
  597   1C11   86 F4                  STX   XREG
  598   1C13   BA                     TSX
  599   1C14   86 F2                  STX   SPUSER
  600   1C16   20 88 1E               JSR   INITS
  601   1C19   4C 4F 1C               JMP   START
  602                         ;
  603   1C1C   6C FA 17      NMIT     JMP   (NMIV)   NON-MASKABLE INTERRUPT TRAP
  604   1C1F   6C FE 17      IRQT     JMP   (IRQV)   INTERRUPT TRAP
  605                         ;
  606   1C22   A2 FF         RST      LDX   #$FF     KIM ENTRY VIA RST
  607   1C24   9A                     TXS
  608   1C25   86 F2                  STX   SPUSER
  609   1C27   20 88 1E               JSR   INITS
  610                         ;
  611                         ;
  612   1C2A   A9 FF         DETCPS   LDA   #$FF     COUNT START BIT
  613   1C2C   8D F3 17               STA   CNTH30   ZERO CNTH30
  614   1C2F   A9 01                  LDA   #$01     MASK HI ORDER BITS
  615   1C31   2C 40 17      DET1     BIT   SAD      TEST
  616   1C34   D0 19                  BNE   START    KEYBD SSW TEST
  617   1C36   30 F9                  BMI   DET1     START BIT TEST
  618   1C38   A9 FC                  LDA   #$FC
  619   1C3A   18            DET3     CLC            THIS LOOP COUNTS
  620   1C3B   69 01                  ADC   #$01     THE START BIT TIME
  621   1C3D   90 03                  BCC   DET2
  622   1C3F   EE F3 17               INC   CNTH30
  623   1C42   AC 40 17      DET2     LDY   SAD      CHECK FOR END OF START BIT
  624   1C45   10 F3                  BPL   DET3
  625   1C47   8D F2 17               STA   CNTL30
  626   1C4A   A2 08                  LDX   #$08
  627   1C4C   20 6A 1E               JSR   GET5     GET REST OF THE CHAR
  628                         ;                      TEST CHAR HERE
  629                         ;
  630                         ;
  631                         ;
  632                         ;
  633                         ;
  634                         ;       MAKE TTY/KB SELECTION
  635                         ;
  636   1C4F   20 8C 1E      START    JSR   INIT1
  637   1C52   A9 01                  LDA   #$01
  638   1C54   2C 40 17               BIT   SAD
  639   1C57   D0 1E                  BNE   TTYKB
  640   1C59   20 2F 1E               JSR   CRLF     PRT CR LF
  641   1C5C   A2 0A                  LDX   #$0A     TYPE OUT KIM
  642   1C5E   20 31 1E               JSR   PRTST
  643   1C61   4C AF 1D               JMP   SHOW1
  644                         ;
  645   1C64   A9 00         CLEAR    LDA   #$00
  646   1C66   85 F8                  STA   INL      CLEAR INPUT BUFFER
```

```
CARD # LOC    CODE       CARD
 647  1C68  85 F9                STA   INH
 648  1C6A  20 5A 1E   READ      JSR   GETCH     GET CHAR
 649  1C6D  C9 01                CMP   #$01
 650  1C6F  F0 06                BEQ   TTYKB
 651  1C71  20 AC 1F             JSR   PACK
 652  1C74  4C DB 1D             JMP   SCAN
 653                        ;
 654                        ;    MAIN ROTINE FOR KEY BOARD
 655                        ;    AND DISPLAY
 656                        ;
 657  1C77  20 19 1F   TTYKB     JSR   SCAND     IF A=0 NO KEY
 658  1C7A  D0 D3                BNE   START
 659  1C7C  A9 01      TTYKB1    LDA   #$01
 660  1C7E  2C 40 17             BIT   SAD
 661  1C81  F0 CC                BEQ   START
 662  1C83  20 19 1F             JSR   SCAND
 663  1C86  F0 F4                BEQ   TTYKB1
 664  1C88  20 19 1F             JSR   SCAND
 665  1C8B  F0 EF                BEQ   TTYKB1
 666                        ;
 667  1C8D  20 6A 1F   GETK      JSR   GETKEY
 668  1C90  C9 15                CMP   #$15
 669  1C92  10 BB                BPL   START
 670  1C94  C9 14                CMP   #$14
 671  1C96  F0 44                BEQ   PCCMD     DISPLAY PC
 672  1C98  C9 10                CMP   #$10      ADDR MODE=1
 673  1C9A  F0 2C                BEQ   ADDRM
 674  1C9C  C9 11                CMP   #$11      DATA MODE=1
 675  1C9E  F0 2C                BEQ   DATAM
 676  1CA0  C9 12                CMP   #$12      STEP
 677  1CA2  F0 2F                BEQ   STEP
 678  1CA4  C9 13                CMP   #$13      RUN
 679  1CA6  F0 31                BEQ   GOV
 680  1CA8  0A         DATA      ASL   A         SHIFT CHAR INTO HIGH
 681  1CA9  0A                   ASL   A         ORDER NIBBLE
 682  1CAA  0A                   ASL   A
 683  1CAB  0A                   ASL   A
 684  1CAC  85 FC                STA   TEMP      STORE IN TEMP
 685  1CAE  A2 04                LDX   #$04
 686  1CB0  A4 FF      DATA1     LDY   MODE      TEST MODE 1=ADDR
 687  1CB2  D0 0A                BNE   ADDR      MODE=0 DATA
 688  1CB4  B1 FA                LDA   (POINTL),Y GET DATA
 689  1CB6  06 FC                ASL   TEMP      SHIFT CHAR
 690  1CB8  2A                   ROL   A         SHIFT DATA
 691  1CB9  91 FA                STA   (POINTL),Y STORE OUT DATA
 692  1CBB  4C C3 1C             JMP   DATA2
 693                        ;
 694  1CBE  0A         ADDR      ASL   A         SHIFT CHAR
 695  1CBF  26 FA                ROL   POINTL    SHIFT ADDR
 696  1CC1  26 FB                ROL   POINTH    SHIFT ADDR HI
 697  1CC3  CA         DATA2     DEX
 698  1CC4  D0 EA                BNE   DATA1     DO 4 TIMES
 699  1CC6  F0 08                BEQ   DATAM2    EXIT HERE
 700                        ;
 701  1CC8  A9 01      ADDRM     LDA   #$01
 702  1CCA  D0 02                BNE   DATAM1
 703                        ;
 704  1CCC  A9 00      DATAM     LDA   #$00
 705  1CCE  85 FF      DATAM1    STA   MODE
 706  1CD0  4C 4F 1C   DATAM2    JMP   START
 707                        ;
 708  1CD3  20 63 1F   STEP      JSR   INCPT
 709  1CD6  4C 4F 1C             JMP   START
 710                        ;
 711  1CD9  4C C8 1D   GOV       JMP   GOEXEC
```

```
CARD # LOC    CODE       CARD
   712                   ;
   713                   ;
   714                   ;       DISPLAY PC BY MOVING
   715                   ;       PC TO POINT
   716                   ;
   717  1CDC  A5 EF      PCCMD LDA   PCL
   718  1CDE  85 FA            STA   POINTL
   719  1CE0  A5 F0            LDA   PCH
   720  1CE2  85 FB            STA   POINTH
   721  1CE4  4C 4F 1C         JMP   START
   722                   ;
   723                   ;      LOAD PAPER TAPE FROM TTY
   724                   ;
   725  1CE7  20 5A 1E   LOAD  JSR   GETCH    LOOK FOR FIRST CHAR
   726  1CEA  C9 3B            CMP   #$3B     SMICOLON
   727  1CEC  D0 F9            BNE   LOAD
   728  1CEE  A9 00      LOADS LDA   #$00
   729  1CF0  85 F7            STA   CHKSUM
   730  1CF2  85 F6            STA   CHKHI
   731                   ;
   732  1CF4  20 9D 1F         JSR   GETBYT   GET BYTE CNT
   733  1CF7  AA               TAX            SAVE IN X INDEX
   734  1CF8  20 91 1F         JSR   CHK      COMPUTE CHKSUM
   735                   ;
   736  1CFB  20 9D 1F         JSR   GETBYT   GET ADDRESS HI
   737  1CFE  85 FB            STA   POINTH
   738  1D00  20 91 1F         JSR   CHK
   739  1D03  20 9D 1F         JSR   GETBYT   GET ADDRESS LO
   740  1D06  85 FA            STA   POINTL
   741  1D08  20 91 1F         JSR   CHK
   742                   ;
   743  1D0B  8A               TXA            IF CNT=0 DONT
   744  1D0C  F0 0F            BEQ   LOAD3    GET ANY DATA
   745                   ;
   746  1D0E  20 9D 1F   LOAD2 JSR   GETBYT   GET DATA
   747  1D11  91 FA            STA   (POINTL),Y STORE DATA
   748  1D13  20 91 1F         JSR   CHK
   749  1D16  20 63 1F         JSR   INCPT    NEXT ADDRESS
   750  1D19  CA               DEX
   751  1D1A  D0 F2            BNE   LOAD2
   752  1D1C  E8               INX            X=1  DATA RECORD
   753                   ;                    X=0  LAST RECORD
   754  1D1D  20 9D 1F   LOAD3 JSR   GETBYT   COMPARE CHKSUM
   755  1D20  C5 F6            CMP   CHKHI
   756  1D22  D0 17            BNE   LOADE1
   757  1D24  20 9D 1F         JSR   GETBYT
   758  1D27  C5 F7            CMP   CHKSUM
   759  1D29  D0 13            BNE   LOADER
   760                   ;
   761  1D2B  8A               TXA            X=0  LAST RECORD
   762  1D2C  D0 B9            BNE   LOAD
   763                   ;
   764  1D2E  A2 0C      LOAD7 LDX   #$0C     X-OFF KIM
   765  1D30  A9 27      LOAD8 LDA   #$27
   766  1D32  8D 42 17         STA   SBD      DISABLE DATA IN
   767  1D35  20 31 1E         JSR   PRTST
   768  1D38  4C 4F 1C         JMP   START
   769                   ;
   770  1D3B  20 9D 1F   LOADE1 JSR  GETBYT   DUMMY
   771  1D3E  A2 11      LOADER LDX  #$11     X-OFF ERR KIM
   772  1D40  D0 EE            BNE   LOAD8
   773                   ;
   774                   ;      DUMP TO TTY
   775                   ;      FROM OPEN CELL ADDRESS
   776                   ;      TO LIMHL,LIMHH
```

```
CARD # LOC    CODE       CARD
777                      ;
778    1D42   A9 00      DUMP    LDA    #$00
779    1D44   85 F8              STA    INL
780    1D46   85 F9              STA    INH      CLEAR RECORD COUNT
781    1D48   A9 00      DUMP0   LDA    #$00
782    1D4A   85 F6              STA    CHKHI    CLEAR CHKSUM
783    1D4C   85 F7              STA    CHKSUM
784                      ;
785    1D4E   20 2F 1E   DUMP1   JSR    CRLF     PRINT CR LF
786    1D51   A9 3B              LDA    #$3B     PRINT SMICOLON
787    1D53   20 A0 1E           JSR    OUTCH
788    1D56   A5 FA              LDA    POINTL   TEST POINT GT OR ET
789    1D58   CD F7 17           CMP    EAL      HI LIMIT GO TO EXIT
790    1D5B   A5 FB              LDA    POINTH
791    1D5D   ED F8 17           SBC    EAH
792    1D60   90 13              BCC    DUMP4
793                      ;
794    1D62   A9 00              LDA    #$00     PRINT LAST RECORD
795    1D64   20 3B 1E           JSR    PRTBYT   0 BYTES
796    1D67   20 CC 1F           JSR    OPEN
797    1D6A   20 1E 1E           JSR    PRTPNT
798                      ;
799    1D6D   A5 F6              LDA    CHKHI    PRINT CHKSUM
800    1D6F   20 3B 1E           JSR    PRTBYT   FOR LAST RECORD
801    1D72   A5 F7              LDA    CHKSUM
802    1D74   20 3B 1E           JSR    PRTBYT
803    1D77   4C 64 1C           JMP    CLEAR
804                      ;
805    1D7A   A9 18      DUMP4   LDA    #$18     PRINT 24 BYTE CNT
806    1D7C   AA                 TAX             SAVE AS INDEX
807    1D7D   20 3B 1E           JSR    PRTBYT
808    1D80   20 91 1F           JSR    CHK
809    1D83   20 1E 1E           JSR    PRTPNT
810                      ;
811    1D86   A0 00      DUMP2   LDY    #$00     PRINT 24 BYTES
812    1D88   B1 FA              LDA    (POINTL),Y GET DATA
813    1D8A   20 3B 1E           JSR    PRTBYT   PRINT DATA
814    1D8D   20 91 1F           JSR    CHK      COMP CHKSUM
815    1D90   20 63 1F           JSR    INCPT    INCREMENT POINT
816    1D93   CA                 DEX
817    1D94   D0 F0              BNE    DUMP2
818                      ;
819    1D96   A5 F6              LDA    CHKHI    PRINT CHKSUM
820    1D98   20 3B 1E           JSR    PRTBYT
821    1D9B   A5 F7              LDA    CHKSUM
822    1D9D   20 3B 1E           JSR    PRTBYT
823    1DA0   E6 F8              INC    INL      INCREMENT RECORD CNT
824    1DA2   D0 02              BNE    DUMP3
825    1DA4   E6 F9              INC    INH
826    1DA6   4C 48 1D   DUMP3   JMP    DUMP0
827                      ;
828    1DA9   20 CC 1F   SPACE   JSR    OPEN     OPEN NEW CELL
829    1DAC   20 2F 1E   SHOW    JSR    CRLF     PRINT CR LF
830    1DAF   20 1E 1E   SHOW1   JSR    PRTPNT
831    1DB2   20 9E 1E           JSR    OUTSP    PRT SPACE
832    1DB5   A0 00              LDY    #$00     PRINT DATA SPECIFIED
833    1DB7   B1 FA              LDA    (POINTL),Y BY POINT AD = LDA EXT
834    1DB9   20 3B 1E           JSR    PRTBYT
835    1DBC   20 9E 1E           JSR    OUTSP    PRT SPACE
836    1DBF   4C 64 1C           JMP    CLEAR
837                      ;
838    1DC2   20 63 1F   RTRN    JSR    INCPT    OPEN NEXT CELL
839    1DC5   4C AC 1D           JMP    SHOW
840                      ;
841    1DC8   A6 F2      GOEXEC  LDX    SPUSER
```

Operating Principles of the KIM-1 Monitor and On-Board I/O Hardware 527

```
CARD # LOC    CODE        CARD
 842   1DCA   9A                  TXS
 843   1DCB   A5 FB               LDA   POINTH    PROGRAM RUNS FROM
 844   1DCD   48                  PHA             OPEN CELL ADDRESS
 845   1DCE   A5 FA               LDA   POINTL
 846   1DD0   48                  PHA
 847   1DD1   A5 F1               LDA   PREG
 848   1DD3   48                  PHA
 849   1DD4   A6 F4               LDX   XREG      RESTORE REGS
 850   1DD6   A4 F5               LDY   YREG
 851   1DD8   A5 F3               LDA   ACC
 852   1DDA   40                  RTI
 853                          ;
 854   1DDB   C9 20       SCAN    CMP   #$20      OPEN CELL
 855   1DDD   F0 CA               BEQ   SPACE
 856   1DDF   C9 7F               CMP   #$7F      RUB OUT (KIM)
 857   1DE1   F0 1B               BEQ   STV
 858   1DE3   C9 0D               CMP   #$0D      NEXT CELL
 859   1DE5   F0 DB               BEQ   RTRN
 860   1DE7   C9 0A               CMP   #$0A      PREV CELL
 861   1DE9   F0 1C               BEQ   FEED
 862   1DEB   C9 2E               CMP   #'.       MODIFY CELL
 863   1DED   F0 26               BEQ   MODIFY
 864   1DEF   C9 47               CMP   #'G       GO EXEC
 865   1DF1   F0 D5               BEQ   GOEXEC
 866   1DF3   C9 51               CMP   #'Q       DUMP FROM OPEN CELL TO HI LIMIT
 867   1DF5   F0 0A               BEQ   DUMPV
 868   1DF7   C9 4C               CMP   #'L       LOAD TAPE
 869   1DF9   F0 09               BEQ   LOADV
 870   1DFB   4C 6A 1C            JMP   READ      IGNORE ILLEGAL CHAR
 871                          ;
 872   1DFE   4C 4F 1C    STV     JMP   START
 873   1E01   4C 42 1D    DUMPV   JMP   DUMP
 874   1E04   4C E7 1C    LOADV   JMP   LOAD
 875                          ;
 876   1E07   38          FEED    SEC
 877   1E08   A5 FA               LDA   POINTL    DEC DOUBLE BYTE
 878   1E0A   E9 01               SBC   #$01      AT POINTL AND POINTH
 879   1E0C   85 FA               STA   POINTL
 880   1E0E   B0 02               BCS   FEED1
 881   1E10   C6 FB               DEC   POINTH
 882   1E12   4C AC 1D    FEED1   JMP   SHOW
 883                          ;
 884   1E15   A0 00       MODIFY  LDY   #$00      GET CONTENTS OF INPUT BUFF
 885   1E17   A5 F8               LDA   INL       INL AND STOR IN LOC
 886   1E19   91 FA               STA   (POINTL),Y SPECIFIED BY POINT
 887   1E1B   4C C2 1D            JMP   RTRN
 888                          ;
 889                          ;   END OF MAIN LINE
 890                          ;   SUBROUTINES FOLLOW
 891                          ;
 892                          ;
 893                          ;
 894                          ;
 895                          ;   SUB TO PRINT POINTL,POINTH
 896                          ;
 897   1E1E   A5 FB       PRTPNT  LDA   POINTH
 898   1E20   20 3B 1E            JSR   PRTBYT
 899   1E23   20 91 1F            JSR   CHK
 900   1E26   A5 FA               LDA   POINTL
 901   1E28   20 3B 1E            JSR   PRTBYT
 902   1E2B   20 91 1F            JSR   CHK
 903   1E2E   60                  RTS
 904                          ;
 905                          ;   PRINT STRING OF ASCII CHAR FROM
 906                          ;   TOP+X TO TOP
 907                          ;
```

```
CARD # LOC    CODE        CARD
908    1E2F  A2 07    CRLF    LDX     #$07
909    1E31  BD D5 1F PRTST   LDA     TOP,X
910    1E34  20 A0 1E         JSR     OUTCH
911    1E37  CA               DEX
912    1E38  10 F7            BPL     PRTST       STOP ON INDEX ZERO
913    1E3A  60       PRT1    RTS
914                   ;
915                   ;       PRINT 1 HEX BYTE AS TWO ASCII CHAR'S
916                   ;
917    1E3B  85 FC    PRTBYT  STA     TEMP
918    1E3D  4A               LSR     A           SHIFT CHAR RIGHT 4 BITS
919    1E3E  4A               LSR     A
920    1E3F  4A               LSR     A
921    1E40  4A               LSR     A
922    1E41  20 4C 1E         JSR     HEXTA       CONVERT TO HEX AND PRINT
923    1E44  A5 FC            LDA     TEMP        GET OTHER HALF
924    1E46  20 4C 1E         JSR     HEXTA       CONVERT TO HEX AND PRINT
925    1E49  A5 FC            LDA     TEMP        RESTORE BYTE IN A AND RETURN
926    1E4B  60               RTS
927                   ;
928    1E4C  29 0F    HEXTA   AND     #$0F        MASK HI 4 BITS
929    1E4E  C9 0A            CMP     #$0A
930    1E50  18               CLC
931    1E51  30 02            BMI     HEXTA1
932    1E53  69 07            ADC     #$07        ALPHA HEX
933    1E55  69 30    HEXTA1  ADC     #$30        DEC HEX
934    1E57  4C A0 1E         JMP     OUTCH       PRINT CHAR
935                   ;
936                   ;       GET 1 CHAR FROM TTY
937                   ;       RETURN FROM SUB WITH CHAR IN A
938                   ;       X IS PRESERVED AND Y RETURNED = FF
939                   ;
940    1E59  86 FD    GETCH   STX     TMPX        SAVE X REG
941    1E5C  A2 08            LDX     #$08        SET UP 8 BIT CNT
942    1E5E  A9 01            LDA     #$01
943    1E60  2C 40 17 GET1    BIT     SAD
944    1E63  D0 22            BNE     GET6
945    1E65  30 F9            BMI     GET1        WAIT FOR START BIT
946    1E67  20 D4 1E         JSR     DELAY       DELAY 1 BIT
947    1E6A  20 EB 1E GET5    JSR     DEHALF      DELAY 1/2 BIT TIME
948    1E6D  AD 40 17 GET2    LDA     SAD         GET 8 BITS
949    1E70  29 80            AND     #$80        MASK OFF LOW ORDER BITS
950    1E72  46 FE            LSR     CHAR        SHIFT RIGHT CHARACTER
951    1E74  05 FE            ORA     CHAR
952    1E76  85 FE            STA     CHAR
953    1E78  20 D4 1E         JSR     DELAY       DELAY 1   BIT TIME
954    1E7B  CA               DEX
955    1E7C  D0 EF            BNE     GET2        GET NEXT CHAR
956    1E7E  20 EB 1E         JSR     DEHALF      EXIT THIS RTN
957                   ;
958    1E81  A6 FD            LDX     TMPX
959    1E83  A5 FE            LDA     CHAR
960    1E85  2A               ROL     A           SHIFT OFF PARITY
961    1E86  4A               LSR     A
962    1E87  60       GET6    RTS
963                   ;
964                   ;       INITIALIZATION FOR SIGMA
965                   ;
966    1E88  A2 01    INITS   LDX     #$01        SET KB MODE TO ADDR
967    1E8A  86 FF            STX     MODE
968                   ;
969    1E8C  A2 00    INIT1   LDX     #$00
970    1E8E  8E 41 17         STX     PADD        FOR SIGMA USE SADD
971    1E91  A2 3F            LDX     #$3F
972    1E93  8E 43 17         STX     PBDD        FOR SIGMA USE SBDD
```

Operating Principles of the KIM-1 Monitor and On-Board I/O Hardware   **529**

```
CARD # LOC    CODE         CARD
 973   1E96  A2 07           LDX   #$07      ENABLE DATA IN
 974   1E98  8E 42 17        STX   SBD       OUTPUT
 975   1E9B  D8              CLD
 976   1E9C  78              SEI
 977   1E9D  60              RTS
 978                       ;
 979                       ; PRINT 1 CHAR  CHAR=A
 980                       ; X IS PRESERVED  Y RETURNED = FF
 981                       ; OUTSP  PRINTS 1 SPACE
 982                       ;
 983   1E9E  A9 20    OUTSP  LDA   #$20
 984   1EA0  85 FE    OUTCH  STA   CHAR
 985   1EA2  86 FD           STX   TMPX
 986   1EA4  20 D4 1E        JSR   DELAY     10/11 BIT CODE SYNC
 987   1EA7  AD 42 17        LDA   SBD       START BIT
 988   1EAA  29 FE           AND   #$FE
 989   1EAC  8D 42 17        STA   SBD
 990   1EAF  20 D4 1E        JSR   DELAY
 991   1EB2  A2 08           LDX   #$08
 992   1EB4  AD 42 17  OUT1  LDA   SBD       DATA BIT
 993   1EB7  29 FE           AND   #$FE
 994   1EB9  46 FE           LSR   CHAR
 995   1EBB  69 00           ADC   #$00
 996   1EBD  8D 42 17        STA   SBD
 997   1EC0  20 D4 1E        JSR   DELAY
 998   1EC3  CA              DEX
 999   1EC4  D0 EE           BNE   OUT1
1000   1EC6  AD 42 17        LDA   SBD       STOP BIT
1001   1EC9  09 01           ORA   #$01
1002   1ECB  8D 42 17        STA   SBD
1003   1ECE  20 D4 1E        JSR   DELAY     STOP BIT
1004   1ED1  A6 FD           LDX   TMPX      RESTORE INDEX
1005   1ED3  60              RTS
1006                       ;
1007                       ; DELAY 1 BIT TIME
1008                       ; AS DETERMEND BY DETCPS
1009                       ;
1010   1ED4  AD F3 17  DELAY  LDA  CNTH30    THIS LOOP SIMULATES THE
1011   1ED7  8D F4 17        STA   TIMH      DETCPS SECTION AND WILL DELAY
1012   1EDA  AD F2 17        LDA   CNTL30    1 BIT TIME
1013   1EDD  38        DE2   SEC
1014   1EDE  E9 01     DE4   SBC   #$01
1015   1EE0  B0 03           BCS   DE3
1016   1EE2  CE F4 17        DEC   TIMH
1017   1EE5  AC F4 17  DE3   LDY   TIMH
1018   1EE8  10 F3           BPL   DE2
1019   1EEA  60              RTS
1020                       ;
1021                       ;                 DELAY HALF BIT TIME
1022   1EEB  AD F3 17  DEHALF LDA  CNTH30    DOUBLE RIGHT SHIFT OF DELAY
1023   1EEE  8D F4 17        STA   TIMH      CONSTANT FOR A DIV BY 2
1024   1EF1  AD F2 17        LDA   CNTL30
1025   1EF4  4A              LSR   A
1026   1EF5  4E F4 17        LSR   TIMH
1027   1EF8  90 E3           BCC   DE2
1028   1EFA  09 80           ORA   #$80
1029   1EFC  B0 E0           BCS   DE4
1030                       ;
1031                       ; SUB TO DETERMINE IF KEY IS
1032                       ; DEPRESSED OR COMDITION OF SSW
1033                       ;     KEY NOT DEP OR TTY MODE   A = 0
1034                       ;     KEY DEP OR KB MODE        A NOT ZERO
1035                       ;
1036                       ;
1037   1EFE  A0 03     AK    LDY   #$03      3 ROWS
```

```
CARD # LOC    CODE       CARD
1038   1F00   A2 01             LDX     #$01        DIGIT 0
1039                      ;
1040   1F02   A9 FF      ONEKEY LDA     #$FF
1041   1F04   8E 42 17   AK1    STX     SBD         OUTPUT DIGIT
1042   1F07   E8                INX                 GET NXT DIGIT
1043   1F08   E8                INX
1044   1F09   2D 40 17          AND     SAD         INPUT SEGMENTS
1045   1F0C   88                DEY
1046   1F0D   D0 F5             BNE     AK1
1047                      ;
1048   1F0F   A0 07             LDY     #$07
1049   1F11   8C 42 17          STY     SBD
1050                      ;
1051   1F14   09 80             ORA     #$80
1052   1F16   49 FF             EOR     #$FF
1053   1F18   60                RTS
1054                      ;
1055                      ;      SUB    OUTPUT TO 7 SEGMENT DISPLAY
1056                      ;
1057   1F19   A0 00      SCAND  LDY     #$00        GET DATA SPECIFIED
1058   1F1B   B1 FA             LDA     (POINTL),Y  BY POINT
1059   1F1D   85 F9             STA     INH         SET UP DISPLAY BUFFER
1060   1F1F   A9 7F      SCANDS LDA     #$7F        CHANGE SEG
1061   1F21   8D 41 17          STA     PADD        TO OUTPUT
1062                      ;
1063   1F24   A2 09             LDX     #$09        INIT DIGIT NUMBER
1064   1F26   A0 03             LDY     #$03        OUTPUT 3 BYTES
1065                      ;
1066   1F28   B9 F8 00   SCAND1 LDA     INL,Y       GET BYTE
1067   1F2B   4A                LSR     A           GET MSD
1068   1F2C   4A                LSR     A
1069   1F2D   4A                LSR     A
1070   1F2E   4A                LSR     A
1071   1F2F   20 48 1F          JSR     CONVD       OUTPUT CHAR
1072   1F32   B9 F8 00          LDA     INL,Y       GET BYTE AGAIN
1073   1F35   29 0F             AND     #$0F        GET LSD
1074   1F37   20 48 1F          JSR     CONVD       OUTPUT CHAR
1075   1F3A   88                DEY                 SET UP FOR NXT BYTE
1076   1F3B   D0 EB             BNE     SCAND1
1077   1F3D   8E 42 17          STX     SBD         ALL DIGITS OFF
1078   1F40   A9 00             LDA     #$00        CHANGE SEG
1079   1F42   8D 41 17          STA     PADD        TO INPUTS
1080   1F45   4C FE 1E          JMP     AK          GET ANY KEY
1081                      ;
1082                      ;      CONVERT AND DISPLAY HEX
1083                      ;      USED BY SCAND ONLY
1084                      ;
1085   1F48   84 FC      CONVD  STY     TEMP        SAVE Y
1086   1F4A   A8                TAY                 USE CHAR AS INDEX
1087   1F4B   B9 E7 1F          LDA     TABLE,Y     LOOK UP CONVERSION
1088   1F4E   A0 00             LDY     #$00        TURN OFF SEGMENTS
1089   1F50   9C 40 17          STY     SAD
1090   1F53   8E 42 17          STX     SBD         OUTPUT DIGIT ENABLE
1091   1F56   8D 40 17          STA     SAD         OUT PUT SEGMENTS
1092                      ;
1093   1F59   A0 7F             LDY     #$7F        DELAY 500 CYCLES APPROX.
1094   1F5B   88         CONVD1 DEY
1095   1F5C   D0 FD             BNE     CONVD1
1096                      ;
1097   1F5E   E8                INX                 GET NEXT DIGIT NUM
1098   1F5F   E8                INX                 ADD 2
1099   1F60   A4 FC             LDY     TEMP        RESTORE Y
1100   1F62   60                RTS
1101                      ;
1102                      ;      SUB TO INCREMENT POINT.
```

Operating Principles of the KIM-1 Monitor and On-Board I/O Hardware

```
CARD # LOC     CODE       CARD
1103                      ;
1104   1F63    E6 FA      INCPT  INC   POINTL
1105   1F65    D0 02             BNE   INCPT2
1106   1F67    E6 FB             INC   POINTH
1107   1F69    60         INCPT2 RTS
1108                      ;
1109                      ;      GET KEY FROM KEY BOARD
1110                      ;      RETURN WITH A=KEY VALUE
1111                      ;      A GT. 15 THEN ILLEGAL OR NO KEY
1112                      ;
1113                      ;
1114   1F6A    A2 21      GETKEY LDX   #$21            START AT DIGIT 0
1115   1F6C    A0 01      GETKE5 LDY   #$01            GET 1 ROW
1116   1F6E    20 02 1F          JSR   ONEKEY
1117   1F71    D0 07             BNE   KEYIN           A=0 NO KEY
1118   1F73    E0 27             CPX   #$27            TEST FOR DIGIT 2
1119   1F75    D0 F5             BNE   GETKE5
1120   1F77    A9 15             LDA   #$15            15=NO KEY
1121   1F79    60                RTS
1122   1F7A    A0 FF      KEYIN  LDY   #$FF
1123   1F7C    0A         KEYIN1 ASL   A               SHIFT LEFT
1124   1F7D    B0 03             BCS   KEYIN2          UNTIL Y=KEY NUM
1125   1F7F    C8                INY
1126   1F80    10 FA             BPL   KEYIN1
1127   1F82    8A         KEYIN2 TXA
1128   1F83    29 0F             AND   #$0F            MASK MSD
1129   1F85    4A                LSR   A               DIV BY 2
1130   1F86    AA                TAX
1131   1F87    98                TYA
1132   1F88    10 03             BPL   KEYIN4
1133   1F8A    18         KEYIN3 CLC
1134   1F8B    69 07             ADC   #$07            MULT (X-1) TIMES A
1135   1F8D    CA         KEYIN4 DEX
1136   1F8E    D0 FA             BNE   KEYIN3
1137   1F90    60                RTS
1138                      ;
1139                      ;      SUB TO COMPUTE CHECK SUM
1140                      ;
1141   1F91    18         CHK    CLC
1142   1F92    65 F7             ADC   CHKSUM
1143   1F94    85 F7             STA   CHKSUM
1144   1F96    A5 F6             LDA   CHKHI
1145   1F98    69 00             ADC   #$00
1146   1F9A    85 F6             STA   CHKHI
1147   1F9C    60                RTS
1148                      ;
1149                      ;      GET 2 HEX CHAR'S AND PACK
1150                      ;      INTO INL AND INH
1151                      ;      X PRESERVED  Y RETURNED = 0
1152                      ;      NON HEX CHAR WILL BE LOADED AS NEAREST HEX EQU
1153                      ;
1154   1F9D    20 5A 1E   GETBYT JSR   GETCH
1155   1FA0    20 AC 1F          JSR   PACK
1156   1FA3    20 5A 1E          JSR   GETCH
1157   1FA6    20 AC 1F          JSR   PACK
1158   1FA9    A5 F8             LDA   INL
1159   1FAB    60                RTS
1160                      ;
1161                      ;      SHIFT CHAR IN A INTO
1162                      ;      INL AND INH
1163                      ;
1164   1FAC    C9 30      PACK   CMP   #$30            CHECK FOR HEX
1165   1FAE    30 1B             BMI   UPDAT2
1166   1FB0    C9 47             CMP   #$47            NOT HEX EXIT
1167   1FB2    10 17             BPL   UPDAT2
```

```
CARD #  LOC     CODE        CARD
1168    1FB4    C9 40       HEXNUM CMP   #$40         CONVERT TO HEX
1169    1FB6    30 03              BMI   UPDATE
1170    1FB8    18          HEXALP CLC
1171    1FB9    69 09              ADC   #$09
1172    1FBB    2A          UPDATE ROL   A
1173    1FBC    2A                 ROL   A
1174    1FBD    2A                 ROL   A
1175    1FBE    2A                 ROL   A
1176    1FBF    A0 04              LDY   #$04         SHIFT INTO I/O BUFFER
1177    1FC1    2A          UPDAT1 ROL   A
1178    1FC2    26 F8              ROL   INL
1179    1FC4    26 F9              ROL   INH
1180    1FC6    88                 DEY
1181    1FC7    D0 F8              BNE   UPDAT1
1182    1FC9    A9 00              LDA   #$00         A=0 IF HEX NUM
1183    1FCB    60          UPDAT2 RTS
1184                        ;
1185    1FCC    A5 F8       OPEN   LDA   INL          MOVE I/O BUFFER TO POINT
1186    1FCE    85 FA              STA   POINTL
1187    1FD0    A5 F9              LDA   INH          TRANSFER INH- POINTH
1188    1FD2    85 FB              STA   POINTH
1189    1FD4    60                 RTS
1190                        ;
1191                        ;
1192                        ;     END OF SUBROUTINES
1194                        ;
1195                        ;     TABLES
1196                        ;
1197    1FD5    00          TOP    .BYTE $00,$00,$00,$00,$00,$00,$0A,$0D,'MIK'
1197    1FD6    00
1197    1FD7    00
1197    1FD8    00
1197    1FD9    00
1197    1FDA    00
1197    1FDB    0A
1197    1FDC    0D
1197    1FDD    4D 49 4B
1198    1FE0    20                 .BYTE ' ',$13,'RRE',' ',$13
1198    1FE1    13
1198    1FE2    52 52 45
1198    1FE5    20
1198    1FE6    13
1199                        ;
1200                        ;     TABLE HEX TO 7 SEGMENT
1201                        ;       0  1  2  3  4  5  6  7
1202    1FE7    BF          TABLE  .BYTE $BF,$86,$DB,$CF,$E6,$ED,$FD,$87
1202    1FE8    86
1202    1FE9    DB
1202    1FEA    CF
1202    1FEB    E6
1202    1FEC    ED
1202    1FED    FD
1202    1FEE    87
1203                        ;       8  9  A  B  C  D  E  F
1204    1FEF    FF                 .BYTE $FF,$EF,$F7,$FC,$B9,$DE,$F9,$F1
1204    1FF0    EF
1204    1FF1    F7
1204    1FF2    FC
1204    1FF3    B9
1204    1FF4    DE
1204    1FF5    F9
1204    1FF6    F1
1206                        ;
1207                        ;
1208                        ;
```

Operating Principles of the KIM-1 Monitor and On-Board I/O Hardware

```
CARD # LOC       CODE       CARD
 1209                       ;
 1210                       ;      INTERRUPT VECTORS
 1211                       ;
 1212  1FF7                    *=$1FFA
 1213  1FFA   1C 1C         NMIENT  .WORD NMIT
 1214  1FFC   22 1C         RSTENT  .WORD RST
 1215  1FFE   1F 1C         IRQENT  .WORD IRQT
 1216                               .END

END OF MOS/TECHNOLOGY 650X ASSEMBLY VERSION 4
NUMBER OF ERRORS =    0,  NUMBER OF WARNINGS =    0


        SYMBOL TABLE

SYMBOL    VALUE   LINE DEFINED       CROSS-REFERENCES

ACC       00F3       76      587   851
ADDR      1CBE      694      687
ADDRM     1CC8      701      673
AK        1EFE     1037     1080
AK1       1F04     1041     1046
CHAR      00FE       90      950   951   952   959   984   994
CHK       1F91     1141      734   738   741   748   808   814   899   902
CHKH      17E8       97      158   265   289   299   301
CHKHI     00F6       82      730   755   782   799   819  1144  1146
CHKL      17E7       96      156   262   288   297   298
CHKSUM    00F7       83      729   758   783   801   821  1142  1143
CHKT      194C      295      234   237   242   244   256   308
CHT1      1982      336      344
CHT2      198E      341      338
CHT3      1991      342      340
CLEAR     1C64      645      803   836
CLKKT     1747       65     ****
CLKRDI    1747       66      355   361   378   384   499   505
CLKRDT    1746       67      459   471
CLK1T     1744       62      358   364   381   387   501   508
CLK64T    1746       64      461   473
CLK8T     1745       63     ****
CNTH30    17F3      101      613   622  1010  1022
CNTL30    17F2      100      625  1012  1024
CONVD     1F48     1085     1071  1074
CONVD1    1F5B     1094     1095
CRLF      1E2F      908      640   785   829
DATA      1CA8      680     ****
DATAM     1CCC      704      675
DATAM1    1CCE      705      702
DATAM2    1CD0      706      699
DATA1     1CB0      686      698
DATA2     1CC3      697      692
DEHALF    1EEB     1022      947   956
DELAY     1ED4     1010      946   953   986   990   997  1003
DETCPS    1C2A      612     ****
DET1      1C31      615      617
DET2      1C42      623      621
DET3      1C3A      619      624
DE2       1EDD     1013     1018  1027
DE3       1EE5     1017     1015
DE4       1EDE     1014     1029
DUMP      1D42      778      873
DUMPT     1800      121     ****
DUMPT1    1814      131      134
DUMPT2    1833      148      177
DUMPT3    1854      163      166
```

SYMBOL	VALUE	LINE DEFINED		CROSS-REFERENCES							
DUMPT4	1865	173	152								
DUMPV	1E01	873	867								
DUMP0	1D48	781	826								
DUMP1	1D4E	785	♦♦♦♦								
DUMP2	1D86	811	817								
DUMP3	1D96	826	824								
DUMP4	1D7A	805	792								
EAH	17F8	106	151	791							
EAL	17F7	105	149	789							
FEED	1E07	876	861								
FEED1	1E12	882	830								
GETBYT	1F9D	1154	732	736	739	746	754	757	770		
GETCH	1E5A	940	648	725	1154	1156					
GETK	1C8D	667	♦♦♦♦								
GETKEY	1F6A	1114	667								
GETKE5	1F6C	1115	1119								
GET1	1E60	943	945								
GET2	1E6D	948	955								
GET5	1E6A	947	627								
GET6	1E87	962	944								
GOEXEC	1DC8	841	711	865							
GOV	1CD9	711	679								
HEXALP	1FB8	1170	♦♦♦♦								
HEXNUM	1FB4	1163	♦♦♦♦								
HEXOUT	196F	323	314	316							
HEXTA	1E4C	928	922	924							
HEXTA1	1E55	933	931								
HEX1	1978	328	326								
ID	17F9	107	140	224	226						
INCPT	1F63	1104	708	749	815	838					
INCPT2	1F69	1107	1105								
INCVEB	19EA	397	176	258							
INCVE1	19F2	400	398								
INH	00F9	85	647	760	825	1059	1179	1187			
INITS	1E88	966	600	609							
INIT1	1E8C	969	636								
INL	00F8	84	646	779	823	885	1066	1072	1158	1178	1185
INTVEB	1932	281	123	185							
IRQENT	1FFE	1215	♦♦♦♦								
IRQP27	1BFE	519	♦♦♦♦								
IRQT	1C1F	604	1215								
IRQV	17FE	113	604								
KEYIN	1F7A	1122	1117								
KEYIN1	1F7C	1123	1126								
KEYIN2	1F82	1127	1124								
KEYIN3	1F8A	1133	1136								
KEYIN4	1F8D	1135	1132								
LOAD	1CE7	725	727	762	874						
LOADER	1D3E	771	759								
LOADE1	1D3B	770	756								
LOADS	1CEE	728	♦♦♦♦								
LOADT	1873	183	231								
LOADT4	18B5	216	221								
LOADT5	18D7	233	225	228							
LOADT6	18EC	241	230								
LOADT7	18F8	247	239	259							
LOADT8	1915	261	250								
LOADT9	1929	270	252	263	266						
LOADV	1E04	874	869								
LOAD10	192B	271	268								
LOAD11	18C2	223	218								
LOAD12	190F	258	182								
LOAD13	18FA	248	254								
LOAD2	1D0E	746	751								

Operating Principles of the KIM-1 Monitor and On-Board I/O Hardware

SYMBOL	VALUE	LINE DEFINED	CROSS-REFERENCES
LOAD3	1D1D	754	744
LOAD7	1D2E	764	****
LOAD8	1D30	765	772
MODE	00FF	91	686 705 967
MODIFY	1E15	884	863
NMIENT	1FFA	1213	****
NMIP27	1BFA	517	****
NMIT	1C1C	603	1213
NMIV	17FA	111	603
ONE	199E	353	336 339
ONEKEY	1F02	1040	1116
ONE1	19A1	355	356 368
ONE2	19B0	361	362
OPEN	1FCC	1185	796 828
OUTBT	1961	309	141 157 159
OUTBTC	195E	308	144 146 174
OUTCH	1EA0	984	787 910 934
OUTCHT	197A	333	132 138 155 164
OUTSP	1E9E	983	831 835
OUT1	1EB4	992	999
PACK	1FAC	1164	651 1155 1157
PACKT	1A00	413	251 405 407
PACKT1	1A0F	421	418
PACKT2	1A15	426	429
PACKT3	1A22	433	414 416
PADD	1741	59	970 1061 1079
PBDD	1743	61	128 496 972
PCCMD	1CDC	717	671
PCH	00F0	73	594 719
PCL	00EF	72	591 717
PLLCAL	1A6B	493	517 518 519
PLL1	1A75	498	499 511
PLL2	1A84	505	506
POINTH	00FB	87	170 272 595 696 720 737 790 843 881 897 1106 1188
POINTL	00FA	86	169 271 592 688 691 695 718 740 747 788 812 833 845 877 879 886 900 1058 1104 1186
PREG	00F1	74	589 847
PRTBYT	1E3B	917	795 800 802 807 813 820 822 834 898 901
PRTPNT	1E1E	897	797 809 830
PRTST	1E31	909	642 767 912
PRT1	1E3A	913	****
RDBIT	1A41	457	200 441 458
RDBIT2	1A53	467	468
RDBIT3	1A50	464	465
RDBIT4	1A63	476	478
RDBYT	19F3	404	223 233 236 241 243 261 264
RDBYT2	19F9	406	****
RDCHT	1A24	439	209 216 248 404 406
RDCHT1	1A29	441	446
READ	1C6A	648	870
RST	1C22	606	1214
RSTENT	1FFC	1214	****
RSTP27	1BFC	518	****
RSTV	17FC	112	****
RTRN	1DC2	838	859 887
SAD	1740	58	615 623 638 660 943 948 1044 1089 1091
SAH	17F6	104	145 283
SAL	17F5	103	143 281
SAVE	1C00	587	****
SAVE1	1C05	590	****
SAVE2	1C0F	596	****
SAVX	17E9	98	198 201 202 203 204 233 334 345 346 427 430 439 442 443 444 448 451

SYMBOL	VALUE	LINE DEFINED	CROSS-REFERENCES								
SBD	1742	60	126	195	360	366	383	389	457	467	494	503
			510	766	974	987	989	992	996	1000	1002	1041
			1049	1077	1090							
SCAN	1DDB	854	652									
SCAND	1F19	1057	657	662	664							
SCANDS	1F1F	1060	****									
SCAND1	1F28	1066	1076									
SHOW	1DAC	829	839	882								
SHOW1	1DAF	830	643									
SPACE	1DO9	828	855									
SPUSER	00F2	75	599	608	841							
START	1C4F	636	171	273	601	616	658	661	669	706	709	721
			768	872								
STEP	1CD3	708	677									
STV	1DFE	872	857									
SYNC	1891	197	211	220								
SYNC1	1896	200	206									
SYNC2	18AB	209	213									
TAB	1871	182	189	191								
TABLE	1FE7	1202	1087									
TEMP	00FC	88	684	689	917	923	925	1085	1099			
TIMH	17F4	102	1011	1016	1017	1023	1026					
TMPX	00FD	89	940	958	985	1004						
TOP	1FD5	1197	909									
TTYKB	1C77	657	639	650								
TTYKB1	1C7C	659	663	665								
UPDATE	1FBB	1172	1169									
UPDAT1	1FC1	1177	1181									
UPDAT2	1FCB	1183	1165	1167								
VEB	17EC	99	122	148	150	173	184	188	190	192	235	238
			257	282	284	286	397	399				
XREG	00F4	77	597	849								
YREG	00F5	78	596	850								
ZRO	19C4	376	341	342								
ZRO1	19C7	378	379	391								
ZRO2	19D6	384	385									

```
INSTRUCTION  COUNT
       ADC     13
       AND      9
       ASL      7
       BCC      4
       BCS      5
       BEQ     26
       BIT     12
       BMI      9
       BNE     44
       BPL     15
       BRK      0
       BVC      0
       BVS      0
       CLC      8
       CLD      1
       CLI      0
       CLV      0
       CMP     38
       CPX      1
       CPY      0
       DEC      2
       DEX     14
       DEY      8
       EOR      2
       INC      7
       INX      5
       INY      2
       JMP     31
       JSR    115
       LDA    108
       LDX     29
       LDY     25
       LSR     22
       NOP      0
       ORA      6
       PHA      5
       PHP      0
       PLA      5
       PLP      0
       ROL     18
       RTI      1
       RTS     28
       SBC      5
       SEC      3
       SED      0
       SEI      1
       STA     81
       STX     14
       STY      7
       TAX      3
       TAY      3
       TSX      1
       TXA      3
       TXS      2
       TYA      4

# SYMBOLS =  204 (LIMIT =  400)     # BYTES  = 1690 (LIMIT = 4096)
# LINES   = 1242 (LIMIT = 1500)     # XREFS  =  646 (LIMIT =  900)
STOP         0
```

INDEX

Accumulators, 27
Address(es), 25, 31
    maps and organization, 272
Addressing modes, 31, 32, 196
    absolute, 32, 197
    current page, 34
    deferred, 32
    direct, 32
    immediate, 32, 197
    implied, 33
    indexed, 33, 197
    indexed indirect, 34, 197
    indirect, 32, 197
    indirect indexed, 34, 197
    paged, 33
    relative, 33
    zero-page, 33, 34
Alphabet
    print on Teletype, 166
Alphanumeric values, 196
ALU, 31
American Standard Code for
   Information Interchange
   (ASCII), 38, 42, 43, 257
Analog
    /digital converters, 23, 296
    units replacement, 5
Application expertise, 8

Arithmetic, 36
    instructions, 37
    /logic unit, 29
    operations, 49, 51
A-registers, 27
ASB, 475
ASCII, 38, 42, 257
    serial data streams, 267
ASO, 475
Assemble, 476
Assembler, 179, 183, 188
    directives, 182
Assembly
    language, 35
    language programming, 188
    manual, 45
    mode, 462, 472
Auxiliary carry (AC), 38

Base, 44
    address, 33
    8 (eight), 45
Baudot code, 261
BCD strings, 47
Binary
    coded decimal (BCD), 29, 52
    digit, 42
    mode, 425

number system, 44
"pure", 44
Bipolar microprocessors, 64
Bit, 42
    manipulation, 37
    slice, 14
        configuration, 30
        processors, 64
BPNF code, 269
Branch, 39
    absolute, 39
    instructions, 26
    relative, 40
Breakpoint(s) (B), 38, 223
Broadway type display
    moving, 164
BRK, 480
Buffers, 66
Bugs, 181
Byte
    .BYTE directive, 195
    manipulation, 37, 474

Canon AE-1 camera, 24
Capacitance, 42
Carry (C), 39
CA2
    as interrupt inputs, 154
    output modes, 155
CB2 output modes, 156
Central processing unit (CPU), 26
Central processor hardware elements, 26
Character manipulation, 38, 47
Check sum, 270
Chip
    select, 274
    size, 61
Clock, 20
    circuit, 20
CMOS, 63
Comments, 194
Communication, 8
    systems configuration, 267

Compiler, 180, 183
Complement
    arithmetic with binary numbers, 49
    representation, 48
Complementary MOS, 63
Computer organization, 9
Computer systems
    economic classification, 17
Computing systems
    large-scale, 14
Condition-code register, 27
Connector pin, 266
Consumer product applications, 5
Control, 7, 47
Controllers
    microcomputer-based, 6
Crystal oscillator, 20
Conversions, 46
Cost effectiveness, 4, 184
Counters, 66
Cross assembler mode, 474
Cross-reference symbol, 179
Crystalline defects, 62

Data
    bus, 22
    collection, 16
    monitoring, 47
    movement, 36, 37
    processing, 6
    transmission, 263
    values, 31
.DBYTE, 195, 474
Debug, 223
    cycle, 181
    phase, 181
DEC RT-11 editor, 213
Decimal (D), 38
    adjust (DAA), 29, 53
    and binary representation, 46
    arithmetic in microcomputers, 51

flag flip-flop, 53
mode, 425
multiplication, 43
Decoders, 66
Design constraints, 244
Diagnostic techniques, 249
Digital/analog converters, 23
Direct memory access (DMA), 59
Displacement, 33
Display-management output program, 24
Division of programming, 179
DMP, 487
DO-WHILE or DO-UNTIL, 176
DSP, 481
Dynamic
device, 64
mode, 63
versus static systems, 64

Economic factors, 183
Edit mode, 462, 470
Editing example, 218
Editor, 462
commands, 181, 219
Educational
challenge, 10
demands, 10
'EE', 163, 169
Efficiency, 184
Eight-bit systems, 41
Electro-optical couplers, 23
Element density, 61, 62
.END, 474
"End-around carry", 51
Engineer
changing role, 8
Equate directives, 191
Error messages, 181
Execute mode, 25
Execution mode, 464
Expressions, 198
Extended simple microcomputer, 281
External references, 205

False, 43
Fetch mode, 25
File-handling, 173
Firmware, 246
Flags, 38
Floppy disc, 179
4-bit
"nibble", 53
systems, 41
Full duplex, 259
Function generator, 277
Fundamental units of information, 43
Fusible-link, 274

Games, 5
Gate propagation delays, 272
General purpose register set, 27
GO, 481
GO TO statements, 176

"Hands-on" experience, 11
Hardware design, 18
Hardware/software tradeoffs, 245
Hewlett-Packard Interface Bus (HPIB), 7
Hewlett-Packard 1611A, 236
Hexadecimal
dump formatted for KIM, 169
representation, 45
Hierarchical modularity, 174
High-noise immunity, 65
Human operator, 20

ICE-80, 225
emulation and trace capability, 227
IEEE 488, 265
I8080 microprocessor, 347
architecture, 349, 350
characteristics, 349
data paths, 352
8X8 bit multiply, 391

extended block move, 392
electrical, 394
instruction, 353, 354, 356, 358
multiple byte decimal add, 392
multiple byte decimal subtract, 393
pinpoint, 394
programming model, 349, 351
programs, 391
16-bit signed compare, 392
16-bit unsigned compare, 392
status, 396
system example, 408
timing, 390
IF-THEN-ELSE logic, 176
"Images", 276
Implementation levels, 249
In-circuit emulation, 224
In-circuit emulators, 173
Index, 28
  registers, 28
  true registers, 28
Industrial experience curve, 2
Information flow, 25
Information processing, 41
Initialization program, 23
"Input" operation, 22
Input/output, 270
Instruction
  register, 25, 30
  sets, 35
Instrumentation, 6
Integral "on-chip", 21
Integrated-injection logic (I^2L), 63
Intel 8080/8055 assembler, 205
Intel MDS-800, 179
Intel UPM (Universal Prom Mapper), 238
"Intelligent" terminals, 6
Interconnection system, 22, 24
Interface adapters, 23
Interfacing
  to keyboard, 282
  to the Teletype, 252

Internal control
  "hard-wired", 30
  logic, 30
Interpretation, 183
Interpreter, 212
Interrupt(s), 53
  enable (I), 38, 59
  handling, 24, 56, 57, 58
  in I/O management, 24
  masking, 59
  multiple inputs, 59
  non-maskable (NMI), 59
  priority, 60
  program, 56
  request, 57
  return from (RTI), 59
  routine linkage, 60
  vectors, 60
I/O
  device speed constraints, 23
  interface, 22, 24
  interrupts in management, 24
  isolated, 23
  selection, 270
IRQ, 59
ISIS editor commands, 219
ISIS-II
  assembler, 205
  operating system, 205
ISIS-II PL/M-80 compiler, 206
I^2L, 63

JSR, 54
Jump(s), 39
  absolute, 39
  and branches, 39
  conditional, 39
  instructions, 26
  relative, 40
  subroutine, 40
  unconditional, 39

Keyboard-monitor input program, 24

Key pad scan subroutine, 283
KIM-1 microcomputer, 23, 411, 412
    assembly language, 416
    audio tape recorder, 438
    display, 450
    input/output modes, 428
    memory map, 417
    monitor program, 174
    paper tape, 433, 436, 438
    prompting message, 427
    record and play back, 445
    single-step execution, 423
    "source code", 416

Large scale systems, 14
"Library", 174
LIFO, 54
Limiting case testing, 247
Linkage, 204
Linking capacity, 205
Listing, 192
    controls, 199
    file, 179
Load mode, 462, 465, 470
Location, 25
Logic
    design, 9
    state analyzers, 236
Logical, 37
    instructions, 37, 39
Long operands, 65
Loop, 28
    control, 28
LSI, 16
    components, 251
    design, 61
    partitioning, 63
LSI-11, 16
LST, 487

Machine language, 36
Macro, 203
    call, 203
    libraries, 204

Magnetic, 42
Marking, 255
Masking, 37, 59
Matching skills to prog
Matching skills to problems, 248
MCS6502, 69
    accumulator and arithmetic unit, 77
    addressing modes for, 82
    alphabet, 166
    broadway type display, 164
    characteristics, 69, 132
    checkerboard test, 168
    compare and bit test, 91
    control register bit designation, 153
    data paths, 73, 74
    decimal to hexadecimal conversion, 160
    'EE', 163, 167
    flag and status register, 83
    hexadecimal to decimal conversion, 160
    indexed addressing, 94
    indirect addressing, 94, 97
    input/output with the, 83
    instruction, 75, 76
    internal architecture, 75
    interrupt(s), 129, 130, 133, 134, 153
    jump and branch, 85, 87
    maximum ratings, 130
    multiple byte decimal add, 160
    non-indexed addressing, 93
    operation codes, 102
    paper tape compared to memory, 164
    PIA register selection/function, 153
    pinouts, 124, 125, 141
    programming model, 73, 74
    programs, 160
    relative branch table, 90

shift and memory modification, 100
specifications, 70
stack, 98
3 byte values, 162
MCS6520, 147
characteristics, 148
external connections, 136
internal architecture, 149, 153
MCS6530, 136
characteristics, 136
internal architecture, 137
MDS-800 development system, 205
MDT-650, 213, 461
execute mode, 477
output mode, 486
Medium-scale integrated (MSI) circuits, 61
Memory, 274
function, 64
mapping, 225
units, 64
Memory-mapped vs. isolated I/O, 23
Metering functions, 7
Microcomputer
-based design, 252
definition, 13
interfacing, 243
major system components, 20
systems, 16
Microcontroller, 14
Microinstructions, 30
"Microoperations", 30
Microprocessor
application(s), 3, 4
-based systems, 18
cost, 13
definition, 13
instruction sets, 35
word length, 40
Microprogram, 30
Microprogrammed mode, 65
Minicomputer, 415
Minicomputing systems, 14

Modem, 261
Modular programming, 174
Modulus, 49
Monitor, 462
Motorola EXORCISOR, 179
Motorola 6800, 27
programming model, 36
MPL, 206
MSI, 61
M6800 microprocessor,
characteristics, 299
data paths, 306
8X8 bit multiply, 342
electrical, 335
extended block move, 341
instruction set, 306, 311
microcomputer example, 339
multiple byte decimal add, 341
multiple byte decimal subtract, 344
opcode, 308
programming model, 304, 305
programs, 341
Multiple-sourcing, 251
Multiple stacks, 56
Multiplexes, 66

NANO
NAND gate
TTL, 65
Negative (N), 38
numbers, 48
zero, 51
NMI, 59
Number systems, 44
conversions between, 46
Numeric
information, 43
machine control, 7
Non-numeric information, 43
NUL, 475

Object, 188
    program, 181
Octal representation, 45
1's complement arithmetic, 51
Opcode, 25
    table, 191
Operand(s), 25, 31
Operation(al) code(s), 25, 31
    classification of, 36
Optical, 41
Option directives, 199
.OPT, 196, 474
Origin directive, 191
Output
    mode, 464
    operation, 23
Overflow (V), 38, 49

.PAGE, 474
Pages, 34
Paper, 42
Parity (P), 38
Partitioning, 63, 245
PASCAL example, 212
PASS 1, 191
PASS 2, 191
PDP-8 minicomputer, 34
"People cost", 185
Peripheral interface chips, 136
Personal computer, 4
"Personality modules", 23 28
PIA
    connection to KIM, 154
    example using KIM, 154
PL/M, 206
PL/M-80, 208
PLuS, 206
Pointer, 27
Poll(ing), 22, 60
Popped, 54
Pop instructions, 54
Positional notation, 43
Positive zero, 51

Power
    down, 21
    interrupt, 21
Process
    control, 7, 14
    yield, 61
Processing units, 7
Processor module, 224
Program
    counter, 26, 29
    interrupt, 56
    state, 29, 55, 58
    status (PS), 58
Programming
    model constituents, 35
    structured, 176
PROM programmers, 173, 237
Pseudoinstructions, 182
Pushed, 54
Push instructions, 54
Pushdown list, 54

Radix, 44
    point, 44
    10, 44
    16, 45
RAM, 20
Read-only memory system, 20, 21
Read-write memory, 20, 22
    MCS6530 RWM checkerboard tester, 165
Ready/wait control mechanism, 23
Recreational exercises, 5
Redundant systems, 3
Reentrant, 55
Refresh logic, 64
REG, 481, 483
Register
    file(s), 27
    restore operation, 59
    save operation, 59
Reliability, 1
Relocatable format, 269

Relocatability and linkage, 204
Return from interrupt (RTI), 58
Rockwell SYSTEM 65, 179
ROM, 237
RS-232 interface, 260
RS334, 265
RT-11 editor commands, 220
RTS, 54
RUN, 481, 483
RWM, 20

Segmentation, 244
Seiko printer interface, 287
Selector
    cam, 258
    magnet, 258
Service routine, 59
Set Carry (SC), 39
Shift/rotate, 36, 38
SI, 481, 484
Sign
    bit, 47, 50
    magnitude representation, 48
Signed numbers, 47
Simulators, 222
Single-chip unit, 16
Single-step function, 59
.SKIP, 474
SLO, 482, 485
Software
    design, 11, 18, 174, 179
    development, 9
    /hardware integration, 181
Source, 188
    file, 179
    program, 181
SRC, 475
Stack, 54
    management of linkage, 54
    mechanization, 56
    pointer, 54
    pointer register, 28
    principles, 54

Start
    bit, 254
    -of-word, 265
Static unit, 64
State transition, 401
Status
    flags, 27
    register, 27
    testing, 38
    word, 395
STOP function, 59
STP, 482, 483
Subroutine(s), 53
    basics, 53
    handling, 57
    jump, 54
    linkage, 54
    nested, 55
    nesting, 55
    return (RTS), 54
Subtraction, 29
    hardware, 49
SYCLOPS, 206
SYM, 475
Symbol table, 179, 191
Symbolic representation of
    information, 41
Symbolism, 41
Synchronization with memory
    devices, 24
Syntax errors, 179
System
    controller, 395
    design, 243
    interconnection, 251
    interfacing, 9
    maintainability, 250
    stack, 40

TAB, 475
Tables, 33
Tabular form address, 276
Target computer, 188

Technological factors in
   microprocessors, 61
Teleprinter, 426
Teletype
   functions, 254
   interfacing to, 253
   Model ASR33, 411
   typical times, 254
10's complement, 48
Text, 465
   editor(s), 179, 212
3 byte
   multiplies two to 12-digit, 162
Top-down, 174, 244
"Totem pole" output
   configuration, 65
TRACE, 480
Transistor-transistor logic
   (TTL or T^2L), 65, 270
      bipolar logic, 65
      high-speed, 65
      low power, 65
      Schottky, 65
Translation levels, 181
      assembly language, 182
      high-level language, 182
      language levels, 182
      machine language, 182
      microprogramming, 182
      operating system machine, 182
      problem-oriented language, 182
      source language, 183
      target language, 183
Translator programs, 183
Transmitting distributor (TD), 258
Transport attributes, 268
Transportability of programs and
   data, 265
Triangular wave generator using KIM, 169
True, 43
TTL (or T^2L), 65, 271

TTY, 482
2-s complement arithmetic, 29, 49, 50
Two-valved elements, 41
Typical system, 18

United States of America
   Standard Code for
   Information Interchange, 255
USASCII control code
   identification and
   generator, 256
UV erasable ROM, 274

Volatile, 20

.WORD, 194, 475

Yield, 61

Zero (Z), 38
Zilog Z-80, 64